This new volume of the letters, spe
press conferences, and journal ent
Adlai Stevenson is at once a continua
a widely praised documentary biography
and a testimony of the changes that molded
the United States and the world between
1957 and 1961.

During the uneasy years of Dwight
Eisenhower's second term as President,
Stevenson traveled extensively in Africa, the
Soviet Union, and Latin America in the
hope of better understanding the needs of
other countries and improving America's effectiveness in foreign relations. His candid,
compassionate descriptions of these journeys provide important insights into the
character of such key international figures
as Nikita Khrushchev, Dr. Albert
Schweitzer, Richard Nixon, and John F.
Kennedy, as well as vividly recreating the
scenes and sentiments of emerging nations.

As a result of his travels Stevenson continued, with characteristic eloquence, to call
for changes in American governmental policy: for nuclear disarmament, for an improved and more equal system of education,
for an end to the cold war, and for a system
of government that serves the well-being,
dignity, freedom, and survival of all individuals. Sensing the complacent attitude of the
country under Eisenhower's administration,
Stevenson urged Americans to strive for the
principles of liberty and justice that are right-
fully theirs, and not to be lulled by political
propaganda or lies.

After two previous unsuccessful attempts
to gain the Presidency, Stevenson did not actively seek office in 1960, but the support of
ministration.

Walter Johnson's, Carol Evans's, and C.
Eric Sear's careful editing of *The Papers of
Adlai Stevenson* has produced a full-scale
portrait of a man whose warmth and
generosity with his friends and family was
carried into his concern for the welfare of all
men, and a just peace among nations. These
collected papers also reflect an accurate,
sensitive view of a troubled period in the history of the United States — one which has
had a continuing impact on national and
foreign policy. This journal is the legacy of a
man who elevated the political dialogue in
America, and whose moral conscience and
style set a standard by which to judge all
future politicians.

Books by Walter Johnson

THE BATTLE AGAINST ISOLATION

WILLIAM ALLEN WHITE'S AMERICA

THE UNITED STATES: EXPERIMENT IN DEMOCRACY
(*with Avery Craven*)

HOW WE DRAFTED ADLAI STEVENSON

1600 PENNSYLVANIA AVENUE: PRESIDENTS AND THE PEOPLE, 1929–1959

THE FULBRIGHT PROGRAM: A HISTORY
(*with Francis J. Colligan*)

Edited by Walter Johnson

SELECTED LETTERS OF WILLIAM ALLEN WHITE

ROOSEVELT AND THE RUSSIANS: THE YALTA CONFERENCE
By Edward R. Stettinius, Jr.

TURBULENT ERA: A DIPLOMATIC RECORD OF FORTY YEARS, 1904–1945
By Joseph C. Grew

THE PAPERS OF ADLAI E. STEVENSON
Volume I: Beginnings of Education, 1900–1941
Volume II: Washington to Springfield, 1941–1948
Volume III: Governor of Illinois, 1949–1953
Volume IV: "Let's Talk Sense to the American People," 1952–1955
Volume V: Visit to Asia, the Middle East, and Europe —
March–August 1953
Volume VI: Toward a New America, 1955–1957
Volume VII: Continuing Education and the Unfinished Business of
American Society — 1957–1961

The Papers of Adlai E. Stevenson

WALTER JOHNSON, *Editor*

CAROL EVANS, *Assistant Editor*

C. ERIC SEARS, *Editorial Assistant*

The Papers of

Advisory Committee

George W. Ball
Julian P. Boyd
William T. Hutchinson
Mrs. Ernest L. Ives
Carl McGowan
The late Allan Nevins

Adlai E. Stevenson

VOLUME VII

Continuing Education and the Unfinished Business of American Society

1957–1961

LITTLE, BROWN and COMPANY • *Boston* • *Toronto*

308.0973
St 48 P
v. 7

LIBRARY OF CONGRESS CATALOGING IN PUBLICATION DATA (REVISED)
Stevenson, Adlai Ewing, 1900–1965.
  The papers of Adlai E. Stevenson.

  Includes bibliographical references and index.
  CONTENTS: v. 1. Beginnings of education, 1900–1941.
—v. 2. Washington to Springfield, 1941–1948.—
v. 3. Governor of Illinois, 1949–1953. [etc.]
    1. United States—Politics and government—20th
century—Collected works. 2. Stevenson, Adlai Ewing,
1900–1965. 3. Statesmen—United States—Correspondence.
I. Johnson, Walter, 1915–   ed.
E742.5.S747   973.921′092′4   73-175478
ISBN 0-316-46751-0 (v. 2)

                  FIRST EDITION

                    T09/77

The editors gratefully acknowledge the permission of the following authors, publishers, individuals and institutions to reprint selected materials as noted:

Martin Agronsky, the Associated Press, Atheneum Publishers, the Atlanta *Journal*, the Auckland *Star*, Boston *Globe*, Stuart Gerry Brown, the Chicago *Daily News*, the Chicago *Sun-Times*, Alistair Cooke, Jonathan Daniels, Doubleday & Company, Inc., James T. Farrell, Field Enterprises, Inc., Margaret Halsey, *Harper's Magazine*, Harper & Row, Brooks Hays, Ben Heineman, Houghton Mifflin Company, Lady Barbara Jackson, Alfred A. Knopf, Inc., the *Listener*, *The Times* (London), Leonard Lyons, Macmillan Company, the *Manchester Guardian*, Bill Mauldin, Hans Morgenthau, William Morrow & Company, Inc., the *New Republic, Newsday*, the New York *Herald Tribune*, New York *Post*, New York *Times*, Random House, Inc., Harrison Salisbury, Time Inc., United Feature Syndicate, Clara Urquhart, the *Wall Street Journal*, the Washington *Post*, Whitney Communications Corporation, Willard Wirtz, Yale University Library, and Paul Ziffren for all items from their publications and writings as detailed in the footnotes.

Atheneum Publishers, for excerpts from *The Making of the President 1960* by Theodore H. White. Copyright © 1961 by Atheneum House, Inc.

The Rand Corporation, for excerpts from *Impressions of Russia in 1958: A Trip Report* by Robert C. Tucker.

Random House, Inc., for excerpts from *Putting First Things First* by Adlai E. Stevenson. Copyright © 1960 by Adlai E. Stevenson.

The Virginia Quarterly Review, for Adlai E. Stevenson's Founder's Day speech published in the Summer, 1960, issue (Vol. 36, No. 3). Copyright © 1960 by The Virginia Quarterly Review.

Little, Brown and Company, for an adaptation of lines from the poem "Next!" from *The Private Dining Room and Other New Verses* by Ogden Nash. Copyright 1953 by Ogden Nash.

Foreword

A dlai E. Stevenson brought the quality of distinction to American public life.

But he did more than that. Lord Harlech[1] remarked:

> The character of America is extraordinarily complex and there are times when one aspect and then another of her character seems to be dominant. Sometimes to the rest of the world she seems to be the prime example of materialism run-riot, a voracious consumer of goods and services and indeed of people, a country disfigured by violence, and a brash military power not above bullying smaller nations. In all, an unsympathetic figure.
>
> But those of us who are her friends know that there is another America.[2] The America of the Declaration of Independence, and the Bill of Rights. The America of the Gettysburg Address. The America that inspired the words inscribed on the Statue of Liberty.
>
> It was to this America that Adlai Stevenson belonged, and while he lived he embodied her aspirations.[3]

Between 1957 and 1961 Adlai Stevenson — as he had done since 1952 — continued to define the issues, to set forth guidelines for achieving a more humane America and a more humane world. Elmo Roper wrote in 1957: "The new shape of the Democratic party is not yet wholly deter-

[1] As David Ormsby-Gore, British ambassador to the United States, 1961–1965.

[2] Senator J. W. Fulbright has written: "There are two Americas. One is the America of Lincoln and Adlai Stevenson; the other is the America of Teddy Roosevelt and the modern superpatriots. One is generous and humane, the other narrowly egotistical; one is self-critical, the other self-righteous; one is sensible, the other romantic; one is good-humored, the other solemn; one is inquiring, the other pontificating; one is moderate, the other filled with passionate intensity; one is judicious and the other arrogant in the use of great power." *The Arrogance of Power* (New York: Random House, 1966), p. 245.

[3] Inauguration speech at the Adlai Stevenson Memorial Library of the English-Speaking Union, London, England, October 14, 1970, p. 3.

mined. But Stevenson gave it a strong push in the direction of responsible, dedicated, progressive leadership."[4]

Through speeches, articles, and his support of and participation in the Democratic Advisory Council, Stevenson helped shape the position of the national wing of the Democratic party on the issues confronting his society. He also, through his advice to Secretary of State John Foster Dulles and President Dwight Eisenhower in November and December, 1957, tried to reorient their thinking about the North Atlantic Treaty Organization and economic assistance to the underdeveloped world.

By the time of the 1960 Democratic Convention, as Theodore White observed, Stevenson "left behind the virus of morality in the bloodstream of both parties."[5] And James Reston wrote: "He elevated the political dialogue in America and he contributed much to the style and the policies later adopted by Presidents Kennedy and Johnson."[6]

Numbered among the writers who helped Stevenson shape new concepts — and who later would contribute to the thinking of President Kennedy — were John Kenneth Galbraith, Seymour Harris and Arthur Schlesinger, Jr.

Schlesinger wrote:

> And in a sense, Stevenson had made Kennedy's rise possible. The Democratic party had undergone a transformation in its eight years in the wilderness. In the last days of Truman the party motto had been, "You never had it so good." The essence of the party appeal was not to demand exertions but to promise benefits. Stevenson changed all that. His lofty conception of politics, his conviction that affluence was not enough for the good life, his impatience with liberal cliches, his contempt for conservative complacency, his summons to the young, his demand for new ideas, his respect for the people who had them, his belief that history afforded no easy answers, his call for strong public leadership — all this set the tone for a new era in Democratic politics. By 1960, the candidates for the Democratic nomination, and Kennedy most of all, were talking in the Stevenson idiom and stressing peril, uncertainty, sacrifice, purpose. More than either of them ever realized or admitted, Kennedy was emerging as the heir and executor of the Stevenson revolution."[7]

In addition to reshaping the Democratic party and elevating the political dialogue in the United States, Stevenson continued his own educa-

[4] *You and Your Leaders: Their Actions and Your Reactions* (New York: William Morrow, 1957), p. 232.

[5] *The Making of the President, 1960* (New York: Atheneum, 1961), p. 168.

[6] *Sketches in the Sand* (New York: Alfred A. Knopf, 1967), p. 81.

[7] *A Thousand Days: John F. Kennedy in the White House* (Boston: Houghton Mifflin, 1965), p. 23.

tion by trips to Europe, Africa, the Soviet Union, and Latin America. In numerous articles he explained what he had observed and learned from his experiences.

In addition, he was head of his own Chicago law firm Stevenson, Rifkind, & Wirtz — and a member of the New York firm of Paul, Weiss, Rifkind, Wharton & Garrison. In a speech to the Association of the Bar of the City of New York in 1966, Francis T. P. Plimpton said:

> From time to time there have been whisperings to the effect that Stevenson was not outstanding as a lawyer. There are, of course, various definitions of legal outstandingness, and there is no doubt that he did not rejoice (or surpass) in the La Salle Street–Wall Street 16-hour a day process of churning out indentures and registration statements. . . .
>
> But there can be no doubt that as an all-around lawyer of wide experience and wide good judgment he *was* outstanding. Those New York lawyers who worked with him on international negotiations in Africa and elsewhere and in appellate matters before the Supreme Court of the United States can and will so testify.[8]

In this volume — as in the previous volumes of *The Papers of Adlai E. Stevenson* — Stevenson's own words are presented in letters, postcards, speeches, press conferences, and his abortive attempts at keeping a diary. These volumes are a documentary biography of Stevenson and, at the same time, a documentary history in his own words of the extraordinary, and often bewildering, changes that remolded the United States and the world during his lifetime from 1900 to 1965.

In selecting the materials from Stevenson's papers to be published in these volumes, the editors decided to emphasize the material that helped answer such questions as: How did he educate himself? How did he become the man he became? What were the key influences in his life? How did he understand his times? How did he articulate the problems of his times?

Because of the large volume of mail Stevenson received it was impossible for him to acknowledge or properly respond to it without the help of his secretaries and law partners. Stevenson authorized them to draft letters over his name, to be signed by his personal secretary, Carol Evans, without going over his desk. Phyllis Gustafson signed when Miss Evans was absent. Although he dictated and signed an impressive number of letters himself, he once told Carol Evans that he did not think his signature was important or added anything to a letter. Incoming letters

---

[8] Association of the Bar of the City of New York, *Memorial Book* (1966); reprinted in the *Harvard Law School Bulletin*, January, 1967, p. 3.

of great importance frequently went first to one of his law partners, depending on the nature of the matter, and were brought by them to Stevenson's attention.

When letters were written over Stevenson's name by an aide, the author's initials with those of his secretary were typed in the left-hand margin of the carbon copy to identify the writer and the person who typed the letter. For example, if on a carbon copy of a letter the initials WWW/AH are found in the left-hand margin, this indicates that it was dictated by W. Willard Wirtz and typed by his secretary, Arlene Huff. If Mr. Wirtz deemed it unnecessary to clear the letter with Stevenson before it went out, the letter was signed by Carol Evans. If the letter was considered important enough to be read by Stevenson before mailing, it was usually presented to him first in draft form, then typed in final form and signed by Miss Evans or by Stevenson himself.

When Stevenson dictated a letter, his initials with those of the secretary were placed on the left-hand margin of the carbon copy. Some of these letters were then returned to his desk for one reason or another (he sometimes added a postscript by hand; or he might redraft the letter), and were signed by him. The others were signed, usually, by Carol Evans.

Because the collection of Stevenson's papers consists mainly of carbon copies it is impossible to know whether he or one of his authorized associates signed them. It is, of course, possible to determine whether he was actually their author. But whether he composed and signed them personally or not, the letters and memoranda are considered to be his because he authorized them to be done in his behalf.

When we have made deletions from letters, speeches, or other papers, we have indicated this by ellipses. We have provided editorial comment on any item where it was necessary for clarity or continuity.

The editors had a large collection of papers available for Volume VII. This volume is, therefore, highly selective. Stevenson provided in his will that material about his governorship be deposited in the Illinois State Historical Library and the remainder be deposited in the Princeton University Library. Stevenson's most important correspondence was at his home in Libertyville when he died. The editors selected some of the material for this volume from the material at Libertyville before the collection was divided between the two depositories. Some items are still in the possession of Adlai E. Stevenson III.

The editors of these volumes searched widely for handwritten documents. Stevenson enjoyed writing by hand — he must have, since he wrote so many letters and postcards. Some people, particularly before Stevenson became governor of Illinois, failed to save them. Many people were most cooperative, placing all their Stevenson items at our disposal. Some preferred to send us only selections from their collections. A few refused to send us any material at all.[9]

After reading the typescript of Volume VI of *The Papers of Adlai E. Stevenson*, Willard Wirtz, Stevenson's law partner and Secretary of Labor under President Kennedy and President Johnson, wrote the editors about the personal letters included in that volume. His remarks are equally pertinent to those in Volume VII.

> A few of us know how much the Governor said beyond what he actually meant, or believed. He played a game, in conversation and on paper. Some of it was just manners. Friendliness. And this included a good deal of exaggeration. Some more of it was part of trying ideas on for size even when he knew they didn't fit, often for the purpose of getting the other side of the idea (which appealed to him more) developed. He was short, in both respects, on discretion. There was also a common element of complaining, going considerably beyond what he felt. And he over-personalized, especially in the first person.
>
> Perhaps this is all a part of what his "papers" are supposed to reveal. But I shudder a little about the extent to which strangers are going to misinterpret.

Some letters, which would cause unnecessary anguish to people still living, the editors have not included in these volumes, or they have made appropriate deletions within such letters. These deletions are indicated by ellipses.

Over the years Stevenson wrote many letters to Mrs. Edison Dick and her family. Some were dictated and transcribed on the typewriter, and some were handwritten. Mrs. Dick submitted extracts to the editors from handwritten letters she received from Stevenson. She has indicated with ellipses material that was deleted by her. The originals of all the handwritten letters are in her possession.

The location of other handwritten letters, postcards or originals of typewritten letters is given in the footnote references. Since the majority of the papers in Volume VII are in the Princeton University Library (some in the distribution, probably inadvertently, went to the Illinois State Historical Library in Springfield), the editors identify the location of only those papers that are *not* in the Princeton collection. Papers at

---

[9] Katie Louchheim wrote: "These were [some of] the women who owned a share in Adlai's destiny." *By the Political Sea* (Garden City, New York: Doubleday, 1970), p. 108.

the Illinois State Historical Library will be identified as "in A.E.S., I.S.H.L."

Most of Stevenson's letters were signed with his full name; those signed "AD" or "ADLAI" were to close personal or political friends. Because we have had to work, in most cases, with carbon copies, it is impossible to know how these letters and memoranda were signed. Hence, signatures have been omitted from such items. Whenever we have located the original letter, and he signed it otherwise than with his full name, we have included the signature.

When he wrote by hand, Stevenson had several idiosyncrasies. He spelled "it's" without the apostrophe; he used "thru" for "through," etc. We have left them as he wrote them and have not added a *sic*.

When references in a letter were not clear the editors wrote to the recipient of the letter (or to his heirs) to seek clarification. The responses — many of them reflected in the footnotes — have been extremely valuable and have added a dimension that would not have been possible to achieve unless these volumes were edited shortly after Stevenson's death.

The editors generally have not included letters written to Stevenson. Publishing letters written by people still alive or recently deceased requires obtaining formal permission — a time-consuming task. Instead, the editors have summarized the contents of an incoming letter where necessary in order to make Stevenson's reply understandable.

Adlai E. Stevenson, as those who knew him well realize, corrected copies of his speeches up to the minute or second of delivery. Moreover, many of these last-minute-corrected speeches the editors have been unable to locate in the depositories. Stevenson sometimes gave these to reporters and they apparently were not returned to him. The editors decided, therefore, to rely on the texts of Stevenson's speeches that he himself approved for publication in *Putting First Things First: A Democratic View* (New York: Random House, 1960). Of the speeches used that were not included in this publication, the editors indicate whether the text was taken from a press release, carbon copy, or some other source.

Under the legal agreement between Walter Johnson and Adlai Stevenson III, Borden Stevenson and John Fell Stevenson, Adlai III agreed to read each volume before publication. In the event of disagreement as to the inclusion of any item of his father's papers, the matter was to be referred to Judge Carl McGowan for final — and irrevocable — decision. Adlai III objected to nothing included in this volume.

Contents

Illustrations

Part One

Oxford and Africa

On May 16, 1957, Adlai E. Stevenson flew to Paris on legal business. While in France, however, he discussed public issues with a number of French officials, including Prime Minister Guy Mollett.

In Belgium, Stevenson discussed some of the activities of Leon Tempelsman & Son of New York, one of his legal clients, with officials in charge of the Belgian Congo. In London, on May 21, he discussed his client's business with Sir Ernest Oppenheimer, of the Diamond Development Corporation. During the next few days he and William Benton, chairman of the board of directors of the Encyclopaedia Britannica, attended a press conference and reception sponsored by the Encyclopaedia Britannica, as well as a board meeting of the directors of the Britannica. Stevenson also met with Prime Minister Harold Macmillan, Foreign Secretary Selwyn Lloyd and other Conservative Party leaders and the leaders of the Labour Party and the Liberal Party.

On May 24, 1957, Stevenson received an honorary degree from Oxford University. Mr. and Mrs. Ives, Adlai III and Nancy Stevenson, and several friends attended the ceremony. One of them, author and lecturer Barbara Ward (Lady Jackson), wrote to Mrs. Edison Dick and Carol Evans:[1]

> The celebrations began at 4 P.M. with a tea at the Vice-Chancellor's lodgings. I may say it was a day as bitterly cold as only an English May can produce, a day you would have thought daunting to audiences in the vast unheated spaces of the Sheldonian Theatre. But the Public Orator at tea said that none of his family could go because every ticket had been disposed of weeks before. The Vice-Chancellor, Mr. [J.C.] Masterman, is the archetype of the University Don — gentle, elderly, urbane, witty, a bachelor.

[1] A shortened version was published in "Affection and Always Respect," in *As We Knew Adlai: The Stevenson Story by Twenty-two Friends*, edited and with preface by Edward P. Doyle, foreword by Adlai E. Stevenson III (New York: Harper & Row, 1966), pp. 220–221.

[3]

(When a colleague of his was asked: "Has he a wife?" the answer came: "No — (pause) — he has a mother.") He was already in academic dress, morning coat, Geneva bands and voluminous gown. He complained of his mortarboard. On his first official occasion, he had to raise it 193 times in thirty minutes. "And," he added, "I have arthritic fingers." The Public Orator[2] was also arrayed in white bands and robe and he circulated to the few guests the Governor's citation — the Latin praises which are read out before the conferring of the degree and record why the University has decided to accord the honour. You will no doubt see this citation — I haven't a copy — but I'll only say that it is one of the warmest and most flattering that I have ever read in a University not over given to enthusiasm. While we struggled over the Latin, the Governor was tried out for length in his scarlet academic gown and for (mental) breadth in his flat black velvet Tudor bonnet. He looked like one of Henry VIII's rather less staid advisers.

Just before five, we were driven to the Sheldonian, a large covered amphitheatre in shape. The academic community sat on the floor of the hall facing the tiers arranged in a semi-circle. In the centre of the tiers was the Vice-Chancellor's throne. The rows on each side of this were reserved for invited guests — and you needed the agility of a mountain goat to climb them to your seat. Behind and above were public galleries filled to overflowing. In fact, two Asian gentlemen had climbed on to a sort of pulpit arrangement on one side of the amphitheatre and two clerical students on the other. The faculty sitting in solid ranks below, wearing black and scarlet gowns, the women dons in our appalling academic bonnets, varied from the infinitely old to baby fellows just out of the egg, from the extremely somnolent to the eager, the talkative and the gay.

We waited about ten minutes, perched on our high benches. Then a hush fell and we all rose to our feet for the Vice-Chancellor's procession. This entered from a side door. Four macebearers came first, carrying heavy golden maces, then two unidentified dons — possibly proctors — in academic dress, then the Vice-Chancellor look-ing remarkably shy. He raced through the arena and with quite remarkable agility hoisted himself up to his steep chair. He then raised his mortarboard to the company and I found myself com-pulsively keeping count (The final score was poor — only a dozen). The proctors and macebearers sat down below and we all sat again and waited. There were confused sounds outside, a certain amount of cheering and, to the trained eye, the unmistakable flash of light-bulbs in the grey afternoon light. The great doors at the end of the arena — facing the tiers — opened once and a cautious face looked in. Through the crack, we could see the distant figure of the Gov-

[2] T. F. Higham, of Trinity College.

[4]

ernor, gorgeous in scarlet, standing beside the Public Orator and surrounded by a bedlam of press photographers. This only added to the hush and decorum within. The face that peered in must have been satisfied, for, a moment later, the Proctors arose and marched back between the rows of faculty members and once again we all got to our feet. The great doors swung open, the Proctors righted about and stamped slowly back followed by the Governor, looking pale and moved, and the Public Orator. There was absolute silence until the procession reached the open space before the throne. There, in clear Latin, the Public Orator read out the citation, very gracefully, savouring every phrase (and why not, for he wrote it) and then the Governor advanced and climbed the excessively abrupt steps to the throne. The Vice-Chancellor (I need hardly say) raised his mortarboard, then grasped the Governor by the hand & declared him Doctor Honoris Causae.

Thereafter a really very surprising thing happened — for Oxford at least. The assembled audience raised the roof. They clapped, they stamped, they banged the benches and the hurricane went on for at least two minutes. Many of the dons were visibly surprised — and as visibly delighted. I am told that all over the upper tier, where the undergraduates were thickest, there appeared a rash of Stevenson buttons. The four conspicuous gentlemen perched in their pulpits almost fell to the arena in their excitement. It was a wonderful demonstration of affection and respect and, I believe, unique in Oxford, at least in these last cynical, unemotional decades.

The Governor then lectured for nearly an hour and was listened to with deep attention. I doubt if the acoustics of the Sheldonian are any too good, certainly not for the benches where we sat since the lectern was immediately to the right of the Vice-Chancellor's throne and slightly below it. But in spite of the fact that perhaps half the audience had to strain to hear, there was none of that coughing and restlessness which comes when people lose interest or lose heart. At times, there was that hush of complete communication when an audience is literally conscious of nothing but the speaker's words. And — since it was the Governor speaking — there were some enchanting moments of humour and impromptu reaction, too. He won all hearts at the beginning by referring to the saying that Oxford is reputed the home of Lost Causes. Whom, then, could they more fitly distinguish than the man who was probably the world's greatest living exponent of the Lost Cause? Later, just as the Governor mentioned a figure for foreign aid — $750 millions or some such — a roll of coins fell from some listener's pocket and bounced noisily to the ground. The Governor paused just long enough to say: "Now, see you retrieve them" and went straight on with his text. The audience gave a howl of pleasure.

At the end, the ovation was as warm as at the start — a test, indeed, after 55 minutes of oratory — and when the Governor left in procession with the Vice-Chancellor, a small army of students followed him until he was finally retrieved and bundled into a University car. Only, I think, those who know the normal temperature of Oxford's academic occasions will realise how warmly and decisively the faculty and the students demonstrated their appreciation of the Governor's role in domestic and international politics. And the demonstration was all the more remarkable in that 1957 is not, alas, a year in which America is much loved in Britain. The Oxford occasion turned into a reaffirmation of our deeper links and only the Governor could have achieved this.

The citation was delivered by the Public Orator's deputy, the Principal of Jesus College, John Traill Christie.

This is a time when England extends to all American visitors an especially warm welcome, because we wish to leave the rest of the world in no doubt of the strong links which still bind our country to theirs: our common heritage of culture, our traditional tie of kinship, three centuries old this very year, and not least our fundamental friendship which allows us the privilege of friends, an occasional difference of opinion. Moreover, the eminent American citizen, whom we are happy to see with us today, is particularly welcome to a University audience. We all know his distinguished record in his own political arena and among the dissensions of the United Nations, and we see in him one who has never failed to exemplify just those virtues which it is the duty of a University to foster, the passion for truth, sound learning spiced with charm, wit without rancour, eloquence without self-advertisement.

Small wonder that with such endowments he was twice chosen as candidate for the supreme office of President; he "failed in the high emprise, yet greatly failed." Throughout the campaigns he preserved his rectitude, his courtesy, his charm and at the very height of the election, his equanimity. We could tell from his courage in defeat what a great President he would have been, had the victory fallen to him. Our admiration might find expression in Addison's famous lines:

> " 'Tis not in mortals to command success,
> But we'll do more, Sempronius; we'll deserve it."

But why delay you longer by commending his great qualities, his learning and his eloquence when we are all eager to listen to his address as soon as our Convocation is dissolved?

I present to you, for the degree of Honorary Doctor of Civil Law, Adlai Stevenson, amid the strains and stresses of national and international politics, the champion of humanism in word and deed, and himself the source.

Stevenson delivered the following speech:[3]

I suppose no greater honor can befall a scholar than an honorary degree from Oxford. But what of one who makes no pretense to scholarship? And who is an American? And even a politician; and an unsuccessful one at that! Indeed, I am reminded that Oxford is said to be the mother of lost causes, and I am also reminded that my political patron saint, Thomas Jefferson, said that ". . . a retired politician is like a broken down courser, unfit for the turf and good for little else."

So you will see how happy I am, how honoured I am, and how very grateful I am — to the Chancellor, the Vice-Chancellor, to the Hebdomadal Council, and to this whole community of scholars which is the source and treasure house of so much of what we call Western civilization.

Such kindness deserves a better fate than is in store for you, I regret to say. Indeed, while I was recording these words it occurred to me, as Voltaire observed long ago, that speech is certainly a very effective means of concealing thought. It also occurred to me how very fortunate I was to receive your degree *before* I spoke. At least I am assuming, Mr. Vice-Chancellor, that your degree, honoris causa, is irrevocable — irrevocable, or should I say even honoris sine causa.

This is not my first visit to Oxford, but it recalls the first. When I was a student at Princeton I came here one vacation with some college friends and took lodgings for a week.[4] One of our number had a theory of non-sightseeing travel. It so far prevailed that we never quite knew which college was which or where we were — except the day our punt capsized on the Isis.

It was a grand week. And if I gathered few facts and figures, I like to think that at the age of 19, at timeless Oxford, I too absorbed some respect and reverence here for the common heritage of the English speaking peoples, and the language, in Walt Whitman's words, "of all who aspire."

It was spring then, as it is now. The first war was over. Its wreckage strewed the continent and the homes of England. But it was the fresh,

[3] The text is based on a mimeograph copy prepared for release to the press.
[4] See *The Papers of Adlai E. Stevenson*, Vol. I, p. 82.

[7]

bright dawn of a new day. Here at Oxford national pride, conflicting interests, mistrust and jealousy between our countries seemed to me petty and impossible on that happy threshold of a new day of universal and perpetual peace.

I felt that way then, so many years ago, and I feel that way now — that what unites us is far more important than what divides us.

But that is easier for *me* to say and to feel than for *you*. When only last week I asked a friend just returned from England if I should talk about the Anglo-American alliance, which has suffered so much of late, his reply was: "There isn't any!" And then when I asked a prominent American historian what I might say to you, he reminded me that the barrier of dialect is the most formidable of all: "I have a hunch that you could speak in Thailand with a much better chance of being understood than you will have in Oxford. We are so near to complete understanding that the slight difference is ignored, with disastrous results. As long as an American wears braces on his teeth and an Englishman on his pants, how shall they ever agree?"

Despite all this good advice I want to talk to you a little about that unmentionable subject — Anglo-American relations. But it is of the *future* that I want to speak, because I did not come here to criticize or counsel *my* government or *yours* about Suez[5] and the unfortunate events of the recent *past*. I have done that rather freely about my government at home — for several years, as some of you may have noticed!

The importance of our Western alliance had not been made clear of late to most Americans, nor the whole truth about our foreign relations. How the American people can be kept honestly informed about their foreign affairs — which are their most important affairs these days — is, I think, one of our most pressing problems. And how truth can prevail against a vested interest in presenting a situation in one guise is still more difficult in this era of mass communication and mass manipulation of the public mind.

I hope we Americans have learned a lesson about the hazards of subordinating foreign policy to domestic politics from recent experience, just as I hope our French and British friends have learned some lessons about the conditions of successful coalition. The magnitude of our common misfortune is measured by the fact that, in the first place, Russia,

[5] For the British, French, and Israeli attack on Egypt in October, 1956, following Egypt's nationalization of the Suez Canal, see *The Papers of Adlai E. Stevenson*, Vol. VI, especially pp. 309–319 *passim*.

after a hundred years of frustration, has obtained a foothold in the Middle East. In the next place, she has attained her first post war objective of weakening our Western alliance. Finally, British-French prestige and influence have been grievously wounded, and we can ill-afford any diminution in our common store of influence in the world.

It is not for me to assess the responsibility for this misfortune; it is sufficient for present purposes that loss of mutual confidence is one of its most grievous consequences. But meanwhile other problems, new problems, arise in all directions to override preoccupation with our grievances. The changes in the Middle East should be enough, but there are plenty of others. Indeed, everywhere one looks it is apparent that the combination of British and American power, prestige and ideals can benefit the free world.

So I do not like what I hear in Europe about our crumbling alliance and it seems more imperative than ever. But the task of fostering it is different now in one very significant respect. In the past, the battle for and against the Alliance has been fought out mainly in the United States; British and European opinion, save for the Communists, has been all for it. Now the position is almost reversed. There is still plenty of criticism of Europe to be heard in America — the *Chicago Tribune* has not fallen silent — but there has never been a time when there was less criticism in principle of the policy of alliance. Looking back, Suez did astonishingly little harm to that idea, and perhaps some growing realization of our partial responsibility for what happened there explains why the anger and criticism evaporated so quickly in the United States.

On the other hand, there is some skepticism about the alliance on this side of the Atlantic. Those of us in America who, through the years, have helped to bear the burden of the fight for the alliance have perhaps acquired the right to ask our British friends, who also believe in it, whether they are quite sure they are not letting the case for it go by default. Perhaps the need for the alliance is too obvious, and its place in the hearts of your people too secure, to require argument or reaffirmation. It would nevertheless be heartening to your American friends, and would help to keep isolationist pressure down, if there were more frequent approving sounds from this side.

And your best friends are disturbed too, by the evidence reaching us that some Europeans regard the brighter prospects for the greater integration of Europe not so much as a means of strengthening our trans-Atlantic alliance but escaping from it. A "Third Force" I think is the catch phrase. I see nothing wicked about the idea of a Third Force. But it does seem to me a little foolish. There is no such margin of strength on our side of the Iron Curtain that we can afford to split up. The pages of history are sprinkled with examples of men who thought they could play the role of umpire and finished up in that of victim.

Now what are some of these urgent missions and these challenges rushing at us that we must meet together? They are not all caused by international communism. Some are the product of the equally startling technological and political revolutions of this dramatic century. Some are old tasks that are ever new. Even as Western man led the way first to political and then to economic freedom and security for the individual, I wonder if he is not summoned again to save the individual from extinction in the massive, collective society that is engulfing us.

As I see it, all the jobs we have to do, whatever they are — social, political, military — and wherever they are — at home, in Europe, Asia, Africa — spring from one concept — the supreme worth of human personality — and have one ultimate goal and common justification — the well being, the dignity, the survival of the individual. The freedom of the individual is the great goal of government. All the political devices we have contrived have that justification.

And it looks to me as though that poor fellow, the individual, was being squeezed from all sides at home and abroad. The world is growing at the rate of 40 million a year. Everything is getting bigger — farms, factories, business, labor, government. And as everything else gets bigger the poor fellow gets smaller. To paraphrase a familiar jingle:

> Everything is so big and I am so small
> I do not like it — at all, at all!

The growth of bigness and what it may be doing to individual enterprise and opportunity will concern us more and more I daresay. Probably what differentiates economic societies today is less whether there is capitalism, but whether there is room for the small enterpriser.

As populations grow, as it becomes harder and harder to extract our sustenance from the earth, be it corn or copper, and the complexity and vulnerability of industrial society increases, there will emerge greater and greater pressures for increased efficiency, bigger units, more elaborate organization and I suppose, ever more regimentation of the individual. We hear more and more about the problems of mass society — mass education, mass communication, mass production, mass consumption, and the massive dangers of massive conformity and manipulation of the mass mind.

The twin forces of automation and atomic energy are racing to revolutionize production. (At one British refinery, I am told six men per shift can now distill 5½ million gallons of crude oil a day.) As machines replace men and nuclear energy traditional fuels, the implications are immense, exciting and frightening. What happens to the displaced workers? Will the gap between developed and undeveloped nations be widened or narrowed? What will we do with the new leisure? Will production outrun absorptive capacity? Can man manage his creations without automating or atomizing himself? Is the individual destined to sink deeper into faceless conformity and obscurity? Are we creating Frankenstein — or a golden age?

Hand in hand with the spread of industrialization and atomic energy goes the power to manufacture the instruments of war and nuclear weapons. Yet we live in a state of international anarchy where there is no control whatever over the means of monstrous devastation, and where there appears to be a double standard of law observance — the United Kingdom obeys the United Nations, and Russia and Egypt don't.

I've attempted to suggest a few of the great and common tasks and opportunities we face. On the political front there are many more. I would like to mention two joint missions to which I think common consent gives priority if we are going to save our hero, the individual, from the worst fate of all — one is a settlement with Russia in Eastern Europe, and the other is our relations with the free peoples and new nations of Asia and Africa.

Walter Lippmann[6] echoes the view of many that: "The greatest question in the world is whether Europe can cease to be divided and can become united by negotiation and peaceable means." With Russia's empire in Europe bruised by the series of explosions in East Germany, Poland and Hungary,[7] the hour for a general European settlement may be approaching.

But it was not of Europe that I wanted to speak here today. This is Empire Day, and in the twilight of the imperial age I as an American wanted to express my admiration for Britain's historic accomplishments in the preparation and emancipation of subject peoples. I am confident that in the age to come the new nations of Asia and Africa will need and get her guidance in the great adventure of national life. Their well-being is, I believe, our greatest task together.

This year has seen the fixing of the timetable for independence in

[6] Columnist and author of numerous books on political subjects.
[7] Riots occurred in East Germany in June, 1953, in Poland in June and October, 1956, and in Hungary in October, 1956, all of which were quelled by Soviet troops.

Malaya and Singapore[8] — and with it virtually ends the period of direct British colonial rule in Asia. And the year has also brought the independence of Ghana, the first Negro colony in Africa to advance to full statehood.[9] A chapter ends in Asia. A chapter begins in Africa, and both bear the same stamp — the substitution of partnership and inter-dependence within a free association of peoples for the earlier phase of imperial control. Here surely is food for our reflection.

It is true, I admit, that the theme of empire and colonialism has not precisely gone by default in recent months. We have heard the diatribes of those expert imperial practitioners, Messrs. Bulganin[10] and Khrushchev,[11] roaring out, above the gunfire in Budapest, their warnings against Western colonialism. We have listened to Middle Eastern leaders who seem to find denunciation of Western imperialism quite compatible with dreams of empire of their own. A powerful voting bloc has been formed in the United Nations, whose single cohesive purpose appears to be the ending of Western colonial rule. In America, for good measure, voices have been raised to denounce the continuance of colonialism as a key issue of our present crisis.

But in this welter, one crucial fact is somehow overlooked. It is that the horse they flog is dead. In the last decade the colonial system in its old form has all but vanished from the face of the earth. The exceptions — in Algeria[12] or Cyprus[13] or tiny Goa[14] for instance — only prove the rule. In fact, one might say that Britain has been the most effective anti-colonialist of all. And while Britain has been liberating an Empire voluntarily, the Soviet Union has been creating one involuntarily.

It is painful to end imperialism in hatred and anger and bloodshed — the last chapter of so many empires in the past. The real achievement is to bring colonialism to an end, as the British have done in the last ten

[8] Malaya signed a pact ending British rule as of August 31, 1957. In April, 1957, Singapore reached an accord with Great Britain providing for a form of self-rule; the country, to be known as the State of Singapore, was to remain within the British Commonwealth, and Britain retained strong controls over the island.

[9] See *The Papers of Adlai E. Stevenson*, Vol. VI, especially pp. 453, 515.

[10] Soviet Premier Nikolai A. Bulganin.

[11] Nikita S. Khrushchev, First Secretary of the Communist Party, who ousted Bulganin in 1958 and replaced him as premier.

[12] Warfare between the Algerian National Liberation Front began in 1954, and resulted in France's granting Algeria a free government in 1958.

[13] Greek Cypriot guerrillas began a struggle against British rule in 1955, which culminated in the island's becoming an independent republic in 1960.

[14] India was disputing the claim of Portugal to Goa, an enclave on the West Coast of India that Portugal had held since 1510, and in 1961 invaded the territory. The following year Goa and two other Portuguese holdings became Union territories under Indian rule.

years, by a peaceful transfer of authority from metropolitan power to emergent nation — a transfer which preserves a living desire for continued cooperation and leaves a certain sense of shared history and destiny intact.

Perhaps it has been the peacefulness, the apparent painlessness of the transition that has led a part of world opinion to lose its perspective on this issue. We are unhappily so constituted that we write up the wifebeaters and forget the golden weddings.

And I think it especially important for an American not to forget that it was not only British Trade that flourished and grew during the imperial period. A world economy came into being. The Americas developed behind oceans guarded by British ships. More and more nations were drawn into the web of trade and development. It was a time when unimpeded growth seemed the order of nature, international payments were self-balancing, capital went where it was needed most; the Hidden Hand seemed effortlessly at work. And the Hand, though hidden, was largely British.

Not the least of the ironies of history is the fact that the 19th and early 20th centuries, to which, even today, many of my fellow countrymen look back as to a Golden Age, was an era underpinned, even for republican, anti-colonial America, by the workings of Britain's imperial power.

I hasten to add that in making my tribute to the high achievements of British imperialism, I do not want it revived. Nor, I think, do the people of Britain. For these transfers of power were rooted in principle — in the profound belief of our Western political faith that nations like men have the inalienable right to govern themselves. This is not a sudden latter day conversion. Burke stated the principle in Parliament almost 200 years ago,[15] while American colonists vindicated it in the field of battle.

The peoples of Asia and Africa, once exposed to British education, learned, as Americans had learned before them, that there is no place for servitude in the British constitution. They derived from their British governors the principles through which British government would be superseded. In the end, independence could be celebrated by *both* sides — as it was celebrated a few weeks ago in Ghana — as a consummation, not a separation; as the working out of principles and procedures held and revered in common, not as a rejection or a breaking away.

[15] Stevenson probably refers to Edmund Burke's speech "On Conciliation with the American Colonies" (1775).

There are also, I believe, strong economic reasons for ending the direct imperial rule. On the side of Britain herself, the burden of empire could no longer be safely, let alone comfortably, borne. With modern welfare policies and modern concepts of investment and expansion, the financing of dependent territories has become steadily more costly. At the same time, after two World Wars fought from the first day to the last, Britain's own capital reserves have been desperately depleted. In the last twelve years your countrymen have attempted with superb discipline to carry, Atlas-like, the burden of world-wide responsibility. The equivalent of the whole Marshall Plan aid to Britain was passed on to India through the release of sterling balances. Colonial welfare and development funds have been poured into Africa. Britain is a partner to the Colombo Plan for Asian expansion.[16] As banker to the whole sterling area it has, with fantastic skill, underpinned 50 per cent of the world's trade with a dollar reserve no larger than that of America's Ford Foundation.

But the strain has told. The recurrent crises of sterling — which certain critics in my country have been only too happy to blame on Britain's experiments in welfare, on "creeping Socialism" and the like — have been evidence of a weight of world commitments heavier than the economy can bear. The free nations, America not least among them, have purchased a considerable measure of stability as a result. But the price, for Britain, has been high.

For the subject peoples, too, the time had come for the transition. In growth and expansion, there seems to come a moment when only heroic efforts of energy and self-discipline can achieve the transition from a static to a dynamic economy. If the measure is — as economists inform me — the nation's ability to raise the share of annual income devoted to productive investment from, say, 5 to 12 per cent, this act of saving, this diversion of present needs to future hopes, requires a leadership, drive, and energy which foreign rulers, however well-intentioned, cannot provide.

Nor, for the sake of perspective, can one forget the less attractive features of colonialism — the arrogance, the social prejudices, the ruthlessness of some economic exploitation. This side of imperialism has been widely publicized. It is still much remembered by ex-colonial peoples. It is still live ammunition in the politician's arsenal. "Psycho-

16 The Consultative Committee for Economic Development in South and Southeast Asia, begun in 1950 and 1951 as an organization of British Commonwealth countries to aid in the financing of economic development in those areas of Asia, and later broadened to include other countries as members, including the Philippines, Thailand, Japan, and the United States.

logically speaking, the evils of colonialism have lived after it, and much of the good has been interred with its bones," as Grayson Kirk[17] has said.

Yet the problems the imperial age helped to solve still remain. The new nations of Asia and Africa are not less, but more than ever, in need of administrative stability, economic growth, and international security. They are all under steadily mounting popular pressure to show results in terms of economic expansion and human welfare. The whole post-colonial world is caught up in what I have called "the revolution of rising expectations." The belief, so widely held, that the ending of colonial rule would somehow automatically bring vast immediate benefits gives these aspirations an added urgency and impatience. So now, without imperial support, results have to be even better and quicker. Yet all the while, the explosive rise in population which modern health measures have brought about threatens even existing standards of well-being. Like Alice and the Red Queen, the new nations of Asia and Africa have to run faster even to stay where they are.

Moreover, Communism is at work to exacerbate and exasperate every tension, to widen each rift of ignorance and prejudice, to enflame already passionate nationalism, to spread a universal sense of resentment and mistrust. In a world already shaken to its foundations by technological change and political upheaval, the chief purpose of international Communism appears to be to frustrate any force of healing or pacification or patience or constructive wisdom.

This, then, is the background of our present post-colonial age — an age of massive change, of giant expectation, of ubiquitous, malevolent penetration and propaganda. It is hardly the world to which any of us looked forward, and, in some measure or another, the old needs are more pressing than ever. Social and economic advance even of a modest kind — let alone the peoples' dreams of grandeur — still demand administrative stability, trade and capital and international security. The imperial system no longer provides them. What is to take its place?

The answer of the emergent nations is naturally that they can provide these conditions themselves. Nationalism, newly crowned, can hardly give any other answer. But all the nations without exception are in fact in urgent need of trade and capital. Some of them — Indonesia comes to mind — need help to hold even a primitive administrative structure together. And the problem of security is the most baffling of all.

Here, I suggest, is the central problem in the great task of establishing new and better relations with Asia and Africa in the new post-colonial

[17] President of Columbia University.

phase. It is to devise ways of restoring some of the props provided by the old order while avoiding any semblance of domination. It is to assist in the search for internal stability, economic growth and external security without interventions which outrage national feeling and lead to a greater vulnerability to Communist agitation. It is a task of immense delicacy and immense urgency and on it turns, I believe, the future of the uncommitted world.

Denis Brogan[18] says: "We are living on borrowed time in Asia and Africa, and speed — with all the risks of disaster — is safer than delay with certainty."

Obviously the accomplishment of this great mission must depend in large measure on Anglo-American cooperation. And I would add that I am not one who believes that the United States, by virtue of its anti-colonial record in the Philippines and elsewhere, can expect a special acceptability among ex-colonial peoples. Sometimes this may be the case. But, in general, our wealth, military power and central position in the Western community expose us to much the same type of suspicion as the ex-colonial powers have to face.

Moreover, I don't share the illusion of some of my fellow countrymen that the cooperation and support of the Afro-Asian nations depends on our relations with Britain and France, and that we can somehow win new friends in Asia by losing old friends in Europe.

In the last ten years, I believe we in the West have become more aware of the gap created — in administration, in technical competence, in capital for expansion — by the passing of the old order and the immense growth in scale of the new needs. And I have heard about the proposals to establish a general overseas service as a successor to the various colonial services. Possibly here is the nucleus of a new type of service, drawing on the training and experience of your Commonwealth as a whole and ensuring that the more needy members of the family can get assistance from other nations in the Community.

But for many of the new nations, the most acceptable form of assistance is likely — for as long as it is needed — to be organized within a strictly international framework. In this field, too, a start has been made through the various agencies of the United Nations, and the Secretary General has suggested that a form of permanent International Civil Service might be set up to give the sustained effort and assistance the emergent nations need.

The provision of better qualified officials is only half the picture —

[18] Professor of political science at Cambridge University and author of numerous books and articles on the United States.

facilities for training them are also needed. But here too a start has been made on a large scale. The British record in the building of new universities in their overseas territories is impressive indeed, and I have visited several of these remarkable new institutions. And today there are, I believe, some 20,000 foreign students in America and 40,000 here in Britain. Yet I question whether we are yet thinking on a sufficient scale. How many there are in Russia and China I don't know.

But technical and educational expansion in the new nations, like everything else, must depend upon their economic development and expansion. We know that this process cannot be left wholly to the unguided promptings of private profit or the enterprise of private capital. Our hope is that private enterprise will play a major part in economic development, but it cannot do it all. The scale is too large. In many underdeveloped areas, the pre-conditions of industrialism — ports, communications, utilities — are lacking. Many governments do not wish to accept foreign private investment in key sectors of the economy. Yet it is on these sectors that expansion in other fields depends.

The United States has been concerned, one way and another, with this problem since the end of the war. There are many Americans who feel that foreign aid at the taxpayer's expense should stop. Yet probably most of our citizens still accept some economic assistance as a reasonable element in America's foreign relations, and certainly all the thoughtful studies support that conclusion. But there is much controversy about the scale, type and conditions of aid — whether it should be tied to military programs, whether it should be given only to reliably anti-Communist nations, whether neutrals and uncommitted states should be helped, whether the money should be in grants or loans or agricultural surpluses, whether national or international channels of administration are to be preferred.

It seems to me that the discussion has underlined certain conditions of success. The first is that a program cannot be fully effective unless it is sustained from year to year. It is, no doubt, for this reason that the government has sensibly proposed a program which can be operative for at least ten years and sets aside in each year some $750 millions for development loans. I am glad to say an approving word for the Eisenhower administration on this issue — (an infrequent experience for me!) — because a development program on the fiction that it is always going to end next year combines the maximum of potential waste with the minimum of effective forethought and planning.

As one outstanding recent study of the problem suggests, I think the aim should be to assist the new states to break through the "sound barrier" of capital formation, to increase their annual investment to the 12 per cent of national income needed to secure a continuous expansion in their means of production. The Communists, with their methods of forced savings, have here a short term advantage over democratic communities, which must lead and persuade and can't coerce the voter. China can "afford" an annual level of saving of 20 per cent of its national income, for it can deal drastically with the consequences of very low current consumption. But India cannot follow that pattern, and as a result may fall behind in terms of strict economic advance.

So if the new nations can supplement their own efforts to create savings with assistance in capital and trained personnel from the West, the Communist advantage could be balanced and the full advantage reaped from political freedom, from tolerance, decency and the spirit of cooperation.

Such an approach has the further advantage of giving a focus and an objective to aid which does not depend upon the cold war or the Communists' activities or the risk of this or that nation slipping away under the Iron Curtain. All these negative reasons for giving aid have the supreme disadvantage of being unattractive to the peoples concerned and of treating them as pawns in a Great Power game — and this is, for them, the essence of imperialism. And for this reason, too, I believe foreign aid would have a far more beneficent impact if a large part of it could be directed through such international channels as the Colombo Plan, or the various agencies of the United Nations, or multilateral regional development agencies.

By the same token, all nations, East or West, who can afford to should contribute in some degree to the capital needed. The United States, as the wealthiest and largest creditor nation, should no doubt give the lead, in its trading, its lending, and its tariff policies. But support for an enlightened international economic outlook among American voters is much more likely to be sustained and consistent if other nations are doing their share.

I think sound, sustained, rational assistance, uninvolved with the world's current battle lines, will make some contribution to another compelling and complex problem of our post-colonial phase — the search for external security.

I think we tend to forget that the Suez crisis, the instability hanging over the Arab oil lands, the Indonesian debt repudiation[19] or the high

---

[19] The Indonesian independence movement, in existence since the turn of the century, intensified after World War II under the leadership of Sukarno. In 1949 the Dutch transferred sovereignty to the Republic of Indonesia, leaving unsettled

handed liquidation of foreign interests in China[20] represent in a real sense a resurgence of the risks and uncertainties which led to the establishment of imperial control in the 18th and 19th centuries.

Our problem today is not — I would underline this point once more — to reimpose external control, but to prevent others from doing so and to develop another stability which permits peaceful, mutually advantageous relations and commerce to be carried on.

I think we can assume that the issue is not one of direct attack by either of the two Communist giants. The danger of universal thermonuclear destruction is now clear to all. But how about local disturbance and disorder, or the risk that local troubles — as in the Balkans before 1914 — will finally spread into general disaster?

You will not expect from me a panacea for this the most baffling, delicate, involved and dangerous of our immediate problems. All I can hope to do is to suggest possible lines of advance. In the first place, I do not believe that we can use force unilaterally to counter what one might call civil torts in international relations. To the uncommitted world, the gunboat sent to recover debt is the very essence of imperialism. But in the present state of law and order we dare not wholly renounce the use of force unilaterally either. Nor can a nation one day renounce force and the next exert it, and command much confidence.

It is, of course, a grave weakness of our international society that redress for wrongs should be so dubious. And the recent spectacle of Russia sitting in judgment on Britain while brutally violating the law in Hungary, or of President Nasser seeking justice before a tribunal whose decree he ignores, will haunt our memories and temper our reliance on the machinery we have created for years to come.[21]

Yet surely the answer is not more anarchy, but less. Don't we have to try to build up a generally respected body of law to cover the rights of

---

the question of control of the western part of New Guinea. A union was set up to regulate the relationship between the two countries, which Indonesia abrogated in 1956 as a result of the continued delay in settling the New Guinea question; and later that year Indonesia repudiated its debt to the Netherlands. In 1957, Dutch property was nationalized and Dutch citizens were expelled.

[20] Following Chinese Communist intervention in the Korean war, the United States imposed economic sanctions against the People's Republic of China, which retaliated by seizing American properties in China and freezing official bank deposits.

[21] In the UN Security Council in October, 1956, both Russia and the United States condemned the Anglo-French attack on Suez following Egyptian President Gamal Abdel Nasser's nationalization of the canal. Britain and France had filed a complaint in the UN over the seizure, and Egypt filed a counter-protest, which was placed on the agenda after the United States had cast the deciding vote in favor of consideration.

investors and the obligations of governments, rather than to seek compensation by force?

Force is legitimate to resist force. And is it not the proper principle that the United Nations, through a properly established police force, has the right to intervene in a local breach of the peace to maintain order until a settlement has been accepted? Is it not a sound principle that in any crisis involving invasion or border clashes, the United Nations should be challenged to instant intervention? And only if it proves unable to act have other powers the excuse, or rather the responsibility, to intervene to prevent further violence? Should intervention then be hedged round with explicit guarantees that it is simply and solely to end the local conflict?

The risk remains that any intervention on the Western side in the fluid, unsettled ex-colonial areas could invite a counter-intervention on the Soviet side and thus set in motion the widening spiral of general war. For this reason, I wonder if we should dismiss all thought of ways and means of withdrawing areas lying between the great centers of Western and Communist power from the larger tensions of the Cold War. We instinctively draw back from such phrases as "neutralism" or "uncommitted areas" or "buffer zones." Yet if in such a region as the Middle East the arming and counter arming of rival groups of small states by rival Great Powers could be replaced by an internationally supervised arms embargo and frontier control, not simply the Middle East but the whole community of nations would gain in security. Probably the Russians prefer things as they are. But our security would hardly be lessened and the explosive possibilities might be radically reduced if we made a direct attempt to find out. The effort would at least expose the Russian propaganda which depicts them as the pacifiers thwarted only by Western determination to divide the area with alliances and blocs.

The passing of the old colonial age has been so sudden and the emergence of the new post-colonial phase so fraught with new risks and dilemmas that it is not surprising to find the Western powers uncertain and fumbling in this first decade of the new era. The changes in thought and habit which it demands on both sides of the Atlantic are vast and, in the normal rhythms of history, would have demanded scores of years, even centuries, to emerge. Now they must be learned overnight. Small wonder, then, that we blunder and hesitate.

In the United States we need to recover from the illusion of effortless security and wealth which a fortunate nineteenth century, shielded by British power, has taught us to regard virtually as a natural right. We have to learn that there is no safety now in isolation, no safety in drift or self deception, that no single "solution" or formula or declaration will rid us once and for all of the need of having a foreign policy at all.

You in Britain have the opposite task — to recognize that British power today is not adequate to all the tasks of international order in the post-colonial phase and that some of the great achievements of British imperialism — stable administrative order in Asia and Africa, world-wide economic advance and a high measure of international security — must now, as it were, be placed in trust and shared with other like-minded states.

In a sense, both our nations face the same challenge — to give up a dream of isolation — for us, isolated inaction, for you, isolated responsi-bility. And we each have to avoid an opposite temptation — the Ameri-cans to rush to the further extreme and attempt isolated leadership, the British to seek withdrawal and irresponsibility within their island fron-tiers. In fact, both nations face the far more exacting challenge of ac-cepting years of joint responsibility, of working patiently with other nations in pursuit of joint solutions, not despairing at early setbacks, not rejoicing too soon, but recognizing with realism and courage that world order is not made in a day, or sustained with half thoughts and half measures.

And I must say frankly — and finally — that since the war, since Potsdam,[22] I don't think we in the West have lifted our sights to the level of our new dangers and obligations and opportunities.

I say "since Potsdam" because on the first day of that conference Secretary Stimson[23] handed Winston Churchill a piece of paper on which was written "Babies satisfactorily born." In other words, the [atom] bomb had exploded in New Mexico, and with the babies a new age was born in a violence undreamed of.

Nothing could ever be the same again. The old Europe was gone forever. The heir to the Western Empire, which had for so long dis-posed almost absentmindedly of the destinies of far away peoples, was now a center of weakness. None of the old terms of reference really made sense any more. Yet we went on talking of Europe, France, Ger-many, as if everything was the same, as if we knew what they meant now. But the old meaning was gone and we had no notion of what their new meaning would be. And most of our leaders didn't even know that they didn't know.

[22] The Potsdam Conference of Stalin, Churchill (supplanted by Clement Attlee), and Truman in July and August, 1945, at which Allied plans for reestablishing European peace were discussed and a demand for unconditional Japanese surrender was issued.
[23] Secretary of War Henry L. Stimson.

War, too, has lost its immemorial meaning. When conquest is the equivalent of suicide, then it is no longer a means of imposing decisions.

And ten years after Potsdam came the conference at Bandung,[24] where the "voiceless ones" found a voice and the imagination of half mankind was released. In a few decades we of the West — the guardians of that divine fellow I talk so much about — the individual — will not even be heeded unless we lift our tired minds to originality, invention, daring. If our armor, our military might, is inadequate, if it can never be adequate again — must our spirits, our minds, our imagination be inadequate too — we who have proclaimed and died for the greatest, noblest values of human freedom and of respect for every individual child of God?

With these things ahead of us, it would be my prayer that the British, who have weathered so many tempests and not been shaken, who have lived through so many crises that have seemed to strike to the foundations of their national life, should not, for any passing misunderstanding, crisis, dislike or pique, withdraw themselves from the great enterprise of our time and seek an isolation which will be as illusory for them as American isolation proved for us.

These are days when British steadfastness, shrewdness, balance, imagination are more needed than ever before. I recall what my fellow countryman, Ralph Waldo Emerson, wrote of you just one hundred years ago. "This aged England . . . pressed upon by transitions of trade and . . . competing populations — I see her not dispirited, not weak, but well remembering that she has seen dark days before — indeed, with a kind of instinct that she sees a little better in a cloudy day and that, in storm of battle and calamity, she has a secret vigor and a pulse like a cannon."

Britain's greatest days were still ahead of her then. I think they still are.

On June 1, Stevenson and his law partner, William McC. Blair, Jr., flew to Lisbon en route to Ghana.

[24] Twenty-nine African and Asian nations met in April, 1955, in Bandung, Indonesia, with the aim of promoting economic and cultural cooperation among the participants, who were all strongly opposed to Western colonialism.

To Carol Evans[25]

June 2, 1957

Dear Carol —

We're stalled here in Lisbon for a few extra hours & I'm sending along some stuff for filing* as I gradually clean up my brief case in preparation for the sun, sweat and confusion of Black Africa.

It has been a busy journey so far and thanks to Bill's expert mgt [management] we haven't missed an appointment yet. I can't say the same for sleep, however! After seeing all the Prime Ministers, Foreign Ministers, etc. etc. I'm reminded again & again that my diary collapsed on the second day! — which is exactly on schedule for the adventures of the last 17 years!

Oxford was beyond description, however, and the dinner at All Souls [College] the pinnacle of academic exaltation. When finally after wining, dining, des[s]erting and coffeeing in 4 s[p]lendid, ancient rooms I could keep silent after toasts no longer, I struggled to my giddy feet and mumbled thru the wine that I had dined with the great, near and far, but this was the first time I had dined with the Warden of St. Anthony, the Principal of All Souls and the Master of Jesus! It worked; tho I wasn't too sure of the gaitered Rector of Christ Church who was sitting close by.

You may receive an incredible scarlet gown and huge Tudor hat — (and probably an incredible bill!) They are not a fancy dress costume, but the paraphanalia of my new estate — D.C.L., Oxon.

Bill is well and weary after working all day (2 full time girls in London) and prowling all night, while I talked, ate and rushed from place to place — also as usual. Tell the boys[26] that if I haven't got a client, I don't think I've lost one!

Yrs
AES

P.s. I worry about the house, the children, the office, my affairs and an occasional report would help.

* regular mail

[25] This handwritten letter is in the possession of Miss Evans.
[26] His law partners in Chicago, W. Willard Wirtz and Newton N. Minow. Early in 1957, the law firm of Stevenson, Rifkind & Wirtz was formed in partnership with the New York firm of Paul, Weiss, Rifkind, Wharton & Garrison. The Chicago partners were Stevenson, Wirtz, Minow, and William McC. Blair, Jr. Edward D. Mc-Dougal was counsel and John Hunt became an associate.

Stevenson spent June 3 and 4 in Ghana, and on June 5, he and Blair arrived in Johannesburg.

To Walter L. Rice[27]

June 6, 1957

Dear Walter,

Bill Blair and I spent Monday and Tuesday in Ghana staying in "the castle" with Prime Minister [Kwame] Nkrumah and I have drafted this "report" hurriedly on the airplane en route to Johannesburg.

While there Sir Robert Jackson[28] made my appointments and drove us around and, of course, I had ample opportunity to talk with him, as well as Dr. Nkrumah, who left just before me for the Prime Ministers' Conference in London, Mr. [K. A.] Gbedemah, Minister of Finance, Mr. [Kojo] Botsio, Minister of Commerce and Labour, Sir Arku Korsah, the acting Governor General, a number of other Ministers, as well as the American Chargé d'Affaires and his Economic Officer, Sir Leslie Mc-Carthy, Chairman of the Commercial Bank of Ghana, John Eggleston, Chairman of the Bank of Ghana, Sir Patrick Fitzgerald, head of Unilever for West Africa, and sundry other knowledgeable people.

I shall not attempt here to summarize the political situation or even make a brief estimate of future prospects for stability and responsibility. While the situation leaves much to be desired and isn't as good as I expected to find, due to the decline in cocoa prices and the rise in political foolishness, it is certainly still good enough and hopeful enough to warrant active promotion of the Volta project. (Actually the completion of the Volta project could well spell the difference between the success or failure of Ghana as an independent "Western" state.)

Instead let me here just report on Volta:

1. Nkrumah gave Leith[29] (who was unknown to him, to Jackson, or to anybody!), Utah Construction Co. and another contractor, an exclusive option to "negotiate" for financing the whole project to July 18. Jackson was in England when it was done and much put out by it all and Nkrumah was a little sheepish about the "option" when I talked to him and told him, incidentally, that Leith was *not* representing Reynolds. He assured me that he gave them the option only "to stir things

---

[27] Vice president and a director of Reynolds Metals Company, one of Stevenson's clients.

[28] A British planning consultant who served from 1953 to 1956 as chairman of the Preparatory Commission of the Volta River Project, which proposed to dam the Volta River in Ghana in order to provide hydroelectric power for local industries and to operate a smelter for the production of aluminum.

[29] Unable to identify.

up." He professed to be irked by all the carpet-baggers that have turned up since Independence, altho I suspect the African Ministers are a little flattered and pleased by the new commercial *courtship*. Also there are plentiful rumours about corruption, and no doubt money like music hath charms, especially to some of these gents who are more familiar with the latter than the former.

2. On July 1 Sir Robert [Jackson] becomes head of the Development Commission of Ghana and ceases to be an employee of the British Treasury. After that and after the expiration of this "option" to Leith et al on July 18 he will feel freer to negotiate and to press ahead for a showdown on the project within the two years which he thinks should be the maximum for a decision, because so much is in suspense pending a decision on the Volta.

3. In view of the "option" and all the confusion about who speaks for who, I asked Nkrumah point blank who he would want Reynolds to deal with in the future and he said without hesitation "Sir Robert and myself and no one else."

4. The present plan is for Nkrumah to make it clear in Whitehall at the Commonwealth Prime Ministers' Conference that he wants to know promptly if the U.K. has any further interest in the project. Then in October, Mr. Gbedemah, Minister of Finance, means to call for a decisive conference between the four partners (U.K., Ghana, Alcan, and British Aluminum Ltd.) before the end of the year. If they are not ready to go ahead on some acceptable basis then the inference is that Ghana will hope to proceed with other partners, presumably a larger group including Americans.

We should have ample opportunity to follow changes in this scheduling thru Jackson and also Nkrumah who talked to me about coming to New York in September to make Ghana's first appearance before the General Assembly of the United Nations. I think he will do it and Gbedemah will be there in September or October for the International Bank and Fund meetings.

5. As to access to the bauxite which has been conceded to Alcan and Aluminum Ltd., Mr. [Peter] Thorn[e]ycroft, Chancellor of the Exchequer, assured me in England that there would be "no trouble" if American capital was included and he hoped it would be. (A changing attitude, by the way, that I found even more pronounced in Brussels with respect to the Congo.) There is much confusion and uncertainty about the concessions in Ghana and tho the legal rights are not too clear, Gbedema[h]'s idea is that the bauxite should be included in the project and therefore owned or rather enjoyed in the ratios of investment or on some negotiated basis. Others say, with a fine show of

[25]

sovereign arrogance, that the concessions will all be cancelled, or, at least, those that have not been exploited.

To sum up: Unless the mysterious option group performs some miracle, I think the matter will be back on the tracks after July 18; *that Reynolds' interest has been made emphatically clear to all concerned;* that Robert Jackson can be counted on to keep us informed and, indeed, might hope that Reynolds could take some leadership in organizing a capital group to help with the project. I have asked him — when the proprieties permit — to put on paper some alternative schemes for financing the project with possible governmental and private sectors indicated and price tags attached, because I'm sure whatever is done it won't be much like the original concept.

I think the suggestions in your letter of giving Mr. Leith no encouragement is correct, altho I know nothing about him, nor does anyone out here. (Remind me to tell you about my telephone talk with Marriner Eccles, the Chairman of the Utah Construction Co. when I return!)

I can think of nothing more to be done on this for the present. However, I expect to go back to Ghana on June 30 and July 1 on my way north, and if you think of anything else I could find out, let me know by cable or mail care American Consul General at Leopoldville, Belgian Congo, where I arrive June 22 to see the Governor General and the "Inga" dam site.

And now a word or [on] two more matters.

I had to go to Belgium on law business for an American client and to discuss the Congo trip which they are arranging for me. While in Brussels I saw most of the leaders of the Government and also the King and the old Queen Mother, Elisabeth. You must remind me to tell you and Richard[30] about my tea party with that octogenarian enchantress! I found the atmosphere, as you doubtless know, quite different. This time Sengier[31] and his superior officer of the Société Générale, van Straaten,[32] with whom I dined, made their interest in American capital in the Congo emphatically clear. So did the King, who sent for me, and also the Minister for Colonies and the Foreign Minister. I am by no means sure just how to evaluate this interest and part of it was doubtless merely friendliness and protocol in a country where I have old connections and much goodwill. They have laid on an elaborate sightseeing trip for my party across the Congo from Ruanda to Leopoldville and I have promised the Governor General an evening for a party in the latter

[30] Richard S. Reynolds, Jr., president of Reynolds Metals Company.
[31] Unable to identify.
[32] Unable to identify.

place before I leave for Nigeria. We are also arranging to fly over the Inga project site, about which I still know very little more than you told me. If you think of anything I should do in the Congo on your behalf beyond "good public relations," let me know at Leopoldville.

The other matter relates to the concluding paragraphs of your letter of May 27 — the huge aluminion [aluminon?] project in French West Africa which I have heard something about in France and out here. When passing through Dakar, the Governor General of French West Africa came to the airport (at 1 A.M.!) to greet me and urged me to come back on my return to Europe after July 1. I do not know whether there is anything in connection with this project that you would like to know but I suppose the information could be had if I stopped off there. I believe the site in French Guiana [Guinea] is about an hour and a half or so by air south of Dakar. Here, likewise, you should inform me as promptly as possible. I could, of course, go back to Paris very easily as I shall be in Italy and Western Germany and perhaps Scandinavia before returning at the end of July. I suppose whatever information is needed is available there as well as Dakar.

The General Motors West African man, whom I saw in Accra, is confident of a large development in West Africa, and is already at work trying to establish dealer connections. As you know, there is, however, little water power in the vicinity as I understand it, but the use of Volta or Inga water power to process French Guiana bauxite is, I suppose, in everyone's consideration.

It has been a weary journey so far but I am getting used to that and will have an agreeable party with me for the balance of the African trip, including my son and daughter-in-law who will be in Johannesburg today.[33]

With best wishes to you, Richard and Louis,[34]

Cordially yours,

P.S. In view of the mention of various personalities, I think it would be well if this letter were not duplicated or circulated widely. In other words, please treat it in *confidence*.

---

[33] Stevenson's old friends Mr. and Mrs. Ronald Tree and Alicia Patterson, publisher of *Newsday,* Mrs. Tree's daughter Frances FitzGerald, and Mr. and Mrs. Adlai Stevenson III accompanied him on the remainder of the trip.

[34] Louis Reynolds, executive vice president and a director of Reynolds Metals Company and brother of Richard S. Reynolds, Jr.

To Borden Stevenson and John Fell Stevenson

June 6, 1957[35]

Dear Boys:

We have arrived in Johannesburg after a few busy days in Paris and Brussels and an even busier fortnight in England. My speech at Oxford went off well and the honorary degree ceremony was impressive indeed. The dinner at All Souls College in the evening was even more so! I can't wait to exhibit my scarlet robes and huge Tudor hat to your admiring audience.

I saw the Prime Ministers and Foreign Secretaries and all the officials, and found France in the usual crisis, Belgium quiet and prosperous, also as usual, and Britain rapidly emerging from the post Suez depression and bitterness. My only unusual experience so far was the long session with the little King in the Palace in Brussels and I found him a shy, sensitive and insecure and thoughtful lad who seemed more concerned that we see the condition of the native in the bush than the development of the cities in the Congo. His grandmother, old Queen Elisabeth, now going on ninety, sent for me and I went to see her in her little chateau in the country. She was a great hero of the First war period and I found her as beautiful and vivacious as I had expected. She weighs probably less than 100 lbs. but is still a musician, sculptress and painter of talent.

We had tea alone and then she took me on to the terrace and insisted on taking photographs of me, although I am not sure that she got the camera focussed on the target. Finally I insisted on taking photographs of *her* too and we ended up with much merriment surrounded with Ladies and Gentlemen in Waiting. It was all very reminiscent of a royal era that is past.

In Paris I lunched with the Ambassador and Mrs. [Amory] Houghton and they talked of John Fell's visit to Marion [Massachusetts] for their daughter's debut party. In London I did a lot of business for the Encyclopaedia [*Britannica*] and the Film Company and had some interesting and new experiences. Uncle Ernest [Ives] and Buffy were there and also Lady Jackson off and on.

We had a couple of hot steaming days in Accra in the new State of Ghana on the way down where I had some business to transact. We stayed in the old 16th century Danish castle which was formerly occupied by the British Governors and has now been taken over by the new African Prime Minister. If it was a little incongruous it was not uncom-

[35] Beneath the date Stevenson wrote: "(Victory day in Calif. 1956.)."

fortable! And now we are in Johannesburg where we have met the [Ronald] Trees and Adlai and Nancy are due this afternoon. Evidently they took a side trip to see Nairobi and a little of Kenya on the way down from Cairo. I am glad they did it although it will take a day or so off the time here.

This week-end we go down to Cape Town for sight seeing and then start through the Rhodesias to commence the trip through the Congo, which should be very interesting. The Belgian Governor has taken charge of this and arranged the itinerary, cars, guides, etc. From there we go up to see Dr. [Albert] Schweitzer, unless his wife's death prevents it, and then to Nigeria, where the British have arranged three full days of sight seeing from one end of that huge country to the other.

I will also stop in Liberia for several days and perhaps in French West Africa before I say goodbye to Adlai and Nancy in Lisbon on July 7.

I wish I knew where you were and what you are both doing and I am hopeful that this brief report of my adventures will reach you before you are both sailing or flying out the Golden Gate.[36] Certainly we couldn't have contrived to keep further apart!

I pray that all will go well and that you will not forget that an occasional note is helpful — indeed *imperative!**

I think it best to write me in care of Miss Evans and let her forward it in view of my schedule, and I hope Borden will have a chance to stop off and see some of my friends in San Francisco on his return from Hawaii as per my earlier letter. It can't hurt and it might be useful in the future.

With much, much love from a wandering Father to his wandering sons,

DAD

* Miss Evans will forward whatever you send.

While in Johannesburg, Stevenson discussed clients' business with Harry Oppenheimer, an executive of the Diamond Development Company and the Anglo-American Mining Company, and he and his party visited the Premier Diamond Mine near Pretoria. Stevenson discussed the Nationalist government's policy of apartheid, or institutionalized racial discrimination, with many people, including the Anglican Bishop, and visited the segregated slums where the Africans lived.

On June 12, at a press conference before leaving for Southern Rhodesia, Stevenson stated: Honesty compels me to say that the policy of

36 John Fell had a summer job with American President Lines aboard the S. S. *President Polk,* and Borden was contemplating a trip to Hawaii.

*total racial separation does not seem to me either practical or realistic in
a modern state where white and nonwhite are interdependent." He
added that the march of time could not be halted and "repression, fear,
and indignity will only increase racial consciousness and solidarity and
hasten the day of reckoning and reconsideration."*[37]

*From Southern Rhodesia, Stevenson and his party flew to Albert Na-
tional Park in the Belgian Congo.*

To Mrs. Eugene Meyer[38]

June 15, 1957

Dear Agnes —

At the moment I'm exactly astride the Equator — lying in a sleepless
bed by a rushing stream at the foot of the Ruenzari, the Mountain of the
Moon, in full moonlight! Today we spent in this incredible game park
and were within 50 feet of this very lion or a close relative!

Love,
ADLAI

To Mr. and Mrs. Ernest L. Ives[39]

June 21, 1957

Dear Ernest and Buf,

We have reached Leopoldville at last after ten days of incessant
travel from Johannesburg through Rhodesia and all across the Congo. I
think we have seen every kind of indigène, pygmy and giant, and every
kind of scenery, jungle, savannah, mountain and marsh, that the world
offers.

And certainly we have enjoyed the most remarkable hospitality and
concern from the Belgian officials in city and bush all along the way.

---

[37] Chicago *Tribune*, June 13, 1957. Stevenson's traveling companion, William
McC. Blair, Jr., recalled: "The Governor's quiet fury one day in Johannesburg
when the concierge of the hotel refused to permit a young African who had an
appointment with the Governor to enter the hotel. The Governor descending to
the hotel entrance and then walking around the block with the young man, who
wanted nothing more than some help in persuading his government to let him
accept a medical scholarship in the United States. The African's desperation equaled
only by that of the Governor, who was unable to help him." "A Dazzling Decade,"
in *As We Knew Adlai*, p. 241.

[38] Lecturer and writer on problems of education, wife of the chairman of the
board of the Washington *Post*, and a close friend and confidante of Stevenson's since
1955. This handwritten postcard is in the Agnes Meyer files, Princeton University
Library.

[39] The original is in the Elizabeth Stevenson Ives collection, Illinois State Historical
Library (E.S.I., I.S.H.L.).

No one is sick but everyone is exhausted, I fear, and tomorrow we set off in the French Governor's plane up into Equatorial Africa to see [Albert] Schweitzer, and on and on and on!

It has been a delight to have Adlai and Nancy. He is writing articles for "The Boston Post"[40] as we go along and his industry warms my heart. Nancy is delightful and gentle and wise as always. The [Ronald] Trees and Alicia [Patterson] are having the time of their lives and little Frankie [FitzGerald] is bearing up like a veteran. Bill [Blair]'s good humor, of course, never changes and his management has kept us on schedule without a hitch every step of the way. The Government has provided us with motors and couriers and courtesy galore and this evening we dine with the Governor General, the Provincial officials, and the African Regional Councillors.

South Africa was beautiful and depressing, more so even than before. The tension is mounting and the anxiety is just beneath the surface of the Whites, both British and Afrikaans. We had a good visit on the Cape, but it was pouring rain and the sight-seeing was disappointing although we did see a couple of the magnificent old Dutch estates and, of course, I had a long session with the Prime Minister.

After visiting Schweitzer we go on to Nigeria, Ghana, Liberia,* and Europe where I had planned to travel about until the end of July after visiting the Plimptons[41] for a week in Italy.

A letter awaiting me here from Carol Evans reports that Borden did not go to Hawaii. I hope that he has been down to Bloomington to see you and has looked in at the Pantagraph.[42] I will send him a telegram on his birthday July 7, from Lisbon, which reminds me of yours on July 16 too! I am afraid we are getting awfully old but I seem to have a good time and keep interested all the same. I pray that you do likewise and if I did not succeed in telling you how much it meant to have you in England with me, let me do so now! That experience and having Adlai and Nancy along this time have reminded me more poignantly than

* A message from the Reynolds Aluminum Co. now looks as tho I should also go to French Guinée & Dakar to check into the Bauxite possibilities. I'm tired and don't relish the thought of more.

[40] Adlai III wrote several articles which appeared in the Boston *Globe* June 3, 6, and 16 and July 4 and 16, 1957.

[41] Mr. and Mrs. Francis T. P. Plimpton. Mr. Plimpton, a New York lawyer, had been Stevenson's Harvard Law School roommate, and Mrs. Plimpton, the former Pauline Ames, had been among their friends at the time. See *The Papers of Adlai E. Stevenson*, Vol. I.

[42] The Bloomington, Illinois, *Daily Pantagraph*, in which the Stevenson family held a substantial minority interest. See *The Papers of Adlai E. Stevenson*, Vol. I, especially Part Five.

ever how much of my life and travels have been alone, without kith or kin.

Much love,

AD

On June 22 Stevenson and his party flew to visit Dr. Albert Schweitzer at Lambaréné, French Equatorial Africa, Dr. Schweitzer recently had issued a statement warning that the testing of nuclear weapons was endangering mankind. When Stevenson stepped from the airplane and asked Schweitzer whether he felt the world was facing a grave crisis, Schweitzer pointed to the grass and replied: "That grass is probably already radio-active, and certainly could be made so. Cattle eat such grass, and become radioactive. The milk we drink becomes radioactive. . . . The very air is already, and can easily be further poisoned by fallout. . . . Can you imagine such a thing? . . . Never — I repeat Never — has the whole world faced such a danger; nothing to approach it; never since the beginning of time. . . ."[43]

During the next two days, in addition to visiting the hospital and the surrounding area, Stevenson and Schweitzer spent a great deal of time in discussion. Frances FitzGerald noted in her diary, "The Doctor and Mr. Stevenson sat in a corner discussing their views on how best to stop the hydrogen bomb tests."

Stevenson made the following notes of his visit to Lambaréné.

Schweitzer Hospital — Is it like Abraham? *goats bleating, dogs barking, hens cackling, babies crying, chattering noise arising from hospital; not a quiet place!*

1st — Must stop nuclear testing. (Story of his radiologist who had two monster children).

2nd — *Then talk about danger of wastes from atomic reactors;* explosion; radioactive cooling water, disposal of wastes. Teller[44] knows all about it!

Shouldn't talk now — testing first — then dangers of peaceful use discussion.[45]

[43] Memorandum of Stevenson's visit by Clara Urquhart, dated June 24, 1957. Mrs. Urquhart, a longtime friend of Dr. Schweitzer, acted as interpreter during the visit.

[44] Edward Teller, professor of physics at the University of California and an atomic scientist who helped develop the hydrogen bomb.

[45] Dr. Schweitzer said to Stevenson, "The Pope in his naivete talks calmly of the peacetime use of nuclear energy, and does not realize that with the present means of utilising such energy, the dangers inherent in its peacetime use, are as great as if

If eliminate uranium & use just Hydrogen — could tell Arabs to drink their oil!

———

Squalor of hospital explained by staff.

1. *As identical as possible with life of people* — if too good can't adjust to village or won't go home.

2. *Allays suspicion* — still think make "lot of money," & that staff all have lot of money. "All white men have." *Don't seem to understand concept of charity — why should they do this?*

3. Stoicism of Sch[weitzer]. — wantless — hates rocking chairs — burn — no backs on his stools — practices what he preaches.

S[chweitzer]. believes can't understand meaning of life — have to go beyond thought — with pain, suffering — whats meaning of it all — beyond thought is mysticism, to somehow *feel* that it is alright.

In heart & soul is urge to do good, to create; gulf stream of warm water in cold sea. Not to be explained but to be sensed.

Suffer with a sense of purpose; that it is alright.

Believes benevolent & enlightened despotism is best & thats what he practices! But must be both; have lately seen too many who were just enlightened — Hitler & Muso! Doesn't rail against world — just lives & works as he pleases in his little corner of it.

Hosp. — built by hand! — poverty — close ink [?] — not important — "Awe & respect for life" — his philosophy — what is important. Hospital just his expression of that faith.

Stevenson made the following statement in Brazzaville, French Equatorial Africa, on June 24, 1957, after returning from his three-day visit with Dr. Albert Schweitzer and a survey of the dam site and natural resources of the Gabun River.[46]

Dr. Schweitzer is gratified by the world's reception of his declaration in April on the dangers of testing atomic devices. Heretofore man has had to obey nature. But now he has learned how to subjugate nature and Dr. Schweitzer considers this the most dangerous period in history. He commented that his views were not as widely reported in the United States, Britain and France as elsewhere. But he feels that his declaration

---

one megaton bomb were tested every day." Memorandum by Clara Urquhart, June 24, 1957.

[46] The text is based on a Xerox copy of Stevenson's handwritten statement.

may have encouraged scientists to express their views more freely, and he was much pleased by the recent petition signed by two thousand American scientists calling for an end of nuclear bomb tests.

His information agrees with the reports I brought him, and he feels that public opinion, led by scientists who know the facts, is now moving rapidly in the right direction and will soon influence governments.

He sees the issue of nuclear tests as a challenge to moral forces in the world. In that connection he detects some hopeful signs of a new spiritual awakening, and that the spirit of a true culture based on human concern for one's own life and for the life of everything that lives is increasing.

It was a great privilege to visit Dr. Schweitzer, to see his famous hospital in that steaming jungle, to meet his staff of remarkably selfless, dedicated people, and to talk at length with a great soul and a wise and good man.

He has no present plans to visit America but he does not exclude that possibility in the future. Meanwhile he has much important writing to complete, an enormous correspondence to handle and he must arrange affairs at Lambarene so that the future of his work there is assured when he can no longer carry on.

Finally, I and my party are deeply grateful to the High Commissioner for providing us an airplane to facilitate our journey and observation of the resources of Gabun, and also to Mr. and Mrs. Le Nicault, Minister of Mines for accompanying us. I was particularly impressed with the enormous water-power potential at the dam site and with the uncalculated wealth of minerals and oil in this country.

While in the Congo, French Equatorial Africa, Nigeria, Ghana, and Liberia, Stevenson discussed with the appropriate government ministers the Reynolds Metals Company's interest in investing in these countries. On July 8, Stevenson and Blair flew from Dakar to Paris.

To Carol Evans[47]

July 9, 1957

Dear Carol:

I reached Paris yesterday after an all-night trip from French Guinea, and go on this afternoon to [Francis T. P.] Plimpton. Meanwhile I have taken advantage of Bill Stoneman's[48] office to catch up with correspondence. . . .

[47] The original is in the possession of Miss Evans.
[48] Foreign correspondent of the Chicago *Daily News*.

[34]

I am weary as can be after the journey but the aluminum developments toward the end were very encouraging and perhaps Reynolds and [Walter] Rice will come to Paris to resume negotiations the end of the month before I return. After a visit to Plimpton and Stanley Woodward[49] in Austria, I don't know what I will do but I will keep you informed. I probably will come back the end of the month, returning through England to see Barbara Jackson and Robert. As you know, she has had a major operation but I talked with her on the phone and she is cheerful and recovering rapidly.

I hope all is well with you and the children — and also that Bill [Blair] will find some enlightening mail in Rome.

Hurriedly,
A.E.S.

Stevenson rested at Balbianello, the villa of Mr. and Mrs. Francis T. P. Plimpton at Lake Como, Italy. The following postcard undated was written while he was there.

To Mrs. Ernest L. Ives[50]

[no date]

Dear Buff —

Thanks *so much* for your letters and what a relief to hear good news about Borden — I havent heard a *word* from him since I left, but there may be a letter from him in Rome where my mail was sent. I'm distressed to hear about the frailties of Lila[51] & Ernest [Ives] but we will have to reconcile ourselves to the advancing years, and certainly he has been surprisingly well, if not vigorous, most of his life. I will be here with the Plimptons a few more days and then probably join Mary Lasker[52] & Flo. Mahoney[53] and drive over to the [Stanley] Woodwards in Salzburg before returning to Paris on aluminum business toward the end of the month. May come back thru England to see

[49] Ambassador to Canada, 1950–1952, and treasurer of the Democratic National Committee, 1953–1955.

[50] This handwritten postcard is in E.S.I., I.S.H.L.

[51] Miss Lila Ives, Ernest Ives's sister.

[52] Widow of advertising executive Albert D. Lasker and president of the Albert and Mary Lasker Foundation. She was at her home in the south of France at the time this postcard was written.

[53] Mrs. Florence Mahoney, a Washington socialite active in Democratic party affairs and an associate of Mrs. Lasker in the Lasker Foundation. She was visiting Mrs. Lasker at this time.

Barbara [Jackson] — she's had a major operation . . . & is doing well but despondent — Home early in August —

Love to the Ives & Alverta[54] —

AD

To Mrs. Eugene Meyer[55]

July 11, 1957

Agnes dear —

Do you know this villa built by a Cardinal and the Viscontis around a 14th century chapel and monastery? Certainly there can be few more beautiful private places in the world — and don't dismiss lightly the observations of a responsible politician who is also a veteran of the vale of Kashmir, Hong Kong, the Mountains of the Moon — not to mention Mt. Kisco!![56] I will have a week's rest here with my friends the Plimptons of N.Y. after the African adventure, which was exciting and rewarding beyond account, but too strenuous for a weary old man!

I *pray* you are well, beloved Agnes, and I *know* you are busy. Perhaps there is a letter from you in Rome where I was supposed to go and didn't. Bill Blair is there now & will join me soon here — "with the mail," which, on the whole, I need with its reminders of the other world I've escaped from the past six or seven weeks in darkest Africa — where the light is now beginning to penetrate and the sleeping to stir.

From here I may go next week to visit the Stanley Woodwards in Salzburg — where I have never been — for a few days. After that I don't know. I had thought to go to Germany & look about a little — with a furtive view to clients! — before returning to Paris for a couple of days of business before coming home the end of July or early August. I feel quite carefree & careless for once — and I'm afraid my law partners think so too!

I yearn for your news, my great, noble and beloved friend —

ADLAI

To Carol Evans[57]

July 12, 1957

Dear Carol:

I'm at Villa Balbianello at last! And it is even more beautiful than I

---

[54] Alverta Duff, housekeeper in Stevenson's Bloomington home during his youth and an employee of the family since that time. See *The Papers of Adlai E. Stevenson*, Vol. I.

[55] This handwritten letter is in the Agnes Meyer files, Princeton University Library.

[56] The Meyers' home in New York.

[57] This handwritten letter is in the possession of Miss Evans.

expected. But how much rest I'll get what with all the correspondence, the visitors, etc. etc., I don't know. Because of interesting developments in French Guinea I have sent long reports to [Richard] Reynolds and Mr. [Walter] Rice may come to Paris to negotiate later on. If so, I'll have to join him, therefore it is hard to make firm schedules or plans. I think I'll stay here until next Wed — the 17th — and then go on to Salzburg, thence maybe for a day or so to Vienna to see something of the Hungarian refugee situation which I've heard about here a good deal and may want to say something about at home. After that, depending on Reynolds, I'll probably go back to Paris, perhaps by way of Bonn. I don't believe I'll try to do the Scandinavian junket this time.

Please send copies of this letter enclosed to the following . . . at the S[an]. F[rancisco]. Chronical promptly by air mail — with a note from you saying that I directed you to send copies of this handwritten letter from Italy to them for their information.

So glad you're making some progress with the papers at Newberry and the House.[58] This is so important to me to get all this stuff in some kind of order so I don't have to worry about it and can find things if need be.

Bill [Blair] is in Rome where he evidently had the mail sent but is coming here to join me today. I suppose Ad & Nance are settled in at Libertyville and I hope they have Bea's[59] mother living there and looking after them. And now, more letters to write — when all I want to do is loll in the sun and drink in the beauty after this exhausting journey.

Best to all,

AES

The Aga Khan, spiritual leader of the Ismaili Muslim sect, died on July 11, 1957. Karim Khan, who had roomed with John Fell Stevenson at Harvard University, was named the new Aga Khan.

To Karim Aga Khan[60]

July 13, 1957

Dear Karim:

First, my congratulations! And not least of all because of the digni-

---

[58] The Newberry Library in Chicago was storing Stevenson's campaign records, while many of his most important papers were kept at his home in Libertyville.

[59] Beatrice Holland, wife of Stevenson's farmer. Her mother had been asked to help out until a full-time housekeeper could be found. See *The Papers of Adlai E. Stevenson*, Vol. VI, pp. 460, 520.

[60] This handwritten letter is in the possession of the Aga Khan IV.

fied, simple and forthright way you have handled yourself in this difficult situation. It has made an excellent impression that has reached even
this lovely retreat where I am visiting some friends! Moreover it is an
accurate reflection of you yourself — and *being yourself*, if I am not
mistaken, will be one of your hardest tasks.

An Associated Press man called me from Milan to report some nice
things you said about John Fell and me, but I could hardly understand
him. Anyway, I'm most grateful and John Fell will be too. I've had some
amusing letters from him. He's enjoying himself immensely and his
duties as an apprentice purser are not exactly burdensome!

I'm returning to America thru Paris & London the end of the month
and if there is anything I can do for you don't hesitate to let me know. *I
mean it.*

I'm confident that you are going to make a great success of your
responsibility —

Yours,

*After the stay with the Plimptons, Stevenson, Blair, Mrs. Mary Lasker
and Mrs. Florence Mahoney visited Mr. and Mrs. Stanley Woodward at
Salzburg, Austria. Then Stevenson and Blair flew to Bonn, Germany,
where Stevenson had a series of talks with U.S. Ambassador David
K. E. Bruce, Chancellor Konrad Adenauer, cabinet ministers, and
German industrialists. At a press conference Stevenson described Germany's postwar recovery as a "miracle." He said that he had proposed
to German leaders that they might repay the United States for its aid,
"without which Germany's present prosperity would have been impossible," by helping take some of the foreign aid load off the American
taxpayer. He recommended that the United States, Britain, and France
and perhaps other countries create an international agency to help build
the economies of underdeveloped countries.*

*When asked at the press conference what he thought of Senator John
F. Kennedy as a potential Democratic candidate for President, Stevenson replied: "I am sure he, like a number of other Democrats, commands close scrutiny at the next Democratic convention. I think well of
him."*[61]

The following letters were written in Paris.

[61] Chicago *Tribune*, July 28, 1957.

To Mr. and Mrs. Stanley Woodward

July 30, 1957

Dear Stanley and Shirley:

I am mortified that I haven't written you a proper note long before this. Our journey northward was agreeable, despite the rain, and we had a little glimpse of some lovely country and of the phenomenal German recovery. The gals[62] deserted us at Coblentz to return by air. There followed three happy, informative and exhausting days with the [David] Bruces in Bonn. I am not sure who was most exhausted, but I am afraid I don't bring serenity to my hosts.

We talked often of our days with you in that enchanting place. I loved it in spite of the adverse weather, and pray that I didn't exhaust my welcome. How kind and patient you were to submit to such an invasion without protest and with such infinite thoughtfulness and courtesy.

With affectionate regards to both you and that wonderful staff.

Cordially,

P.S. After a few days here in Paris, I am going to London and thence home — to work — and how I dread it!

To John Fell Stevenson

July 30, 1957

Dear John Fell:

. . . I have had a fascinating journey in Austria and Germany and am now again staying with friends in a splendid villa near Versailles, in a manner to which I am almost getting accustomed. In a few days I go on to England and then home, arriving about the 7th. After a few days in New York, I will go on to Libertyville and get things ready for your return!

I suppose you have kept up with the news about Karim [Khan] but I am enclosing some clippings from a Paris magazine in case you haven't seen them.

I yearn to see you and hear all about what you have seen and heard — and learned!

Love,

---

[62] Mrs. Mary Lasker and Mrs. Florence Mahoney, who had joined Stevenson in Italy.

On August 6, Stevenson held a press conference in New York City. He urged Americans to declare a "six months moratorium on self-righteous moralizing and preaching." ("Anti-Americanism," he observed, was "much too common in Europe and Africa.") He advocated a "sustained, consistent policy of constructive foreign aid and investment — not just military aid — to insure that the underdeveloped countries can develop." He added: "And I think the burden should be shared by others, above all, Germany."

Stevenson remarked that he wished the Soviet Union had accepted Secretary of State Dulles's proposals for aerial inspection[63] but "all is not lost and I hope we will press on, for the burden of arms is intolerable and nuclear war unthinkable. I believe we should now concentrate on ending nuclear weapons tests and production, for that is the world's greatest danger, and there is, I think, some hope of Russian agreement to suitable safeguards in that direction."

In reply to a question, he criticized the civil rights bill pending in the Senate as not strong enough but he stated he would rather have this bill than "none at all."[64]

When asked for his opinion of the defeat in the House of Representatives of a bill to provide federal funds for school construction, Stevenson stated that the failure to assure an adequate education for all children constituted not only a "national extravagance" but "criminal negligence." "I wish," he said, "President Eisenhower had talked as loudly to the Republicans in Congress as he did to the voters last year."[65]

Alistair Cooke wrote in the Manchester Guardian, August 8, 1957:

> . . . Mr. Stevenson's press conference was pleasant, as it always is. But the lively interest of it was in his manner. Politicians, defeated politicians especially, are not unlike other men in trimming their figures to fit their next suit. Mr. Stevenson may say in all conscious honesty that his national political career is at an end. But his natural destiny is now more than ever what a close friend or two has imagined it to be from the beginning. He is the obvious choice as

[63] A week earlier in London, Secretary Dulles had presented the Western proposal for "open skies" inspection zones to guard against surprise attacks. See the New York Times, August 1, 1957.

[64] The bill called for the creation of a Civil Rights Division in the Justice Department, the granting of powers to seek injunctions against obstruction of voting rights, and the creation of a Civil Rights Commission, which was appointed November 7.

[65] The President, honoring a campaign pledge, submitted a bill authorizing a four-year, $1.3-billion program for school construction, $750 million for purchase of school bonds, and authority to back the bonds' credit. School desegregation problems and zeal for budget-cutting led to its defeat in the House on July 25 by a vote of 208–203, with the Republican vote 111–77 against.

Secretary of State in the next Democratic Administration, if it should come in 1960. Yesterday he acted as if he knew it.

Mrs. Hermon Dunlap Smith wrote Stevenson inviting him and anybody he wished to bring with him to a vacation at the Smiths' summer home at Desbarats, Ontario.[66]

To Mrs. Hermon D. Smith

August 9, 1957

Ellen dear:

Africa is behind me — and Desbarats in front! Your note welcomed me to New York, and I am already aching to fall off the dock. I talked to Borden by telephone and it looks as though we might come up Sunday, August 25, and stay until after Labor Day if that is convenient. I doubt if he will want to bring anyone, but I have written a note to Alicia [Patterson] reporting that she would be welcome if she cared to come. I saw her the other night, but neglected to talk about it in the confusion.

Because I want to be with Borden without too much diversion, I think I won't press him to bring anyone with him.

With love to you all, and especially my godchild,[67]

Yours,

To John Kenneth Galbraith[68]

August 9, 1957

Dear Ken:

After three months in Europe and Africa and a few hours in New York, I am convinced (1) that no one is interested in Europe and Africa, and (2) everyone is interested in hard money and inflation.

Certainly this problem, plus the rising needs for social investment, must be emerging as the great issues for the present. If you and Seymour[69] think this is correct, couldn't we get together for a talk here in New York September 9 or 10? My partner, John Wharton, would like to sit in and I've assured him that you and Seymour could explain the

---

[66] See Hermon Dunlap Smith, "Politics and R & R," in *As We Knew Adlai*, pp. 28–41.

[67] Her son, Farwell Dunlap Smith.

[68] The original is in the Galbraith papers, John F. Kennedy Memorial Library.

[69] Professor Seymour Harris, Mr. Galbraith's colleague in the Department of Economics, Harvard University.

mysteries of hard money and inflation, which seem to bedevil Europe as well as America.

I'm leaving now for Chicago and will be there until September 9. If you could come down for an evening around that time, I would be free either the 9th or 10th.

My love to Kitty,[70] and I pray you are both well.

> Yours,
> ADLAI

To Sam Rayburn[71]

August 9, 1957

Dear Sam:

I am back this week after three months abroad. And if you were not so busy, I would come to Washington and demand an evening and unload a couple of hours of uninterrupted talk about my adventures. But I'll restrain myself, and perhaps by the time I see you again I'll have forgotten what I was going to say, anyway, and you will be spared.

Meanwhile, however, I must pass on something that has come to my attention during my few days in New York. I understand there is pending before a conference committee a supplemental appropriation for the United States's participation in the Brussels International Fair of 1958, to the amount of about $3,000,000. I was in Brussels not long ago and heard a great deal about the Fair from the Prime Minister, the Foreign Minister, et al., and a good deal from the Belgians and Americans and others about the efforts that the Russians and the Iron Curtain countries are going to make.

I would hope very much that the United States would not suffer too much by contrast with them, let alone our allies abroad. The Soviet Union will spend between fifty and sixty million dollars. I gather this is a lively concern in many quarters, and therefore I am taking the liberty of adding my voice to the many you must have heard in behalf of the passage of this little appropriation.

Now forgive me for annoying you, and affectionate regards.

> Yours,

On August 10, Stevenson returned to Libertyville. At the Chicago airport he repeated to reporters many of the statements he had made in New York City. He remarked that it was going to be good to be home

---

[70] Mrs. Galbraith.
[71] Speaker of the House of Representatives.

after visiting sixteen countries. "This trip reminded me," he stated, "that the best way to study our foreign policy is to see for yourself. Next to that is good newspaper reporting." He expressed the hope that the Eisenhower Administration would end its ban on U.S. newspapermen visiting the People's Republic of China. "The Administration defeats our own best interests and puts a premium on ignorance instead of information."[72]

Waiting for Stevenson was a letter from Samuel Brightman, deputy chairman for public affairs of the Democratic National Committee and editor of the Democratic Digest. Mr. Brightman enclosed a copy of the three brief paragraphs that the Washington Post gave to Stevenson's New York press conference and a copy of the fifteen paragraphs given to Hollywood star Jayne Mansfield's visit to Washington, D.C. Brightman wrote: ". . . I am thinking of starting the Volunteers for 40-18-35 for the 1960 campaign."

Stevenson sent the copy of the three paragraphs on his press conference to Mrs. Eugene Meyer, whose family owned the Post. He also enclosed the lengthy story about Miss Mansfield and Brightman's letter, writing at the top of the letter: "Agnes — You'll love it!

AES

p.s. But the UP discourages me — not for the first time!"

To Mrs. Eugene Meyer[73]

[no date]

Agnes —

It is so discouraging! After saying many thoughtful things about Africa & Europe — important things — this is what gets printed — the answer to some question.

AES

---

[72] Chicago *Sun-Times*, August 11, 1957.
[73] This handwritten letter is in the Agnes Meyer files, Princeton University Library.

Part Two

Law and Public Service

Columnist Gerald Johnson thanked Stevenson for his review in the
New Republic, August 12, 1957, of Johnson's book, The Lunatic
Fringe. *Mr. Johnson predicted a boom for Stevenson for 1960.*

To Gerald W. Johnson

August 13, 1957

Dear Gerald:

Thanks for that good letter and your charitable comments about my
comments on you. . . .

As to my future, I seem to be less interested than my friends. As for a
boom, I am sure you know it would be as unauthorized as scarlet fever.
And I am not trembling with apprehension that that sheriff's posse
bristling with shotguns is likely to come and get me. For me it will be
the law business, with an occasional utterance and some concentration
on foreign affairs, which was my first interest. I hope the crystal ball also
has more of Gerald Johnson in it.

Warmest regards.

Cordially yours,

James Eldridge wrote in the Indianapolis News *about Stevenson's
recommendation that West Germany assist with aid to underdeveloped
countries. Mr. Eldridge informed Stevenson that he had discussed the
matter with Robert Lasch of the* St. Louis Post-Dispatch *and Paul
Ringler of the Milwaukee* Journal.

To James Eldridge

August 14, 1957

Dear Jim:

Thank you for your note. I am glad you did not overlook the sugges-

[47]

tion that Germany could do something herself for the free world as well as expiation of sin with her present abundance. I doubt very much that they will for a variety of reasons, expounded to me by Adenauer[1] at great length, and others, notably the Finance Minister;[2] but the Ruhr barons (and the Middle Ages produced nothing rougher, tougher and abler) thought well of the idea. Some of them, like Krupp, are doing some major projects, probably at a loss. Here it went unnoticed, but that I have become quite accustomed to.

I am glad you spoke to Bob Lasch and Ringler. There are many aspects to this and I would be glad to talk with you about it when you come here in October. I am not sure that bilateral transactions are always the best, a la Marshall Plan, and especially for Germany. You have probably heard of the Commission for Technical Cooperation in Paris for Africa to study needs and then distribute the assignments among participating countries.

There could also be a little enlightened writing about the practicalities of so-called independence in Algeria. I think our anti-colonialism sometimes runs away with our understanding and our judgment and inflaming it unrealistically does us no good.

Cordially,

Congressman Brooks Hays of Arkansas wrote Stevenson that he and others were building national loyalties into the Democratic party structure. "We need your help and advice," he said, and declared: "We cannot survive as a Congressional party."

To Brooks Hays

August 14, 1957

Dear Brooks:

I find your letter of May 17 on my return from three months travel in Africa and Europe. I think you are right — we cannot survive as a Congressional party. And if the country feels about the President and the administration the way the rest of the world does, we won't have to after 1960.

I yearn to see you.

Yours,

---

[1] Konrad Adenauer, chancellor of West Germany.
[2] Fritz Schäfer.

To John Fischer[3]

August 14, 1957

Dear Jack:

I have talked to Jane Dick, who has brought me up to date about the Oxford speech. Of course you are at liberty to use any part of it in an article that you wish.

I count it as one of my more important utterances, but it had, I understand, virtually no press here although it attracted considerable attention in Britain. This was to emphasize the indispensable role of the English speakers toward the preservation of the individual and a world in which he can survive. This seemed to me to afford an opportunity to talk about the much misunderstood subject of colonialism, what the British had done and the future of the ex-colonial territory. There are too many people expounding emphatic views about colonialism and imperialism who haven't travelled in the ex-colonial world, in my opinion.

I look forward to seeing you soon, I hope.

Yours,

To Francis T. P. Plimpton

August 14, 1957

Dear Francis:

I am afraid I still owe you and Pauline a bread and butter letter — and what bread and butter, wine and cheese it was! But I propose to deliver my thanks in person — and soon I hope. Which brings me to the business at hand.

You will shortly have a call from one of my New York partners, John Wharton, asking you to act as independent counsel to the Field Foundation in connection with some decisions that will have to be made in a matter in which this firm finds itself in the embarrassing position of dual representation. I don't think the work will be onerous, and that you will consent to do it is the fond wish of Hermon Dunlap Smith and

Your obedient servant,

P.S. I will be in New York for a meeting which you will be requested to attend the week of September 9, and I hope to have an explanation of all your misdeeds since I left you at Balbianello without food, shelter, raiment or wine!

[3] Editor of *Harper's* magazine.

While in New York City en route to Chicago, Stevenson had spent an evening at the farm of Mr. and Mrs. Eugene Meyer at Mt. Kisco, New York. Mrs. Meyer sent Stevenson two editorials from the Washington Post *praising Senator Lyndon Johnson's achievement in steering the civil rights bill through the Senate without a filibuster. She also enclosed a review of her book,* Education for a New Morality (*New York: Macmillan, 1957*).

To Mrs. Eugene Meyer[4]

August 15, 1957

My dear Agnes:

Thanks for your letter and the enclosures. Certainly the Post went to town for Senator Johnson as I have seldom seen it, and I am afraid I am a little perplexed by all this.

The review of your book enchants me and I am delighted that it is attracting the attention it deserves, at least among the understanding.

The evening at the farm wasn't enough, but it was a wonderful aperitif, and I am grateful to both dear friends who have come to mean so much in my life. Eugene was so interesting and helpful to me. . . . What a remarkable man and what a fruitful life. As to his lady, well, she will never relax and tend her laurels — and I hope she doesn't.

Blessings and much love,

ADLAI

Wilson W. Wyatt, who had been Stevenson's campaign manager in 1952, wrote him about Kenneth S. Davis's A Prophet in His Own Country: The Triumphs and Defeats of Adlai E. Stevenson (*New York: Doubleday, 1957*).

To Wilson W. Wyatt

August 15, 1957

Dear Wilson:

I am back from my endless journeys and find your letter of July 20. I hope the book is all right but these highly personal accounts make me very uncomfortable, I confess.

I am eager to see you. Have you any plans to be here or in New York during the autumn? I shall be back and forth and perhaps we can arrange something, soon I hope.

[4] The original is in the Agnes Meyer files, Princeton University Library.

I did a prodigious amount of work for the Reynolds Company during my travels in Africa and think I may have started something in French Guinea that interests them. Walter Rice met me in Paris and we had some negotiations about which I want to tell you. The scramble for bauxite in West Africa is well advanced and they should have a position, I think, unless large deposits develop closer at hand.

I pray that all is well with Ann[5] and the children.

Yours,

Loran B. Cockrell wrote that the Reverend Richard Paul Graebel of Springfield, Illinois, who had been Stevenson's pastor during his term as governor, had been recommended for their church in Madison, Wisconsin. He asked Stevenson to express his judgment of Mr. Graebel.

To Loran B. Cockrell

August 19, 1957

Dear Mr. Cockrell:

I have your letter of August 13. My regard for Reverend Richard Graebel is limitless. He is not only a forceful preacher but an original and imaginative thinker. And what minister can sing Stille Nacht in German better than anyone in the choir! He is much beloved by everyone in his congregation in Springfield and commands an enviable respect in an even larger community.

I can recommend him on all counts most unreservedly.

Sincerely yours,

Senator Lyndon B. Johnson sent Stevenson a copy of the speech he delivered the night before the civil rights bill passed the Senate. He added that there was an effort to kill the bill on the basis that it did not go far enough.

To Lyndon B. Johnson

August 19, 1957

Dear Lyndon:

I am back at last after the long journey in Africa and Europe and find your good letter of August 14 on the top of my mountain.

---

[5] Mrs. Wyatt.

The civil rights debate certainly has been another major test of your extraordinary management of our Democratic majority. And I emphatically agree that the bill as it appears to be emerging has merits which, happily, seem to be better perceived now from day to day. As I attempted in my ignorance to say on my return, if the President vetoes it it will certainly be evidence that he wants an issue more than legislation.

I know you haven't spared yourself during the session and I pray you haven't abused yourself.[6]

Cordially yours,

To Walter Reuther[7]

August 19, 1957

Dear Walter:

In Sunday's paper I saw the announcement of your proposal to the auto manufacturers to modify contract demands in exchange for price reductions. This is the kind of leadership we must have. I'm glad it came from labor, in the present climate of opinion, and I'm not surprised that it came from you. Congratulations, and I hope we can have a talk some day. I have some idea how trying these days have been for you.

Cordially yours,

To Lady Barbara Jackson

August 19, 1957

My dear Barbara:

Thank you for your sweet note from London and the wonderful enclosure (which I promptly loaned and have now lost!).

If our London encounter was good for you it was even better for me and I have prayed anxiously that I didn't exhaust you what with theatres, parks and motoring. . . .

I assume you and your forces are settled into the Ghana trenches once again and that MacDuff[8] is exploring the garden which, as I recall, needed some of your attention. Even if it is hot, consider yourself blessed with all those servants. At home our Nancy [Stevenson] is in the kitchen with only distant hopes of reinforcement.

This likewise doesn't count as a letter but when such a thing will happen I can't foretell with the mountain accumulated in my absence still unscaled. Please tell Robert that I have his excellent letter which

[6] Mr. Johnson had suffered a heart attack in July, 1955.
[7] President of the United Automobile Workers.
[8] Her son, Robin.

marshals the situation with perfect clarity and I will acknowledge it presently.[9]

Much love to you all,

To Humphrey Waldock[10]

August 20, 1957

My dear Sir Humphrey:

I am sending you with unbecoming immodesty a book which I could hardly recommend as I opposed its publication.[11] Anyway, some professor friends of yours at Harvard have published this account of my last campaign. I suspect it is "for the record" as I can hardly envision a raid on the bookstores when it comes out.

My other sons have been duly impressed with my Oxford robes, but, skeptical always, demanded to see my "diploma" — but I have none. Perhaps Oxford does not bother with such trivia. But if it does, I am begging!

I think often of that happy day and when I do I think of the many kindnesses of you and your wife.

All good wishes.

Cordially yours,

Novelist James T. Farrell wrote Stevenson a lengthy letter analyzing the decline in individuality and remarked that "patient and steady explanation, coupled with continuing thought and observation" would in time alter the conformity of the present.

To James T. Farrell

August 20, 1957

Dear Jim:

I am sorry that your letter of August 10 has only now reached the top of the heap that awaited me after a long journey abroad. It is a most interesting letter, and some time we must talk about the problem of

[9] Sir Robert Jackson had described investment possibilities for the Reynolds Metals Company in Ghana.

[10] Chichele Professor of Public International Law and fellow of All Souls College, Oxford University.

[11] Adlai E. Stevenson, *The New America*, edited by Seymour E. Harris, John Bartlow Martin, and Arthur Schlesinger, Jr. (New York: Harper, 1957). In fact, Stevenson approved publication of the book and cooperated in its compilation. See *The Papers of Adlai E. Stevenson*, Vol. VI, pp. 486–487, 501, 524.

individuality. I agree that there has been little inducement to individuality and I think you have said something wise and true, that is, examples before us make it clear to youth that there is little need to sacrifice yourself to the anguish of thought, the risks of experiment and error, and the discipline of clarity in order to be a success.

I must thank you for a great phrase — "the institutionalization of banality." Of course it is dangerous. Any exaltation of ignorance and conformity and mediocrity is subtle, sinister poison in a growing, changing, boiling world. I suppose, too, that patient explanation, steady patient explanation, is not only necessary but the only solution. I am afraid I don't have the patience, nor am I too sure of my lance or the location of the windmill.

It is always good to hear from you.

Cordially yours,

William Benton sent Stevenson a draft of a statement commenting on Connecticut Congressman Thomas J. Dodd's announcement of his candidacy for the Democratic senatorial nomination. Mr. Benton asked Stevenson to make suggestions. He praised Dodd's record in Congress and said he would be a strong candidate, as would Mayor Richard Lee, of New Haven, and Chester Bowles. He added, "As to my own intentions, I can only say that anyone who has had the privilege of representing Connecticut in the United States Senate, as I have done, knows well what an honor and opportunity it is. No one can deliberately turn his back on such an opportunity — and that includes me. I would welcome the opportunity to serve again."

To William Benton[12]

August 20, 1957

Bill —

I think this is OK — and my scratchings are not important. It is spontaneous, friendly and guileless — makes every one happy and you *distinctly* available & interested, but not an aggressor. I think it also preserves your value as weight in someone's direction if you are eliminated —

See you soon —

ADLAI

[12] The original is in the possession of the estate of William Benton. Mr. Benton died on March 8, 1973. At the time this volume went to press, his widow and four children had indicated that they wished to deposit his papers at the University of Chicago.

Had Geoffrey's[13] daughter for weekend and arranged Lincoln trip for her to Springfield and Louisville.

AES

Clara Urquhart sent Stevenson some photographs taken during his visit to Dr. Schweitzer. She also quoted from a letter from Dr. Schweitzer to her: "To talk of serious matters with Stevenson did me good; I became fresh again; I appreciate Stevenson as a sincere, [illegible] and serious man and consider it important that he has a future in public affairs before him."

To Clara Urquhart

August 22, 1957

Dear Clara:

I should have thanked you long before this for your parting note in London with some more of Enrico's[14] lovely pictures — this time of moi meme. I think you are right that he has done an excellent portrait but I am a little self-conscious about showing it around.

Which is not to say that I am a spring, reluctant to drip in a briny ocean! What an exquisite verse that is, and I am grateful to you for sending it to me. If you compared me to a brook in your notes, I will be delighted, of course, but your excellent reputation for truth and veracity, as we lawyers say, will suffer, with me at least.

I have been keeping your notes until I could get off on a little holiday with my son Borden, to read them in leisure and tranquillity. The chaos about my office and home, with children but no servants, and the accumulation of three months, has even frustrated newspaper reading; and what a delight that has been!

In a very interesting piece that Adlai [III] wrote about his visit to Schweitzer appears this paragraph:

"There is irony at Lambarene. Few of Schweitzer's manuscripts are prepared for publication. Few ever will be. The world will never know the reason in the Doctor's ideas because the Doctor wants only to prepare his hospital for the day he dies. That will be the day when

---

[13] Geoffrey Crowther, editor of the *Economist.*
[14] Enrico Pratt, an Italian artist, poet, and musician and a friend of Mrs. Urquhart's.

his ideas are lost to man, and electricity finally comes to his hospital."[15]

Adlai tells me that you were his source. But it conflicts with the understanding that I had that he had two priorities: the future of the hospital and the conclusion of "The Kingdom of God," a synthesis of his philosophy.

I have imposed on you so much and for so long I hate to do it again!

With warm regards to Enrico and everlasting thanks to you, I am

Cordially yours,

P.S. My staff gets a lot of letters asking for comments on my visit to Schweitzer and in desperation I have hastily dictated something that might be mimeographed and slipped into form letters. May I ask still another favor — your blue and red pencils and general improvement!

Stevenson enclosed the following draft in his letter to Mrs. Urquhart.

MY VISIT TO DR. SCHWEITZER AT LAMBARENE SUMMER OF 1957 — ADLAI E. STEVENSON

In June I spent three days with Dr. Albert Schweitzer at his primitive hospital deep in the steaming jungle of equatorial Africa. They were days I shall never forget. He is well, magically strong and vigorous for a man of 83 who has spent so much of his life in relentless toil in such an unhealthy place. Even today he refuses a chair and perches on a wooden stool at the work table in his small, crowded room. His day is almost twenty hours of exertion with the running of the hospital, correspondence, manuscripts, visitors, heartening his heroic staff, and each and every day doing physical labor about the place.

Visitors to Lambarene do not always understand why his hospital is so primitive — without electricity, running water and modern comforts. Perhaps they don't fully understand how a relatively little money has to go a long way, for so many thousands of patients each year, or why he wants primitive natives from the forest to feel at home in his hospital. He believes that changes in a way of life must come gradually. A reverence for life must not be confused with indulgences that soothe the body and atrophy the spirit.

Now in the evening of his crowded life of music, theology, philosophy

15 Boston *Globe,* July 4, 1957.

and humanity, he has two principal preoccupations: the future of his hospital on the banks of the jungle stream, and the completion of a work on Christianity and possibly some further volumes on his philosophy of reverence for life. He counts this the most dangerous period in all human history, because men, heretofore controlled by nature, has now learned to control nature. But will he, has he, the wisdom and restraint to master the nuclear forces he has released?

To Queen Mother Elisabeth of Belgium

August 21, 1957

Your Majesty:

I have just had a visit from the Belgian Consul in Chicago, who has delivered to me your note of August 8 together with the photographs. The latter are a happy and permanent reminder of a visit with you that I shall never forget, and I am deeply grateful to you for sending them to me. Let me also add that I am deeply impressed with your talents as a photographer!

My journey through the Congo was a fascinating experience, made comfortable and enlightening by the infinite courtesies of the Belgian officials along the route. My visit with Dr. Schweitzer at Lambarene enhanced my admiration for that sainted man — even if it didn't enhance my admiration for his very primitive hospital. The latter, I am afraid, shocks many people because it so little resembles modern Western hospitals. But there "le grand docteur" has ministered to the suffering for more than forty years, and only the blind could be indifferent to the immensity of his service to humanity over those trying years of poverty and improvization under difficult circumstances.

I talked to him about your proposal for a conference of some of the world's leaders of thought, theology and philosophy and a declaration about the crisis of mankind in the atomic age. He said that this was the "most dangerous period in all human history" because man, who has always been subservient to nature has now learned to command nature — but not how to *control* the forces he has released. However, he was disinclined to take the initiative in convening a meeting such as you suggested. I think he is anxious to withdraw from the area of public controversy and to devote himself to arranging for the future of his hospital and the completion of a final book.

But I am writing you at unnecessary length and he may have written you himself as I suggested. Please forgive me.

I shall hope very much that if I can return to Belgium for the Exposition next year I may have the privilege of paying my respects. I almost did so with your charming grandchild, the wife of Prince Alexander of Yugoslavia. They were good enough to invite me to fly with them to Brussels for [from] Versailles not long ago, but I was obliged to come home.

With profound gratitude for your thoughtful note and the precious photographs, I am

Most respectfully yours,

To Robert Kintner[16]

August 21, 1957

Dear Bob:

I am no television expert, or even fan. I haven't had time! But one of the really whimsical, charming things I have seen on this medium, and for which I blame you exclusively, is Kukla, Fran and Ollie.[17] Besides, Burr Tillstrom, its creator, is a client of my small but recherché law office!

But the purpose of this is to inform you that for reasons wholly incomprehensible to me this charming bit of satire, wit and fantasy — good for young and old as the medicine man says — is, I understand, about to go off the air. Surely such assassination, murther, and mayhem cannot be permitted in this enlightened land of culture and sophistication.

So what are you going to do about it? Surely your fertile and well paid mind will have relief and remedies for such public ills.

Besides, how is my godson[18] and my girl?

Cordially yours,

To Richard S. Reynolds, Jr.

August 23, 1957

Dear Richard:

In my innocence I had thought that one of the compensations for a twice defeated Presidential candidate was at least absolution from raising money! But no such luck.

And I must add that I am full of hope for the [Democratic] Advisory Council, which I have had something to do with organizing and for

---

[16] President of the National Broadcasting Company.
[17] A pioneering television show, originating from Chicago, that featured puppet characters and actress Fran Allison.
[18] Mr. Kintner's son Michael.

which I have ruthlessly induced Tom Finletter[19] to serve as guide, philosopher and friend.

I would hope very much that you and the family might give this indispensable brain trust some thought, and then if you agree that it is our best hope for a better party job also give it some tangible encouragement.

Forgive me for harassing you when you have French Guinea, the Volta and other miscellaneous things to think about.

Sincerely yours,

P.S. I earnestly hope that you and the brethren will conclude to do something really helpful to this enterprise.

To Herbert Lehman[20]

August 23, 1957

Dear Herbert:

Thank you so much for your letter of August 12, inviting me to become an honorary Co-Chairman of the Committee for the Observance of the 10th Anniversary of the founding of Israel. I accept gladly, and I am delighted that you are undertaking this assignment which can prove so significant as the situation in the Middle East deteriorates further.

With affectionate regards to you and Edith,[21] I am

Cordially yours,

To Mrs. Eugene Meyer[22]

August 25, 1957

My dear Agnes —

We are off — Borden & I — in a little while for Canada and tranquility — a commodity in short supply for me in Africa, Europe or Libertyville. Nancy is in the kitchen with the new non-English speaking Czechs I've acquired, the phone is ringing, the baby bellowing, the dogs snarling, Borden can't find [h]is camping clothes — and it's just the time to write you a thoughtful note!!

But you see, dear Agnes, I *don't* overestimate the intelligence or ability of the average reporter. I *did* write out statements on disarma-

---

[19] Thomas K. Finletter, former Secretary of the Air Force. For the informal group formed by Mr. Finletter after the 1952 election to discuss issues and prepare policy statements for Stevenson, see *The Papers of Adlai E. Stevenson*, Vol. IV, especially pp. 267, 462.

[20] Retired U.S. senator from New York.

[21] Mrs. Lehman.

[22] This handwritten letter is in the Agnes Meyer files, Princeton University Library.

ment (suggesting a change of emphasis from aerial inspection to nuclear suspension — which Ike has *now* done!)[23] on civil rights bill, on Europe (suggesting a German foreign aid program, which will also come!!) on Africa, on Gluck[24] etc etc. And I had them mimeographed and *distributed* at the press conference so there would be no danger of misquoting me, at least on those questions which I knew they would ask.

No — what I *do* overestimate is the anxiety of newspaper management to educate reporters, to assign them thoughtfully, to give importance to important news as well as *spot, hot* or hard news.

But you are right; my job isn't to lecture the press but to be a lawyer specializing in international work where I have something special to offer in the form of unequalled good will most everywhere — except the Middle East! (And I have some ideas on how the *buyers* of aid have a power they haven't used on the *sellers* if only America & Europe could talk reasonably and trustfully which is impossible with [Secretary of State] Dulles) But I can't say the clients have been exactly crowding my door!

The fury, the silent, stubborn purposefulness, of the deep South is really frightening. I saw it so well in the primary in 1956 — and now Martin[25] in his book "The South Says Never,"[26] shows how far we've receded since the Sup[reme] Ct decision. But I hate to think you're getting this "dirt by mail" — with which I'm so familiar! Yet — I'm not much worried, because you're no weakling, you *are* remarkable and you know it as well as I. And what's more you are *right* — and is there any better armor! Whats more, in time you will emerge as a sensible moder-

---

[23] On August 21, 1957, President Eisenhower announced that the United States had offered to suspend the testing of nuclear weapons for two years provided the Soviet Union would agree that during that period there would begin a permanent cessation of the production of fissionable materials for military purposes. The *Democratic Digest,* August, 1957, reprinted excerpts from editorials, quoting the Atlanta *Constitution,* which commented, "All this makes Adlai Stevenson look more and more the prophet"; the Trenton *Evening Times,* which said that Stevenson "was right on a major issue of the last campaign"; and the Chicago *Tribune,* which said, "Adlai is entitled, at least, to a good, broad smile."

[24] Maxwell H. Gluck, a clothing chain executive, whose appointment as ambassador to Ceylon had been attacked by a number of senators on the grounds that he was unqualified for the post and had received it primarily because he had been a large contributor to the Republican campaign. See the New York *Times,* August 9, 1957.

[25] John Bartlow Martin, author of a number of books including *Adlai Stevenson* (New York: Harper, 1952).

[26] *The Deep South Says "Never,"* with foreword by Arthur Schlesinger, Jr. (New York: Ballantine, 1957), a description of Southern resistance to racial desegregation following the 1954 Supreme Court decision that held "separate but equal" schools unconstitutional.

ate — not one of our intolerant northern liberals that irritate me so much with their irresponsibility. I think its dreadful the way we're talking about desegregation of schools in terms wholly of racial justice, equality & sociology, instead of *education*. Bravo — me brave gal! Don't pull down the whites to raise the blacks — or both lose.

I pray that Eugene has recovered from his set back; I wonder if he should even go to large meetings where the confusion of many voices and views is confusing & raises tensions and pressures.

What with Eugene and all the writing and speaking work you have to do I think you have a perfect right to resign from Cultural Center C[ommi]ttee.[27] After all you've done what you set out to do — and then some!

Last night I had the best talk with Borden — who has just returned from Harvard — I've ever had. His progress toward self confidence & self understanding is incredible! . . . He has also developed a religious curiosity and interest I never before detected and talks about a man who has given away a large fortune and is studying for the Trappist order as his "best friend." It is all so baffling, and I never expected to hear Borden say he might like to do social welfare work!

But I'll report again when I get back. Now to the woods — and blessings to you &

Mille pensées
ADLAI

Forgive this horrid, hurried scrawl!

In disarmament talks in London, the United States proposed a five-part agreement: (1) establishment of inspection zones; (2) a two-year suspension of nuclear weapons testing; (3) cessation of production of further nuclear weapons; (4) cutbacks in levels of forces and conventional arms; and (5) moves to stop development of outer-space missiles. On October 28, in the face of impending collapse of the talks, President Eisenhower issued an appeal to the Soviet Union, saying in part: "It would be tragic if these important first-stage proposals, fraught with such significance for the peace of the world, were rejected by the Soviet Union even before they could have been seriously studied and before the Western presentation is complete. Such a Soviet attitude would condemn humanity to an indefinite future of immeasurable danger."

[27] Mrs. Meyer was chairman of a committee to raise $36.6 million by private subscription to build an auditorium and cultural center in Washington, D.C., with only the cost of the site to be borne by the federal government. On August 8, the House defeated a bill to purchase a site.

To Dwight D. Eisenhower[28]

August 29, 1957

Dear Mr. President:

I write to express my warm approval of your August 28 statement and the broader developments this week on the disarmament front. As you know, I believe that the world wide danger of the nuclear arms race demands that we pursue a solution relentlessly. And even if, as now appears likely, no agreement is reached in London, at least America has demonstrated again that we are not unmindful of the responsibilities of civilized leadership — which are moral as well as political and military.

Respectfully yours,

The public relations officer of the Anglo-American Corporation, a holding company of major mining interests, wrote from South Africa inviting Stevenson to write an article for their house organ, Optima. *Somewhat revised, Stevenson's article also appeared in the* Sunday Times (*London*), *December 29, 1957. The following letter and memorandum were dictated before Stevenson left for Canada.*

To A. N. Wilson

September 1, 1957

My dear Sir:

Re: PR/ANW/MID

I have your letter of August 20 and very much hope to be able to send you something in early October. I will advise you definitely before long, after I have had a little time to canvass my thoughts and my schedule.

I do not want to write about South Africa. I cannot without criticism of public policy there, and of that there has been enough from me. Nor am I eager to write for your magazine about sub-Sahara Africa and its evolution because many of your readers know far more than I, in spite of my two journeys about that vast area.

I think I will try to send you something, therefore, of a broader pattern — relating to the common tasks of Western peoples in this era of nationalist revolution and the twilight of colonialism. For years I have been disturbed by the unqualified and uninformed hostility of most Americans to "colonialism," and, in turn, the hypersensitivity of Western

[28] This letter was written from Desbarats, Ontario.

Europeans. Your issue will be just a year after Suez and its sequel which was the peril point of Western disunion. Things are better now but there is still little popular understanding of the vacuum left in the wake of imperial power, especially British. Perhaps an appreciation of this from an American would not be without interest to your readers, which I gather are largely in the U.K., Canada and here.

At all events, let me first see what, if anything, I can squeeze out of a busy schedule, and if you don't like it please don't hesitate to send it back. The fee is quite all right.

Sincerely yours,

To William McC. Blair, Jr.

September 1, 1957

Please see the letter I've written the P.R. man at Anglo-American. I should think we could do a piece of that £1000 for the firm without too much trouble.

I suggest that you convert the *uncut* version of my Oxford speech into an article entitled "A Year After Suez" — or what you will — the point being that we of the West, and especially the British Commonwealth and the U.S., still have tasks to perform together, and the greatest of these is to save the individual from being gobbled up in collectivist conformity.

A year after Suez — the lead might be — it is a fitting time to take stock.

The Anglo-French intervention in Egypt a year ago, right or wrong, evoked in the U.S. a burst of self-righteous anti-colonialism. Vice President Nixon shouted exultantly: "Isn't it wonderful to be independent at last from those imperialists" (check quote). And America's indignation obliterated reason and masked our own large part in provoking the crisis.

Now, a year later, while the ravages to the grand alliance of Western democracies have been somewhat repaired and there has been a lot of second thoughts — and second speeches! — in the U.S. things are not going too well in the ex-colonial areas where the individualist and collectivist societies are competing for the souls of millions who hardly know the difference. In Indonesia there is confusion and communism; in India there is trouble with the huge development program (check on this?); Russian influence is rising in the Middle East; the nationalism and bloodshed in Algeria is enfeebling our great and ancient ally, France; misgivings are mounting about democracy in Ghana, the youngest member of the family; and race tension is rising in South

Africa. And wherever economic development is the surest attitude to force and collectivism there is a shortage of capital for development.

The empires are gone, but the problems remain. For Americans, especially, who have been more concerned with the empires than their problems, perhaps a backward look may be instructive.

(Oxford stuff about empire and its evolution.)

I think it might fit to get in, at the conclusion or elsewhere, something about Britain serving notice that there would be no more government aid for the newly independent nations of the Commonwealth (Cf. White Paper attached)[29] just when needs are increasing. And here I think it would be well to express some reservations about the new policy. (Cf. Sir Edmund Hall-Patch's[30] letter attached.)[31]

Who will fill the vacuum — Germany? The United States? New international development agencies? Maybe time has come for a major German foreign aid program. Certainly America has a large stake but after spending $60 billion abroad since the war, unmistakeable signs of taxpayer revolt in U.S. But some encouraging evidence of increasing awareness of importance of emerging Africa. (Cf. clipping attached.)[32]

Query: Should a paragraph be inserted re advantages of multilateral development agencies to limit bilateral deals, and penetration!, be it by Russians or Germans??? (Cf. Speech to ASNE April 1956.)[33]

And how should it end?

To Carol Evans[34]

September 6, 1957

Have for me to read when I come to the office on Friday everything I said on H-Bomb in 1956, i.e. the passages in ASNE speech in April, American Legion in Sept. and later ones.[35]

Get me a ticket to N.Y. for Monday, Sept. 9 around 10 AM — preferably from O'Hare.

Let me see my statement of last Dec. about not running again.[36]

---

29 The editors do not have a copy of this White Paper.

30 British diplomat and economist, until his retirement in 1954 United Kingdom executive director of the International Monetary Fund and the International Bank for Reconstruction and Development.

31 The editors do not have a copy of Sir Edmund's letter.

32 The editors do not have this clipping.

33 See *The Papers of Adlai E. Stevenson*, Vol. VI, pp. 110–121, for Stevenson's speech to the American Society of Newspaper Editors.

34 This handwritten memorandum is in the possession of Miss Evans.

35 For Stevenson's most important statements on the H-bomb issue, see Stevenson, *The New America*, pp. 17–27, 44–58.

36 See *The Papers of Adlai E. Stevenson*, Vol. VI, p. 376.

Have I enough money for the Sept. 15 income tax installment?
Did Marshall Field cash the check I sent him for the deep freeze?

C. K. McClatchy, who had been on Stevenson's campaign staff in 1956, wrote that he was working for the Washington news bureau of the American Broadcasting Company. He added that he was returning to Sacramento, California, to work on the family's newspaper, the Bee.

To C. K. McClatchy

September 11, 1957

Dear C.K.

I was delighted to have your letter and all of your news. Somehow I had thought to see you long before this, and I hope that will come to pass in New York or Chicago. If not, I shall see you in Washington when I come down there for the Democratic Advisory Committee meeting in mid-October.

I am sure the TV experience will be valuable, and what with presidential campaigns and TV, you must have mastered the distasteful but necessary art of politics by this time.

I am so glad to hear that you decided to go back to California in the spring. What an opportunity you have! It makes me a little jealous, and also very happy to think of you in a position of growing authority and influence in that vast community.

My travels through Africa this spring were "fabulous and fascinating," to borrow your felicitous expression, and I wish I could tell you all about them. And I am sure Bill [Blair] and Adlai [III] wish they could show you all of their pictures.

Cordially yours

Miss Carol Hardin, Stevenson's second cousin, wrote him that she had just become a secretary at the Foreign Policy Association. She expressed the hope that he would attend the dedication of the Warren Austin Auditorium on October 19.

To Carol J. Hardin

September 17, 1957

My dear Carol:

I was so very glad to have your sweet letter and to hear that you are working for FPA. I can imagine no better place, and I am sure you must be envied by all of your friends. Only yesterday I had a visit from the charming granddaughter of a former American Ambassador to half a dozen countries who speaks half a dozen languages, hoping that she can get similar kind of work in New York. If you need such a gal, let me know and I will send her around for an interview with my charming cousin Carol!

I regret, however, that I can't attend the reception because I must be in Washington that day. And now you have magnified my regret a thousand fold.

Much love to you and the family.

Yours,

Mayor Richard J. Daley of Chicago wrote that at the Conference of Mayors, Mayor Thomas F. J. Quigley, of Stamford, Connecticut, had given him a key to that city for Stevenson.

To Richard J. Daley

September 17, 1957

Dear Dick:

Thank you so much for sending me the key from Mayor Quigley of Stamford. My belt now looks like the keeper of the Tower of London — I almost said Saint Peter!

Of course I would like to have lunch whenever you are free. Just let me know, with an extra option in case I am stuck with a conflict.

Yours,

Columnist Doris Fleeson wrote Stevenson from California, where she was vacationing. She sent him a description of the Eisenhower Adminis-tration that included these words: "The mess is not tragic because the inhabitants of the mess do not really suffer from it, they wallow in it." The mess, she continued, "derives quite simply from the abolition of character, intelligence, morals." She asked Stevenson about the recently elected senator from Wisconsin, William Proxmire.

To Doris Fleeson[37]

September 18, 1957

My dear Doris:

I enjoyed your letter so very much, but I cannot say that it filled me with an irresistible desire to take wing at once to California. I have been on my wings long enough for a while and I would like nothing more than to sit in undisturbed serenity on my green acres and read and reread your exquisite definition of the Eisenhower administration. I used to get some secret and unworthy satisfaction out of opaque leadership, confused diction, and even major mistakes. But no longer! This trip abroad has revealed to me in stark outline America's emaciated prestige, influence and even credibility. I wonder if our people have any realization of the estate to which we have fallen in the esteem of the world's leaders. Nor can I speak of it even to the friendliest souls without their suspicion, mistrust, even dismay, that I should be so "bitter."

I only hope that some more of the colleagues of your trade will begin to put our posture in proper perspective before we suffer all of the unhappy consequences of blithe ignorance.

Proxmire is okay. I have known him and his family for years, and he has been down here since the election. I think you will like him. If there is any frailty it is solemnity and sobriety. But aren't those sometimes in short supply among us Democrats?

I yearn to see you.

Yours,
ADLAI

Professor Seymour Harris urged Stevenson to accept an invitation to speak to the presidents and deans of New England colleges. He expressed the hope that Stevenson would visit Harvard University frequently even though his son Adlai III and his grandson Adlai IV had now departed.

To Seymour E. Harris

September 18, 1957

Dear Seymour:

I can't tell you how grateful I am to you for making that long journey

[37] The original was in the possession of Miss Fleeson at her death on August 1, 1970.

for our evening in New York. I felt so wretched I concluded to leave without interrupting that enlightening conversation.

I must decline Dean Kerby-Miller's[38] invitation, only because I am already at the point of exhaustion and the autumn has not even begun. I don't know how I can manage a law practice, a complicated family, incessant travel, and all of the vestigial public responsibilities that seem to linger on. I hope you will understand. Perhaps if I had been a college professor I would always know what to say and how to say it!

So many thanks for your piece on inflation for the [Democratic] Advisory Committee. I shall take it home and read it at once.

Yours,

p.s. My links with Cambridge are still strong. John Fell will be in his senior year and my son Borden, who has had the hardest time . . . wants to stay in Boston, although he has now finished college. So I shall be there to see them from time to time I hope — and you and my beloved friends too! Borden is returning now to look for a job somewhere "around Harvard" or in Boston. I hope he finds something interesting and useful and educational, because it is important that he start to do something on his own after a difficult and complicated career so far.

Mrs. Paul B. Reno, of Oakland, California, wrote Stevenson that the Democratic party would be much better off without the likes of Senator Allen J. Ellender and Senator Lyndon B. Johnson.

To Mrs. Paul B. Reno

September 19, 1957

Dear Mrs. Reno:

I think I know how you feel! But it seems to me the great strength of our nation is that our institutions — including our political parties — are designed to reconcile extremes in our society, permitting a growth that is stable, though at times perhaps maddeningly slow. We must not forget that among our Southern Democrats are some of the finest liberals in the country. Patience and understanding on our part will be needed if they are to be able to continue making progress towards a solution of the South's racial problems.

Cordially yours,

[38] Wilma A. Kerby-Miller, dean of instruction at Radcliffe College, lecturer on English at Harvard University, and president of the New England Association of Colleges and Secondary Schools.

Mrs. Bonnie Rothe, an educator, asked Stevenson if he could tell her why he believed that "integrity, creativeness and development of one's potential as an adult human being" could survive in a world "as deeply enmeshed in apathy as ours."

To Bonnie Rothe

September 19, 1957

Dear Mrs. Rothe:

I can only answer your question this way: There have been many times in history when the world seemed "deeply enmeshed in apathy." But there has *never* been a time in history when the world did not need "integrity, creativeness, and development of one's potential." How else to combat the apathy? How else to work effectively toward the ultimate good?

Of course there will be complete conformity and universal mediocrity if we *all* conform, if we all "settle for" mediocrity. But you yourself do not. And I do not. And there are millions of others, like us, who do not. We work constantly for better education, for enlightenment in place of ignorance, for freer communication among peoples — all aimed at the ultimate goal of building a better world. It may be a thankless task, but it is not a hopeless one!

Cordially,

Frank Lloyd Wright asked Stevenson if he would take on a case for his architectural foundation since the state of Wisconsin had challenged its real estate tax exemption. He asserted that the issue was important enough for a lawyer of Stevenson's caliber and added, "I can think of none better."

To Frank Lloyd Wright

September 20, 1957

Dear Frank:

I have seldom been more flattered! That you would want me to undertake this case for you pleases me a great deal. It means that you not only remember and trust me but respect my competence, and that would gratify even a less vain mortal.

But, alas!, I cannot do it. In the first place I find that my commitments long since made are going to keep me away most of the autumn. And, secondly, I really doubt if it would be wise at this stage to bring in "an outsider," especially one who might attract undue attention, to the embarrassment and irritation of the local court.

All the same, I think from my superficial understanding of the controversy, that you are on sound ground and that the Foundation should be exempt, certainly, from Federal taxes as an educational institution. I had supposed that you had specific exemption from the Bureau of Internal Revenue. I believe the question of real estate taxes may be somewhat less distinct, but here also, under the usual tests of purpose to which the property is devoted, I should think the equities were strong on your side.

I yearn to see you again. I follow you, of course, through the public prints, but that's not enough! Please give your wife my regards, and believe me,

Most gratefully and affectionately yours,

P.S. I have heard on my return from abroad of your charitable comment about me on a TV program.[39] Bless you, my dear and honored friend!

To Paul A. Dever[40]

September 23, 1957

Dear Paul:

The other day I was talking to some of our more thoughtful Democratic friends about future leadership of general appeal in our party around the country. The name of Chubb Peabody[41] of Boston came up as a good example of the best type.

It caused me to wonder about him and his difficulties in making progress in the Democratic party in Massachusetts. Someone said that he was probably going to run for Attorney General; and I wish you could let me have, in strict confidence, your estimate of his prospects and whether encouragement from the party leadership is likely to be forthcoming.

I am making some similar inquiries about other people elsewhere, and you may be sure it will be for my personal use only.

But more than the foregoing, I would like to know about you and your state of mind and state of health. I pray that they are both good.

---

[39] The editors have been unable to identify this program.

[40] A Boston lawyer and governor of Massachusetts, 1949–1953.

[41] Endicott Peabody, a Boston lawyer, brother of Mrs. Ronald Tree, and later governor of Massachusetts, 1963–1964.

And I shall look forward to at least a word with you when I come there this autumn to see my offspring. And with any encouragement I would even give you a few hours on Africa!

Cordially yours,

Columnist Leonard Lyons sent Stevenson a piece that Mrs. Lyons had written, and he asked, "With both Eleanor Roosevelt and my wife stuck on you, what is there about you that endears you to a female columnist?"

To Mrs. Leonard Lyons

September 23, 1957

Dear Sylvia:

Leonard has confessed! And high time too. I always thought I knew — even if the silly reading public didn't — where the talent, the perception, the sensitivity, the distinction, the style, really was in your remarkable family (I mean your generation of that remarkable family) — and now I know! And now I know how silly the reading public is — for sure.

If Lennie and his pals had endeared the [New York] Post, you've addicted me! And how's that for some fresh made English.

Respectfully, and out of my mind, dear Sylvia,

Gerald Johnson wrote on September 14, 1957, that columnists like Frank Kent and David Lawrence were trying to portray Stevenson as another Al Smith, too embittered by defeat to deserve serious attention. Johnson suggested that a pleasant word about Eisenhower would lend weight to Stevenson's criticism of serious mistakes.

To Gerald W. Johnson

September 23, 1957

Dear Gerald:

Help! — I am caught between cross fires. Your note suggesting that I say a good word about the President every now and then arrived along with a batch of letters from disgruntled Democrats berating me for having said a couple of approving words about him on the FACE THE

NATION[42] program recently. But you have a good point and I will keep it in mind, although the opportunities are rare!

Cordially,

When the schools opened in September, 1957, Governor Orval Faubus of Arkansas posed a serious challenge to federal authority by calling out the National Guard on September 3 to prevent nine Negro children from attending Little Rock's Central High School, thereby "interposing" state authority against an order of the federal district court to proceed with integration.

On the television program Face the Nation, *on September 8, Stevenson stated: "It appeared to me that here was a case where the National Guard was called out to prevent compliance with the law rather than to enforce it. I was deeply grieved." Stevenson added that he applauded President Eisenhower's statement that he would do everything in his power to see that the Constitution was upheld. Asked what he would do to enforce the court decision if he were President, Stevenson replied: "At this point the President doesn't have much that he can do."[43] Stevenson recalled that in a campaign speech in Little Rock the year before — a speech that was cheered — he had stated "The Supreme Court . . . has determined unanimously that the Constitution does not permit segregation in the schools. . . . I believe that decision to be right." At that time Stevenson urged the President to exercise the "great moral influence and great prestige" of his office "by calling together white and Negro leaders from the areas concerned in the South to explore ways and means of allaying this [the] rising tensions."[44]*

On September 20, 1957, Federal District Judge Ronald N. Davies issued an injunction against Governor Faubus enjoining him from interfering with the integration plan, and Faubus withdrew the troops. By this time, however, he had provoked the mob. The Negro students had to enter the school through a howling crowd of whites. As the crowd grew, newspapermen were manhandled. At noon the Negro students were removed from the school by the authorities. That evening President Eisenhower denounced the "disgraceful occurrence" and stated

[42] See the editorial introduction to the next document for Stevenson's comments on President Eisenhower's response to the Little Rock, Arkansas, school desegregation crisis.

[43] Chicago *Sun-Times*, September 9, 1957.

[44] See the New York *Times*, September 9, 1957; and for a discussion of Stevenson's views on civil rights, see Stuart Gerry Brown, *Conscience in Politics: Adlai E. Stevenson in the 1950's* (Syracuse, New York: Syracuse University Press, 1961), pp. 76–111.

that a federal court order "cannot be flouted with impunity by any individual or mob of extremists." He issued a proclamation directing those who had obstructed federal law "to cease and desist therefrom and to disperse forthwith." But the next day a crowd gathered again about Central High School. The President thereupon federalized the National Guard and ordered paratroops to Little Rock. On September 25, the nine Negro students reentered the high school and the mob was dispersed.[45]

On September 24, Stevenson issued the following statement.

At this point the President had no choice. The combination of lawless violence and the Governor's irresponsible behavior have created a crisis which Arkansas is powerless to meet. Federal force must in this situation be used to put down force.

But this is only a temporary solution. We have suffered a national disaster and I hope the President will now mobilize the nation's conscience as he has mobilized its arms.

To William Benton[46]

September 24, 1957

Dear Bill:

Of course I have no objection to your proposed distribution of Britannica Film stock. Indeed I wish I knew half as much about building companies and creating incentives as you do.

At the moment I am sharply in need of some incentive to write a mighty address to the educators of North Carolina. I hope the fog that seems to envelope me is not the long shadow of Central High School in Little Rock.

I will be in New York on the evening [of] Monday, September 30 for a few days. If your apartment is free I should like to use it; if not, I shall bivouac in your neighborhood.

Sincerely yours,

ADLAI

---

[45] See Anthony Lewis, *Portrait of a Decade: The Second American Revolution* (New York: Random House, 1964), pp. 46–56.

[46] The original is in the possession of the estate of William Benton. See note 12, above.

On September 28, 1957, Stevenson spoke to the State Citizens Committee for Better Schools, at Chapel Hill, North Carolina.[47]

This Committee was set up, I understand, by Governor [Luther] Hodges to provide "A layman's approach to North Carolina's educational problems and our opportunities in the general field of education."

Well, my only qualification for being here is, I fear, that I am a layman! So I am all the more honored to have this opportunity to talk with a group which is inspiring the people of North Carolina to new achievements in your long struggle for realization of the goals which Governor Aycock[48] set a long time ago and which Governor Hodges supports with such dedication and sincerity.

But I too learned something of the urgent problems of education when I was Governor of Illinois. Indeed, confronted with those baffling needs, it was then that I developed an interest that has grown since in the better use and development of our educational resources of all kinds — human, financial and physical — including films and audio-visual aids to enliven instruction and to communicate with large numbers of students in a vivid, enjoyable and understandable form.

But my interest in education is probably more an inherited than an acquired characteristic. Certainly it was latent during the period of my own formal schooling! Yet my great grandfather[49] was primarily responsible for the founding of the first teacher's college[50] in Illinois just a hundred years ago. It was there, I think, that he said: "The plow will break the prairie, but only schools can cultivate it."

Perhaps you will forgive me if I also invoke the shade of an even more remote ancestor[51] who came in 1763 to the community which is now Statesville, North Carolina. His principal distinction, I find, was, in a biographer's words, that "though small in size, he was great in voice and could pray with a fervor, a fluency, and a volume amazing to all who heard him."[52] In fact, he was called "Little Gabriel," which I suspect is as close as the Stevensons have come to the angels.

[47] The text is taken from a copy of a press release that contains deletions marked by Stevenson and is probably, therefore, identical to the text he delivered.

[48] Charles Brantley Aycock (1859–1912), who as governor of North Carolina from 1901 to 1905 received nationwide attention as a result of his campaign to upgrade the state's public educational system, which was plagued by poor equipment and organization, inferior personnel, and low attendance.

[49] Jesse Fell.

[50] Normal State Teachers College (now Illinois State University), at Normal, Illinois.

[51] William Stevenson, the first of the family to come to America, in 1748.

[52] Kenneth S. Davis, *A Prophet in His Own Country: The Triumphs and Defeats of Adlai E. Stevenson* (Garden City, New York: Doubleday, 1957), pp. 20–21.

Yet I have come here not to unbury my ancestors, but to talk about our children, and their education.

I once heard it said that Harvard University "humanizes the scientist"; and that Massachusetts Institute of Technology "simonizes the humanist." But what such levity suggests is more than a joke. In this nuclear age it is every day more apparent that we must achieve a humanism that is scientific and a science that is truly human.

I say we "must" — why?

We live in an age of revolution, as we know; a political revolution that has brought the end of empire and independence overnight to a score of nations and perhaps a billion people; an ideological revolution that has confronted western civilization with the greatest challenge since the Turks fell back from the walls of Vienna in the 17th Century; and a technological revolution that has decimated distance, unlocked the fury of the atom and brought all people in all stages of development cheek to jowl on this shrunken planet.

All these revolutions have converged in this dramatic century and revealed nothing more sharply than the necessity for education and understanding for a people charged with the responsibility for civilization and the good society that is ours.

I visited that great and good man Dr. Albert Schweitzer at his hospital at Lambarene in the fetid jungle of Equatorial Africa this June. He said to me that this was the most dangerous period in human history — not modern history, not even Christian history, but in all history. Why? Because heretofore man had been controlled and ordered by nature; but now man, with the release of the atom, could control nature, before he had learned to control himself. Those weren't his exact words but that was their purport.

Now how are we going to achieve a humanism that is scientific and a science that is truly human? How in society radically transformed by violent political, ideological and scientific revolution can we reconcile the conflict between humanism and science?

Certainly we can't do it by educational practices dominated by philosophies of the pre-scientific age. But certainly the schools will have to do it through our unique system of public education. There is no other way.

The two most immediate issues are, of course, those of integration and of federal aid to education.

There is no point or profit in reopening here the federal aid to education issue. That program has just gone down again in Congress for the second time.[53] I spoke in its behalf as strongly as I could — *before* it

---

[53] On July 25, 1957, the House of Representatives, by a vote of 208–203, had killed a bill that would have authorized federal assistance to states and local

was defeated. President Eisenhower spoke out in its behalf as strongly as he could — *after* it was defeated.

Of the matter of integration in the schools I say only — lest my silence be misunderstood — that if I thought it in my power here today to advance by anything I could say or do the solution of this problem I could speak of nothing else.

I have realized, thinking through what I might say here this morning that whenever, for ten years now, I have spoken about education in recent years it has been about the classroom shortage, the teacher shortage, the things that government can do for education — the bricks and the mortar, the faculties and the personnel, the arithmetic of education, about, in general, its quantitative side.

And always on these occasions, I have had the feeling that what I was talking about was some way wide of the real mark. For the heart of educational progress will never be reached by any federal aid to education bill. It does not lie in either the newness or the number of our classrooms. Nor is it measurable by any of the statistics that flood the literature of this subject.

What counts, of course, is what is going on in our classrooms, what the teachers of America are teaching its children. And if you say, that what teachers are doing itself depends upon the adequacy of their facilities, I would still insist that the central question is what, regardless of the odds, the teachers are *trying* to do.

If our educational purposes are unclear, if the curriculum is chaotic and cluttered with distractions, if the teaching staffs are overburdened with indiscriminate responsibilities well beyond their reasonable capacity to carry, we must expect our children will be educated for mediocrity instead of for something better.

We are well advised, I think, to take very seriously the admonition that education for *all* may come to mean real education for *none*. The struggle is very real today between massiveness, standardization and conformity on the one hand, and on the other, the spirit of individualism which has given freedom and democracy and life itself their meaning.

In the years ahead the task of improving the *quality* of education will be made doubly difficult by the great enrollment bulge which has already overwhelmed our elementary schools, and is now upon the high schools. When the youngsters now in first grade are ready for college, there will be twice as many of them as there are college students now!

---

communities in financing school construction to alleviate a national shortage of classroom space. The defeat followed adoption of a controversial amendment that prohibited such aid to any district where schools were operated in violation of the Supreme Court's 1954 decision forbidding racial segregation in public schools.

We must recognize that this battle of the bulge is going to have to be fought by the teachers with inadequate ammunition. There will be more schools, more teachers, but not nearly enough of either. The odds will get worse, very possibly, before they get better. (We are still spending more on beer than on our public schools, and for more dog food than for audio-visual materials.) There will be a natural tendency for teachers to throw up their hands, to say — quite rightly indeed, that not they but the parents caused this bulge and that unless those who are responsible are willing to do something about it, it's not the teachers' concern. One of the most dangerous possibilities will be that the teachers will accept the evils of mass education as inevitable, convinced that assembly line uniformity is the inescapable consequence of mass production in man as in automobiles; that we can never have diversity again.

This must not happen, not even if the people of America fall behind in matching as taxpayers this rising production as parents.

This is going to place tremendous demands — greater, to be sure, than the rest of us have any right to make — upon the resourcefulness, the ingenuity and the courage of school teachers and local school administrators.

And you've *got* to accept every child who comes to the door, whatever their numbers. But you are entitled to say, "All right, we'll take these children, all of them. But we'll have only half as much time for each of them as we used to have, and so we can't do some of the things for them we used to do. This means that you parents have got to help out on this job."

I have wondered sometimes how much of the typical teacher's time is spent on parts of this job which could be turned over to less highly trained assistants or even to volunteer mothers — yes, and fathers — in the community. Does the teacher have to go along on the field trip to the dairy and the bank? And if some parents want a course in driver training added to the curriculum, couldn't you fairly say you'll be glad to if that group will also bring forward some volunteer instructors for that course?

I am suggesting that there is probably in most communities a substantial waste today of teacher time on parts of the teaching job that untrained people could handle.

There's another "no" you're going to have to say. I understand that there were roughly 3 million young men and women who tried to get into college this year. Most of them did. Just 13 years from now, in 1970, there will be 7 million trying to get in. A lot of them won't — and all the wordage in the world about equality of educational opportunity isn't going to change that hard fact. There's another hard fact which is that a very appreciable number of those 7 million won't be equipped to *use* a college education. Just this week Dr. Carroll Newsom, President of New York University, said that many students not properly suited for advanced study are applying for admission to colleges and universities.

Somebody is going to have to say that the only reasonable equality of educational opportunity is the equality of children's opportunity to get all the education, not that they *ask* for, but that they can *use*. I think this is what North Carolina's Governor Aycock meant when he said fifty years ago, that it is every child's right "to burgeon out all that there is within him." Somebody is going to have to be unpleasantly ruthless in setting up a system that says that Susan Anderson can go to college because she will *use* that opportunity but that John Blankton can't go because he isn't equipped for it even though he — or his father — says he wants to and that he can afford it. And this somebody is going to have to be you school people, because everybody else — including, particularly, parents and politicians — are going to talk the cliches instead of the facts of democracy.

We must make that "no" group as small as possible, however, which means better preparation for college work under even more difficult circumstances.

I'd like to refer very briefly to another kind of ingenuity that I think you are going to have to exercise. I have become, as I said, especially interested in the better exploitation of our teaching resources by the use of visual and audio aids to education — aids which will go a very long way toward helping the too few teachers educate their too many pupils. We are still in the infancy of the development of educational films, television and the like. Badly used, even over-used, they could result in the sterilization of education. But already there has been such progress made along these and related lines that the discriminating administrator and the resourceful teacher can now do a better job for more children with less of his time and at less cost than was true before. And a most spectacular recent contribution is the full introductory course in physics on film by Dr. Harvey White, of the University of California, which has attracted such attention here and abroad, and may well point the way to the solution of our national embarrassment in the teaching of the sciences.

I remember, from the twenties, the popular song "Frigidaire Will Never Replace The Iceman." I also remember that it did. But it is plainly true that there is no substitute for good teaching. Yet it has become equally plain that an intelligent use of these devices can greatly enrich the educational offering and can release the teacher's fuller energies for the performance of that essential part of the teaching job which demands his, or her, best self.

But these are matters of ways and means, and claimed descent from the founder of a teacher's college is too little license for my having gone into them even this far!

Nor do these matters of administrative policy and of teaching techniques go to the center of the mark. It isn't just a question of the "how" of teaching. It is more a question of the "who" — for surely there can't be good teaching without good teachers. But it is most of all, of course, a question of "what" is taught.

I know the storminess of the sea I now embark on. The abuse of one another by politicians is poetry compared with the violence of the conflicts between you pedagogs. And perhaps you will indulge me the observation that there is more to be said for a two-party political system than for a two-party division in the field of educational theory. In both cases it tends to magnify essentially minor differences and to drown out the new voice which may well be carrying the truer message. With you people there is apparently no surcease. And I get the feeling, frankly, that there is so much to be said both for "adjusting the child to life" and teaching him how to read that I rather suspect someone may soon come up with the heresy that we perhaps ought to try to do both!

What should be taught? Why, a very great many things, of course, but it is most important of all that no one man, or any one group of men — or women — should ever be in a position to say what should be taught.

Yet that each of us should bring to this question whatever suggestion our own experience prompts. Mine is a quarter century — I acknowledge with a shudder and a sigh — in public affairs, on and off, mostly off! And it prompts me to beg you to: Teach our children how to join in the making of great decisions.

I mean the great decisions on which life and the quality of living depend. I mean decisions on questions so vast that they are only partly understood by those who have to decide them. I mean decisions so crucial that no one man or group of men can be safely entrusted with them, decisions that must be made by a collective wisdom that has to be infinitely greater than any of its individual parts, a wisdom that rises above its source.

There came across my desk just last week a publisher's blurb for a new book about America as a Civilization.[54] It includes a brief checklist

---

[54] Max Lerner, *America as a Civilization: Life and Thought in the United States Today* (New York: Simon & Schuster, 1957).

of some of the changes in our social landscape just in the past decade. Let me read it to you.

"There are the automatic factory, the electronic eye, the feed-back, and nuclear energy; there are the public relations men and motivational research; there are the 'new leisure,' the new suburbia and exurbia, the guaranteed annual wage, and (coming very fast) the four-day work week; there are the 'baby boom,' steady dating, the servantless family, the split-level home, the barbecue pit; there are the young people storming the gates of the colleges as never before in history; there are the paper-backs, the big money quiz shows, the 'confidential magazines,' the 'mutiny of the young,' the 'revolt of the middle-aged man'; there are the new military elite, and the 'expense account elite,' the new elite of corporate and trade union executives; there are the new stimulants and new tranquilizers, new cures and new diseases, new lives being led and new deaths being died."

And this is only what is happening here in America. We must add to this list the impacts upon us, some already felt but others not yet sensed, of the convulsions of awakening Islam, the continued reaching out from the Communist citadel of what Kipling called The Bear with the Face of a Man, the explosive and sudden emergence from the quiet past of the nationalist revolution in Asia and Africa.

I do not say that today's problems are harder (although I think they are) than those our fathers met. I do say that they are of a kind and that they are coming so fast that they place new and very different demands upon those who are called upon to meet them. In a democracy this means on all of us. And these new demands are accordingly placed directly on the schools.

The political processes cannot, I am convinced, meet these demands without an increased help from the schools. Ralph Waldo Emerson once wrote that:

"Politics is an after-work, a poor patching. We are always a little late . . . We shall one day learn to supersede politics by education. Let us make our education brave and preventive."

I hope not to be misunderstood when I say that the one disappointment I have had in politics is not in losing an election. (Perhaps I should say two disappointments!) It is rather in the feeling of frustration, of disillusionment, in not being able to get across in a political campaign ideas that have seemed to me part of the very warp and woof of civilization's survival. Partly this has been because of my personal shortcomings. Partly it has been because of the triumph of "public relation" over debate and discussion. Partly it is the fault of that part of the press which conceives of its function as being only to tell people what it says they want to hear.

But whosever fault it is, it will remain for the schools to administer the cure. And if you say, how in the world can we do it, I can only answer. Well, who else is going to? You are not the carriers of the waters of mankind, which cannot raise it above the source. You *are* the source.

How far can these statements of elevated educational purpose be translated into specifics? I confess again my limitations; yet there are a few observations that seem worth timid advance.

We hear about "adjusting to life." If I understand what this means, I am all for it. But what is "life"? If you mean a child's learning to live easily with the other members of his family and the rest of the people in the block, fitting smoothly into his environment, his country club, his church, feeling at ease with the people he sees from day to day, then I think you've drawn the circle dangerously small. For distance and time and space have shrunk, "life" is never again going to be a local island for any man or woman in the world; and whoever tries to make it so will not only defeat his own purpose but will deny his obligation as a member of civilized society.

Yes, adjust children to life — to life in the *world* in which they live — a world where, among other things, the vast majority who are poor, the vast majority whose skins are dark, the vast majority who are uneducated, are now demanding their birthrights as children equal in the sight of God.

There is no point in more than mentioning, because it is obvious, the new demands that are being made upon the schools in terms of what men and women *must* know. We are acutely aware of our shortage of trained scientists, of engineers, chemists and physicists. Yet the shortage is equally, perhaps even more, desperate, of men and women who understand and can handle the problems of the new social and human relationships.

You will remember that the writers of the Book of Chronicles (1:12:32) list the groups that came to David's support. Among them were "the children of Issacher, men that had understanding of the times, to know what Israel ought to do." Surely the need is as great today for men — and women — with "understanding of the times."

There will have to be much more than increased factual knowledge brought into the educational bloodstream. It is perhaps one of the ironies of progress, perhaps even one of the dangerous dilemmas of democracy, that the harder the world's problems become, the more they are going to have to be met by people who know less and less about them.

A man was reasonably well equipped, fifty years ago, to vote on issues relating to war and peace and defense and preparedness on the basis of his first hand knowledge and understanding. War was mostly an enlargement of what he had seen over the gunsight of his own rifle. Today, total war would be something beyond comprehension either in its immediate manifestations, or, much more, in its effects upon the bodies and minds of people thousands of miles, or even a generation, removed in time and place.

Yet the children in today's classrooms will have to decide what to do with nuclear weapons, if we can't.

It wasn't too difficult to give a child in the seventh grade in 1857 the essential facts which would be a basis for his deciding later whether the Monroe Doctrine represented a good or a bad foreign policy. Yet today a general education can give only a small percentage of America's children more than a little bit of equivalent understanding of the implications of the United Nations, NATO, SEATO, the Baghdad Pact and a dozen other vitally important world compacts.

Yet the children in today's classrooms will have not only to decide tomorrow what to do about these compacts, let alone how to deal with the great revolutions of Asia, Africa, and the Middle East which comprise so much of the world in which they must live.

There is no need to extend this list. It is, I think, the sombre fact that the problems of life are becoming increasingly hard to understand.

But there is neither room nor reason here for despair. And I am not proposing the addition to the curriculum of a course in How to Make Decisions.

There are, however, some implications for the educational process in the vastness of the decisions tomorrow's citizens are going to have to make.

What they cannot supply in complete understanding they will have to supply in other ways.

We must safeguard, to begin with, against the danger that they will simply turn the decision making over to somebody else. Part of the protection against ultimate error will be the participation of enough decision makers that their collective reactions, feelings, even hunches, will add up to wisdom. There is reason to question whether the schools are doing all that *has* to be done to excite young men and women, even while they are boys and girls, to participate in the public decision process. It isn't just an obligation.

The importance of independent thinking is always real. But it is especially important in a season of history when the world faces new problems, problems for which the popular notions have proved inadequate, problems which demand new ideas, problems we know we haven't met yet to our own or to the world's satisfaction. These problems won't be settled, or they won't be settled wisely by any generation that is afraid to think new thoughts or which jeers at intelligence and independence of mind, and which finds emotion easier than reason.

Surely it is in our oldest tradition for the schools to teach that to think free, and not just to conform is the truly American way. "The home of the brave" has never meant just brave in deeds; it means, too, brave in ideas. And I think of William James' statement of what it is that the schools seek essentially to impart:

"The feeling for a good human job anywhere, the admiration of the really admirable, the disesteem of what is cheap and trashy and impermanent — this is what we call the critical sense, the sense for ideal values. It is the better part of what men know as wisdom."

Yet there are disturbing symptoms, if they are to be credited, that the young people in this country today seem to be accepting a distressingly different set of values. I am thinking of the poll of thousands of high school students recently conducted by Purdue University. One in four of the students polled stated that "More than anything, I want to be accepted as a member of the group that is most popular in school," and 38% said that "there is nothing worse than being considered an 'odd ball' by other people." Over half of these young men and women expressed the conviction that "Most people are incapable of deciding what is best for them," and that our political system is a "dirty" game which is out of ordinary people's hands. A majority of the students say that they favor censorship of books, movies, radio and television, and 41% that they would cancel or substantially restrict freedom of the press.

Perhaps these studies are subject to substantial discount. These are hard things to measure. And yet you have the suspicion from your own knowledge that there is a tendency in too many minds today to pull back from the frontiers of new thinking, new ideas.

Related, I think, to this urge to conform to the habits of the herd, is the human desire for security. And I suspect that there are elements in the public school setup which tend, often quite strongly, to make the schools agencies for promoting what may become a very false sense of security. It is much easier for teachers, like politicians, to preach the gospel that things are all right, that if we can just keep going along about as we are there won't be too much to worry about. History seems to be on this side. So, most likely, are many of the town's leading citizens.

It is right, I think, that the schools should err a little on the side of being conservative, especially I suppose at the primary and elementary levels. But there is no excuse for their being timid, and none for being afraid. To face squarely the facts of life is to face the fact that there is no longer any security at all — for individual or nation — in standing still. We will be derelict if we do not prepare children for the shock of discovery that the world is in a tumult of change, and that you can't sit it out.

Surely it is right that the schools must supply the technical, scientific training which is necessary to keep this nation at the front of man's discovery into the secrets of nature. But no emphasis on the technology of man's survival or his material progress must be permitted to lessen the intensity of our search for mankind's way to the achievement of his higher destiny.

If peoples are ever to speak to peoples, the language will not be that of guns and bombs. It will be the language of mutual concern. It will be the message that free people should be sending out to show what is meant by freedom.

The verities are still the ends, the acts of survival only the commoner means; and knowledge of the truths, not the flash of hydrogen bombs, must bring the light by which we walk into the future, unafraid.

Nothing I have said here has been meant in criticism. I know full well how easy it is to talk in broad generalities about the state of the world and the role of the individual, about the ideals of education. And then you return to a noisy, crowded classroom where the problem is just keeping your head above water, meeting the daily demands, just coping with what comes along. Whether Johnny will be ready to make great decisions for himself as a man seems some way secondary to whether Johnny will be able to put on his own rubbers and get on home and out of the way.

And yet it is in the trying, more than in the accomplishment, that life's satisfactions come, and the consciousness of high purpose never achieved that makes bearable the humdrum of daily detail. No one could ask more.

I hope that you will find in these remarks only an expression of our common task, an expression of the conviction of the layman and the teacher that there is nothing more important than the education of our children, as generous in heart as in hand, as independent in mind as in body, as courageous in thought as in deed, so that we may as a people walk straight and sure and proud.

While in North Carolina, Stevenson stayed with Governor Luther Hodges. At a press conference on September 30, Stevenson was asked to comment on President Eisenhower's announcement that he had just called a conference of Southern governors to the White House to discuss the Little Rock situation and integration of schools. Stevenson stated:

It is no secret that almost two years ago I urged such meetings as President Eisenhower has arranged for next week with the Southern Governors. I wish he had conferred with them and leaders of both races long ago. If he had done so and his position had been clearly expressed I don't believe we would have suffered this national misfortune which has been so widely exploited by our enemies.

It is time now to bind up our wounds. I hope the soldiers can be quickly withdrawn from Little Rock, and that local authorities and law-abiding citizens everywhere will see to it that they are never needed again anywhere.

To Luther Hodges

October 7, 1957

My dear Luther:

After scrambling around the country for a week, I am home at last — and full of happy memories of my visit with you and those charming ladies. Your courtesy touched me deeply and I only wish I might have been a little more helpful in this difficult interval in your life. I am sure the respect which your conduct has commanded in these recent weeks has not gone unnoticed and must comfort you.

I wish there were more opportunities to discuss this grave cleavage in our country and our party. Surely the future must rest with reason, not passion, law observance and not violence. The question is how. In this temper I am sure you and a few of your moderate Southern colleagues are on the right track. I only wish we could help you more. Our greatest need seems to be better white leadership in the South, and perhaps one could say better Negro leadership in the North.

I was happy, too, that you had an opportunity to see something of the work that the Encyclopaedia Britannica Film company is doing for education. I hope that the counsels of Dallas Herring[55] and so many

---

[55] Chairman of the North Carolina State Board of Education.

others will prevail and that more funds will be available. Certainly if a shortage of technically trained people inhibits industrial location in North Carolina, such things as the physics films should be an effective stimulant to students.

Please give my affectionate regards to Martha.[56]

Yours,

On October 3, Stevenson spoke to the Council on Foreign Relations in New York. Mrs. Eugene Meyer wrote that her husband had "told me your discussion of African problems was absorbing and highly instructive," and she expressed her disappointment that Stevenson had not joined in a theater party arranged by their mutual friend Roger Stevens.

To Mrs. Eugene Meyer[57]

October 7, 1957

My dear Agnes:

Thanks for your note. I wish I had been with you at Roger Stevens' play. But I wasn't invited! In fact, I didn't even know about it.

I was never more flattered than by the presence of Eugene Meyer at my unorganized remarks on Africa. I agree that the audience was attentive and cordial but I can't understand why! I prepared nothing but a few pencil notes — reminders — about some of the countries we visited, or of course I would send it along.

But I am sending along a copy of the speech I made at Chapel Hill in case you want to see the whole ponderous text.

How I wish I could come out for lunch on the 13th. I returned to Chicago Sunday instead of going up to see the boys this past week-end and must go back to Boston en route to New York next week-end.

I had a fascinating week-end with Luther Hodges in North Carolina, and a luncheon with Bill Douglas[58] and Earl Warren[59] in Washington, all of which I yearn to tell you about — not to mention a long telephone talk with Sherman Adams.[60]

Much love,
ADLAI

[56] Mrs. Hodges.
[57] The original is in the Agnes Meyer files, Princeton University Library.
[58] Associate Justice William O. Douglas of the United States Supreme Court.
[59] Chief Justice of the United States.
[60] Assistant to the President. The purpose of Mr. Adams's call was apparently to explore the possibility of Stevenson's membership on the Civil Rights Commission. See Stevenson's statement of October 28, 1957, below.

Stevenson attended a party given by Mrs. James F. Oates, Jr., at the Onwentsia Club in Lake Forest, Illinois, to celebrate the ninetieth birthday of her father, Frank G. Wright. Stevenson was seated next to the Oateses' daughter Rosalind. James F. (Jimmy) Oates III acted as toastmaster.

To Mrs. James F. Oates, Jr.[61]

Thank you, thank you, thank you!! I'm glad it was supper too; and I *was* "st[r]ategically" seated indeed! She's more diverting than ever — and your father gets better with the decades — and Jimmy's a block of the old chips — and I had a wonderful time —

ADLAI

To Richard J. Daley

October 9, 1957

Dear Dick:

At luncheon the other day you mentioned the railroad terminal consolidation program about which I used to hear so much while I was a Director of the Illinois Central. I was minded during our conversation, and somehow forgot, to tell you that one of my law partners, Newton Minow, has been interested in this subject for a long while, and participated in some research while at Northwestern Law School which resulted in a comprehensive analysis of the problem, published in the Illinois Law Review while he was its editor in 1950.

It has occurred to me that for several reasons he might be a helpful addition to the Commission if you could use him. As I believe you already know him well, I will not burden this letter with his background. I think you know enough about his extraordinary talents, energy, enthusiasm and good judgment to appreciate his possible value in this important work.

I don't want to trouble you about this but if you care to talk about it further I will be available any time.

Cordially yours,

Mrs. Kenneth S. Bates, of Hampton, Virginia, wrote Stevenson about her concern over the use of force to achieve integration. She said the country needed his guidance and she knew his advice would be wise and unbiased.

[61] This handwritten postcard is in the possession of Mrs. Oates. It is postmarked October 7, 1957.

To Mrs. Kenneth S. Bates

October 21, 1957

Dear Mrs. Bates:

So many thanks for that very thoughtful and perceptive letter. I share your concern over the situation in the South but I am hopeful that the type of incidents we have witnessed of late in Little Rock will not be repeated.

As you perhaps know, I have opposed the use of force in connection with the Supreme Court's decision on the desegregation of schools, but I think that some people forget that it was Governor Faubus who first used force to interfere with a decision of a Federal Court and, under those circumstances, I felt that the President had no choice other than to send troops to Little Rock, although I wish that long ago he had marshaled the nation's conscience in support of the Court decision.

Sincerely,

Harry S. Ashmore, editor of the Arkansas Gazette, *who had served on Stevenson's 1956 campaign staff, wrote powerful editorials opposing Governor Faubus's action at Central High School. When federal troops arrived, Ashmore wrote that this shock might prompt Arkansas to "regain perspective, restore peace, sustain the law."*

To Harry S. Ashmore

October 21, 1957

Dear Harry:

If anyone has gotten anything except misfortune out of Little Rock it is thanks to you. I have been wanting to say this to you since they caught you with your dukes up.

Blessings.

Yours,

To Lady Barbara Jackson

October 22, 1957

Dearest Barbara:

This is still not the letter I am planning to write you, but it is the best I can do ad interim.

I found Sir Robert fit and wise and balanced in spite of his manifest distress about developments there.[62] I wish he might have come to the

---

[62] Stevenson had conferred with Sir Robert Jackson on the situation in Ghana.

conference at Princeton,[63] which was attended by many of the business, academic and professional African experts of America (program enclosed). I found it extremely enlightening, and if the Jackson ears have been burning of late it was due to frequent references to them there as well as Stephens College, Boston, New York and Washington, which have all been on my itinerary in the past two weeks.

[John] Kenneth Galbraith's assurances that he has made suitable arrangements for your 1958 winter-spring visit are comforting.[64] If there is anything more that needs attention, let me know. From my observations of young Goheen,[65] at Princeton, I have a feeling that he would like you there for the winter, but I wasn't sure whether it was to speak or teach!

Ken has sent me your paper,[66] but I haven't read it yet — or written mine, or read the New York Times piece,[67] or caught up with my mail — or lost any weight — so you can see my record for not doing is better than my record for doing — which is also as usual. What amused me is that I told CED[68] some time ago that I would try to do a piece for them on my idea of the most important economic problem facing us in the next twenty years, which is to keep the underdeveloped territories out of trouble — a doctrine I have learned and espoused from guess who. And then guess who comes along and says — according to Galbraith — that the problem is 40 million more Americans! All this persuades me that our communications are breaking down and makes the time to February longer.

I shall be writing Robert soon along the line he suggested; and how I yearn to see MacDuff[69] and his courtiers — and I don't mean Krobo Edusei![70]

Much love,

P.S. Word is coming from here and there that the time is approaching for me "to speak" again. Fear is spreading in this land and disillusion on

63 The Princeton University Conference on Emerging Sub-Sahara Africa, held on October 15 and 16, 1957.

64 Lady Jackson was to be a visiting scholar and lecturer at Harvard University.

65 Robert F. Goheen, president of Princeton University.

66 Lady Jackson does not recall what paper Stevenson refers to. Letter to Eric Sears, October 5, 1975.

67 The report of Lady Jackson's Harvard Commencement speech of June 13, 1957, in which she urged a revival of the spirit of the Marshall Plan to stop the disintegration of the Atlantic community. See the New York *Times*, June 14, 1957.

68 The Committee for Economic Development, a nonpartisan group of businessmen and scholars founded in New York in 1942 to conduct research and formulate policy recommendations on major economic issues.

69 Her son, Robin.

70 Minister of the Interior of Ghana, 1957–1958. Lady Jackson notes that his "relative extremism made him a somewhat difficult partner for his more moderate colleagues" in Nkrumah's cabinet. Letter to Eric Sears, October 5, 1975.

the right is mounting. At the center there is anxious dismay, at the left a sort of joyous anticipation of doom and disaster. I think we may be pretty sick and only beginning to notice the symptoms. Anent Sputnik[71] and putt-nick an Italian told me he could not decide whether Ike's putter more resembled Chamberlain's umbrealla or Nero's fiddle. But you have heard them all.

A.E.S.

P.P.S. But the real purpose of this letter was to remind you to remind Robert that my very dear friends Harold and Mary Hochschild (Chairman of American Metals Company, which owns Rhodesian Selection Trust, etc.) are arriving at Accra from Liberia at the end of a long journey through Africa and that I hope you can do something about them. These are some tourists I can unqualifiedly recommend, and indeed guarantee. She is the daughter of Alan Marquand, the founder of the school of Art and Architecture at Princeton and a famous patron of his time. And he is a liberal big businessman if I ever saw one. I hope you can see that they meet the Prime Minister, et al.

To Lester B. Pearson[72]

October 22, 1957

Dear Mike:

Nothing has pleased me more in these trying times of Sputnick and putt-nick than the news of your Nobel Prize.[73] And what a happy event in the life of an ex-Foreign Minister. Somehow, such recognitions for such as you seems to me all too few. But, then, such as you are all too few!

My congratulations and warmest wishes.

Cordially yours,

P.S. Perhaps I was the more pleased because I hollered about putting UN patrols along the Israeli border two years ago, and you did it — and then some!

---

[71] The first artificial earth satellite, launched into orbit by the Russians on October 4, 1957.

[72] Canadian Secretary of State for External Affairs, 1948–1957, and later Prime Minister; senior adviser to the UN charter conference in 1945 and president of the UN General Assembly, 1952–1953.

[73] It had been announced on October 14, 1957, that Mr. Pearson was to receive the Nobel Peace Prize on December 10, 1957.

To Alfred Hayes[74]

October 22, 1957

Dear Mr. Hayes:

I enjoyed my luncheon with you and your associates so much, and I hope I shall have other opportunities to hear what is going on and its meaning in those mysterious caverns of lower New York. It reminded me again of what I have thought so often — that a little more direct communication between some of the major influences in our society could be helpful to all concerned. I think especially of the importance of more talk with the sophisticated labor leaders.

My New York office is at 575 Madison Avenue, and the telephone is Murray Hill 8-5600. When you are in that vicinity some day, and hungry, let me know!

Cordially yours,

To E. J. Ryan[75]

October 23, 1957

Dear Jack:

I was delighted to have your letter. Somehow it brought back to me vivid, indelible memories of that brief visit with you high above the jungle and the sea. There is much to talk about in this season of Sputnik — and putt-nik — as the humorists say, and I find the alarm, anxiety and disillusion that are spreading through this country disquieting, and also, and I hope I say it without bitterness, overdue! What with the loss of our political prestige, Little Rock and our moral prestige, the earth satellite and our scientific leadership gone, and now cracks appearing in the economic armor, it is little wonder that people are beginning to ask if we have been slipping. We Democrats are not loathe to offer an answer!

I saw Walter Rice and Richard Reynolds in the East not long ago and have been talking with them about some project in Africa. They told me how well your operation had progressed and how little you had been troubled by the Haitian revolution[76] so far. I pray that continues to be the case; and I shall hope for an early opportunity to see what is happening in person. But the hope looks quite forlorn just now.

[74] President of the Federal Reserve Bank of New York.
[75] Manager of Reynolds Metals Company mines in Haiti.
[76] On June 14, 1957, the Haitian army had ousted provisional President Daniel Fignola. An election in September chose François Duvalier, who took office on October 22, 1957, and the military junta resigned.

Adlai and Nancy send their best. He has finished at Harvard Law School and is now law secretary to one of the judges of our Supreme Court.[77] They have even bought a small house on the edge of the slums,[78] and it looks to me as though he might be thinking about politics as well as saving money!

It was good to hear from you.

Cordially yours,

To Mrs. Franklin D. Roosevelt[79]

October 24, 1957

My dear Mrs. Roosevelt:

Alas! I will not be here on November 16. I expect to be in New York several days that week, and on the 16th I had planned to go to the Princeton-Yale football game at Princeton, my first appearance at such a ceremony in many years. I shall try to see you during the week in New York, however.

Affectionately,

ADLAI

Mrs. Eugene Meyer asked to borrow a picture she had given Steven-son. On October 19 she wrote him that he was a man whom millions of people looked to for political, moral, and mental guidance, and as a result he was not free to marry carelessly for companionship. She added that all great human beings were lonely.

To Mrs. Eugene Meyer[80]

October 25, 1957

My dear Agnes:

I am just leaving for Bloomington for a couple of days of family and public affairs. Before I leave, I must report, however, that I have made a complete inventory of my "Agnes photos," as follows:

Two by Louise Dahl (?) at your desk, one inscribed very prettily!

One on the peak of Mount Whitney.

One done in Paris of a plaster model.

[77] The Illinois Supreme Court.
[78] In Chicago.
[79] The original is in the Franklin D. Roosevelt Library, Hyde Park, New York.
[80] The original is in the Agnes Meyer files, Princeton University Library.

But the "youthful" photo to which you refer I cannot find, nor can I even recall it. Isn't this dreadful? Are you sure you sent it to me?

I know the death of your groom after so many years must have touched one who feels personal relationships so deeply.

Your great and helpful letter I will not here attempt to answer, but I'm afraid you set an importance, both to me as well as to others, on my "career," which I do not wholly feel or believe. Of all this we must talk another time.

Affectionately,
ADLAI

Stevenson issued the following statement on October 28, 1957.

I gave the matter prayerful thought but concluded that I could not accept membership on the Commission on Civil Rights proffered to me by the President through Sherman Adams for several reasons:

First and foremost, my best judgment as to how I can be most effective in this and other areas of national and world concern seemed to me to preclude my accepting this appointment.

I also believe I can be of more service to improve race relations if I am free to do and say what I think not restricted by the proprieties of an official position on this Commission.

We Americans must adjust to the changing times quietly and sensibly and consistent with our traditions of lawful behavior, morality and social justice. I think I could be of more use preaching this gospel which I devoutly believe as I could serving on this Commission within the limitations of the statute creating it.

All the same, I am grateful for the opportunity the President afforded me, and I am sorry I did not feel I could take advantage of it.

To Mrs. Ernest L. Ives[81]

October 30, 1957

Dear Buff —

If you could check into that colored general[82] before you leave in detail and let me know all about her — including salary — it would be helpful. I doubt if this couple is educable and I have so little time or patience. Moreover after Nancy & A[dlai III] move into town one

[81] This handwritten letter is in E.S.I., I.S.H.L.
[82] A maid for Stevenson's home in Libertyville, where he was having servant problems.

person should be enough. Of course I could keep these people until after the holidays I suppose & look around then.

Also I wish you would check up in detail on that couple or the availables in SP[Southern Pines] after you get back there. This domestic management business is really tough for anyone as busy & preoccupied as I am!

I have a plaintive plea from Foster[83] now to come to Wash[ington] for 6 weeks to work up some means of restoring confidence before the NATO meeting in Paris in Dec. I've agreed to go to Wash. to see him (in secret) tomorrow night. Then back here Friday for a week — then Boston & N.Y. — and maybe Wash indefinitely if he gets the best of me! Don't talk about this — I don't want to embarrass them, *or me!*

LOVE

AD

To Kwame Nkrumah[84]

October 30, 1957

My dear Dr. Nkrumah:

After consultation with Sir Robert Jackson in New York recently, Reynolds Metals Company is sending you a letter formally recording its continuing interest in the bauxite and water resources of Ghana and its anxiety to be kept informed of developments to the extent that propriety permits.

Sir Robert has been extremely helpful in keeping us so advised in the past and in interpreting the Government's position. I hope this can continue, against the time when the Government may want or need some other interests in addition to those already involved in the Volta project. I have reported to Sir Robert that meanwhile Reynolds Metals Company *may* go ahead with a substantial investment in alumina in French Guinea along with French and other foreign companies. But such an investment is not to be interpreted as a loss of interest in Ghana, especially if that enormous project can be approached in steps.

As a friend and admirer of yours and of your country — (after two or three visits, I am now considered a Ghana expert!) — I am going to take advantage of this opportunity to say that I have thought much about you and your problems during the recent trying months which have brought Ghana so much publicity in the press.[85] Sir Robert has

---

[83] Secretary of State John Foster Dulles.

[84] A carbon copy is in the possession of Carol Evans.

[85] Nkrumah's government deported two Ashanti Moslem leaders on the grounds that their presence was "not conducive to the public good." Then Ghana's Parlia-

enlightened some of us in this country immensely and put things, I believe, in better perspective. I only wish he might have felt free to attend the Conference on Sub-Sahara Africa at Princeton University a couple of weeks ago where he could have been so useful among so many Americans interested in Africa and concerned about recent developments in Ghana.

The interest in Ghana continues great and people are by no means wholly skeptical. Every move that you and your Ministers make seems to be watched closely, even here in the Middle West. It is for that reason and the importance to Ghana of good world "public relations" (a phrase I don't like!) that some of Ghana's most hopeful and vocal friends have been uneasy recently. I am sure you are quite aware of how sensitive the world is to developments there, especially in cautious capital investing circles.

I have expressed repeatedly my confidence that Ghana's good will and identification with the West and the principles we preach (even if we don't always practice them wholly!) is a deep conviction with you and your principal associates.

I can sense, and Sir Robert has helped me to understand, some of your difficulties, and my prayers are very much with you. I hope you will not hesitate to let me help if I can in any way.

With my esteem and warm good wishes, I am

Cordially yours,

To Sir Robert Jackson

October 30, 1957

Dear Robert:

I have finally gotten around to dictating a letter to Prime Minister Nkrumah and enclose a copy herewith. I have not yet heard from Reynolds but assume the draft letter I prepared for them has also gone forward. A copy is enclosed.

I am also enclosing copies of some correspondence with the J. Henry Schroder Banking Corporation which you may recall was hoping to be appointed as Ghana correspondent. I should have thought it might be better for Ghana to use a company so experienced in foreign trade and with British connections, such as Schroder.

I hope the letter to the Prime Minister will be helpful and not mis-

---

ment passed a bill authorizing the deportations. When the issue was brought to court, Nkrumah's attorney general contended that Parliament had "absolute and complete power to legislate on any subject whatever" and no court could review any act not specifically forbidden by the constitution. See *Time,* October 14, 1957.

understood. I also enclose a clipping from this morning's New York Times about AlCan's cutbacks,[86] which has doubtless already come to your attention.

My life continues in disorder and incessant motion. You and Barbara will be interested to hear (in confidence) that the President asked me to be Chairman of the Civil Rights Commission created by the last Congress. I declined, I think for obvious and sufficient reasons. Foster Dulles is now asking me to help out before the NATO meeting in an effort to devise new machinery and, I suspect, new confidence! It all keeps me very much off my legal balance! And tell the dear Barbara that it also makes me yearn for some of that calm and wise counsel of hers.

I am off to Washington again today, thence to New York and home; then back East next week, including Boston. The Jackson ears should burn all around my circle — heavens, I almost said my orbit!

Yours,

To Mrs. Eugene Meyer[87]

November 2, 1957

Agnes dear —

. . . I was in Wash. Wed. night on a very hush mission at the request of the Secretary of State[88] (*not to be mentioned!*) and thought to telephone you (but it was so, so late when my conference was over) to say please, please don't think badly of me about the picture. I *do* remember it perfectly; kept it on the table behind me for many months and Miss Evans put it away when I was gone for a long time and now can't find it. But we'll continue the search in my new office at 135 *South La Salle St.* to which we moved while I was conveniently absent these past few days.

And please, please don't say you are not going to write to me any more. I *do* have the time and inclination to listen; I've been listening and learning — more attentively, more profitably, more admiringly —

---

[86] President Nathanael Davis of Aluminum Limited of Canada announced on October 29, 1957, in Montreal that his company "had decided to postpone certain phases of its expansion program," a move reflecting "our expectation that new production coming into operation during the next year or two in the industry as a whole will take time to be absorbed." New York *Times*, October 30, 1957.

[87] This handwritten letter is in the Agnes Meyer files, Princeton University Library.

[88] Secretary Dulles had asked Stevenson to accept a post as special assistant to the President, with the responsibility of helping to develop the United States position for the forthcoming NATO talks. See the editorial introduction to the next document.

more lovingly — than you evidently realize my gifted and beloved friend —

ADLAI

Saturday afternoon
Nov. 2 1957

(I think of a year ago as I write that date — a year the world won't soon forget, worse luck. Hope you will toast it in a Sputnik coc[k]tail — ½ vodka ½ sour grapes.)

Russian success in placing Sputnik I in orbit around the earth jolted the "illusion of American omnipotence." The elaborate tranquilizing by the Eisenhower Administration was dealt a serious blow. After the launching of the first Sputnik, British Prime Minister Harold Macmillan flew to Washington for conferences. The President agreed to convert the December meeting of the North Atlantic Treaty Organization into a conference of Allied heads of state. Secretary of State John Foster Dulles persuaded President Eisenhower that a dramatic step was needed to demonstrate American unity.

On October 30 Dulles met with Stevenson. They discussed a "secret" six-page memorandum entitled "Terms of Reference for Mr. ―――― for Summit NATO Meeting." Stevenson would be designated Special Assistant to the President and "receive political guidance from the Secretary of State. His office would be in the State Department. . . . He would be furnished an appropriate staff of officers from the Departments of State and Defense and the Atomic Energy Commission." Stevenson's mission would be:

> (a) To develop the US Government position on the points covered in paragraphs 5 and 6 of the US-UK "Declaration of Common Purpose" of October 25, 1957. (b) To coordinate this position in advance of the NATO meeting with the United Kingdom, France, Germany, and Italy. (c) To assist in developing public understanding and support for the U.S. position. (d) To participate in the presentation of this position to the North Atlantic Council in December.

Stevenson scribbled some nearly illegible notes on his copy of the memorandum. Above (b) he wrote: ". . . need better understanding in Asia, in Am[erican] states — not pressing not threshold." Under (c) he wrote: "Have dependable allies; can share with them. U.S. people think we can do it alone. Cant!"

The memorandum also contained a section headed "Comments On Functions." Number 1 stated that development of the U.S. position would involve substantial "missionary" work since the main concepts of the "Declaration of Common Purpose" were in general terms and probably not well understood in "some quarters of the Executive Branch." On one side of the page Stevenson wrote, "Pres[ident's] job," on the other side this cryptic statement: "Confid[ential] Strauss[89] secretive! Feared McM [Macmillan] would think we'd deceived him, mutiny. Strauss — resign."

Number 3 stated that development of the U.S. position involved methods of "getting across" to our NATO allies the facts of U.S. nuclear capability available for their defense and methods of "assuring our NATO allies that this nuclear capability will in fact be employed in their defense." Stevenson wrote opposite this: "Can't be done by this Adm[inistration]! Asking me to say you can trust Ike! Deeds not words and machinery."

On the top of page 4 Stevenson wrote: "Must have group here to talk to; before action they would have access to Pres, will be heard!"

The next day Dulles wrote Stevenson, ". . . I hope that your response will be affirmative. It would symbolize at home and abroad solidarity with respect to a sector of our international policy where, I think, there cannot be any serious difference of opinion. . . ."

The Administration wanted Stevenson's help because of his prestige. The proposal, however, meant that although he was to prepare the American position, the Secretary of State and the President were free to use it or not, as they saw fit. Stevenson asked the advice of members of the Democratic Advisory Council, Senator Lyndon B. Johnson, Speaker Sam Rayburn, Thomas K. Finletter, George W. Ball, and other close friends.

To John Foster Dulles

November 3, 1957

PERSONAL AND CONFIDENTIAL

Dear Foster:

I appreciate your letter which I find on my return to Chicago. I have thought long and anxiously about our discussion. Reluctantly I have come to the conclusion that it would be a mistake for me to attempt to formulate policies for presentation by the President at the Summit Meeting of the North Atlantic Treaty Council in December, even if we could restrict the scope of my work to matters relating to the NATO

---

[89] Lewis Strauss, chairman of the Atomic Energy Commission.

area alone and to the subjects covered in the U.S.–British Declaration of Common Purpose of October 25. The problems are so many and so complex, I do not believe I could organize a staff to consider them adequately and recommend proposals with supporting detail in time for the NATO meeting, let alone in time for the President's meeting with the Congressional leaders on December 1.

I recognize fully the gravity of the situation and the crucial importance to the Alliance of the tasks which you and the President are facing, and I am flattered that you want my help.

However, I believe that policy formation, in the circumstances, is not only the responsibility of the President and you, but that no one else is or could be in the same position to do it, what with the vast resources of the Federal [Executive?] Branch and familiarity with the personalities and conflicts available to you. I doubt, moreover, if this responsibility should be assumed or could be performed by an "opposition" leader (if I can still claim that title!) as a temporary member of the Executive Branch, no matter how highly placed.

But I do not want to leave it there. I would be glad to review and discuss your proposals from time to time before they are put into final form. And where we are in agreement, I will do such "missionary" work as I can and give such policies all the support, private, public and political, as I can, both here and abroad.

Indeed, if advance consultation with our Allies would be helpful or contribute to greater solidarity and confidence, I would undertake to make such a journey as a special envoy of the President.

What I am trying to say is that in this situation, I don't believe I care to assume the responsibility for formulating United States policy and position. I believe that is for the President to do. But I have both a duty and a desire to do what I can to strengthen the Atlantic Community and to be as helpful to the President and you as I can.

I don't believe I need to repeat my gratitude for your confidence or assure you I have tried not to let partisanship or personal convenience influence my decision in a matter of such urgency and consequence to our country.

I wish the President and you the greatest possible success at the Council meeting.

Sincerely yours,

P.S. When I can get it typewritten, I will send you some of the matters which occurred to me during my travels the last few days that the United States should consider in an effort to strengthen the Alliance.

A.E.S.

PRELIMINARY MEMORANDUM RE: U.S. POSITION AT NORTH ATLANTIC TREATY COUNCIL MEETING IN DECEMBER 1957

November 4, 1957

CONFIDENTIAL

As I understand it, our objective is to increase the strength of NATO by restoring mutual confidence and enlarging the sense of an interdependent community among its members.

With the loss of U.S. monopoly in the air-atomic weapons and for other reasons, uncertainty has been increasing about our capabilities and our resolution to use our capabilities in defense of our friends at the risk of nuclear retaliation. Britain is developing its own nuclear defenses and expensively learning things we — and Russia! — already know. France is threatening to follow suit; others will too, and the danger of these weapons some time falling into irresponsible hands is increasing. Irrational nuclear armament is also an extravagance the Atlantic community can ill afford when its combined resources are needed for the common defense and for the economic development of the retarded areas.

NATO was a response to the necessity of concerting the power of the Atlantic Community to meet the menace of post-war Russian truculence, ambition and power. With the U.S.S.R. still aggressive and able to frustrate collective defense measures in the U.N. by veto or defiance, the NATO concept of community security is still valid. But the *power* and *purpose* of the Atlantic Alliance must be quickly and vigorously refreshed to arrest neutralism, restore mutual confidence among the allies and reassure the larger world about Western intentions and capabilities. The urgency has been dramatized for us by the demonstrated scientific prowess of the Soviets.

How can this be done? It cannot be done by the U.S. alone, but it cannot be done at all if the U.S. doesn't take a strong and prompt initiative.

The Declaration of Common Purpose of the President and Prime Minister of October 25, 1957, suggests some objectives:

(a) Pooling scientific resources and sharing tasks.

(b) More knowledge of the military capabilities of the Alliance.

(c) Confidence that it will be available in case of need for the common security.

(d) Confidence that it will not be misused for purposes other than self-defense.

(e) Economic action to support the cooperative security effort.

The emphasis of this communique was almost exclusively military. Accepting this as a first priority, if by no means the whole answer, the following are some of the areas of action at the December meeting that occur to me as *means* to the declared *end:*

(1) Reaffirm the non-aggressive purpose and character of NATO; that its purpose is peace in a world divided by two systems — freedom and Communism, that NATO does not propose to destroy the Communist system by force, and that it will resist — *with appropriate weapons* — any attempt to destroy *it* by force; but that it welcomes competition in the economic and social fields.

(2) Create a committee (under the Secretary General?) to pool scientists and scientific research, at least as to allies with tolerable security systems. We need all the brains we have and can borrow from one another.

Propose to amend our secrecy laws. It is widely said that our "secrets" are better known to the scientists of our enemies than our friends. Certainly it seems ridiculous for Britain to be spending heavily to discover what is already known to us — and the Soviets.

Genuine rationalization of research and development here and abroad and appropriate redistribution of scientists has important practical and psychological advantages — *if* it is possible.

Should NATO undertake the stimulation of scientific education among member states?

(3) Empower some group to decide from time to time what weapons should be produced where. Some weapons can and should be made in Europe. And Europe should make its contribution to the cost. How much better for the U.K., for example, to spend money on weapons for the common defense than in duplicating research and facilities.

Perhaps a sufficient start would be to confine weapon production generally to the U.S., Britain and France.

(4) Offer to arm NATO with tactical nuclear weapons. (I am not informed about what means of delivery of *strategic* weapons our allies have but presumably ours should remain with SAC.)[90]

Doubtless many security and other reasons will be advanced in opposition, but while asking our Allies to have confidence in *us* they are asking the U.S. to prove that *we* have confidence in *them,* and both will take more than words.

[90] The Strategic Air Command, the command of the United States Air Force responsible for long-range bombers and intercontinental ballistic missiles.

(5) Create a "Nuclear Council" of NATO in Washington to keep all members fully informed about capabilities in being and in prospect of U.S. and all NATO states.

Some such new machinery situated here where the bulk of our power is located may be necessary to keep abreast of developments and allay uncertainties in member states.

(6) Agree to the creation of a "political high command" charged with deciding where nuclear weapons should be used by NATO or member states.

How should it be comprised? How constituted to function quickly? What preliminary soundings at home and abroad?

(7) I am not sure that NATO is a suitable instrument for collective economic development programs in the retarded countries — a responsibility and mechanism of defense that is of equivalent or greater importance than military strength.

But the NATO Council should be able to devise machinery for prompt consultation and action in cases involving member states, like the Iceland fish and Lebanon apples.

In addition to the foregoing obvious points with which the December meeting must deal, there are some other considerations which I am hastily recording without regard to priority, relative importance or attempting to exhaust the list.

(1) If we don't — *in fact* — have balanced or better military capabilities than the Russians, et al, then candor with our allies becomes the first condition of confidence.

(2) Our people have lived in complacent ignorance so long they have little conception of the dimensions of the battle or the greater effort required. This public information job — in which the President is a major factor — must avoid the extremes of foolish defeatism and hysteria, on the one hand, and half measures and easy outs on the other. The major component is the truth!

(3) The main threat is *not military aggression,* but subversion by propaganda, economic bribery and political penetration. Have we any common plans to counter such ambiguous aggressions?

(4) If the Atlantic Community had multilateral economic and trade development plans it would mean a lot more to many people than its purely military anti-communism does now.

Is an experimental plan to stabilize some raw material prices, which is so important to the underdeveloped areas, beyond the capacity of a league of the principal industrial states like NATO?

(5) Is the administration prepared to reverse itself on the debt limit and the budget ceiling?

(6) Is the reliance on air-atomic retaliation a realistic deterrent to "nibbling" aggression? Doesn't NATO need highly mobile striking forces — plus determination to *use* them! — for quick response to smaller clashes before they get out of hand? Who will furnish them?

Obviously we will have to do a large part of this job and we should be ready to say so at this meeting.

(7) We must get across the idea that each must do his part; none of us can do it all himself — including the U.S.!

(8) I *repeat* that more flexibility and more initiative toward disarmament, at least nuclear disarmament, is imperative. We must be ready for new Russian proposals which may be extremely effective as propaganda. I have often said that suspension of nuclear testing with suitable monitoring posts to safeguard against violation should not be made conditional on cessation of production of nuclear materials. It would be an important first step; it would break the deadlock and halt or slow down the dangerous race which at best leads only to stalemate and a balance of terror.

(9) The concluding words of the Eisenhower-Macmillan Declaration seems to repeat Secretary Dulles' familiar thesis that Russia is in disorder and if we hold fast the Communist system will break down or be modified. While this may be true, it is a premise that few leaders I know accept, with the exception of Chancellor Adenauer, and therefore should not be constantly repeated as a reassurance.

(10) In this connection, I must say, too, that I have found *no one* who agrees with our rigid China policy and *many* who credit it with much of our lost confidence.

(11) Nor, if our allies consent, does it seem wise to refuse to discuss any hope of peace bilaterally with the Russians. From my meager experience more could be accomplished by asking questions and reconnoitering the areas of possible accommodation alone and face to face in the traditional manner of diplomacy.

But this "brief" memo of first impressions is neither brief nor altogether relevant!

To Thomas K. Finletter[91]

November 4, 1957

Dear Tom:

On November 11 I have to attend and probably speak at a banquet at the Waldorf-Astoria at which one of the principal contributors is being

---

[91] The original is in the possession of Mr. Finletter.

honored. If I get out in time I will come to your house to see Bevan.[92] I would like very much to talk with him, quietly and without a crowd, and not knowing how to reach him have asked Gunther[93] to ask him if he could have lunch with me on the 13th. Gunther had written me about some other things. Perhaps you could also ask him, if you know how to reach him.

I was unable to reach Nitze[94] by telephone because he was on the way to Boston. I will wire him from here.

I think the meeting would be more productive if everyone had their views as to what should be accomplished at the NATO meeting, and how, on paper. I will try to get my thoughts sorted out and recorded. I have promised a preliminary memo to Dulles, whom I have written as per the enclosed copy, and also talked to him by telephone.

Yours,
ADLAI

P.S. . . .

P.P.S. — And this is *my* lunch!

P.P.P.S. In my telephone talk with Dulles yesterday he was very agreeable and suggested that maybe I was right in feeling that policy formulation could not and should not be delegated. He also indicated that he would want to take advantage of the opportunity to consult.[95]

[92] Aneurin Bevan, a Member of Parliament and treasurer of the British Labour Party.

[93] John Gunther, author of *Inside Europe* (1936), *Inside Asia* (1939), *Inside Africa* (1955), and numerous other books.

[94] Paul Nitze, former director of the Policy Planning Staff of the State Department under President Truman.

[95] Secretary Dulles wrote Stevenson on November 5:

"I thank you for your letter of November 3, confirmatory of our telephone conversation of that date.

"I had not meant to suggest that you would be responsible for policy formation but rather, as indicated in the draft paper I gave you, to develop our position under paragraphs 5 and 6 of the Eisenhower-Macmillan "Declaration of Common Purpose" whereby our basic policy is established. Also as that memorandum suggested, I had assumed that you would in this respect receive political guidance from the Secretary of State. What I had envisaged was very much like what I undertook for President Truman and Secretary Acheson when I negotiated the Japanese Peace Treaty, with broad guidance from the President and Secretary of State. However, I accept the conclusion you have come to in this respect.

"I welcome your offer to review and discuss our proposals from time to time before they are put into final form. Just how this is physically arranged and what we say publicly will call for a little thought.

"The matter of advance consultation abroad with our Allies would, I think, best be dealt with after our ideas are somewhat further advanced as to what of substance we might propose. It can then be better determined, I think, how this had best be conducted. I appreciate, as does the President, your offer in this respect.

". . . I shall await with interest the memorandum of suggestions referred to in

Chakravarti Rajagopalachari, former governor general of India whom Stevenson met in India in 1953, wrote deploring the armaments race with the Soviet Union and expressing his concern that the course followed by the United States and the Soviet Union could lead to "world suicide." He asked, "Can't the great minds of the United States grasp the sword of Christ instead of running after Khrushchev?"

To Chakravarti Rajagopalachari

November 7, 1957

My dear Friend:

Yes, it seems senseless, this ludicrous dance of death that costs so much and should go into productive development where it is needed, all over the earth. And it can only lead to stalemate at best and a balance of terror. But at worst it leads to the power of coercion, threat, and conquest by intimidation. So what do we do? Well, we keep chasing one another, the democracies lagging behind and then spurting forward, goaded by anxiety, the Soviets pressing relentlessly on to a goal I daresay they perceive no better than ours. But how and when does reason triumph? To borrow your exciting phrase, when and how does the United States grasp the sword of Christ?

I keep telling our politicians of both parties that we *must* yield a point here and there on disarmament to persuade the Russians to come along and take a first step. But it is all very hard when they manage to foul every nest with their truculent talk and manifest power.

I wish I could write your kind of "wrote"!

With all best wishes, I am

Cordially,

Stevenson spent the week of November 11 in New York City on legal matters and in discussions with associates, including Thomas K. Finletter and Paul Nitze, about his recommendations to Dulles and Eisenhower for the NATO meeting. On November 12, presidential press secretary James C. Hagerty told reporters that Stevenson had rejected a White House invitation to "take part in the work of preparing an American program" for the NATO meeting. Hagerty stated that Stevenson

---

your postscript. This, I know, will be very welcome and then we could again talk together.

"I am disappointed that your participation will be somewhat more limited than I had first envisaged. I greatly appreciate, however, the sympathetic thought you have given to our suggestion and am glad that you may be willing to help."

did, however, offer to comment on the U.S. program once it was sub-
mitted to other NATO countries. When asked what "comment" meant,
Hagerty replied, "Public comment."

Stevenson, after reading Hagerty's remarks, talked to Dulles on the
telephone. A record was kept of part of the conversation.

STEVENSON: If you would rather let me put this out and you could put
   out both of the letters. It's making a hell of a mountain out of it. The
   present posture is I am trying to find an area in which I could help if
   you want me to and I've tried to indicate what that area would be.

DULLES: I told him [Hagerty] that without attempting to formulate policies, or something like that. I would be glad to discuss them, however, if you say. Yet I think we could let it go at that.

STEVENSON: What language do you have in mind?

DULLES: I would say that without attempting myself to formulate policies, or something like that.

STEVENSON: Without attempting. I offered him my full cooperation in
   reviewing and discussing our government's proposals before they are
   put into final shape without attempting myself to formulate those
   policies.

DULLES: Yes, something like that. "I told him that" — How does that
   sentence start?

STEVENSON: That invites a lot more inquiries as to just what proposals
   were formulated. Let me see if I can put something like that in there
   without assuming responsibility for formulating. Can you follow this
   up by indicating that this reflects the understanding and position we
   are now in?

DULLES: Yes.

STEVENSON: I will get out something here and if we want to put out
   these letters it is entirely all right with me.

DULLES: I would rather not put out the letters; that will open up widespread discussion. I would rather shortcut it if I could. There will be
   great arguments about them; the press tries to stir up trouble. That's
   the way they like to handle these things. We can shortcut that by a
   statement of yours. It is better than to give out letters.

STEVENSON: I will see what I can do and get it out promptly.

At 12:15 P.M. on November 12, 1957, Stevenson received the follow-
ing telephone call from James C. Hagerty.

STEVENSON: Hello.

HAGERTY: This is Jim Hagerty, how are you, sir?

STEVENSON: Fine, thank you.

HAGERTY: I tried to get you this morning. Tried you at the Savoy Plaza and left word for you to call.

STEVENSON: What time did you try? I usually leave before 9:30. This morning I left at 9:15.[96]

HAGERTY: I didn't know where you were. I didn't want to call you if you were in Chicago and wake you up at 8 o'clock; that was the reason I delayed. I put the call in, as I recall it, about 9:30.

STEVENSON: What are you calling me about?

HAGERTY: I was calling you to tell you what I was going to say. I assume you had seen the stories that first came out of Chicago.

STEVENSON: What does that mean? I haven't been in Chicago since last Thursday.

HAGERTY: From the AP and UP last evening — as a result of stories carried in the Chicago papers. That was the first time I got clearance. Last night I said I had no comment but this morning, in answer to [a question at the] press conference I said you had been invited in participation of the work on NATO to comment on whatever program would be developed.

STEVENSON: This is about as long as it could be. That is no surprise to me now.

HAGERTY: That was all I had to say.

STEVENSON: All right, thank you very much.

After talking with Hagerty, Stevenson issued the following statement the same day.

As a matter of courtesy to the President and Secretary Dulles, I have declined to comment on recent press stories about my possible partici-pation in the NATO meeting.

In view of Mr. Hagerty's statement I must now say that I have had no direct contact with President Eisenhower whatever. At Mr. Dulles' re-quest I have discussed the NATO meeting with him and possible assis-

[96] At the end of the typewritten transcript Stevenson wrote, "This is all wrong!" with an arrow pointing to this place in the text.

tance in preparation for it. A week ago I assured him, orally and by letter, that while I could not undertake to formulate the President's policies, I would gladly review and discuss our government's proposals before they were put into final shape.[97] Where we were in agreement I offered to do such "missionary" work and provide such support as I could — privately, publicly and politically — both in this country and in Europe among our Allies. I have also given the Secretary of State a memorandum of my first impressions of the problems we must confront.

In view of the gravity of our situation in the world I have both a desire and a duty to assist our government, regardless of partisanship or personal convenience.

Shortly after launching the first Sputnik on October 4, 1957, the USSR successfully orbited Sputnik II, carrying a live dog, on November 3. Although the United States was able to launch a satellite of its own less than three months later, on January 31, 1958, the Russian achievement had considerable impact on American public opinion for some time afterwards. The demand for excellence was heard everywhere and appeared to affect every aspect of American life. One notable result of the furor over Sputnik was a rush to expand and strengthen science education programs; another was the beginning of another upward spiral in the arms race.

On arrival in Washington on November 17, Stevenson issued the following statement.

Sputnik has awakened us. I am glad it has. But simply a greater effort in scientific research and missile development is not a sufficient response to the challenge which is now apparent.

We must rebuild mutual confidence between the United States and our allies. They need us and we need them more than ever. And I am here to help if I can to bring about a closer military and political association through NATO. Genuine partnership means more than pooling our military and scientific resources. We must also work out joint policies in areas of common interest and common danger *before* crises like Suez arise.

[97] Shortly after Stevenson's statement, Hagerty explained to reporters that he had been in error that morning. Stevenson would present his comments to the Administration on its program as it developed: "These comments will be more in the nature of consultations while the program is being prepared, not just public statements after the program is completed." See Doris Fleeson, Chicago *Daily News*, November 15, 1957, for her analysis of the situation.

More likely than the unlimited nuclear-missile war is limited Communist aggression, as in Greece, Korea, Indo-China and Malaya. A stand-off in weapons of mass destruction will not prevent limited wars. And we must have highly mobile forces and the means of their delivery any place to prevent or confine brush fires before they spread.

But the measure of the emergency is not merely military. A danger quite as great as Soviet domination by long range missiles is a Communist economic breakthrough in the under-developed areas. If sustained economic growth under democratic auspices fails, people will turn to the Russian example. I believe we must mobilize the productive resources of all of us to demonstrate that voluntary democratic methods can be more efficient as well as more humane in economic modernization.

I believe that disarmament, at least nuclear disarmament, is the best hope for survival and that we must never be diverted from that goal.

Finally, I believe that the pursuit of life, liberty and happiness is going to take a lot more public understanding, self-discipline and effort than we have put forth lately.

President Eisenhower wrote Stevenson, "I am delighted that you and Foster will be getting together on Monday to discuss our preparations for the NATO meeting in December. . . . I share his view that you can be of real help to us in this work." He added that he did not expect to be in Washington on November 18 but later there would be conferences at which "we can both be present."

To Dwight D. Eisenhower[98]

Sunday Night, November 17, 1957

Dear Mr. President:

I am grateful for your kind letter of November 14 which arrived in New York yesterday as I was leaving town.

I hope that my discussion with Secretary Dulles and his staff may prove of some help in preparing for the NATO meeting, which I trust is not timed too soon to explore with our allies what can be usefully accomplished at Paris next month.

Perhaps [I should] take this opportunity to say what I am sure we all understand — that while I must be free to seek advice in my informal consultative capacity from persons outside the Department, including

[98] The text is from a typewritten copy of Stevenson's handwritten original.

leaders of my party, and also to express my views, even where they may differ from the administration, I shall strive to promote national unity in furtherance of the great tasks before us.

With apologies for this handwritten note and every good wish, I am

Respectfully yours,

Stevenson spent three days in Washington. On November 18 he and Dulles talked at length and Dulles gave him a number of proposals to study. After his three-day visit, Stevenson returned to Chicago to attend to business affairs.

To Mrs. Ernest L. Ives[99]

November 21, 1957

Dear Buff:

It has been a trying fortnight, but I had a wonderful week-end with the boys in Cambridge. Borden's progress is good even if employment looks as distant as ever.

I shall do the best I can with this miserable assignment. I felt there was no choice but to respond within the narrow limits proposed, and they accepted. To refuse to do anything would have been bad citizenship and therefore maybe bad politics. But it is a melancholy job, surrounded by people who mean me no good.

Florence Mahoney, who is in Hong Kong, has loaned me her house,[100] which may be more convenient than a hotel or guesting. I will probably have Bill [Blair] and Tom Finletter there with me, off and on. I will also have a lot of help in Washington from George Ball, Paul Nitze, etc. outside the Department.

Adlai and Nancy have moved into their house,[101] which still looks chaotic to me, but they seem content. Alverta is bringing the new woman up for a look Saturday and I think I will let my aliens depart if she looks all right.[102] I must go back East soon, probably for two weeks, then perhaps on to Paris, although that I shall avoid if I possibly can because of the danger of too great involvement.

LOVE,
ADLAI

P.S. Thank Ernest for his heartening wire.

[99] The original is in E.S.I., I.S.H.L.
[100] In Georgetown.
[101] In Chicago.
[102] The friend Alverta Duff brought with her from Bloomington to be Stevenson's housekeeper found it too lonely at Libertyville and stayed only a short time.

To Dean Rusk[103]

November 21, 1957

Dear Dean:

Thank you for coming to luncheon the other day and also for the splendid pieces, most especially the one on China[104] which helps me a great deal.

I will go back to Washington on Monday next after a few hours in New York and stay there for a fortnight working over the Department's papers. If you have any ideas for me as your thought matures on what can and should be done to give the NATO meeting a lift, I hope you will get in touch with me either at the Department of State, or at the house where I will be staying at 3600 Prospect Avenue, Adams 2-6888.

Cordially yours,

To Chakravarti Rajagopalachari

November 21, 1957

My dear Friend:

Your beautiful letter has travelled back and forth across the country with me during these last difficult weeks. Little by little our land is becoming aware of what we have long known and the unhappy posture of our affairs, not only do I mean just unhappy in the sense of being behind the Russians in some weapon development, but rather in the loss of confidence and prestige and moral respect. I agree with you that a response to a weapon challenge with greater weapons effort is doomed to failure. Not alone can the Russians, who can subordinate the people's standard of living to the State's objective, probably out-produce us in the long run, but I fear that what we call freedom, which is so wonderfully good, will not inflame the loyalty of peoples who know little about it, democracy and consent and a lot about hunger and want.

There is much to write about all this and I wish I had both the time and the talent to put the "agonizing reappraisal" through which we are now passing in proper context for you. It can be both good and bad. The effort to avoid the truth goes on and our response therefore will be less than total and more military than mighty I fear. But there are many who perceive, as you do, the realities. I hope their tribe increases — and a lecture tour by you, Sir, would light the right fires in the highlands.

With very warm, respectful regards, I am

Cordially yours,

---

[103] Former Assistant Secretary of State.

[104] Mr. Rusk had prepared a memorandum on relations with the People's Republic of China.

Dr. Albert Schweitzer wrote Stevenson on November 15, criticizing the West for not discussing the cessation of nuclear tests proposed by the Soviet Union. He also expressed concern over the American government's response to the Sputniks by increasing nuclear armaments.

To Dr. Albert Schweitzer

November 22, 1957

My dear Dr. Schweitzer:

I have your letter, and for it I shall be everlastingly grateful. I share wholly and with acute anguish your dismay about our military response to Sputnik. But there are other voices in this country, that perhaps are less audible to you, and I am not inaudible in the State Department, either!

But I would be less than candid if I didn't express my hope that, while calling upon America not to pursue this mad course, you do not overlook the proposals the West has made and the Soviet Union has rejected — total suspension of tests and discontinuance of production of fissionable materials for weapons, safeguarded by inspection. It would seem to me that those who pray for deliverance from nuclear bondage could well call upon the Russians, and very loudly, to evidence their sincerity by accepting our proposals. While personally I would go further toward meeting the Russians' lesser offer, I cannot believe that we must bear all the criticism for the deadlock when they won't meet our better proposal — better, that is, for mankind, because it includes the ending of production as well as testing.

I wish so much that I could have another talk with you soon — with the exquisite assistance of Clara [Urquhart]!

With my respect and affection,

Cordially yours,

P.S. I have been thinking that maybe you should some day call upon both the East and the West to accept one proposal or the other; that the great imperative is no more testing, which means no more development of thermonuclear weapons of any size, and the elimination of those we have. I may write you again further in this regard, if you will forgive me.

A.E.S.

To J. William Fulbright[105]

November 22, 1957

Dear Bill:

I hope when you get back to Washington you will let me know. I would like to have a little time with you in connection with my melancholy task.

Yours,

P.S. You can reach me at "home" — 3600 Prospect Ave., N.W., telephone Adams 2-6888, or the State Department, telephone Republic 7-5600.

To Lloyd K. Garrison

November 22, 1957

Dear Lloyd:

I do not anticipate any problems under the federal conflict of interest statutes, but for the full protection of both my partners and myself should any question ever arise as a result of my position as a temporary consultant to the State Department, I want you to take whatever steps may be required to separate me from all firm activities and earnings for a period of one month, including my $3,000.00 a month draw, retroactive to November 20, 1957, the date I was sworn in as a consultant.

Cordially,

Emily Morison Beck, of the Atlantic Monthly Press, sent Stevenson a copy of the latest edition of Bartlett's Familiar Quotations.

To Mrs. Brooks Beck

November 23, 1957

Dear Mrs. Beck:

Thank you, my dear friend, for the new Bartlett's — and for that page of Stevenson. I wonder how long it will last in such formidable competition! But you have launched my little Sputnik of immortality, and I am grateful indeed.

I enjoyed so much my two brief glimpses of you.

Cordially yours,

[105] U.S. senator from Arkansas.

Stevenson, accompanied by William McC. Blair, Jr., and Carol Evans, returned to Washington on November 25 to work at an office in the Department of State. Miss Evans worked at the Washington office of the Stevenson law firm since she could not be given a security clearance in time to work at the State Department. On arrival Stevenson issued the following statement.

I am constantly asked about the political implications of my temporary service to the President and Secretary of State in preparation for the NATO meeting. I also hear that there is some resentment among my friends about the way I have been greeted by the administration.[106]

I wish to say that I am not interested in ceremonials, titles or manners. I came to Washington not for fun or fanfare but to help out — to lend what experience, influence and confidence I have to my country in a critical hour. I have had a cordial welcome and full cooperation from the Secretary and the State Department.

No limitations on my freedom of speech have been imposed or even suggested. Likewise, I do not want to interfere with anyone's freedom to criticize. I do not speak for the Democratic party, but for myself alone. And to avoid any possible embarrassment I will not participate in purely party activities until my service is terminated.

The salary provided by law in my case I intend to give to Charity.

And now I want to get to work. The time is short and there is much to do.

Stevenson attempted to keep a diary. He succeeded — for one day.

Monday, November 25, 1957

I returned to the Department of State in Washington on Monday, November 25, and was assigned very adequate room on the sixth floor, with Arthur Compton, Jr. as my assistant, and two secretaries. The accumulated scores of letters I sent over to my law office for Miss Evans to manage. New position papers on scientific and technical cooperation, weapon development production and economic cooperation were delivered to me. I had lunch with ex-Congressman [James P.] Richards (South Carolina), former Chairman of the House Foreign Relations

---

[106] Doris Fleeson had noted in her column that on Stevenson's visit to Washington the week before, "he was not met at the airport Sunday night by any administration official and he was left to make his own arrangements. . . . The President has still to speak to Stevenson. . . ." Chicago *Daily News*, November 21, 1957.

*Committee and now Special Assistant to the Secretary, to discuss
political liaison. He thought I should talk to [Lyndon] Johnson, [Sam]
Rayburn, and not worry too much about the House and Senate committees or the conferees summoned by the President for the NATO
briefing on December 3. He suggested Mansfield[107] and [J. William]
Fulbright as good members of the Senate Committee and Morgan[108]
and Cannon[109] in the House. He was very forthright about his disappointment over Southern Senators on foreign aid and the growing
patriotism. When I asked him why he was for it he said he knew and
that the Secretary knew how serious the situation was and how important it was to reassure the Europeans that even if there was a change
of administration in Washington our basic policy was constant. He felt
that this was more on their minds than domestic bipartisanship, etc.*

*At two o'clock I met with Secretary Dulles to review his meeting with
[Heinrich] Von Brentano, the German Foreign Minister, over the week-
end. The latter put great emphasis on political consultation, even as
Foreign Minister Pineau[110] had done. He also assured Dulles that the
German economic structure was "fragile," the effective interest rate was
10 per cent, new expenses were on the suffering refugees, new housing,
military effort, etc. Evidently the Germans are not going to be too helpful with economic assistance.*

*Brentano made some point of the importance of emphasizing at the
NATO meeting that NATO is a permanent association, not expiring in a
few years or with the expiration of the Soviet threat but a natural
regional association that must continue for the benefit of order. I talked
with Dulles about this before and he asked me to prepare some paragraphs for the President's speech for the summit meeting communique.
Dulles again pointed out that the Strategic Air Command was useful
until about 1960 and then would be superseded by missiles, that by that
time we would be ready for deliveries so that if our allies commence
now with the intricate training, financing, launching site development
we would be ready by the time they are ready. Dulles again expressed
his anxiety about the Joint Chiefs who don't accept the principle of
"allied interdependence" and are concerned with the trustworthiness
of the allies.*

*Von Brentano emphasized that the non-military aspect of the NATO
alliances should be emphasized because it makes it easier to accept the
military commitments in Germany.*

[107] Senator Mike Mansfield, of Montana.
[108] Representative Thomas E. Morgan, of Pennsylvania.
[109] Representative Clarence Canon, of Missouri.
[110] French Foreign Minister Christian Pineau

After reviewing the draft paper on scientific and technical coopera-tion, weapons development and production and related matters, I was visited by Randolph Burgess, Ambassador to NATO, prior to attending the long session of Task Force II. Burgess said he would return to Paris on Saturday and wanted to take with him a paper setting forth our views in principle at least, so that the member nations will have a little while to review our proposals before the meeting.

General Cutler[111] Assistant to the President, was Chairman of the Task Force II meeting, which lasted three hours. Dr. Killian,[112] of Massachusetts Institute of Technology, proposed a number of changes in the portions relating to scientific cooperation and money. When we reached the questions of who would "trigger" the bomb, Secretary Quarles[113] of the Defense Department, expressed the view that this matter should not be exaggerated as it had been in fact settled: the President alone can do it and he has indicated that his authority is implicit in the NATO Commander in the event of attack and that through him he exercises his authority.

There was prolonged discussion about ways and means of cutting our allies in on the production of certain weapons abroad, the deployment of delivery systems and warheads, and their control, and amendments to the law required to share weapons and nuclear science information.

I had a feeling that the atmosphere in the room with representatives of the services, the AEC [Atomic Energy Commission], the Bureau of the Budget, as well as the State Department, was more one of concern with how we made a profession of good will and confidence than the reality. But I was pleased to note audible declarations that the meeting had to have more than a military content.

To Mrs. Edison Dick[114]

November 28, 1957

My dear Jane:

It is Thanksgiving Day and we are hard at it — as usual! How I wish I were sharing the festivities on Woodland Road.[115]

---

[111] Robert Cutler, a Boston banker and special assistant to the President for national security affairs.

[112] James R. Killian, Jr., president of Massachusetts Institute of Technology, special assistant to the President for science and technology, and chairman of the President's Scientific Advisory Commission.

[113] Secretary of the Air Force Donald A. Quarles.

[114] The original is in the possession of Mrs. Dick.

[115] The Dicks' home in Lake Forest, Illinois.

I enclose a quote I happened to see in the Washington Post that should be added to the Christmas Card possibilities.

I am not sure when I shall be home to resolve — among many other questions — this small problem, but it might be around December 10.

Have I thanked you and Eddie properly for taking in my family and in-laws for Thanksgiving? Of course not. Like everything else, my thanks can never catch up with my gratitude.

Affectionately,

ADLAI

To John Foster Dulles

November 29, 1957

PERSONAL AND CONFIDENTIAL

SUBJECT: NATO Heads of Government Meeting

I have been here a week and this is an interim report of my reactions. I will give you another in a fortnight, when the preparation for the meeting will be over and my work finished.

The paper work I have seen seems to be good and with much of it I agree. To make these comments as brief as possible I will emphasize my criticisms:

1. A meeting of heads of state on December 16 seems to me too early for proper preparation and Congressional concurrence. Hence the President is in the undesirable position of making conditional or uncertain proposals.

In addition, I fear that the advance disclosure of the nuclear stockpile, scientific exchange and weapon production in Europe has anticipated much of the significant business of the meeting, and also lost the value of prior diplomatic exchange with enhanced sense of participation and some domestic prestige and support among our partners.

For these and other reasons I regret that the meeting must proceed as a heads of state meeting with the risks of anticlimax.

2. I am troubled by the lack of a sense of urgency. I came to Washington to work first in 1933, again early in 1941;[116] both times the atmosphere was different. I wish it was now.

The response to Sputnik, etc. doesn't seem to meet the measure of the emergency. It seems to be compounded largely of more missiles and more reassurances. But it is obvious to the informed that a much greater

116 For Stevenson's service in Washington during the New Deal, see *The Papers of Adlai E. Stevenson*, Vol. I, Part Eight; for his wartime service as special assistant to Secretary of the Navy Frank Knox, see *The Papers of Adlai E. Stevenson*, Vol. II, Part One.

effort is required all along the line, and that firm and far-reaching decisions in principle should be made promptly within the Executive Branch. If it is made clear now that Congress will be asked for a comprehensive program to reverse current trends, I believe public and Congressional support would be better assured.

This basic decision is related to NATO. I doubt very much if it will be possible to communicate much sense of urgency and determination to our allies in Paris if we have not made the measure of the emergency clear at home.

3. *Political Consultation.* The political differences between the NATO states are dangerously enfeebling. Our allies want more than just military reassurances, they want political reassurances. I think we would too.

You have stressed the dilemma of choice between close collaboration with our Atlantic allies and winning support among Asian and African states. But I do not believe that we have interests in the Middle East and in Asia which differ materially any longer from those of our NATO partners. I doubt whether our interest in the survival of a democratic India is any greater or any less than Europe's. Collapse of the Western position in the Pacific would be as fatal to Europe as to us. Who can say whether we or our NATO partners have been more seriously damaged by the deteriorating situation in the Middle East? Our differences with our allies have not been so much differences of interest as differences in judgment as to the wisdom of actions.

I hope we can say and do more to make it clear that in our view the members of an alliance must have a due concern for the special interests of each, even as each must have a due concern for the interests of all — the alliance itself; that we want to and will, if possible, help to make NATO a more effective agency for the solution of enfeebling internecine conflicts, like Algeria, Cyprus and Tunisia.[117] These are not merely problems of Great Britain and France; they are problems in which we are all deeply concerned. Similarly, our problems with South Korea, Taiwan, Jordan, etc. are problems in which our NATO allies suffer with us.

In meeting the threat presented by our highly organized opponent, successful resistance on the periphery is possible only if there is unity at the core. What we are faced with is the monolithic menace of the Soviet Union and its satellites — a menace which can be effectively met only by a solid resistance on the part of the West.

[117] Tunisia complained that France was violating her airspace and territorial rights as a result of skirmishes with Algerian rebels who, France claimed, had taken refuge in Tunisian territory.

I know your concern about flexibility for prompt action, but I do not think it incompatible with a greater anxiety to harmonize political action than the papers prepared for the meeting suggest.

4. *Limited War Capability.* Since nuclear standoff and the deterrence of nuclear war is the best we can hope for from our nuclear defenses, it is obvious that we must take timely steps to provide the other necessary military supports for our policy.

In the position papers I have seen, I don't find clear evidence of an intention to build up the conventional strength of NATO to resist a limited Soviet aggression. It would appear that the intention is to use tactical nuclear weapons as the automatic answer to Soviet aggression.

The Soviet Union is more likely to create an ambiguous than an unequivocal aggression. What we may well be confronted with on the Eastern front is a challenge to Berlin or to Yugoslavia or to Warsaw — a challenge resulting not so much from Soviet tanks or guns as from a subversive local Communist movement. I am not at all sure that such an "ambiguous aggression" can be adequately met by the forces now available to the Western Alliance.

At the same time, can any aggression be met by the use of tactical nuclear weapons, in a crowded industrial area such as Western Europe without precipitating general war?

My doubts are more of a caveat than an imperative. I think we have accepted the proposition too quickly that no conventional defense can be interposed to a possible Soviet aggression in Europe.

Outside the NATO theatre I see an even greater need for a conventional force availability, including airlift, to cope with small wars and keep them small. I am sure a lot of people want reassurance that with all the talk of missiles and nuclear weapons we are not neglecting our conventional capability and tempting the enemy to nibble at the edges of the free world. I wish it was clearer from what I have read and heard that the U.S. had taken steps to enable it to deliver an effective conventional force wherever needed.

5. *Economic Development.* I find the suggested position paper (PRS Memo 104a) on economic assistance inadequate.

Just now the hottest war is the cold war. I think the United States should take a strong affirmative lead to organize and enlarge the financial and technical resources of the capital countries to accelerate the economic development of underdeveloped areas. By announcing his intention to ask Congress for the means to increase our own efforts, the President will be in position to ask for a larger measure of effort from our allies, especially the Germans.

The purpose of the meeting in Paris is to strengthen not only NATO but the free world as a whole. We should make it clear that in the American view the military defense of Europe and the winning of the economic battle for the improvement of the conditions of life of the uncommitted peoples are not alternative imperatives for the NATO countries — they are both necessary. Moreover, the tasks of military policy are negative and an insufficient expression of the common aspirations of our peoples and of peoples throughout the Free World.

With these considerations in mind, I recommend that the United States take the following three actions:

(1) Announce that we are asking Congress for a substantial enlargement of our foreign development funds.

(2) Call upon the other NATO countries to make increased resources available for underdeveloped countries.

(3) Propose a special meeting of the OEEC[118] to be held in January to (a) determine a scale of effort for foreign economic development; and (b) improve coordination among the participating countries.

These actions would moderate the impression that the NATO meeting was concerned almost exclusively with military matters. And, they would reassure underdeveloped countries that the West was mindful of their first concern (which is *not* the Soviet threat) and that they could secure capital to be used productively, independent of military commitments.

I am, of course, not in position to suggest with precision what should be the magnitude of the American effort. But over and above existing efforts, the United States might seek to expand its economic development loans by about $500 million per annum, including, say, $200 to $250 million for India for a few years. The other countries of NATO, together with such other parts of the Free World as are capable of making contributions — I include Switzerland, Australia and even some of the richer Latin-American states — might be asked to contribute an additional $200 million per annum.

I use the figure of $500 million. This assumes that Congress should be asked to appropriate about $600 million for the Development Fund, together with something more for the Indian Five-Year Plan, although part of the India aid may come from the Export-Import Bank.

A meeting of the countries of the Western World capable of aiding the underdeveloped areas could have great impact as a demonstration of the pacific and constructive intentions of the West. While the proposal should be made at NATO, I do not suggest that the participants be

[118] The Organization for European Economic Cooperation, established in 1948 by subscribers to the European Recovery Program.

limited to NATO countries. Certainly Switzerland, Canada, Australia and New Zealand, and possibly Argentina or Cuba, should be added to the invited countries now members of the OEEC.

At a later stage a general meeting of potential contributing and receiving nations might well be organized. And I would gladly amplify my reasons for suggesting OEEC as the appropriate agency.

6. *Trade Policy.* Our NATO partners continually criticize us for our failure to liberalize our commercial policy to an extent commensurate with our position as the leading creditor nation. Hence, I would suggest that the U.S. make a statement which would contain the following points:

(1) An expression of gratification at the initiative taken by the Six Nations in bringing into being the common market.[119]

(2) An expression of hope for the success of negotiations looking towards the creation of a free trade area.

(3) A reaffirmation of our belief that a strong and integrated Europe is essential to a strong free world and that the peaceful purposes of NATO will be served by increasing the momentum toward the unification of Europe.

(4) An expression of hope that the nations participating in the common market and in the free trade area will move as rapidly as possible toward the liberalization of external tariffs and other trade barriers.

(5) A statement of the President's intention to ask Congress to extend the U.S. Trade Agreements legislation for a period of five years and to move as vigorously as possible under the legislation toward the liberalization of trade throughout the whole free world.

7. *NATO's Larger Meaning.* The exclusively military emphasis in NATO has not enhanced respect in the cold war areas. It would be well to vigorously call attention to its wider meaning and potential significance. None of the papers seem to do this.

NATO is more than a temporary military alliance. Although it was born of the urgent necessity to defend our free institutions and cultural traditions, the roots of our great community of interest are much deeper than common defense. And the community of interest will outlive the threat which brought NATO into being.

We have reached the stage where the historical developments which unify our nations — our recognition of the dignity of the individual, the

[119] The European Economic Community, established in 1957 by Belgium, France, Italy, the Netherlands, Luxembourg, and West Germany, whose initial purpose was to eliminate economic barriers such as tariff systems and restrictions on movement of capital and labor, leading eventually to political solidarity.

responsibility of government to the people, the universality of certain basic human rights, and the love of God embodied in our religions — must begin to give us the strength to forge an even greater unity of purpose. The atom and the supersonic missile have made us realize our proximity and our vulnerability. We must now seize the opportunity to agree on common goals and find common paths to reach them.

NATO's greatest goals are to compose outstanding differences with our adversaries, to normalize and turn into fruitful channels the relations of the West with the East. As far as America is concerned, NATO is our promise to participate in a joint search for a better future.

NATO commits North America permanently to sharing in the solution of the problems of the Atlantic Community and the reconciliation of differences between its members. And beyond its frontiers, NATO must serve to extend to others the advantages of the modern industrial society which we enjoy.

The achievement of our goals is not only the task of governments; a major role must be played by the voluntary cooperation of our peoples. The Bruges Conference on the Atlantic Community and the Parliamentarians from the NATO countries who met last month[120] declared the need to further the cultural strength of the Community, its spiritual values and the realization of its social ideals.

That we have not realized the greater values for mankind in this closer association of the Western community is due to the relentless Soviet military threat. But in solving the immediate problems which face us in the military and the political arena, we must not lose sight of the fundamentals which give meaning to our great Community. For it is these fundamentals which make worth while the many sacrifices which we have had to make, and will have to make, to defend our civilization and all that it stands for.

8. *The President's Principal Speech.* I believe this document has acquired more heart and balance during the past week. I am not sure how it reads now, but I suspect the weapons emphasis needs more dilution and that it will still appear to most of the earth's inhabitants that the U.S. is busily preparing for war.

Although it is necessary, of course, to reassure the members of the Alliance that their defenses will be modern and adequate, it is likewise necessary to convince the world at large that the purpose of NATO is to maintain peace and not to wage war.

Instead of starting with a reaffirmation of our treaty pledge to fight in defense of a NATO partner, it might better start with a reaffirmation of

[120] Stevenson apparently refers to a meeting held in Paris November 11, 1957, of one hundred and fifty representatives drawn from all fifteen NATO member countries.

the non-aggressive, peaceful purpose of NATO which came into existence not to destroy the Communist system but only because we cherish freedom more than peace. And I think equilibrium in the speech between the military and non-military ways of seeking peace would be improved by more passion and urgency in the treatment of disarmament — in language anyone could understand.

I suggest starting on the note of the peaceful purpose of NATO and ending on the idea of lifting the armament burden and the horror of nuclear war as the central objective of the NATO powers.

9. *Disarmament.* I don't believe the disarmament papers I have seen do justice to the subject or the opportunity to recover some lost ground among the bystanders at the armament race. I suspect that because of the charges and counter charges and the technical character of the disarmament proposals the world at large is confused about our position, and that by calling for the prohibition of nuclear weapons and the ending of nuclear tests Russia has assumed, in large areas of the world, the mantle of the one great power which is desirous of taking immediate steps toward peace.

I should think it would be possible for the allies to state their position in simple terms again, and to make it resonantly clear that arms control, at least nuclear disarmament, is the only certainty of survival. I would carefully refrain from any appearance of obstinacy about our present proposals and welcome a resumption of negotiations and new initiatives. Indeed, I would, as you know, offer some ourselves!

10. Finally, if only the communique — they are always so ponderous — could end with a brief and ringing statement summing up NATO policies in simple language — "Arms only for defense. Aid for the needy, underdeveloped nations. Cooperation with all states, including the Communist nations, to promote world peace and progress."

I am sorry that this comment is so long. As I said at the outset, what concerns me most is that the crisis is larger by far than our response. As Pericles said when Sparta was frightening the Athenians: "I am more worried about our own faults than about the plans of our enemies."

Governor Luther Hodges praised Stevenson for becoming an adviser on the planning for the NATO meeting but admonished him to be watchful of the group he was working with.

To Luther Hodges

December 3, 1957

Dear Luther:

Many thanks for your letter which has finally caught up with me here. It has been a trying interlude, but knowing something of the situation and how dismal it is I did not feel that I could in personal comfort and perhaps even party esteem decline to do anything. It is a melancholy task and full of hazards, with which you are so familiar. But I am glad you approve of what I am trying to do.

With my thanks for your thought of me, and warm wishes to you and your charming lady, I am

Cordially yours,

On December 3, Stevenson met with the President for their first discussion since he had assumed the NATO advisory role. Dulles and he talked with Eisenhower for about ten minutes. The President, according to a statement Stevenson made to reporters, indicated "he would be very happy if I would go" to Paris. But in going over the same ground for television, Stevenson said, "I don't know whether I have been invited or not." A little later James C. Hagerty told newsmen, "The President did ask Mr. Stevenson to go to the NATO Council meeting and that decision is now up to Mr. Stevenson."

To John Foster Dulles

December 3, 1957

The inquiries from the press about the Paris meeting and the confusion appears to be endless. I would like to end the speculation and I am sure you would too.

I have drafted this little statement which I would like to put out forthwith if you have no objection.

Stevenson enclosed the following statement.

December 3, 1957

As I have said before I expect to complete my consultation on the U.S. proposals for the NATO meeting in about a week. I undertook this task as a patriotic duty, and I will consider my assignment completed after I have studied all the proposals, expressed my views and made my recommendations to Secretary Dulles.

Unless there are compelling developments I will not attend the Paris meeting. I would be without authority and necessarily identified with decisions I might not always agree with and could not publicly oppose. I do not wish thereby to inhibit or mislead my friends here or abroad.

While, of course, there are differences between us, I do not wish to leave the impression of disagreement with our proposed positions at the meeting. On the contrary I agree with most of them.[121]

I am grateful to the President and the Secretary of State for this opportunity to be of service and for the further confidence implicit in the President's suggestion that I attend the NATO meeting in Paris.

To Pierre Mendès-France[122]

December 3, 1957

My dear Friend:

Robert F. Goheen, President of Princeton University writes me that they have asked you to do the Walter E. Edge Lectureship in Public and International Affairs at Princeton in April.

I hope very much that you will find it possible to accept this lectureship. You will enjoy Princeton and some of the men you will meet there, and I am sure they will profit immensely from your visit. And besides, it may give me a chance to see you, and that would be welcome indeed!

I am not going to accompany the President or the Vice President to NATO. I am sure you will understand the embarrassment of a situation without authority and the necessity to accept positions in silence of which I might not approve. I have worked, however, with satisfaction and some success with Secretary Dulles and his associates in preparing for the meeting and I regret that I cannot follow it through. I count the meeting of great importance and I pray that it will draw this country and France closer together.

With my esteem and regards, I am

Cordially yours,

---

[121] Robert J. Donovan reported in his syndicated column that sources close to Stevenson said that he felt that the "American proposals place too much stress on military measures and too little on political and economic measures for the strengthening of NATO and the rest of the anti-Communist world." Chicago *Sun-Times*, December 4, 1957.

[122] A member of the French Chamber of Deputies and former Prime Minister and Foreign Minister of France.

Mrs. T. S. Matthews, the former Martha Gellhorn, who was married to Stevenson's Princeton classmate, urged Stevenson to visit them in London when he attended the NATO meeting. It was not clear on December 4 that President Eisenhower, who was recovering from a stroke, would be able to attend the meeting.

To Mrs. T. S. Matthews

December 4, 1957

Dear Martha:

Thanks for your note. And how I wish I could come for tea! But I am not going to NATO, that is if I can possibly help it. I am sure you can envision some of my difficulties and embarrassments, especially if Mr. Nixon is my senior partner! I have told the President that I wouldn't care to go unless there is some compelling reason, and I can't imagine what that would be.

We are having more trouble with the French just now about suspending the nuclear tests than anyone else. They seem to be determined to become a nuclear power too. Then will come the Germans, I suppose, and on and on until . . .

I pray you are well and I yearn to see you. Best to Tom.

Yours,

To Joseph E. Johnson[123]

December 5, 1957

Dear Joe:

As you know, I have been looking forward to joining you on Saturday to pay tribute to Warren R. Austin at the dedication of the Auditorium in his honor. I now find that my present duties will require me to remain in Washington this week-end.

Although greatly disappointed, I am comforted by the awareness that no one could so completely understand my situation as Ambassador Austin.

Staunch Vermont Republican and Assistant Minority Leader in the Senate, he unhesitatingly accepted President Truman's invitation to represent the United States in the United Nations. He saw clearly the importance of demonstrating to the entire world the dedication of *all* the American people to the United Nations ideal of peace and justice.

He kept that vision before him constantly and resolutely kept the voice of the United States in the United Nations from acquiring any

[123] President of the Carnegie Endowment for International Peace.

note of partisan disharmony. He set a glowing example of service that it is especially appropriate to recall on December 7th — the anniversary of adversity surmounted by unity of effort and sacrifice.

Now, as then, the nation needs to manifest its willingness and ability to mobilize the power of its unity and to join with its allies in seeking a more peaceful, more secure, and more abundant life for the peoples of this small planet.

At the outset of this new effort, Warren Austin's ideals and patriotism should provide inspiration and guidance to us all.

Sincerely yours,

To John Foster Dulles

December 5, 1957

Memorandum Number 2
SUBJECT: NATO Heads of Government Meeting
ECONOMIC DEFENSE COORDINATION

You asked yesterday for some further explanation of the proposals set forth in my Memorandum No. 1 of November 29 for a more effective and dramatic Western economic effort in the cold war.

The suggested U.S. position that has gone forward to Ambassador [W. Randolph] Burgess is all right as far as it goes, but it does not go anywhere — beyond expression of "interest in an enlargement of the resources available to the less developed areas." The *action* portions which I suggested have been deleted.

I have urged that we

(1) Announce that we are asking Congress for a substantial increase of our foreign development funds;

(2) Call upon the other NATO countries to make increased resources available for underdeveloped countries;

(3) Propose a special meeting of the OEEC [Organization for European Economic Cooperation] to be held in January to (a) determine a scale of effort for foreign economic development; and (b) improve coordination among the participating countries.

I. Argument:

The maintenance of sufficient military strength to deter aggression is essential to the security of the peoples within the NATO Community and of peoples everywhere not under Communist rule.

But we recognize — you have said it repeatedly — that the tasks of military policy are negative and an insufficient expression of the common aspirations of peoples throughout the free world.

[127]

In our proper concern with the need to redress the military balance, I am fearful that we will under-emphasize, or appear to under-emphasize, our concern for the economic and political contest throughout the world. *I think we agree that the political and economic contest is the hot war now and the greatest danger.* We have been losing ground in the under-developed countries which Lenin and Stalin both believed to be the decisive stepping stones, first to the domination of Europe and ultimately, the world. The progressive weakening of our position in Asia and Africa in the next few years, coupled with dramatic Soviet advances in the military field, will further the neutralist movement among many of our friends in Europe and Latin America.

You have pointed out that Soviet foreign economic aid is already pressing us closely, and that their effort is on an ascending curve while ours is descending.

Of course, arguments can be multiplied indefinitely for more aggressive moves in the political-economic contest with the Soviet, and the enhancement of Soviet prestige in these uncommitted areas as a result of Sputnik cannot be exaggerated.

Hence it is manifest from the figures and the facts on Egypt, Syria, Afghanistan and elsewhere not to mention the rising Chinese pressures in Asia, that the political and economic penetration of the Communist bloc must be arrested. I think it calls as imperatively for a combined Western effort as the Soviet bloc's weapon capability.

II. Scale of Enlargement:

I proposed in Memorandum No. 1 an enlargement of our foreign development funds, including $200 to $250 million for India, and that we should call upon our NATO partners to do likewise.

I understand the Administration has decided to ask Congress for the $625 million authorized for the Development Loan Fund. An intensive effort must, I think, be made to explain to Congress and the country why an American effort on at least this scale must be sustained in the national interest. I am sure the Administration will have the support of many leading citizens and many voluntary organizations on a non-partisan basis if it is prepared to lead and stay the course.

I suggested that at least $200 million more, over and above existing efforts, should be forthcoming from Western Europe, Canada, Australia and others — especially Germany. Western Europe will claim, with a degree of justice, that they are already making greater net contributions than the United States, via colonial loans, sterling balances, etc. All attempts to establish equivalent contributions by examining existing flows (public and private, military and non-military, colonial and non-colonial) are bound to break down. The sensible way to proceed is to establish existing levels of effort as a floor; and commit all participating industrialized nations to an increase. There will undoubtedly be a certain amount of fun and games in switching funds from "existing" to "additional" categories; but if a serious commitment is made in principle, the bookkeeping can probably be handled.

I fear the tendency for Western Europe to channel all capital exports into residual colonial areas — and to induce Germany to back this effort is not altogether wholesome. The present proposal represents an occasion to begin the gradual move of more Western capital to, say, the Colombo Plan area, and more American capital into Africa.

With respect to Germany and — perhaps — with respect to other Western European countries, the United States ought to be prepared to bargain hard for an increase in capital exports under the proposed arrangement. Because others, like ourselves, are suspicious of international funds, it will have to be made clear that what is contemplated is the coordination of sovereign national efforts.

The case of India needs special mention. $200–$250 million from the U.S. may see them through this year. But, unless the five-year plan goals are going to be cut back, they will need reasonable assurance that the whole $2 billion, including about $800 million to $1 billion from the U.S., will be available over the four years and assurance can only come, obviously, as the result of an international effort.

The U.S. financed about $400 million in development assistance in fiscal 1957. On the basis of the funds appropriated and requested for the Development Loan Fund the two-year average provides for little more than a continuance of the old rate of economic development assistance. Hence, as I understand it, a loan of $200 million to India this year would be possible only if Congress appropriated the further $200 million which was authorized for the Development Loan Fund for fiscal 1958.

It may be said that any such amount of money from the Development Loan Fund to a particular country is too large. But the population of India represents a large fraction of the under-developed areas within the Free World (about 40 per cent). Beyond this, however, India has, for a variety of reasons, prepared herself to absorb effectively much more capital per head at this stage than most of the other underdeveloped countries. It is appropriate, therefore, that the Fund should initially allocate a disproportionate share of its resources to Indian development.

This should be done, however, in such a way as to carry to all other underdeveloped countries the clear implication that the reason India is getting so much is not that the United States favors India politically but that India has demonstrated that she has prepared herself to make effective use of the loan.

In short the India case should be regarded as an instance of the purposes for which the Loan Fund was created rather than as an *ad hoc* political whim of the United States.

III. Mechanics:

Partnership in development of less developed countries clearly represents a common interest and responsibility of the Western nations who have banded together in NATO. In order to create and to express a feeling of partnership among contributing nations a meeting should be held under the auspices of the Organization for European Economic Cooperation (OEEC) to agree on general principles of aid — including commitment to continuity over several years — and to give assurance to under-developed countries of the Free World that they can secure capital to be used productively on the basis of economic criteria, *independent of military arrangements*. The meeting should establish the approximate goals, taking into account present contributions and capacities of countries, without attempting to create new machinery or fixing any rigid pattern of administration. Bilateral aid within a multi-national framework and also the pooling of funds should be discussed with a view to the best means of coordinating the activities of the participants.

I am not here suggesting that the United States agree in advance to pooling any of our aid funds. Rather, I am proposing a method through which activities of the participating nations could be coordinated, agreement reached in fields or areas of endeavor and final allocation of funds left to each nation on a bilateral basis. But there may be cases in which a multi-lateral effort is more effective. I understand there are many people in Europe who feel that the political effect of European aid will be greater if it *is* "European" and not French, German, etc.

The arguments for and against international funds are familiar. If there is flexibility of method the choice may depend on many factors including political objectives or economic development for its own sake on the theory that it has an automatic relationship to stability and democracy. It should also be noted that even the larger European nations find difficulty in mounting the kind of machinery that we have to determine needs throughout the world and to allocate money, technicians and capital goods wherever they will be most effective. Their efforts need at least the coordination here proposed and they need to be coordinated with ours. Too often, I suspect, the absence of suitable machinery has been a perfect excuse for the people who, for financial and other reasons, want to do nothing.

To start out with a conference under the auspices of OEEC seems sound because it is a flexible and comprehensive instrument. Most of the countries with higher national per capital [capita] incomes are already members. By adding Australia and New Zealand the list of potential contributing nations would be complete except for Latin America.

Two other reasons make OEEC a particularly suitable agency to conduct the meeting and organize our economic defenses. First, it is important at this stage to strengthen not merely the feeling of transatlantic partnership but also of Europe's continued capacity to play a major constructive role on the international scene. Two, European know-how and established business relations could clearly increase the efficiency of aid. Moreover, various proposals for Western European action in underdeveloped countries which might use mixed United States and European funds could be considered in this context (cf. the Pella plan to use repayments on Marshall Plan dollar loans, augmented by additional European contributions). A further reason for the suitability of OEEC is that it is established as an organization which coordinates efforts of various sovereign nations without any of them having to surrender any part of sovereignty. OEEC is without military flavor, includes two relatively rich countries (Sweden and Switzerland) which are not in NATO and would seem to constitute the best available framework for such a meeting and the coordination of the Western economic development effort.

At later meetings of potential contributing and receiving nations I envisage recourse to the Colombo Plan for South Asia; to the Organization of American States and the Economic Commission for Latin America; and, possibly to the United Nations Economic Commission for Africa, which will be constituted in 1958 or 1959, etc.

I can conceive of a Joint Middle East Development Agency as a logical extension of economic cooperation into the Mediterranean area and a demonstration of our willingness to commit technical and financial resources to sound development without political strings. The development of the Jordan River valley with consequent resettlement of some of the refugees might be a task of this Agency, as well as borrowing and channeling some of the oil revenues into regional development projects.

Finally, I think OEEC is indicated because it is established, has a Secretariat accustomed to serve such meetings, and because it would best dramatize the extent to which dignified, constructive and responsible relations with the old colonial areas are still possible, despite Suez, Cyprus, Algeria, etc.

I hope very much that at NATO the U.S. can express something more than "interest" in the less-developed, uncommitted areas where the cold war is hot. I can think of nothing more effective than a serious, thoughtful proposal to mobilize the resources and skills of the democratic "haves" for the development of the "have nots."

To John Foster Dulles

December 6, 1957

SUBJECT: President's Opening Statement
You asked my views on the draft of December 2, 1957.
I don't like Section I.
I like Section II, the first paragraph in Section III and Section IV.

The balance of Section III seems to me an unnecessary declaration of our total reliance on nuclear defenses. If a comparison of our virtues and Soviet vices is desirable I should think Section V might be recast into a more effective brief.

I like the stern realism of Section VI and the resolution to face the larger tasks of a larger challenge. Although it needs smoothing and editing I think it is the right note for the President to strike.

I prefer the Secretary's draft for the conclusion, except for the last paragraph, which is a little anemic. The last paragraph of Mr. Smith's[124] draft seems to me stronger and better.

But let me say again that I wish the President in this speech could loudly declare that he thinks NATO has a larger purpose than defense; that its purpose is peace and progress; that as free nations have gathered together to protect themselves they should also mobilize their resources and skills to help the less fortunate in the human family to advance; that in this shrinking world, as in our communities, the rich must help the poor; and that this is a higher, better goal for NATO than the accumulation of nuclear weapons, however necessary.

To William McC. Blair, Jr.

December 10, 1957

I have acknowledged the attached.[125] It indicates what I said yesterday. We must get out the fact: that I was not wanted in Paris.

---

124 Unable to identify.
125 A letter criticizing Stevenson for not going to Paris, arguing that his lack of authority was no excuse for refusal to go. The editors have been unable to identify the writer.

Premier Nikolai A. Bulganin of the Soviet Union wrote a letter to each member of the United Nations asserting that as a result of activities by NATO countries, the danger of a nuclear war had increased. The forthcoming NATO meeting, Bulganin further stated, would increase tensions by working out plans "for extensive use" of atomic weapons, supplying West Germany with nuclear weapons, and increasing the number of American bases in Europe. Bulganin recommended that the great powers "could already now take upon themselves an obligation not to use atomic and hydrogen weapons of any kind and immediately cease the tests of such weapons, or at least suspend the test for two or three years with the establishment of a necessary international control over the implementation of such an agreement." Bulganin also proposed a summit conference of the heads of the British, French, Soviet and American governments to discuss these proposals and other important questions, including the situation in the Middle East.[126]

To John Foster Dulles

December 11, 1957

SUBJECT: President's Speech in Closed Session.

I am submitting herewith some revisions in the draft of the President's speech in closed session which I have seen this morning.[127]

While I am gratified by the increased emphasis on economic development, I am, of course, disappointed that the United States is not prepared to propose some concerted *action* in this field, such as I have suggested in my memorandum of December 5.

---

[126] For the text of Bulganin's letter, see the New York *Times*, December 13, 1957.

[127] On draft No. 3 of the President's speech, Stevenson made a number of handwritten suggestions in the text. On page 1, for instance, the draft read: ". . . We ought, however, always to make it abundantly evident that we seek with perseverance, resourcefulness, and flexibility to end the need for greater military establishments."

Stevenson recommended instead: ". . . We ought, however, always to make it abundantly evident that we will seek patiently and everlastingly to end the need for greater military establishments and to release huge resources for the greater welfare of mankind."

On draft No. 4, to which Stevenson's Memorandum of December 11 refers, the draft on page 5 read: ". . . And by 'peace' I know we do not mean merely that barren concept of a world where open war is prevented by human beings struggling to create war machines which neutralize each other. The peace we seek is a positive state of justice and joy, where individuals exercise their inalienable rights, and pursue and gain happiness."

Stevenson suggested instead: ". . . And by 'peace' I don't mean a balance of terror of modern weapons. I mean a positive state of security in which individuals can freely exercise their inalienable rights to life, liberty and the pursuit of happiness."

In my attached revision I have included (at least for fun!) some counter-proposals to Bulganin. I wish there was a possibility of the President's taking some initiative even at this late date. The Russians have hit us again where it hurts most — in the cold war — and I think there must be some *better* response than "foul!"

To John Foster Dulles

December 11, 1957

SUBJECT: Secretary's Speech in Closed Session

I neglected to say to you this afternoon that in one of his speeches I think it might be wise for the President to pay his respects to Soviet science and applaud the satellites as the beginning of a new epoch, the Space Age, which confronts us with the challenge not of this earth alone, but of the illimitable distances and mysteries of the universe.

With respect to your speech:

Page 1, Paragraph 1: To say that long range missiles will help to maintain SAC's superiority seems to me more likely to provoke ridicule than reassurance. I would omit this sentence.

Paragraph 2: I don't find the limited war or local action capability very convincing.

Page 8, top: I should think that our insistence that the other NATO nations do *their* share in force contributions might be stated more emphatically.

Page 10: No one likes the phrase "clean" nuclear weapons. Can't we call them "non-fallout type" weapons, "non radio-active" weapons, or at least "cleaner" weapons?

I would strongly recommend against mentioning them at all and am in favor of omitting b) and c) or substituting something about "the characteristics of nuclear weapons."

Actually, I would prefer to see the whole grisly inventory from a) to h) omitted.

Page 12: As I said in a previous memorandum I understand that when controlled thermonuclear energy production becomes possible its impact on the rest of the world will make Sputnik look feeble. I have an impression also that the USSR is quite likely to achieve this controlled reaction before the West.

Would it not be well to include a sentence at the end of this section at the top of Page 13 proposing that our Western scientists work with Russian scientists in achieving this goal of unlimited energy production which will have much to do with relieving international tensions?

Page 12, Section H, Economic Cooperation in NATO: Is not this the place to suggest the necessity for some permanent arrangements to meet the Iceland fish cases in the future?

Stevenson issued the following statement on leaving Washington on December 12, 1957.

I am returning to Chicago after several weeks in the State Department in connection with the NATO meeting in Paris next week.

Soviet political penetration and scientific progress, and other developments of recent years all make a solid Atlantic Alliance more necessary than ever.

I hope and confidently believe that this meeting will be more than a spectacle, and that it will rebuild mutual confidence and determination among the NATO partners. In my judgment the cold war in the less developed countries poses the greatest present peril, and demands the attention of the Atlantic community as urgently as our military strength.

While I trust that this meeting will harden our resolve to resist Soviet threats, blandishments and penetration, I also hope it will not harden the division of the world. The great purpose of all of us is peace, not by capitulation but by agreement.

I like to think that Bulganin's letter is a good omen. But if they want to ban the use of nuclear weapons, for example, why won't they agree to ban production? Our experience with fine Soviet promises has been very disillusioning but all the same we must leave no stone unturned to reach settlements, and I hope our response to Bulganin's letter will be affirmative in spirit. I have made some suggestions myself.

If I have been of any service I am happy and well rewarded. My hopes and prayers accompany Secretary Dulles and the President on this mission.

I urge my friends in Europe to believe that we Americans are undivided in our resolve to do our utmost in our common protection and in our search for peace.

Finally, I take this means of thanking the many people who have sent me their good wishes and counsel in this assignment.

Eric Sevareid in a broadcast on December 6, 1957, reviewed Stevenson's attempts to inject new thinking into the American plans for the NATO meeting, particularly in the economic field, and then stated: "But Mr. Stevenson has found no evidence that the Administration will make such attempts in Paris. He apparently has concluded that while Paris will be useful in tying up some loose ends, it will not provide a truly creative and inspiring new lead for the Western alliance. He did not wish to be formally associated with minor measures only, and he would run the risk of European journalists and politicians using him as a foil against the American delegation. . . ."[128]

While some of the spirit Stevenson had desired in the American position appeared in President Eisenhower's speech on December 16,[129] Stuart Gerry Brown wrote: "But the little success was lost in the big failure. Neither at Paris nor afterward was American effort devoted to augmenting NATO for positive, nonmilitary purposes."[130] In fact, not until Under Secretary of State C. Douglas Dillon signed articles in December, 1960, setting up the Organization for Economic Cooperation and Development was another recommendation of Stevenson's accepted by the Eisenhower Administration.

Ten days after Stevenson ended his Washington assignment, John B. Oakes of the New York Times published an article entitled "Stevenson: Back in the Limelight."[131] Mr. Oakes wrote, "From the relative obscurity that followed his political defeat a year ago, [Stevenson] . . . has suddenly re-entered the limelight. . . . Adlai E. Stevenson is very much alive." After describing Stevenson's participation in the preparations for the NATO meeting, Oakes wrote, "Whether Mr. Stevenson still has any political ambitions is anybody's guess. He gazes at you with amazement if you put the question; and it is hard to imagine so sensitive a man who went through what he went through twice wanting to do it a third time. However, any experienced politician will tell you that the Presidential virus is harder to get rid of than the Asian flu." Oakes added, "A few months ago a Stevenson renomination for a third term would have been unthinkable; now the speculation is that it's at least thinkable. . . . In any event, he is more frequently spoken of by his admirers as a future Secretary of State than as a Presidential possibility."

Benjamin Buttenweiser, a New York banker, organized a dinner in honor of Lloyd K. Garrison to raise funds for the Democratic Reform Movement.

[128] "Mr. Adlai Stevenson and NATO," *Listener*, December 12, 1957.

[129] See paragraphs 11–20 of the speech in *North Atlantic Treaty Organization Meeting of Heads of Government*, Paris, December, 1957 (Washington, D.C.: Department of State Publication 6606, International Organization and Conference Series, 1, 35), pp. 35–41.

[130] *Conscience in Politics*, p. 187. Stevenson furnished Mr. Brown with the documents that he prepared for Dulles and the President, and he read Brown's book in manuscript and made suggestions by hand in the margins.

[131] *New York Times Magazine*, December 22, 1957.

To Benjamin J. Buttenweiser[132]

December 12, 1957

Dear Ben:

I am distressed that work in Washington, commitments in Chicago and acts of the enemy — I don't mean *just* the Republicans! — make it impossible for me to get back to New York in time for the dinner for Lloyd Garrison.

You will know better than I can tell you how disappointed I am because Lloyd is my law partner, and what a chance it would have been to say a nice word about *his* firm!

But even more disappointing is the lost opportunity to tell what everyone knows who knows him — that you are honoring tonight as fine and brave and good a man as most of us will ever know. He has enriched, en[n]obled and honored his friends beyond what his friends can ever do for him.

On another visit to New York I will hope to see you, too!

Cordially,

William Stoneman wrote on December 9 that he did not know why Stevenson was not coming to Paris but that it was a prudent decision. Stoneman said that NATO commander General Lauris Norstad was critical of proposals for economic cooperation and extensive political consultations.

To William H. Stoneman

December 16, 1957

Dear Bill:

Thanks for your letter. I had three lively weeks of pre-NATO consultation, drafting, and fencing with the press. The reasons for not coming were, I assumed, fairly obvious — I didn't want to go, and wasn't wanted (this letter, obviously, in the utmost confidence). I am sorry Norstad feels that way about an enlarged and coordinated effort in the economic, political, propaganda field. I think he's 100% wrong, and that it will do little good to have everything he wants and more in Western Europe, even if you could get it, while losing Asia, the Middle East, and the less developed areas. The latter we are doing very rapidly, I

---

[132] This handwritten letter is in the possession of Lloyd K. Garrison.

assure you, and the sooner we address ourselves to that war with equal resolution and realism, the better.

My proposal to Eisenhower-Dulles et al. was for the NATO meeting to accept the challenge of economic competition and suggest OEEC carry on from there. So far as I know, it is doing nothing of interest or importance outside of Europe, and what's of interest and importance *is* outside of Europe in this field. I thought it a suitable agency to coordinate the Western effort with the Colombo Plan, the World Bank, the Ex-Im [Export-Import] Bank, the UN, etc., etc. And I still do, faute de mieux.

. . . My love to that Norse gal.[133]

Yours,

P.S. I hear you said something nice about me in your paper the other day. I'll have to start reading it again.

On December 5, Chakravarti Rajagopalachari wrote from India urging Stevenson to speak out against equipping the NATO allies with nuclear weapons since it would end hope of relaxing tensions.

To Chakravarti Rajagopalachari

December 18, 1957

My dear Friend:

Your further letter has come, and moves me deeply. But I wish somehow that you in the distant places could bring the same moral pressure to bear on the Soviet Union that is addressed to us. After all, it is *they,* not we, who refuse to prohibit production of nuclear weapons. And if they are ready, as they say, to ban the *use* of weapons, why aren't they willing to ban the *production!*

I have been pleading for two years for the discontinuance of testing and further development, and I wish our Government would agree to that now in exchange for suitable inspection and monitoring. But even more important is production, because testing now has the effect of refinement and diminishing the radioactive hazards. In all this we suffer here, as well you know, from all the disadvantages of a democracy in a goldfish bowl, and our propaganda is the most serious victim.

The Administration — and you know they have something less than my esteem! — has come a long way toward removing the horror of nuclear weapons. Even the United Nations has almost unanimously

133 Mrs. Stoneman, the former Maj-Lis Rissler.

approved the disarmament proposals of last summer. For my part, as I say, I would go still further, but certainly the Russians must agree to security of some kind or one cannot expect the West to disarm its nuclear component and leave us at the mercy of the much vaster Communist conventional forces.

I think Bulganin's letter has wounded us deeply in world opinion, and I wish our response to these things was more affirmative and less distrustful. All the same, the experience, and I'm sure you agree, with Russian proposals and promises has been disillusioning at best. Why aren't they called upon by all the Asians to fulfill their Geneva agreements for free elections in Germany, etc., etc.?

I wish we could talk face to face of ways and means to arrest this ghastly dance of death and restore respect and understanding for our position in Asia.

With warmest regards and Christmas greetings, my dear and honored friend, I am

Cordially yours,

Walter Selove, professor of physics at the University of Pennsylvania, sent some suggestions about nuclear matters while Stevenson worked on his proposals to Dulles and Eisenhower.

To Walter Selove

December 18, 1957

Dear Mr. Selove:

I was delighted with your letter, which I used to good purpose, I think!

I am quite satisfied with the attentive audience my recommendations in Washington had, but not too well satisfied with the consequences. I had hoped so much that we might make even more rapid progress in converting our negativism to something more affirmative.

I suppose the rumors that I have heard for a long time about British progress with the extraction of heavy water from sea water is in the direction of unlimited energy production to which you refer. Is it possible that the British will be ahead of the Russians!

I have heard much from my friend Cyrus Eaton[134] about the Pugwash Conference,[135] and I am sure that you are right that meetings of

[134] Cleveland industrialist, farmer, and philanthropist.
[135] Mr. Eaton, deeply concerned over the menace that nuclear weapons posed to the survival of mankind, sponsored the first Pugwash Conference at his Nova

that kind, as individuals without official responsibility, present opportunities we should exploit to the fullest.

With my thanks and warm regards, I am

Cordially yours,

To Mrs. Eugene Meyer[136]

December 22, 1957

Dearest Agnes —

I am flying back to Chicago after 3 frenzied days in N.Y. of business, firm parties and seeing my wonderful John Fell and his Belgian friend off for Switzerland for the holidays. (I wish I didn't dread alpine skiing with that knee of his!)[137] And now — settled on the plane — on a brilliant, flashing cloudless winter day — I've opened your letter at last. And what a superb and feeling letter it is! But so they all are, and each reminds me how fortunate I am to have not only your friendship, but your love and confidence, dear Agnes.

I'm glad you sent me that Chinese bowl[138] and I shall open it this very day when I get back to my prairie pastures — and I'll hold it in my hand and repeat your lovely words. And then I'll thank my maker once more at this Christmas time of beginning for giving me such a brilliant, exciting and comforting friend who has sharpened my values and nourished my self respect — even if she has been much too tolerant of my frailties. And you have done something else for me too — quickened and restored my respect for learning and for a passionate sense of justice — and — and — and!

But enough of the comforts and excitements you have given me — and there have been *dis*comforts too. For you have also made me envy your scholarship, your courage and your amazing vitality and usefulness. I am not mindless of my own shortcomings and somehow you & Eleanor R[oosevelt] (she waltzed gaily & lightly at a dance the other night!) have a way of unconsciously reminding me of my limitations! You are indestructibly youthful not just because you are always learning but because you are also always brave.

Scotia home in July, 1957. Scientists and scholars from many countries attended. Mr. Eaton announced that the participants agreed that "if nuclear warfare was ever indulged in, both aggressor and the defender would perish and the devastation would be unspeakable." A second conference was held in Quebec, March 31 to April 11, 1958. See the Chicago *Sun-Times,* May 25, 1958.

136 This handwritten letter is in the Agnes Meyer files, Princeton University Library.

137 John Fell Stevenson had been injured in an automobile accident in December, 1955. See *The Papers of Adlai E. Stevenson,* Vol. VI, pp. 27ff.

138 Mrs. Meyer had written on December 18 that she was sending Stevenson an eighteenth-century Chinese porcelain for Christmas.

I suppose I'll miss your call today — there may be no one at my house and [I] won't get there until mid-afternoon just in time to go out to a party with some old friends. I've let my hopeless Czechs[139] go and have acquired a colored "widder woman" who may or may not have arrived in my absence. On Tuesday Adlai [III] & I go to Louisville where Borden joins us for Christmas with Nancy's parents[140] and where I'll see the Binghams[141] et al — and doubtless talk of you.

I'm troubled about Feb 5–7 at Libertyville. I have to be in N.Y. Jan 30–31 and Wash[ington] (for the Democratic Advisory Council) *Feb 1 and 2*, and had sort of planned to go up to Boston or back to N.Y. for birthday with John Fell (mine is Feb 5 and his Feb 7) as I have done for several years. But let us see; maybe it will work out.

I wish I could send you a proper Christmas present, I wish I could do something, somehow to make you know how grateful I am and how much you mean to your loving

ADLAI

P.S. YES please send me more good quotes, like Pericles!

To Mrs. Franklin D. Roosevelt[142]

December 23, 1957

My dear Mrs. Roosevelt:

While I am not positively certain, it seems quite likely that I shall return to New York for a few days about January 3. In that event I would be delighted to dine with you on the 4th or 5th of January, preferably the latter.

However, if the uncertainty of my return to New York at that time causes you any inconvenience perhaps you had best not include me. I will wire you definitely as soon as I can.

Meanwhile, I am putting the 22nd on my calendar for lunch with you in Chicago.

Affectionately,
ADLAI

Gerald W. Johnson wrote Stevenson that he wanted to see him President but in view of two defeats the only way to gain the office was "to

---

139 Servants at Libertyville.
140 Mr. and Mrs. Warwick Anderson.
141 Barry Bingham, president and editor of the Louisville *Courier-Journal*, and his wife, who were old friends of Stevenson's.
142 The original is in the Franklin D. Roosevelt Library, Hyde Park, New York.

play to lose it." He urged Stevenson to get an issue — perhaps an eco-nomic one — and criticize the Administration in season and out of sea-son. If his criticism cost him the nomination, it would make him Secre-tary of State. But Mr. Johnson characterized himself as the worst political adviser around, "bar Sherman Adams alone."

To Gerald W. Johnson

December 26, 1957

Dear Gerald:

And the "worst political advice" I get from you is better than the *best* political advice I get from anyone else. Your letter delights me, not just because it is *good* political advice but because it is what I have wanted and needed to hear. And incidentally, I am fortified by not *wanting* it, — the job — which makes it easier to play to lose it. So the real question is an issue that needs a reckless rider. Here I am per-plexed. There are so many things that need saying and that are wrong here and abroad, that I am in my old trouble — selectivity.

There is truth — simple truth. If the basic assumption of democracy is an understanding electorate, how in the hell can you have a successful democracy when the public is cozened and deceived, and likes it? Sput-nik revealed what many of us had long known but couldn't sell — against peace and pomposity!

Then there is the really big, looming, brooding fact that we will have to spend more for defense and foreign development, and domestic so-cial expansion thanks to an explosive population, and all of that means inflation. I know of only one way to stop it or to meet it — increased production. If I am not mistaken, the next 20 years are going to be capitalism's greatest challenge. Can it expand productivity to head off a fatal inflation?

I can mention a baker's dozen of other mighty, majestic issues. But which one needs ventilation most? If your New Year isn't exactly happy, it will certainly be exciting!

Affectionate regards.

Yours,

Cyrus Eaton wrote to ask if Stevenson had seen the full text of Premier Bulganin's letter of December 10 to President Eisenhower. Mr. Eaton said it was a statesmanlike utterance to which the United States should respond. He also praised an article, "Christmas Thoughts In 'A World Gone Mad,'" by Raymond Fosdick in the New York Times Magazine, December 22, 1957.

To Cyrus S. Eaton

December 30, 1957

Dear Mr. Eaton:

Yes, I read the text of Bulganin's note the day it arrived, while I was working in the State Department. Indeed, I even drafted some language for the President to use in Paris in connection therewith. He saw fit not to use it and the result was that our NATO partners took the initiative and forced us to make the proffer of negotiation. That our response was so negative instead of affirmative did us no good abroad, as you well know.

And I have also read Raymond Fosdick's excellent article. Unhappily, like so many of them, it states the case but not the remedy, which is always so much harder.

I wish for you the best of everything in the New Year, and send you my congratulations on your most recent and spectacular achievement.[143] I hope you will tell Mrs. Eaton that I look forward to meeting her, too.

Cordially,

To Henry Luce[144]

December 30, 1957

Dear Mr. Luce:

While I do not expect any change in your magazine's distaste for me, I still continue to hope for reasonable accuracy in its reporting. Hence I enclose this recent example of what an anonymous reader, who sent it to me and evidently heard the speech, calls "*Time's* style."

Time says I posed the problem of inflation caused by new expenditures and then "avoided" it facetiously.[145] I didn't. I said it would require expanded production. I even suggested an international effort, more self-discipline, etc.

I don't mind if your editors don't like my ideas, but don't you think they should at least report them honestly?[146]

---

[143] Mr. Eaton had recently married Anne Kinder Jones.
[144] Editor in chief of *Time* and other magazines.
[145] See *Time*, December 23, 1957.
[146] Mr. Luce replied on January 18, 1958, that it was *Time* policy to report any speech only briefly and the question was whether the normal brief summary was unfair. He noted, "Perhaps it was unfair to say that you 'avoided' the problem of inflation, but you *did* say 'that's another speech.' " Mr. Luce added that it was not a question of not liking Stevenson's ideas in the speech because *Time* itself was in

What I said was fully reported in the New York Times, and a copy is enclosed.

Sincerely yours,

Pierre Mendès-France wrote that he understood why Stevenson had not attended the NATO meeting. He said that the meeting did not create the impression of a determination to seek a détente with the Soviet Union. He called Stevenson's attention to his proposal in 1954 that armaments should be reduced in Central Europe as an avenue to a détente.

To Pierre Mendès-France

December 31, 1957

My dear Friend:

Your excellent letter has come, and I am deeply grateful for your comments on the [NATO] Conference. I gather that our views are very close together — which comforts me! I had very much hoped that the President would take some initiative in the direction of a detente, and I made specific recommendations in that regard. I also urged a proposal for an enlarged and *coordinated* economic development effort by the Western powers, using OEEC as a planning and coordinating agency. I was disappointed that so little attention was given to the economic-political-psychological war in Asia, the Middle East, Africa, etc.

I remember well your recommendations in 1954, and disengagement at the center of Europe still interests me very much. I wish, however, I could see Germany's future with more clarity.

You have had a difficult year, and you will have more. But I hope there will be moments of peace amid the tumult in the New Year, and look forward to a glimpse of you in Paris in the spring.

Cordially yours,

To George W. Ball[147]

December 31, 1957

Dear George:

The attached letter from Mendes-France may interest you.

---

favor of them. Mr. Luce continued that he hoped *Time* in the not too distant future could present a meticulous, accurate report of Stevenson's thoughts within the limits of the space available.

147 A Washington lawyer who had been a longtime friend and associate of Stevenson and his campaign aide in 1952 and 1956.

I have been asked (secretly!) by Senator Green[148] to testify before the Foreign Relations Committee in Executive Session on my recommendations re NATO. I have not yet given him my answer. What do you think?

Yours,

P.S. I should add that just the day before they left for Paris, after the arrival of Bulganin's note, I urged that the President accept the challenge to negotiate in his opening statement and even submitted language on concessions and disarmament. Had he done so he would have anticipated the European demand for the detente.

Beginning in 1952, Stevenson received many hundreds of messages and cards during the Christmas season. He responded by sending a New Year greeting on a card designed by him and bearing a message reproduced in his handwriting, with a poem or quotation that he found appropriate and appealing.

December 31, 1957, Libertyville, Illinois

At the darkened doorway of another year I think you will like this ancient plea for a little light on a stony path "along which one goeth leaping."

I send it to you with my heartfelt thanks for your Christmas kindness to me — and with my hopes for your happiness in the New Year.

ADLAI E. STEVENSON

The inside of the card bore this poem:

> Grant me, Lord, a little light,
> Be it no more than a glow worm giveth
>   Which goeth about by night,
> To guide me through this life,
>   This dream which lasteth but a day,
> Wherein are many things on which to stumble,
>   And many things at which to laugh,
> And others like unto a stony path
>   Along which one goeth leaping.
>
> — Prayer of an Aztec Chief

[148] Theodore Green, of Rhode Island.

To Lady Barbara Jackson

January 2, 1958

Dear Barbara:

I have been trying to find an opportunity to write you a proper letter but the situation is, as usual, aggravated now by several thousand Christmas messages, two sons at home, one grandson, one daughter-in-law, one new law firm, and one thousand interruptions of assorted varieties from students writing Ph.D. theses to visitors from Ghana! I have just finished entertaining His Honor Arku Korsah[149] and his Lady at luncheon with a few judges of our courts. What a nice man — of many words. We spoke of you, but that seems to happen whoever passes this way.

I have carefully clipped your last piece from the Times Magazine,[150] which I will doubtless use as the basis of my next public address, with very moderate accreditation — which is also as usual!

My next "effort," by the way, will be soon — when I must testify before the Foreign Relations Committee of the Senate on NATO and my recommendations. Doubtless the interrogation will go on from there, and I hope to be able to use the occasion for upgrading the development of countries in the uncommitted areas and for a posture of greater flexibility vis-a-vis negotiation with the Soviet Union. As for the latter, I am afraid [John] Foster [Dulles] will evade for reasons he considers sufficient and is almost disqualified anyway.

My next speech is in New York on January 30. I had thought to talk about larger spending, the inflationary consequences and the necessity for increased production, but I am afraid it is too much content for a single speech, and in the present state of recession I am having trouble selling the necessity for planning a vast increase in production to meet the coming inflation. So I suppose I will go back to economic development and foreign policy.

The time of your arrival is drawing closer and it will be my best birthday present. I yearn to see you, and so do Adlai [III], Nancy and their entry. And, by the way, they announced at Christmas in Louisville another present to be delivered the end of June.

The holidays are over — thank heavens. But it has been a gay and busy time, in which my accomplishments and production have struck an

149 Chief Justice of Ghana.
150 "For the New Year: New Visions," *New York Times Magazine,* December 29, 1957.

all time low. I am sure you have managed things better — including the weather which, at the moment, is hovering somewhere around zero.

I have read your piece for the Atlantic,[151] and need I add that it is excellent — also as usual! I liked especially the line about the player boooming the plaything. The ending is superb.

I yearn to see you.

> Affectionately and I send much love ad interim,

Clement Davies, a Liberal Member of Parliament, wrote Stevenson that at the NATO Parliamentary Conference, which preceded the NATO meeting of the Heads of Government, there was unanimous agreement that cooperation economically and socially had to receive more urgent consideration in the future. He was critical of the British Government for not cooperating more closely with the European Common Market.

To Clement Davies

> January 3, 1958

My dear Clement:

I have just reread your letter of December 9. Now with the NATO Conference behind us our mistakes and failures are the more apparent. But so is the future challenge which somehow we must meet — together.

While I agree entirely that our economic safety depends upon close Western cooperation, I wonder if that cooperation must not extend far beyond the boundaries of NATO. Having pressed Secretary Dulles and the President hard to upgrade and equate the Communist economic-political threat to Asia, the Middle East, etc. with the military threat, I was naturally disappointed that so little happened in this direction at Paris. Foster Dulles reported to me by telephone when he returned that none of our allies had manifested any interest in coordinating and marshalling our financial and technical resources to meet this danger which seems to me hotter than the military danger in the West. I had suggested that the President should ask the NATO meeting to call upon OEEC [Organization for European Economic Cooperation] to summon a meeting of all the capital rich countries to launch an enlarged and coordinated campaign in this area. My purpose was (1) it was necessary, and (2) it would dilute the over-emphasis on missiles and nuclear weapons.

---

[151] "Can the West Regain the Initiative?" *Atlantic*, February, 1958, pp. 33–37.

I agree with you that it seems a pity that Great Britain is not leading, but actually protesting the irresistible movement toward greater unity in Europe. Moreover, I don't wholly understand it, although I can envision the reluctance of big business to take any chances even for a greater goal — even as here!

Things are not good in this country, as well you know. But it is certainly no time for despair and the fact that people are catching onto the facts of life which have been so successfully concealed for so long is wholesome. Our response to emergency in the past has been noble, and I believe it will be again. The trouble, of course, is the total failure of leadership.

It is always good to hear from you and I am happy that your resourceful mind and brave spirit is ever at work.

I send you best wishes for the year ahead.

Cordially yours,

To Mrs. Franklin D. Roosevelt[152]

January 10, 1958

Dear Mrs. Roosevelt:

I now find that I will probably have to be in New York on Wednesday, January 22 — when you are in Chicago. My misses are multiplying, and I don't like it. I had hoped this time I might even entice you out to Libertyville for a leisurely talk. But I shall try to catch you in New York during that week, if you are there, and if even only for tea.

Affectionately,
ADLAI

To Mr. Gordon Dean[153]

January 10, 1958

Dear Gordon:

So many thanks for your letter and the report.[154] I have read the accounts in the newspapers and hope to have an opportunity to examine the document in detail at once.

From my first impression I quite agree that it has said a lot of things that needed saying very badly. I am constantly irked by the fact that they are things that should have been said several years ago and that

---

[152] The original is in the Franklin D. Roosevelt Library, Hyde Park, New York.

[153] Former chairman of the Atomic Energy Commission, 1950–1953.

[154] "International Security: The Military Aspect," released to the press on January 6, 1958, by the Rockefeller Brothers Fund.

the situation has changed but little. Evidently it took Sputnik to do what all of our clamor could not do and our press wouldn't do. I wish the Rockefeller Brothers Fund was also doing a report on the importance of truth as a fundamental condition of a successful democracy!

I still hope for that visit with you in New York.

Cordially yours,

To Mrs. Eugene Meyer[155]

January 16, 1958

My dear Agnes —

I read it[156] coming down on the plane, murmured Hurrah! — clipped it for hot eyed northern friends — and thought, a little wistfully, of my ill starred speeches about gradualism etc just two years ago — that no one wanted to hear.

You've said what needed saying — and Oh so well! Now read Harry Ashmore's Epitaph for Dixie.[157]

Ever —
ADLAI

Professor Stuart Gerry Brown was writing a book entitled Which America? *It was an analysis of Eisenhower and Stevenson since 1952 which, as Brown wrote to Stevenson on January 22, 1958, "tries to show not only that Ike has given no leadership but why, and to show that in certain crucial respects you, though out of office and in opposition, have provided it." Brown sent his manuscript to Professor Arthur M. Schlesinger, Jr., for comment. On December 16, 1957, Brown wrote Schlesinger, "You interpret the book, or assume that others will interpret it, as an opening gun in a new campaign for Adlai. When I was writing early this fall I did not have this in mind. . . . It is not the purpose of the book to 'nominate' Adlai, but to show that in crucial ways he has in effect been President all along." Brown added that of course he did favor the renomination of Stevenson.*[158]

---

[155] This handwritten letter is in the Agnes Meyer files, Princeton University Library.

[156] Agnes E. Meyer, "Race and the Schools: A Crisis North and South," *Atlantic*, January, 1958, pp. 29–34.

[157] Harry S. Ashmore, *An Epitaph for Dixie* (New York: Norton, 1958).

[158] This letter is in the Stuart Gerry Brown papers, Syracuse University Library.

To Stuart Gerry Brown[159]

January 18, 1958

Dear Stuart —

Your letter to Arthur has fallen into my hands. I am proud — pleased — honored! — that *anyone* should entertain such views — let alone *you*, a political scientist, historian and practical politician!

But, dear Stuart, wouldn't it be more practical and profitable for the country and our party to search and find an unscarred leader, fresh and eager for the contest, *and* the task? Besides, I have done it twice, not because I *wanted* it or fancied myself worthy of Olympus (now called the "Summit"!) but because I was persuaded my party wanted me. I don't believe our Democratic friends should be encouraged to want me that much again — and *you* will understand, I'm sure, that after two such traumatic experiences it will take *some* encouraging to persuade *me* again!

I don't expect the people to understand my distaste for further political consideration and I've long since given up trying to convince them — especially our press which so often equates wisdom and perception with cynicism.* But I am sure *you* will understand.

I wish I could send you some quail[160] — instead, *blessings — thanks* from a full heart, and let me know when you come my way, please.

Cordially,
AES

* I've just read a batch of clippings — editorials — which said I consulted on NATO last month just long enough to get back into the newspapers! Ho Hum!!

Returning from his South Carolina vacation, Stevenson spent January 19–24 in New York City before going back to Chicago.

To Elmo Roper[161]

January 22, 1958

Dear Elmo:

Devereaux Josephs[162] has sent me a copy of "You and Your

159 This handwritten letter is in the Stuart Gerry Brown papers, Syracuse University Library.

160 Stevenson was on vacation at the home of Mrs. Marshall Field III in South Carolina.

161 Marketing consultant and public opinion researcher.

162 Devereux C. Josephs, chairman of the board of the New York Life Insurance Company.

Leaders."[163] I shall take it back to Chicago with me and may even read about Stevenson first!

My congratulations — I am told it is admirable!

Cordially yours,

Chester Bowles, former governor of Connecticut and former ambassador to India, sent Stevenson a draft of a statement he had sent to former Secretary of State Dean Acheson for consideration by the Foreign Policy Advisory Committee of the Democratic Advisory Council.[164] Bowles warned that in attempting to redress the military balance with the Soviet Union, we might lose sight of the political, economic, and ideological factors in foreign policy making. He added that at a recent Democratic political meeting in Connecticut a small businessman had commented, "As I read the news from Washington the sole difference between us and the Republicans is that we advocate $2 billion more than they do on missiles. I am all for that. But have we nothing more to offer?"

To Chester Bowles

January 22, 1958

Dear Chet:

Your letter of January 10 has followed me around the country. I think your statement is admirable, and I am getting very anxious about Dean [Acheson]'s leadership and military emphasis. I believe I will make that comment by the small businessman at your political meeting the text of my speech here at the ADA [Americans for Democratic Action] dinner next week.

May I suggest that your statement that at the NATO conference the administration insisted that the only question of importance was missiles, etc., is not quite accurate. While they would not accept my proposals about taking the initiative on negotiation, they *did* try to put a good deal of emphasis on the economic-political war while rejecting my proposals for specific action. But Dulles told me afterward, and I think it true, that they got little attention from our Allies.

Could I also suggest that it is not that the administration has refused to *trust* the American people so much as it has *misled* and

163 *You and Your Leaders: Their Actions and Your Reactions, 1936–1956* (New York: William Morrow, 1957).

164 For the differences between Acheson and Bowles and Stevenson over foreign policy, see Bowles's *Promises to Keep: My Years in Public Life, 1941–1969* (New York: Harper & Row, 1971) and *The Papers of Adlai E. Stevenson*, Vol. VIII.

deceived the people. It seems to me that this is becoming apparent and that we should charge them with deceit, not with a refusal to trust the people. They seem to me quite different in meaning in this context.

I am distressed that I missed you during your trip to Chicago and I hope that we can remedy that soon.

I am going to talk about your statement with Tom Finletter in advance of the meeting, with the hope that it will have some effect on the Committee draft which I suppose Dean will prepare.

Cordially yours,

Mrs. Eugene Meyer wrote Stevenson and expressed the hope that his speech on January 30 would furnish the inspired leadership that was not forthcoming from the President and the Secretary of State. She enclosed clippings and notes for the speech.

To Mrs. Eugene Meyer[165]

January 23, 1958

My dear Agnes:

Your letter arrives just as I am leaving for Chicago. It is most welcome, and especially the notes and clippings for my speech next week. As to the latter, I have done little or nothing so far and have crowded days ahead of me. I am afraid that it will fall far short of "the great opportunity," but that won't be *your* fault!

I think I will try to concentrate on "the other war" — economic-political penetration. As usual, the military, which is non-controversial, seems to be getting all the concern and attention, and I am afraid trade and aid are faring little better in the press and public than in Congress. Yet here, of course, is both our best opportunity to *really* help and do something constructive and at the same time our greatest danger.

I had a visit with Eleanor Roosevelt the other night and found her keener than ever. What extraordinary gals you are!

Affectionately,
ADLAI

To Mrs. Ernest L. Ives[166]

January 24, 1958

Dear Buff:

I am just back in Chicago after some lobbying for education — and

[165] The original is in the Agnes Meyer files, Princeton University Library.
[166] The original is in E.S.I., I.S.H.L.

educational films! — in Washington,[167] five wonderful days of crisp weather hunting at Ruth Field's in South Carolina, and a few frenzied days of work, entertainment, etc. in New York.

Now I must write a speech, clean up things here and return to New York the end of next week (to give the speech), and then go to Washington for the Democratic meetings. Thereafter I will spend a few days working in New York and go to Boston for a birthday party with John Fell on the 8th at Aunt Lucy Porter's,[168] returning here the first of the following week for a proper stretch of time at home.

I see no point in your going to the dinner in Washington on the 22nd. I may have to go myself, just for appearance sake, although I get dreadfully bored with those fiestas and my everlasting travels. I assume I shall be here on your way to Bloomington on Monday, February 24, and I am noting that you will stay with me a few days that week.

I am elated about the new people on your farm. And from what little I have seen of her, I am elated about the new lady in my kitchen. Carol Evans and Nancy [Stevenson] both give her high marks, and I pray that my problems are resolved for the present at least.

I wish I were going to be with you in Florida . . . but there are too many complications hereabouts to take off any time now. . . .

Love,
AD

To Lady Barbara Jackson

January 29, 1958

Dearest Barbara:

Welcome![169]

I'm afraid I must reach you this way instead of in person, because I must be in Washington on Monday, New Jersey on Tuesday, returning to New York on Wednesday. My office telephone number is Murray Hill 8-5600, and I stay at the Savoy Plaza, telephone Eldorado 5-2600.

The joint birthday party, which Borden is organizing, is a sort of cocktail-supper business at Aunt Lucy Porter's on Saturday afternoon. I am sure afterwards we can cook up something to do, and maybe even have a good talk. In any event, Sunday should afford an opportunity for that, if you have any time. I had planned to stay over Sunday night to

---

[167] Stevenson's testimony before the Senate Foreign Relations Committee was postponed, but he talked to a number of congressmen about Encyclopaedia Britannica Films.

[168] Mrs. A. Kingsley Porter, of Cambridge, Massachusetts, Ellen Stevenson's aunt.

[169] She had just arrived in Cambridge, Massachusetts.

be with Borden and John Fell, but if the Puseys[170] *really* wanted me for dinner, of course I could gladly come, and all the more gladly if I could bring Borden. We can talk of that by telephone from New York, I suppose.

A copy of the letter from Rettaliata[171] is on my desk this morning, but the date is disturbing — the middle of John Fell's vacation, when I had in mind taking him down South.

I have conferred with Jane [Dick] about the 22nd [of February], when I must, I suppose, be in Washington. But I shall be back the next day and she has promised to deliver you to my doorstep, and we may even be able to have a night on the town on the 21st.

As to the future, the March 5th weekend looks hopeful, and if I can rearrange a speaking engagement in Miami I may be able to get back for April 26th, too.

Enough of plans for now. I have a speech to write, "and miles to go before I sleep."

Love,

P.S. If convenient, please send your Cambridge telephone number to me at my New York office (575 Madison Avenue).

P.P.S. . . .

A.E.S.

Margaret Halsey sent Stevenson a copy of her recent article, "Beware the Tender Trap,"[172] in which she commented on the current belief that Vice President Nixon had "matured" and there was a "new Nixon": "The word 'new' . . . concedes tacitly that the Vice President was absent from Sunday School the day they were teaching the Golden Rule and other restraining amenities. But the word 'new' also suggests that the subject has reformed, and that where he was formerly bad, he is now good." Then, she added: "Until some absolutely unmistakable portent comes along — such as Mr. Nixon resigning his office and going to Africa as a missionary — common sense requires the working hypothesis that he has not changed and is not going to." Mrs. Halsey also wrote: "The highest office in the land wobbles like a spent ping pong ball between a Kansas Hindenburg and a character assassin. . . . What is actually involved, in the tender trap about a 'new' Nixon, is an attempt to debase the moral currency."

170 Nathan M. Pusey, president of Harvard University, and Mrs. Pusey.
171 John T. Rettaliata, president of the Illinois Institute of Technology. The editors do not have a copy of his letter to Lady Jackson.
172 *New Republic,* January 13, 1958.

To Margaret Halsey

January 29, 1958

My dear Friend:

I had already seen it; indeed, I had already distributed it; indeed, I had already suggested to certain friends that reprints by the hundred thousand should be distributed. I hope they "get going," or is it cracking?

I suppose it's a landmark in literature. Certainly, it's a landmark for AES. I would like to comment brightly, but I can't decide which scalpel or exposure I like the best, and they come so fast!

I hope we can meet sometime, although I confess it frightens me a little. You might suspect the truth!

With admiration and gratitude,

Cordially yours,

P.S. My only comment has been that with this one piece you have done more than the Democratic Advisory Council in a year and with a lot of money.

A.E.S.

On January 31, 1958, Stevenson spoke at the tenth annual National Roosevelt Day Dinner, sponsored by Americans for Democratic Action.[173]

I am happy to be here tonight at your annual celebration and to see so many old friends. To many of you I am indebted for a loyalty I must have often sorely tried, for counsel which I have not always taken and for gallantry in hopeless combat more than once.

And it is an honor to be invited to speak at your commemoration of a great American who embodied the whole meaning of political leadership — Franklin Roosevelt. I am honored, too, by the presence of our glorious countryman — Mrs. Eleanor Roosevelt.

Last night I saw the opening of Dore Schary's play about Franklin Roosevelt — "Sunrise at Campobello." It is not about politics; it is a play about the triumph of one man and one family over disaster. It moved me deeply, not alone because of the human drama it portrays but also because of the image of leadership in many crises it brought to mind —

[173] The text is from the New York *Times*, February 1, 1958. Typographical errors have been corrected by the editors.

his paralysis and personal crisis, the lonely courage, the proud decision; then the crises of depression and war and the courage and skill with which he lifted our nation to great, decisive deeds.

We need such qualities to conquer the crisis of today. Ours is not simply a crisis of ballistic missiles, and it cannot be repaired just by weapons. It has been long in the making; it stretches across the whole front of our national policies and back to the roots of our national life. Its final location, I believe, is in our minds and hearts.

To meet it we will need a radical alteration in our national spirit and a radical reconstruction of our national policy.

A famous European flattered me the other day with the statement that no one had a better right than I to point out the price America and its allies are paying for five years of "Peace, Prosperity and — Pomposity."

And I have thought of late that perhaps the last survivor would be pomposity, for Sputnik scattered the doves of peace that obscured our vision a year ago and recession has replaced prosperity. I looked up "recession," by the way, the other day and hit upon "recessional," which was defined as a piece of music played near the end of a performance when the people were moving out.

The best of all the reasons for the people to move out — the first item in my indictment — would be the Administration's systematic withholding and misrepresentation of the truth about our situation. Could there have been more frightening proof of the lost confidence and desperation of our oldest, best allies than the Suez disaster? Yet were we told? And how far behind would we have fallen in arms and education if the Russians had not launched the Sputniks?

A well-known scholar, Hans Morgenthau,[174] wrote the other day:

"The Administration has consistently concealed . . . information in both the most vital and most trivial matters and misrepresented the truth known to it. . . . Its most eminent spokesmen have assured us time and again that our strength vis-a-vis the Soviet Union was unimpaired if not actually increased.

"We witness the beginning of a crisis of confidence in the Administration, and we must beware lest it turn into a crisis of confidence in the democratic process itself."[175]

But the task, now, isn't to count the chickens coming home to roost. And I haven't come here tonight to abuse the Eisenhower-Nixon Administration and Secretary Dulles. The task, now, is to face the fact that our lease on leadership is fast running out and to find — wherever it is to be

[174] Professor of political science at the University of Chicago.
[175] "The Decline of American Government," New Republic, December 16, 1957.

found, in whatever party, section or group — the vision, the energy, the courage and sacrifice to save the free world from disintegration. This, I know, is the mission of this organization, without reference to party, and I honor you for it.

Happily, America has been awakened at last — by the Russians! Sputnik has opened a door to the truth at last. Its somber implications in education, in military capacity, in world influence, have punctured our fog of comfortable complacency — as some people I know never could!

Sputnik has, as Dr. Johnson said of the prospect of being hanged, tended to concentrate the mind marvelously. But, unhappily, the concentration seems to be largely on missiles. After the President's heartening State of the Union message,[176] I expected a program of national revival, a mighty response to a mighty crisis. Instead, the budget message proposed a program for contraction. It told us, in effect, that we would try to achieve those grand objectives some other year.

Even on the purely military side the proposal is for just a little more money. But the increase doesn't even meet increased costs, and it is a smaller proportion of our gross national product than any year since 1951.

On the domestic side there is not even an illusory promise of more strength. Instead of expansion and enrichment of the aims and capacities of our way of life, the program is to roll back, cut down, contract, all along the line from school construction to cancer research, at a time when a rapidly growing population is multiplying the needs. As Walter Lippmann puts it: "The basic conception of the program is that this nation, challenged as never before in history, is to reduce and contract its national responsibility for the internal development and welfare of the nation."

For my part, I don't think two and a half cheers for America and survival is enough!

But what I wanted to talk about is not our well-being nor our military stature. As to the latter, you cannot build strength through joy.[177] And there is little doubt that our military deficiencies, at least, will get a lot of sympathetic attention from Congress. For we must jealously guard our military strength lest our adversary gets too far ahead and puts his advantage to use. But when use by either side means retaliation and destruction of both, then clearly nuclear war becomes less likely, and we must look for other instruments of national policy in our quest for peace and security.

[176] See the New York *Times*, January 10, 1958.
[177] This was a Nazi Party motto dating from 1933.

[157]

The Soviets have already done so in the drive to their goal of universal domination. And they have found another mighty weapon in education and scientific achievement. We have been repeatedly warned about their progress by Senator William Benton and others I could name. But, as Lloyd Berkner[178] recently wrote, "In the complacency of our assumed technological lead, we have confused our high standards of living and material prosperity with intellectual stature. It is an extravagant and dangerous mistake."

But there are encouraging signs that at last we may be going to do something about our education. And certainly the current amnesty for intellectuals and eggheads must be very agreeable to many of you!

The Communists have moved quickly in another direction, too — the political, economic and psychological penetration of the backward, underdeveloped areas where freedom from external control is new, economies are weak, governments unstable, and the people yearn for material improvement. I am confident that the Russian-Chinese bid by aid, trade and propaganda for influence and allegiance in these areas is far more dangerous than Soviet missiles or manpower. For these areas of Asia, the Middle East, Africa and Latin America with their vast populations and resources are decisive in the world struggle. We need them and they need us. To help these countries develop so they can better produce what they sell so that they can better buy what we sell, and so that they can better preserve their independence, is the best investment we can make.

We have been losing the "cold war" in these areas as well as in weapons. To measure Communist success in political penetration by economic aid and subversion we have only to look around — at Egypt, Syria and Southeast Asia. If this goes on, the consequence will be progressive isolation for the United States.

So I am emphatically in favor of the Administration's program for economic assistance and also freer foreign trade. I'm told that both are in danger in Congress. But espousing unpopular causes seems to be my specialty and I want to say a word about aid — not military aid but funds to loan, to invest in economic development in these countries where shelter, food, clothing, disease are more interesting than democracy or communism or the great world contest that concerns us.

Many Congressmen will gladly vote billions for arms and military assistance abroad, but balk at millions to help the new, underdeveloped countries stand on their own feet.

It has always seemed to me since President Truman announced the

[178] President of Associated Universities, which operated the Brookhaven National Laboratory for the Atomic Energy Commission.

Point IV idea[179] that we Americans who believe so passionately in the ways of peace and commerce and have such industrial skill should welcome a contest with communism with weapons that construct and develop instead of kill.

The Russians saw that Point IV, economic assistance, was what these countries wanted and went for it in a big way. But our emphasis has been largely military — so much so that the world has begun to suppose that America thinks only in terms of military solutions. Our diplomacy has been addressed primarily to the promotion of military coalitions around the Communist periphery. Ninety per cent of our foreign aid, so called, has been allocated on military grounds. Meanwhile, nations which were unwilling to join us in military pacts have had relatively little economic assistance. This has played directly into Moscow's hands. And I am not sure how effective our huge military assistance expenditures have been.

Meanwhile the Communist bloc has rapidly increased its long-term low-interest credits to strategic countries for economic aid. They have a clear-cut strategy for dealing with the surging nationalism of the new nations — to keep it aimed forever against their old colonial masters and by skillful penetration and subversion to gradually chain these decisive regions to their victorious chariot.

As for us, what do we want of the people who live in these regions? We want them to remain independent; to modernize their ancient societies; to develop their countries economically; to take a role of increasing responsibility on the world scene; to succeed for their sake, which is also ours.

And we should know they can preserve freedom and contribute to world order only by fulfilling the aspirations of their peoples for human dignity and a tolerable standard of living. For that they need help — loans and credits mostly — and ultimately they are likely to take it where they can get it.

Let me call particular attention to India where the great economic development plan may have to be cut back for lack of foreign loans. India is the key to Asia. It is the major area in the underdeveloped world where the energies of nationalism have been channeled into constructive tasks by democratic means. If democratic methods fail there, our cause will suffer grievously elsewhere. Nowhere will "too little and too late" prove more costly than in India.

[179] So called because it was the fourth point of a program, outlined in President Truman's 1949 inaugural address, under which American knowledge of technology, public health, public administration, and business techniques was to be shared with underdeveloped countries. The program also encouraged the flow of private investment to these countries.

In this session of Congress the Economic Development Fund created last year should be radically expanded and put on a long-term basis. We must be able to hold out to the leaders this offer: if you are prepared to guide your nation along paths of social and economic modernization, we are prepared to look ahead with you for many years. We are prepared to loan you money to help you develop sensible programs; and we are prepared to help you find the foreign capital to bring them to life.

We have awakened just in the nick of time to the fact that our adversaries are outdoing us in education and the weapons of the future. I hope we also realize, in time, what is at stake in these vast uncommitted, under-developed areas where the Communist dictators with their large pool of technicians, their greater facility with languages, their austere standards of living, their closer identification with life in these poor countries, their lower costs, shameless propaganda and flexible government have great advantages.

We must find ways to commit the full weight of Western financial and technical resources to this cause. This was a principal purpose of my late service in the State Department. Many of the industrial nations are engaged in technical assistance and lending for economic development. As we have coordinated our military defense in NATO, I think we must coordinate, combine and enlarge the efforts of the "haves" to help "have not" nations. We must be able to make clear to the needy quickly what should be done, what can be done, how and when.

Perhaps it is not beyond the genius of Western capitalism even to help stabilize commodity prices. The present decline, according to the United Nations figure, has cost the primary producers, who are mainly uncommitted, $600,000,000 to $700,000,000 in export income in 1957, which wipes out our economic aid program, and then some!

With the vast Western economic and technical powers harnessed for constructive tasks, many possibilities come to mind. One can think, for example, with a certain zest of taking on Mr. [Nikita S.] Khrushchev with his plan for "catching up" — challenging him on housing statistics, on cars and durable goods and food; of welcoming the competition in foreign aid and urging the Russians to meet us on a matching basis. "We'll provide half the capital for Nile development, Come on, Mr. Khrushchev, what about the other half? You will? Good — we'll do it together through the World Bank. You won't? Well, we understand that communism isn't yet productive enough, so we'll do it ourselves. Better luck when next we try — which we shall do next year and the year after that, and on and on until kingdom come, because we believe that our competition in peaceful development will one day create a world in which we can all live together without the present grimaces and name-calling and general offensiveness which are an insult, Mr. Khrushchev, to the common humanity we all share."

Of course, we can expect no quick miracles. Moralizing, cursing communism, proclaiming containment will be no substitute for day-to-day actions which demonstrate that our interest in these regions transcends military support and loyal votes in the United Nations. For if these nations can make the transition from stagnation to growth by the methods of consent it will give democracy and peace new impulses which may safeguard free society for generations.

It is both harmful and inaccurate to present our interest in these areas as "economic warfare." We defeat ourselves and deface our best instincts by disavowing all generous motives where foreign investment is concerned. Of course self-interest is involved. Developed countries are stronger countries and better customers too.

But there is another element. Both foreigners and our own people — even Republicans! — would like it better, I think, if we didn't act as if we were ashamed to admit to a degree of natural brotherly compassion. I haven't seen any repeal of the command to love your neighbors. And neither Christ nor Santa Claus is regarded as subversive by the average voter.

I have tried to suggest that our task is twofold, that a bold, sustained Western economic development effort is just as imperative, just as urgent, as missiles and nuclear weapons — and much less expensive! The United States expenditure I'm talking about is only 3 or 4 per cent of what we plan to spend on military defense, and much of it will be repaid.

Deterioration of economic standards and failure of hope is the classical recipe for unrest, disorder and final war. So let us take care not to lose the earth while we are trying to win the sky.

But, finally, there can be no safety for anyone as long as there are hard, inflexible divisions between East and West and nuclear weapons anywhere. We must break the stalemate. And if there are always risks in trying to strike bargains, there are greater risks in not trying to. I think our position has been too rigid, and theirs more so. But rigidity is rigor mortis nowadays, and I am glad that our Government, even if reluctant, is negotiating about negotiating.

Under present conditions I doubt if any major political settlements are possible. We don't get anywhere for the very good reason that nobody trusts anybody. And I doubt if confidence can be restored by propaganda letters, a little meeting at the summit or a town meeting of all the nations. I suspect that confidence can be built only brick by brick, item by item, agreement by agreement. So I welcome with cheers the cultural exchange agreement concluded this week,[180] for intercommunication is certainly one way to understanding and confidence.

I would be surprised, too, if the Soviet leaders are prepared to end the arms race on acceptable terms just now. But I would be even more surprised if there are not men in the Kremlin who know the arms race is insane and world domination impossible in the twentieth century.

We must keep up a steady dialogue with these men. We must break the arms deadlock. As you know, I have long thought that we might take a big first step and get inspection started by agreeing to end nuclear bomb tests if the Soviets would agree to genuine safeguards against violation.

And I would like to lay before you another thought. Suppose the Secretary General of the United Nations appointed a commission to examine all the proposals that have been made to mitigate the arms race. This committee would be composed of private citizens, top men of affairs and science, chosen by the Secretary General from anywhere and everywhere and acceptable to the nuclear powers. It would work in private. It would render an advisory report.

What purpose would the report serve?

First, it would take the great life and death issue of our age out of the realm of competing propaganda.

Second, it would give the non-nuclear world some degree of responsibility for breaking the vicious circle. At the moment most people are frightened bystanders, cut off from any responsible connection with this problem. Understandably they tend to back any move, no matter how impractical, that would seem to bring the Soviet Union and the United States together.

Third, the Committee's report at a minimum could clear the air of all the bunk and phony proposals. By clarifying and narrowing the issues, it could provide a businesslike basis for serious negotiation among the nuclear powers.

This is but one proposal. I am sure there are many other better ones. The point is to give positive and convincing evidence of our determination to explore every path to peace.

A final word — I hear the cynics say that comfort and wealth have corrupted us, that America has grown soft, that we can't even understand the dimensions of the national effort required of us. Well, I've heard all that before and I don't believe it. I don't believe our nation has lost the capacity for heroic response to great demands.

---

[180] On January 27, 1958, Russia and the United States signed an agreement which increased cultural, technical, educational, and sports exchanges between the two nations.

But certainly the time has come to break through the thinning fog of complacency and affirm our conviction that American society is so varied, so inventive, so flexible, so abounding that problems exist to be overcome — that danger is also opportunity and our community becomes healthier and happier in the performance of great tasks.

That, I believe, was the innermost faith of our friend and abiding inspiration — Franklin Roosevelt.

On February 1, 1958, Stevenson attended a meeting of the Democratic Advisory Council in Washington, D.C. He then returned to his New York City law office for the week. Governor G. Mennen Williams of Michigan wrote Stevenson that he felt substantial progress had been made at the council meeting in getting peace to the top of the Democratic foreign affairs program.

To G. Mennen Williams

February 7, 1958

Dear Mennen:

I am sorry we didn't have more of a talk in Washington. I hear you did very well at the banquet and I only wish I had had an opportunity to hear you.

As to suggestions for the themes we should develop as a Party, I think our discussion there was revealing. I hope we can keep enough emphasis on disarmament, economic development, negotiation and the positive elements to at least balance our military friends in the Senate. The hazard[s] of carrying the "War Party" label any longer are too obvious to need mention.

For your information, I enclose a copy of a speech I made here in New York last week, although I can hardly recommend the investment of much time in reading it.

It was good to have a glimpse of Nancy[181] too.

Cordially yours,

Miss Edith Gifford, who worked for a press clipping service, put together many attractive scrapbooks on Stevenson. She presented them to him as gifts from time to time.

181 Mrs. Williams.

To Edith Gifford[182]

February 7, 1958

My dear Edith:

Even my birthday does not pass unnoticed! What a splendid addition to my enormous library of Giffordiana. The trouble is I am getting fascinated by scrapbooks about *myself* — which must be a sign of rapidly advancing age!

Bless you, my dear friend, and affectionate wishes.

Cordially yours,

After his visit to Cambridge, Massachusetts, where he celebrated his fifty-eighth birthday party with his sons Borden and John Fell and friends, Stevenson returned to Chicago.

To Jacob M. Arvey[183]

February 10, 1958

Dear Jack:

I am just back from the East and find your beautiful barometer. What a splendid gift! I am grateful indeed. Moreover, it's high time I knew what the weather was. I've lived in ignorance too long!

Cordially,

George F. Kennan, professor at the Institute for Advanced Study in Princeton, New Jersey, and former ambassador to Russia, delivered the Reith Lectures over the British Broadcasting Corporation. They were published in the United States under the title Russia, the Atom and the West *(New York: Harper, 1958). Dean Acheson, among others, criticized Kennan in* Life, *February 3, 1958, for his proposal for the disengagement of military forces from Germany and Eastern Europe.*

[182] The original is in the possession of Miss Gifford.

[183] Democratic National Committeeman from Illinois, who had been instrumental in the party's support for Stevenson's nomination for governor in 1948. See his "A Gold Nugget in Your Backyard," in *As We Knew Adlai: The Stevenson Story by Twenty-two Friends*, edited and with preface by Edward P. Doyle, foreword by Adlai E. Stevenson III (New York: Harper & Row, 1966), pp. 50–65.

To George F. Kennan

February 11, 1958

Dear George:

I have been meaning for some time to send you a word to express my dismay and distress about the recent altercation. Regardless of the merits of disengagement, I have felt that your contribution to thought and inquiry in the Reith Lectures was significant and distinguished, and commanded our congratulations and warm respect. I hope you don't feel too upset about some of the developments. A politician has to have a thicker skin than a statesman, but it's useful for both!

I hope you approve of your daughter's engagement[184] as much as I do!

With warm good wishes,

Cordially yours,

Gilbert Harrison, editor and publisher of the New Republic, *asked Stevenson to comment on Margaret Halsey's article "Beware the Tender Trap," which had appeared in the issue of January 13, 1958.*

To Gilbert Harrison

February 12, 1958

Dear Gil:

I don't want to comment *publicly* on the Halsey-Nixon piece for obvious reasons. I have had a delicious correspondence with her about it, however. And certainly, "lest we forget" about him is as important political business as there is.

But I would like very much to have and pay for some 50 reprints of her article if your office has them.

Cordially yours,

Mrs. Margaret Munn, who had been a secretary to Governor Stevenson in Springfield, sent him birthday greetings.

---

184 Grace Kennan was to be married to C. K. McClatchy, of Sacramento, California.

To Margaret Munn[185]

February 14, 1958

Dear Margaret —

Thank you for remembering "that day" once again. I'm ready to forget it now! I pray you are well and dream of the old days —

Yours
AES

By February, 1958, the most serious economic recession since World War II was in full swing. Cyrus Eaton wrote Stevenson that President Eisenhower's current golfing vacation with Secretary of the Treasury George Humphrey —"Chief Architect of the Recession" — was a tragedy, but the Democrats should take full advantage of the fact.

To Cyrus Eaton

February 14, 1958

Dear Mr. Eaton:

I hope they *can* make use of your reminder that the President is vacationing again with George Humphrey, and what the latter gentleman did to the country, thanks to his pliant chief.

As I understand it, I am not going to speak at the meeting in Washington on the 22nd, but I shall see that someone else doesn't overlook this interesting opportunity!

It would be nice to see you sometime, and you must let me know if you come here.

Cordially,

To Harry S. Truman

February 17, 1958

Dear Mr. President:

I thought if you were sharpening your knives for the Washington party, [186] you might enjoy the enclosure from Cyrus Eaton, who probably knows the former Secretary of the Treasury better than either of us.

Yours,

[185] This handwritten note is in the possession of Mrs. Munn.
[186] A dinner to be held on February 22, 1958, in honor of President Truman, which Stevenson was planning to attend.

To Mrs. William Attwood[187]

February 17, 1958

Dear Madam:

Word has come to the remotest recess of the prairie about your recent elevation.[188] Please know that the most torpid hearts of the democracy are stirred* by the news.

Thanks to you, our hopes are boundless!

Faithfully,

* Mine is still in liquid form from too much stirring.

Margaret Halsey replied to Stevenson's letter of January 29, 1958, expressing her delight that he had enjoyed her article on Nixon. She said it was an anguish to her to see "The Abominable Snow Man so easily and successfully transmuted into a sort of Tennysonian politico . . . 'icily regular, splendidly null'" She wrote that she suspected that what was carelessly labeled as anti-intellectual in American life was in "reality anti-moral." She concluded that she would be the one to quail if they met: "In propria persona, I am a paramoecium."

To Margaret Halsey

February 17, 1958

My dear Friend:

Yes, perhaps you are right and that what passes for anti-intellectuality is in reality a form of anti-morality — because intellectuality is hard and so is morality.

But must we strain very hard to see the explanation for the transmutation of your "Abominable Snowman?" Isn't the alchemy no more magic than an eagerly helpful press, a shrewd, indefatigable politician who has discovered that there is mileage in integrity, and a preoccupied public, incapable of sustained indignation unless continually reminded? Could it be that some would even call it Christian forgiveness; could it be that so many are *particeps criminis* when it comes to witch hunting?

Be all that as it may, what the press can do *for* or *to* someone with a people as conditioned to advertising as ours is all too familiar. I notice,

[187] Wife of the foreign editor of *Look* magazine, who had joined her husband and Stevenson on part of their world tour in 1953.

[188] Mrs. Attwood had recently been elected secretary of the Democratic Committee of New Canaan, Connecticut.

for example, that in spite of Sputnik, Suez, and all the revelations of the duplicity, deceit, and concealment of the past five years, the polls still report that Eisenhower is overwhelmingly the most "respected" man in the world.

Are you really a paramecium! I can hardly wait to see you — and hear it.

Cordially yours,

Stevenson went to Washington on February 22, 1958, to attend a dinner in honor of Harry S. Truman. Three days later Stevenson spoke at a Conference on Foreign Aspects of U.S. National Security.[189] At the request of President Eisenhower, Eric Johnston, the President's special representative to the Middle East, convened the conference. Among those who spoke were Eisenhower, Truman, John Foster Dulles and Stevenson.

To Mrs. Ronald Tree[190]

February 23, 1958

M T — Sunday again (what long weeks!) — and I'm sitting in Paul Magnusons[191] study trying to write my "keynote" for the "White House Conference" on foreign aid — as you can see!

Last night — "Truman dinner" — was a sell out, so they took another ball room, switched speakers tables after dinner and I had to make a speech. "Truth" was my text — and it worked very well, I think. I would send you a copy — if I had one at hand — but you already have too much to read and do and say — and you are there to sit and dream in the sun and recharge.[192]

Truman's speech came into the room where I was by closed circuit TV and was pungent, sharp and politically effective, for the multitude, as long as he was giving 'em hell, but not so good when he tried to get affirmative. He went way over his TV time and some people said his articulation was a little indistinct and "old." I didn't notice it particularly. He was extremely cordial with me, and Bess even more so. I sat

---

[189] For the text of this speech, see *Foreign Aspects of U.S. National Security: Conference Report and Proceedings* (Washington, D.C.: Committee for International Economic Growth, February 25, 1958).

[190] This handwritten letter is in the possession of Mrs. Tree.

[191] Dr. Paul B. Magnuson, a well-known orthopedic surgeon, and his wife, Laura, old friends of Stevenson's at whose Washington home he often stayed.

[192] Mrs. Tree was in Barbados.

next to Lyndon [Johnson] who complained incessantly about Butler,[193] NDC [the Democratic National Committee], DAC [the Democratic Advisory Council], his health, his trials etc etc.

I suppose you've heard that with the Governorship in the bag Dilworth[194] has made some mistakes and announced that he won't be a candidate — and now they[195] can't agree on anyone else, and [Harold] Stassen looks better every minute! But Mat McCloskey assured me that with a few assassinations he would get it all straightened out.

Helen Meyner[196] sat at my feet as I spoke — beautiful as the night — and burbled happily about your visit Saturday March 8. I arrive from Dallas — [William] Benton's apt. — Friday mid-afternoon Mar. 17 and will expect a message or call — if I live that long!

There is so much to say, to hear, to know, to believe — and so little time for anything — and almost *none* now for my foreign aid effort. And, God! I must go to Perle Mesta's[197] for lunch, etc. etc. (Last night — after the dinner — I stopped to see C. K. McClatchy and fiancee at their very gala dance, but eschewed the Phil Sterns[198] and ten other fiestas and crept off to bed like a good boy, or was it an old man.)

Plus que hier — A.

P.S. Taken by surprise — when the chairman asked me to greet the multitude before changing rooms last night, I gulped nervously, mumbled and said out in Illinois once a long time ago the Democratic Methodist preacher in a small town and the Reps were having a meeting in the Presbyterian church, so he slipped in the back pew to hear what was going on, but the chairman spied him and asked him if he wouldn't come forward and pronounce the invocation. "No," he said, "I must humbly ask to be excused; I don't want the Lord to know I'm here." But, I said, I *do* want the Lord to know I'm here to pay my respects to Harry Truman — etc. etc. It worked — and how! But *what* strength it took *not* to tell the one about the Ky. [Kentucky] moonshiner Grandfather S[tevenson]. told about who was sentenced for the 10th time and the exasperated judge said, "Johnson (why do I say Johnson!), you've caused this court more trouble than anyone ever did before; have you

---

[193] Paul Butler, chairman of the Democratic National Committee.

[194] Richardson Dilworth, mayor of Philadelphia.

[195] Pennsylvania leaders, including Matthew H. McCloskey, treasurer of the Democratic National Committee and a fund-raiser for Stevenson in the 1956 campaign.

[196] Wife of Governor Robert B. Meyner of New Jersey.

[197] A well-known Washington hostess and party-giver, and former minister to Luxemburg.

[198] Philip Stern had worked on both of Stevenson's presidential campaigns, in 1956 as codirector of research.

anything to say before I sentence you again, and good & plenty!" "Only this, Judge; that *you've* caused me just as much trouble as I've caused you!" — and thats the way I feel about our beloved guest of honor: HST etc etc.

To Mrs. Eugene Meyer[199]

February 28, 1958

Dear Agnes:

I am just back from Washington, where I have been uttering again — copies enclosed — and find the exquisite reminders of your Chinese period awaiting me.[200] I shall take them home to improve the weekend, and to be reminded again and again how much I have to thank you for — visual, educational, ornamental, and useful!

While in Washington, I called up Kay,[201] hoping to visit with them, but unfortunately Phil was working that evening. While I was disappointed, I am sure the work is a good sign. She sounded cheerful and friendly, also gave me a very reassuring report.

The Democratic clambake was the best in my recollection from the point of view of program, and an unexpected success in the box office. The foreign aid extravaganza was almost too much of a good thing and may, I fear, have created some resentment in Congress — excess pressure, etc. But certainly a lot of people, who came in unexpectedly large numbers from such distant points as Alaska and Hawaii, and at their own expense, must have been enlightened with the feast of oratory. My contribution was received with reverberating applause, but Eisenhower and Truman got the press, as they should. Nixon gave me a couple of unctuous greetings that I could have got along without, but otherwise the meeting and my bipartisan exposure was all quite agreeable, and I hope useful. Certainly the response to the speech was generous beyond its merits.

Affectionately,
ADLAI

P.S. A letter has just arrived, which I am stuffing hurriedly in my pocket for later attention.

---

[199] The original is in the Agnes Meyer files, Princeton University Library.
[200] Stevenson apparently refers to Mrs. Meyer's gift of Chinese porcelain.
[201] Mrs. Meyer's daughter Katharine, wife of Washington *Post* publisher Philip Graham.

*Senator Joseph Clark, of Pennsylvania, wrote that the February 25
speech was "Stevenson at his very best — and there is none better than
that." He enclosed a copy of a letter to Eric Johnston urging organization at the congressional level to influence congressional sentiment on
foreign aid.*

To Joseph S. Clark

February 28, 1958

Dear Joe:

Thanks for your letter. I am very much flattered. I suppose you are
right about the necessity for a grassroots organization. I have been a
little skeptical about this method of bringing pressure to bear on Congress, and I hope it does not create more antagonisms than it resolves.
While no one can be sure what the "people" think, I have a feeling that
the issue of "foreign aid" has been resolved long since and that they are
ahead of the Congress.

For myself, I wish I was as convinced about the utility of the military
assistance program and expenditure as I am about the necessity for a
much more effective economic effort by the United States, in combination with its allies and the other capital-rich countries of the West. I
wish we had had more time to talk.

Cordially yours,

To Alicia Patterson

February 28, 1958

Dear Alicia:

I have the hardest time keeping track of your whereabouts, and
henceforth will write all letters duplicate, sending one to *Newsday* and
one to Kingsland.[202]

It is important for me to know whether you are coming here on the
20th and 21st of March, as my schedule indicates. I wish I could go with
you and Marietta [Tree] to Barbados, but it is unhappily beyond my
horizon this year. Do let me know about the 20th and 21st, or I shall be
obliged to give someone else my precious time. So there!

Love,

P.S. I will be in New York for a few days from the 10th to the 13th,
and perhaps we can confer by phone, at least. Meanwhile, I have to go
to Texas, so I'm afraid any trip out here will be futile.

AES

[202] The town near the Guggenheims' plantation in Georgia.

Professor Esmond Wright, of Glasgow University, reviewed Kenneth S. Davis's A Prophet in His Own Country: The Triumphs and Defeats of Adlai E. Stevenson.[203]

To Esmond Wright

February 28, 1958

Dear Mr. Wright:

I have just seen a copy of your review of Mr. Davis's book about me, which was published in "International Affairs." And if I am "the most admirable American of his generation," I must say at once that you are undoubtedly the most admirable Englishman of your generation!

Thank you, sir, for such grace.

Cordially yours,

Although he had recently traveled abroad several times, to various parts of the world, Stevenson had not been to the Soviet Union since 1926, just before he began his law career. Now, perhaps chiefly to further his self-education, he decided to plan a trip to Russia. Among a number of people, he consulted the Soviet ambassador to the United States about arrangements.

To Mikhail A. Menshikov

February 28, 1958

Dear Mr. Ambassador:

I have just returned to Chicago, and want to say as promptly as possible how very, very grateful I am to you for your hospitality and interest in my forthcoming journey to the Soviet Union. As our plans develop, Mr. Blair and I will take advantage of your kindness and impose on your staff for assistance, if necessary. I look forward most eagerly to revisiting the Soviet Union after more than thirty years.

With best wishes and my respect, I am

Cordially yours,

P.S. And I shall not soon forget that splendid lunch — from which I am recovering slowly!

Former President Truman wrote on Februrary 27, thanking Stevenson for his remarks at the February 22 dinner.

[203] *International Affairs*, January, 1958, p. 128.

To Harry S. Truman

March 5, 1958

Dear Mr. President:

So many thanks for your very thoughtful letter. I thought you were in your usual excellent form at the Democratic dinner and I was glad to have been able to play a part in a well deserved tribute to you and your administration.

I certainly hope that I can stop by sometime in Independence to see you and have a look at your library.[204] I have been trying to give a little more attention of late to my law business on the theory that unless I give it a little more concentration my meagre clients may conclude that my oratory is better than my advice!

I was delighted to see both you and Mrs. Truman looking so well.

Cordially yours,

P.S. . . .

Between March 5 and 13, Stevenson visited Dallas, Texas; Washington, D.C.; Princeton, New Jersey; and New York City. On March 12 he participated in a transatlantic radio program with Hugh Gaitskell and Pierre Mendès-France, the opposition leaders of the United Kingdom and France, respectively. The discussion centered on whether easing of tensions could be expected from a summit conference. Stevenson stated that the Eisenhower Administration was too rigid in its insistence that substantial progress be made by negotiating at lower levels before the leaders met at the summit. On the other hand, he warned against raising expectations too high over what could be accomplished at such a meeting. He said:

As to this forthcoming meeting it would be a pity if our expectations were too high. There is, however, a reason for hope and optimism that we might accomplish something on a less exalted scale. Proposals have been made from time to time — as long as two years ago in this country by myself, by Mr. Gaitskell and others abroad — with respect to the discontinuance of the testing of hydrogen weapons (we believe with suitable inspection here — that that's a necessary precaution). At least if this could be accomplished at the summit this time, this would establish

204 The Harry S. Truman Library had opened in 1957.

the principle — the mechanics, perhaps — of an inspection system — at least look in that direction. And this would break the arms deadlock which seems to me is the most terrifying aspect of our contemporary scene. This would be a very substantial achievement, and from there we could go on to the consideration of outer space, and so on.

To Luther H. Hodges

March 13, 1958

Dear Luther:

I was most disappointed not to have had a proper talk with you in Washington. . . .

Aside from politics and race relations — both of which will be with us for a long time! — I had something else I wanted to mention.

A message . . . reports that a new curriculum study is being undertaken in North Carolina. This is good news and I am delighted, but not surprised, that your progressive state is in the forefront of the effort to repair some of the misplaced emphasis in education. It prompts me to speak again about audiovisual education and its tremendous potential in promoting and enriching our teaching. You may remember seeing one of the films from an introductory physics course while I was visiting you last fall. Since then a study has been made in the Chicago public schools in which 700 students taught by these films were tested against 900 students taught physics in the conventional manner. Obviously if the films when used the first time proved even nearly as effective as a class room teacher they would be extremely valuable and comparatively inexpensive instructional materials. The report of the division of student examinations showed that the students taught by films had an average of 72.0 as against an average of 66.7 for the students receiving usual instruction.

This, the school people say, is an event of first importance. It means that we now have a new type of instructional technique which may well prove one of the most revolutionary developments of this generation in the educational field.

I suspect this will be welcome news in view of the interest in North Carolina where they felt they could make effective use of a number of sets of this physics course. However, I gather . . . that the allocation of emergency funds by the Governor is the only way to take immediate action. The rapidity with which some of the most enterprising school districts have taken these films into the curriculum prompts me to remind you that North Carolina may wish to do likewise. It has also prompted the Fund for the Advancement of Education, created by the

Ford Foundation, to underwrite the cost of another similar course in chemistry. It is in course of production now at the University of Florida, and more such major developments are in progress, including a history series by Arnold Toynbee[205] now in production at Washington and Lee.

I find on my incessant travels that prescribing remedies for our educational deficiencies has become almost as popular a pastime as prescribing for our foreign policy — and I am no exception! But I am reassured by the rapidly growing interest and the attention the Committees of Congress are giving to these methods in the hearings on current school legislation. And I hope that emergency funds available to you will enable North Carolina to take greater advantage of the film too.

I still have hopes of a visit with the [Mr. and Mrs. Ernest] Ives at Southern Pines this spring, and perhaps even a brief glimpse of you.

Cordially yours,

Benjamin E. Mays, president of Morehouse College, a predominantly black college in Atlanta, invited Stevenson to speak at its commencement in June.

To Benjamin E. Mays

March 27, 1958

My dear Benjamin Mays:

I have your letter, which has awaited my return to Chicago. It pleases me a great deal. I remember vividly our enlightening meeting in New York. Your loyalty and encouragement, then and always, has comforted me — but please don't suggest a third time!

I wish I could come to Morehouse for Commencement. It tempts me as I have seldom been tempted before. Unhappily, however, I have a son finishing at Harvard that very day,[206] and also a trip abroad shortly thereafter. All in all, my schedule in early June admits of no additions, and I must ask you to excuse me, with profound thanks for your flattering invitation.

Sometime if you have a chance, I wish you would let me have your views about what fields of work among Negroes and whites alike merit the greatest concern of private philanthropy at this time. Is it collapse of communication between the two communities; is it a failure of leader-

[205] British historian and author of the multivolume *A Study of History* and numerous other works.
[206] John Fell received his degree from Harvard on June 12, 1958.

ship; is it the new problems caused by the rising tide of immigrants into the Northern cities, etc., etc.? I am consulted often about what to do in the field of race relations, by people of good will with money, and confess my perplexity.

It was good to hear from you.

Cordially yours,

Marquis Childs wrote an article for the St. Louis Post-Dispatch, March 2, 1958, on the possibility that Nelson Rockefeller might run against Averell Harriman for governor of New York. At one point in the article, Childs wrote of Harriman, "His break with Adlai E. Stevenson after the 1952 campaign was largely a result of Harriman's conviction that Stevenson compromised on issues on which the Governor believes there can be no compromise."

To Marquis W. Childs[207]

March 17, 1958

Dear Mark:

Noting this story, which is as excellent as I have come to expect, I am taking the liberty of sending along a comment in enlargement, but not contradiction — which is something I would never dare to do with you!

Actually, as you will recall, there was no "break" with me until late in the summer of 1955. Until the time of the Governors' Conference in August, Averell had frequently repeated his intention to support me.[208] Even then, I didn't fully understand his ambiguity, and he never positively indicated his own ambitions until after the President's heart attack — in the television interview about a week later, I believe.[209] It was not until December that he made a critical remark about a phrase I

[207] The original is in the possession of the State Historical Society of Wisconsin.

[208] Cf. Stevenson's letters to Harriman and Mrs. Eugene Meyer in *The Papers of Adlai E. Stevenson*, Vol. IV, pp. 547–548 and 558.

[209] Governor Harriman appeared on the CBS program *Face the Nation* on October 9, 1955, and declared that his response in the past when asked whom he supported — "I'm for Stevenson" — was "only a partial answer." He said that he was "not entirely a free agent" in the matter, since he expected to be a member of the New York delegation, which would decide whom to back, and he added that he could not take time off from his duties as governor to enter any primaries. It was conjectured that this indicated that he thought of himself as a potential candidate but was avoiding confrontation with Stevenson or Senator Estes Kefauver in the primary elections, the loss of which might destroy his chances of nomination. See "Harriman Denies a Pledge to Back Stevenson in 1956," New York *Times*, October 10, 1955. Harriman did not actually announce his candidacy until June 9, 1956, the day after President Eisenhower was stricken with ileitis.

used in a speech before a Democratic fund raising dinner here in Chicago. I believe the sentence, referring to the Republicans, was something like this: "While moderation is the spirit of the times, we must not confuse moderation with mediocrity."

Please don't acknowledge this. The point is that there was no break whatever until he decided that he was a candidate.

I hope you and your charming ladies are all well.

Cordially,
ADLAI

Mrs. Walter Baumgarten, Jr., Stevenson's cousin, sent Stevenson the news that her son had been elected secretary of his class at Yale University.

To Tad Foote[210]

March 17, 1958

Dear Tad:

I can't understand why my intelligence service reports so many unimportant things and overlooks important ones. At all events, I've only now become aware of the fact that a member of my family has been elected President, or at least its constitutional equivalent in Yale terms! Like anyone on whom such recognition and responsibility has fallen, your classmates are to be congratulated and you, too, in that order of felicitation.

I hope very much that you will come to see me if you ever get in my vicinity. It has been a long time, and besides congratulating you I should like to hear what you are planning to do after college — if you have decided. My youngest son, John Fell, confronts that decision when he finishes at Harvard this spring.

With my congratulations and affectionate best wishes,

. Cordially yours,

To Margaret Halsey

March 17, 1958

Dear Margaret Halsey:

I have been carrying your letter of February 7 around with me exhibiting it discreetly to fellow admirers of Halsey and fellow feelers — or is it feeling fellows — about Nixon.

210 The original is in the possession of Mrs. Walter Baumgarten.

Why is it I like to read your letters better than answer them? Or is this true of everyone? I think it has to do with the fact that you have ideas and I don't. Perhaps that is the difference between politicians and certain paramoeciums.

Cordially yours,

Sir Edmund Hall-Patch sent Stevenson a speech by Oliver Franks, chairman of the board of Lloyds Bank, analyzing the position of sterling in the world economy. Sir Edmund praised Stevenson's efforts in Washington on February 25 in support of foreign aid.

To Sir Edmund Hall-Patch

March 17, 1957

My dear Sir Edmund:

I am happy to find your letter of the 11th this morning, enclosing Oliver Franks' report, which I will read promptly. And in due course I will impose on you some utterances of my own in the areas of trade and aid. While the perspectives for neither are good, something will be done on both, I am sure. The foreign aid bill will be reduced, unhappily, I fear, in the economic rather than the military sections. The Reciprocal Trade Agreements Act will be renewed, but with some further debilitating amendments and probably for only a couple of years. Meanwhile, however, the struggle does not abate.

I have just had a delicious visit from our charming girl friend,[211] who has captivated one and all, as usual. Somehow her schedule looks formidable and exhausting to a hardened campaigner, but I can detect no ill effects nor any diminution in her taste for gaiety, conversation, and champagne!

My plans now indicate a week or ten days in London commencing about the 17th of June. If you are there at that time, I will hope for a visit of some kind.

Cordially yours,

Enc. Halsey reprint on Nixon.[212]

---

[211] Barbara Ward.
[212] "Beware the Tender Trap," *New Republic*, January 13, 1958.

To Mrs. Franklin D. Roosevelt[213]

March 18, 1958

My dear Mrs. Roosevelt:

This morning I read your column about educational TV. It reminded me that educational *films* is another of the myriad things I never have time to talk to you about. To me, a more hopeful development in teaching techniques than educational TV is the educational film, which can be used to enrich almost any subject in the humanities and sciences.

Too little is known of the enormous progress that has been made in the production of such films both here and abroad. Actually, they constitute much of the program material for educational TV, but can be used in any classroom at any time by a teacher competent to manage the equipment. Moreover, in all the standard textbooks there is a film correlation so the teacher can know precisely what films are available with reference to the course, and at what point they can be best used.

This technique has now reached the stage of an entire course in introductory physics on colored film, which is quite remarkable and can bring to any classroom, with or without a physics teacher (most of them, unhappily, are without a *qualified* teacher), the best teacher in the country, Dr. Harvey White of the University of California.

But this must stop! Sometime I hope we can have a more leisurely and uninterrupted talk about a lot of things. Grandsons are nice, and so are visitors, but they *do* interfere!

Affectionately,

ADLAI

P.S. I was so glad you spoke a good word for Tom Finletter!

Senator Richard Neuberger, of Oregon, wrote that more Republicans than Democrats supported his amendment to control billboards on federal interstate highways. He expressed the hope that Democrats outside of Congress would speak up in support of the amendment.

[213] The original is in the Franklin D. Roosevelt Library, Hyde Park, New York. The postscript was added by hand.

To Richard L. Neuberger[214]

March 19, 1958

Dear Dick:

Lest there be any misunderstanding as to my position, I want to make it emphatically clear that I support wholeheartedly your billboard control amendment to the Highway Bill.

My reason for supporting this amendment is that I consider it to be not only in the public interest, but absolutely essential to preserving for American motorists their vast investment in the new Federal Interstate Highway System.[215]

With best wishes, I am

Sincerely yours,

Endicott Peabody, who was seeking the Democratic nomination for governor of Massachusetts, wrote on March 18, suggesting that if former Governor Paul Dever supported him it would secure the nomination.

To Endicott Peabody

March 20, 1958

Dear Chub:

Thank you so much for your letter. I know the difficulties which you still confront, but the news is encouraging. I shall be sure to resume my counsel to Governor Dever when the opportunity presents itself.

With affectionate regards to Toni.[216]

Yours,

To Alicia Patterson

March 25, 1958

Dear Alicia:

I have to entertain, somehow, for Mr. and Mrs. Harry Oppenheimer of South Africa, in New York on April 7. Could you come to dinner with

---

[214] A carbon copy of this letter was sent to Charles Tyroler, of the Democratic Advisory Council.
[215] Senator Neuberger read this statement into the *Congressional Record, Senate,* March 24, 1958, p. 4544.
[216] Mrs. Peabody.

them? Indeed, maybe you would like to have them at your house —
thereby paying your social debts to them and improving your standing
with me. I have in mind the Canfields,[217] [Lloyd K.] Garrisons,
Tempelsman,[218] and Marietta Tree if she is back from Barbados.

I leave tomorrow to make another one of those "administration
speeches" in Washington, this time on foreign trade; thence to New
York for Herbert Lehman's 80th birthday, a speech on education at the
Waldorf on Saturday, and a broadcast with Agronsky[219] on Sunday. I
must be crazy! Then on Monday the 31st, or Tuesday April 1st, I will go
down to Southern Pines, I hope with John Fell, and stay with Buffy
(Mrs. Ernest Ives, telephone 2-7451) over Easter, going to New York
again on Monday the 7th.

Ever,

*Stevenson was in New York City on March 24 and 25 to attend a
meeting of the Field Foundation and to work at his law office.*

To Stanley Frankel[220]

March 25, 1958

Dear Stan:

I quote as follows from a letter which I received recently:

"I have been thinking about long playing records and their application in political campaigns, and the more I think about it the more
enthusiastic I become over the great possibilities that are presented by
this form of communication.

"During a campaign, when a candidate makes a major speech over
TV or radio and a voter for one reason or another misses that speech, his
chances of knowing just what the candidate said are very remote. The
number of newspapers in this country which reprint major campaign
speeches in full could be counted on the fingers of one's hands; and by
the time the speech is 'interpreted' by the local editorial writer the
reader gets a sadly distorted picture of what the speaker really said.
Months after the election is over and a book of the candidate's speeches

[217] Cass Canfield, chairman of the executive and editorial committees of Harper
& Brothers, and Mrs. Canfield.
[218] Maurice Tempelsman, a dealer in industrial diamonds and one of Stevenson's
clients.
[219] Martin Agronsky, Washington correspondent of the American Broadcasting
Company.
[220] Editor of *Coronet* magazine. A carbon copy of this letter was sent to Charles
Tyroler, of the Democratic Advisory Council.

appears, many people read for the first time what they should have known before voting.

"I've been thinking that long-playing records of campaign speeches could be sold and distributed to large groups for replaying in local community gatherings, in homes and on local radio stations where time can be purchased more cheaply than on networks. Of course, tape recordings serve much the same purpose except that a tape-recording machine is available to fewer listeners than record players are. A record played in the quiet of one's home is impressive to a listener, too.

"The Liberal Party here in New York sold many of the Arnold Michaelis' record interview with you late in 1956[221] and it would be interesting to know how that may have influenced voters.

"Well, anyway, it is a thought to keep in mind for 1960."

It may be there is an idea here that could be developed with a little thought; and certainly, as you have said, we need some ideas badly.

Cordially yours,

On March 26 and 27, Stevenson was in Washington, D.C., where he spoke at an international trade policy conference on the 27th. On the next day he attended a dinner in New York City in honor of Senator Herbert Lehman and worked at his law office. On March 29, he spoke to the annual conference of the United Parents Association of New York.[222]

On March 30, Stevenson appeared on the National Broadcasting Company's television program Look Here. *On the program he said that he still believed it was wise to have proposed in 1956 the suspension of nuclear tests in the atmosphere even though it cost him votes. "We originally could have taken the initiative in proposing that we save mankind from the horror of nuclear weapons," he stated. "We didn't do it. We thought it better not to. I think that was wrong. Then the Russians seized the initiative and they proposed it."*

Stevenson was asked on the program whether he was a candidate for the 1960 presidential nomination.[223] He replied: "Let me just say once more what I have said repeatedly, and that is that I haven't been a candidate, I am not a candidate and I will not be a candidate."

[221] *Portrait of Adlai Stevenson in Conversation with Arnold Michaelis* (Spoken Arts 770), taped in June, 1956.

[222] This speech, revised and adapted, appeared as "Dual Education Problem: School and Home," *New York Times Magazine*, April 6, 1958.

[223] A Gallup Poll had reported that as between Nixon and Stevenson the results were: Stevenson 46%, Nixon 42%, Undecided 12%. Chicago *Sun-Times*, February 9, 1958.

On March 31, Stevenson attended the funeral of James A. Finnegan, who had managed his 1956 campaign. Governor Frank Clement of Tennessee had wired Stevenson expressing his sorrow over the death of Mr. Finnegan.

To Frank G. Clement

April 2, 1958

Dear Frank:

Thank you for your wire about Jim. I went to his funeral in Philadelphia on Monday and I have seldom seen a more moving public recognition of a useful and respected citizen. He will be missed in wider areas and especially in our party.

I am distressed that I missed you on your visit to Chicago. I would like to do something about that!

Cordially yours,

To Alex Rose[224]

April 2, 1958

Dear Alex:

I was disappointed that I had no opportunity to talk with you during the late festivities in New York. I am grateful indeed for being included in the tribute to Herbert Lehman. Certainly what the Liberal Party did for him did you both proud.

I have been quite disturbed by some rumors I have heard about Governor Harriman's feelings toward Tom Finletter. Certainly there are few better qualified Democratic possibilities for the U.S. Senate in the country. I should think that our party should be honored and happy to have him for a candidate if it were possible. I dare say you feel the same way, and I hope we can have a talk about it and what can be done to that end soon. I also hope that the rumors I have heard are unfounded. I suspect they are.[225]

Cordially yours

[224] Head of the Liberal party in New York.
[225] In September, the Democratic State Convention nominated New York City District Attorney Frank S. Hogan instead of Mr. Finletter.

To Mrs. Eugene Meyer[226]

April 3, 1958

Dear Agnes:

So [Lyndon] Johnson is my rival. I was afraid of Humphrey,[227] Gore,[228] [J. William] Fulbright, et al. But your "lovely soul and spirit" and your "gentle kindness" and talk of "wonderful mother"—(what has happened to you?) — have enraptured a tall, lean Texan. So what chance has a short, bald, bulgy Illinoisan? Alas! But what the hell did you write him to elicit this creaking gallantry?[229]

Ever,

ADLAI

P.S. The letter was waiting.[230] I shall put it away on a bed of rose leaves under a blanket of immortelles.

Stevenson had been commissioned by the Authors' League of America to try to persuade Soviet authorities to pay royalties on American books that they published.

To Joseph S. Iseman[231]

April 3, 1958

Re: Author's League of America, Inc.

The following reports and miscellaneous intelligence were gathered in Washington, D.C. this week:

I met with Fred Merrill[232] (an old friend), who is in charge of

[226] The original is in the Agnes Meyer files, Princeton University Library.

[227] Senator Hubert H. Humphrey, of Minnesota.

[228] Senator Albert Gore, of Tennessee.

[229] Mrs. Meyer replied on April 6 that she had written Johnson that the picture of his mother that appeared along with a story about him in *Time* explained more about him than the article did. Mrs. Meyer added that this comment had touched Johnson deeply and he wrote her the letter she sent to Stevenson.

[230] Mrs. Meyer's letter of March 30, 1958, noting that Roscoe Drummond, Washington columnist of the New York *Herald Tribune*, predicted Stevenson would be nominated. Mrs. Meyer, among other things, said that she planned to talk to Mrs. Franklin D. Roosevelt, Senator Herbert Lehman, Roger Stevens and others about it and that Stevenson need know nothing about her activities.

[231] A member of Stevenson's law firm, Paul, Weiss, Rifkind, Wharton & Garrison.

[232] Frederick T. Merrill, director of the East-West contacts staff in the State Department.

implementing the Cultural Relations Treaty with the USSR, and with Carroll Woods, Economic Officer in the Bureau of Eastern European Affairs (Ext. 5435). Their objective is to break through the iron curtain with exchanges of all kinds, and they make it clear that they are concerned more with this objective than fighting over royalties for injured authors. However, they were profoundly interested in our problem and eager to cooperate in any way.

They showed me the message that had been sent by Dulles to the Soviet on January 11, 1956, asking most of the exact questions posed by your memorandum with respect to pirated works in the Soviet Union. There has never been an acknowledgement of that note, probably due to the fact that it followed closely on the heels of the Geneva Foreign Ministers' Conference. Adherence to the Copyright Convention was one of the seventeen points advanced in the East-West negotiations, and the USSR turned down the whole package. Their guess was that the Russians might be on the eve of a general thaw and that some royalties might be forthcoming *in the future*. They were not too sanguine about recovery for the past.

They have little to offer in the way of sources of information other than those you have already thought of. They pointed out that the Russians take a moral position and refuse to deal with publishers, preferring to deal with authors. They hope to exchange a delegation of writers this year and have already completed a music exchange, and Shostakovitch will come this year with this group. They hope to send [William] Faulkner, [Ernest] Hemingway, [John] Steinbeck and others to Russia, but the Russians have not yet agreed to a writers' exchange. They have also completed negotiations for an exchange of sculptors and painters for this autumn and are working on radio and TV exchanges.

They explained to me that Consultants Bureau, Inc., 222 West 17th Street, New York City, Earl Coleman, President, claims to have a contract with the Russians to translate and market Russian books in this country.

Their suggestion is that they address another note to Moscow and they would raise the matter for discussion in the East-West negotiations any time I suggest would best coincide with my representations. Certainly there is no policy objection to what we are contemplating.

I also met with Quincy Mumford, the Librarian of Congress, and Arthur Fisher, the Register of Copyrights, John Lister Nolan,[233] Daniel

---

[233] John Lester Nolan, associate director of the Reference Department of the Library of Congress.

C. Mearns,[234] Robert Land[235] and a Mr. Gorikov, the Russian expert from the Library staff, later. They referred to Robert Frase of the American Book Publisher's Council, 812 17th Street, N.W. (Republic 7-7031), as knowledgeable in this field.

Fisher gave me a long dissertation on the copyright situation, culminating in the report that they were having a meeting of the International Copyright Committee on August 18 at Geneva. He said there was some expectation that the Russians, or a satellite acting on their behalf, might come as a preliminary step toward a copyright convention. When they joined UNESCO they sent in full information immediately afterward, and they might do the same thing in this case. The Russian expert showed me a guide to Soviet Russian translations of American literature published in 1954 by Columbia University, which you doubtless have. Fisher felt that we should proceed with talks about reciprocal exchange of books with royalties as we are doing with films. The Russian reply is that they don't want to give money to publishers, but only to authors, which is a little anamolous in view of their control of everything. Robert Frase is familiar with this situation.

These gentlemen were likewise not too optimistic about recovering back royalties because the Russians take the position that under their law they have done nothing wrong. Translations are not copyrightable, which is calculated to encourage translation and dissemination. They also point out some weaknesses in our position, as we were historically pirates until the Copyright Convention of the 1890's.

The Russians are abstracting and also photostating and reproducing American scientific journals.

Our moral position may be weakened by our refusal to pay royalties for our armed services broadcasts. We talk about protecting our citizens abroad and don't even protect them from copyright violation by our own broadcasting or compensation distribution societies abroad. . . .

Enclosed is a memo from a Russian publication of books published in the USSR translated from English. Where the word "books" is used it means printings and not separate volumes. A book in two volumes is treated not as two books in these statistics.

[234] Chief of the Manuscripts Division of the Library of Congress.
[235] Assistant chief of the General Reference and Bibliography Division of the Library of Congress.

To K. A. Gbedemah[236]

April 3, 1958

Dear Mr. Minister:

I have just had word from my friends at the J. Henry Schroder Banking Corporation that an account has been opened with them by the Government of Ghana. Naturally they are very pleased, and in view of my intervention on their behalf I, too, want to express my thanks to you. As I understand that this is only a temporary arrangement, permit me to say again that I think this old and enterprising Anglo-American banking house could be very useful to you because of their exceptional experience and activity in world trade. Hence I believe it would be mutually advantageous if the present arrangement ripened into something permanent.

Here, as you well know, the portents of the future are confusing. While there are many encouraging factors, they are balanced by unfavorable factors, and unemployment continues to rise contra the seasonal trend. My own guess is that there is more trouble ahead and that we will be lucky if we turn the corner conclusively this year.

I will make my annual business trip to Europe and Britain in June and I am planning to spend a few weeks "sightseeing" in the Soviet Union. It will be my first visit there in more than thirty years. I understand there have been some changes!

I will, accordingly, miss the Prime Minister when he comes here in July, to my great regret. But I hope to see Sir Robert Jackson in late May before my departure, and it would be nice to see you in Europe if you are to be there at the same time.

With esteem and warm regards, I am

Cordially yours,

J. Edward Day, who had been director of the Illinois Department of Insurance while Stevenson was governor and who was now an insurance executive in California, sent Stevenson a feature story on the Day family — including a picture of Mr. and Mrs. Day and two of their children, James and Geraldine — that had appeared in the Los Angeles Times, March 9, 1958.

---

[236] Minister of Finance of Ghana.

To J. Edward Day

April 3, 1958

Dear Ed:

Thanks for your letter and the grand piece from the *Times*. It is the best and most accurate account of anything I have ever read in "that paper"! In fact, I recognized everything in the story — except the picture of the family. It is hard for me to believe that little Jerry is that big, beautiful debutante on the arm of Mary Louise's[237] chair. But, alas, I am afraid I would still recognize you — and still playing with cats!

What a superb family it is and how happy you all look. I wish you were all here this very minute.

I am glad to hear that the Republicans are in bad shape in California. I told Pat Brown[238] he should know you, and you can be sure he will. Bill Blair was out there last week and brings back the same comforting reports — also that the Democrats have a lot of money for the campaign. That is a crisis I never confronted!

When are you coming this way? I hope it is soon and that you will plan to stay a night with me. I will be here off and on until we leave for a journey abroad the middle of June. I must wait to celebrate Jane Dick's graduation from the University of Chicago![239]

Much love to you all.

Yours,

John A. Hannah, president of Michigan State University, invited Stevenson to give an address at its commencement exercises on June 8, 1958.

To John A. Hannah

April 7, 1958

Dear Dr. Hannah:

I have your letter and would be happy to accept both your invitation to speak at commencement and the honorary degree. But may I defer for the present a decision about coming on Saturday? I must leave on a

237 Mrs. Day.
238 Edmund G. Brown, attorney general of California.
239 Mrs. Dick, who had left college before graduating, completed her credits for a degree at the University of Chicago in 1957–1958.

long trip abroad the following week and may be badly pressed at that time. But I would much enjoy a longer visit with you and I shall certainly come on Saturday if I possibly can.

Will you also let me know how long I should speak. And if you can give me any counsel as to preferred subjects it would be most welcome. *This is not a perfunctory request!* Fifteen to thirty thousand people at an academic gathering staggers me, I confess, and I don't know how to holler at that many people thoughtfully at all, let alone for half an hour.

And I may have to ask you to give me a good character with some of your Presidential colleagues whose invitations for that week-end I had declined due to a trip abroad that has now been postponed!

With thanks, and my esteem and best wishes, I am

Cordially yours,

P.S. Shall I wear my resplendent scarlet Oxford D.C.L. robes? I've been wondering if they would ever be unpacked!

From April 8 to 10, Stevenson was in New York City attending meetings of the board of directors of the Encyclopaedia Britannica *and of the advisory board of Encyclopaedia Britannica Films. He hosted — at the home of Alicia Patterson — a dinner in honor of Mr. and Mrs. Harry Oppenheimer of South Africa.*

V. Y. Dallman, editor of the Springfield Illinois State Register, *wrote that all members of his family renominated Stevenson for 1960. In his column on March 31, 1958, Mr. Dallman described him as the "losing winner with a sense of humor, the truth and a smile."*

To V. Y. Dallman

April 8, 1958

Dear Vin:

Thank you so much for that thoughtful and flattering letter. Of the flattery, I have had so much from you I shall be tempted to take myself seriously!

But please, my beloved friend, do not encourage the 1960 talk. Surely two ordeals is enough!

Besides, I want to keep that humor, truth and smile that you so graciously talk about, and running for President is a hazard to all three!

With affectionate regards to Mrs. Dallman, I am

Cordially yours,

On April 4, after having lunch with Stevenson, Senator Richard L. Neuberger told the press, "Adlai E. Stevenson continues to be the best hope of the Democratic Party for the Presidential nomination in 1960."

To Richard L. Neuberger

April 10, 1958

Dear Dick:

Thanks so much for your visit and your note — and that graciously flattering statement to the press. But I really don't want to be considered for that ordeal again. I know the friendship and charity that animated you — but I wish it didn't!

Affectionate regards to Maurine[240] — and come again.

Yours,

Miss Edith Gifford had just sent the most recent of the scrapbooks of newspaper clippings about Stevenson which she compiled over the years.

To Edith Gifford[241]

April 10, 1958

Dear Edith:

The enormous box has come with all those new volumes, and again I am at a loss to thank you for such incredible and sustained effort. I think I had better withdraw from all public life to give you a rest. That might be a good excuse to give myself one too. Shall we make a compact?

Anyway, I am as grateful as ever, and if a permanent record of me has any value you are entirely responsible.

Bless you, my dear friend, and my utmost thanks.

Cordially yours,

ADLAI

On April 10, Stevenson and his son Adlai III attended a dinner honoring Joseph Bunting, general manager of the Bloomington Daily Pantagraph, on his retirement. Stevenson attended meetings of the board of

[240] Mrs. Neuberger.
[241] The original is in the possession of Miss Gifford.

directors of the Pantagraph Corporation, which was owned by the Mer-
wins and Stevenson and Mrs. Ives.[242]

To Mrs. Ernest L. Ives[243]

April 14, 1958

Dear Buffy:

Adlai and I spent a couple of happy days with Tim and Adrienne [Ives] in Bloomington, to attend the Bunting farewell dinner and the Pantagraph meetings. They are well and the reports from all quarters are most gratifying about their easy adjustment to the community, popularity, etc. The babies are beautiful and healthy, and what more could you ask! We visited the farm, saw the neighbors, played tennis and sat in interminable meetings at the Pantagraph.

I also conferred at length with Joe Bohrer[244] about the [Unitarian] church situation. He agrees emphatically on the following priority (1) restoration, and (2) a new building on the present site. Before I finished I convinced Loring[245] of this and the proposal of the Pantagraph Foundation will be a gift of $35,000 for restoration and $25,000 for a new building on the present site with nothing offered, at the present time, for a new building on a different site.

I will not go into detail, which I suspect is quite familiar to you, but I gather the hazards of restoration and the uncertain expense are a contributing factor to great reluctance to move in that direction, not to mention the anxieties about future maintenance and upkeep cost. So I rather suspect that the struggle in the church meeting will center around a new building at the present site and the financial advantage of selling the site and starting elsewhere with a lot more money to spend. If you want any more dope, call me and I will try to fill you in. Tim and Adlai sat through the Foundation meeting.

The condition of the paper is healthy and prudent provision is being made for the million dollars we will have to spend in another five or six years on new presses, etc. Although I would prefer to retain more of the money in the business, the pressure for income by Davis[246] and Hes-

[242] For the relationship of the Stevenson and Merwin families to the *Pantagraph*, see *The Papers of Adlai E. Stevenson*, Vol. I, pp. 153–155; Davis, *A Prophet in His Own Country*, pp. 145–146; John Bartlow Martin, *Adlai Stevenson of Illinois: The Life of Adlai E. Stevenson* (Garden City, New York: Doubleday, 1976), pp. 74–76.

[243] The original is in E.S.I., I.S.H.L.

[244] Joseph F. Bohrer, a Bloomington lawyer and friend of Stevenson's since 1905.

[245] Stevenson's cousin Loring "Bud" Merwin, publisher and president of the *Pantagraph*.

[246] Davis Merwin, Loring Merwin's older brother and former president of the *Pantagraph*.

ter[247] is incessant and a proposal to distribute $30,000 this year and a like amount next year, in addition to the regular dividend, was carried in spite of my protest — which could not be very persuasive in view of the circumstances. Tim and Davis, Jr. were added to the Board and Adlai III had an opportunity to learn something about the business. I have transferred five shares of stock to each of the three boys.

Love,
ADLAI

To Sam Rayburn

April 15, 1958

Dear Sam:

I hear that you are running for a 24th term and while I don't ordinarily interfere in primaries and I am not sure you will have any opposition, this is just a note to say that I will be glad to help out if necessary!

Cordially,

Harry Golden, publisher of the Carolina Israelite, *who had just visited with Stevenson in Chicago, sent him several memoranda. One concluded, "A 1960 campaign without Governor Stevenson would be a most bitter anti-climax not only for America but for the entire Western World. . . ." Another analyzed the question of Southern Negroes communicating with the white power structure. Another stated that Mr. Golden was urging Governor Luther Hodges to call a conference of Southern governors to get agreement on obeying the law based on the reality that the Supreme Court was not going to reverse itself on its 1954 school decision.*

To Harry Golden[248]

April 16, 1958

Dear Harry:

Thank you for your letter and the memos which were a solid useful sequel to the light and joy you shed hereabouts, and on me especially.

I wish I *wanted* to run for President again, especially when I get such reassuring and thoughtful encouragement as yours. But the fact is, I don't!

---

[247] Hester Merwin Ayres, sister of Loring and Davis Merwin.
[248] The original is in the possession of Mr. Golden.

Let us then turn to your memorandum about communication. I find it extremely reassuring, sensible and provocative. But how do we commence communication with "the power structure" which is now possible? What steps can we take? Is there any general pattern? How could a Foundation explore the possibilities and further them? It sounds to me mostly as though some communities were coming to their senses after the emotional excesses of the immediate past. But can such a process be "helped"?

I am afraid you have a very exacting friend as well as a great admirer in Illinois!

Yours,
ADLAI

p.s., I neglected to say that I think your suggestion to Governor Hodges to quietly take the lead in promoting the idea of obedience and acceptance of the doctrine of inevitability is very sensible. I think he could do not only himself but the country a lot of good, and I hope you will send me a copy of the memorandum you prepare for him. Indeed, I would like to attend the meeting, but I suppose it should be confined to southern leaders.

Chester Bowles wrote praising Stevenson's recent speeches as clear and constructive. Mr. Bowles then explained his deep concern that he and William Benton, his former partner in the advertising business, were both seeking the Democratic senatorial nomination in Connecticut.

To Chester Bowles

April 16, 1958

Dear Chet:

Thank you so much for your letter and your charity about some recent utterances. I often wonder why I go on uttering, which is such painful work!

I, too, have been troubled about the competition between you and Bill. I have long known how much you mean to one another and have often heard him talk with pride about his identification with you.

Only the other day I expressed again my anxiety about this, not only from my own point of view but from the point of view of your countless mutual friends as well as the party and your future value to it. Again he assured me that he would avoid any personal collision at any cost. I am sure that is your purpose too.

From the fragments of Connecticut news that come my way, I would gather that you are doing very well indeed. And ever so many thanks for sending me your new book.[249] I had previously read the *Encyclopaedia Britannica Year Book* piece and I gather that this has some of the same material.

Yours,

Mrs. Eugene Meyer wrote on April 15 that she had just had an interview with former President Truman. She found that Truman was opposed to Senator John F. Kennedy as a presidential candidate in 1960, on the grounds that the country was not ready for a Roman Catholic as President. Mrs. Meyer wrote that she sensed that Truman thought Stevenson would be the best candidate for 1960. Truman had stated that he bore Stevenson no ill-will, though he was still displeased that Stevenson had refused his offer of the 1952 nomination.[250] Furthermore, following the 1952 draft, he felt that Stevenson wanted to dissociate himself from him; what had most hurt Truman, Mrs. Meyer wrote, was Stevenson's reference to "the mess in Washington."[251] Truman also told Mrs. Meyer that he had asked Stevenson in 1955 to announce his candidacy but that Stevenson could not make up his mind. Therefore, Truman said, he had decided to support Governor Harriman.[252] He now felt that Stevenson's strength had grown remarkably since his cooperation with Secretary of State John Foster Dulles over the NATO meeting and his subsequent speeches. Stevenson could not be an avowed candidate for 1960, Truman added, but he had to have "friends."

When Mrs. Meyer asked Truman if he minded if she reported the conversation to Stevenson, Truman replied that he would be happy if she did so. She observed that Truman would be pleased to talk to him but that the first move would have to come from Stevenson. Mrs. Meyer urged him to get over all the "remnants of snobbishness" in his system and to phone Truman and not be "haughty" with him. She added that she had told Truman that Stevenson had "terrible marital difficulties" when the President first knew him but that as the result of disappointments that would have crushed most people, Stevenson had grown.

---

[249] *Ideas, People and Peace* (New York: Harper, 1958).

[250] See *The Papers of Adlai E. Stevenson*, Vol. III, pp. 490–491.

[251] For a discussion of this, see Davis, *A Prophet in His Own Country*, p. 415; Martin, *Adlai Stevenson of Illinois*, pp. 644, 680. See also Stevenson's letter to Truman, in *The Papers of Adlai E. Stevenson*, Vol. VI, pp. 35–37.

[252] See *The Papers of Adlai E. Stevenson*, Vol. VI, p. 180.

To Mrs. Eugene Meyer[253]

April 18, 1958

Dear Agnes:

Your interesting report has arrived and I find the Kennedy part the most interesting of all. HST's comments are the same ones I have been over with him orally and in writing several times. I will tell you all about it on Monday next, I hope. Remind me to comment on the following points he made to you:

(1) Why I could not in good conscience accept his proposition in 1952 when I was already a candidate for reelection as Governor.

(2) The "mess in Washington" letter to the Oregon editor.

(3) Why I refused to announce my candidacy in 1952 [1955] when he asked me to.[254]

Finally, I beg you to believe that I have never been "unkind," "haughty," "snobbish" to him — never, never, never! On the contrary, I have championed him when the going was tough in many places and as a candidate for Governor in 1948.[255] Why he clings to these illusions I think I know, and I think along with several friends I also know who has constantly influenced his recollection and attitude.[256]

I remind you that I had *no* marital difficulties when we first talked in 1952. They were three years behind me.

On May first I am afraid I can't possibly get to Washington for that tempting dinner in view of the fact that I have declined a very important function in New York that night, among other reasons. On the 11th I shall be in New York between a case before the Court of Appeals in Albany and a fund-raising dinner on Monday, May 12. We have the damnedest luck! And I have the damnedest time trying to earn a living, and practice statecraft, politics and perpetual travel.

Affectionately,

ADLAI

[253] The original is in the Agnes Meyer files, Princeton University Library.

[254] See Stevenson's letter to Truman of July 18, 1955, in *The Papers of Adlai E. Stevenson,* Vol. IV, pp. 529–530; Davis, *A Prophet in His Own Country,* pp. 444–445.

[255] Truman's unpopularity in Illinois was so great that leading Democrats in the state feared that their entire 1948 ticket was in jeopardy if he was the presidential candidate that year, and several of them, including Jacob Arvey and Paul H. Douglas, attempted to draft Dwight D. Eisenhower instead. Stevenson refused to join in this movement, and many of his gubernatorial campaign speeches contained praise of Truman. See *The Papers of Adlai E. Stevenson,* Vol. II, Part Five, *passim.*

[256] It is not clear whom Stevenson alludes to.

Stevenson was in New York City and Washington from April 18 to 21. He attended a meeting of the Field Foundation, lunched with Arthur Hays Sulzberger of The New York Times, *attended a party for newspaper people given by Alicia Patterson, and a reception for Sam Rayburn and other congressmen sponsored by Katie Louchheim, vice chairman of the Democratic National Committee.*[257] *On April 21 he flew to Palm Beach, Florida, to visit Mrs. Albert Lasker and on April 24 spoke to a meeting of the Florida Educational Association. He returned to Chicago the following day.*

Harrison Salisbury, of the New York Times, *wrote that he understood Stevenson had picked Robert Tucker, who had worked at the U.S. Embassy in Moscow for six years, to accompany him on his forthcoming trip to the Soviet Union. Salisbury said that he and Thomas Whitney, foreign news analyst for the Associated Press and author of several books on Russia, were to see Tucker soon and the three of them would pool their advice. Salisbury expressed the hope that Stevenson would return from Moscow full of ideas for solving our problems and ready to stimulate us into action.*

To Harrison Salisbury

April 28, 1958

Dear Harrison:

I am most grateful for your letter. . . .

I shall certainly see you before I leave, and I am sure my three advisers can multiply the values of my trip enormously. I think I shall appoint you chief brain squeezer forthwith — and be sure to collect all the juice!

I wish I thought my visit might yield some of those ideas you suggest for solving our troubles and firing their enthusiasm for greater exertions. I will do my best, but I will need a lot of help, and I think I know where I am going to look for it!

Yours always,

Miss Eleanor Kask, of the World Publishing Company, asked Stevenson for a statement about Harry Golden's forthcoming book, Only in America.

[257] See Katie Louchheim, *By the Political Sea* (New York: Doubleday, 1970), pp. 82ff., for her analysis of Stevenson.

To Eleanor Kask[258]

April 30, 1958

Dear Miss Kask:

Harry Golden could happen only in America!

Where else could a Jew from New York's lower East Side turn up in such a place as Charlotte, North Carolina, with his effervescent *Carolina Israelite!* Mr. Golden's lively personal journal always leaves me in a gale of mirth or with a knitted brow — or both! This heavy thinker with a light heart is one of America's secret weapons, and I commend his book "Only In America," to all who seek light and joy.

Cordially yours,

To LeRoy Collins[259]

April 30, 1958

Dear LeRoy:

While the memory is fresh, let me say how much Maurice Mitchell[260] and I enjoyed our breakfast in Miami and what a pleasure it was to see you again. An even greater satisfaction was the repeated evidences of the affection and respect that you have earned so quickly throughout Florida. While I know what a satisfaction this is to you, I also can understand the burden of responsibility that accompanies it.

I am delighted that you share my enthusiasm for the educational film. I hope you can become even more familiar with some of the developments in this field which have convinced me of its enormous potential value in instruction. I am sure the Encyclopaedia Britannica Film people would be delighted to show some more examples at your house at any time. I hope Florida can get that man from Ohio and enlarge its activity in this field.

And I hope — even more — that I shall have more frequent opportunities to *see* you. I have no doubt that I shall hear about you a great deal.

Cordially yours,

Martin Agronsky wrote that he had received a "tremendous" amount of mail as a result of Stevenson's appearance on his television program

[258] The original is in the possession of Harry Golden.
[259] Governor of Florida.
[260] President of Encyclopaedia Britannica Films, Inc.

Look Here *on March 30. He stated: "It will always remain an insoluble paradox to me that the American public can have so tremendous a regard for your wisdom, perception and statesmanlike qualities, while twice negating the opportunity to place you where these qualities would constantly be available for the national good." He added that he and other reporters were grateful that nothing Stevenson had ever said in public or private diminished his stature in their eyes and expressed the hope he would report another Stevenson presidential campaign.*

To Martin Agronsky

May 1, 1958

Dear Martin:

That was a very kind letter indeed. I could say some comparable things about correspondents and commentators, and for all these things I don't need to tell you where your name would be.

I am glad that the broadcast had a favorable response, and I would relish collaboration with you on any project — except another Presidential campaign.

Cordially yours,

Mrs. Eugene Meyer had just testified before the Education Committee of the House of Representatives on the Federal Aid to Education bill.

To Mrs. Eugene Meyer[261]

May 2, 1958

And that was a bold, gallant and arresting thing you did before the house committee — gal! They, we, needed a shock and you shook!

How the devil do you get so much done??? But don't tell me; I'm tired enough as it is!

Off to N.Y. now for a week of law. This business of having to earn money for which I have no aptitude is such a chore!

Love ever —
ADLAI

Stevenson was in New York City on legal business from May 3 to 13. He presented a case to the Court of Appeals in Albany on May 8. On

[261] This handwritten letter is in the Agnes Meyer files, Princeton University Library.

May 12 he attended a dinner meeting of the Democratic Advisory Council.

To Robert S. Benjamin[262]

May 14, 1958

Dear Bob:

I tried to call you Tuesday morning before my hurried departure for Chicago to say the following:

(a) Thanks for a good time.

(b) My apologies for a lousy speech.

(c) My quadruple apologies for departing so unceremoniously.

(d) My thanks to you, Marietta [Tree], et al, for your heroic services to DAC.

I shall look forward to your visit here on May 28 with that charming little girl.

Cordially yours,

P.S. The dinner Wednesday evening, May 28, for Justice [Earl] Warren, the Lord Chancellor, etc. is black tie, in the Grand Ballroom of the Palmer House at 7:00 P.M., preceded by a reception at 6:00 o'clock. Afterward we will drive to my house on the remote prairie for the night.

To Lady Barbara Jackson

May 14, 1958

Dear Barbara:

Your letter and the formidable manuscript[263] have arrived — and I have relaxed! I have not had an opportunity to read either and I will do so tonight in the beauty and tranquillity of Libertyville. And this is the first time I have enjoyed said beauty and tranquillity in two weeks.

I find on my return a cable from John Armitage[264] of Encyclopaedia Britannica advising me that they have changed the date of my meeting in Oxford to Saturday the 21st. I hope, therefore, that we can proceed with the Stratford plan for that night. I will surely have the two boys, unless Borden has to go off on some business project of his, and may

---

262 Chairman of the board of United Artists and a member of the Democratic Advisory Council with responsibility for fund-raising.

263 Lady Jackson conjectures that this "may have been a memorandum on prospects for the American economy which I believe I may have written for him at some point." Letter to Eric Sears, October 5, 1975.

264 London editor of the *Encyclopaedia Britannica*.

feel I should bring along my cousin, Lady Mildred Bailey,[265] if I can't contrive another visit with her. We can plan about Sunday and our return route later I suppose.

. . . Isn't the South American fiasco frightening?[266]

Affectionately,

p.s. Did I tell you that Mary Lasker and Bob Tufts[267] would like to meet with you on Monday or Tuesday, June 2 or 3, when I gather you will be in New York at the St. Regis on your way home. If you could let Mary know which day and what time would be convenient I am sure a further talk would bring our negotiations to some finality and coherence.

And would you tell Robert [Jackson] that I am grateful for his letter from Ghana of May 2, and that I will look forward to a talk with him in New York on Monday, May 26, or on the following morning before his departure for Syracuse.

To Mrs. Eugene Meyer[268]

May 14, 1958

Thank you, dear Agnes, for that good letter.[269] I feel better!

My argument in Albany was *good* — if I do say so. But winning a "hopeless" case is something else.

I'm working hard at the law & doing reasonably well, considering the distractions — and HST isn't one of them![270]

Much love & blessings!

ADLAI

---

[265] The former Mildred Bromwell, a first cousin of Stevenson's father.

[266] The previous day, mobs in Caracas had stoned a car carrying Vice President Nixon, who was on a goodwill tour of South America. President Eisenhower demanded that Venezuela provide for Nixon's safety, and he ordered troops to Caribbean bases as a "precautionary measure."

[267] Robert Tufts, professor at Oberlin College and a speechwriter for Stevenson in the 1952 and 1956 campaigns.

[268] This handwritten letter is in the Agnes Meyer files, Princeton University Library.

[269] It is impossible to identify the letter Stevenson refers to, since Mrs. Meyer did not always date her letters to him.

[270] Stevenson enclosed a clipping from the Chicago *Daily News* of May 8, 1958, quoting Mr. Truman as saying that Stevenson had to be prevented from winning the 1960 presidential nomination.

To Lady Mildred Bailey

May 15, 1958

Dear Millie:

Britain and Claridge's are to be blessed with my presence for a week commencing Monday, June 16. If you are there at that time I hope I can have a glimpse of you and perhaps the children. Borden will be with me and John Fell arrives the 19th or 20th, I think. I will have business engagements much of the week in London, and I am planning to go up to Oxford for a luncheon on Saturday, June 21st, thence to Stratford for a Shakespeare play (and the cultural elevation of my young), returning to London Sunday.

I hope you are well and that you will not be too distant at this time.

Affectionately,

To Fletcher Knebel[271]

May 15, 1958

My dear Knebel:

I have just read your piece in LOOK on the draft[272] — with much interest, warm approval and unhappy memories. I set forth most of these reasons for a new approach to our military manpower problem in a speech at Youngstown in October 1956.[273] I am glad to note from what you say that the light is spreading at last. Certainly the alchemy by which the Republicans converted my proposals to increase our strength and security into an effort to win votes by undermining our security was and continues to be one of the more aggravating mysteries of that campaign for me.

With my congratulations and best wishes, I am

Cordially yours,

To Lloyd K. Garrison

May 16, 1958

Dear Lloyd:

I had a visit today from Sid McMath, former Governor of Arkansas. Bill Blair has been helping him raise money in support of the candidacy of Judge Lee Ward, who is running against [Orval] Faubus for Gover-

[271] Washington bureau correspondent of Cowles Publications.
[272] "The Fight to Kill the Draft," *Look*, May 27, 1958.
[273] See *The Papers of Adlai E. Stevenson*, Vol. VI, pp. 287–298.

nor of Arkansas. While the prospects are hardly brilliant there is a possibility of a runoff with the supporters of the several opposition candidates ganging up to defeat Governor Faubus.

McMath is going to be in New York soon. I have asked him to call you. He is, as you know, a liberal minded man as Southerners go on the race question. He is coming to New York in search of funds, and I have suggested that he call on you — not for money but to talk generally about the race problem in Arkansas, especially with respect to the NAACP [National Association for the Advancement of Colored People] about which we have talked so often. I hope you can spare him a few minutes. I think you will enjoy him.

Yours,

On May 21, Stevenson spoke at the University of Louisville and stayed with Mr. and Mrs. Barry Bingham.

To Mrs. Eugene Meyer[274]

May 22, 1958

Dear Agnes:

Thank you for your dear letters and the enclosures. But I think I shall not attempt to convert that subject, however important, into a commencement speech especially one that must be given in a stadium to 20,000 people. I shall have to contrive something a little bit more lively than the menace of bureaucracy I fear me.

I am bold enough to include the speech I made at Louisville last night, which like most of my speeches will get little or no press I suspect. I think it is the only important thing I have said since the proposal for a non-governmental armament study last January.[275] I don't think we can afford to drift this way much longer, and this is one of the things that will certainly be done a year or so from now. Why not now?

Only the latter part is important.

Affectionately,
ADLAI

Commentator and author Elmer Davis, head of the Office of War Information during World War II and an adviser to the U.S. delegation

[274] The original is in the Agnes Meyer files, Princeton University Library.
[275] See p. 162, above.

*to the San Francisco conference of the United Nations in 1945, had just
died after a long illness.*

To Mrs. Elmer Davis

May 22, 1958

Dear Mrs. Davis:

What can I say? Nothing that will help, I suppose. You had a long
and distressing preparation yet I know what a shock it is, even then.

But I would like to say this: You had the privilege of sharing the life
of one of the truly great and good men of our time. You are a fortunate
woman, and some time you will be a happy one again.

My sympathy and affectionate regards.

Sincerely yours,

*Congressman Stewart Udall published an article, "Why Adlai Steven-
son Haunts the Democrats," in the New Republic, May 19, 1958, noting
that "it might be ill-reckoning to count him out early" for 1960. Udall
wrote that among his reasons for this statement were the "character and
qualities of his mind" and added: "Stevenson's maturity has served him
well." "A further explanation of the Stevenson phenomenon is that he
has worn well as a person," Mr. Udall noted, and added that he "talks
sense." Udall indirectly urged the Democrats to nominate him and
Stevenson to accept the bid.*

To Stewart L. Udall

May 28, 1958

Dear Stewart:

I have just now seen your piece in the May 19 New Republic. I am
not haunted, but I am excited, flattered, grateful, and inflated beyond
recognition. And what a graceful and puncturing pen you have too!

If talk about 1960 leaves me a little uneasy and uncomfortable, talk
about the past with such perception and sympathy as this pleases me
mightily.

Speaking of "haunting," I hope you can find a moment to look at the
suggestions in the latter part of the enclosed lecture. We will be
haunted again — and how! — unless early steps are taken to convene a
meeting of the free world experts to consider new foundations for world
trade and development. The old ones are crumbling. Must we again
wait until we have to take some leadership? And certainly we Demo-

crats don't need to wait. But so far as I know, there wasn't even a comment in the press that I made the lecture, let alone what I proposed.

I wish you would stop and see me in Chicago on your travels back and forth across the country once in a while.

Cordially and gratefully yours,

To Gilbert A. Harrison

May 28, 1958

Dear Gil:

Stewart Udall's piece has inflated me beyond recognition. Some might say that I was that way already. And doesn't he write extraordinarily well too! But talk about that future in that vein leaves me a little uneasy, as you know.

I think the suggestions toward the end of the attached lecture will also haunt Democrats and Republicans alike if we don't do something about it and promptly. So far as I know there wasn't even a newspaper comment, but surely a "royal commission" of experts to consider new Western foundations for world trade and development will become more imperative with each passing month.

Love to Nancy,[276]

To Llewellyn E. Thompson[277]

May 29, 1958

Dear Tommy:

I want to bring you up to date on our plans for the trip to the Soviet Union. To have seen you and your wife would have been one of the best parts of this adventure, but I hope, for your sake, that your holiday at home proceeds on schedule.

My party includes my two sons, Borden and John Fell, Bill Blair whom you know, Robert Tucker, formerly of the Embassy in Moscow, and some very old friends: Alicia Patterson, and Mrs. Marshall Field, of New York, and the latter's daughter Fiona, age 20. The ladies join me in Helsinki.

Ambassador Menshikov, on behalf of his Government, has invited me and my party to be guests of the Government during this journey but I have declined this courtesy, feeling that it might impair the objectivity and conviction of any reports I make on my return.

I expect to leave on June 16, spend about ten days in London and Brussels on business, and then two weeks or more in the four Scandi-

[276] Mrs. Harrison.
[277] United States ambassador to the Soviet Union.

navian capitals. We plan to leave Helsinki for Leningrad on July 12, remaining in Russia until August 8. According to the present itinerary we will be two days in Leningrad and proceed by overnight train to Moscow, arriving there July 15. On July 17 the men in the party will set out on a trip to Central Asia and Siberia, which will take about two weeks. A tentative itinerary for this part of the trip is enclosed. The ladies, meanwhile, will travel in the Ukraine, the Crimea and the Caucasus. Afterwards we shall all rejoin and stay in Moscow for a week: July 31–August 7, and then, we hope, travel by Intourist[278] automobiles to Warsaw.

My office has been working on preparations for a discussion in Moscow on the question of royalties for American authors. I have promised to send a copy of it to Ambassador Menshikov within the next few days, together with a request that he forward it to the Minister of Culture, [Nikolai A.] Mikhailov, in Moscow. Your suggestions for handling this matter have been most helpful. I am requesting, through the Ambassador, an interview with Mikhailov on my arrival on July 15. I presume that the discussions can be continued after our return to Moscow on July 31. My associates have been discussing the whole complex question of copyright and royalties with . . . the State Department and other government agencies, and we are well aware of the difficulties that may be expected. We will keep your Embassy informed of the nature and results of any talks we have with the Russians in this regard and will welcome any suggestions and assistance which it may be able to provide on the spot.

I would also welcome any information that is available regarding the new diamond production in Russia, mostly, Ambassador Menshikov tells me in the Yakutsk area. I also hope to find out what I can about the aluminum industry in the Soviet Union. As you know, concern is spreading in the West about Soviet capacity and intentions in both these fields. Any information your Embassy can give me either here or when I get there will be most helpful.

With warm regards to you and your wife, I am

Cordially yours,

To Mikhail A. Menshikov

May 29, 1958

My dear Mr. Ambassador:

First let me thank you once again for that delightful evening with you and Mrs. Menshikov and the Moscow dancers in Chicago. Their visit

---

278 The Soviet state-run travel agency for foreign visitors.

was a memorable event in our cultural life, and after seeing that remarkable performance I am looking forward even more eagerly to our visit to the U.S.S.R. this summer!

We have worked out our plans as suggested in my letter to you of April 30, and are now able to give you a little more details of where we would like to go, whom we would like to see and what we would like to do. Mindful of your kind suggestion that I keep you informed, I should like to outline our trip as we see it now.

First, however, a further word about the memorandum mentioned in my previous letter with regard to the matter of royalties for the American authors who have asked me to represent their interests. The memorandum expressing our views on this question will soon be completed and I shall take the liberty of sending you a copy. In this connection, Mr. Allan Ecker, of my firm, and Mr. Robert Tucker had a most helpful conversation last week with Mr. Juri Gvosdov of your Embassy.

I presume that Mr. Mikhailov, Minister of Culture, would be the proper person for me to talk to about the royalty issue. I would be grateful if you would inform him of my desire, and also if you would forward my forthcoming memorandum to him. It would be most convenient for me if I could meet with Mr. Mikhailov and his associates on either Tu[e]sday, July 15, or Wednesday, July 16, for a preliminary discussion of the questions raised in my memorandum. If necessary, we could then resume our talks upon my return to Moscow around July 31.

As mentioned in my previous letter, my party of eight will arrive in Leningrad by air from Helsinki on July 12, and we plan to proceed by train to Moscow on the evening of Monday, July 14. While in Leningrad we would, of course, look forward to a tour of this historic city. If it were possible for some of us to spend a day visiting Novgorod I should think it might be interesting. Among institutions I might like to see, if the short schedule in Leningrad permits, is your Academy of Sciences.

Our first stay in Moscow will be very brief. If Andre[i] Gromyko[279] is there at the time, and can spare a few minutes from his busy schedule, I would be happy to pay my respects to an old friend. I should also like to take advantage of this first stop in Moscow to see something of the city and, time permitting, the university and the offices of one of your newspapers, such as Pravda or Izvestia. However, my primary concern during this time will be, as I have indicated, to meet with Mr. Mikhailov and his associates to discuss the questions raised in my

[279] Soviet Minister of Foreign Affairs. For his service on the United Nations Preparatory Commission while Stevenson was a member of the United States delegation, see *The Papers of Adlai E. Stevenson,* Vol. II, Part Four, *passim.*

memorandum. I believe my sons and the other members of my party will wish to see as much of the city and the people as time permits.

On Thursday, July 17, I would like to leave with Mr. Blair, Mr. Tucker and my two sons, on the trip to some of the eastern areas. A provisional itinerary is enclosed, Any advice you have regarding it would be most welcome. The ladies in my party, Miss Patterson and Mrs. Field and her daughter, have decided to travel during this time to the Ukraine, the Crimea and Caucasus. I believe the Cosmos Agency in New York is arranging the itinerary for them.

At Tashkent, our first stop on the trip East, I hope to learn as much as time permits not only about this important center but about Soviet Central Asia as a whole. I would like to get a clearer picture of the position of a constituent republic in the Soviet state system, of the nationality policies being pursued by the Government, of the economic and cultural development of the region, and so on. An opportunity to speak with officials of the Uzbek Republic would be welcome, but only if quite convenient. I am sure it would be interesting to visit some typical institutions in Tashkent, such as a people's court, an educational establishment, etc.

In Samarkand I hope to speak with representatives of the Moslem faith about religious activities, as well as to see the historic sites of this ancient world center.

In view of the time limitation, I am afraid that we will not be able to include Alma-Ata on our itinerary, unless it proves practicable to stop there for a few short hours on the way from Tashkent to Novosibirsk. At Novosibirsk, I would like to see something of the industrial development in that area, and visit the new regional Economic Council and the local branch of the Academy of Sciences. Possibly a short excursion along the River Ob would give us an impression of the development of the region.

We had originally thought of stopping in Northern Kazakhstan en route from Tashkent to Novosibirsk to see a sample of the "virgin lands" project, but a study of the regular air schedules suggests, I fear, that this may not be practicable. Accordingly, our itinerary now calls for a side-trip of a day and a half from Novosibirsk to Barnaul for this purpose. At Barnaul I would welcome an opportunity to visit one or two of the new state farms and to speak with officials in charge of the development of the virgin lands.

During our visit in Sverdlovsk it would be of interest to see the Urals Heavy Machinery Works and to speak with officials in the regional Economic Council and other local institutions. Perhaps there would be time to visit a collective farm at this point on our trip. I also understand that in Sverdlovsk the Home of Pioneers is well worth seeing. The marker at the traditional dividing point between Europe and Asia is something I suppose everyone sees.

We had originally planned to stop for a day or two at Gorky or Kazan in order to see something of the Volga region. But if it can be arranged, we would like to start out from Kuibyshov [Kuibyshev] (where I would hope to see the great new hydro-electric power station) and travel upriver on one of the regular steamers as far as Kazan or even Gorky, stopping at Ulyanovsk. From Kazan or Gorky, we would fly back to Moscow, arriving there on July 30 or July 31.

During the ensuing week in Moscow, I would, as mentioned in my previous letter, welcome an opportunity to speak briefly with a few of the leaders of the Soviet Government. If entirely convenient for him, I would like, of course, to pay my respects to Premier Khrushchev. And, if their convenience permits, I am sure a visit with Deputy Premiers [Anastas] Mikoyan and Koslov[280] or [Mikhail] Suslov would be very informative. I will fully understand it, however, if their busy schedules make it impossible. It would also be enlightening to me to speak with the head of the new State Committee for Foreign Economic Ties, Mr. S. A. Skachkov. And of course I would welcome the opportunity to speak informally with some representatives of your scientific and literary communities, and to visit various places of interest in and around Moscow, including Tolstoy's home in the country.

If it can be arranged, we would like to proceed on August 8 from Moscow to Warsaw by automobile.

I was much interested in what you said about the diamond discoveries in the area of Yakutsk. I should like very much to have any available information about diamond production and marketing. Perhaps such information could be better obtained in Moscow, however. I have friends who manufacture diamond tools, mostly for drilling oil wells. I have thought, too, that instead of all of us covering the same ground, Mr. Blair and perhaps one of my sons might go on from Tashkent to Irkutsk for a brief survey of the Lake Baikal development. If it would be possible and informative for him to proceed from there to Yakutsk to see something of the diamond development I think we might want to make some such alteration in our plans.

I plan to depart from the United States on June 15 and to spend some time in Western Europe and Scandinavia before leaving Helsinki for Leningrad. If in the meanwhile you have any further suggestions for me

280 F. R. Kozlov, First Vice Chairman of the Presidium of the Supreme Soviet of the U.S.S.R.

with regard to our itinerary or activities while in the Soviet Union, please communicate them to me here in Chicago.

May I take this opportunity to express to you once again, Mr. Ambassador, my sincere appreciation for your interest and your help in connection with the trip, and please give your wife my warm greetings.

Respectfully and cordially,

To John L. Burling[281]

May 30, 1958

My dear Mr. Burling:

I feel as though I should call you "Jack" because I have known your father and mother and brother for so many years.

Your letter has come and the most generous enclosure. Because I believe the Democratic Advisory Council serves a useful and necessary purpose which can increase as time goes on and the principle becomes better established, I have been bold enough to solicit funds for it. Hence, as "trustee," I am putting your contribution to work through the New York Committee.

I would welcome an opportunity to tell you more about the problem of formulating a program and maintaining any political coherence and continuity in an institution as diverse and as large as the Democratic party. It is in an effort to fill, even in an exploratory way, some of these voids of which I have become so conscious that I took some initiative in setting up this project in the first instance a year and a half ago.

You are more than good to entrust this money to me, and for the present I think I know of no better way to use it.

With all good wishes and my thanks, I am

Cordially yours,

To Lady Barbara Jackson

May 30, 1958

Barbara, dear:

. . . I haven't done a thing about my Michigan State commencement speech but I am sure I will at least *look* well in my Oxford robes.

By all means give me any thoughts you have about utterances in Europe. I have decided to avoid any formal speech, but I will have to face the press everywhere and should have consistent themes to echo on

[281] A New York lawyer and former counsel to the Senate committee investigating organized crime.

all occasions. It would be an enormous help if you could contrive something for me when I get there.

I have heard nothing from my cousin, Mildred Bailey, and let's count her out on the Stratford engagement. I can see her for tea in London. Shall I plan to meet you in Oxford Saturday morning? I must call on the Vice Chancellor[282] and [Humphrey] Waldock and Goodhart,[283] if I haven't seen him already.

The news about MacDuff[284] is comforting. I was fearful that you would find him frail and thin. I would encourage the balancing act. You know how important after dinner entertaining is, especially in the United States where we have ceased to talk!

Love,

Ross P. Game, feature editor of the Waukegan, Illinois, News-Sun, submitted a list of questions to Stevenson: Did he intend to campaign for Democratic congressional candidates? Was he willing to run for President again? Would he accept a draft? Did he believe the Democrats would win in 1960? How would he appraise the Eisenhower Administration's record?

To Ross P. Game

June 2, 1958

Dear Mr. Game:

I have your letter and only wish that I could do justice to your questions.

Let me say first that I plan to take a somewhat active role in the campaign for Democratic candidates for Congress this fall, although this will depend to some extent on the amount of time I have available. I have already made three or four speaking commitments commencing in the latter part of September.

As for 1960, I have said repeatedly that I am not a candidate and have no intention of becoming a candidate for the Democratic nomination.

You may be surprised to learn that I believe that a Democratic President will be elected in 1960 — and I am not interested in any political or governmental positions.

I am afraid that I haven't the time to give you my appraisal of the

282 J. C. Masterman, Provost of Worcester College.
283 Arthur Goodhart, Master of University College.
284 Her son, Robin.

Eisenhower Administration to date, but I would be glad to send you a few dozen speeches if you would care to have them! Seriously, I am afraid that I just cannot answer that question in a letter, but I am enclosing a short talk I made at a dinner in Washington last February which you may not have seen. Also enclosed are two speeches which I made in Washington, one before the Conference on Foreign Aspects of U.S. National Security and the other before the National Conference of Organizations on International Trade Policy.

With every good wish, I am

Cordially yours,

To Adnan Menderes[285]

June 3, 1958

My dear Mr. Prime Minister:

I hope you will recall our meetings during my visit to Turkey in 1953.[286] Your courtesy and conversation I shall long remember. Indeed, I have often thought of the misgivings you expressed about the future in the Middle East as the sorry events of the past few years unfolded. I wish I could talk to you now!

But the purpose of this letter is to advise that a client of mine (Pan American Land & Oil Royalty Company of Dallas, Texas) is filing an application with the Turkish Petroleum Administration to obtain licenses for oil and gas development in Turkey. Pan American Land is also discussing an agreement with Turkish Petroleum Corporation for development on a joint basis of certain properties of Turkish Petroleum Corporation.

Pan American Land is an American company organized to explore for and develop oil and gas outside the United States. Its Board of Directors include some very distinguished citizens of this country. The company is backed by very substantial interests which can increase its modest capital as necessary from time to time. This company is closely associated with the well known geological consulting firm of DeGolyer and MacNaughton, which has already done a considerable amount of geological work in Turkey.

I am interested personally because I think a small company, with adequate backing available as needed, excellent leadership and scientific advice will have many advantages in developing oil and gas properties as compared with the major oil companies and none of the disadvantages of the major companies. The Pan American company is

[285] Prime Minister of Turkey.
[286] See *The Papers of Adlai E. Stevenson*, Vol. V, pp. 322–323.

presently active in Cuba and Colombia and is conducting negotiations elsewhere.

Mr. John C. Jacobs, President of Pan American Land & Oil Royalty Company, will come to Turkey in the next month or two and I hope he may have the privilege of paying you his respects, and mine as well! I only wish I could do so in person and look forward hopefully to that good fortune. He is a young man of fine education and business experience.

Respectfully and cordially yours,

To Mrs. Eugene Meyer[287]

[no date]

Agnes Dear —

Don't you dare stop giving me hell! I'm isolated — and you're about the only wise, worldly and loving one who knows it. Pour it on! I like it! Thank Eugene for all those reprints and for his interest. I so wish we could be *ahead* of a crisis for once! I'm so distressed about your battle wounds — are dogs necessary? Aren't Senators enough —

Love —
ADLAI[288]

On June 8, 1958, Stevenson received an honorary degree and delivered the commencement speech at Michigan State University.[289]

I once heard it said that a commencement speech should be aimed halfway between student and faculty, thereby assuring, I assume, a perfect miss. Whether the aim is poor or whatever the reason, after long experience with commencement orations I have concluded that they don't — or at least mine don't — communicate much of enduring value at this watershed in your lives when you pass from the brief interval of academic education to the long interval of education by action and experience.

I said to the students at Princeton once upon a time that "the laws,

[287] This handwritten postcard is in the Agnes Meyer files, Princeton University Library.

[288] Mrs. Meyer replied on June 7, 1958, saying that any man who wrote love letters on postcards could not be civilized.

[289] The text is from a pamphlet published by Michigan State University. Revised versions of this speech appeared in *Vital Speeches*, July 1, 1958, and the *Centennial Review of Arts and Sciences* (published by Michigan State College of Science and Arts), Fall, 1958.

the aphorisms, the generalizations, the universal truths, the parables and the old saws — all of the observations about life which can be communicated handily in ready verbal packages — are as well known to a man at twenty who has been attentive as to a man at fifty.

"What he knows at fifty that he did not know at twenty boils down to something like this: the knowledge he has acquired with age is not the knowledge of formulas, or forms of words, but of people, places, actions — a knowledge not gained by words but by touch, sight, sound, victories, failures, sleeplessness, devotion, love — the human experiences and emotions of this earth; and perhaps, too, a little faith, and a little reverence for things you cannot see."[290]

My feeling of inadequacy on these occasions brings to mind Samuel Butler's remark when he was once asked to talk about how to make the most out of life. I think his reply was: "I don't even know how to make the most out of the next fifteen minutes." And I feel that way about the next twenty minutes!

But, happily, your merciful President has not asked me to enlighten and inspire you with profound philosophy and luminous wisdom, but to talk a little about the role of educated Americans and the desirability of knowing more and more about the peoples and problems of other lands — the people in the other houses of this little village we call the world, if I can put it that way.

And so I will, because to know more — I was about to say "something" — about the world has become a condition of survival. By survival I don't mean only from violent death, but rather from the slow, lingering extinction of all we Americans are and mean as a people. In this age of seething revolution — political, scientific and ideological — the race is to the swift and wise and ready, and we must look to those who have enjoyed the privilege of some education to be swift and wise and ready. You won't find it easy to lift your eyes from the office where you work and the home where you live, long enough to see and fathom what is going on around you. And, unhappily, you can't find out readily from the news reports in most of our newspapers, or from our capsule magazines, or, I regret to say, even from the leaders of our public life who too often like votes better than the truth.

You will have to work at the business of understanding the world beyond your doorstep or your factory gate. You will have no more important work to do. And you will have no harder work to do either, than keeping out of the iron clutches of conformity to the thinking, the prejudices and social attitudes of the group in which you live and work.

[290] See Stevenson's speech of March 22, 1954, in *The Papers of Adlai E. Stevenson,* Vol. IV, p. 339. Stevenson has made minor elisions in this excerpt.

You will find that the truth is often unpopular and the contest between agreeable fancy and disagreeable fact is unequal. For, in the vernacular, we Americans are suckers for good news.

We all know that ours is a perilous period, a time of testing, that the old order is changing, that the sky is overcast and visibility low. And, in this open season for adjectives and for seniors, on a hundred campuses solemn gentlemen, like myself, are reminding the captive graduates how fortunate they are to have an education, and goading, urging, imploring them to accept the great challenge and remake the future — with faith in democracy, humanity and God.

I hope I don't sound either irreverent or uncouth if I ask how these abstract powers manifest themselves, how these wonders are to be wrought. Socrates' answer was brains. And I don't think it has been superseded. But how do you put that idea over to the typical American? For generations he has been indoctrinated with heresies — that you can get something for nothing, that peace and security should be in the bargain basement, that technology is science, that skill is reason, that a politician is a statesman, and that the best proof of intelligence is meeting a payroll.

That is where *you* come in. You haven't been indoctrinated yet. Because stupidity is common you don't have to be stupid too. You can use the brains God gave you and that this University taught you how to use.

We often hear it said that we are the leaders of the free world, the saviors of Western culture and tradition. And so we are and so we must be, because we are the strongest, richest, biggest — and also have the most to lose.

But looking at the condition of the free world we must have been leading we cannot boast about our leadership. Suez, Sputnik, Indonesia, the anti-American outbursts, and now the torment of France, are only more recent milestones on the path to disaster. In each there are echoes of the Communist struggle, but in each there are symptoms of much more — of the frailties of our alliance, of Russia's great achievements, of rising economic unrest, of the nationalist revolution that is sweeping the world, and of the widespread dislike and distrust of the United States.

I could go on, and also suggest why the structure of the free world has deteriorated so badly in the past few years, but it just might sound political — something I always avoid! The point is that the Western world has never been so weak politically, and the urgency of the need for statesmanship, imagination and leadership bold enough to face the stern realities has never been more apparent.

And, speaking of statesmanship and realities, let me say a word about

France, our oldest ally and the center of our defense structure in Europe, which faces the delicate and dangerous task of reforming its constitution and restoring its strength and stability in the next six months. In that interval France can founder on the economic rocks. We can help to prevent that. And we can also help France work out a sensible economic improvement scheme for North Africa — for Morocco, Tunisia and Algeria — and thereby advance order, progress and peace in an area so vital to our security and so vulnerable to Arab nationalism and Communist influence.

What we *want* is a cooperative alliance and I hope what we — our government and our people — will *give* is cooperation, help and hope to tormented France in this crisis, which is also a crisis for all free democratic government.

There are, broadly speaking, two views about how to deal with our unprecedented political weakness and the crisis of the West. One is that the policy of military containment is succeeding. It assumes that if we can keep up the pressure long enough, the Soviet Union will be beset by internal troubles and tensions and in time will change into something we can get along with. This is our present policy. It was inherited from the days of Soviet nuclear, economic and scientific inferiority.

The other view is that military containment has failed, that what is needed is political initiative, new ideas and a change of emphasis from military strength to economic development.

For my part, I think we will need *both* — bolder political and economic initiatives, and also a sustained defense effort — if we are going to arrest the decay of our strength and unity and purpose. I am afraid it will require more effort, much more effort, and more expense, more self-discipline, more restraint by business, labor and all of us. We shall have to push and pull our allies along with us. And we shall have to face the distasteful fact that there is something more important than comfortable family life, a split level ranch house, social security, and three cars in the garage.

Unless we put first things first; unless we take the measure of our challenge and our shortcomings; unless we push through the fog of complacency and self-deceit that still engulfs us our troubles will compound and our perils increase.

I can illustrate what I mean by self-deceit. This week I was reminded by a magazine article[291] that two years ago, having in mind the coming Soviet economic challenge, I said that the rapid growth of the Soviet economy was "probably a more important fact than the development of Soviet military power"; to which a very exalted official of our govern-

[291] The editors have been unable to identify this article.

ment indignantly replied that "such statements of praise for the Soviet economy do the cause of the free world great damage."[292]

I wish I thought such nonsense and deception from high places was over, because, as a prominent columnist[293] wrote this week, "the great measures that are now needed cannot even be considered until the country is firmly and fully undeceived."

So the beginning of wisdom about the world is to face the facts. And then we must do something about them.

In that regard I will presume to suggest a couple of things we might do.

The first is economic and is brought to mind by the fact that this is the tenth anniversary of the commencement of the Marshall Plan. By that vision, by that forethought, and by that vast joint economic effort under American leadership, Europe was saved from a deadly crisis.

I think we are confronted today with a new crisis, a creeping crisis, not as dramatic but maybe more serious and more far reaching.

We are witnessing, I believe, the last stages of the old, world-wide, self-regulating, international trading and investment system which we in America have largely taken for granted. At the same time, as it recedes, we see, expanding, eager to take its place, the new Communist techniques of grants, gifts, loans, trade, aid, barter, technical assistance, raw materials at cost, or plain dumping, all bent to a single political purpose — the reinforcement of Communist power.

And, to give this crisis its full dimensions, it is occurring just at a time when America's need for secure trade abroad and for steady access to foreign materials is growing in proportion to our soaring population and diminishing resources. Moreover, the change comes at a time when the emerging peoples of Asia, Africa, the Middle East and South America are demanding with more urgency than ever before a larger share in the world's wealth. Back in 1953 I called this mood "the revolution of rising expectations."[294] Today I would add "the revolution of frustrated hope."

[292] The editors have been unable to identify the source of these quotations. However, Stevenson more than once in 1956 warned of the probable effect on underdeveloped, uncommitted countries of a dramatic gain in the Soviet economy. See, for example, his speech before the American Society of Newspaper Editors on April 21, 1956, and his campaign speech in St. Louis on September 27, 1956, in *The Papers of Adlai E. Stevenson*, Vol. VI, pp. 115, 241. Following the St. Louis speech, a Republican "truth squad" consisting of Senator Karl Mundt, Senator Frank Barrett, Representative William B. Widnall, and Representative Donald L. Jackson denounced Stevenson's assessment of future Soviet growth, saying: "Selling America short in this wicked world is too dangerous a tactic to be used as a political device in a Presidential campaign." New York *Times*, September 29, 1956, p. 8.

[293] The editors have been unable to identify this columnist.

[294] See *The Papers of Adlai E. Stevenson*, Vol. V, pp. 411, 456.

Yet in spite of two world wars and the almost total disappearance of the old conditions, we still tend to react to problems raised by trade or foreign investment or balance of payment difficulties as though the old 19th Century conditions still prevailed.

The three main elements of 19th Century stability were low tariffs, international lending and adequate trading reserves.

But today tariffs are up, trading reserves are down, and only international investment bears any resemblance to the past, thanks to large investments and spending by Britain and France in their overseas territories, and to the United States' huge post war export of dollars in foreign aid and lending which has been the basic element in the expansion and prosperity of the free world.

Forty per cent of total world trade is conducted in sterling and balanced on funds about equivalent to those of the Ford Foundation. This is a remarkable achievement, but it is also desperately precarious. And the time is fast approaching when Britain's days of massive lending and maintenance of world trade must give way to building up reserves and higher investment in Britain's own resources. We must at least foresee the possibility that France will make a similar policy reversal. Germany has chosen to use its massive American aid and great national effort to rebuild itself and its reserves. In the United States the pressure for higher tariffs and reduced foreign lending bear little relation to our position as the world's greatest creditor. And our programs have a temporary, provisional character, following the rhythm not of need but of Communist pressure and the Congressional fever chart.

The fact is that the free trading system which we desire to live by, and which for others is a condition of survival, cannot function unless steadily and consistently we take up the creditor role which our predecessors in Europe are putting down. And let us not forget that just as the American effort has become overshadowed by recession and doubt, the Russians are advancing. They offer Europe expanded trade; they tempt the fringe countries with long-term, low interest loans. And Russian-Chinese production is expanding; each year there is more on which to draw, more capital to offer, more goods to exchange.

Not only is the old system tottering, but a new, brash, aggressive and powerful competitor is thrusting his way in to complete the overturn and to set up his own controlled, guided and totally political system in its place.

In this atmosphere of growing crisis, I suggest to you, with the utmost urgency, that we cannot permit the present policy of drift and confusion to persist indefinitely. The free nations must be rallied to consider ways and means to a functioning, expanding, free world trading system, and each must accept full responsibility for the policies that are worked out.

I believe that America should now declare its readiness for such a stocktaking.

I believe we should propose that a Committee of Experts be set up comparable to the group which laid the groundwork for the Marshall Plan in 1947. It should be their responsibility to prepare an agenda for the regeneration of the free world economy upon which the nations can agree and act — joint measures to secure sustained growth, joint negotiations for a low tariff or free trade area, joint undertaking of a long-term aid and investment program, and joint agreement on adequate working capital for world trade and convertibility.

Such an agenda for the free world would not only meet the main strains and crises of today, it would go far to revive the conditions under which the old, unfettered, expansive system of free international trade once worked.

Today, make no mistake about it, the drift is all the other way — towards declining production, higher trade barriers, commerce starved for working capital, falling investment, economic frustration and trouble in the underdeveloped areas.

As in 1947, it is to our energy, intelligence and foresight that we must look if this drift is to be reversed. We must start thinking seriously of the new system which must take the place of the old. Let us heed the portents and do so now. For once let us do something before we have to.

The other suggestions I would like to make are political.

The International Geophysical Year has been a great success and brought forth much of value and scientific cooperation. Why don't we now propose an International Medical Research and Health Year as another way for the world to cooperate for survival instead of destruction? Certainly collaboration and exchanging research and resources in the field of medicine and health would be merciful to the human race — which is something we all have in common — and could further reduce tensions and mistrust.

And mistrust is the root of evil in the world — which brings me to the other suggestion I want to make toward a peaceful world.

Nobody trusts anybody; this is the heart of the trouble. The more we search for a new kind of security in law to replace the old security of weapons which are becoming unusable, the more clearly we see that this factor of trust is the foundation stone of the new edifice of peace.

We have a kind of peace today. But it is built not on security but on the worst conceivable insecurity. The nuclear powers can destroy or maim one another and all the innocent bystanders. And as nuclear weapons become more dispersed, the instability of this balance of terror increases. But the nuclear stalemate has bought us a little time to work on the new security that has to take the place of the old security of weapons.

How can we extend this time and use it wisely? One way is to take a small step toward disarmament. Then a second step can be planned, and then a third, and all the while confidence accumulates, the belief that men have in one another and in law and justice. Inspection and controls can reinforce this confidence, but they are not substitutes for it. Mutual security guarantees can strengthen it, but without trust they, too, are not enough.

Because even the testing of nuclear weapons, let alone their use, is incompatible with human welfare, I have urged for years that we take the initiative toward an agreement to end such tests as a first step. Now Russia has taken the lead, and there is reason to hope that we can reach a reasonable agreement on methods of inspection against violation.

This small step would be historic, it would break the disarmament deadlock, it would establish for the first time the principle of inspection on each other's soil; it might arrest the spread of nuclear weapons. And, most of all, it could start building the stockpile of confidence without which progress toward major agreement is impossible.

Another way to create confidence, as Raymond Swing[295] has suggested, might be for us, the West, to accept the principle of Soviet equality in power. I don't see how we could agree to a *political* status quo which would mean rigid spheres of influence. But it seems to me that both sides, seeing that the approximate equality of *power* is what is keeping the peace, might agree to preserve that equality. If both sides are content with power equality, then to reduce forces and limit nuclear weapons become matters of arithmetic and enforcement, not of prestige and political influence in the world.

Such a proposal conflicts with present day policy, I know. But present policy has hardly produced spectacular results. And certainly equality is closer to reality than the concept that the Soviet Union is backward economically and technically and that it is sure to collapse from internal defects. Moreover, the Sputniks have blasted any complacent notion that we are immune to retaliation and they aren't.

I know, too, that this suggestion has many hazards. We could not, for example, advance proposals at the summit that would increase our relative power; neither could they, which would be quite a change from

[295] Radio commentator and author.

their cynical attempts in the past to get and not to give. And I am not suggesting that we can or should do away with competition in science, education and economic development. All I am saying is that rivalry can no longer be decided in battle. If we are not rivals for military superiority our other rivalries are safe, and civilization is safe.

Surely the present nuclear stalemate, this balance of terror, cannot be a permanent security system. New steps are necessary to break the deadlock. I have suggested some for your consideration.

And surely, with the old system deteriorating, it is not beyond the genius of the great democracies to devise new and adequate underpinnings for trade and economic expansion, when not only our prosperity but our security depend upon it. I have made some suggestions for your consideration in that direction.

I hope you will think on the mighty problems of your time.

In St. Luke it is written: "Ye can discern the face of the sky and of the earth; but how is it that ye do not discern this time."

You must "discern this time," for your *own* sake, and for your *country's* sake.

You have had the advantage of education; it is therefore, your right and privilege to sustain the sovereignty of intelligence and imagination against the assaults of stupidity and vulgarity. I hope you can do it with gentleness and humility, with tolerance and good humor.

Finally, after this solemn fare, let me say that the wisest thing I have heard lately was James Thurber's[296] remark that everybody is getting too grim these days!

Take these words to heart; be of good cheer; it's a wonderful, exciting time to be alive. I envy you. And I hope you never have a dull moment!

To Isidore Levy[297]

June 10, 1958

My dear Professor Levy:

Rene Dubos[298] has sent me your fascinating study of the origin of the name "Adlai."[299] I am embarrassed that I have not thanked you for it before, as evidently it was published some time ago in Brussels. Your scholarship awes and amazes me and I am having copies of an English translation prepared for my sons and also my grandson, Adlai E.

---

[296] *New Yorker* cartoonist and humorist.
[297] Professor at the Collège de France.
[298] Bacteriologist and professor at the Rockefeller Institute for Medical Research.
[299] "Adlai," *La Nouvelle Clio,* Vols. VII–VIII–IX (1955–56–57), Nos. 7–10, pp. 465–467.

Stevenson IV, age eighteen months. Some day I hope to have an opportunity to thank you in person for telling me who I am!

Sincerely yours,

Mayor William B. Hartsfield, of Atlanta, Georgia, wrote Stevenson describing the lawsuit he was supporting which challenged the county unit system, under which Georgia's underpopulated rural counties dominated statewide elections. He also spoke highly of growing interest in Stevenson for 1960.

To William B. Hartsfield

June 10, 1958

Dear Bill:

Ever so many thanks for your letter. Your persistence fills me with admiration — if there was any room therefor! I think, indeed I know, what you have been doing and the temperate statements by you and some other Southern leaders have had a lot to do with improving understanding and mollifying the extremists in the North.

This surely is the Lord's work.

I cannot say the same, however, about the prospect of a certain candidate for President. I think he has had enough of all that, although he is profoundly flattered by the regard of friends he esteems as highly as he does you!

Cordially yours,

Gerald W. Johnson wrote that the speeches at the University of Louisville and at Michigan State University convinced him that Stevenson had an important issue in an international committee to plan economic grand strategy. Mr. Johnson added, however, that we needed an expanded humanism more than an expanded economy. But he wondered whether this idea could be explained to the public.

To Gerald W. Johnson

June 12, 1958

Dear Gerald:

I am not sure that economic planning is ever a good issue. I am not even sure that I want an issue. What I do want is to try to say some of the things that damn well need saying.

[221]

And I am sure you are right that what we need most is expanding humanism. But how the hell do you tell the boys in the back room about that?

I think the trouble is that the people are far away, and getting farther away, from government. I hardly know what it is, let alone how to say it — but I'm sure it needs saying and I hope to do so in Europe this summer. Maybe by autumn you'll know how and will tell me!

Bless you for reading all that stuff of mine.

Yours,

To Lyndon B. Johnson

June 13, 1958

Dear Lyndon:

Someone has just sent me the Congressional Record, including my commencement speech in Michigan the other day. It was good of you to bother to have it printed and even better to say such nice things about it!

I am disappointed that I have had so little opportunity to keep in touch with Congress this winter and spring. But the reports of your skillful management from your numberless admirers come almost daily. I think often, however, of your health and the difficulties of the conservation of strength we all confront, especially you. I only hope you think about them too!

I am leaving presently on a long journey and I shall hope for a visit with you on my return in the fall.

Yours,

Part Three

Trip to the Soviet Union, 1958

O n June 15, 1958, Stevenson and his son Borden flew to London en route to the Soviet Union. John Fell Stevenson and William McC. Blair, Jr., joined them in London two days later. Stevenson transacted some legal business for clients interested in Africa. He met with the directors of Encyclopaedia Britannica, Ltd., and talked with British advisers to the Britannica at Oxford University. He met with leaders of the Government and the Opposition. He dined with old friends, including Sir Louis and Lady Mary Spears, Mr. and Mrs. Douglas Fairbanks, Jr., Geoffrey Crowther, Mr. and Mrs. John Gunther, John Steinbeck, Mr. and Mrs. Hamish Hamilton, and Mary, Duchess of Buccleuch. Stevenson, his two sons and Lady Barbara Jackson drove to Stratford to see the production of Romeo and Juliet and spent a day driving through the Cotswolds.

On June 16 he held a brief press conference where he was asked about his political intentions. He declared: "I have no further political ambitions. I have said it before, and I say it every morning automatically at nine o'clock. I have not been, I am not, and I will not be nominated as Democratic presidential candidate."[1]

He explained to the reporters that the Authors' League of America had retained him to try to collect royalties for American authors whose books had been published in the Soviet Union. He also said that he wanted to visit the Soviet Union to observe conditions there and discuss many outstanding issues, including the suicidal nuclear arms race, with Soviet leaders. He told the reporters that Soviet officials had agreed that he could travel to areas ordinarily prohibited to foreigners.

One reporter wrote that Stevenson seemed "much more subdued nowadays. He was never one for clowning or flippancy, but there was a time when you could never expect to spend more than 10 minutes with him without hearing at least one good joke and probably some memo-

[1] The Times (London), June 17, 1958.

[225]

rable epigram. He still smiles a good deal as he talks, but the conversation is sober and serious. No wonder, really, for Mr. Stevenson has many substantial problems to deal with."[2]

On June 24 Stevenson and his party flew to Brussels. Mrs. Marshall Field and her daughter Fiona joined Stevenson there. While in Brussels they attended the World's Fair, and Stevenson conferred with officials and with his client Maurice Tempelsman, lunched with King Baudouin and former King Leopold, and lunched with Queen Mother Elisabeth. Stevenson wrote in his diary, "Flowers at Old Queen's luncheon table — finest I've ever seen! Small arrangements of fuscia [fuchsia] on table cloth in oblique parallel rows."

Stevenson also attended a performance by the Bolshoi Ballet with Ulanova in Romeo and Juliet — "Something to remember!" he wrote in his diary.

On June 27 Stevenson and his group flew to Copenhagen. At the airport he was met by the United States ambassador, Val Peterson. Stevenson noted in his diary that Mr. Peterson "apologized for nasty speech he made in '52 campaign. 'Some stuff prepared by [Harold] Stassen; sorry I made it.'"

Stevenson, an insatiable sightseer, visited the Carlsberg Brewery, the Tivoli Gardens and the Glyptotek Museum, drove to Roskilde castle, and visited the home of Hans Christian Andersen in Odense. Back in Copenhagen on June 30, he wrote in his diary, "What about my 2nd grandchild — due yesterday." He added that he had received a phone call from Chicago but it was from actress Lauren Bacall calling from "the Pump Room at 3 A.M.!"

Stevenson talked at length with the prime minister about the Soviet Union and he visited with atomic scientist Niels Bohr, who explained that the Russians did not have to steal American atomic secrets, since they already knew the scientific facts about the atom. "Gentle lovable old man, with charming sharp wife," Stevenson wrote in his diary.

While in Denmark he had some time for correspondence.

To Mrs. Ronald Tree[3]

June 28, 1958

Long ago I sent a coupon from a magazine with money I earned digging dandelions for a "magic lantern," I think it was. I remember vividly the agony of waiting for the reply. And now I've experienced it again. Brussels will be forever blessed; not one, but three! . . .

---

[2] Auckland, New Zealand, *Star*, July 18, 1958.
[3] This handwritten letter is in the possession of Mrs. Tree.

So much to report — business, politics, lords & ladies, gaiety — and despair. I'm a fellow of Worcester College — and my feet are as tired as Frankie's[4] after the Brussels Fair! After Stratford — magnificent Romeo & Juliet saw Tewksbury Cathedral. . . . Royalties very kind in Brussels — lunched, dined with all — King, Ex King and real King — Lilliane — and beloved Elizabeth, where the photographic frenzy almost submerged John Fell! . . .

There is so much to say about symptoms — and now for a great luncheon where I must make a speech — horrors!

Ruth [Field] and Fiona [Field] joined here — no chance to talk yet. Look well.

Ghastly letter — Goodbye — . . .

A

To Mrs. Edison Dick[5]

June 29, 1958

Dear Jane — a week in London, a few days in Brussels, two days in Denmark — and I'm ready for home and a month's rest! But I've never had a gayer, better, more interesting time. I only hope it has been the same for the boys and of that I'm not too sure. . . . Clearly I don't know how to handle it all and my own appalling schedule too. They've lunched and dined and danced with Lords, Ladies, Kings, Princesses and Ministers and had an opportunity to see and observe and record that is given to few. Do they take it in? I really don't know. But one thing they *did* take in — the best performance of Romeo and Juliet in a generation at Stratford followed by the Bolshoi Ballet in Brussels in — Romeo and Juliet!

Tonight we are at the country estate of some noble and charming Danes . . . and must be up at 6 to shoot a Roebuck before heading back to Copenhagen for the inevitable reception and Prime Minister dinner. It has been a glorious warm, sunny Sunday — the first proper day we've seen since the rains commenced June 14 in Lake Forest, Ill! I'm DELIGHTED you're coming to Moscow. I hope we get there too — without any more damage than excessive hospitality and too good food has already done us!

Affectionate greetings from all the Stevenson boys.

ADLAI

P.S. My grandchild is due today! And no word – A

---

[4] Mrs. Tree's daughter, Frances FitzGerald.
[5] This handwritten letter is in the possession of Mrs. Dick.

To Eugenie Anderson[6]

June 30, 1958

My dear Eugenie — I'm staying the night with Ivar Vind[7] in their old family place on Fyn [Funen]. Before I go to bed I must send you this greeting & report that you are much beloved and badly missed in Denmark. If there is anyone you *didn't* captivate in this charming and hospitable land I haven't met him! It has made me very proud to be able to claim you as a friend. I hope you are well & Bill Blair adds his love to mine.

ADLAI

On July 1 the Stevenson party flew to Oslo. Stevenson was met at the airport by former Secretary-General of the United Nations Trygve Lie, Norwegian officials, and Hayden Raynor, counsellor of the United States embassy. At a press conference at the airport, Stevenson said that the Russians might be sincere in announcing that they wanted an agreement to stop nuclear weapons tests. He also called for the West, and particularly Germany, to make a greater effort to furnish economic assistance to the underdeveloped world.[8]

Stevenson visited the Folk Museum and the museums where Viking ships and Kon-Tiki *were displayed. He met with Trygve Lie, with the foreign minister, and with the prime minister several times, while in Oslo. On July 2 he wrote in his diary, "Still no word on Nancy's baby!" On July 3 he wrote: "Cable with breakfast — Lucy Wallace Stevenson has arrived 8 lbs 1 ounce — Hooray. Woke up boys. Sent cable."*

Before leaving Oslo, Stevenson had time for some correspondence.

To Mrs. Ronald Tree[9]

July 2, 1958

M —

Thanks for cheery news from Scotty R.[10] Always envied those who sit in the gallery cheering, taunting, damning the wretched gladiators who

---

[6] Former ambassador to Denmark, 1949–1953.
[7] A Danish landowner, one of Bill Blair's closest friends and best man at his wedding.
[8] Chicago *Sun-Times*, July 2, 1958.
[9] This handwritten letter is in the possession of Mrs. Tree.
[10] James Reston of the New York *Times*.

do their best for short glory or long oblivion. Tell him I'm going to join *them* — the gallery I mean!

Have staggered from one ghastly, interminable & magnificent feast thru Belgium, Denmark & half a day of Oslo where your message awaited me, also amusing letter to Blair. Thanks for both.

. . . As to *me* — it was all gone too fast; not enough time to stand and stare. But I've had some good bloody, medieval days that I love — from Warwick & Tewksbury to Elsinor[e]. For *politics*, I've made bold efforts at long sustained talks with PMs & FMs in Belgium & Denmark and am deep in it here with both, cum King. Trygvie, bless his soul, says I've made sad mistake to meet with the Executive C[ommi]ttee of the Labor Party, his party in office 23 years! but the Ambassador agreed to it and I'm stuck.

As to the world, as I draw closer to the iron curtain I know less. Is the Kremlin closing its doors again, to be opened only to spew forth more Trojan horses? Is all hope of any common ground of mutual interest lost? I had thought the cost of arms & foreign aid *might* be enough. Or is it pressure from China, as Nye [Aneurin] Bevan confidently assured me?

I would like to talk about these things, but our Ambassador in Denmark — impossible & unpopular. . . . (Tho he did come to the airport & apologize for unkind things uttered in 1952!) In Belgium, good, but wholly a business man.[11] Here — I'll know after dinner tonight. . . . John Fell lost in a curious fog of preoccupation — Borden says its *love!* As to B[orden]. don't feel I'm getting across to him or that he's relaxed.

In short — I'm imposing on you! Ruth & F[iona]. bearing up well; a fine, quiet self sufficient girl with a shy elfin quality that beguiles me, but *not* the boys, I regret to say. Ruth bearing up nobly and appears interested. . . .

And here it is page 4 & I've not started the letter I planned, full of sage observations. Love to your daughters and all — In Norway the moon is *Up* — Affec.

AES

PSS 1 AM — Miss [Frances] Willis — Ambassador — was *grand* & her 89 year old & decrepid mother grander! And both unattached! May stay here longer!! Princess Ranghild [Ragnhild] as disappointing as most Royalties. But Lange,[12] the FM, excellent!!! Trygvie calls him, a little contemptuously, an "intellectual." Why do I always get along best with the wrong people — intellectual men & married women!

[11] John Clifford Folger.
[12] Harvard M. Lange, minister of foreign affairs.

There is so much to say & the purpose of *this* was to tell you the purpose of that — which was supposed to be an essay on *facing* West while *going* East — a difficult but agreeable exercise — and the only way to *go* East, under present circumstances. What with mounting truculence, the pendulum swinging so violently, it is not an agreeable prospect — and then the Bay of Portugal is so, so deep —

> *But,* not by *Eastern* windows only
> When daylight comes, comes in the light,
> In *front,* the sun climbs slow, how slowly,
> But *westward* look, the land is bright!
> And so — Good *night!*

(It is quite bright up here now the midnight sun)

7/2   It is morning now, and lighter still! Lying on my sleepless bed listening to the street noises I thought of another journey — as I always do. A year ago we rose very early & *almost too late* & flew to Monrovia — a flight I won't forget.

Thanks for review of "Ere I forget *Thee*" —

To Mrs. Eugene Meyer[13]

July 3, 1958

Dear Agnes — I am not sure how much you would like the "struggle of life" in Norway! But we are having a "Rest & Recreation" interlude at the moment at Hanko with Mrs. Josephine Bay[14] for a look at the famous yacht races. After the incessant travel and tension of the last weeks in England, Belgium & Denmark this is heaven by the sea. On Sunday we go on to Stockholm & then Helsinki for more dinners, receptions & speeches I fear — before Russia on July 12 — Just as things reach the bottom! Pray you are all well.

ADLAI

On July 3 the Stevenson party motored to Hanko to visit with Mrs. Josephine Bay and see the yacht races. They sailed around the "lovely irregular, unspoiled harbor where all manner of yachts are anchored from all northern Europe. . . . Place so simple; one old hotel in woods, not even a souvenir store — only boats, boats, boats & all beautiful!" he wrote in his diary. On July 5 the party sailed back to Oslo, where the

---

13 This handwritten postcard is in the Agnes Meyer files, Princeton University Library.

14 President and chairman of the board of the New York brokerage firm of A. M. Kidder and widow of Charles U. Bay, former U.S. ambassador to Norway.

next morning Stevenson spoke at the commissioning ceremonies of a lifesaving vessel given by Mrs. Bay to Norway. ". . . I spoke in front of prow on waterfront by city hall. 'Arts of Peace & Preservation' etc. Good speech. Josephine very pleased. . . ."

The Stevenson group flew to Stockholm for lunch on July 6. Stevenson wrote in his diary, ". . . Confusion on arrival — Foreign office had ar ranged for boat to take us to Drottingholm — lunch on board — couldn't find boat! Long cortege of cars with officials & press. J.F. [John Fell] said like campaign caravan.[15] *Got separated. Press conf. on dock! Finally Fields, J.F., one 'guide' and I left on the boat. delicious lunch! Found others, plus 2 officials & more press, at Drottingholm. . . ."*

On July 7 Stevenson visited the Town Hall — "marvelous — had forgotten it since visit with Ellen in 1931," he wrote in his diary.[16] *After other sightseeing that day he spoke at the Swedish-American Foundation. "Speech! Good — (for the first time in Scandinavia)," he noted in his diary. The next day they drove to Ullsberg for lunch and Stevenson returned with Prime Minister Tage Erlander, who was host at dinner that evening. "What food!" Stevenson wrote in his diary.*

On July 9 the Stevenson group flew to Helsinki, where they were joined by Alicia Patterson and her niece Alice Albright. Robert C. Tucker, who had been on the staff of the American embassy in Moscow for eight years, joined Stevenson to serve as an interpreter and expert on the Soviet Union.

Stevenson motored into the countryside to visit consumer cooperatives, visited art galleries, spoke at a reception of the Finnish-American Society, and conversed with the prime minister and other officials.

While in Helsinki he wrote some letters.

To Mrs. Ronald Tree[17]

July 10, 1958

. . . He[18] can't sleep; perhaps its the night[l]ess northern nights. He moves thru the crowded routine of the days with zestless determination. Even markets get only a glassy sidelong glance, as the remorseless

---

[15] John Fell Stevenson wrote: "Our arrival in Stockholm was hysterical. We were met at the airport by a row of black cars which was to take us to a boat on which lunch was waiting. Trailed by 10 press cars we soon found ourselves in a deadend street — No one knew where the boat was. . . ." Letter to Natalie Owings, July 7, 1958, in the possession of John Fell Stevenson.

[16] For the visit of Stevenson and his wife to Mr. and Mrs. Ives in Copenhagen in 1931, see *The Papers of Adlai E. Stevenson*, Vol. I, pp. 221–225.

[17] This handwritten letter is in the possession of Mrs. Tree.

[18] Stevenson refers to himself.

schedule of sightseeing, official palaver and ponderous feasts passes by. Moreover he is testy, irritable, preoccupied, which makes him a poor travelling companion and a worse father, obviously to be shunned by all young men in search of a good time. — A fish become a crab long since, I fear. And morning & afternoon he explosively demands "mail," saying he can't understand why he hasn't "heard from Adlai & Nancy"; which is curious, as J.F. pointed out, following by hours a letter from them both!

But I know whats wrong and it rather serves him right. After all he'd been master of heart & head a long time, and then *thought* he was a long time longer than he was, if you can understand that sort of sentence. But now the defenses are crumbling and the poor fellow is weak with wanting. It would make little difference if it didn't interfere with his mind and disposition — the former being under considerable and sustained pressure, the latter being constantly exposed to public scrutiny. But he did get away with it in Sweden under trying circumstances and occasioned much public mirth by his sallies, all recorded at length in press with photos. . . .

And now I must go again before I've got to all the gaiety & wisdom which I meant to pass on herewith. This afternoon I'll have a Sauna — wonderful de Quinc[e]y like dreams in steaming mists — and then a cold Finnish lake. See you!

A

. . .

On July 12 the Stevenson party flew to Leningrad. The editors decided to publish his diary of the trip rather than the twelve articles he wrote for the North American Newspaper Alliance, which were syndicated to a number of newspapers, including the New York Times. *These articles, with some slight editing, were published in book form under the title* Friends and Enemies: What I Learned in Russia.[19] *While these articles were more reflective than the diary, the diary reflects his immediate impressions on a day-by-day basis.*

Stevenson's diary of his Russian trip is more complete than most diaries he had attempted in the past. Miss Roxane Eberlein assisted the editors in transcribing Stevenson's difficult handwriting. Robert C. Tucker published an account of the trip as a Rand Corporation report.[20]

19 New York: Harper, 1959.
20 *Impressions of Russia in 1958: A Trip Report* (Santa Monica, California: Rand Corporation, November 30, 1958).

The editors have used this report in footnotes to amplify the diary text. Professor Tucker kindly read the following manuscript and helped clarify ambiguities. In order to make the diary more readable, the editors decided to correct Stevenson's misspellings only the first time they occurred.

July 12, Leningrad
    . . . Greeting at Airport — Vice Pres of Leningrad Sov[i]et,[21] other officials, press, including [Henry] Shapiro of UP, [Max] Frankel of NYT. . . . Speech of welcome — & bouquets for ladies. Drive into town with representative of Mr. Zukov of culture cttee[22] sent from Moscow, V.P. of Soviet etc.[23] Enormous wide street; huge ugly stolid apt. bldgs rising out of treeless plain on both sides. Astoria hotel on St. Isaac Sq. Ancient splendor of the 19th Century — I have bedroom, dining room, parlor, office & bath! — gilt, brocade & lace. Met U.S. press. long palaver with our innumerable guides & hosts re plans. Fine dinner — caviar, bortsch, steak & vegs. Lovely twilight walk to Hermitage Sq. along Neva. People poorly dressed, small but seemed cheerful. J.F. [John Fell] gathered a crowd of young ones. very gay.

Leningrad, Sunday, July 13
    Fine breakfast — orange, omelet & tea. Talk with Mitchell Wilson[24] re approach on royalties. A car cortege to Kazan cathedral & tour anti-religious exhibit, Nevsky Prospekt. Alexander Nevsky church for crowded services — deeply impressive devotion! To Tchaikovsky's tomb; drive past Smolny Inst. & cathedral, Admiralty etc to Hermitage & Winter Palace. Remembered a good deal from 32 years ago — but didn't see the famous gold ornaments discovered on Black Sea coast or collection of jeweled boxes, saddles etc. then, nor the living apts. now. French Impressionist collection! By boat to Peterhof — Thousands in

[21] A. A. Ledbedev, deputy chairman of the Leningrad City Soviet.
[22] Yuri Zhukov, chairman of the State Committee on Cultural Relations with Foreign Countries.
[23] The four men who were to accompany Stevenson while he was in the Soviet Union were V. V. Vakhrushev, an official of the press section of the State Committee on Cultural Relations with Foreign Countries; his deputy, V. A. Kuskov; R. P. Grigoriev, an Intourist interpreter; and S. S. Kuzin, also of Intourist, who was to handle arrangements for meals and lodging.
[24] An American writer of science fiction novels that were very popular in Russia, where he was at this time on a four-month tour. He was lionized everywhere, and in a very unusual move, Russia gave him $15,000 as royalties for his book sales, of interest to Stevenson in connection with his representation of the Authors' League of America.

restored park on Sunday afternoon. Back too weary for theatre — but talked & joked with crowds of young people on street after dinner — very friendly & poor. Very little politics. Great interest in U.S. & world.[25] *John Fell great attraction — also Alice! J.F. gave a young man a jazz record. Clasped it to his heart!*

Came back from Peterhof part way on subway — fantastic stations — marble, bronze propaganda palaces below ground — very deep. Talked with merchant sailor returning from holiday with wife & baby. Hard to shake large entourage. All so attentive!

Leningrad, Monday July 14

Smolny Institute — finishing school for girls of nobility — where Lenin set up headquarters — now hq. of Len. Provincial Soviet. Lenin's room — pictures — no mention of Trotsky among heroes.

Smolny monastery church most beautiful bldg. in this beautiful city. . . .

Then to Young Pioneer playground in Park of Culture & Rest — group singing, dancing, games, reading room, swimming; seemed solemn for children, but friendly, even affectionate. The leader — a stern looking bright girl — tied red hank. [handkerchief] around my neck & declared me an honorary young Pioneer! Moving experience! Evening with reps. of Len. Academy of Science — including Kostenko[26] *who presided — great electrical physicist, others — English literature, chemistry, law, architecture, etc. — and a very pleb[e]ian political minded "Hero of*

25 Robert Tucker wrote: "The most interesting experiences were some unplanned and informal conversations with young people in front of the hotel. . . .

"They were friendly and showed the familiar Russian inquisitiveness about all things American. Their questioning was intensive but not hostile. It seemed designed to elicit facts which would help place certain things they had heard about the United States in rational perspective. There were repeated expressions of the desire to travel, and particularly to visit America. On the second evening, when the group had learned Governor Stevenson's identity, there were many requests for autographs and questions about his 1960 intentions. And he provoked general laughter when, answering a question about his planned itinerary, he said: 'I am going to Siberia — and hope to return. . . .'

"But certainly they impressed one as having inquiring and critical minds, as persons who wanted to think for themselves on the big issues and craved not ready-made answers and solutions but materials which would enable them to reach their own independent solutions. When we left for Moscow by the Red Arrow two nights later, two of them appeared unobtrusively on the station platform at the last minute and waved goodbye as the train pulled out. They had constituted themselves as an unofficial deputation of the people of Leningrad to see off Governor Stevenson." *Impressions of Russia*, pp. 1–5.

26 Mikhail P. Kostenko, director of the Institute of Electromechanics of the U.S.S.R. Academy of Sciences and a deputy to the Supreme Soviet.

*Sov. Union." Enormous banquet in the bldg. of the Society of Writers —
many toasts*[27] *&remarkably good speeches, including mine, I hope!
Alicia performed nobly! Boys didn't go — wish they had!!! All full of
wit, humor, learning & friendliness — except 'Hero of Soviet' who
wanted more 'objective' reporting in U.S.! Even these very distinguished
profs. seemed wholly part of system & happy. Are they I wonder?
Midnight train to Moscow. Good Train — "Red Arrow" — painted blue.*

Tues. July 15 — Moscow
    *Arrived early accompanied by our retinue of chaperones from
Intourist & Cttee on Cultural Relations.*[28] *Sovietskaya Hotel — very
Stalinist! another 4 room suite. American tourists, students & NBC team
doing "Youth Wants to Know" programs with Russian leaders. Cam-
bodian Communist delegation. Visit to Intourist Chief re itinerary.
Very cordial & helpful. Invited to party — declined. Visit to Z[h]ukov
— Ch. of Cttee on Cultural Rel. Strong man — comer. Little aloof.
Slight encounter re seeing [Andrei] Gromyko — evidently wanted me
to ask to see him. Said I didn't want to disturb his holiday, etc. To
Kremlin — fantastic collections of jewels, gold, silver, etc of Czars &
clergy. "No wonder there was a revolution," universal comment. Palaces,
churches, Supreme Soviet chamber, Czars bell, cannon, etc. Que[ue]
in Red Square before [Lenin's] tomb — everlasting. Embassy reception
in* PM *— Begum Aga Kahn [Khan] — Orval Dreyfuss*[29] *& family stayed
for family dinner with Ambassador [Llewellyn] Thompson, wife &
children. Much talk about landing of Marines in Lebanon & Sov[iet].*

[27] Tucker wrote: "The theme of the toasts proposed one after another by the
Soviet scientists was the desirability of increased professional contact with their
American colleagues." *Impressions of Russia,* p. 6.
    [28] Stevenson replied to the speech of welcome by saying in part: "At railroad
crossings in the United States there is a sign that says 'Stop, Look and Listen.' And
that describes my purpose. . . . I sometimes think that it might be a good idea
to declare an 'International Stop Look and Listen Day' — a day on which politicians,
officials and diplomats everywhere in the world would pause and look and listen
with eyes and ears and minds open to the desire of ordinary people everywhere
for peace." Tucker wrote: "That evening the *Evening Moscow* front-paged the
news of Governor Stevenson's arrival and accompanied the report with a photo-
graph. The report, a fairly lengthy one, quoted his statement about the sign at the
railroad crossings, but it significantly omitted the conclusion that there should be
an 'International Stop Look and Listen Day' when governments would take account
of the desire of ordinary people everywhere for peace. The reason was evidently
not lack of space but rather lack of desire to permit an American leader to appear
before the Soviet people as a statesman responsive to the popular wish for peace.
Only Soviet leaders are supposed to have "eyes and ears and minds open to the
desire of ordinary people everywhere for peace." *Impressions of Russia,* p. 8.
    [29] Orvil E. Dryfoos, publisher of the New York *Times.*

reaction.[30] (*British & French Ambassadors at reception seemed delighted!*) *Amb. called to Foreign office at 10:30 — me to bed. Boys went to Ballet.*

Wed. July 16 —
  Sharp denunciation of Am[erican] aggression in papers. Called on "Mayor" of Moscow — Hard — able. Housing biggest problem. 9 sq. meters living space[31] *— ex[clusive of] kitchen etc — objective 12. Huge housing dev!! Hideous great yellow brick structures. Can they ever catch up with needs? To Embassy for briefing before seeing Gromyko. Have landed 5000 marines. Hussein*[32] *has declared himself king of Iraq & asked British aid. . . . Line in morning papers about "U.S. aggression" not too disturbing. Called at Gromyko's office at 11. Had come in from Dacha 40 km. [kilometers]. Very cordial reunion — asked for boys — followed my career. Did I want to talk seriously? What did I think of Lebanon etc? Talked one hour; two stenos recorded every word. Familiar line. Aggression: no outside interference, cf. UN report; only pretext. Hussein "empty headed." Const[itution]. of Iraq-Jordan scrap of paper. Who judges legitimacy of Lebanon govt. that asked our aid to protect its integrity. Reminded him of October revol. [in Russia]. Only people can decide legitimacy. Hitler used pretext of menace. Personally friendly but very tense & upset. "Not way to win friends among Arabs." Told Gromyko not to underestimate unity of Am people behind Pres! etc.*
  Back to Embassy to report. Thompson to prepare cable to [State] Dept. Then to [N. A.] Mikhailov, minister of culture, T[hompson] finds very hostile. Presented Grenville Clarks book[33] *& request for Russian*

---

30 On July 14, just before the Stevenson party arrived in Moscow, a military *coup d'état* removed the pro-Western leaders of Iraq, and King Faisal was assassinated. The Eisenhower Administration countered by landing troops in Lebanon at the request of the incumbent but outgoing president, who had been the only Middle Eastern leader to accept the Eisenhower Doctrine, promulgated in 1957 and approved by Congress. The doctrine authorized such use of American forces to assist any nation against aggression from a country controlled by international Communism.
  Tucker wrote: "An air of tension was palpable in the Soviet capital as the big propaganda campaign against 'American and British aggression against the Arab peoples' gathered steam. Ordinary Russians were wondering anxiously what this fresh international crisis portended, and thoughts were centered on one overwhelmingly important question: Will there be war? And at the moment of our arrival, the Soviet government's actions were not calculated to reassure their anxious minds on this point." *Impressions of Russia,* pp. 9–10.
  31 Per person.
  32 King of Jordan.
  33 Grenville Clark and Louis B. Sohn, *World Peace through World Law* (Cambridge, Massachusetts: Harvard University Press, 1958).

*publication first. Then Authors League case — asking if he didnot
believe in equal treatment for authors etc etc. Softened up with some
friendly humor. Said he would examine my memo carefully & talk when
I returned again. Changed subject to movie exchange breakdown —
considered disrespectful of R[ussian]. movies, asked my influence.
Promised full report on Soviet ed[ucational]. movies. Parted in good
spirits. No word of Lebanon.*

*Back to Embassy to approve cable re Gromyko visit, memo re author's
case interview, briefing on trip, mail, etc. Amb. called to F. O. [Foreign
Office] again. Handed formal statement — propaganda plus Soviet
reserves rt. [right] to take steps nec[essary]. to protect independence
of countries against American aggression. Not alarmed yet. T. believes
may be a long time getting out of M. E. [Middle East] result of many
mistakes, plus natural nationalism, religions, ambitions & complexities
mostly acting against West. To Puppet Theatre in evening (Ruth [Field]
rejoined us late last night from London) and about the best entertainment I ever saw!*

Thurs. July 17 — Moscow to Tashkent.[34]

*Off at 11:30 after long ride to airport past fantastic Univ[ersity].
bldg. & new housing construction — in T U 104 [jet] — 1800 miles in
3½ hours! 3 hrs. later, Reception. Long drive thru city (800 000) to
"Dacha of Central Cttee" — an old estate used for VIPs, Huge native
Uzbeck [Uzbek] dinner — Soups, shaslik etc. Good small tomatoes &
cucumbers. Old city — 70% of people some say — officially 30% — very
Asian — mud brick — squalid. People polyglot Mongols, Tartars, Arab,
Persian looking. Wear little embroidered skull cap & mostly western
clothes. Native clothes disappearing everywhere in cities. Even R[us-
sian]. tunic. 75% Uzbeck, 25% Russian.[35] After dinner with our 4 chaperones & local cultural direction & Howard Norton[36] of Balt. Sun who
came along for first visit to Central Asia after 3 years in Moscow went for
drive. Vast transformation of old Asian city evident everywhere, mostly
since Revolution. Huge statue of Stalin at hub of wheel in center of park
in new city. Hot — dry — like So. Calif or Ariz. irrigated cotton around*

---

[34] Just before leaving, Stevenson wrote Mrs. Ronald Tree: "We leave Moscow
for the 'interior' this minute & still no word. . . . I'll pray all is well — and that's
what I said to Gromyko at end of long anguished session yesterday. But he said that
deeds were better than prayers! . . . People friendly — no evidence of crisis, except
in the Embassy & ministries and thats where I've been. . . ."

[35] Tucker reported that the president of the Uzbek Society of Cultural Relations
with Abroad estimated the population of Tashkent as 75 per cent Uzbeks, 11 per
cent Slavs, and the rest non-Uzbek Central Asians. *Impressions of Russia*, p. 17.

[36] Moscow bureau chief of the Baltimore *Sun*.

*city. Insisted on walk in old part against guides who show usual self
consciousness about anything bad. Reminded of "locations" in Johannesburg or refugees in Pakistan. People curious & friendly; no smells! Bright
eyed little Uzbek boy asked if Amerikowski — Yes. "Do you live better?"
Well, anyway, "we are friendly" and as we left ran after us to shout —
"Greetings to children of America!"*[37]

Friday July 18 —

*Bright — Hot — not far from Afghan frontier here. Called on Mayor
— long friendly talk with humorous little man. Like all very defensive on
subject of Russian domination of sovereign Uzbeck Republic. Housing
big problem — city archi. showed us around — Shaved head — Uzbeck
— looked almost Chinese. Hates colorful "old city" — same hideous drab
brick modern bldgs. But wide tree lined streets. Assemblying airplanes
in big Lenin Sq. for air show. Huge statue of Lenin — propaganda signs
over streets — Lenin & Stalin everywhere. Huge stadium — 70,000.
Great banner — "Ardent Greetings to sportsmen of Chinese Republic" —
gymnast tournament about to start. Young girls with teacher having
group calisthenics. Architect & local guides wouldn't let us back into
old city. . . . Pioneer Palace — old house of a black-sheep Romanoff —
sign — "Thanks to Party & Govt. for our happy childhood." Eager
workers showed us around. Wood carving, painting, embroidery, sports,
etc and chess groups. Hysterics over boy not yet 5 who was chess prodigy
— going to Moscow with Uzbeck team — beat editor of "Michigan Telegraph" quickly. "Have detected unusual talent? — "can't practice with
others because he has to take naps" Russian? No Uzbeck — No — Korean!*

*Visited market, of course! Mostly fresh vegetables — privately grown
& sold. Dried apricots — 20 rubles kilo! Old Russian woman spoke few
words of French to me — very eager, but crowd quickly gathered & I
moved on. What story she could have told!*

*Priced skull caps — from 16 to 60 rubles. Shirts with Uzbeck em-
broidery 280. Red Fox pelt — 60! Crowds curious, correct & quickly
responsive to smiles & gestures. Yet Tas[h]kent Pravda this morning*

---

[37] Tucker wrote: "This was the first of many occasions on which Uzbeks encountered on the street, showed a friendliness towards Americans which at times
became demonstrative. Good will toward the U.S.A. is strong among the Russian
population, but I have the impression that it may be even stronger among Moslems
of Uzbekistan. And this impression derives from contacts with them at the height
of the campaign over Lebanon. If these people who smiled and applauded at the
sight of Americans in Tashkent and Samarkand had believed even a good fraction
of what they were reading and hearing about us through every official medium at
that moment, they ought logically to have been in a lynching mood." *Impressions of
Russia,* p. 20.

says "People of Uzbeckstan wrathful about American aggression in Lebanon." Long interview with Chief justice[38] and two lady "jurists." (1) Peoples Courts — elected for 3 yrs — legal ed[ucation]. not required (2) Oblast courts — orig juris[diction] & appeals. Elected by Oblast Soviet. (3) Supreme Court — orig[inal] & appeal juris. Supreme Soviet of Rep. elects — 5 yr terms — 19 judges — 3 on case. "Sup Ct indep[endent]. & resp[onsible]. to no one except law." But ministry of justice verifies work of courts . . . 7 judges sit on appeals. Final appeal to Sup. Ct of Sov[iet] Union in cases of violation of Congress of Sov law or law of another Rep[ublic]. 92 lawyers in Tashkent Oblast. Local law faculty graduates 60–70 — mostly don't practice.

Much talk about "Parasitic Law" passed by Uzbeck Rep. last year which authorizes people to deport anyone who doesn't work or evades social responsibility & can't be "re educated." His neighbors "talk to him"! Warning always enough. C. J. [Chief Justice] said "temporary — in response to public demand" in answer to ques[tion]. about constitution.[39]

To shabby small main mosque thru winding streets of old city to be met by deputy Mufti. Threaded way thru hundreds of moslems at Friday prayers — listened to short sermon about peace. Believers mostly old & ragged men — Uzbecks — all moslem. Dinner with Deputy Mufti — marvelous melons — kind of Casaba — soup, rice, mutton — tea — ripe figs etc. 3 way translation!

Koran says — a lot! — including, believe not what you hear but what you see.[40] Speeches at beginning and end of long meal in strange room of mosque served by 3 slovenly men. Mufti charming pock marked man. Elected every 5 yrs at conclave of delegates from all mosques of "diocese." "In Czarist times — he was selected by govt. & if any protest they were bribed." Only handful of pilgrims to Mecca now. Had to go to Moscow for permission himself. How many went before revol[ution]? "Don't know, because anyone was free to go — but probably only a few." Showed me seminary with 40–50 students of Koran, library of Mosque — with bound volumes of Pravda — and presented each of us a Uzbek

---

[38] Usman Ibragimov, chief justice of the Supreme Court of Uzbekistan.

[39] Tucker reported that the chief justice had explained that the people of a neighborhood constituted themselves a "social court" to discuss such a case. Then, if the person did not mend his ways, this "court" could order his deportation. When asked whether it was consistent with the Soviet constitution to punish people without recourse to the courts of law, the chief justice, replied that this was just "a temporary exception to the Constitution." *Impressions of Russia*, p. 25.

[40] Tucker quoted the deputy mufti as saying in a toast: "[The Koran] bids us to believe not what we hear but only what we see with our own eyes." Ibid., p. 26.

beaded cap and me a silk Uzbek gown that W.B[lair]. priced in store at 750 [rubles]!*

  To a concert in evening — orchestra in white western shirts, black ties & black evening trousers playing only Uzbek string & wind instruments — shrill, rather unpleasant. Very formal with R[ussian]. conductor in tails. Carmen! Then endless singing & dancing to accompaniment of ensembles of 6 plus flat drum held in one hand — all folk songs of central Asia with liberal propaganda themes. "National song of Iraq" — sounded ominous just now but turned out to be a love song with nothing to do with Iraq — "I've counted all the stars and none is as bright as my love for you." Gold or silver teeth prevalent! Audience wholly Uzbek.

  * And when I left the Mosque on the day of "Wrath" the crowd applauded![41]

Sat. July 19 —
  Long interview with PM[42] *— small, swarthy, bright eyed, forthright, nervous little man — Uzbek with 5 phones!*

  Pop. increased 25% in 5 yrs. Claims higher birth rate & lower death rate than USSR or USA. (Always compare the two).

  Council of Ministers (31) meets monthly. Prae. [presidium] of 9 is exec. organ & plans work — includes Gos Plan[43] *Chief, Finance & [the Committee of] State Control.*

  Rep[ublic's]. Sov[iet] subordinates to Supreme Sov. [in Moscow] of 424 which approves Rep Council. "Stalin loved dictatorship & centralization by verticalism." But did great work etc. Since have decentralized & corrected his errors.[44] *How much? Formerly we controlled about 2½ billion of prod[uction] now 24 billion.*

  Natural gas near Bokara — for our 4 Reps. and Afghanistan, our neighbor!

  26 Uzbeks in Council of 31.

[41] Tucker reported: 'The contrast between the official image of a wrathful people and the Uzbeks as we encountered them was total. Nor was there the slightest basis for any Uzbek to suppose that Governor Stevenson, who was identified in the local press there and elsewhere in the Soviet Union simply as 'leader of the Democratic Party of the U.S.A.,' represented anyone other than those very U.S. 'imperialists' who, according to *Pravda of the East,* had torn off their masks in Lebanon. Yet, for example, as we left the main Mosque in Tashkent, a great crowd of people milling in the street around our cars broke into applause when he raised his arm in greeting." Ibid., p. 22.

[42] Mansur Z. Mirza-Akhmedov, chairman of the Council of Ministers of Uzbekistan.

[43] The Soviet state planning commission (Gosplan), which drew up and supervised successive five-year plans for economic and other types of development.

[44] Tucker noted that "it was somewhat surprising to hear Mirza-Akhmedov express himself on Stalin with a critical vehemence which we encountered in no other Soviet official [we] met on the trip." *Impressions of Russia,* p. 36.

Party guidance? By overlap of individuals & parallel organ.[45]

Foreign Minister's functions? Very limited. Cede part of Sovereignty to Moscow. Still hope to be in UN.[46]

Coordination of Econ councils working OK. Regional control — great savings in personnel & automation. Average income 640–1000 [rubles]. Add free medicine for family, vacations etc. Separate schools for R[ussian] & U[zbek] speaking children, also other languages. Teachers colleges in native languages 4000 in Univ. of Central Asia.

PM — son of baker, was a locksmith.

Visit to great Textile Combine — 17 000 workers, 750 medical personnel for workers & families — 400 bed hospital — produces 200 million meters of cloth 89 cm [centimeters] wide. Total USSR 5½ billion yards? Workers 72%, women — most all Russian that we saw. Max[imum] earnings 1700–1800 [rubles] per mo — min. 600. Average 750–800 Value of product about 2 billion.

Visited nursery for babies of workers up to 3 — very good!

The Soviet Union cast its 84th veto in the Sec. Council today!

A solemn day indeed, pictures in the local Pravda of 100 000 people demonstrating before the U.S. Embassy in Moscow yesterday ag[ainst]. "U.S. aggression in Lebanon." And now I must go to an official dinner given by the Mayor!

It took from 8 until 11:30. I spoke about Peace and its first condition according to Kruschev [Khrushchev] — "trust" — & the precondition of trust — truth — that the Voice of America had been jammed for the last two nights, that no US reporter in Moscow could report without censorship — that even my statement had been censored — Didn't they believe in equal treatment in the search for truth? The Mayor said "yes" — and crossed his heart with his right hand in the graceful gesture of the Usbeks [Uzbeks] — that has only one peer — the Indian! A long evening of talk about Central Asia among Usbek nationalists. Algebra came from here. Also Viticulture (the wine has not improved!) as well as Ghengis Kahn, Tamerlane, Baber etc. But their knowledge of their ancient history was refreshing.[47]

[45] Tucker reported that Mirza-Akhmedov was reticent on this point and said he and two other deputies were members of the Bureau of the Uzbek Party's Central Committee. Tucker added: "Reticence on this question of Party control of the government institutions in the Soviet Union was a general characteristic of the Soviet officials with whom we spoke on the trip." Ibid., p. 35.

[46] Tucker wrote that Mirza-Akhmedov had alluded to the foreign ministries of the various republics that were formed in 1945 to facilitate their entry into the United Nations. He said it was regrettable that "sovereign independent" Uzbekistan was not in the UN. Ibid., p. 33.

[47] Tucker observed: "The men around the table began to speak less as Soviet patriots and more as Uzbek patriots." When the discussion turned to Tamerlane,

Back to the villa — the Dacha — to listen to the news from Lebanon, Jordan & Iraq — and Soviet jamming of U.S. broadcasts in Russian & distortion of their English broadcasts. If this has been going on for 10 yrs its a wonder we are still at peace!

Sunday July 20 — Tashkent to Samarkand & return

At last, at 58, the Golden Road to Samarkand, by air! Our chaperones now 6 — plane laid on for us. An hour flight thru green irrigated valley Kolkhozes[48] & towns. Crossed the wide semi dry Syr-Darya that empties into Aral Sea — then across higher plateau of arid wheat lands to Samarkand! — fruit & sugar. Higher & drier than Tashkent — the heat quite bearable. "Mayor" — Uzbek history prof. etc. Observatory of Ulug-Beg,[49] murdered nearby on pilgrimage to Mecca by "reactionary religious plotters" who "opposed spread of knowledge" Mosque & tombs climbing hill — The Living Czar — turquoise domes flashing in the morning sun & blue, green, yellow tile work that can't be reproduced. Large crowd assembled at bottom, applauded when I came down, bowed with right hand on heart after their manner.[50] The Debi-Hanum — great mosque of Tamerlane also in ruins & beyond restoration. . . . Surely the ancient "Registran" — sandy place — is as Lord Curzon said — the "noblest public sq. in the world." Borden picked up some pieces of tile. Good restoration work in progress.

The Gur Emir and Tamerlane's black, simple, narrow tomb of nephrite. Sitting in the crypt surrounded by Uleg-Beg, [Ulug-Beg] Mamhmoud, T's tomb etc listening to the Prof while Bob Tucker translated!! Before the Profs. lecture in tomb of Tamerlane "He is not a national hero of the Uzbecks — We don't approve of his warlike depredations."[51]

---

the successor of Genghis Khan as conqueror of Russia, one of the men declared, "Why, we regard Tamerlane as the great national hero of Uzbekistan." Ibid., pp. 40–41.

[48] Collective farms.

[49] Grandson of Tamerlane and ruler of Timurid who was reputed to be the first astronomer since Ptolemy to compile a star catalogue.

[50] Tucker reported: "As we moved from historical ruin to historical ruin, the crowd of curious onlookers kept growing. And there was no mistaking its friendliness." *Impressions of Russia*, p. 43.

[51] Tucker described this incident: "The climax of the tour was a visit to the tomb of Tamerlane. We entered and descended a flight of stairs to the lower level where the sarcophagus lies. Professor [Kim] Samebaev was in the lead. As he reached the threshold of the inner sanctum, he stopped, turned to face us, and said: 'We are about to see the sarcophagus of Timur. But before we go in, I would like to make one thing quite clear: We do *not* consider him the national hero of Uzbekistan. Soviet historians have researched this question, and they have arrived at the opinion that Timur pursued a predatory policy.' The allusion to the remark made the

Excavations of earlier city Ghengis sacked. Market — wonderful Bazaar — like the best of Cairo, Damascus, Bagdad. Lunch at Central Cttee's dacha with Mayor — outdoors. He was mgr. [manager] of a cannery. Visited Caracul institute[52] *— tea factory — poor shops. Not even post cards! Had 150 tourists last year. What's ahead for this exquisite monument of the glory of Central Asia?*

Monday July 21 —
Goodbye to Tashkent and its shady poplar lined roads — flower lined streets — a city that looks the same everywhere in the new part & even large factories seem to be hidden behind walls or trees. But before leaving we visited the show case collective — Ksyl Uzbeckstan [Kzyl Uzbekistan] — where the Chairman — for 21 yrs! a huge Uzbeck told us all about it — 7500 acres — 2150 able workers etc — & details of purchase of machinery from the MTS. It all sounded as tho prices were going up for the Kolkhoz and the consumer. Visited typical home — two families, mud house, some nice iron beds, grape arbor, old women making bread — plastering pies of dough on walls of mud oven. Very hospitable — insisted on tea & bread. Visited kindergarten —very neat — children singing & dancing. Ch[airman] — "Nat Kabal" — & head nurse — anxious about peace — "Why don't you do something." And when I said "why doesn't Kruschev" — they said "K works for peace — why doesn't Eisenhower." I think these people are mostly content & convinced.
Three hours by Ilusha (jet plane) to Alma Ata — across brown hills & dry wheat lands to green plain at foothills of Ala-Tau Mts —snowy & high. Bracing air. City 500,000, 60–70% Russian etc, 30% Kazakh. Bracing air. Ponderously plush VIP guest house just built, dripping with velvet curtains — by rushing stream & flower strew[n] hills 10 km out of town. Visit with our slatternly looking hosts so full of enthusiasm, to the Oblast Ch[airman]. who received us with cabinet — and strawberries and cherries! If anything Ks [Kazakhs] are more proud than Uzbecks and the miracles they have wrought are something.[53] *Drive around with*

---

previous evening was unmistakable, although nothing whatever had been said by us on this subject. And when I asked the professor what had occasioned his 'explanation,' he replied: 'The comrades consulted with me.' I suspect that it was the 'comrades' from Moscow who did so." Ibid., p. 41.

52 The All-Union Scientific Research Institute for Karakul Sheep-Breeding.

53 Tucker reported: "During a short courtesy call on G. S. Karzhaubaev, the chairman of the Alma-Ata Oblast Soviet, the conversation chiefly dealt with agriculture. Of the 22 to 23 million hectares of virgin lands recently brought under cultivation in Kazakhstan, he said, 560,000 hectares fall in this oblast. Nine-tenths of this is planted with winter wheat." *Impressions of Russia*, pp. 47–48.

city architect. Many parks & trees. Best dinner at our Dacha since we arrived in USSR! No shashlik! Theatre — "gov't. box." Extraordinary performance! Selections from Iolanthe, Barber of Seville & Figaro — in Russian. Marvellous dancing, ballet, chorus singing. Alma Ata — opera house has a R[ussian]. company, a Kazak and a ballet co. Repertoire over 50; personnel 500, season Sept. to July 1, 7 performances a week! Back to Dacha — for mountains of strawberries, raspberries — and Voice of America[54] *on terrace at midnight by rushing stream — on opposite side of world from Chicago. Iraq radio asking for assassination of king of Jordan etc etc — and look where we are!! All U.S. broadcasts in Russian are jammed as usual. How can these people know* anything!

Tues — July 22 —

What a day! 1st — visit with some difficulty to church — nice green & white turnip top 100 yrs old at end of unpaved street. Services — mostly elderly women, some young people — offering before Ikon of rice, bread, raisins etc for "departed loved ones." Ta[l]ked to two bearded priests — town 80% Russian — church attendance increasing. To Market — man ahead of me — cleaning up. (Always unwilling to take us anywhere without notice).[55] *Old flower seller gave me bunch (beautiful flowers in Alma Ata — arranged in old fashioned mélange) Meat inspected, also milk. Amusing drunk "I'm an artist," quickly removed. "Ray of East" kolkhoz — Russian farmer bookkeeper mgr. Son teaches history. If gov[ernment]. wants him to be a farmer he'll be a farmer!*

Second largest earner in Sov. Union — raise everything — 11 000 ac[res]. cultivated 72 000 pastures.[56] *Vegetables fruits most profitable. Exhausting inspection of beet, cabbage, onion fields. How long do the women in the work brigades work? 10 hrs — but in the winter they have nothing to do — "We work!" one muttered.*

Lunch in grove deep in country — even working cabinet carted out and vast variety of foods — with champagne finale! — and toasts to peace, as usual. This again, the paper reports, was a day of wrath & indignation about imperialist aggression.

---

[54] The embassy had furnished Stevenson with a shortwave radio.

[55] In Samarkand, on the drive from the airport, Stevenson saw a crowded market place but the mayor of the city persuaded him to visit a market later that day. When they did so, a table of fruit and vegetables was awaiting them and all the customers were elsewhere in the market. Stevenson did not stop at the table but went to the crowded part of the market. See Tucker, *Impressions of Russia*, pp. 44–45.

[56] The "Ray of the East" collective had 40,000 sheep, 1,500 pigs, 1,100 horses, 2,600 cattle, 35,000 head of poultry, 290 silver foxes, 180 camels, and 500 beehives. There were 6,000 people on the collective.

Visit to P.M.[57] of Kazakhstan while boys went to movie studio which was disappointing. P.M. tall lean ex Elec. engineer. Then visit to Academy of Sciences and long lecture by Pres, surrounded by about 25 members, on institutes of Academy & its purpose — the develop. of K. — which is rich in minerals. When he mentioned a town I said isn't that where Malenkov is?[58] He smiled, hesitated & with affirmative nod from one of his fellows, said "yes." I wanted to say I'm leader of U.S. opposition & am free to speak & travel & look where I am! Vice-Ch — "party member" — asked what I thought of Lebanon — and I let "Em have it quiet[l]y and slowly — I think! When I mentioned censorship he said U.S. reporters don't report "objectively" etc. Visited Observatory in foothills of [mountains?] Prof. V. G. Fesenkov[59] of Leningrad. 6 or 7 telescopic devices. Working evidently mostly on Sputnik. Building another observatory next year. Saw photo of rocket launching one of Sputniks taken there. Could it have been from Kirgizia?

Night of Moscow [tummy?] & 'the disease.' after longest, hardest day of trip.

Wed. July 23 —

Farewell to our happy cheerful hosts & the elegant guest house of Alma Ata & off to Rub[t]sovsk & Siberia in a private plane[60] with our 4 chaperones. Kazakhstan mostly arid & desert as we flew 650 miles north Over Lake Balk[h]ash — flat, salty.

Rub[t]sovsk new pioneer town surrounded by rich farm land & "new lands" in huge Kolkzs [kolkhozes] & State Farms. Tractor plant

[57] Dinmuhammed A. Kunayev, chairman of the Council of Ministers of Kazakhstan. Tucker reported: "Mr. Kunaev maintained that Kazakhstan is 'an independent Soviet state,' having been in pre-revolutionary times a mere borderland of Tsarist Russia. Asked about the relations between the Kazakh government and Communist Party, he became evasive. There are, he said, fifteen equal republics in the Soviet Union, all working under a single plan approved by the Supreme Soviet, but this plan is based on decisions of the Party at its Twentieth Congress. Kazakhstan has its own Communist Party, but it is an 'indissoluble part' of the C.P.S.U. As to his relations with the First Secretary of the Kazakh Communist Party, Mr. Nikolai I. Belyaev, Kunaev confined himself to saying that they had 'common tasks.' Together they work out a 'common line.' "

[58] Georgi M. Malenkov, chairman of the Council of Ministers from 1953 until his resignation in February, 1954, when he became deputy premier. In July, 1957, he was ousted from the Presidium and the Central Committee for anti-Party activities. Tucker was told that Malenkov was alive and at his post in Ust-Kamenogorsk, but noted that in Moscow it was widely rumored that he was dead. *Impressions of Russia*, pp. 49–50.

[59] Professor of astrophysics at Moscow University and director of the Alma-Ata Astrophysical Institute.

[60] The plane was furnished by the Soviet government.

*evacuated from Kharkov in 1941 — now employees 16,000. Women
doing almost every kind of work. (Women motormen on trolleys
everywhere in Sov Union) Even in foundry & on precision machine
tools. Many machines American lend lease. Also farm implement factory
— 3500. Met by typical political 'mayor'*[61] *— go getter, aggressive type
always ready with peace speech — now so familiar — and V. Gordeev*[62]
*— Vice Chairman of Altai Krai — an area larger than all Newfoundland,
and a most unusual & attractive man of 39. Raised at a Kolkhoz, became
school teacher. In many long talks revealed ignorance & mistrust of
Am[erica]. Denied censorship, jamming, restricted areas, Am. armed
forces figures etc. One party enough when all people united. Amused,
incredulous about all we said — and very* intelligent, *parrot of party line.
Discouraging experience.*[63]

*Large crowd of curious people at grass field — what a bump! — air-
port. I'm first important foreign visitor. Although this is another "Day
of Wrath" over Lebanon smiled and clapped when I spoke to them.
Driving along Turk Sib Ry to town across vast flat prairie on soft dirt
road I felt like a boy in Bloomington again. Wail of steam whistles, dogs
barking, chickens crowing, dust on roads, unpaved streets, log cabin
villages spread along roads, calfs grazing on road sides — all reminded
me of frontier life. Visited great state farm, large Kolk[h]oz, tractor
repair station (400 employees) & communities clustered around —
like early west except social life around party club house (ornamented
with Stalin & Lenin) instead of church — and tractors & thousands of
acres instead of horses & hundreds. Big crowds around hotel to see me.
Guides always tried to hustle me thru. Very reserved, but as usual
quick to smile & clap.*[64] *Little chance to talk with* people *— also as usual.
All utterances about peace. No indications of discontent. Hotel primitive
— enormous Lenin & Stalin pictures, usual book stand. Toilet paper —
cut up paper napkins — Mud in tub — but a tub! The Lucullean table
of Alma Ata has suddenly simplified to Borsch, veal & fried potatoes
& the inevitable cucumbers & tomatoes — and raspberries! Raspberry
feast out in fields of Kolkhoz served by farm women.*

[61] Vasily L. Zibarev, chairman of the Rubtsovsk town soviet.

[62] Vasily V. Gordeev, deputy chairman of the Altai Krai soviet.

[63] Tucker wrote of Gordeev: "One of his most noticeable mental traits is a respectful attitude toward state authority as such. He probably takes it as axiomatic that
the social-economic system in "capitalist" countries is doomed — but I doubt that he
has any strong genuine feelings about it." *Impressions of Russia*, p. 81.

[64] Tucker reported: "A little later we came out and found a still larger crowd
standing in a semicircle at the hotel entrance. There was applause when the Governor raised his arm in greeting, and shouts of 'peace and friendship.' As we walked
through the crowd to our cars, I overheard one man say to his wife: 'He's the
future president of a great nation and we ought to have a look at him.'" Ibid., p. 64.

*Wonderful theatre in farm implement factory "Club" in old town —
Aza, the Gypsy Girl, by Ukra[i]nian stock company. Audience workmen
families. Adm[ission] 3–10 roubles. Met & joked with cast afterward.
Very responsive jolly people — all Ukranian. After theatre — ours were
only autos. People walked. Few bicycles.*

*On leaving Gordeev made nice speech — I think you liked it here for
3 reasons 1) it was green, and, lets admit it, we like green too 2)
the children are happy, well fed & cared for, and we have noticed that
you like children 3) Construction — we are building everywhere in the
city, the towns and on the farms, and you appreciate development.*[65]

All were true.

*Huge wheat crop — average 30–35 bu. Corn for silage only. Two
phase harvesting.*

*Everywhere signs — catch up with America. Everyone — "compete."
Tried to explain that we are not competing in food & fiber because we
have too much. Not sure I convinced them! Very proud of achievements.
You are 150 [years old]; we are 40 [years old] — and we have already
overtaken you in some things and will in the rest.*[66]

*Russian carts on roads, log cabins, old Russian stoves — sleep on
top — frost comes in late August only about 100 days growing season —
but beautiful, cool bright summer.*

Hotel room equipped with great Soviet Ency, & books in English.

Friday — July 25 — Robsovsk to Novosibirsk

*Steppe turns more to forest. Novo. on great river Ob — 800 000
[population] from 100 000 in 28 yrs. Old house log — carved woodwork.
New bldgs std. [standard] Sov architecture. Lodged airport "Hotel" —
very comfortable — meals in airport restaurant. "Accommodations in
hotel not satis."*[67]

*Another boom town — "capital" of Siberia — 4 Ry & highway bridges
over Ob-Trans Sib bridge & construction camp originally. Wide main*

---

[65] Tucker observed: " 'Construction' is manifested in the new plants, public buildings, schools, etc., which are going up here and there, but what it essentially connotes
in the mind of a Gordeev is the general process of building up the country over a
long span of time, making it modern and powerful, industrialized and great. . . .
In our contacts with men of the Soviet governing class there were many such
manifestations of the future-oriented mentality. One aspect of it is a kind of positive
delight that many provincial officials seem to take in the obliteration of surviving
traces of old Russia." Ibid., pp. 83–84.

[66] Tucker noted: "The gospel of construction and living for the future belongs
to the outlook of the Party, but the Party outlook and the popular outlook are
divergent. The people are tired of being told that they should work for some future
goal that they themselves will not be here to see and enjoy." Ibid., p. 85.

[67] Novosibirsk normally was a "closed city" not accessible to American travelers.

streets. Side streets unpaved. Huge apt. houses. Many factories — lamps, radio, machines, farm equip, leather, food etc. Center of "culture" — many schools, technicians & city of Culture going up nearby — for 30,000, Univ., Insts. to work on fundamental problems in mathematical, physical, geological natural & econ. sciences — and direct work of all branches of Academy of Sciences in Siberia. Also obviously directed to China.

Visited machine tool plant — arrogant mgr. angry about trade with U.S. "Warned you that if you wouldn't sell to us we would make our own — and we have." They have! Huge drills, presses etc. Visited Mayor — curious about growth of U.S. cities. Saw machine tool trade school; gree[n]houses raising tomatoes, cucumbers, cabbages, lettuce — and grapes! — for town where winters are 8–9 mos. Bathing beech [beach] on river bank — crowds of young people — very informal — no bath houses — ladies in bras & black panties — just like a day 5 yrs ago on Danube at Belgrade.[68] *Crowds quickly assembled — mobs of curious wet little boys & we retreated.*

Theatre! Largest in Sov U. Very handsome — wide foyers. Regular Co. on tour. In smaller auditorium — Siberian Peoples Chorus — doing old & new songs & dances — songs sad, dances exciting. Recruited from neighborhood — now pro. Performing arts in R[ussia]. the best! Went back stage (after audience rose at end — turned to "royal box" & applauded me!!) and joked with jolly, curious caste of 50.

Hydro dam 40 km [south of Novosibirsk] — 400 000 kw 3 generators operating. Power cost to customers of grid will be 4 kopec[k]s or 4 mills [per kilowatt hour]. Financing hard to understand when capital cost doesn't have to be repaid! Great engineering feat in coldest place large dam ever constructed. Lunch on boat on lake with chief of Construction & director of Hydro Station — Chief makes 150,000 to 200,000 [rubles per year].

Large factories all around. Huge communication center (?) — counted 30 tall steel towers. Met with dozen representatives of Siberian Branch of Academy [of Science]. Explanation and drawings of new City of Science — to house 25 000 including 7000 scientists, a university and 15 institutes. No emphasis on humanities — "leave that to institutes elsewhere." Enthusiastic and able men apparently dedicated to development of Siberia for which this impressive undertaking is being created. Anticipate no trouble in getting top men to come out to this pioneer frontier.

Meeting with Sovnark[h]oz — Regional Economic Council — headed by calm commanding confident husky man of about 50–60 formerly

[68] See *The Papers of Adlai E. Stevenson*, Vol. V, p. 339.

*manager of farm implement plant. "I make a lot of money. I can't tell
you how much but my basic salary is 6000 [rubles per month]."*[69] *Short
of labor — Regional Council great improvement over ministerial
system.*[70] *To be consolidated into smaller no. [number]. "Profit necessary
incentive to production." 900 employees in Sovnarkoz for 100 000 in
industries.*

*Banquet with this very big and agreeable business man — ruggedest
drinking bout yet & the American team lost!*

Sunday July 27

*To large airfield 40 km SW of town — 100 fighters etc!! and off to
Sverdlovsk by TU 104 — roomy, luxurious, quiet and over 1000 miles in
2 hours! So much of Siberia under cultivation!*

*Sverdlovsk — Formerly Ekaterinburg where Czar was murdered.
Will they let us see the house? Like Novo[sibirsk]., this town also forbidden to foreigners. (Boys asked for motor boat ride at Novo — but
would not take them thru the town). Usual airport greeting — wretched
old hotel. Drive around ugly booming town that has a more relaxed,
self confident air than Novo. etc. This is 250 yrs old & center of mining
industry.* New bldgs — *prefabricated slag. Huge Polytech — 10,000*
students — to service *heavy industry. Town full of old log houses & some
handsome mansions of past. House where Czar & family shot as
Kolchak's army approached now a party school. A tigress at door
wouldn't let us go thru. Geological museum of Urals very interesting.
Pioneer Palace in famous 18th century house of early gold tycoon. What
remarkable & tireless work they do on children! Puppet show by children
in park. Electronic devices created by children, garden plots — vegetables, fruits, grafting, flowers.*

Went to church — funeral — Sexton said there were 38 — *now 2:*[71]
Old infirm women — also babies being baptized.

---

[69] Tucker quoted the director of the sovnarkhoz, V. T. Zabaluev, as saying that
his salary was seven thousand rubles per month, adding: " 'But you must understand, of course, that my salary and my income are two quite different things' — a
point which the average Soviet official would play down rather than emphasize."
Impressions of Russia, p. 105.

[70] Tucker wrote: "Asked about the reasons behind the decentralization of industrial management, [V. T.] Zabaluev spoke at length about the duplication of
effort and extra expense which resulted under the old ministerial system. For
example, each ministry used to build its own auxiliary services, such as railway
and auto transport. The result was that two different plants in the same district,
subordinate to two different ministries, would have two different systems of services,
whereas a single system is economical. The new setup is breaking down these
'interdepartmental barriers.' " Ibid., p. 102.

[71] Thirty-eight churches in pre-Revolutionary Ekaterinburg versus two in Sverdlovsk in 1958.

Circus! Marvelous acrobatic, juggling & wild riding in tiny ring by tribesmen Ossetian of N. Caucaus [Caucasus]. Best clown ever saw — worked constantly 3 hours — 3rd performance today — Sunday! Gets 100 per perfor!

Rector of Univ. escorted me in Sverdlovsk — sweet, gentle man.

Stevenson mailed the following postcard on July 28.

To Mr. and Mrs. Ronald Tree[72]

Dear Trees — We are on the way "back" from Central Asia & Siberia after great adventures. The press gets hotter about imperialist American aggression in Lebanon but the people greet us enthusiastically and the hospitality is violent. This *is* the new frontier — booming, vital, confident and full of eager pride. It makes you *think* — if you can stay awake after a collective farm, a couple factories, 3 interviews with committees and an evening of dancing, singing — and vodka! The markets in Central Asia were great — you would have loved them! Bill & boys send love — also the "mayor" of Sverdlovsk, whose gold teeth are nipping my ear. — Aff — ADLAI.

Monday — July 28 — Sverdlovsk — Kazan

Bookstores in hotels, airports, offices even Volga river boats! Conferences with 48 yr old head of Sovnarkolz [Sovnarkhoz] of Sverdlovsk Oblast. Looked like prematurely grey N.Y. lawyer! Held ministerial rank in industry — came with 30 from Moscow under reorganization. Party man. Very able — 1500 employees in his Regional Econ. Council supervising 500 enterprises & 600 000 workers. Territory size of UK [United Kingdom] — 4 million. Prod. up 1st half of '58 11%; only 4.5% in '57. 30 billion production. "Some sectionalism but state interest must prevail" — "Your shirt is closer to you than anothers" proverb[73] —

---

[72] This handwritten postcard is in the possession of Mrs. Tree.

[73] Tucker reported that Sergei A. Stepanov, chairman of the Regional Economic Council, told them "that the central government works out the industrial plans for all the regions and that these plans provide for the interrelations between them. He admitted that there are cases of sectionalist tendencies. For example, the Sverdlovsk region is rich in timber, whereas other parts of the country, such as the Ukraine and Uzbekistan, need timber. Some Sverdlovsk officials want to take the locally produced timber for local uses at the expense of consumers in these other places. The tendency to look after one's own interests first is only human ('your own shirt is closer to your body,' according to the old Russian proverb), but the sovanarkhoz strives to keep the interests of the state as a whole constantly in mind and to fulfill its obligations under the plan." *Impressions of Russia*, pp. 118–119.

Object to overtake U.S. in per capita prod. Growing more rapidly than US — proud & candid — 8 hr day reduced to 7 Jan 1 in iron & steel — increased wage of 13%. Policy against wage increases except to keep up with increased productivity — but overall productivity increase took care of loss to budget in iron & steel hour adjustment. Discussed party & labor relations — all fine! Reducing work week in all industry to 7 [hour] day & 41 hr week.

Using plastics to reduce metal. Using more aluminum. Constantly introducing new machinery, technology & procedures to increase productivity. 7% metal cutting tools replaced last yr.

Uralmash — heavy machinery factory — 16 000 employees. Big heavy, workman type mgr., tough, confident & amused. Ed. Ryerson[74] & Am[erican]. steel delegation here month ago. Rolling mill for India, huge presses, 12 000 lbs pressure horizontal, 30,000 vertical, mining machinery largest excavater etc.

Enormous lunch at plant — called it "tea" — speeches.

To country — 40 km — West to Europe-Asia marker & "picnic" at pleasant site by road on edge of forest. More food, vodka, champagne & speeches. Walk in woods — hint of winter in air. Back to city barely in time to throw things in suitcases & rush to airport with our friends. Arrived Kazan 11:30 [P.M.] — met by smiling, delightful "Mayor," historian of city, deputy minister of culture, Prof of law from Univ. Saw lovely Kremlin built by Ivan after defeat of Tartars in 1552 — by full moon. To hotel for another feast & speeches!

To the Volga river boat 46 yrs old and a tiny compartment & bed at 3:30 A.M.

Tuesday, July 29 —

Woke up on the Volga — another place I never thought I'd be! High bank on one side, low on other. Occasional stops at villages on high side including Cheboksary — capital of Chuvash Autonomous Republic. Occasional tugs & tank barges, huge log rafts with huts on top. Boat takes 7 days Astrakhan to Gorky. Old peasants selling cucumbers, eggs, bread ras[p]berries on banks at stops. Movjik [Moujik] [peasant] types getting rare. Country flat and vast. Passed great palace of Cherchaev family — "one of 200 estates." Now a rest home. Villages formless collection of wooden houses climbing up bank and running along bluff. Look very woeful and shabby. Workers going to "rest home" in Cherchaev manor house.

---

[74] Edward L. Ryerson, chairman of the executive committee and former chairman of the board of Inland Steel Company and an old friend of Stevenson's.

*Volga river boats along banks — low gunwales, high, sharp prow.
Children swimming on banks — all in trunks. Women wear regular bras
& black panties. Old grizzled toothless peasant — black bread, dried
fish — "Our Mother Volga" — with great pride.*[75] *Farewell dinner with
our 4 chaperones & talk with Ed Stevens of Christian Science Monitor
who flew out to Kazan to meet us and ride back.*

Wed. July 30 —
   *Gorki — Got up at 5:30 by mistake! Read in sun on deck. Gorki —
former Nizhni Novgorod — 5th largest city — at 9* [A.M.]. *Fine red brick
Kremlin being restored. Large, eager delegation at dock. Up bluff
by auto — thank God — to busy lovely old town & ornate old hotel.
Breakfast, drive around — fine view from old houses of "rich merchants"
on bluff across the flood plain. Good churches here & there — incl.
fantastic baroque private church of Stroganovs.*[76] *Museum, Indus.
exhibit — many children. Across river, past old Fair to Gorky auto plant
— formerly Molotov — hence ZIM car.*[77] *45 000 employees — autos trucks
— "young exec." director. Came to U.S. but wouldn't let him go to
Detroit. They — the Russians — started this travel restriction business &
large areas still closed to foreigners, incl. Sverdlovsk & Novo. But
Rs* [Russians] *don't know it.*
   *Many women in plant again. Wild 65 km drive to Hydro dam. Violent
rain. Boarded Hydrofoil boat, 75 ft — 60–75 kms p.h.! — for trip back to
town. Lunch on board. Remarkable boat. John Fell beside himself
with joy. Long talk with designer. Hotel for enormous dinner, as usual,
with Mayor — excellent, quiet, worldly man and also as usual, an
engineer. Many toasts, speeches & reeling to our private plane to
Moscow at 7:30* [P.M.] *We think very well of Gorky!*

[75] Tucker wrote that an old peasant chatted with them for a few moments, then looked out at the wide river pensively and said, "Our own Volga." *Impressions of Russia*, p. 125.

[76] Tucker wrote: "As we were leaving the Stroganov church (an unscheduled stop), a Russian lad walking by stopped to talk. He seemed excited at the unusual sight of a group of foreign visitors in the city, and asked where we hailed from. When he heard 'America,' he brightened and said: 'You should come more often! We like and respect America. Oh, they write all sorts of things in the papers, but' — and here he ended with a gesture that said: But we don't believe all the things they write. I asked him if he was a student and he replied: 'No, a worker.' He accompanied me to the car, shook hands vigorously and walked away." Ibid., pp. 126–127.

[77] A luxury sedan, used by state officials below the highest echelon, whose name derived from the initials of the factory, Zavod Imeni Molotova (Factory Named for Molotov). The name of the plant was changed to Gorky after the ouster of former Foreign Minister Vyacheslav M. Molotov from the Central Committee in 1957, for alleged anti-Party activities.

Moscow at 10:30 & thru the huge apartment district to the Sovietskaya again — same rooms. No mail at Embassy! Something is wrong! Word from Mr. C.[78] *that some "higher level" talks will be set for tomorrow. To bed — thank God!*

On his return to Moscow, Stevenson told reporters that he had found a "depressing lack of knowledge" by Russians about the United States. "The peoples of the Soviet Union receive a one-sided picture of what's going on in the world," he said. "All Soviet officials emphasize the importance of coexistence and competition with the United States seems the absorbing preoccupation. But I wonder if it is understood that the basis for peaceful existence is mutual trust. A much freer, fuller exchange of information and ideas than now exists will help. As a result of this trip I can see no better place for competition than in the spreading of truth instead of propaganda about each other."

He stated: "That the people of the Soviet Union, like those of America, genuinely desire peace and friendship is certain." He concluded by saying, "I have been struck by the scope and energy of the industrialization everywhere in the eastern areas of the Soviet Union and the drive to bring millions of acres of new land into production."[79]

During the days from July 31 to August 8, Stevenson was so busy with interviews that his diary for those days consists of only one page. He lunched twice with Deputy Foreign Minister Vasili Kuznetsov, who had been ambassador to China — "excellent man," Stevenson wrote in his diary. ". . . China talk interesting — alarming? — significant?"

Stevenson interviewed Minister of Education Yevgeni I. Afanasienko; Minister of Public Health Mariya Kovrigina; the Prosecutor General Roman A. Rudenko; Semyon A. Skachkov, the chairman of the State Committee on External Economic Relations; and Vice Rector Ivanov and some members of the faculty of Moscow University.[80]

On July 31, Stevenson had approximately a two-hour conversation with First Deputy Premier Anastas Mikoyan. The early part of the conversation was concerned with Soviet policy in the field of foreign trade, difficulties in the way of expanding trade between the United States and the Soviet Union, and a discussion of the decentralization of industrial administration within the Soviet Union. Robert Tucker, who

[78] An official of the Ministry of Culture; the editors are unable to identify him further.

[79] Chicago *Daily News*, July 31, 1958.

[80] For a description of these meetings, see Tucker, *Impressions of Russia*, pp. 136 ff.

accompanied Stevenson to this meeting, prepared a memorandum of the conversation. The following excerpt is from this memorandum.[81]

The last part of the meeting was taken up with a lengthy political discussion which Mikoyan began by inquiring why such an educated, informed man as Governor Stevenson found it necessary to include "groundless attacks" on the Soviet Union in every speech. He asked whether this was due to inadequate information or whether conditions in the United States were such that anti-Soviet attacks were mandatory, as had been the case in Russia in the first war when no one ever made a speech without attacking the "entente" as the enemy even though many people did not even know what the entente was, and some thought it a woman.

The Governor replied by saying that there were many reasons for misgivings about the USSR. One of the factors was ignorance of the United States and its motives, which was evidently very extensive in the Soviet Union. Stevenson went on to say that during his trip through the country the papers had been reporting every day on meetings to denounce America's "unprovoked aggression in Lebanon." But he had detected no enmity in the people. Likewise American audiences had just welcomed Soviet dancers with a friendly reception. Perhaps ignorance played a part in American attitudes as well. At the root of the whole thing was the need for deeper mutual understanding than so far existed. However, one great difference between the two countries which had to be understood was the fact that in the Soviet Union everything was run by the government whereas in the United States it was run largely by private individuals. Mikoyan contested this statement, charging that it was the direct opposite of the truth. Not everything was in the hands of the government in the Soviet Union. It had 15 governments and in what way were they worse than the monopoly firms in the USA? These governments represented the people, for in the Soviet Union there was democracy. The monopolies on the other hand were completely arbitrary and did not represent the people. Why, for example, did William Randolph Hearst need so many newspapers? Why did he not keep one and give the rest to the people? What kind of free enterprise did their editors have when they received their orders from the "center"? To this the Governor replied that they were always free to resign their positions. Mikoyan said that they could resign but the alternative would be to starve, and no one wanted to do that.

The Governor said that although no agreement would be possible on the merits of the respective systems, it should be possible to

[81] A copy is in the possession of the editors.

agree on the need for more intimate understanding on both sides of the other's system.

Mikoyan replied by saying that the United States press frequently resorts to distorting the facts, "which we do not find pleasant." To this the Governor replied that he had been reading many things in the Soviet press which he did not find pleasant. For example, he wished that we might have read the real facts in the Soviet press regarding the landing of US troops in Lebanon. Although they had been invited by the legitimate government, the landing had been called "aggression." The Governor considered that a distortion.

There followed a discussion about the Lebanon constitution and whether or not it empowered President [Camille] Chamoun to take the action he had taken. Mikoyan maintained that the Lebanese parliament had opposed the action and said that of course it might always happen that a "bankrupt president or monarch," feeling the soil slipping under his feet, would call in foreign troops to his aid. But this was aggression and "absolutely incredible." The Governor maintained the President Chamoun was acting within the inherent constitutional right of any chief executive of a democratic republic in taking action to protect his country. He had not been opposed by his parliament, but only by the speaker of the parliament. The United States had made it quite clear that under the UN charter it would not permit small nations to lose their freedom through outside interference. Mikoyan replied that he had recently read the constitution of Lebanon and that it gave the President no right to invite foreign troops into the country without the agreement of parliament. He went on to protest that the USA had no right to send troops into a foreign country in order to protect the interests of US citizens there. Acting on that principle, each great power could send in troops to protect its own citizens. Thus, Russia could send in troops to protect Russian citizens, China to protect Chinese citizens, and so forth.

The discussion turned to the question of jamming and travel restrictions, the Governor saying that it was not US practice to jam Russian broadcasts and he did not think that Russia should jam ours or restrict travel. He had taken a portable radio with him on his trip and had witnessed this constant jamming. Further, he understood that the United States had in May renewed its proposal of November 1957 for removal of restrictions on travel in both countries, and he hoped that this proposal would be accepted by the Soviet Government.

As regards jamming, Mikoyan replied that he was happy to hear that the Soviet Union was jamming the Voice of America so well. If the facts the Governor had mentioned were correct then he had only praise for the Ministry of Communications. It was doing good work. America was waging a cold war against the Soviet Union and it was necessary for the latter to take steps to counteract it. Furthermore, the United States officially states that it is waging a cold war. At one time the Soviet Union had not jammed the American broadcasts and such a time might come again. That would be when the cold war ends and normal relations resume. He went on to say that the State Department considers cold war to be its "main line of behavior."

Regarding travel, Mikoyan said that the Governor had traveled extensively in the Soviet Union and that any other American could have taken the same trip. True, an American might not be able to go everywhere but he, Mikoyan, believed that "99% of our country is open to travel." The Governor referred to a map in his possession showing extensive areas of the Soviet Union being closed to travel by foreigners and added that he considered such restrictions to be foolish. Mikoyan replied that as soon as the cold war ended there would be an end to all these restrictions. But all Soviet initiatives to this end "fall off the State Department like peas from a wall."

Mikoyan went on to speak of the Soviet policy of encouraging tourism and spoke of the hospitality of the Soviet people toward tourists. He spoke favorably regarding the abolition of the finger-print requirement for travel in the United States. He complained that there had been no answer to a Soviet proposal of two years' standing for an exchange of parliamentary delegations.

The Governor emphasized his view that the restrictions of which he had spoken should be relaxed all the way around and that such a relaxation would promote confidence and trust. He was in favor of more trade and more communication of all kinds, "even by radio." He hoped that Mr. Mikoyan would be able to hear the Voice of America in the Russian language. Mikoyan replied that it was a "disagreeable voice." To this the Governor said that he himself was against having a cold war and the one way to avoid it was by talking with one another, but one should not suppose that he should always hear what he wanted to hear. Mikoyan agreed that this would be foolish and dull. The meeting concluded in a light vein and good spirits and Mikoyan presented Governor Stevenson, who doesn't smoke, with a large box of all kinds of Russian cigarettes.

On August 5, Stevenson had a meeting with Premier Nikita Khrushchev, who had just returned from a trip to the People's Republic of China. A memorandum of the conversation was prepared for Stevenson's files.[82]

[82] A copy is in the possession of the editors.

The following is a typescript of a conversation between Premier Khrushchev and Governor Stevenson held in Khrushchev's office in the Kremlin on August 5, based on longhand notes taken by Robert Tucker, who accompanied the Governor. The talk lasted two hours and twenty minutes. Present on the Soviet side in addition to Khrushchev were his interpreter Troyenovsky, and Chairman of the Committee on Cultural Relations G. Zhukov, who took notes for Khrushchev.

The Governor began by thanking Khrushchev for the reception and by observing that Khrushchev was a man who traveled a great deal, referring to the fact that he was just back from China. He also said that he had very much enjoyed his trip around the Soviet Union and wanted to express appreciation for the hospitality and courtesy which had everywhere been accorded him. Khrushchev said that he was glad to hear this and that he envied the Governor for being in all those places that he had visited. The Governor said he should have come along with him. Khrushchev said that he would have been happy to accompany the Governor on his rounds of the Soviet Union but that the Governor had not invited him to do so, probably because the Governor had not wanted any witnesses present so as not to be committed to the kind of statement he would make back in the United States. This was "cunning way" (khitrost) Americans had. When the Governor observed that Khrushchev had himself probably been just about everywhere in the Soviet Union, Khrushchev said that there were many places he hadn't yet seen, for example, Samarkand (which the Governor had visited), Turkmenistan, Armenia, and Yakutia. As for Georgia and Azerbaijan, he had been in those places only in 1921 during the Civil War. It was a big country and one life was not enough time to get acquainted with it all. And he also had to do a lot of traveling abroad, the Governor said. "Not so much," answered Khrushchev.

The Governor observed that Acting Foreign Minister Kuznetsov had been talking with him at Lunch today about the rapid development of China, Khrushchev said that this pace of development was "astonishing" (porazitel'noe). The Chinese themselves had not foreseen such a tempo of development.

The Governor remarked that during his trip around the Soviet Union he had had an opportunity to see what was being done in decentralization of industrial control. He had the impression that this step had been met with universal approval.

Agreeing, Khrushchev said that not only had it been approved, but also very good results were evident even though the step had been taken only a short time ago. He went on to say that it was impossible to direct such a big country from one center. There were very highly qualified people working in the localities around the country, but under the previous setup paralysis had resulted while these people were waiting for directives from above. The old system of centralized direction was "impossible." Now we have freed ourselves from routine current work in order to concentrate on the larger problems, and the routine current work is being done locally.

Khrushchev went on to say that, as he had learned, the Governor had expressed to Mikoyan the view that there were more economic administrative regions than there were natural economic regions in the country. He said that they had proceeded more or less along the line of setting up economic regions to coincide with administrative regions, but that was only the "first stage." There would also be a "second stage," in which larger economic regions would be created. However, their purpose would be planning rather than operative direction (*upravlenie*). In a sense, this arrangement already existed in part. For example, the Ukraine had a gosplan which did the planning for several economic administrative regions within the Ukraine, and the situation was the same in Kazakhstan and Uzbekistan. So in a sense such larger economic regions were already in existence. However, similar arrangements in a second stage would be worked out within the Russian Federation. For example, there would be established a Urals economic region embracing the several oblasts in the Urals. However this larger region, as well as others to be set up on similar basis, would be for planning purposes only and not for administration. (The inference appeared to be that the existing regional economic councils would remain in existence in the second stage.) The Governor said this sounded sensible, and that such a step might reduce conflicts as between economic councils. To this Khrushchev replied that it would also result in a certain reduction of freight shipments, for it would make possible a better specialization of production.

The Governor went on to raise the question of trade, observing that some of the chairmen of the economic councils and plant managers had spoken of a desire to increase trade between the two countries and in particular to buy abroad rather than produce at home certain types of machines for which the need might only be temporary. Personally he was emphatically in favor of more U.S. Soviet trade. As Mr. Khrushchev must be aware, he could not speak for the United States Government. However, he had the impression that there was no obstacle to negotiations between the Soviet Union and U.S. private firms in the vast majority of cases. The problem of government credits for the Soviet Union was a different matter, however, especially in view of the fact that the Lend Lease account remains unsettled[83] and that political relations have been so strained. If Mr. Khrushchev did not mind receiving a very friendly suggestion, he would suggest that some new and reasonable offer might be put forward in connection with the Lend Lease settlement because old accounts must be settled before new credits could be granted. He understood that the COCOM[84] list was to be very substantially reduced by the middle of this month and he felt that with a better political climate the field of trade could vastly expand.

Khrushchev agreed with the Governor that there must be a settlement of the Lend Lease question. But this was not the main problem. Under any Lend Lease settlement the U.S. would receive only a very small part of what it was — spending on propaganda against the Soviet Union and on credits extended to its allies in order to maintain strained East West relations. The Americans were a very practical minded and calculating (*rashchetlivy*) people. If they were to tally up these expenditures just referred to, it would turn out that America has been spending several times more on these purposes than it spent on Lend Lease in the war. Further it was necessary to consider the comparative sacrifices during the war. No sums of money could pay for the loss of lives of all the fathers, sons and brothers who died in the war.

The Governor inquired whether the last statement was meant to signify that the Premier did not recognize any further obligation under Lend Lease.

Khrushchev replied that he had not meant to say that, but merely that if all the circumstances were to be taken into account, this would help us to reach agreement. America had been contributing to the development of industry in West Germany, for example, showing that these things were not so much a matter of expenditure as of political policy. But here, he went on, he and the Governor had come to an area of differences. Let the diplomats exchange opinions on the question. He and the Governor could agree that the development of trade was a most desirable thing. He had sent a letter to President Eisenhower about trade between the two countries, and though[t] the President's reply "rather good." They had wanted to publish the President's reply but could not do so for "prestige reasons" since no American paper had published the text of the letter to the President. The Governor observed at this point that he thought he recalled having read the text of Khrush-

---

[83] Talks on settling Russia's $11 billion Lend-Lease debt were reopened in January and February, 1960, but again broke off without an agreement.
[84] The Coordinating Committee of the Department of State.

chev's letter in full in the *New York Times*. Khrushchev said that he had checked up on this matter, that he had instructed the Foreign Ministry to speak to the State Department about reciprocal publication but the State Department had not agreed to this proposal, and probably what had appeared in American papers were reports based on the Soviet press. No American paper had published the text in full.

As to the Soviet aim in dispatching the letter to the President, Khrushchev went on, we did not expect credits. I was quite sure that we would not get the credits. And now I would like to tell you a secret. The United States press and public figures have long been accusing the Soviet Union of concentrating its economic development in the field of heavy industry and slighting the development of consumer goods. Now there is a program for the development of the chemical industry in order to increase the supply of consumer goods. So we wrote to ask whether the Americans would not help us here. Of course the result was nil. And now our people see that when the Americans express solicitude for the development of consumer goods in the Soviet Union, they do this not because they are really concerned about the welfare of the Soviet people, but because they are pursuing certain political aims of their own. This we have proved.

The Governor said that he was not aware of any "accusations" having been made, but only of reports of the American press regarding Soviet concentration on heavy industry. It was not a question of accusation or approval or disapproval. The Governor said that he thought the Premier had mis-read the American attitude, and added that he personally would very much like to see the Soviet Union succeed in raising the living standard of the people with American help. However, to repeat, there were some obstacles to the extension of new credits until the settlement of the old ones, but he wished to reemphasize that negotiation with private firms was almost entirely open to the Soviet Union, and that, given an improvement of political relations, he hoped that trade would expand.

KHRUSHCHEV: How shall we improve political relations? Your firms want to trade with us. I just saw the Deputy Chairman of Gosplan who has been in the United States. He brought back many interesting propositions in his briefcase.

S.: In connection with the chemical industry, I believe.

K.: Yes. He was received by a Minister, either of Economics or of Commerce, I forget which, who said that the U.S. Government would not hinder deals made with private firms. So apparently we will consider the propositions made by these firms with a view to inviting their representatives to come here for talks.

s.: The Prime Minister asks: How can we improve political relations? I wish I knew the answer. The Prime Minister thinks that the answer lies in Washington, while we on the other hand think the answer lies in Moscow.

k.: We have been carrying on a correspondence with the President. Evidently we both want to improve the atmosphere, but it is just the opposite of this that happens.

s.: I personally thought that things were going to get much better, that the Prime Minister's liberal attitude, his suggestion, for instance, that there are "many roads to socialism," indicated that some alteration had taken place in the old Soviet position that had frightened the United States. But now there seems to be a turn backwards. Revisionism, for example, is no longer tolerated, and that is too bad. The U.S. under my Party made much progress in a liberal direction. But is not the Soviet Union becoming rigid again?

k.: Do you think that the main reason for the tense situation lies in our dispute on ideological questions? That sounds rather strange. Since when have U.S. business circles been taking an interest in these disputes, and what difference can it make to them who is right and wrong in these disputes, since the capitalists do not consider it possible in general to build a Communist society? And if we cannot agree with certain Communist Parties on these questions, how can we agree with you?

s.: It is not a question of what the "capitalists" — since the Prime Minister used that term — think, but rather a matter of what all humanity wants, and in no country more than mine. The point is that we feel that all nations should have the right to go in any direction they wish, and when we see this right interfered with, even within the Communist world, it frightens us.

k.: Let's write that rule down and approve it at a Summit Conference. It's what we wanted to establish all along. We want to establish it and hold it sacred, no interference in the internal affairs of other countries, for these affairs should be settled by the peoples concerned.

s.: Has that been the Soviet Union's position in regard to the things that disturb us, as for example, Yugoslavia and Hungary?

k.: What troubles you in regard to Yugoslavia and Hungary?

s.: The intervention of two years ago in Hungary, and the recent attack on Tito for going the way he pleases.[85] I am disturbed when I hear it said that the objective of the Soviet State is to communize the world. I think we should let the world go the way it pleases.

к.: You draw a correct conclusion just now, and we think that the question of which road is to be followed is an internal matter of the people concerned. The trouble with the Americans is that they poke their noses where they shouldn't. Why on earth should they send their troops to Guatemala or to Lebanon, or why should British troops be sent to Jordan, or why should the Americans send troops to Cuba to support such a well known democrat as [President Fulgencio] Batista who beheads those who oppose him. Who asked the Americans to perform the function of a gendarme to Lebanon.

I am sure that neither Tito nor Kadar[86] authorized Mr. Stevenson to raise this question, for those are sovereign states. If I wrote to Comrade Tito about this, he would undoubtedly be deeply shocked, and all the more so would Comrade Kadar be deeply shocked, for these are internal matters. The Americans must learn why the peoples of the world can decide these questions without the help of the U.S.A. We have decided to spend our vacation with Kadar this summer. I'll tell him about your solicitude, but, I am afraid that he might not welcome it. Let's go together and we will speak to the Hungarian people together and set forth our respective positions to them, and then we'll see which position the people will support.

s.: I am afraid that the Hungarian government I am talking about cannot speak any more.[87]

I had not been aware that American troops had landed in Cuba. Are there any there? And I don't want misunderstanding, I don't come here on behalf of Tito, but as a private citizen to express appreciation for the hospitality accorded me everywhere on this trip.

к.: In that event it would be better not to raise questions which would relate solely to us and the foreign Communist Party concerned. We and Tito are communists and somehow we will settle this affair. It is an internal affair, and in any event you couldn't help us. Let's rather talk about questions of how best to improve the relations between us and the United States.

s.: I started to discuss this matter in order to explain why relations are bad. Now that I know that the Prime Minister agrees that there

---

[85] In June, Russia had criticized President Tito of Yugoslavia for accepting American aid.

[86] Hungarian Minister of State Janos Kadar.

[87] Stevenson refers to the execution in June, after a secret trial, of four leaders of the 1956 revolt, including former Premier Imre Nagy.

should be no interference in other's internal affairs, I think our discussion can profitably continue.

к.: We have said this dozens of times, but in response we see the Sixth Fleet being moved up near the Soviet frontier and ships sometimes entering the Black Sea and we see ourselves surrounded by military bases, while all the while you in the United States say that we are bad because we don't respect the rights of the United States. How can we take a different attitude toward you if we are encircled by your bases? Or if the U.S. sends warships near to a country which shows dislike for the Vice President of the United States?[88] If a country shows disrespect for us, we simply wouldn't go there — but we would not send troops.

s.: The Prime Minister apparently does not realize the basis of the difficulty between us, and why the U.S. and, I think, other countries are fearful of the objectives of the Soviet Union. Actually, there should be no conflicts for we have enough territory and resources. All our troubles arise from outside us. After the war, in which we fought side by side, the U.S. believed in cooperation and disarmed almost totally. Then came a whole series of unhappy events, the pressure in Greece, Turkey and Czechoslovakia, the war in Korea, the pressure on all the countries from the Baltic to the Black Sea. Our policy has been defensive, not aggressive or expansive. We relinquished the Philippines, and we have tried only to ensure security of such country to go its own way. I am sure that the Prime Minister would not agree with me, but I am trying to tell him what we think. I am sure that we have all of us made mistakes, but the important question is how we get along from now on. As far as I and many of my fellow countrymen are concerned, we are very eager to find a way to settle the conflicts that divide us.

к.: This I believe, and thank you for your words. I have read your speeches, some things in them are wrong or even offensive. But on the whole I think that you stand on a platform of improving relations and we welcome it. So far as the Korean question is concerned, the Soviet Union has no troops there but America does. Again, there are no Soviet troops in the Near and Middle East. The Americans have bases in England, Turkey, Greece, and I don't know where they don't have them, and yet you want us to respect you. But how can we applaud this? What would the Americans think if the Russians set up bases in Mexico or some other such place? How would you feel?

[88] Some of the marines and paratroopers dispatched to Caribbean bases following the stoning of Vice President Nixon's car in Caracas in May had been transported by ship.

The policy of Dulles is one of rollback (the word used was *sderzhi-vanie,* and all through the interview it was mistranslated by Troyan-ovsky as "containment" — Robert Tucker). But history will roll him back, or throw him out rather than roll him back (*ili vybrosit a ne othrasit*). There has not been a single Russian soldier in Czechoslo-vakia and there is not now a single Russian soldier in Czechoslovakia. Do you really recognize the right of every people to arrange its des-tiny in its own way? This is the whole question. You must understand, Mr. Stevenson, that we live in an epoch when one system is giving way to another. When you established your republican system in the eighteenth century, the English did not like it. Now, too, a process is taking place in which peoples want to live under a new system of society, and it is necessary that one agree and reconcile himself (*miritsa*) with this fact. The process should take place without out-side interference. But you are playing the part of a gendarme in the Middle East. You are turning the Arabs against yourselves, while we, having no troops there, are applauded because we are not interfering. If this principle were accepted, it would improve the international climate and we would welcome it.

s.: The bases represent only a response to the fear of post-war Soviet policy. Regarding Lebanon, we went in there to protect the indepen-dence of a small country. I am amused that we both charge each other with offending the very principle of noninterference which we both approve of. But our points of view are very far apart, and all we can do is to take up our differences one by one. And I hope that there will be an open mind here in the Soviet Union, just as I for one will try to keep an open mind in my country.

к.: Our people have an open mind toward (literally: no prejudices against — R.T.) the Americans. Tourists here will never meet any hostility, as Governor Stevenson can probably testify from his experi-ence on his trip through the Soviet Union in the recent weeks.

s.: There is universal friendliness. Peace and friendship are dear to the heart of every Russian. The question is how we are going to achieve it, and I hope that some progress will be made in the Security Council in New York.

к.: We do not intend to sit in the Security Council as the President proposed.[89] We do not intend to sit with the corpse of Chiang Kai-

[89] Following the Iraqi coup of July 14, President Eisenhower called for an emergency meeting of the UN Security Council, and on July 19 Khrushchev countered with a proposal for a five-power summit meeting to prevent war in the Middle East. Finally, at the request of the United States, an emergency session of the General Assembly met on August 8 to consider the situation.

shek. Will I sit at the same table as Chiang Kai-shek? No, I'll never do it.

s.: But the mechanism exists and we cannot make it conform to our desires.

k.: But America is acting capriciously. It is not China but Chiang Kai-shek that is represented in the United Nations, and how about the Cuban representative? Am I to sit there with the representative of that General?[90] And the representative of the old Iraqis sitting there. I won't sit there. Let Sobolev[91] do it if need be. But the Prime Minister of the Soviet Union won't sit down there with them.

s.: The Iraqi Republic has been recognized by most of the powers, and I have never heard anything about Chiang Kai-shek coming there.

k.: It would be his representative.

s.: So the Prime Minister wants the machinery to be reformed to his views before it can be used?

k.: The machinery should be conformed not to my wishes but to the real state of affairs. There could be a conference outside the Security Council. But no one will drive us into the stable for a conference with Chiang Kai-shek. We won't do it; we don't like the smell.

s.: I regret what you've said. This situation concerns everyone, and sometimes it is necessary to adjust oneself to the general interest.

k.: True, but in this matter no self-interest of ours is involved. The forum of which you spoke was proposed in order to torpedo the conference. It is no accident that De Gaulle[92] does not agree.

s.: I am sure that there are two points of view here.

k.: [Walter] Lippmann is against it. What party does he belong to?

s.: Neither, but he is a great friend of mine.

k.: I don't always agree with him, but I am a reader of his and he writes quite intelligently. He is a reasonable man.

s.: I'd like to say a final word.

k.: I don't want you to be offended. I have respect for you.

s.: Thank you. When the Chief Executive of one of the biggest countries can spare so much time, he must be quite a big man. I will not impose any longer upon his time but would like to say one thing. I attended the founding meeting of the United Nations in San Francisco as a

90 Major General Fulgencio Batista, president of Cuba.
91 Arkadi A. Sobolev, the Soviet permanent representative to the UN.
92 French President Charles de Gaulle.

member of the American delegation. The Americans, like the Russians, had great hopes then. I worked with Gromyko and later with Vishinsky, and with Molotov for months in the setting up of the United Nations.[93] One problem ran all through it: the Soviet attitude that the great powers, because they had the power, could organize the world. Now this is true and even if you consider that it is right, still that is not the way in which the organization was worked out. So I have felt and hoped that we could work within the organization as set up, especially in such crises as this one. But here I trespass on the field of the diplomats and had better not say anymore save to express the sincere and earnest hope the Prime Minister will exercise restraint as regards any actions which would prevent this meeting from taking place.

к.: We are for the conference, but as a summit conference, a conference of the heads of government, and evidently — this is my view — the conference should not only deal with the Near and Middle East but with the whole range of questions that had been anticipated. It would not be sufficient to consider the Near and Middle East alone, because any such discussion could not but lead to still greater tension. And we cannot reconcile ourselves to the presence of troops in Lebanon and Jordan. We will mobilize the peoples and public opinion against it, and any meeting on that one problem always will lead to further tension. So the reasonable thing would be for the Americans to withdraw the troops from Lebanon, Jordan, and Turkey, and withdraw the Sixth Fleet from the Mediterranean or at least from the shores of Syria and Lebanon, and then there would be a better atmosphere and hope for agreement and we could meet and confer. And we could help people to live, as the late President Roosevelt once put it, without fear.

s.: A meeting to discuss everything would take a long time. But the meeting to which I have been referring might lead not to greater tension but to withdrawal of the troops, if we could get the Arab States to agree among themselves. And this, as you say, would reduce tension.

к.: Conference or no, you will have to act sensibly and withdraw the troops unless you want to antagonize the peoples still more. We will never reconcile ourselves to their remaining there. Of course, if a country wants to go to war, then it can ignore public opinion. But if one does not want war, then one must take account of public opinion.

s.: The American troops are there not to please the Arabs but to protect

[93] See *The Papers of Adlai E. Stevenson,* Vol. II, Part Four, *passim.*

a small country at its request. Peace depends upon the security of *all* nations from outside interference. When this nation no longer feels menaced, the troops will be withdrawn. But I had better not discuss Lebanon any further, or I might get in trouble with Secretary Dulles!

K.: But this point of view is not far from that of Dulles. I am astonished that you say American troops will stay there regardless of Arab opinion. Why, they will throw them out. How can Americans arrogate the right to decide how long to keep its troops there? If America supports a bankrupt President or king afraid to face his people, world opinion will be antagonized. How can one fail to reckon with this? I am surprised at you, Mr. Stevenson. Public opinion must be respected. See how far we stand from one another — at opposite poles.

S.: I am disappointed that the Prime Minister does not want to discuss Lebanon separately.

K.: It should be discussed at the General Assembly with all countries participating, and for the purpose of bringing about condemnation of the aggressors and the demand for the withdrawing of their troops.

S.: Maybe the General Assembly would be a proper forum, but I thought that the Prime Minister had expressed his readiness to go to New York or Geneva to the Security Council.

K.: I was ready to go, but all this time has passed and there has been no solution. This correspondence is just a way of gaining time to cover up the actions that are being taken. De Gaulle says that he will not go to New York. Eisenhower would prefer not to go to Geneva and [Harold] Macmillan takes still a third position. This is quite a field for discussion, and I do not exclude the possibility that there is some kind of collusion (*degovorennost*) between them.

S.: I have the impression that they all agreed to meet at Geneva.

K.: I read the press, but I have not seen that anywhere.

S.: The President said that he would be willing to meet anywhere by the 12th of August, except in Moscow.[94]

K.: I don't recall his saying that but I do recall that he said something about Moscow. Moscow is the most secure place in the world, as Mr. Stevenson can tell the President.

S.: I believe that the [Prime] Minister is mistaken. I have the impression that the President said that he would be willing to meet anywhere by the 12th of August. I suggest that the Prime Minister look into this.

94 See the New York *Times,* August 2, 1958.

K.: But within the framework of the Security Council. According to normal Security Council proceedings.

S.: It is a question of making use of the machinery which exists for this very purpose.

K.: There is no need for that. We all have our representatives there. Dulles has indicated that even unofficial talks would be excluded unless they took place by accident in the men's room.

S.: Perhaps they ought to put me on the payroll for representing my government's position.

K.: There appears to be no difference in foreign policy between your party and Mr. Knowland's[95] party.

S.: There are great differences.

K.: You have not shown it.

S.: I hope that my Party can show it after 1960. But we can't let the whole world wait.

K.: I must say that in my last elections I cast my vote for you. I have no objection to Mr. Eisenhower and indeed have great respect for him, as I have publicly stated. But fate has drawn him so close to another person whom I will not name[96] — a person who, if brought together with a saint, would make the saint look like a sinner. When there is a new President, there will be a new sputnik[97] of the President, and only then will there be a better atmosphere. You know we have a way of joking when representatives of the socialist countries get together. We say: we will regret it if that sputnik of Eisenhower's leaves the State Department, for he is very helpful to us. He helps us so. We'll hardly get a more helpful opponent than he.

S.: We Democrats may have to deprive you of that advantage; but in the United States it is all up to the people.

K.: Does the Constitution permit a third term? But I suppose that the President's health would make it difficult anyway.

S.: The Constitution excludes it.

While there are differences, please do not underestimate the anxiety that all Americans feel regarding the dangers in the world today, or their solidarity regardless of party in wanting to reduce tension and arrange settlements.

[95] William Knowland, Republican senator from California and a strong supporter of Chiang Kai-shek.
[96] Khrushchev refers to John Foster Dulles.
[97] I.e., a satellite.

к.: I believe that. I follow the United States press a great deal and as I see it — what can the Americans have against us or we against them? But that sputnik of the President is embittered (*ozloben*) and is artificially keeping up a state of tension. We statesmen have no right to carry on relations in the way he is doing. Common people relate themselves to one another at the promptings of their feelings, their hearts. But politicians do so by a calculation (*rashchet*) of the needs of their countries. A man may have an unpleasant personality, but we have no right to say whether or not we like the color of his hair. We have to ignore personal feelings, and cannot subordinate policy to those feelings. And our political aim is friendship and peace among the nations. I recently received the Premier of Austria. Here was he, a "little capitalist" as he called himself, and here was I, a communist, and yet we could find common ground and we had a useful talk. We parted with the very best feelings of mutual respect after having improved relations between our countries. Why cannot the same be true of our relations with the United States? We in this country have always respected America and American culture.

s.: This is the reason why I came to the Soviet Union. I believe that it is imperative to improve our relations but this is a two-way street. We have our views and our fears regarding the Soviet Union and the Prime Minister has expressed similar fears regarding the United States. Somehow we have to find a means of allaying these fears. This is a business of give and take.

к.: (Pointing to a spot midway on the table). Let's meet here. As [Winston] Churchill said, half-way.

s.: We, on our part, have already gone pretty far. We want to be able to talk without polemics, without invective, and abuse, without charges and countercharges. But if we always try to appeal to the peoples over the heads of the governments, it only makes things worse. Maybe the Prime Minister does not understand everything about us just as we do not understand everything about the Soviet Union.

к.: Two or three years ago Mr. Gartz,[98] a representative of the American farmers, came here to talk about corn. We sat and drank together and had pleasant talks. He is a very good man. We bought some of his corn. We drank cognac in the Crimea. There were no disputes and the meeting went profitably to both sides.

s.: I know him. He is a corn expert.

[98] Roswell Garst, of Coon Rapids, Iowa. On Khrushchev's visit to the United States in 1959, he and Stevenson met again at Mr. Garst's farm.

s.: (Laying on the table a copy of *World Peace through World Law*). Before I leave I would like to present this book to the Prime Minister at the request of Grenville Clark, one of the most respected jurists in the United States. I have already given copies to the Minister of Culture, Mr. Mikhailov, with the urgent request that it be translated and published in the Soviet Union. It expresses the most advanced thinking of jurists in the United States about the problem of world peace through world law.

k.: I shall ask our specialists to study it.

At this point the Governor said he had another favor to ask and mentioned a personal matter involving permission for the Russian mother of Mr. Tucker's wife to join her family in the United States. K. said he would look into it and took a memorandum from Mr. Tucker.[99]

k.: But how shall we improve our relations? Shall I vote for you again in the next election or not? I favor a President who will stand for improvement of our relations on the basis of reciprocity. But the policy of rollback must be rolled back. You cannot roll us back from our country. On that basis there not only cannot be friendship, there cannot even be good relations. What is needed is the recognition that there are countries with a socialist system and other countries with a system of private property.

s.: Live and let live — freely and sincerely fulfilled — that is the principle which ought to be followed. But I feel that I have come here under false pretenses, for the Prime Minister cannot vote for me. I will not be a candidate again.

k.: But how does Mr. Stevenson *know* that he will not be a candidate?

s.: But I think that we will win, although that is uncertain and for the future.

I believe in conclusion, Mr. Prime Minister, that we should proceed from the idea of equality of power on the two sides. Neither rollback by us nor expansion by the Soviet Union. Then we can recede by disarmament, for the arms race is an awful waste. "And an awful danger too," Khrushchev said, together with an expression of emphatic approval of this concept of power equilibrium.

The Governor thanked Khrushchev for the interview and apologized for taking so much time. K. said that he had enjoyed it and anxiously hoped that he had said nothing to offend Stevenson.

[99] Mrs. Tucker's mother was granted permission to emigrate at the end of 1958.

Stevenson said K. was forthright and he liked that; that he came from Illinois, where they raised larger corn than that — pointing to a glass case of ears of field corn at the end of the room — and that they should hold a summit meeting in a corn field. K. laughed his approval with a string of "Da, Da, Das."

At the close of the interview the Governor brought in his sons, Borden and John Fell, and introduced them to Khrushchev. They and the TASS representative took photographs while K. beamed and bantered. K. asked how old the Governor's sons were. He said his son, age 29, had just graduated from an institute. His field was automatics of rocket launching. The Governor said he hoped K. had another son who would launch doves of peace. K. said he had lost his other son, a flier, in the war. He had been shot down in the first days of the war, had recovered from broken legs suffered in the crash, returned to the front and was shot down again and killed. K. asked if the Governor's sons were married and when told that they were still single, suggested that they ought to come back and marry Russian girls — "that would be a contribution to Russian-American cooperation."

The farewell was very cordial, with K. laying both hands on the Governor's.

On Sunday morning Stevenson attended the service at the Baptist Church in Moscow — a visit not arranged through official channels — and afterward called on the chief rabbi of Moscow. Robert Tucker described the visits:

About two thousand worshippers, mostly older people and in their great majority women, were packed into the church. Reverend Nicholas Vysotski gave the sermon and then introduced Governor Stevenson to the congregation and invited him to say a few words. He spoke of the present gathering as a sign of the continuing vitality of religious feeling in Russia, and said that Americans generally consider a rich spiritual life to be one of the essential ingredients of a rich national life. This evoked an audible response of approbation from the intensely interested audience, some of the members of which were weeping. They struck up a hymn of parting as the Americans left the church. . . . One had the feeling that, despite all adverse conditions created by the political authorities, the Russian Baptist movement is a very live one among the religions of the country. A visit to the synagogue and the interview with the chief Rabbi of Moscow later that same day did not yield the same impression with regard to organized Judaism. This, however, might be a reflection, more than anything else, of the especially adverse conditions of Russian Jewry and of the extreme reluctance of the Rabbi (for whatever reason) to say anything which might indicate the nature of these conditions."[100]

Stevenson had some time in Moscow to catch up on his correspondence.

To Mrs. Eugene Meyer[101]

[no date]

Dear Agnes —

Back from Central Asia & Siberia — alive! It was a great adventure & extraordinary opportunity to see, hear & feel across a vast area of this huge, strange land. People friendly, eager, proud — hospitality violent! Conferring with people here in Moscow, on to Warsaw & Prague on Aug. 8, home early Sept — and none too soon. I'm getting tired! Pray all is well in your precinct —

Affec regards to [illegible]

ADLAI

To Paul Ziffren[102]

August 4, 1958

Dear Paul:

I hear nothing but good — even at this distance! — about the prospects for all Democrats in California this fall. I am glad you reminded me of the [State] Convention, which will be taking place just as I am starting for Western Europe after my stimulating, if baffling, weeks in the Soviet Union. And I shall keep on traveling west until I land in California the end of September!

I look forward eagerly to a happy reunion with all of you very soon — and to the most successful Democratic campaign California has ever seen! Meantime I send my warm greetings to the delegates who will gather at Sacramento to prepare for that glorious event.

Cordially,

ADLAI

---

[100] *Impressions of Russia*, pp. 163–165.
[101] This handwritten postcard is in the Agnes Meyer files, Princeton University Library.
[102] The original is in the possession of Mr. Ziffren.

To Mrs. Ernest L. Ives[103]

August 6, 1958

Dear Buff —

This has been a frightful rat race from first to last — and its almost the last! 2½ hours with K[hrushchev] yesterday. Also Foreign minister, Education minister, Culture minister — and now another ordeal with the latter in re my authors.

Leave Friday, Aug 8, for Warsaw by air, (c/o Am Embassy), thence by auto to Prague Tues Aug. 12, thence to Bellevue Palace, Bern on 14th and to Florence on 18 — I hope! Will wire you from Bern time of my arrival. Boys may come in advance, but not clear about leaving Prague yet!

Thought you would enjoy these reports from home!

Love —

IVAN THE WEARY

Following a meeting with Minister of Culture N. A. Mikhailov to discuss the question of royalty payments, Stevenson issued the following statement on the evening of August 7, 1958.

Mr. Mikhailov, the Minister of Culture, and his staff have been very cordial. But the official position regarding the payment of royalties to American authors and dramatists whose works are published in the Soviet Union was not encouraging.

That an author is entitled to payment for his work is a basic principle of Soviet law, and one hears many proud boasts about the protection of human beings from exploitation. Yet the works of defenseless foreign writers is being constantly exploited, and they even point with pride to the huge numbers of foreign books published without compensation in virtually all cases.

When compared with the major questions that divide our two great countries, this is a small matter indeed. But recognition of the rights of creative writers and artists would be a significant forward step on the highway to mutual understanding.

But the Ministry of Culture is studying the matter. And I will continue to hope that here, where there is such emphasis on education and

[103] This handwritten letter is in the Elizabeth Stevenson Ives collection, Illinois State Historical Library.

culture, the demands of common justice, the accepted standards of international conduct and recognition and respect for intellectual labor, will prevail at last.

In his book Friends and Enemies: What I Learned in Russia (*New York: Harper, 1959*), *Stevenson presented the following conclusions on the Soviet Union in the last chapter.*

Not long ago Soviet Russia was lightly discounted in America as a serious competitor in atomic energy, industrial production, scientific development, education and political influence. More recently we have been told from high places that the Soviet system is shaky and that if we hold fast its own obvious ills will destroy it.

So I went to Russia to see for myself. . . . Now I should like to record a few of my conclusions.

The first is that we have been badly informed and are badly mistaken. The Soviet Union is a stable power system and is not on the brink of internal collapse. The reasonable hope is not that it will disintegrate but that it may evolve into something less aggressive and menacing to peace and human freedom.

The second is that Russia is not the largest question mark in America's future. It is number two. Our number one problem is China — and so is Russia's. But the lengthening shadow of China is another subject.

Our emotional reaction to the rise of Communism has been to reject reality, aided and abetted of late by our political leaders. We were not prepared for sputnik or the Soviet economic challenge. But the illusion of our superiority in everything, together with the denial of unpleasant realities, is a bad basis for foreign policy. I hope we are fast approaching the end of this era of innocence and ignorance.

When I say the Soviet regime is stable I don't mean there is no internal dissension. I have no doubt there is bitter controversy over policy and sinister plotting for power in the Kremlin. One of the worst indictments of the Soviet system is that after forty years they have not worked out a means of transferring power without conspiracy, exile and violence.

What I mean by stability is that if life is austere and hard, at least it is getting better and there are no signs of rebellion. That does not mean that all Russians are devout Communists. Actually, only a fraction of the adults belong to the party. But if they are not the mass of indoctrinated zealots, the 200,000,000 enthusiastic Communists that some have portrayed, neither are they the mass of sullen, terrorized helots, seething with rebellion, that others have pictured. They seemed to me like most people — loyal, obedient and patriotic, proud of Russia as a great nation and of her achievements to which they contributed.

The industrial development, as I have said, has been spectacular. Even the chronic lag in farm production shows signs of responding to new remedies. While two-thirds of our output goes to the consumer, in Russia the consumer has had to do without and two-thirds has gone to industrial development, with a high priority for military strength and foreign aid and trade. The economic goal is to catch up with America in per capita production. And the new seven-year economic plan confidently predicts that the Soviet Union will pass us in total and per capita production and give the Russian people the world's highest living standards by 1970 or before.

The political goal is to displace the United States as the foremost world power, and, as it always has been, to make the whole world Communist. And the leaders confidently expect to do that too, although the timetable is elastic.

The jolly, agile and able boss, Nikita Khrushchev, talked earnestly about better Russian-American relations and agreed with me that non-interference with other states was a good place to start. But his interpretation seemed to be non-interference by everybody — except the U.S.S.R. And his testy talk about Hungary, Poland and Yugoslavia echoed the stresses and strains in the satellite empire where the peoples have long histories of freedom and independence and are ruled by uneasy minority Communist governments. Russia's satellites in Europe are a perpetual source of insecurity.

And I have no doubt that they will try to eliminate the dangerous free island of West Berlin in the heart of East Germany, because, as Hungary showed, they are resolved to keep their uneasy empire intact.

But internally the Soviet Union appears to be stable, strong, and getting stronger. Khrushchev's Russia is not static. However, for all the developments and changes in industry, agriculture and other fields there is no alteration of the totalitarian structure. And my guess is that Mr. Khrushchev has no intention of presiding over the dissolution of the Soviet dictatorship — not, as he vividly puts it, "until the shrimps whistle." Rather the purpose of these capital repairs on the dictatorship seems to be to modernize and adapt the administrative system to the needs of a dynamic, growing industrial economy, to make the country economically more productive, militarily more powerful, administratively more efficient, more modern in appearance, more normal in atmosphere — and thereby give the dictatorship a new lease on life and strengthen the one-party system.

The Soviet challenge is formidable, and it will be with us for a long time to come. I think they have given up trying to take over the advanced countries, like France and Italy, and the greatest danger is not in Europe but in Asia and Africa. Already Soviet technicians and salesmen have established economic beachheads in many poor countries struggling to develop, and without any military strings attached. The Soviet example of rapid and successful industrialization of an illiterate, backward country has a great attraction for the newly developing people who live like Russian peasants and are demanding a better life. And of course the irrelevance to them of the Soviet example, the brutality of the means and the heavy price in democratic values are not at first apparent.

Five years ago I wrote and have often repeated that Soviet economic growth was "a more important fact than the development of Soviet military power, and to many people in the underdeveloped countries it is the single most impressive fact about the Communist world." And a year ago I urged our government to give economic development equal priority with defense at the NATO meeting in Paris, because if sustained economic growth under democratic auspices fails, people will turn to the Soviet example.

I came away from the Soviet Union more convinced than ever that the battle of the future is economic and political and the major battleground is in Asia and Africa. They are trying to persuade the neutrals to secede from the capitalist system and will exploit to the fullest their enormous appeal as a backward and non-colonial country that has "made good."

There were other disturbing conclusions. Perhaps the single most disturbing thing about Soviet Russia is the ignorance of these friendly, warmhearted people about us.

"Why do you have two parties?" an intelligent ex-schoolteacher and district boss asked me. "Here we are not antagonistic; we all have the same goals; we all work for one another." I said something about the people having a choice of men and measures. "But here," he said, "the Communist party includes the best and knows what's best. So how could there be any question of choice?" It all seemed a little hopeless — especially while careening across the Siberian steppe from mudhole to mudhole.

They know little of our life and motives, most of them, I suspect, sincerely believe that we made the Iron Curtain and for some mysterious reason may attack them at any moment, as the incessant propaganda proclaims. How the ordinary people can continue to be so friendly, hospitable and admiring about America baffles me. Their instincts are good, and it is depressing that they can't know that ours are, too.

It is important, I believe, for us to make every possible effort to lessen their ignorance of our country and its democratic way of life. But likewise we need to study them hard and try by every means for better understanding and deeper appreciation of the conditions of life, attitudes, values and ideas, of the Russian people and their Communist masters. We need to know much more than we do about the mind of this 200,000,000-strong people, who are destined to play a very big part in history and with whom we must hope to live as peaceful neighbors on a shrunken planet. In short, we should do everything we can to increase contact and to encourage Russians to come here and Americans to go there.

Russia is only now emerging from a revolution that stretches far back of the Bolshevik Revolution. What individual freedom under law means is hard for people who have never had it to understand, but it is our most precious possession and we should be proud and eager to exhibit it; besides, it is the best hope for the future.

I wish all the Soviet bosses — the Ministers, the members of the party Presidium and even Mr. Khrushchev himself — could come to this country, because most of them seem to be imprisoned by their own propaganda and laboring under many delusions. Even if they are not deluded, but cynical and insincere, it is harder to be that way after you have come to know something of a country and a people.

My happiest conclusion is that the Russians don't want war any more than we do. The people, who suffered so horribly in the last war, don't want it for obvious reasons; the leaders because it would interrupt their great development program, and because they believe the manifest destiny of Sovietism is to inherit the earth from "decadent capitalism" anyway.

Khrushchev's phrase was "We will bury you." But he did not mean they would kill us first. On the contrary, I concluded that they would use their arms cautiously, knowing from experience that any further expansion by force means war because we would intervene. I suspect they realize, too, that Stalin was the principal architect of NATO because he frightened us.

I wish I felt that our defensive bases in Europe, North Africa and the Middle East did not provide Khrushchev and Co. such a convenient peg for propaganda about America's offensive threat. But while it has been an article of Communist faith that dying capitalism would fight its way out, I also concluded that the Soviet leaders may no longer believe in the inevitability of war. The reasoning is that the Soviet system will be so strong the West won't dare to fight. Even if this vision of a supine, expiring capitalism seems psychotic to us, a change of heart about the inevitability of war would be significant and hopeful.

And there are other encouraging signs. One is the decline in fanaticism. Many of the younger rising Soviet leaders have been trained as engineers and economists and spend their careers in administration. In this new managerial elite, ideology gets more lip service than passion. They are not doctrinaire gamblers and revolutionaries trying to seize power, but realistic practical people trying to make the Soviet system work better. And I think they will be easier to deal with as they replace the older generation of combat Communists.

A related hope is that with economic improvement and better living conditions in Russia we will have more in common and the enmity of inferiority will diminish. With more self-confidence it is not unreasonable to expect that the areas of scientific, economic and political co-operation will broaden and reduce the divisions and tensions. As Russia becomes a modern, industrialized and rich society it will move along a path similar to that traversed by the other industrial societies of the West. It may not be the same path, but, like other nations, Russia, too, must evolve. And we know that in highly developed societies it is not so easy to fool, frighten and mislead the people.

Once Soviet policy and politics focus on economic welfare and the Russian people have a taste of the mass consumer's age (even automobiles!) there will be no turning back from the welfare state and all that implies for Bolshevism as we have known it.

A wise Pole said to me last summer that the changes in Western capitalism and the changes in Soviet Communism are bringing us imperceptibly together in the center. The day is not far distant, he said, when only a few politicians on both sides who are chained to the old semantics will still be talking about two totally opposed worlds.

We laughed together about the prospect of capitalism subverting Communism, and Russian officials struggling with toll roads, suburbia, gas stations and the rest.

But all that is for the future — if not the birds.

Meanwhile the reality is the remorseless Soviet challenge which we have too long ignored and underestimated. They will use their greater flexibility to keep us off balance and on the defensive. They will continue to picture us as menacing and rigid to the Afro-Asian bystanders. They will make agreements only when it serves their purpose. Suspending nuclear tests with inspection is a hopeful possibility and would be the first break in the armaments deadlock. But I am less hopeful of Soviet agreement to larger measures of inspection of their territory because it would tend to convert their closed system into an open one and thus endanger the basis of Soviet control.

While I think the intensity of the Soviet system will decline in time, I see little hope for early change. On the other hand, there is the constant danger that we will fall asleep again.

If we can't do much with Moscow, we can do a lot with ourselves. The free world must set its house in order and keep it in order, and not just sit around, bickering, postponing and waiting for total peace to break out. Moscow will be more likely to talk seriously if the Western alliance is vital and viable, the residual colonial problems being dealt with (while the reality of Soviet imperialism becomes more obvious), and above all the free world making a concerted effort to unite the advanced and retarded areas in common economic enterprises.

I think we must plug patiently away at stopping the arms race, with international supervision, and forego any lingering ideas of military superiority which will only accelerate the arms race. I think it would be most realistic and helpful if we recognized the principle of equality with the Soviet Union. And we should always be ready to talk with them at all levels, but with little hope of quick success. Time is of no importance to them, as it is of no importance to Orientals, and the hope is that little by little we can break away from the concept of each other as the enemy and reduce fear and distrust.

I have seen the Russians close up. They are tough, fearful and going places. But they are also very human and friendly. Their hopes and desires are for peace — and an apartment. The leaders are scornful of "capitalism," yet even Khrushchev wants to attain the American standard of living more than anything else. And we still have the supreme advantage of living under the system most people want if they can get it and afford it.

This should give us calm and final confidence.

On August 8, 1958, the Stevenson party left Moscow for Warsaw. His diary of the trip follows.

Aug 8 — To Warsaw
    . . . *Farewells, press statement, champagne at airport. Warsaw — freer feeling, civilized people, tension lower. 90% destroyed,*[104] *gripping*

104 During World War II.

*motion picture of destruction by city arch[itect]. who showed us in-
credible ruins & great recovery — Rebuilding as was! Still Police State.
[William] At[t]woods waiting after auto trip behind Iron-Curtain. I
have Paderewski's*[105] *suite in Bristol [Hotel] which he owned! Long
talk with Rapacki*[106] *at office, also lunch party. Dinner with Ambassador
[Jacob] Beam. Concert at Chopin's birthplace 50 Km West. Cocktail
party by press. Interviews with leaders, but Gomulka,*[107] *the boss, out of
town on holidays. Great improvement since 1956 — and advent of
Gomulka; agri[culture] de-collectivized; private trading restored. Many
small private shops in Warsaw.*

Execution places all over — fresh flowers, names of victims[108] *on
plaques. Don't like ancient enemies — Russians; Hate Germans! East
Ger. "our insurance."*

*Went to a Russian circus; presented surgical instruments for CARE
at fine orthopedic hospital — inspection. Ghetto — memorable reminder
of horrible massacre of ½ million Jews. Want more U.S. credits — without
declarations of anti-communism & USSR that make acceptance dangerous. Ambassador discouraged my trying to see Cardinal Wyzsinski.*[109]
*No doubt Church influence too great for any modern state. Churches
on Sunday jammed. (Tank battle took place in ruins of cathedral —
now restored). Most catholic country in Europe.*

*While in Poland, Stevenson wrote his law partner Joseph Iseman,
reporting on his talks with Soviet officials about the payment of royalties
to American writers.*

To Joseph Iseman

August 11, 1958

Dear Joe:

We are in Poland at long last but this letter may not get mailed until
we reach Prague. I believe that Bill Blair has already sent you a sum-

[105] Ignace Jan Paderewski, pianist and prime minister of Poland, 1919.

[106] Foreign Minister Adam Rapacki.

[107] Wladyslaw Gomulka, who had become first secretary of the Polish Communist
Party at the time of the 1956 crisis in Soviet-Polish relations, when he won a
number of concessions giving Poland greater independence from Russian control
and established a greater degree of internal freedom, while avoiding the armed
conflict that had resulted from the revolt in Hungary.

[108] Of the Germans during World War II.

[109] Stefan Cardinal Wyszynski, Roman Catholic primate of Poland, who had been
imprisoned from 1953 to 1956 as a result of his anti-Communist stance and the
hostility of the Polish government to the Church. He was released eight days after
Gomulka came to power.

mary of my first conversation with Mr. Mikhailov. I am enclosing a summary of further discussions we had on my return to Moscow from Siberia. I was irked no end by my talks with the Minister and issued a statement, copy of which I am enclosing, in Moscow on the evening of August 7. A few minutes later I went to a farewell party which was given for me by Mr. Z[h]ukov, Chairman of the Committee on Cultural Relations. Present at the party was Mr. Sobolof,[110] head of the Writers Union of the Russian Republic — a very influential man whom I had met a few nights before. He was cordial in the extreme as in our previous meetings and was fully informed about what had happened. He was very conciliatory and eager to reassure me that the matter of royalties was not dead. He made repeated long speeches about "starting fresh," "beginning again," "wiping the slate clean" and similar expressions, and in response to an inquiry as to how I felt about such things, I said it sounded to me like a repudiation of accumulated indebtedness. He said that indebtedness could never be ascertained and that many Russians as well as Americans had never been paid. He said that he did not like the word "repudiate" and I said that I didn't like the word "cancellation" but that if that was the best they could do we would consider the matter of course — still I could hardly believe that Russian writers could feel comfortable with such a solution. He said in very good humor that perhaps we could start *almost* over and go back part way if not all the way. He asked me if I would write him about all this and I promised to.

I am confident that Sobolof was acting with authority and this undoubtedly puts the matter in a brighter light than my statement left it. Please consider what sort of a letter or proposal we could make, given the situation, and we can talk about it on my return to New York Sept. 8.

I am strongly under the impression that we touched a deep and sensitive cord and that they want to do something both to clean up the account and to restore respect among intellectuals as well as to encourage the publication of Soviet works abroad. But to make good for past royalties is probably beyond either their means or intention. So perhaps you will have to come up with some logical commencement date in recent years.

Hastily,

Aug. 12

Motored to Crakow — 3 cars and bus with luggage! — Lovely rolling country — intense cultivation, grain and dairy. Crakow for lunch with Prof of history from ancient Univ. & Mayor. Delightful Prof — 4th

[110] Leonid S. Sobolev.

generation of teachers at the Univ. — guided us about fascinating ancient city — castle, churches, tombs, square, galleries (fine small Leonardo removed by Germans, restored by Americans) and 14 Century Univ. including Dr. Faustus laboratory — complete with dried cat chasing dried mouse and the devil's hand print on ancient door. Prof. — "Poland is half free." Alicia [Patterson] & boys drove to Aus[c]hwitz to see death camp — Dicks[111] *& [Robert] Tucker & I drove on to Zakopane in high Swiss like Tatras in time for finicular [funicular] ride to mountain top & splendid view.*

Aug. 13 —
   On to Prague — long delay at border & then at lovely hotel in high pass at noon discovered it would take 10 hrs more to Prague! Revolted! and eager Czech deputy minister of foreign trade staying in hotel — arranged for airplane to come to pick us up. Thus ended the motor trip — thank God. Greeted in Prague at 4:30 by usual officials and John Allison — U.S. Amb[assador]. and old friend who took boys & me to stay in Embassy — most elaborate and absurd U.S. Embassy in world! Private house of coal magnate — indoor swimming pool govt. has never filled. A little sight-seeing of [illegible] Prague — and marvellous view from chancellery garden. Staff dinner party at Embassy. No govt. interviews — P.M. away, F.M. at [UN] Gen[eral] Ass[embly]. in N.Y. & Pres. afraid to see me in absence of his rival the P.M. Czechs — docile, submissive compared to Poles. Highest standard of living in E. Europe. Great Palace of kings of Bohemia, "street of alchemists" — medieval remnants.

   Off to Zurich by Swiss air at 11:30 — beautiful flight. Changed at Zurich — with help of Federal Counsellor, Municipal & airport & consular officials! Can I ever be alone? (And how will I like it when I am!) Boys stayed in Prague with the group at Ambassadors & I arranged for them to go on to see Vienna en route to Buffy [Ives] at Florence. . . .

   Bern, spic, span, prosperous — my rooms at Bellevue Palace overlook the river and on horizon are the Jungfrau, the Eiger, the Monch etc — now dazzling white, now pink, now wreathed in pastel clouds.

To Mrs. Ronald Tree[112]

August 14, 1958
Arrived here this PM via Warsaw, Cracow, Slovakia & Prague. Some

111 Mr. and Mrs. Edison Dick had joined the group in Moscow.
112 This handwritten letter is in the possession of Mrs. Tree.

clutch of intelligentsia gathered — and how tiresome all the talk has become! I feel like a soldier just out of trenches at a university seminar on war, or is it peace? Can't escape before Monday; then to Italia after a visit with Andre Meyer[113] at Gstaad re. business. . . .

Here must sit and talk, stand and speak and write two articles re. R[ussia] & K[hrushchev] to meet early deadline. There –??

Lines from Moscow – A-bomb age – 1958.

> At midnight in the music Hall
> The fossils gathered for a ball
> Amid the mastodonic wassail,
> I caught the eye of one small fossil:
> "Cheer up, sad world," he said and winked;
> "It's kind of fun to be extinct."[114]
>
> IVAN THE TIRED

August 14-18 — Bern —

Mostly locked in rooms writing Krushchev articles with help of Bob Tucker who came with me from Prague — and attending some of sessions of "working party" on relaxing tensions arranged by Paul Hoffman.[115] Good group — [G. L.] Mehta, former Indian amb[assador]. to U.S. presided — and proposals agreed after 3 days of talk and sub-committee drafting were good, if not original, and I felt candid talk about one another and what "non-interference" means would have been more useful. Suspect Paul Hoffman will pick up this idea — he loves meetings and travel! On Saturday night I had to talk to a group about Russia. On Sunday "World Brotherhood" Conference people began to arrive — . . . and I had to conclude the speaking. . . .

Monday — Aug. 18 —

First article finished and mailed, second almost finished; speeches finished, thank God. Andre Meyer sent Geiger, "the hero of Switz," alpine reserve pilot over to pick me up and fly me across the breathtaking mountains to Sion for lunch at his chalet high up at Crans. Madame de Murville, Editor & owner of Journal de Geneve & the Meyers quiet, modest, brilliant scientist son & charming, dignified Chilean wife were there. After marvellous lunch, talk about Russia.

---

[113] Senior partner of Lazard Frères & Company, one of Stevenson's clients.

[114] These lines are an adaptation of the poem "Next!" from Ogden Nash, *The Private Dining Room and Other New Verses* (Boston: Little, Brown, 1953), copyright 1953 by Ogden Nash, and are used here by permission.

[115] Chairman of the board of Hoffman Specialty Manufacturing Company and former chairman of the board of Studebaker-Packard Corporation.

Some business talk re Allied Bldg. Credits. I flew back from Sion in the valley below with baskets of fruit presented by Mayor etc to Bern in time to catch train for Florence.

Beautiful ride threading thru Alpine passes in twilight to Brig — changed trains, ghastly night on wagon lit. Up at 5:30 — Firenze. Ernest [Ives], the U.S. Consul, Mr. [Samuel W.] Lewis, & USIA John Stoddard & police commissioner to meet me.

Aug. 19 — 24 — Florence — *and the beautiful 15th century Capponi villa high on the hill called Arcetri crowned with Gallileo's tower — and golden Firenze beneath the terraced gardens, olive groves and cypress walled pool. Buffy in heaven, at last — and why not! Borden & JF already here. John & Margaret Farwell[116] arrived in evening.*

A week of sightseeing, wining, dining & work in Florence.

Day with PM — Amintore Fanfani at Camaldoli — (Report to State Dept on long talk with this forceful man). Ancient Monastery.

Lunch at Valambroso with Bernard Berensen[117] — caustic about Eisenhower — Chairman of Charm School — distrusts Generals & Military heroes — have learned to reconcile conflicting views for a single simple purpose — win war. Politics & govt. much more. Delightful talk about Harvard, Education — "Intellectuals of the world arise — unite." Very feeble — 93 — tended by famous Nicky Mariano[118] & his sister from Santa B—— [illegible].

Aug 25

Flew to Nice by way of Rome for visit at Villa Fiorentina — Lady Kenmore's beautiful place at end of Cap Jean — with Mary Lasker. Borden joined later; also John Fell drove his new Mercedes down from Stuttgart on way to visit Karim Kahn [Khan] at Cannes. [J.F. gets $10 000 for his Russian pictures, or $6 000 net!)[119]

To Paris — *Sat. Aug 30 for business and reunion at Ritz. Saw [Charles] De Gaulle for long visit, lunched with Couve de Murville,[120] F. M. [Foreign Minister] Guy Mollet. Saw Mendes-France,[121] hordes of journalists etc. De Gaulle impressed me! Very candid.*

[116] Friends of Stevenson's from Chicago.

[117] Bernard Berenson, art critic and author.

[118] Mr. Berenson's longtime companion until his death in 1959.

[119] John Fell had arranged to sell the photographs he took on the trip to Russia to Magnum Photos.

[120] Maurice Couve de Murville, French ambassador to the Federal Republic of Germany.

[121] Former Prime Minister Pierre Mendès-France.

Much political talk — as usual in Paris.

. . . Business done, left with Stanley Woodward, Bill Blair & John Fell on

Saturday, Sept. 6 — *for Algiers en route to Hassi-Mess[a]oud oil fields in Sahara as guest of Compagnie Francaise des Petroles.*[122]

Occupied same room in St. George Hotel where I presented my credentials from FDR, Frank Knox and Henry Stimson to Gen Bedell Smith, Ike's chief of Staff in Oct. 1943.[123] *The past rose before me like a dream — for here Ellen & I also stayed just 30 yrs ago — 1928 — on our wedding trip.*

Sunday Sept. 7

Flew with Co. officials 700 km into the desert to Hassi-Messoud — a field that promises to rival W. Texas. Great achievement; Tommy gunners as everywhere in Algiers. Heat! Food! Swimming pool at camp; close barbed wire at night. Air conditioned, portable house. Visited installations — camel snubbed me!

Monday Sept. 8

Flew to oasis of Gardaia [Ghardaïa] where M'Zabites have lived since 1000. Fascinating towns in cruel, rubble desert. On to Touggourt end of great date palm gardens stretching 125 km to Biskra. Beginning of rail line to Mediterranean. Saw beginning of 24" pipeline to link up Hassi-Messoud field and sea.

On to Algiers where I had talk with General Salan[124] — *who remembered our visit to Indo-China. Optimistic about revolt; "Tunisian border now closed." I wonder!*

To N.Y. with John Fell by TWA that night — and so ends 3 months of almost incessant travel thru England, Belgium, Denmark, Norway, Sweden, Finland, USSR, Poland, Czechoslovakia, Switzerland, Italy, France, Algeria — and if I missed anything or anyone — well I'm almost glad! How tired I am! — and now the accumulation of months at home — and Lucy Wallace Stevenson!

---

[122] Stevenson was investigating possible investment opportunities for a client.

[123] See *The Papers of Adlai E. Stevenson*, Vol. II, p. 169.

[124] General Raoul Salan, who had been French commander in chief in Indochina, 1952–1953. For Stevenson's visit to Vietnam and Cambodia in April, 1953, see *The Papers of Adlai E. Stevenson*, Vol. V, Part Seven.

Part Four

The Moral Challenge

S tevenson wrote out in longhand the following statements for a press
conference held on his arrival in New York City, September 9, 1958.

New York I think A H [Averell Harriman] has been a good Governor
and I am confident that he will be reelected.

It is no secret that with Mayor [Robert] Wagner unavailable, I was
for Tom F[inletter] for Senate, He offered N.Y. an unusual opportunity
to send a man of distinguished qualifications to the Senate at this critical
time.

But Mr. [Frank] Hogan has had an excellent [record] as District
attorney and I have no doubt will make a fine senator.

Campaign — I hope to be as active as possible. But after 3 months away
I will have to first pay attention to the accumulation of personal and
professional work that awaits me.

There have been many invitations to speak and I hardly know what
my obligations are. I know that I am going to Calif the end of the
month to do what I can for the Dem. ticket.

Far East — *China* I donot care to talk about Quemoy & Matsu.[1] I
expressed some views about them in a speech to the Am[erican] people
when the crisis first arose 3 years ago[2] and on the basis of my limited
information my views are unchanged.

But I don't believe we can talk about them any longer apart from
Formosa itself because Comm[un]ist China has made it clear that its

[1] The People's Republic of China had begun a heavy bombardment of these off-
shore islands near Taiwan on August 23, 1958. On August 28, President Eisenhower
called the islands more important than three years earlier to the defense of Taiwan
and ordered additional warships to the area, while Secretary of State Dulles announced a week later that U.S. forces would help defend the islands if necessary.
On September 7, U.S. ships escorted a Nationalist convoy carrying supplies to
Quemoy; the Communists withheld their fire.

[2] See Stevenson's speech of April 11, 1955, in *The Papers of Adlai E. Stevenson*,
Vol. IV, pp. 468–476.

objective is to capture Formosa and the little islands are only incidental to that.

To use force to accomplish its purpose does violence to the UN charter and to all modern concepts of international intercourse. This, however, was Comm[un]ist China's method in Korea and appears to be its purpose again.

Nor has Comm[un]ist China a good legal title to Formosa which was Japanese before the war, not Chinese.

A very dangerous situation which calls for negotiation, not violence. Unhappily the Chinese have disclosed no disposition to negotiate.

Whether these little islands so close to the China mainland ever should have been occupied and defended as part of Formosa is hardly relevant now. The U.S. can and must fulfill its commitments.

Stevenson arrived back in Chicago on September 12, 1958.

To Leonid Sobolev

September 12, 1958

Dear Mr. Sobolev:

Upon my return to the United States, I write you to recall our meetings in Moscow and your suggestions at the delightful farewell party Mr. [Yuri] Zhukov gave me.

I have conveyed to the Authors League of America my impression that Soviet writers (and in particular yourself!) would like to see this situation which has caused such unhappiness among American authors, dramatists and intellectuals resolved. And I am taking advantage of your suggestion, that I write you if some other basis of settlement seems possible to us.

I recall your observation that it might be difficult to compute the royalties due to American writers in the U.S.S.R., and to Soviet writers in the U.S.A., for publications and dramatic performances which have already taken place.

I have reviewed this matter, since my return, with the Authors League of America, and I am confident that the League could make a prompt and accurate computation of any royalties due to Soviet writers from the major American publishing houses. Instances of unpaid royalties are few, and in several cases, at least, I am informed that royalties have been set aside for payment to the Soviet authors as soon as there is agreement on payments to American writers for use of their works in the U.S.S.R. I believe that such a computation would be sufficiently precise for all practical purposes.

As for the computation of Soviet royalties due to American authors, I believe that the matter is also not as difficult as might at first appear. Much of the information (derived from *Knizhnaya Letopis*, and other Soviet sources) is available in this country, and is set forth in the appendices to my memorandum of June 14, 1958, and the supplement of July 7, 1958, which I submitted to the Ministry of Culture prior to my visit. (It occurs to me that you and the other members of the RSFSR Writers Union may be interested in reading that memorandum, and I am accordingly sending you a copy under separate cover.) However, in view of the widespread use of American works in the U.S.S.R., and the fact that Soviet royalties have only rarely been paid to American writers and on no ascertainable basis of computation, I recognize that the task of compiling what is due to each author might still be difficult.

But I am without specific authority to make any proposal other than that set out in my memorandum. Nonetheless, in view of the practical difficulties mentioned above, I would like to explore with you the possibility of an agreement in principle as to some date as of which the royalty obligation on both sides would be deemed to have commenced. I suggest that August 14, 1945, the date of the termination of hostilities in World War II, which initiated a new chapter in the relations between the U.S.A. and the U.S.S.R., after a long period of comradeship in arms, would be an appropriate date from which to commence our royalty understanding.

I will await with great interest an expression of your reaction to this suggestion. If it is favorable, I would recommend it promptly and it might well be that we could reach a solution of this vexatious situation quickly, at least in principle.

Finally, as you doubtless know, John Hersey and Bruce Catton, two friends of mine, and of William Faulkner, all of whom are distinguished American writers, are going to visit the U.S.S.R. soon. I am apprising Mr. Hersey, who is a member of the Executive Council of the Authors League of America, of my talks with you on the subject of royalties.

I shall long remember my happy visits with you in Moscow, and I wish there was going to be a return visit here. Why not? But let's get this publication royalty business worked out first, and please bear in mind that all we are asking for is equal treatment — our publishers treat your authors like any foreign authors, and you, in turn, treat Americans just as you would an author in the Soviet Union writing in some language other than Russian.

With best wishes to Mrs. Sobolev, I am

Cordially yours,

To Walter Lippmann[3]

September 12, 1958

Dear Walter:

I am just back from a too long journey and must hurriedly thank you for months of enlightened writing which enabled me to struggle through every press conference from Siberia to the Sahara. And now we have Quemoy again and, as usual, I must thank you again for putting perspective in the picture.

In this connection someone in New York urged me to send you a copy of a speech I made in April 1955 — when things were just the same!

Affectionate regards to Helen. . . .[4]

Yours,
ADLAI

Alicia Patterson published articles on the trip to the Soviet Union in Newsday, *September 10, 11 and 12, 1958.*

September 12, 1958

Dear Alicia:

I hear your articles are great, and I am ashamed that you got ahead of me, but I should have foreseen that. Come to the Desplaines as soon as you can.

As though Siberia and the Sahara were not enough I now have Quemoy coming at me from all quarters. I was reminded of a speech I made in 1955 on this same subject, which still seems pertinent. Maybe you will be interested in it.

Love,

To Robert W. Dowling[5]

September 15, 1958

Dear Bob:

My son, John Fell, has reported to me his interview with you in New York, thanks to Roger Stevens, about that remarkable hydrofoil boat on which we traveled on the Volga. While I know nothing of the develop-

[3] The original is in the Lippmann papers, Yale University Library.
[4] Mrs. Lippmann.
[5] President of City Investing Company of New York City.

ment of similar craft in this country, I think the one we were on has great potential for transportation, especially on our rivers and sheltered waters, not to mention its potential value for recreation. John Fell said you wanted the name of the engineer: Rostislav E. Alexeev, Krasny, Sornovo Shipbuilding Yards, Gorky, U.S.S.R.

Alexeev is a large, agreeable and enthusiastic man, and has been working on this boat, I believe he said for fifteen or twenty years. The principle is, of course, the same as the air cushion created by an airplane wing.

John Fell plans to be back in New York this week and seems to be more concerned with promoting this boat than getting a permanent job! Or maybe he thinks they are the same thing, and perhaps they should be. Certainly it fascinated me, and I am sure it won't be long before somebody exploits the idea in this country. I shall be glad to talk to you about it.

With all good wishes to you, I am

Cordially yours,

Chester Bowles wrote that after losing the Connecticut senatorial nomination to Thomas Dodd, partly as a result of the candidacy of William Benton, he had decided to run for the House of Representatives. He added: "Many of the proposals that you made are now being adopted by the Administration, but late in the day and with their usual clumsiness." He urged Stevenson to speak out sharply on the Administration's errors on Quemoy and Matsu.

To Chester Bowles

September 15, 1958

Dear Chet:

I was delighted to find your letter on my return and touched that you took the time to write me in such detail about that horrible business in Connecticut. Somehow this seems to me the worst of our party's failures, and the circumstances of you and Bill being involved make it even worse. I'm sure that for the future peace of mind of both of you, *that* situation *must* be restored.

I was delighted to get the news abroad that you have decided to run for Congress, and I am not surprised to hear that you are running like hell already! May I send you the enclosed check as a very modest expression of my enthusiasm? I shall try to get some more. I am sure that you can be enormously helpful in the House, where the paucity of foreign policy intelligence is obvious.

I have been baffled as to what to say about Quemoy, beyond the misgivings expressed at every airport I have passed through in the last two weeks. In April 1955 I made a nationwide speech which I have just reread, and which says all the right things. But I hesitate to jump in again now, and the Administration appears to be so far committed, it may have negotiations afoot about which I am not informed. Anyway, I am sure you are right to hit it constantly.

I yearn to see you and Steb.[6]

Yours,

To Robert C. Tucker

September 22, 1958

Dear Bob:

Enclosed are the two texts I have prepared. As might be expected, I have been delayed on the trade and aid piece and will try to send you that tomorrow. Please telephone any corrections on these to me at the office (Financial 6-5180) collect.

I enclose the list of articles as I have given them — tentatively to NANA.[7]

I promised them 6, 7 and 8 by mid-October or before, and the balance before the end of the month. I will work on your drafts 6 and 7 when conditions permit, but conditions are awful, and aggravated by this damned Congressional campaign and necessary commitments there. You are a friend in need!

Does Russia have some former Chinese territory which could be a source of trouble between them? If so, should I mention that point in the first paragraph, page 5, of #4?

Sincerely,

Simon and Schuster, the publishers of Washington Post cartoonist Herblock's forthcoming book, asked Stevenson to write a statement about it.

[6] Mrs. Bowles.
[7] The North American Newspaper Alliance, which syndicated Stevenson's articles.

To Nina Bourne

September 25, 1958

Dear Miss Bourne:

You may say this, or any part of it for me:

"Herb Block's *Special For Today* ought to be required reading — except that would take the immense fun out of it. This man isn't just funny; every time he tickles our funnybone he stiffens our backbone. His sense of humor is knowing what has to be taken seriously and what (and who) shouldn't be. Everything he says makes good common sense, and uncommon good reading."

And tell the author for me that he writes even better than he draws — which is the highest compliment I can think of.

Cordially yours,

Walter Lippmann wrote that he had just read Stevenson's April 11, 1955, speech on Quemoy and Matsu. "I did not realize until I reread it this morning how perfectly clear the problem was to you away back in 1955. One of the notions it leaves in my mind is the wonder as to whether the Democratic leaders in Congress have done their full duty as an opposition party." He added that he and Mrs. Lippmann were about to visit Moscow.

To Walter Lippmann[8]

September 25, 1958

Dear Walter:

Thanks for your note about that Quemoy speech back in 1955. And I wonder if the opposition in our society can ever really do its duty in the foreign affairs field when the ignorance is always so great and the initiative always with the Executive.

Have a good time in Moscow. You will find a warm welcome awaiting you; and I hope we can have a talk shortly after you return.

Best to you and Helen.[9]

Sincerely yours,
ADLAI

[8] The original is in the Lippmann papers, Yale University Library.
[9] Mrs. Lippmann.

Ralph McGill, editor of the Atlanta Constitution, *printed excerpts from Stevenson's April 11, 1955, speech on Quemoy and Matsu in the issue of September 23, 1958, and commented: "It is tragic that the nation has not had the intelligence, experience and understanding of Adlai Stevenson in some high place of government decision. . . . In 1955 and 1956 the nation wasn't ready to listen to common sense. It wanted to be reassured that all was well. And the fact that the 'impractical man' of 1955 is revealed today as perhaps the most practical thinker among the nation's political leaders heartens his friends, but reminds us of the melancholy fact that he is, incredible though it is, a crying in the wilderness."*

To Ralph McGill[10]

September 25, 1958

Dear Ralph:

A friend in Atlanta has sent me your column about my 1955 speech — and my self-esteem has risen dangerously! Thanks for resurrecting it. I think it is probably good for people to realize sometimes how we slip into unfortunate situations so heedlessly and in spite of better counsel.

But what do we do *now?*

Yours,
ADLAI

On September 30, 1958, Stevenson flew to California to campaign for the Democratic ticket. He campaigned there for five days. In Los Angeles on September 30, Stevenson said in a speech delivered at a fund-raising dinner for Congressman Clair Engle that the United States should defend Formosa but had no business fighting for Quemoy and Matsu. Vice President Nixon, who was campaigning in California for the Republican ticket, called Stevenson's statement "well intentioned, but unrealistic and unworkable." Nixon added: "The major test of success of a foreign policy is — does it keep the peace with honor?"[11]

Mrs. Eugene Meyer wrote Stevenson that she was sad that his Los Angeles speech received so little publicity, but she accounted for it by his not releasing it on time for the East Coast papers. She added, "Yours is the only influential voice in the opposition."

---

[10] The original is in the possession of Mrs. Ralph McGill.
[11] Chicago *Tribune*, October 1, 1958.

To Mrs. Eugene Meyer[12]

October 7, 1958

Dear Agnes:

I am just back from California and find your letter of October 2. By this time I trust you have received the full text of the speech I made in California. I am also distressed that it had so little publicity. I worked on it somewhat more than usual and tried to make it affirmative and programmatic as well as critical. From much I heard this summer I have come to the conclusion that China is and will be a larger problem for us than the Soviet Union, and thus far we have handled it with appalling ineptitude. Moreover, this speech was available in the morning here in Chicago of the day that I delivered it in Los Angeles, which was certainly "on time."

You know I would rather come out to Mt. Kisco than anything I can think of, but I am afraid it will be impossible that weekend because I must speak in Milwaukee for the Democrats on the night of the 18th and am planning now to return here on the 15th. This whole trip is only for Tom Finletter's benefit.[13]

Affectionately,

ADLAI

P.S. . . .

Benjamin Swig, owner of the Fairmont Hotel in San Francisco, advised Stevenson regularly on investments.

To Benjamin F. Swig[14]

October 10, 1958

Dear Ben:

While in San Francisco you told me about a building you and your associates were purchasing in Washington and suggested that I participate in the group providing the equity capital.

I have reviewed my situation on my return from California and I am

[12] The original is in the Agnes Meyer files, Princeton University Library.
[13] Mr. Finletter had organized a committee to support Governor Harriman and senatorial candidate Frank S. Hogan. Stevenson was to speak at a fund-raising affair in New York.
[14] The original is in the possession of Mr. Swig.

enclosing my check to your "Clients' Fund" for $25,000 for this purpose. In due course please send me the documents evidencing my participation, and also whatever data is available on the building for my files.

I am grateful for your thought in this connection. It was good to see you again and to find you as animated and lively as ever.

Cordially yours,

ADLAI

Stevenson campaigned in New York on October 14, spoke at a fund-raising dinner for Chester Bowles, and visited with Mrs. Franklin D. Roosevelt, Walter Lippmann and Allen Dulles, the director of the Central Intelligence Agency. He also did some legal work before he returned to Chicago on October 16. On October 18 he spoke at a labor rally for the Democratic ticket in Milwaukee. Among other things, he said: "The tragedy of the Eisenhower Administration is that its only weapons seem to be platitudes or paratroops. And this seems to be true whether the situation is Little Rock or Lebanon, South America or Quemoy." After the Milwaukee speech, Stevenson spoke at a number of Democratic rallies in Chicago, and on November 1 he addressed a rally in Minneapolis for senatorial candidate Eugene McCarthy and gubernatorial candidate Orville Freeman.

To Harry S. Truman

October 20, 1958

Dear Mr. President:

I expect to be in Kansas City on November 20 to speak at the annual meeting of the National Association for Mental Health. The following morning I hope to satisfy my long standing desire to see the [Truman] Library — and its founder if you are to be in Independence at that time.

Margaret and her very attractive husband[15] came out for luncheon with me in Libertyville not long ago and we laughed and laughed, regardless of the Chinese, the Russians — and the Republicans!

With warm wishes to you and Mrs. Truman, I am

Cordially,

P.S. I think your speeches have been effective, and I marvel at your endurance!

15 Mr. Truman's daughter had married Clifton Daniel, of the New York *Times*.

To Mrs. Eugene Meyer[16]

October 23, 1958

Dear Agnes;

"Science and the Democratic System"[17] has just landed on my desk. How the hell do you do it! I struggle around with my wretched speeches and nothing much happens, and look at you.

I was in New York for a couple of days (imagine my raising money for [Averell] Harriman!), but they had me loaded with chores and there was no time to call you, let alone come out to Mount Kisco which I wanted very much to do.

There is much to talk about. However, I shall be nailed here until the end of November when I will probably go East again, but I suppose by that time you will be in Washington.

Do let me hear from you. I miss your letters — even if I don't answer them.

Affectionately,
ADLAI

Earl Mazo, who had interviewed Stevenson for a book he was writing about Vice President Nixon,[18] asked for permission to quote him as follows: "1. (Your antipathy toward Nixon) '. . . goes to lots of things — to Voorhis,[19] to Helen Douglas,[20] to the horrors of his 1952 campaign . . . to his exploitation (of issues) by emotion, by propagandizing and by passion, which offends everything his office stands for.'

"2. 'Nixon's change in tactics and methods in the campaigns between 1952 and 1956 was conspicuous, but it was mostly technical. He has not stopped distorting issues or demeaning his office.'

"3. (Nixon's use of the Stevenson deposition in the Hiss case was) 'vile and contemptible, and obviously intended to mislead.'

"4. 'The idea of Nixon being a candidate for President of the United States is something I find hard to face.'"

[16] The original is in the Agnes Meyer files, Princeton University Library.

[17] An address delivered by Mrs. Meyer before the forty-fourth annual conference of the Michigan Welfare League in Detroit, October 23, 1958.

[18] *Richard Nixon: A Political and Personal Portrait* (New York: Harper, 1959).

[19] Former Representative Jerry Voorhis, of California, whom Mr. Nixon defeated in 1946.

[20] Former Representative Helen Gahagan Douglas, of California, whom Mr. Nixon defeated for U.S. Senator in 1950.

[299]

To Earl Mazo

October 23, 1958

Dear Earl:

Could we just settle for the following quotes? I think you know how distasteful this personality talk is to me, and in our talk evidently my grammar was as bad as my English!

3. (Nixon's use of the Stevenson deposition in the Hiss case was) "vile and contemptible and obviously intended to mislead. Moreover, I think it is the duty of everyone, especially lawyers, to give honest testimony in a court of law when called upon to do so. To decline to do so for fear the defendant might ultimately be found guilty is contemptible timidity and would corrupt the judicial process."

4. "The idea of Nixon being a candidate for President of the United States, the most exalted office on earth, is something I find hard to believe possible."

Sincerely,

Mrs. Eugene Meyer wrote Stevenson that she had just talked with Walter Reuther, who stated that Stevenson was the best choice for the 1960 nomination.

To Mrs. Eugene Meyer[21]

October 28, 1958

My dear Agnes:

Thanks for your letter. I'm glad the pipeline is flowing again! I hope I can have a talk with Reuther before long. I share your admiration — but not his choice for that awful chore!

I have been campaigning a bit here and there and also trying to finish up my wretched articles on Russia. Together with occasional interruptions to practice a little law, it has been a difficult month and I hope for better things after the election. And the best would be a visit with you! . . .

Affectionately,
ADLAI

---

21 The original is in the Agnes Meyer files, Princeton University Library.

To Arthur Schlesinger, Jr.

November 4, 1958

Dear Arthur:

Thank you so much for the material you sent for the Minneapolis speech, and you will note that I used some of it. The occasion was happy, boisterous and typical Minnesota. By the time [Orville] Freeman, [Hubert] Humphrey and [Eugene] McCarthy had all introduced me and each other and the Negro bands had paraded, the radio-TV time was gone. So everything was as usual. But the speech seemed suitable for the audience and I hope you find merit in it.

I share your views about McCarthy. He is undoubtedly one of the rare ones, and God knows they are rare. . . .

Love to Marian.[22]

Yours,

P.S. . . .

To Eugene Burdick[23]

November 4, 1958

Dear Bud:

You were awfully good to send me *The Ugly American*,[24] which I have already dipped into and keep in three rooms in my house so that I can proudly say to my guests "I know the guy." And now I can put an autographed copy in the guest room — and what an autograph!

Thank you, Sir; and affectionate regards to that lovely and charitable Carol.[25]

Cordially yours,

Philip Noel-Baker, a member of Parliament with whom Stevenson had worked during the formation of the United Nations, wrote that he expected to visit Premier Khrushchev soon and asked Stevenson what Khrushchev had said to him about disarmament.

---

[22] Mrs. Schlesinger.

[23] Author and associate professor of political theory at the University of California at Berkeley.

[24] Eugene L. Burdick and William J. Lederer, *The Ugly American* (New York: Norton, 1958).

[25] Mrs. Burdick.

To Philip Noel-Baker

November 5, 1958

Dear Philip:

I was so glad to have your letter and the Labor Party policy statement which I shall read with much interest.

I made a calculated decision *not* to talk about disarmament with Khrushchev or the other principals in Moscow. My reason was, of course, that the answers were reasonably foreseeable unless I was to give the matter much of the interview time at the expense of other items where his public views have been less audible.

I shall be much interested in what you uncover at your meeting with him in December.

It is always a comfort to know that you are busy and bold.

Cordially yours,

The Democrats increased their margin of control in both houses of Congress in the November 4 election. Stevenson sent a number of telegrams to victorious congressional candidates, including George McGovern and Kenneth Hechler. To Senator John F. Kennedy, who was overwhelmingly reelected, Stevenson wired: "You only got what you deserved. Congratulations and warmest regards." Congressman Brooks Hays of Arkansas, however, was defeated by a segregationist.

To Brooks Hays[26]

November 6, 1958

I have been hoping and hoping for better news from Little Rock. It never occurred to me that this was possible, and I feel injured and indignant. The Congress won't be the same without such wise counsel in our foreign affairs and such understanding of the great problems that confront us at home, including race relations on which your views commanded wider respect than most anyone.

But you won't be idle long, and I am confident that your service to your country and your fellow man is in no wise impaired by the election.

Respectfully and affectionately yours,

[26] A telegram.

The Palos Verdes Peninsula Democratic Club wired Stevenson on November 4: "Six years ago the Palos Verdes Peninsula Democratic Club was organized by a small group of your admirers who gathered to watch your campaign on TV. This evening we are celebrating California victory and our club's sixth birthday party. While our candidates have won there are many of us who feel that the real victory belongs to you for it was your candidacy which gave us the inspiration to join together to work for the Democratic party. We wish to salute you as the inspiration for the clubs which have brought about the Calif swing to the Democratic party."

To the Palos Verdes Peninsula Democratic Club

November 7, 1958

My dear friends:

I just want you to know how much I appreciate that very kind and thoughtful wire — and I feel well rewarded if my campaigns played any part at all in building Democratic strength in California.

I am profoundly grateful.

Cordially yours,

To Mrs. Franklin D. Roosevelt[27]

November 14, 1958

Dear Mrs. Roosevelt:

I understand that two young friends of mine, Norman Ross and David McElroy, have invited you to appear on their television program V.I.P. here in Chicago on Sunday evening, December 14.

The only purpose of this letter is to say that I have known both of these gentlemen for some time and think very well of them and their program. As a matter of fact, I am appearing myself on V.I.P. on the 23rd of this month.

The interview is conducted by Mr. Ross who is an extremely alert and intelligent young man. He has traveled extensively abroad and returned only recently from a trip around the world under the auspices of CARE.

I know you will be here on Monday, December 15, for the dinner of the U.N. Universal Declaration of Human Rights and it occurred to me that if you were coming in the night before and were willing to appear on this program, you might like to know that you would be among friends — and great admirers!

With every good wish, I am

Sincerely yours,

ADLAI

[27] The original is in the Franklin D. Roosevelt Library, Hyde Park, New York.

To William Benton[28]

November 17, 1958

Dear Bill:

Thanks, old man, for the new Encyclopaedia [*Britannica*]. I was getting along fine with the old one until you reminded me that it *was* old. But I won't give it to philanthropy; I'll give it to John Fell or one of the boys with the hope that it will yield even more profit there than a tax deduction.

Thanks — come again — I've got some other things to show you that need replacement!

See you Thanksgiving.

Yours,
ADLAI

George McGovern wrote that, in addition to his own senatorial victory, South Dakota elected the first Democratic governor in twenty-two years and the Democrats captured control of the state Senate. He concluded that Stevenson "must be our standard bearer" in 1960.

To George McGovern

November 17, 1958

Dear George:

And no one in South Dakota should take more satisfaction in that incredible transformation than — George McGovern!

But let's not talk about 1960 — at least not that way.

Blessings and warmest thanks for your kind words.

Cordially yours,

To Cass Canfield

November 20, 1958

Dear Cass:

Now that these ghastly articles have been written, published, and read, I wonder what you think about a book.[29] As the Russians say, are your views positive or negative?

28 The original is in the possession of the estate of William Benton. See note 12 to Part Two, above.
29 These articles were published as *Friends and Enemies: What I Learned in Russia* (New York: Harper, 1959).

Stevenson with Dr. J. T Christie, then Principal of Jesus College, Oxford
University, where Stevenson was awarded the degree of Honorary
Doctor of Civil Law on May 24, 1957.

Traveling in Africa in 1957 were, left to right, Clara Urquhart,
Adlai Stevenson, Mr. and Mrs. Cass Canfield, and William Blair.

Stevenson and Albert Schweitzer. Lambarene, Africa, 1957.

With Secretary of State John Foster Dulles. December 11, 1957.

Stevenson during his 1958 Russian tour. On his right in sunglasses is
Alicia Patterson; behind her is Edison Dick. At far right are
William Blair and Borden Stevenson.

Mrs. Marshall Field III, Stevenson, and his son John Fell
relax during Russian tour, 1958.

A family gathering in the spring of 1960. From left to right:
Adlai Stevenson III, the Aga Khan, Nancy Stevenson holding Katherine
Randolph Stevenson, Adlai Stevenson holding Lucy Wallace Stevenson,
Borden, and John Fell. The Aga Khan was John Fell's college roommate.

1960 campaign appearance at the Morosco Theater in New York. From left: Senator Herbert Lehman, Melvyn Douglas, Stevenson, and Anthony Quinn.

Bill Attwood —

I'm afraid this is pretty
meat — little punch and
spirit. But I guess it will
have to go, unless you have
something else in the bag.

We need some new speeches
badly, I fear!

Handwritten note to campaign speechwriter William Attwood
in the spring of 1960.

Hard to speak.
Came to one before — Lincoln's confession
Don't hurt — better start laughing — embarrass

Can't prove what is in my heart
Been together before — When Rep. friends
Time for change" —
Irony — "stood still
In '56 — "Peace Party" — Disarray — Groping

Which club to use — ?
"Speak Softly — —"
Don't talk about problems while putting
U — 2 can make a foreign policy.

"changed slogan this year
Time for a "change" — Revolving

Being here reminds me — Wilson —
"Great outpourings like this not in
compliment to an individual; they are
the demonstration of a purpose. And
all I have to say is that, whoever
the candidate, I pray God he may
not disappoint the expectations of the people

And he won't

We believe — Politics is important business
Want to be part of something bigger — to
give meaning to ourselves — democracy, —
make it work — for us as individuals
for the country
Partly too — whole future depends on
political decisions here in USA
We want to make them
Don't want to drift
Shipwrecked on other reefs.

20th Century — We need world —
Decisions made together
Speech coming on!
Thanks — warm feeling — comps
Proud — Calif — Angelinos

Stevenson's notes jotted down during the flight to Los Angeles
for the 1960 Democratic National Convention. His speech
upon arrival was based on these notes.

Watching the television as the 1960 Democratic National Convention
nominated Senator John F. Kennedy as its candidate. Seated on floor from
left are Adlai III, Borden, Nancy, and John Fell Stevenson.
Mrs. Ernest L. Ives is behind the governor.

Stevenson in his Chicago law office, January, 1961, before he left to assume
his post as U.S. Ambassador to the United Nations. His partners,
from left to right, are: Edward D. McDougal, Jr., William
Blair, Willard Wirtz, Newton N. Minow, and John Hunt.

I will be in New York for ten days and will hope for a word with you then.

Cordially yours,

Hugh Gaitskell, leader of the Labour Party, sent Stevenson his congratulations over the Democratic victories and added that it was "tremendously encouraging" to them in England.

To Hugh Gaitskell

November 20, 1958

Dear Hugh:

I was delighted to have your note and to hear that the election results did not pass unnoticed in Britain — or unsung in some quarters.

It may have been a little too good for our partisan health, a reflection which doubtless reveals my age and sobriety. It seems to me things get messier by the day, and I wish there were more opportunities for quiet talks across the sea. I will hope for another come the spring, in any event.

Cordially yours,

To the Reverend Martin Luther King, Jr.

November 21, 1958

Dear Dr. King:

I just want you to know how very grateful I am to you for your thoughtfulness in inscribing for me that copy of your new book *Stride Toward Freedom*.[30] I have not yet had an opportunity to read it but I shall hope to settle down with it sometime next week.

Together with your legion of friends and admirers I have been concerned over your recent misfortune, but I am relieved to learn that you have been making such good progress.[31]

I note that we have the same publisher which puts me in very good company!

With respect and warm good wishes, I am

Cordially yours,

[30] New York: Harper, 1958.

[31] Dr. King was autographing copies of his book in Harlem on September 19, 1958, when a deranged woman stabbed him in the chest. Letter, Mrs. Martin Luther King, Jr., to Walter Johnson, January 22, 1971.

Richard Powers, of the Associated Press, wrote Stevenson asking him which person actually was his personal choice for Vice President in 1956. Powers also asked for Stevenson's reaction to the talk about nominating him in 1960.

To Richard P. Powers

November 24, 1958

Dear Mr. Powers:

I have your letter and only wish that I could be helpful, but the truth is that I maintained complete neutrality as far as the nomination for the Democratic Vice Presidential candidate was concerned in 1956. I expressed no preference and had none.

My decision with respect to letting the delegates select the candidate for Vice President was made prior to the time I met with my party leaders at the Stadium.

As for 1960, my position is what it has always been and that is that I am not and will not be a candidate.

You were good to think of me and I am grateful indeed.

Sincerely yours,

On November 24, 1958, the Motion Picture Pioneers held a dinner in honor of Robert S. Benjamin and Arthur B. Krim of United Artists Corporation. Max Youngstein was chairman of the dinner, Harry Belafonte sang, and Stevenson and Bob Hope spoke.

Mr. Youngstein said in introducing Stevenson: ". . . In 1952, I, among many others, among many millions, was electrified by a voice over the radio and television stating simply: 'When the tumult and the shouting die, when the bands are gone and the lights are dimmed, there is the stark reality of responsibility. . . . Let's face it. Let's talk sense to the American people.' To have fulfilled that promise with integrity, with intelligence, with a compassion and understanding for the aspirations of men all over the world, and to have cemented that promise with the God-given and ever-present gift of wit and humor makes our next speaker for me not only the voice but also the conscience of America. Gentlemen, may I now present to you the Honorable Adlai Stevenson."[32]

[32] The text is from a tape recording in the possession of Arnold Picker, United Artists Corporation.

Mr. Youngstein, Mr. Benjamin, Mr. Krim, and gentlemen, I am deeply moved by your flattering introduction. I think that speech was pretty good myself now that I have heard it for the first time. (Laughter) . . . You know, I have heard a great deal here in the past few minutes about the Pioneers and the beat generation. Well, I am not sure whether I qualify as one of the Pioneers, what I have heard of the motion picture industry in the last few months I wonder whether the word is "pioneers" or "survivors." (Laughter and applause) But I am very sure, indeed, if I may say so, Mr. Chairman, that I am a senior member of the beat generation. (Laughter and applause)

Now I know it is customary and usual in cases like this to start off by saying how glad one is to be here among the survivors of the motion picture industry. I'm not so sure that I am glad to be here, really (Laughter) — sandwiched between Belafonte and Hope (Laughter), with not even an award to look forward to as the evening wears on. (Laughter and applause) The last time I spent an evening with any of you gentlemen was some nine or ten years ago, and what did you do to me then? You sandwiched me between Jack Benny and Fred Allen. At that time I think it was Fred Allen who spoke first, and then it was my turn. I had to tell the simple truth that during dinner he was so exquisite when he spoke people stood on their chairs, threw their napkins in the air, hollered and shouted, and then the master of ceremonies said: "Now we have another speaker, Governor Stevenson of Illinois." And I got up and I said but the simple truth, that during dinner Mr. Allen had said to me: "What are you going to say?" and I said: "Well, I have prepared a manuscript," and he said: "let me see it." "Gentlemen, you have just heard my manuscript. As far as his was concerned, I read it and I can't remember a word of it." And now you've done it to me again, and I'm getting suspicious.

I suspect this organization is dominated by Republicans. (Laughter) I don't know whether they are Nixon Republicans, Rockefeller Republicans, modern Republicans, or Old Guard Republicans. You know, it doesn't make any difference to me any longer because the only thing they can agree upon is me. (Laughter and applause)

Really, I haven't the remotest idea what I am supposed to do here tonight. Mr. Youngstein said: "You are the open end speaker." (Laughter) Reminding me of something I heard from my grandfather a long time ago — a definition of a politician. "A politician," I think he said, "is a gentleman who meets every problem with an open mouth." (Laughter) Well, I hope my friends Arthur Krim and Bob Benjamin haven't been deluded by this award gimmick. It must be one of the oldest gimmicks in America now. It's a sure way to get a speaker for a dinner, and a sure way to get a crowd, because, who can tell, maybe you'll be the next man who will want the crowd to come and hear you, and therefore you come and hear him. But I am glad for their sake that you have done this honor to them. They are old friends of mine — Bob Benjamin and Arthur Krim. Moreover, they're clients. (Laughter) We are all familiar with their great contributions to the law, to philanthropy, to the motion picture industry, and what two lawyers have done for United Artists has become one of the dramas, one of the romances, of this period of our business industry. You know what it does, gentlemen, it just goes to show what a good lawyer can do if he's elected President. (Laughter and applause) But the law has lost the two again.

And I am happy also — glad to be here also — to have had an opportunity to hear again Harry Belafonte, an old friend and a great artist, who has brought pleasure to countless people in many places. I last saw and heard him in Monte Carlo on the Riviera last summer. I don't think he was any happier among those rich Republicans than I was. (Laughter) You know, I've read in the paper out in Illinois of the difficulty he has had of finding a place to live in New York. In [inaudible] ourselves he might have had the same trouble in most any other Northern city, but it's worked out well, I understand, to his satisfaction, and I suppose all's well that ends well. But for my part, and I think I express the views of all of you here tonight, I endorse and share emphatically the views that Mrs. Roosevelt expressed when she said that she would be happy and honored to have Harry Belafonte as a neighbor of hers. And so would I. (Applause)

And I also think it very nice to have Bob Hope here tonight. You know, we have more in common, perhaps, than many of you realize. I am told he made three appearances for the Republicans this fall,[33] and they only lost by something over a million votes. (Laughter and applause) Well, I made two appearances for the Democrats in New York and they only lost by 500,000 votes. (Laughter and applause) It's a good thing I didn't come back a third time.

You know, we first met, Bob Hope and I, at the Executive Mansion in Springfield when I was Governor of Illinois, and he arrived in Springfield — this was almost ten years ago — and he came to present his compliments to the Governor, and he arrived at the door with an orchid in his hand, and when I flung open the door he was so surprised when he discovered that the Governor of Illinois — Adlai — was a man — (Laughter) — that he forgot to give me the orchid.[34] (Laughter)

[33] In California.
[34] For another version of this story, see *The Papers of Adlai E. Stevenson*, Vol. III, p. 560n.

Some troublemaker said as I came in here tonight he thought it was an outrage that Stevenson spoke in the middle and Hope spoke last. But I want you to know that I don't think so — I think it's exactly right. I remember a politician once saying to me long ago that when an audience claps before the speech it's faith, when they clap during the speech it's hope, and when they applaud at the end it's charity. (Laughter) But he should be last — he's a great man, and this has been recognized for a long time. Someone — I hope reliable — told me that even his fifth-grade teacher in Cleveland recognized his greatness a long time ago. She said: "That boy will go down in history." Well, he did — he went down in history, spelling, geography and arithmetic. (Laughter) Now, Hope has done a lot of traveling, as you have noticed, of late — some people inquire why he travels so much. Well, I think you have to see his show to understand why he travels so much, and then you'll know. (Laughter) But I travel, too, a great deal. I've never been sure whether I was trying to catch up with him or Eleanor Roosevelt. (Laughter) But he's done a great job, to which I can personally testify, and so can some of the rest of you who have been there recently, as a Good Will Ambassador to the Soviet Union. And I have some news for you, Bob. They told me that all is forgiven and that you can come back.

You know, as I listen to myself going on here, I think this must be the ultimate proof that I am not running for anything. (Laughter) What candidate on God's earth would leave himself so vulnerable, so wide open, with Hope coming on after him? (Laughter)

Finally, I am glad to be here for another reason. I, too, have made some films. Perhaps you are not aware of that. They weren't conspicuous box office attractions. In '56 I spent some two days in Hollywood. The Democrats had a great idea — it lasted for a few minutes — a great idea, that I would make some five-minute shorts, and then they would preempt the concluding minutes of some of the most popular TV programs and put on these little films. Well, the day came; the show went on; I was great. At least all my friends told me I was great. Then they had a party, and then the telegrams started to come in. The first one I will remember always. It said: "I like Ike. I love Lucy. Drop dead." (Laughter)

But you've been very good to me, and I have many happy memories of the kindness of many people in the motion picture industry in my political campaigns and otherwise. Often they would bring in the crowds, transfix them until we could lock the doors and I could start to speak. And I am deeply grateful to many of you here tonight, too.

I was reminded here tonight, by the way, of one of the greatest compliments — perhaps the greatest — that ever befell me. It was when

I was Governor of Illinois and I happened to be in California, and I was invited to the first party in Hollywood that I ever went to. In the course of the evening some lighthearted fellow asked me to please stand on a chair and say a few words to the crowd, and I did. And someone said down in front: "How could a man be so charming and not be Jewish?" (Laughter)

I would like, because I have had some opportunity to see for myself, to talk to you about the international communion of the arts and their enormous imporance. I think we are all conscious, we who travel, of the good that was done by many of our travelers abroad from your fraternity — by Van Cliburn to Moscow, by the Porgy and Bess Company, by Louis Armstrong, even the Harlem Globetrotters, even the Bob Hope globetrotting. All of these things have been of enormous value to us. I believe, like you, that if people can laugh together that is the first step, perhaps, toward living together. And certainly this is the most important unfinished business of the generation in which we live. I think it is time that we all stopped shivering with fear about what is going to happen to us and started thinking about what we are going to make happen to us. Just as you have built this little organization to relieve the sorrows of some people, so all of us who are unafraid of translating good will into action can do so much to bring to reality the golden promise of this century. And I wonder who could do more than the clever and the good — people like Bob Benjamin and Arthur Krim — but it is so rare that you find the clever and the good embodied in the same person. You remember an old verse:

> *If all the good people were clever,*
> *And those that are clever were good,*
> *This world would be nicer than ever*
> *We dreamed that it possibly could.*
>
> *But it seems as though seldom, if ever,*
> *Do the two hit it off as they should —*
> *The good are so harsh to the clever,*
> *And the clever so rude to the good.*

These gentlemen are an anomaly — to be both clever and good is to assume not only the burdens of the contemporary business society but responsibilities much larger than that.

I am very grateful to you tonight for inviting me here to join you in paying homage to these two dear friends. Thank you. (Applause)

To Gerald A. Billen

December 3, 1958

Dear Mr. Billen:

You will perhaps recall our correspondence regarding your mother, Mrs. Teresia Bilezka. While in Moscow this past summer I mentioned your mother's case to the Soviet authorities, and particularly to Mr. G. Zhukov, Chairman of the State Committee on Cultural Relations with Foreign Countries. I have just seen Mr. Zhukov here in New York and he informed me that your mother has been given permission to leave the Soviet Union.

Needless to say, I am delighted that you will now be reunited and I hope and pray that she has already left the Soviet Union and arrived safely in this country.

Sincerely yours,

Stevenson was in Washington, D.C., from December 5 until December 8, 1958. While there he attended the Gridiron Club dinner, lunched at the Soviet embassy, and attended a meeting of the Democratic Advisory Council.

To Mikhail A. Menshikov

December 9, 1958

My dear Mr. Ambassador:

After our delightful luncheon the other day and my visit with your accomplished son, I talked to Senator Joseph Clark, of Pennsylvania. He in turn assured me that he would make arrangements for Stanislav to visit some friend of his in a northern Pennsylvania town, possibly Bradford, outside the restricted area.

Senator Clark told me that he or his friend would communicate directly with Stanislav in care of the Embassy in Washington. I hope very much that this can be arranged, and I am sure that Senator Clark will be highly sensitive to your son's anxiety to see something of the community's life with as much anonymity as possible. But if I am not mistaken, that able young man is going to find anonymity a problem for the rest of his life!

With my thanks for your hospitality and best wishes, I am

Cordially yours,

To Paul G. Hoffman

December 10, 1958

Dear Paul:

I have just seen John Cowles' editorial of December 6th about your new job.[35] It reminds me that I have shamefully neglected a message of congratulation. I am sure this influential area of transcendant importance will stretch wholesomely and lengthily beyond the assignment itself.

While in New York last week, I had lunch with Pearl Buck[36] (Mrs. Richard J. Walsh, R.D. 3, Perkasie, Pa.) to discuss her proposal for an effort to marshal the thought and moral influence of leading scholars, thinkers, philosophers, scientists, etc. A similar project was proposed to me several years ago by the old Queen Mother of Belgium. I think there may be an idea here worth further exploration, and consistent with the idea which we share of using the non-governmental resources of the world in the quest for peace.

At all events, I told Pearl Buck — a wonderful woman — that I knew of no one better equipped for such a task than Paul G. Hoffman. Hence I am enclosing the memorandum she gave me, which is obviously extremely preliminary. I hope you can see her sometime.

Cordially yours,

Stevenson's Dalmatian, King Arthur, who had wandered frequently from the executive mansion throughout Springfield while Stevenson was governor, had recently died.

To Margaret Munn[37]

December 11, 1958

Bless you, Dear Margaret, for sending me the Artie picture and Vincent Dallman's[38] wonderful column. I had no idea that Artie's passing was a matter of such public note in Springfield.

Merry Christmas!

THE GUV!

[35] Mr. Hoffman had just been appointed director of the new United Nations agency for economic and technical development. See the Minneapolis *Morning Tribune,* December 6, 1958.
[36] Nobel prizewinning author and president of the East and West Association.
[37] The original is in the possession of Mrs. Munn.
[38] Editor of the Springfield *Illinois State Register.*

To Mrs. Franklin D. Roosevelt[39]

December 12, 1958

My dear Mrs. R.:

On the eve of another departure from Chicago, I am reminded that I shall miss you here next week. But I am going to see you in New York at the dance if I have to come disguised as a waiter.[40]

Love,
ADLAI

Chester Bowles, who had been elected to Congress, wrote that he and Mrs. Bowles had found a house in Washington, D.C., and that Thomas L. Hughes, who had formerly worked for him, would join his congressional staff.

To Chester Bowles

December 12, 1958

Dear Chet:

So many thanks for your good letter of December 8. I am delighted to hear that you have found a house in Washington, which must be a relief and doubtless one of any Congressman's greatest achievements.

Tom Hughes I have known for a long while and I think you are fortunate to have him back in your service.

I will be in Washington over the week-end of January 18 and will hope for a visit with you then. My mission is a formidable one — the first A. Powell Davies Memorial Lecture, and I shudder at the thought of it.

With affectionate regards to you all,

Yours,

To Pearl S. Buck

December 12, 1958

Dear Miss Buck:

FRIEND TO FRIEND[41] has arrived, together with your gracious

[39] The original is in the Franklin D. Roosevelt Library, Hyde Park, New York.

[40] Mrs. Roosevelt replied on December 16 that an invitation for the party on December 22 should have reached him, so that he need "not worry about a disguise!"

[41] Pearl S. Buck, *Friend to Friend: A Candid Exchange Between Pearl S. Buck and Carlos P. Romulo* (New York: John Day, 1958).

inscription. I hope I can have a go at this, and very soon. Certainly Asia is more important to America than America to Asia just now, and who can tell us more about it than you.

The suggestion of your trip to China really awakes my own yearning to go. I think it important that you do if you think you can manage it. Certainly the new leaders of China need to know something more about us as well as we about them.

Cordially,

En route for a holiday at Chelsea Plantation, the winter home of Mrs. Marshall Field in South Carolina, Stevenson dined at the Atlanta airport with Mr. and Mrs. Ralph McGill and their son. He wrote the following letter aboard the airplane to Savannah.

To Ralph McGill[42]

December 14, 1958

Dear Ralph — En route to Savannah —

I'm afraid I imposed on you — but I DID enjoy it! — and am most grateful. That boy, Ralph Jr., warmed my heart, and you gave my confused thinking new balance & direction. *Thank you* — and my apologies for spoiling your Saturday evening.

I meant to speak to you about that advisory committee for research grants. I think the educational film has limitless possibilities for enrichment of the curriculum, especially at the primary level and in the sciences. But watch out for the educational TV people — whose claims exceed their accomplishments — and who seem to dominate most committees these days. And watch out for grants to individual members of the committee itself — except the Atlanta Constitution, of course!

I wish I could see you more often — and even find words to tell you how grateful I am for so much for so long.

If you & your wife could come over to Chelsea for a night this week — it would be *wonderful!!*

Yours,
ADLAI

P.S. . . .

Mrs. Eugene Meyer suggested that she hold a reception in Stevenson's honor after he delivered the first A. Powell Davies Memorial Lecture.

---

[42] This handwritten letter is in the possession of Mrs. Ralph McGill.

To Mrs. Eugene Meyer[43]

December 18, 1958

Agnes dear —

I've been so busy pursuing duck, quail, doves and snipe — and then sleeping off the effects of such abnormal exertions — I've had no moment to write you until now — when I'm leaving this 18th century fragment for the frozen North.

The Powell Davies lecture chills me — and your letter about my audience — "all the brainiest people in Washington" — does nothing to reassure me! Write a paragraph or two — pertinent & soaring! — I beseech you, so that somewhere there will be a heart in my utterance. Your description of him and his virtues is helpful — bless you, and now some more please!

Yes, of course, I would be delighted to come to a reception at your house afterward — altho I know now how I'll feel — like crawling off & dying quickly in a dark corner. But don't do it if it is awkward in any way or too much of an exertion for Eugene. Which reminds me that sometime I hope you will let me know when you are going to Florida & when it would be conv[en]ient to come for a few days — to lie on the hot sand with my eyes shut and listen to the wisest woman of my life. You can even talk, lecture, about my weight — unless you are too late for I've started, thanks to your merciless assault!

Of course what I wanted to say was that your letter about what "I had done for you" — exhausted me. But can it be true — what you say about *me.* What you say about you — yes, "self-actualizing" ever. But — well, perhaps when there is time, if ever, you will tell me more. And be sure to repeat that I am one of the few men you ever knew who was not afraid of you — because I think I really am & need reassurance.

But *can* you do it all — think, write, speak, manage & even time for *me.* I marvel, and love you —

ADLAI

Stevenson was in New York City from December 13 to 23, when he returned to Chicago and then spent Christmas with Mr. and Mrs. Ernest Ives at their old family home in Bloomington, Illinois.

[43] This handwritten letter is in the Agnes Meyer files, Princeton University Library.

To Sam Rayburn

December 22, 1958

Dear Mr. Sam:

I can imagine the number of requests about committee assignments you must be receiving from newly elected members of Congress — and I hesitate to add to these requests. But I understand that John Brademas of South Bend [Indiana] is anxious to serve on the Education and Labor Committee, and I just wanted you to know that I think he would be exceptionally well qualified for that particular Committee.

As you may know, John worked closely with me during the 1956 campaign, and his interest and background in the problems of education and labor were of great value to me.

John is a remarkable young man, and I know he will be helpful to you and the Democratic leadership in every possible way.

Warmest wishes to you for Christmas and the New Year.

Cordially,

To Thomas J. O'Brien[44]

December 24, 1958

Dear Tom:

I hope you will pardon this intrusion, but I am writing to say that I hope very much that some way will be found to put Chester Bowles on the House Foreign Affairs Committee. I don't suppose there is anyone more experienced in the field of foreign relations and I am sure that Chet would be enormously useful were he to get such an appointment.

With warmest good wishes to you for the Holiday Season, I am

Sincerely yours,

Stevenson's message at Christmastime was a "foldover" card. On the front was reproduced the following in his handwriting.

Thank you for your Christmas message — and the comforting reminder it brought that "no man is useless while he has a friend."

I wish you good fortune and a peaceful New Year. And I hope these

---

[44] U.S. representative from Illinois and former sheriff of Cook County, 1939–1942.

words of Boris Pasternak will hearten and refresh you as they have me.

ADLAI E. STEVENSON

Libertyville, Ill.
December 1958

The inside of the card bore this quotation from Doctor Zhivago, *by Boris Pasternak: "If the beast who sleeps in man could be held down by threats — any kind of threats, whether of jail or of retribution after death — then the highest emblem of humanity would be the lion tamer in the circus with his whip, not the prophet who sacrificed himself. But don't you see, that is just the point — what has for centuries raised man above the beast is not the cudgel but an inward music: The irresistible power of unarmed truth, the powerful attraction of its example."*

To Joseph S. Clark

December 29, 1958

Dear Joe:

Please thank Noel[45] for her letter and tell her I look forward eagerly to dinner with you on the 17th.

I have your letter.[46] I think the trouble between the DAC and Congress relates more to leadership of the latter than members generally. But you would know best whom to include for any such discussion. I always have respected the views of Anderson[47] and Gore.[48] And outside the staff of the DAC (Murphy,[49] Perlman,[50] Tyroler,[51] etc.), the

[45] Mrs. Clark.

[46] Senator Clark had written Senate Majority Leader Lyndon B. Johnson a letter on November 18, 1958, stating that the increased group of Democratic liberals in the Senate wanted stronger representation on the Steering and Policy Committees. Alfred Steinberg wrote: "Johnson boiled with rage at Clark's audacity, and his anger increased when Clark's letter appeared in the newspapers. Nor did his vehemence decline when the Stevenson, Truman, etc., Democratic Advisory Council demanded that a big package of liberal legislation go through Congress in the Eighty-sixth Congress so that the party would have legislative achievements to boast about in the 1960 campaign." *Sam Johnson's Boy: A Close-up of the President from Texas* (New York: Macmillan, 1968), p. 494.

[47] Senator Clinton Anderson, of New Mexico.

[48] Senator Albert Gore, of Tennessee.

[49] Charles S. Murphy, presidential counsel and principal speechwriter for President Truman.

[50] Philip B. Perlman, Solicitor General under President Truman.

[51] Charles Tyroler, executive director of the Democratic Advisory Counsel and former special assistant to Secretary of State George C. Marshall.

[317]

best informed about its operations and — what is more important — its possibilities are Tom Finletter and Marietta Tree.

As to our party's position generally, it might be interesting to hear what people as far apart as Muskie[52] and the Western Senators, Clair Engle,[53] McGhee,[54] etc. think about the state of things. Among the Southerners, as you know, I have always thought John Sparkman[55] enlightened and sensible. But you will know best about them and how we can bridge that even bigger gap.

As to Presidential candidates, I am eager to hear your assessment but I am afraid there is little I can contribute. I have tried to keep as far away from that and from the plans and ambitions of the candidates as I could, for obvious reasons.

Happy New Year to you and Noel, and please don't go to any trouble about our meeting. It will be quite enough for me to see *you*.

Yours,

p.s. I wish I had a lecture for the Powell Davies affair!

David Lawrence, governor-elect of Pennsylvania, wrote expressing his admiration for Stevenson's leadership and raising the question of the presidential nominee for 1960.

To David Lawrence

December 30, 1958

Dear Dave:

Thanks for "them kind words," my dear and loyal friend. But you have long since fulfilled any obligations to me — and how!

As for me? I'm for anyone, except Stevenson. And most of all, I'm for a good talk with you. When your ordeal is over and you are shaken down in Harrisburg send for me — please.

Happy New Year — to Mrs. L[awrence]. too.

Yours,

William C. Baggs, editor of the Miami Daily News, *asked Stevenson to write an essay on the prospects for 1959.*

---

52 Edmund S. Muskie, senator-elect from Maine.
53 Senator-elect from California.
54 Gale McGee, senator-elect from Wyoming.
55 Senator from Alabama, who had been Stevenson's running mate in 1952.

To William C. Baggs

December 30, 1958

Dear Bill:

I said I couldn't send you anything. And this *isn't*, but it's *something* — if you want to use it. I will be neither hurt nor surprised if you don't.

Happy New Year!

Sincerely yours,

It is always easy to talk about our hopes, especially for a distant future. But you ask me what we should expect to settle for in 1959. That's a good deal harder.

There won't be this year, we know, the Peace the herald angels sang so hopefully almost two thousand years ago. Yet it seems a reasonable expectation that there won't be War this year either, even if for the bitterly ironic reason that the world is so ready for war and knows so well and so recently its terrifying meaning.

At another perilous time of doubt and suspicion in the world, a great writer, Heinrich Heine, concluded a New Year's message with these words: "But above all, I wish that we may hurt each other as little as possible in the New Year." At the gate of 1958 [1959], I feel the same way.

The year will be a wasted one if we don't make some progress toward the fuller Peace. I think we will.

It seems reasonable to expect that an accord will be reached regarding the testing, perhaps the development, possibly even the use, of nuclear bombs.

I would guess that history's account of 1959 may be written in terms of the free world's facing or not facing the hard practicalities of increasing national consciousness — with its potential both for good and for evil — along that huge strip of the Earth lying on both sides of the equator and ringing the world. We must move faster than we have been on this front if we value freedom enough to press its values against the cynical competition of the communist powers.

China, probably more even than Russia, represents the long range threat to the free world's ideals. I wish there were more reason to hope, too, that 1959 might be the year of decision to do whatever is necessary to lay a basis for the future relationships between the peoples of the Western World and those of China.

Our year's biggest test here at home will be whether we falter again, stand still, or continue to move forward in putting into living fact our professed ideals about the essential equality of all men — and particularly all children. I think there has been progress on this in 1958, despite some of the tragedies we have had to witness. Surely our resoluteness as a people has been made clear to any who might have doubted it before.

To Nikita Khrushchev

January 5, 1959

My dear Mr. Prime Minister:

Just a short note to tell you that I appreciate your kind assistance in the personal matter involving Mr. [Robert] Tucker's mother-in-law which I mentioned during our visit together last August.

He informs me that Mrs. Pestretsova has arrived safely in the United States. She and her daughter are happy to be reunited once again, and the whole family is of course very grateful.

And may I take this opportunity to tell you once more of my own gratitude for the friendly, courteous and hospitable reception which I and my sons and friends were accorded wherever we went in the Soviet Union.

With very best wishes,

Sincerely yours,

To William Benton[56]

January 8, 1958

Dear Bill:

I am putting down breakfast Wednesday A.M., January 21st, at 8.30 at 1734.[57] If it is inconvenient for you, it will make no difference to me.

Yours,

P.S. I keep hearing you quoted as saying that I am for [Hubert] Humphrey. As you know I've been trying so hard to avoid public involvement. Help! Help!

On January 18, 1959, Stevenson delivered the first annual lecture in memory of the liberal Unitarian minister A. Powell Davies. He spoke in

[56] The original is in the possession of the estate of William Benton. See note 12 to Part Two, above. The postscript was added by hand.
[57] Stevenson's room in the Savoy-Plaza Hotel.

Constitution Hall to an audience of four thousand people. The address was widely quoted in editorials, and the Saturday Review, February 7, 1959, *published a condensed version of it.* Life, February 9, 1959, *published a full-page editorial "The Cost of Easy Options," quoted a number of sentences from the lecture, and called it "the best recent statement of this informed worry." Stuart Gerry Brown devoted a chapter to this speech in* Conscience in Politics *and observed: "This address, more than any other of his many speeches and writings, explains why Adlai Stevenson could not have been elected to the Presidency of the United States in the 'Age of Eisenhower.' But it explains, too, why he had established for himself a high place in the history of his time and his country, and why, on transcendent issues, he could and did articulate the will and the vision of America as no other of his contemporaries could do."*[58]

THE POLITICAL RELEVANCE OF MORAL PRINCIPLE[59]

I am profoundly flattered by your invitation to inaugurate these annual lectures in memory of Dr. A. Powell Davies. It is an honor to be asked to help in any way in the commemoration of a man so eminently worthy of being remembered. But it is hard indeed to pay adequate homage in words to a man whose own words were so fresh, so apt and fitting to the important issues of the day.

But I am encouraged by one fact. Dr. Davies did not feel that his office as a minister of religion debarred him from comment upon contemporary problems. On the contrary, he saw that he could make his message relevant to his people only by showing it at work in the concrete issues of their daily lives.

I think of a story my grandfather Stevenson, a devout Scotch-Presbyterian of Southern descent, told about the preacher who was driving along a back road when he espied a parishioner wearily clearing up a poor, stony field. "That's a fine job you and the Lord have done cleaning up that rocky field," he shouted. "Thank you, parson," the man replied. "I wish you could have seen it when the Lord had it all to himself."

[58] *Conscience in Politics: Adlai E. Stevenson in the 1950's* (Syracuse, New York: Syracuse University Press, 1961), p. 256.

[59] The text is that released to the press. With slight changes this speech was reprinted in Adlai E. Stevenson, *Putting First Things First: A Democratic View* (New York: Random House, 1960), pp. 27–43; Stuart Gerry Brown, *Adlai E. Stevenson: A Short Biography, The Conscience of the Country* (Woodbury, New York: Barron's Woodbury Press, 1965), pp. 201–215; *An Ethic for Survival: Adlai Stevenson Speaks on International Affairs, 1936–1965,* edited with introduction and commentary by Michael H. Prosser (New York: William Morrow, 1969), pp. 235–250.

Dr. Davies believed that God is dependent on man, as man is on God. He believed that the clergy above all were responsible for making a reality of the bond between God and man, and he was fearless in letting his congregation and the world know the truth as he saw it. He had a sensitive awareness of peril to the individual in our day of bigness, of statism and conformity. Therefore he was impelled to fight for the oppressed and the persecuted; to fight for equal justice for all and the rights inherent in our citizenship. Ardently he defended freedom of the mind, free speech, the right of the dissenter to speak and the duty of the conformist to listen. And his compassion was boundless.

It was the tardiness of the American social conscience in understanding the severity of its ordeal with authoritarianism that made Dr. Davies impatient, that made him work so hard to awaken us to the perils. He literally wore himself out trying to mobilize public opinion and induce every American to hold himself personally responsible for the preservation of freedom.

From the mountain of vision, Dr. Davies constantly proclaimed the political relevance of moral principle and of religon as a "judgment of righteousness." From the dusty plain of politics I would like in my turn to reaffirm this relevance. I like to believe that there may be some value in echoing testimony from a layman who has spent his middle life in the press and confusion of great events in government service, in diplomacy and in politics.

All politics is made up of many things — economic pressures, personal ambitions, the desire to exercise power, the overriding issues of national need and aspiration. But if it is nothing more, it is without roots. It is built on shifting, changing sands of emotion and interest. When challenged, it can give no account of itself. When threatened, it is in danger of collapse.

Today, when the threat and challenge to free society seem more total and powerful than ever before, it is not a political luxury or fruitless pedantry to re-examine our fundamental principles. I think it more likely to be the condition of survival.

There is a phrase of Dr. Davies that stays in my mind. I do not know when I have heard a more terse and pregnant summing up of our predicament. "The world," he said, "is now too dangerous for anything but the truth, too small for anything but brotherhood." This I believe to be in broad measure a correct estimate of the condition of the human society, which is now capable, with a few hydrogen bombs, of extinguishing itself. Today we can all be killed by the same bombs or atomic fallout. In that sense we have attained a desperate physical solidarity. But moral and social solidarity in the family of man is still to be found.

Not so long ago I visited Dr. Albert Schweitzer in his primitive jungle hospital in French Equatorial Africa, and he told me he considered this the most dangerous period in history, not just modern history, but all human history. Why? Because, he said, heretofore nature has controlled man, but now man has learned to control elemental forces — before he has learned to control himself.

Many of us seem to rely on some mythical God-given superiority of the white Western world to save us. And my concern is that there is more evidence that the Communists accept the reality of the human condition than we do.

It is impossible to spend weeks travelling around the Soviet Union as I did this summer without taking away an overwhelming impression of thrust and purpose in most aspects of Soviet life. The revolutionary ardor has cooled with time but even the very pragmatic political leaders seem to believe profoundly in the truth of their way of life, and they are quietly confident that it will sweep the world in time. I think they sincerely believe that their methods, their aspirations, their dreams, make up the final truth about the nature of man and society; that collective man in the collective state is the ultimate unfolding of human destiny, the end of history, the "far off divine event" for which mankind has been in long travail, the vision of "all things made new" that has haunted men's minds ever since Christianity thrust into human thought the intoxicating ideal of a perfected humanity.

From this conviction, if I have not overstated it, flow two consequences. The first is that no effort, no dedication, no sacrifice is too great that may help to realize the Communist party's goals in Soviet society. The second is that no corner of humanity can be a matter of indifference to the Communists, because the whole human race is destined to become one in communist brotherhood.

These are not abstract generalizations. Russia is a vast powerhouse of energy all harnessed to the communal task of building the Soviet dream. The thrust of economic growth which adds a nine or ten per cent increase each year to industrial expansion is one aspect of this energy. The vast sums available for science and research are another. The self discipline and long hours put in by school children to train themselves as the scientists, technicians, administrators and linguists of the new world order are perhaps the most significant measure of the resources of energy, work and skill upon which Soviet leaders hope to draw. In Moscow, Serge Obraztsov, the brilliant director of the famous Puppet Theatre, said: "I visited China five years ago. It was the most extraordinary experience of my life. People in China have had nothing — nothing! Now several hundred million people are dreaming of tomorrow. I cannot describe to you the feeling of excitement there — much, much more even than here in the Soviet Union."

The energy, the drive, the dedication in the USSR spill over into international affairs. In part, of course, this is the restless concern which all imperial powers must exercise, especially when the peoples they control are as restive and unreliable as the captive peoples in Russia's European empire. But communist activity, planning and efforts in trade and aid are not confined to areas of communist control. They are world-wide, and there is no corner of the earth's surface which they think too insignificant for their attention. While trade missions are busy in Latin America trading Soviet machinery and oil for coffee and wool, academic representatives are touring West Africa, Arab and Asian students are being trained in Moscow, technical advisers dispatched to India and Burma and Indonesia, and the glossy flood of propaganda depicting the Soviet millennium of bumper harvests and happy workers is pumped out all round the world.

All this we know — or begin to know. But I wonder how often we try to grasp the scale of dedication that lies behind it. Why should they be so busy? Why so much work and thought? Why such diversion of resources? Why such patience through every setback, such forward thrusts through every point of Western weakness? Heaven knows, we only want to stay home. Why don't they? Why do we never meet an isolationist Communist? These are the questions that haunted me while I confronted at first hand this iron, forceful and formidable way of life.

And I don't think there is any doubt about the answer. Part of it is simply needed foreign trade. Part is fear, the search for security through friends. And part is the historical centrifugal forces in Russia that have been pressing outward for a hundred years — to the Pacific, the Balkans and the Middle East. But the important thing is that the Soviet Russians believe in their truth, as the men of the Western world once believed in theirs. They, not we, are firing the shots heard round the world — and also the satellites that orbit above it. The fact that their faith is in many ways an evil perversion of the great propositions that once made the blood course in our Western veins does not alter the fact that their tempo is dynamic and ours sluggish — even, I think, to ourselves.

The reason cannot be that we Americans have lost our vision of truth and brotherhood. No country on earth owes the sense of community more explicitly to the fact that it is united not by race or nationality but by fidelity to an idea. We were born "dedicated to a proposition" and our greatest leaders — the Jeffersons, the Lincolns, the Woodrow Wilsons — were not great because they achieved purely American purposes, but because they were able to speak for humanity at large and extend their vision to the whole family of man.

Nor, I believe, can we find fault with the American dream. Its truths are still "self-evident." The possession of liberty and the pursuit of happiness — rightly understood   have not been overthrown as the highest goods of human society. Indeed, the ferment of our freedom works inexorably and dangerously in the communist world. No one can have visited Poland without seeing how little the Polish people accept their servitude and how they look beyond their neighbors to the free world as the reservoir of power and hope.

But, alas, on the basis of the record, one would hardly suspect that the Western world possessed so powerful a weapon. All our talk — in diplomacy, in strategy, in aid and trade, in all the intricacies of our worldwide relations — has been to a depressing degree purely defensive. We have offered aid not to help others but to shield ourselves. We have reacted to countless Soviet initiatives; acted on our own initiative barely at all. We watch the skies for other people's sputniks and listen to the telegraph wires for other people's moves. Yet we are the free men of this universe, the children of liberty, the beneficiaries of unequalled abundance, and heirs of the highest, proudest political tradition ever known to man!

Why this lack of initiative? Why this paralysis of will? What have we done to our truth and our brotherhood — the supreme truth of freedom, the Christian truth of brotherly love? Have they failed? Or have we?

There is no more urgent duty than to discover why we have failed and to get back into the arena, aspiring, striving, fighting once more for what we believe. An examination of what you might call our collective conscience is to my mind far more important than particular projects or programs. You can have a perfect assembly of pieces for your watch, but they are worthless if the mainspring is broken. I am not basically worried about our various pieces — our technology, our science, our machines, our resources. But I am concerned, desperately concerned, about our mainspring. That it has run down, we know. But is it broken beyond repair? In the last analysis, no question is worth more consideration in America today.

And I would like to suggest some of the ways in which it seems to me we have enfeebled the great central pulse of our freedom, the great truth of liberty, which, more than any other nation, we first set working in the modern world.

The great German poet, Goethe, who also lived through a crisis of freedom, said to his generation: "What you have inherited from your fathers, earn over again for yourselves or it will not be yours." We inherited freedom. We seem unaware that it has to be remade and re-earned in each generation of man. One reason for this failure is, I believe, passing at last. In recent years we were stifled with complacent self-confidence. We believed ourselves dominant in every field. We talked of "the American Century." We forgot the ardors and efforts that had given us a measure of pre-eminence. Complacency made us impervious to ideas, even the obvious idea that we are in danger. So we assumed that all we needed was to sit still and enjoy the "peace and prosperity" that was our right.

I believe that phase is passing. Our foolish languor has been shaken, if not shattered. We are more ready to examine ourselves and our record. And it is a privilege of our society that every citizen should make his own inquiry. If I stress one or other aspect of our problem, this is simply my angle of vision. You have yours. The urgent thing is to feel the need for re-thinking and to set to work the ultimate energies of free society — which cannot be done by the fiat of government but only by the troubled conscience of responsible men and women.

It is simply as a citizen as concerned as you are that I want to suggest what seems to me to be the obstacles to a full understanding of our great mission in this time of testing.

I believe — as I have said before — that we have confused the free with the free and easy. If freedom had been the happy, simple, relaxed state of ordinary humanity, man would have everywhere been free — whereas through most of time and space he has been in chains. Do not let us make any mistake about this. The natural government of man is servitude. Tyranny is the normal pattern of government. It is only by intense thought, by great effort, by burning idealism and unlimited sacrifice that freedom has prevailed as a system of government. And the efforts which were first necessary to create it are fully as necessary to sustain it in our own day.

He who offers this thing we call freedom as the soft option is a deceiver or himself deceived. He who sells it cheap or offers it as the by-product of this or that economic system is knave or fool. For freedom demands infinitely more care and devotion than any other political system. It puts consent and personal initiative in the place of command and obedience. By relying upon the devotion and initiative of ordinary citizens, it gives up the harsh but effective disciplines that underpin all the tyrannies which over the millenia have stunted the full stature of men.

But of what use is escape from external restraint if given the opportunity men simply stunt themselves? If freedom means ease alone, if it means shirking the hard disciplines of learning, if it means evading the rigors and rewards of creative activity, if it means more expenditure on advertising than education, if it means "bachelor cooking" and "life adjustment" courses in the schools, and the steady cult of the trivial and the mediocre, if it means — worst of all — indifference or even contempt for all but athletic excellence, we may keep for a time the forms of free society, but its spirit will be dead.

I believe we have had enough of adjustment, conformity, easy options and the least common denominator in our system. We need instead to see the "pursuit of happiness" in terms which are historically proven and psychologically correct. The dreary failure in history of all classes committed to pleasure and profit alone, the vacuity and misery accompanying the sole pursuit of ease — the collapse of the French aristocracy, the corruption of imperial Rome, the decline and fall of the resplendent Manchus — all these facts of history do not lose their point because the pleasures of today are mass pleasures and no longer the enjoyments of an elite. If we become a nation of Bourbons, numbers won't save us. We shall go their way. Vacuity and indifference are not redeemed by the fact that everyone can share in them. They merely restrict the circle from which regeneration can come.

I say this — I hope you will believe me — in no Puritan or pleasure-hating spirit. On the contrary, there is no boredom or misery to equal the pursuit of distraction alone. We do not slip into happiness. It is strenuously sought and earned. A nation glued to the television screen is not simply at a loss before the iron pioneers of the new collective society. It isn't even having a good time. No society has ever spent as much as we do on drink and tranquillizers. Can one argue that this is evidence of universal fun? I ran across a quotation of La Bruyere on the court of Louis XIV that struck me as relevant: "Les joies sont visibles, mais fausses, et les chagrins cachés, mais réels" — its joys are visible, but artificial, and its sorrows hidden, but real.

But perhaps this misunderstanding of the true nature of happiness and of the conditions of its pursuit is simply an aspect of something else — our misunderstanding of the real nature of freedom. I recall the words of the wise Judge Learned Hand, who warned us that freedom would not survive in our Constitution if it had already died in the hearts of the people. We shall not have a free society unless we have free men.

And how often do we reflect upon what this inner freedom entails? "Give me the man," cries Hamlet, "who is not passion's slave." But this is what we are in danger of becoming, slaves to a tyranny more intimate and inescapable than any Stalin or Mao Tse Tung could impose. We can be made slaves simply by the clutter and complexity of modern living —

which notoriously leaves no time for serious thought and offers every means of distraction so that we can avoid such thought. Between aircraft that take us everywhere more rapidly, newspapers that grow in weight and coverage, news that flashes round the globe, ceaseless and competitive entertainment, fashions — God help us! — that change from sack to trapeze and back again, we can fill up every "unforgiving minute" with enough trash and preoccupation to still forever the deeper voices of the soul. Like Matthew Arnold, we can

> ". . . *see all sights from pole to pole,*
> *And glance and nod and bustle by,*
> *And never once possess our soul*
> *Before we die."*

How are we to defend freedom if, for the tyranny of external control we substitute the clattering, cluttering tyranny of internal aimlessness and fuss? This freedom for our souls, freedom at the profoundest level of our being, is not a gift to us by our contemporary way of life. On the contrary, much of this life is a direct conspiracy against it. And if we cannot — by a certain discipline, by readiness for reflection and quiet, by determination to do the difficult and aim at a lasting good — rediscover the real purpose and direction of our existence, we shall not be free. Our society will not be free. And between a chaotic, selfish, indifferent, commercial society and the iron discipline of the communist world, I would not like to predict the outcome. Outer tyranny with purpose may well triumph over the inner, purposeless tyranny of a confused and aimless way of life.

I doubt if any society in history has faced so great a moral challenge as ours, or needed more desperately to draw on the deepest sources of courage and responsibility. Ours is the first human community in which resources are so abundant that almost no policies lie beyond our capacity for purely physical reasons. What we decide to do, we can do. The inhibitions of poverty — lack of resources, lack of capital, lack of power — do not hold us back. We can accomplish what we aim at. Thus, perhaps for the first time in the world, choice, not means, ends, not instruments, are decisive.

Then again we have proved — drably and dangerously — over the last decade that defensiveness is not a sufficient reason for action. All the policies we have pursued in self-defense have left us still on the defensive. But if we do not act from fear, we must find some other motivation. In free society there is no other alternative but to tap the vigor, faith and imagination of the people themselves. We must find out once more who we are, as the psychologists say. And I would earnestly appeal especially to the women of America to organize an "Operation Wisdom" and to lead the way to a new self-examination and self-discipline.

But perhaps the most urgent reason why the quality of our moral response has become the decisive issue in politics is quite simply that most of the major problems of our day present themselves in moral terms, and are probably insoluble without some stirring of generosity, some measure of vision. Let me give you three instances. In the wealthiest nation in the world, at least 5 million families still live in squalid but remediable poverty. They are a minority. They don't have the votes to force the issue of their misfortune into the front rank of public issues. They depend, for remedies, upon the alert conscience of the majority. But how do we keep the conscience sensitive and alert? By concentrating on our own concerns and adding the dishwasher to the television set to the air conditioner? By griping over taxes and attacking that great bogey we call "the welfare state?" By closing our minds every time our shiny car takes us through a slum? No — we shall have the dedication and drive to wipe poverty out of this rich land only if the well-to-do majority of today do not repeat the selfish indifference which, in many communities, has been the epitaph of yesterday's wealthy elite.

Or take the issue of the rights and status of our colored citizens. This is our small share of a worldwide problem. The four hundred years' dominance of men of white skin is ending. The vast colored majority of mankind are seeking the opportunity and the respect which white people have been lucky enough to enjoy for so long — sometimes at the colored people's expense. But, within this worldwide crisis, we in America, with our colored minority, have a major role to play — for good or evil. "The unfinished work" which Lincoln left us, of creating a society in which all men can hold up their heads as equals and self-respecting citizens, can never be accomplished unless there are enough white men and women who resist in the core of their being the moral evil of treating any of God's children as essentially inferior.

Nor is this simply a question of our own national community. I come back to the painful fact that the communists show a worldwide concern which is largely lacking among the men of the West. The whole human race is their horizon. Their "brotherhood" is materialist, collectivist, atheist, and we dislike it, but it embraces everybody, and it is the framework of policies which take the missionaries of their new order to the ends of the earth. I say with all the emphasis I can command that we have no corresponding commitment to our fellowmen. For hundreds of years, we have preached the Christian promise of brotherhood, but today, when vanishing space and scientific revolution have turned our planet into a single neighborhood, the ideal means little in terms of concern or conviction, in terms of policy or action.

Here we are in the Atlantic world, 16 per cent of the world's peoples consuming 70 per cent of the world's wealth. We cannot be indifferent to the moral implications of this gap. I do not know how we can gain a new perspective about the narrow world of plenty and poverty in which we live unless moral insights of justice and compassion stir us to understand the privileged position in which we live.

We are not going to be stirred to action by our own needs. We are the cushioned, protected, fortunate minority. It is not the measure of our morals or the lesson of our history to be spurred on only by fear of Russian encroachments. What we have done has largely had this motivation, and it has left us on the defensive. Our hope is to accept the implications of our own faith, make concrete the image of brotherhood which we profess, and set to work to express our dedication in whatever effort or sacrifice the world's needs may dictate. And, if we must always think in terms of contest with the Soviets, the ability to create the good life for the greatest number will be decisive.

This age has been defined in many ways — as a time of conflict in ideology, as a time of ferment in technology, as a period of revolution in science, as an era when at last the means lie at hand to free mankind from the ancient shackles of pain and hunger. It is all these things — but I believe the true crisis of our times lies at a deeper level. We have indeed conquered means and resources unknown to earlier ages. We have had thrown open to us frontiers of choice which would leave earlier ages stupefied by their scale and scope.

But all this freedom and elbow room only thrusts onto us with more force the fundamental issue of the faith that is in us. We can use our wealth and capacity for some vision of truth, some ideal of brotherhood, or we can imprison ourselves within the selfishness of our own concerns and the limitations of a narrow nationhood. This is the dimension of our crisis.

You may argue that these qualities — of dedication and selflessness — are pretty remote from the realities of politics. They are all very well for private life, but what part can they play in the rough and tumble of partisanship, of primaries, conventions and election campaigns? Ambition, drive, material interests, political skills, the art of maneuver — all these, you say, have their part, but do not let us pretend that the democratic process is primarily a school of virtue or an arena of moral combat.

And yet, I wonder. It has been the view of great philosophers and great statesmen that our system of free government depends in the first instance upon the virtue of its citizens. Montesquieu made virtue the condition of republican government; Washington declared that it could not survive without it. We have had a hundred and seventy-five years of it since their time and no one can deny that the system has survived a remarkable amount of skulduggery. In fact, it is probably a tougher system than its founders imagined. Yet I believe they are right. For no democratic system can survive without at least a large and active leaven of citizens in whom dedication and selflessness are not confined to private life but are the fundamental principles of their activity in the public sphere.

Naked interest and naked ambition will carry a lot of people naturally and inevitably into politics. We do not need societies for the promotion of lobbies. Interests, good and bad, will promote themselves. Nor, in any generation do we lack politicians whose only principle of action is the advancement of their own career — the starry-eyed opportunists and all the other eager men in a hurry to the top. But into what state must politics degenerate if that is all we find active in the political arena? That and sectional interests played upon by personal ambitions? There have been such periods — the roaring nineties, the time from Harding to the Wall Street crash — but our democratic system survived because such epochs were followed and cleansed by periods of disinterested reform.

But there has never been any disinterested reform without disinterested reformers. And here we come to the essential contribution made by dedication and selflessness to the public good. No one ever did any good in politics without readiness for endless hard work — for the grinding, boring, tedious work, as well as the glamorous, high sounding, headline hitting work. The painstaking hours collecting the facts, the hours in committee and conference, the hours in persuasion and argument, the hours of defeat and disappointment, the hours of disgust and revulsion at the darker sides of human behavior — these cannot be supported without energy and devotion. No reforms come easy; even the most obvious will have its entrenched enemies. Each one is carried to us on the bent and weary backs of patient, dedicated men and women.

They are not only dedicated in their readiness to give energy and hard work to the cause; they must also have sufficiently clear sight and open minds and hearts to see the need for reform in the first place. But clear sight and an open heart for others' needs is again something that hardly "comes naturally." We have so many needs of our own — our families, our jobs, our homes, and fortunes, our prospects. We are hemmed in with needs and interests, weighty, urgent, honorable, human needs and interests, even if they are exclusively our own. It takes an extra dimension of vision to see beyond our inner circle of interest. Most people, most of the time, do not possess it — which is one reason why self-regarding interests make up so much of the stuff of politics. And this, I suppose, is why the men and women of genuine, imperturbable public spirit seem so few and far between.

I sometimes think there is a danger of this element of vision vanishing almost wholly from our political life. In the main we are so comfortable; so many evils of the past have shrunk in size and almost out of sight. At the same time, people marry much younger, have larger families and are profoundly involved in earning a living, making careers and safeguarding the future of their children. It is more difficult, they say, to give time to public affairs when private life is so urgent and absorbing.

Yet is it, I wonder, more urgent and absorbing than a hundred years ago when young men not only married young, had large families and built up careers, but also opened up the new frontiers, created new cities from the wilderness and gave to new states and communities the framework of active political life?

If one reads the life of young Abe Lincoln, it is hard to believe that his struggles as a young lawyer and his difficulties as a young parent were less than those of young men today. Yet there was no time when the deepest issues of the day did not occupy his mind or the call of statecraft make itself heard above the claims and clamor of everyday life. Nor was he alone or exceptional. Stephen A. Douglas' life was no different. The prairie towns were filled with earnest, active citizens deeply, profoundly concerned with the great issues of a nation "half slave, half free." When the multitudes gathered, a hundred years ago, to listen in rapt attention for hours to the Lincoln-Douglas debates, had they fewer responsibilities and duties than the citizens of today to many of whom the great issues of politics seem to be most usefully conveyed in 15-second television flashes of subliminal advertising?

Is it not possible that the pressures of personal responsibilities are not greater but that the dedication and selflessness needed to discern and influence public issues have shrunk? In a century in which so many of the mentors of the public mind — from the psychiatrists to the ad-men — speak to us in terms of "what we owe to ourselves," may there not indeed have been a slackening of devotion compared with those days, not so long distant, when what man owes to God and his neighbor was a common theme of public discourse?

If so, this is a dangerous hour for our politics and for government by consent of the governed. For at no time have so many of the great issues of the day demanded clear, real moral vision to bring them into focus —

the vision of A. Powell Davies, who loved the truth and believed in man's capacity and right to govern himself.

On January 26, 1959, Stevenson spoke to the National School Boards Association in San Francisco. After visiting a few days in the Bay area, he vacationed at Aspen, Colorado, with Walter Paepcke, chairman of the board of the Container Corporation of America, and Mrs. Paepcke until February 6 when he returned to Chicago.

To Estes Kefauver

February 7, 1959

Dear Estes:

Thanks for your letter. I wish I was a little more exhilarated, being a President at last![60] Actually my relations with the Field Foundation are not changed in the least by the new circumstances.

I hardly need tell you that your suggestion that the Foundation help the NATO Parliamentarians' Conference interests *me*. However, the Foundation is devoted exclusively to work in the field of race relations and child care, and related fields. Hence there is no possibility that they could respond to your suggestion, much as I would like to.

I look forward to a visit with you and I hope it won't be much longer before the opportunity arises.

Affectionate regards to Nancy.[61]

Cordially yours,

Senator Lyndon Johnson wrote on February 4, 1959, wishing Stevenson a happy birthday and describing his job as Majority Leader as "hectic."

To Lyndon B. Johnson

February 9, 1959

Dear Lyn:

I was flattered by your note on my birthday. I marvel with all you have to do in your frantic days that you can find time for such thoughtfulness. What a guy!

[60] Stevenson had recently been elected president of the Field Foundation.
[61] Mrs. Kefauver.

From where I sit things are going well — and I hope your health is going as well too.

Yours,

Author Taylor Caldwell wrote Stevenson that she was a one-hundred-per-cent old-line Republican, but that she had nothing but praise for the quotations from his lecture in memory of A. Powell Davies that were published in Life, *February 9, 1959. She mentioned that she had been reading "eulogies" of him in the publications of patriotic organizations and concluded that he had never been fairly presented in the national press. She also wrote that she was sending him a copy of her forthcoming novel.*

To Taylor Caldwell

February 11, 1959

My dear Miss Caldwell:

I was delighted with your engaging letter. It was good enough for a Democrat! Indeed, it was too good.

I shall look forward most eagerly to "Dear And Glorious Physician," and I am profoundly flattered that you are going to send me an auto-graphed copy. I will do the same for you with a little volume of news-paper pieces that Harper's is putting out in March.[62]

If you have read eulogies about me I am delighted. Somehow I have missed them, but in a full and busy life I have missed you too, and that I hope to be able to remedy some day — and soon, I hope.

With my warm regards and admiration, I am

Cordially yours,

To Fidel Castro[63]

February 24, 1959

My dear Sir:

I have just had a telephone call from my friend, Congressman Charles Porter of Oregon. He gave me a most interesting account of his recent interview with you in Havana and also mentioned your charitable words about me. I am honored and grateful.

I send you my best wishes and most earnest hopes for the success of

[62] *Friends and Enemies:What I Learned in Russia.*
[63] Premier of Cuba since February 16, after his guerrilla force had ousted the government of General Fulgencio Batista.

[334]

your great undertaking in Cuba. It is not easy for us in America to envision the obstacles you have overcome and the problems you confront. But, at least, some of us try, and with high hopes for the stability, peace and prosperity of your beautiful land

Cordially yours,

On February 17, 1959, Stevenson's aide Bill Blair wrote him in a memo: "I think it is very important for you to plan to attend the Democratic Victory Dinner in Washington on February 28. There will be a lot of talk if you don't and I can't think of any excuse that would make very much sense! Please plan to attend. Your friend and supporter." Stevenson had been objecting that he did not wish to go, and he sent the following telegram in reply to a telegram from the wife of his 1956 assistant campaign manager, in which she said: "What's a cake without the icing, what's a party without the spicing? . . . All we need is you, you, you."

To Mrs. James Rowe

February 26, 1959

THE SIREN'S SWEET SONG LIFTS ME LIKE A TIDE AND WAFTS ME OFF TO WASHINGTON. BUT MY FOOT IS IN A TRAP. LOVE AND THANKS FROM

ME ME ME

Singer Bing Crosby wrote Stevenson that he was impressed by the quotations from Stevenson in the editorial in Life, *February 9, 1959. Mr. Crosby expressed concern that many young people lacked dedication and offered to help in an effort to alter the situation.*

To Bing Crosby

February 27, 1959

Dear Bing:

I was delighted to have your letter of the 18th and I am very much flattered by such charitable comments from what you call "tinsel town" about that lecture. Indeed, I am bold enough to enclose a copy, although I can hardly urge that you read it in toto.

I wish I knew the answers to some of my anxieties about our country in these searching times. Certainly communications, papers, magazines, films, television, radio and books have not kept us fully and truthfully informed or stimulated enough for self-examination and dissatisfaction. But exhorting the truth is easy to say and hard to practice, I suppose, and certainly among my ilk — the politician (although I am a lawyer again, thank God!) — telling the people what they want to hear rather than what they should hear has been standard practice for as long as the history of democracy.

What to do? I am reminded of an old man in an English railroad station whom I overheard say to a group of friends: "I'm going up to London to be diagonized by the doctors." Well, I guess I am better at diagonizing than prescribing, a common frailty of people who talk too much.

I will remember your offer to help if I get some better ideas.

Sincerely yours,

Stevenson attended the Democratic party dinner in Washington on February 28, 1959, and spent the following week at his New York law office. He then flew with Mr. and Mrs. Roger Stevens to Jamaica to vacation at the home of Mrs. Mary Lasker.

Mrs. Eugene Meyer, who had invited him to visit her in Naples, Florida, wrote that the warm sun there, plus the fishing and house guests, made it difficult to concentrate on writing. She added that Mr. Meyer's health was improving.[64]

To Mrs. Eugene Meyer[65]

March 14, 1959

Agnes dear —

Thanks for your good letter. I know how you feel — to write anything, even letters, to think anything, even banalities, takes heroic exertion in these latitudes.

I am so glad to hear Eugene is picking up under your tender direction — food, drink & women! I like that prescription too — but as the character in that wonderful Gothic Tale of Isak Dinisen [Dinesen] says — "The love of eating is a heavy cross." and I'm *really* unloading that burden down here — *really!!* So don't tempt me too far. I plan now to leave here on BOAC flight 402 on March 22 — arriving Miami at 2:25 PM. Evidently I have to wait there 3 horrible hours until I can get

[64] Mr. Meyer died on July 17, 1959.
[65] This handwritten letter is in the Agnes Meyer files, Princeton University Library.

Naples Airlines flight 417 at 5:30! which arrives at Naples at 6:15. There seems to be no other way to do it — altho motoring across the Everglades is a temptation. But it is hard to organize that from here. I will plan to stay with you the 23rd & perhaps the 24th and then go down to Captiva to see some relatives and home folks for a day or so — all of which will be contrived from your house.

And now — to sea, to rum and then to sleep — again!

Affec —

ADLAI

[Later]

Dear Agnes — Signals changed! I am now arriving *Saturday* by Naples Airlines at 6:15 PM instead of Sunday. I hope it isn't inconvenient — and if it is you can stretch me under a palm tree in the garden for the night. I can sleep anywhere at any time; indeed that's about all I can do in this sultry green paradise —

ADLAI

Stevenson returned to Chicago on March 27, 1959. Barry Bingham reviewed Stevenson's book Friends and Enemies: What I Learned in Russia (*New York: Harper, 1959*) *in the* Louisville Courier-Journal, *March 20, 1959. Harrison Salisbury, of the New York* Times, *wrote Stevenson, March 3, 1959, praising the book and stated: "You never should have gotten out of the newspaper business! The more I consider your report the better I like it." The* New York Times Magazine, *March 1, 1959, published Stevenson's introduction to the book, under the title "This Time We Might Get Licked."*

To Barry Bingham[66]

March 30, 1959

Dear Barry:

I have just returned from Florida and the Caribbean, sun-soaked, rum-soaked, plump, sleepy and stupid. But not too sleepy to read your review of the book which Cass Canfield insisted on publishing. And not too stupid to realize that at least you and Harrison Salisbury knew what I was trying to do. I was disappointed that most of the reviews didn't even note the questions I tried to ask about our psychological and structural preparation for the ordeal. I get so many letters saying that

[66] A copy is in the Adlai E. Stevenson collection, Illinois State Historical Library (A.E.S., I.S.H.L.)

my criticism of the American scene in this book and elsewhere is wholly negative; that I say what is wrong without saying what to do about it. But if people *did* know what was wrong there would be no problem of what to do. . . .

Love to Mary.[67]

Yours,

Professor J. Frank Dobie, of the University of Texas, praised Steven-son's book Friends and Enemies: What I Learned in Russia *and stated that it was a tragic deprivation that a man of Stevenson's thinking and reasoning was not in charge of the nation's foreign affairs. Mr. Dobie expressed the hope that the United States would act as if it was civilized and rational and take advantage of Stevenson's abilities.*

To J. Frank Dobie

March 30, 1959

My dear Dr. Dobie:

I was charmed to find your letter awaiting me on my return from a journey. Somehow a letter like that from an American who has earned such esteem from his fellow men does me more good than even a good review!

I am sure you are right that progress to the state of rational civiliza-tion is geological. . . . But it advances! And I am happy to have had anything to do with the advance — *if* I have. And you haven't per-suaded me, my dear and honored friend.

Cordially yours,

To Patrick J. Lucey[68]

April 3, 1959

Dear Pat:

Thank you for sending me your letter of March 11 to "potential candi-dates." I am flattered to be included, but I am sure you know that I am neither a present nor "potential" candidate for the nomination this time!

I keep hearing good things about the growing strength of our party in Wisconsin — which fills my heart with joy and for which we have you to thank in large measure.

With warmest good wishes, I am

Cordially yours,

[67] Mrs. Bingham.
[68] Chairman of the Democratic party of Wisconsin.

C. Scott Fletcher, president of the Fund for Adult Education, sent Stevenson a copy of the fund's proposal "Education for Public Responsibility."

To C. Scott Fletcher

April 7, 1959

Dear Mr. Fletcher:

I welcome your statement of the problem of adult education, or *continuing* education, as I like to think of it. It is good to know that the Fund for Adult Education plans to exert vigorous leadership, both in research into what is most needed to preserve and extend our liberties and those of the free world and in the effort to provide greater educational opportunity for our mature citizens. I fully share your concern and I like the direct way in which you are dealing with it.

I see an imperative need for at least two levels of continuing education. The first is education — through the humanities and the social studies — in awareness and responsibility. I mean training in the ability to read and to listen critically, and to form judgments in the light of the facts and the public interest. The exercise of such responsibilities as voting, participating in public discussion (even paying taxes!) serves democracy and freedom only as it reflects the best use of a citizen's critical powers. At this level of continuing education I should guess almost everyone might be a potential pupil.

The second level I think we need is for education not so much *for* leadership as *of* leaders. I think we could do a great deal more to encourage our citizens who are willing to accept leadership responsibilities in the community — private as well as public. I should think studies of such questions as why people become leaders, what qualities enable them to succeed, what are the sources of discouragement, and others, might provide fruitful materials for leaders to use in continuing their own education.

Finally, I am skeptical of assumptions that Soviet education is simply education for servitude. Of course Communist youth are not taught to criticize the party or its policy. But they *are* well trained for the lower levels of decision-making, and they assuredly acquire a discipline of learning whose fruits are dramatically apparent. I think perhaps we shall do better for our own future if we concentrate more of our energies upon critical study of ourselves and our own civilization and less upon worry about the Soviet future.

I think the Fund for Adult Education is on the right track and I am encouraged by this new initiative in "Education for Public Responsibility." Good luck!

Sincerely yours,

In its April 12, 1959, issue, the New York Times Book Review *published Stevenson's review of* Elm Street Politics, *by former Democratic National Committee chairman Stephen A. Mitchell, with a foreword by former Republican national chairman Leonard W. Hall, published by Oceana Publications, of New York.*

This is a book by the former chairman of the Democratic National Committee about the "political club movement" — and I should be the last person in the world to review it. For I am the author's grateful debtor and no less hopeful for the new-style politics and politicians he writes about; and therefore, a little dizzy already at the prospect of leaning back to keep from leaning forward to keep from leaning over backward — about him and the clubs.

Actually, though, Mr. Mitchell places little strain on the reviewer's objectivity. "The trouble with politics," he says, "is that it is too much of a spectator's sport. * * * The purpose of this book is to encourage more people to take a larger part in politics." Starting from an account of a neighborhood political-club meeting in the Mitchell living room on Elm Street in Chicago, he goes on to report the recent mushrooming of the club movement across the country, endorses this movement with unqualified and non-partisan approval (echoed in a foreword by Leonard Hall, the author's erstwhile Republican counterpart), and concludes with a set of detailed "do-it-yourself" instructions on how the rank-and-file citizen who belongs to or leans toward one party can have his say without losing his amateur status.

This recognition of the important role of the independent but practical participant in American politics is timely. We have been inclined to over-glorify, I think, the voter whose "independence" takes the form of splitting tickets, "voting for the man," switching parties, and staying aloof from what is too commonly considered the griminess of organization politics. Such voters are probably essential ballast against any party's ever moving the vessel too far to one side or the other. But it is equally important to recognize that there are means readily at hand for compounding the effectiveness of independent political *thinking* by organized political *doing*.

These are Mr. Mitchell's principal purposes, and he serves them fully and well. In the process he has written an interesting and useful little review of the transformation of American politics that has accompanied the rapid social changes in this generation. Politicians will find food for thought here, for Mr. Mitchell analyzes what we sometimes only imperfectly perceive in the pattern of growth and change in three separate settings — the big city, the suburbs and rural counties.

He also brings out what is becoming apparent in areas where the "revolt" of the non-professionals has been going on longer — that the new-style leaders and organizations are apt to age rapidly once they achieve supremacy. Does this mean that the club movement that has been spreading so rapidly is just the same old struggle for power of the party "ins" versus the party "outs?" Mr. Mitchell says no, that there is "a strong continuous trend in favor of the new-style politician and new-style party member-worker."

Inevitably Mr. Mitchell raises some broader points and issues on which there will properly be questions and legitimate difference of opinion. For example, I think the case for the clubs goes beyond the fact that there is sometimes good reason for protests against the ward bosses, boys-in-the-back-room kind of politics. Mr. Mitchell sometimes seems to shatter his spear against windmills that are more and more old caricatures of old-fashioned organization politics. And when he finds his epitaph for "the bosses" in the poet's "The old order changeth, yielding place to new" he leaves out Tennyson's explanation: "Lest one good custom should corrupt the world." I hope the generation of the clubs proves as responsive to the political needs of the new times as the much maligned "bosses" were to theirs.

In California where the Democratic club movement commenced, following the 1952 election, and has reached its zenith, it is interesting to note that it arose not as a "boss-antidote" but largely as a consequence of the previous incompleteness of the regular party organization.

Many of the clubs have unquestionably sprung up primarily as receivers in bankruptcy to take over the affairs of local party organizations whose leadership had developed hardening of the arteries or a propensity for embezzling political power. But to oversimplify the explanation for this new institutional development as a protest against "the pros" would have unfortunate consequences. There are other explanations: Mr. Mitchell calls our attention to the anxiety of these times, as well as expanding prosperity, leisure and education.

I wonder, too, if there isn't significant coincidence between the emergence of the clubs and the development of what are larger than usual divisions within both major parties about basic public issues, like segregation, defense, monetary policy, Federal aid to education, right-to-work laws, etc. And there is probably a connection between this new political development and the fact that our country's affairs have not been going so well in the world.

"More and more of us," as Mr. Mitchell notes, "feel an inner need or duty to defend our way of life some way." For some people concern has become positive anxiety, which leads them on to the feeling of wanting to take a hand in doing something or other. I suppose in a sense the club movement is for some people a reflection, on Caesar's side of things, of an attitude which finds its catalyst for others in the revival meeting.

Mr. Mitchell does not overlook the attraction of the clubs for people who shy away from the regular organization out of a concern about getting their shirtsleeves dirty. I read, along with "Elm St. Politics" an illuminating recent book by William Lee Miller, "The Protestant and Politics."[69] Mr. Miller brilliantly analyzes the attitude of too many good churchgoers about politics' uncouthness. He reaches what has always seemed to me the necessary conclusion that trying to make politics a little bit better by actually getting into it is one of the tests of whether a man's religious faith is great enough to take him into the practical, everyday scramble between good and evil.

It does not belittle the movement to ask some questions, as a perceptive California friend of mine has done, about at least the West-Coast type of club development. What are the effects of an almost exclusively "ideological" political motivation? Is some degree of instability the likely price of a lack of the restraint of economic interest and of part-time interest in politics? What are the implications of all-out election campaigning by highly vocal groups who assume little responsibility for legislative follow-up of either their nominees or their programs? What is necessary to prevent hit-and-run politics — even by one's highest minded political friends?

These seem to be worth-while questions. And as I think of the basic differences between, for example, the California Democratic clubs and the form the "independent" movement has taken in New York, it seems to me, too, that what may be viewed as an antibiotic on Elm St. in Chicago may be a vitamin pill in Los Angeles, and a still different miracle drug in New York. Whatever it is appears good for the body politic — but still needing experiment and constructive criticism.

Mr. Mitchell repeatedly recognizes and emphasizes the necessity of making the clubs instruments for increasing the stature and the effectiveness of the two major parties — and not just places for people to ease their consciences by ineffective political setting-up exercises.

It is this matter of the relationship between the clubs and the regular

[69] Philadelphia: Westminster Press, 1958.

party organizations which is the most important part of this whole business, and Mr. Mitchell deals with it extensively and constructively, after he is done belaboring the bosses. He suggests that "people new in politics should use the club as a sort of revolving door connecting the club members with the legal or formal party organization" and notes the possibility and the fact of "a good deal of overlapping of membership between the clubs and the regulars."

It is, of course, through the formal Democratic and Republican parties that the will of the nation's people will be brought to bear in meeting problems which have now assumed the dimensions of crisis, as they have before and will again. Surely it is the first obligation of the newly organized neighborhood club to channel its strength toward meeting them.

The most interesting thing about Steve Mitchell's book is his reminder of how far America had receded from its high point in the arts of self government while reaching its high point in living standards. He summons as his witness that durable authority, De Tocqueville, who in the Eighteen Thirties was amazed at the average American's knowledge of his government. The most comforting thing about the book is Mr. Mitchell's conclusion "that there are many signs of a revival of this American tradition which places on every man and woman the right and duty of taking a share in the government of his community, state and nation."

And Stephen Mitchell's extraordinary contribution is that he is now preaching what he has effectively practiced.

To T. S. Matthews

April 13, 1959

Dear Tom:

Will you be in London in June, and if so could you and Martha[70] be persuaded to make a major contribution to my knowledge of England? The means are as follows: I could arrive from America (on my annual trip) on Friday morning, June 19, instead of Sunday, June 21st, and step into the Matthews' waiting arms and automobile (or my automobile!) and motor to Cornwall, Wales, or whatever you recommend, returning to London on Monday, June 22. If that sounds like too much of me, bring anyone else you like. And if the airport is inconvenient as a starting point, how about Claridge's? After years of travelling in your adopted homeland, each April I am reminded that I know nothing

[70] Mrs. Matthews.

beyond Southampton, London, Oxford and Cambridge and the intervening countryside.

Besides, think what such a journey would do for your health and my greater understanding of people, politics, press and philosophy.

I can't explain the foregoing except that Spring seems to have come to the prairies at last and with it my appetite for the countryside.

Affectionate regards to Martha.

Yours,

p.s. I can lay on a suitable car with chauffeur readily if needed.

Stevenson spent the week of April 20, 1959, as a Chubb Fellow of Timothy Dwight College at Yale University.

To Mrs. Eugene Meyer[71]

April 30, 1959

My dear Agnes:

Forgive this hurried and dictated note in response to so many of yours which have accumulated during my travels around the country.

The latter culminated in a week at Yale, which was harder work but more fun than campaigning. I talked to all and sundry — including 600 at the Divinity School and 3,000 in Woolsey Hall. . . . Among my new professorial friends was the Eugene Meyer professor.

. . . But please let us not talk of my future exposure to the "ghastly tensions of public service and the burden of power" or I shall charge you with a death wish.[72]

When do you go to Mount Kisco? I will hope for a quiet evening there before I leave for Europe the middle of June. There will be business in Washington in between but my trips there always are too hectic.

Affectionately,
ADLAI

Political reporter Edward Folliard wrote in the Washington Post, *April 24, 1959: "Adlai E. Stevenson continues to be a red hot if passive contender for the Democratic nomination for President in 1960. . . . It would be strange, indeed, if 1960 again brought out the old hole in the*

[71] The original is in the Agnes Meyer files, Princeton University Library.
[72] Mrs. Meyer had been urging Stevenson's candidacy for President in 1960.

shoe lapel pins and the 'Madly With Adlai' placards. But it could happen."

To Edward T. Folliard

April 30, 1959

Dear Eddie:

Thanks for your letter and the story. It makes me feel very good, but I am not worrying in spite of your distinguished reputation as a political seer. Old candidates never die — they just wear out — and I am worn out! Hooray!!

Why don't you ever come to see the happiest, contentedest, fattest, freest lawyer you know?

Yours,

P.S. Yes, I remember that day in December 1957 outside the White House.[73] And I still say "What!"

To William O. Douglas

April 30, 1959

Dear Bill:

I had an interesting talk with your charming friend, Dr. James Yen,[74] and we will meet again after his return from Formosa. I remember well visiting some of the rural reconstruction and rehabilitation projects when I was out there, and I am glad you have got this work started in the Philippines.[75] It is a pity the world isn't filled with a few more Jimmy Yens — and a few more Bill Douglases!

I hope you are well.

Cordially yours,

William Baggs wrote Stevenson that Ralph McGill, Harry Ashmore, executive editor of the Arkansas Gazette, *and he had analyzed the political situation and agreed that Stevenson was going to be increas-*

[73] Stevenson had just emerged from a White House meeting and had been talking to reporters when Mr. Folliard told him that he was looking forward to a Stevenson candidacy in 1960, to which Stevenson, somewhat taken aback, replied, "What!"

[74] Founder of rural reconstruction movements in a number of countries, including his native China.

[75] Dr. Yen helped organize a private rural reconstruction movement in the Philippines in 1952, and based on its success, founded the International Institute of Rural Reconstruction, located in the Philippines, in 1960, when he became the institute's first president.

ingly involved in the 1960 presidential situation. Mr. Baggs mentioned that he had attended a small dinner party with Richard M. Nixon and that the Vice President seemed to be trying to become a political philosopher, since he had quoted Hegel and Kant.

To William C. Baggs

April 30, 1959

Dear Bill:

Your letter awaited me after a week of being wise and good — a difficult exercise for me — with the students at Yale. It is a most interesting and disturbing letter on two counts, me and politics and Ashmore and Patterson.[76] Of the latter I know less evidently than you think. Of the former I hope I know more than you suspect.

But I can agree that a good long talk would be fruitful for me and I hope if anything brings you to Chicago or New York between now and mid-June you will let me know. I will be leaving then for Europe for six weeks.

Yours,

p.s. But nothing can reconcile me to Nixon!

Stevenson's nephew Robert Pirie, the son of Mrs. Ralph Hines, wrote that he was applying to the law schools at Harvard University and the University of Michigan, and asked his uncle for advice. He also mentioned that he and his fiancée, Deirdre Howard, were to be married on June 10.

To Robert S. Pirie

April 30, 1959

Dear Bobby:

I am mortified that I have neglected your letter of April 12 which arrived during a long absence. It came as something of a surprise to me, as I thought you wanted to go on and specialize in the rare book field. Indeed I always envied you having such a taste and being in a position to follow it to all of its exciting, if obscure, destinations. However, who am I to ask anyone to stop, look and listen before he goes into the law, and, in any event, I assume that this is precautionary and protective and you have not yet resolved to serve that cruel mistress forever and ever.

[76] Hugh B. Patterson, publisher of the *Arkansas Gazette*.

While I have no special influence at Harvard Law School and would hesitate to use it if I had, I have written Livingston Hall[77] (Adlai tells me he is sort of second in command), as per the enclosed copy. I was loathe to write Dean Griswold[78] directly. I cannot foresee what effect this will have, if any, but if Harvard's doors are closed there must be some others that must be open or can be opened. I think of the University of Virginia in this connection, where the law school enjoys a much better reputation than the college. The others are many and obvious to you, including Leland Stanford where the Dean[79] is a special friend of mine.

I had my first glimpse of Joan[80] on my return yesterday and a very satisfactory glimpse it was.

With love to Deirdre.

Yours,

P.S. The change of the wedding to June 10 is most distressing. That is the day of the semi-annual meeting of the Board of Directors of a company of which I am chairman of the Executive Committee, and I am not a bit sure that I will be able to get to the wedding. Somehow, I had thought it was to be on the 11th.

Mayor Richard C. Lee of New Haven, Connecticut, wrote on April 28, 1959, that Stevenson's visit to Yale University had made an excellent impression on both the faculty and the student body.

To Richard C. Lee

May 9, 1959

Dear Dick:

I have just returned from another journey and find your letter. . . . Certainly you have earned yourself and New Haven a position in the history of urban renewal which is going to get larger and larger, if I am not mistaken.

. . . I must say that the visit to Yale was a strange experience for me and I think a very valuable one, for which I have you to thank. I came away with a feeling that I had performed very badly but that it had been a good lesson and a good reminder of the occupational hazard of

---

[77] Professor of law, vice dean and acting dean of the Harvard Law School.
[78] Erwin N. Griswold, professor of law and dean of the Harvard Law School.
[79] Carl Spaeth.
[80] Mr. Pirie's sister, Mrs. Harry Thayer.

politicians, and too much talking and too little studying and reading. I felt also that they piled too much on me and didn't give me enough time to gather my wits and collect my thoughts between classes, seminars, inquisitions, lunches, dinners, etc.

Your letter is reassuring, therefore, even if I discount it substantially, and I am grateful. The students, their curiosity, thoughtfulness and interest, came as a surprise. In spite of three sons and myriads of young friends, I came away from New Haven with a quite new and enlarged respect. But where are these guys going when they get out of school? I wish I saw more of them in our party meetings and activities. This is something we must think about and work at more than we have done, and right away!

I wish I were going to see you again, and soon.

With renewed thanks for getting me into all that trouble!

Cordially,

P.S. . . .

By the spring of 1959 Stevenson had received a number of letters urging him to be a candidate for the 1960 Democratic nomination. (The editors have included his standard reply to only some of these letters.) There was also considerable newspaper speculation about Stevenson's role in 1960.[81] *Meanwhile, James Doyle, a Madison, Wisconsin, lawyer and former chairman of the Wisconsin State Democratic party, began to sound out his political friends on Stevenson's prospects. Doyle was impressed that no clear favorite for the nomination had emerged in 1957, 1958, and by early 1959. He felt that a Stevenson draft was at least possible.*[82]

To James E. Doyle

May 13, 1959

Dear Jim:

Coming back from the University of Illinois this morning (where I made this lecture for a fee!), I read some clippings Bill Blair had

[81] See, for instance, the Chicago *Tribune*, January 3, 1959; the Chicago *Sun-Times*, January 23, 1959; the Chicago *Sun-Times*, April 20, 1959; the New York *Times*, April 19, 1959.

[82] Donald Murray, "Patronage and the Draft in the Nominating Process: A Case Study of the Stevenson Organization at the 1960 Democratic National Convention" (unpublished mimeographed master's thesis, Brooklyn College, 1962), p. 8. A copy is in the possession of the editors. See also Theodore H. White, *The Making of the President, 1960* (New York: Atheneum, 1961).

slipped into my brief case, including your eloquent endorsement for 1960. Thank you, my dear and loyal friend! But if I emphatically disagree with your conclusions about the party's best interests, my virtues and future, I am sure you will understand that it does not diminish my gratitude for such charity.

And are you really coming to see me? Please do — I want to thank you and to set you right!

Cordially yours,

Mary McGrory, columnist for the Washington Evening Star, *wrote Stevenson that she had recently traveled to California, Washington and Oregon and found that sentiment for him in 1960 was strong. Most of the people she met on her trip, she remarked, were in politics because of him. Miss McGrory added that she had just completed a 10,000-word article about him*[83] *but was concerned that it was pitched too narrowly on her Boston Irish view of life "so alien" to his background.*

To Mary McGrory

May 13, 1959

Dear Bloody Mary:

Thanks! That's the best condensation of a lot of work, a lot of suffering, a lot of frustration, and a lot of fun by a lot of people I have ever had. Who but you can grasp the "Big Picture" and squeeze the pigments to a drop. I was going to say "synthetic drop" but something is wrong with my synthesis.

And while you are cruising around in this shameless way, why don't you stop off and get a Chicago-Irish view of a political life that is *not* so alien?

Please remember me to Mary McGrory.

Yours,

P.S. I am constantly meeting folks who say they get into politics on my account. But why don't they get out on my account?

---

[83] " 'Uneasy Politician': Adlai E. Stevenson," in *Candidates 1960*, edited by Eric Sevareid (New York: Basic Books, 1959), pp. 216–244.

To Archibald MacLeish

May 19, 1959

Dear Archie:

At least I could not quarrel with one of the Pulitzer prizes this year.[84] What a remarkable man you are and how proud I am to call you "friend" — especially to my irreverent young.

I am coming to Cambridge on June 6 to speak at the Harvard Business School and will probably stay the night at Dana-Palmer House.[85] If you and Ada[86] are about at that time I will hope for at least a moment's greeting.

Again my heartfelt congratulations.

Yours ever,

To Mr. and Mrs. Alfred Lunt[87]

May 20, 1959

My dear Friends:

I *may* go up to a memorial affair for Frank Lloyd Wright at Spring Green on Monday, June 8. Taliesen — Spring Green — is west of Madison. And I *may* have with me Alicia Patterson, of New York, and John Allison, our Ambassador to Czechoslovakia.

If Genessee Depot[88] is in the vicinity, I would like so much to call on you briefly, going or coming. But where is Genessee Depot! Ex-politicians don't keep road maps around! And will you be there? And may we stop?

Cordially yours,

Stevenson spent the last ten days of May, 1959, in New York City. On May 29 he delivered the commencement address at McGill University in Montreal, Canada, where he was awarded an honorary LL.D. degree. He then returned to Chicago. At this point, an article appeared by columnist Rowland Evans, Jr., who wrote that Stevenson had told friends that Senator Johnson was the most "capable" of the Democratic

---

[84] Mr. MacLeish had received the Pulitzer Prize for drama for *J.B.: A Play in Verse*.

[85] A Harvard University guesthouse in Cambridge.

[86] Mrs. MacLeish.

[87] The stage actor and his wife, actress Lynn Fontanne.

[88] The Lunts' home in Wisconsin.

presidential prospects, Senator Humphrey next, Senator Kennedy third, and Senator Symington fourth. Evans added: "Stevenson, despite repeated statements that he has no interest at all in getting a third nomination, is widely regarded as a possible compromise candidate if none of the active candidates should get a majority of convention votes."

To Hubert H. Humphrey, Lyndon Johnson, John Kennedy, Stuart Symington[89]

June 1, 1959

On Sunday morning, May 30, a story by Rowland Evans, Jr. appeared on the front page of the New York Herald-Tribune purporting to express my views on the relative merits of the Democratic candidates for 1960.

I was out of town at the time and when Clayton Fritchey finally found me and told me about the forthcoming story I authorized him to promptly issue a statement for quotation that it was a total fabrication and that "I have never discussed the relative merits of Presidential candidates with anybody at any time."

Ho-Hum! And will you now all join me in a toast to the freedom of the press?

To George Cornish[90]

June 1, 1959

Dear Mr. Cornish:

A story by Rowland Evans, Jr. in the Herald-Tribune on Sunday, May 30, states that I have rated the Democratic Presidential candidates. Please be advised that I have written the Senators involved that this story is a total fabrication and that "I have never discussed the relative merits of the Presidential candidates with anybody at any time."

If you have not run this denial in your paper I would appreciate it if you would do so. I suppose it would be too much to expect you to give it the same prominence you gave the original fabrication.[91]

Sincerely yours,

[89] "Blind" copies were sent to Clayton Fritchey, Marietta Tree, and Governor Robert Meyner, of New Jersey.

[90] Editor of the New York *Herald Tribune*.

[91] Mr. Cornish replied that the *Herald Tribune* had published the Associated Press dispatch in which Stevenson denied the story. Mr. Cornish added, however, that Mr. Evans was a "careful and conscientious reporter and he received his information from a source which he believed entirely accurate."

To Rabbi Jacob J. Weinstein[92]

June 9, 1959

Dear Jacob:

I regret more than I can say that I shall be in New York for a meeting of the Field Foundation on June 12 and for that reason will not be able to join the Congregation of K.A.M. in celebrating your double anniversary.[93]

The world that all of us are striving to build is a world founded upon the rock-bottom freedom of all men everywhere to worship as they wish, to think what they please, and to say what they think. It is a world where all men can live in dignity and secure in the knowledge that they have the opportunity to build a full and happy life for themselves and their families. You more than anyone I know have practiced what you preach and all who share in this dream of a better world are enormously in your debt — and none more than

Your devoted friend,

To Paul Ziffren[94]

June 16, 1959

Dear Paul:

I hear that you are the target of a testimonial dinner and while I wish I could be present, I suspect that it will be crowded enough! But you are getting just what you deserve and, if a native-born Californian may be permitted to say just a word, let me thank you both for what you have done to strengthen the image of our Party as liberal, progressive and imaginative, and for all the help and encouragement you have given me in the years of the locust!

But, of course, your greatest service has been to introduce into my life that incomparable Mickey.[95] She is my candidate for everything and anything!

Cordially,

ADLAI

[92] Rabbi of the K.A.M. Temple in Chicago. The original was in the possession of the late Rabbi Weinstein at his death on October 2, 1974.

[93] This presumably refers to the thirtieth anniversary of his ordination in 1929 and his twentieth as rabbi of K.A.M.

[94] The original is in the possession of Mr. Ziffren.

[95] Mrs. Ziffren.

Congressman Byron L. Johnson, of Colorado, wrote Stevenson prais-
ing his recent speeches[96] and declaring that his was one of the voices
sensitive to the deepest needs of the world. He urged Stevenson to
continue to speak out.

To Byron L. Johnson

June 17, 1959

Dear Byron:

I was delighted to find your letter when I returned recently from the
"commencement circuit." Your flattery pleases me enormously. Voices
like yours encourage me mightily, both for our party and for our country. I emphatically agree that the people *are* ahead of most of the
politicians. The difficulty is always getting them to pause, to listen, and
to put complicated things in a form they can understand. Somehow I
feel distressed that political leaders don't do a better job of educating.

. . . But please don't expect me to talk too much. I feel that I have
vastly overdone it this winter and spring both at the price of my own
leisure reading and law practice and also with political consequences
that sometimes make me most uneasy.

I hope it won't be long before we can have a good talk.

Cordially and gratefully yours,

On June 18, 1959, Stevenson flew to England, where he spent two
weeks visiting with old friends, attended board meetings of Encyclo-
paedia Britannica, Ltd., and conferred with contributors to the Bri-
tannica.

To Mr. and Mrs. Douglas Fairbanks[97]

[no date; probably June 30, 1959]

My dear Fairbanks:

I had thought to call or see you before this — and now I'm off to
Lisbon in the grey dawn, full of contrition *and* thanks for that lovely
party and your many kindnesses. I wish we had had a little time for just
talk together — but that seems seldom possible in London.

I have hope for *that* in America, because I count you among the best

[96] His most recent speech, at the Harvard Business School on June 6, 1959, is
reprinted in Adlai E. Stevenson, *Putting First Things First: A Democratic View*
(New York: Random House, 1960), pp. 58–75.
[97] This handwritten letter is in the possession of Mr. Fairbanks.

informed Americans abroad and always marvel at the position of affection and respect you have earned.

Farewell and thanks! thanks, thanks!

ADLAI

At Lisbon, Portugal, Stevenson and his son and daughter-in-law joined Mr. and Mrs. William Benton for a three-week Mediterranean cruise aboard the Bentons' yacht.

To Jawaharlal Nehru

July 10, 1959[98]

Dear Mr. Prime Minister:

Mrs. Eleanor Roosevelt recently has lent her name to a new and great center for cancer research; the Eleanor Roosevelt Institute for Cancer Research, to be located on the grounds of the American Medical Center at Denver, Colorado. The American Medical Center is the only hospital in the United States which accepts far-advanced cancer patients on a free, non-sectarian basis, and for as long as treatment may be required. It is supported entirely by public contributions.

May I ask your special consideration of a very special project. It is our idea that we should ask government leaders and well known men and women the world over to signify their regard for the cause Mrs. Roosevelt represents, by contributing items of interest and historical import. These items will then be auctioned to the highest bidders at an affair of international scope. The funds realized will go wholly toward the building of the Eleanor Roosevelt Institute for Cancer Research.

Any time before the middle of September will serve our plans as far as the arrival of gifts is concerned. This will provide sufficient time for the printing of a formal, illustrated inventory of the "auction" for international distribution.

Mrs. Roosevelt will celebrate her 75th birthday on October 11th of this year, and while the "auction" will be held early in 1960, I should like to think that every gift received in the cause of helping cancer research also will be a gift in honor of her Diamond Jubilee.

Should your interest lead you to ask any questions at all concerning the Institute or arrangements for receipt of the items to be auctioned, I shall be more than happy to try to answer.

Cordially,

[98] This letter was not written while Stevenson was on the Bentons' yacht, but either was prepared in Chicago before he left and typed much later or was written in London and sent to Chicago for typing.

P.S. Since the auction will be held in Los Angeles, please address any gifts you may care to send to my attention at: American Medical Center, 122 South Robertson Boulevard, Los Angeles 48, California.[99]

Mrs. Edwin Winter, of Lake Forest, Illinois, wrote Stevenson that their mutual friend Mrs. Edison Dick had just undergone a serious emergency operation.

To Mrs. Edison Dick[100]

[no date]

Dearest Jane —

A letter from Ruth [Winter] has just arrived with the preoperative details — and I must get this ashore with the tender at once.

While of course you are anxious, I also *know* you are *strong* and *wise* — wise enough to sense the healing medicine in the mind, even in such cases as this. I *know* that everything is going to be alright, that no evil can really befall you, clothed as you are in composure, confidence — and love. Many tenderly devoted people will help you bear this burden until, like most of our crises and fears, it has made you stronger and handsomer than ever and is only an ugly memory.

On and on we sail to new delights and beautiful adventures. Herewith some purloined and altered lines from the blue sea and wild Balearic coasts:

> If I could only see what's there —
> This golden day that makes me stare:
> The climbing walls, aflame with flowers,
> The steady sun that melts the hours,
> The summer sea, blue after blue,
> And islands new, almost in view.

And *now* I'm getting homesick!

Much love —
ADLAI

[99] Nehru sent two sixteenth-century Moghul paintings and a seal over three thousand years old.

[100] This handwritten letter is in the possession of Mrs. Dick. It was mailed in Palma de Mallorca in early July, 1959.

To Mrs. Franklin D. Roosevelt[101]

July 25, 1959

Dear Mrs. R —

I've had three idle, sunny weeks on this lovely yacht with Adlai and Nancy, Bill Benton's family and some friends — and all we've missed is *you!* I think I've relaxed at last, or perhaps "decomposed" is a better word! I pray you are well & getting some *rest.*

Love
ADLAI

After three weeks of cruising on the Bentons' yacht, Stevenson visited with his sister and brother-in-law in Florence, Italy, and then flew to Turkey on business. He completed his vacation with a visit at Mary Lasker's villa in southern France.

To Mrs. Ernest L. Ives[102]

August 20, 1959

Dear Buff —

I'm off for home in a few minutes — and impatient to get back after 2 months of wandering. This visit with Mary has been luxurious and pleasant but a little too much society & people for my taste. Yesterday we went cruising on Onassis'[103] famous yacht and got back at 4 AM! Mary seems well and I marvel at her capacity for self protection by rest — and also for sustained & constructive interest in *all* public questions as well as health.

I've not had a word from Borden since I left him in Rome on the 11th. . . . Thanks for your letter & much love —

AD

P.S. . . .

Gerald Johnson wrote Stevenson that he was wavering in his support of him for 1960 because the Eisenhower Administration's economic pol-

[101] This handwritten postcard is in the Franklin D. Roosevelt Library, Hyde Park, New York.

[102] This handwritten letter is in the Elizabeth Stevenson Ives collection, Illinois State Historical Society (E.S.I., I.S.H.L.).

[103] Greek businessman and shipowner Aristotle Onassis.

icies would lead to an economic depression, and he did not want Stevenson to be saddled with such a situation.

To Gerald W. Johnson

August 27, 1959

Dear Gerald:

I am just home from two months abroad and find AMERICA IS BORN[104] on my table. I am returning it at once, not as a dissatisfied customer, but as a devoted admirer in search of an autograph from his favorite historian, philosopher and wit. Please add your signature to the first page and return it in the enclosed, at your leisure.

I must add, too, that I have been reflecting with alternate smiles and anxiety over your letter of June 20th. I come back home to find that instead of being a half forgotten name I am still politically "hot," and you have added another reason — the impending economic troubles — to my reasons for wishing to be politically "cold."

And how right you are that the enemy is approaching via revolutions in South America (and Asia and Africa) and not over the radar defenses with atomic bombs.

I was, by the way, a little amused and a little wistful when I read that Eisenhower was going to raise the subject of better cooperation with our allies in the field of economic development of under-developed countries. Ho hum! This was what I pleaded with him and Dulles to do in Washington during my month there in 1957. Added to Nixon's sudden discovery that the Russians are tough and their economic development staggering,[105] which I also talked about long ago, gives me a little feeling of weariness with educating Republicans.

I pray you are well.

Cordially yours,

The Greater St. Louis Citizen's Committee for Nuclear Information asked Stevenson to assist them in securing funds from foundations.

---

[104] *America Is Born: A History for Peter* (New York: William Morrow, 1959).

[105] The Vice President had visited Russia from July 27 to August 2, 1959, where he had several meetings with Khrushchev (including the so-called "kitchen debate") and toured several Ural and Siberian industrial centers including Novosibirsk and Sverdlovsk, ordinarily closed to foreigners.

To Mrs. Albert Lasker

September 2, 1959

My dear Mary:

I think I mentioned to you some time ago the St. Louis project to make some measurement of the effect of nuclear fallout and that they had approached me about the possibility of getting Foundation funds. On my return to Chicago I find the enclosed letter and proposal to the Lasker Foundation in duplicate. I am sending one copy to you against the possibility that you might have a chance to look at it before you return — although with all those new models and abstract pictures to look at I doubt it![106] Please bear in mind that I know nothing about the merits of this and my only connection is with a talk last winter with my cousin Judy Baumgarten, a wonderful girl who is passionately interested in this project.

I hope you got away from Fiorentino sober, serene and slim — I didn't! I have not yet struggled through the accumulation of those two and a half months abroad and I am staying at home over the Labor Day week-end to try try try to catch up — doubtless with more interruptions than I would have had had I gone away.

Love,

Chester Bowles wrote that Stevenson's strength as revealed in public opinion polls must be a source of personal satisfaction. (The Gallup Poll, July 22, 1959, for instance, reported 53% for a Stevenson-Kennedy ticket as compared to 42% for Nixon-Rockefeller, with 5% undecided.)

To Chester Bowles

September 2, 1959

Dear Chester:

I was delighted to have your letter. You are right that the continued talk about me is rewarding and a great satisfaction; but all the same I find it very disquieting. Of that I hope we can talk sometime.

. . . Your book[107] has arrived, and I marvel again at your extraordinary productivity. It gives me a feeling of useless futility — and I want to get your vitamin prescription. Of course I will write something for the jacket at the first opportunity and send it along.

---

[106] Mrs. Lasker was in Paris.
[107] *The Coming Political Breakthrough* (New York: Harper, 1959).

Except for the week of October 10–17 I expect to be here most of the month. By all means let me know as far in advance as possible when you come. And if you could spare a copy of Barbara [Ward]'s letter I should like to have it. I find her always most stimulating

Yours,

Stevenson's London publisher and good friend, Hamish Hamilton, wrote that he and Mrs. Hamilton were sorry to have missed him at Florence, Italy. Mr. Hamilton suggested that Stevenson read a new biography of Madame de Staël, Mistress to an Age, *by J. Christopher Herold.*

To Hamish Hamilton

September 3, 1959

My dear Jamie:

I *should* take your letter home and eat it for dessert tonight. But if I did, I should also write you a worthy response. As I couldn't possibly match your charms as a correspondent, I am answering hurriedly by dictation — and also because, with a long holiday ahead, I am in a hurry to let you know how grateful I am for this engaging report from the English-Italian axis, which wins all the battles, and without weapons!

I haven't read the de Staël book and, as you surmise, probably won't. Moreover, such biographical books always give me an unwholesome feeling of being born in the wrong century. Balance is restored, however, when I reflect that in that century I would have been an obscure peasant with vices that would probably be distasteful, and virtues which *certainly* would have been distasteful!

What a lovely journey you must have had. I wish I could have been along to learn and listen — and eat! . . .

While staying with her,[108] I didn't go to see B.B., for the very reason you suggest.[109] I gather it is much too late to communicate. Nor did I have enough of Harold Acton[110] on this visit to Florence. But it was a glorious week all the same, including a memorable journey to Ravenna, Rimini, Caesena, and San Marino, where the Captains-Regent had a wonderful welcoming ceremony in the great hall of the "palace" on top

[108] Mrs. Ives.
[109] Bernard Berenson was ill at the time of Stevenson's visit to Italy and died shortly thereafter, on October 6, 1959.
[110] British author and poet, who made his home in Florence.

[359]

of the rock. Then, led by the band and the entire army (30 men), we marched down the steep little street to Garibaldi Square, and laid wreaths on his statue. When I asked how long he had lived in San Marino, they told me "24 hours."

You are right that Eisenhower and Nixon — the latter now solemnly proclaiming what I have been saying for about five years — have scored heavily for the Republicans with the American electorate, which is both emotional and forgetful, beguiled by a partisan press. When I think of the stupidities, failures, and hazards of the past few years, it revolts me a little — or should I be candid and say a lot! But we shall see how long this utter reversal of the Dulles policy and proclamations persists. John Steinbeck writes me that the question in England is: "Who gave Ike the benzadrine?" Speculation on that subject is interesting here, too! . . .

Warmest wishes,

William Baggs wrote Stevenson that he did not fully appreciate the new popularity of "Curly" Nixon since he had debated Nikita Khrushchev at the American National Exhibition in Moscow.[111]

To William Baggs

September 3, 1959

Dear Bill:

Thank you for that letter. I have no doubt that Curly scored heavily, as you say. Indeed, I have no doubt that he will be a formidable candidate, all of which fills me with a feeling that must be nausea and wonder about the new image of the American hero to inspire our little boys.

Well, as the Spaniards say: Health, wealth, and love, without a mother-in-law!

Yours,

P.S. . . .

The executive secretary to Governor Edmund G. Brown of California wrote Stevenson's law partner Willard Wirtz that the wish not to be a candidate in 1960 was not an adequate reason for Stevenson's failure to

111 This sharp, impromptu running exchange, which covered a wide variety of topics from the merits of washing machines to summit meetings, was videotaped and shown on television in the United States, where it became known as the "kitchen debate" and was seen as enhancing Mr. Nixon's prestige as one who was not awed by the Soviet leader. For Mr. Nixon's version of this event, see his *Six Crises* (Garden City, New York: Doubleday, 1962).

be the leader of the Democratic party and to speak out forcefully on issues.

To Frederick G. Dutton

September 9, 1959

Dear Fred:

Bill Wirtz has let me see your letter of August 28, and I confess I am a little disturbed. While, as you know, I have wanted to avoid becoming a candidate, or even appearing to be a candidate, again, I have also felt a responsibility to the party and certainly my interest is undiminished, not to mention my indignation about the Republicans! How to accomplish these sometimes contradictory objectives has not been easy for me. But I have been faithful in my services to the Democratic Advisory Council and have spoken if anything too frequently. Perhaps my speaking has not been partisan enough to fulfill the responsibility in mind. Or perhaps much of what I have said has not reached the West Coast. I often suspect that that is the case when I get letters from there urging me to say and do things I have already said and done as best I could. All of which prompts me to send you a collection of utterances for the past year, but I will spare you that!

I do feel that the Democratic Advisory Council has missed a chance to sharpen its impact and that we can't win elections by issuing scholarly declarations and pamphlets while Nixon runs away with the headlines.

I also concede that I have necessarily spent a good deal of time on my law practice since 1956. But many would say that I have spent not too much but too little. I could add other things about the difficulty of acting as a leader when the Congress is in session and public attention is focused there. If, however, you were to say that public concentration on Washington only aided and abetted my anxiety to become more obscure, I would have to confess that also! I could add a good deal about the infrequent occasions that I am called upon by our leaders in Washington to confer or express my views.

Please know how grateful I am for your candor and also how flattered. I wish I knew the proper posture and how to make my voice more resonant — and when! It has not been an easy interval, but I am sure I can do it better with more counsel from you. It would be a comfort to have an opportunity to talk all these things over, and please arrange it if you possibly can on your next trip East.

With warm regards to your wife, I am

Cordially yours,

To William Benton[112]

September 10, 1959

Dear Bill:

I am afraid this won't reach you in time for your meeting with Hubert [Humphrey]. I have been disturbed by reports since my return that some of his "young men" seem to think that I am his principal obstacle, that I am running for President, and that I should issue a General Sherman statement to evidence my sincerity. I am sure that he knows what my situation is exactly, but I would like awfully to know what he personally feels.

. . . Your Thanksgiving invitation has arrived, and while it is too early to resolve my annual question with the boys' mother, you may be sure that Southport is their favorite turkey shoot![113]

Yours,

ADLAI

On September 18, 1959, Nikita Khrushchev proposed at the United Nations that all nations abolish their weapons and armed forces, except for internal peace units, in four years and turn to competition in the art of peace. Stevenson issued the following statement later the same day.[114]

Mr. Khrushchev's total disarmament proposal must be taken seriously. The only way to eliminate the scourge of war is to eliminate the means of war. And Mr. Khrushchev has proposed just what we have all preached — a disarmed world.

Whether he means what he says is the question now. We have reason to be skeptical, but we have better reason to study his proposal with an open mind and high hope for progress at last towards arms control with security.

The Soviet Union knows as well as we do that in the Nuclear Age no nation can afford unlimited war. I have often said that a danger greater to us than war is Soviet economic and political penetration around the

---

[112] The original is in the possession of the estate of William Benton. See note 12 to Part Two, above.

[113] Mr. Benton had invited Stevenson and his sons to spend Thanksgiving at his home in Southport, Connecticut.

[114] The text is from a carbon copy.

world. So I do not dismiss Mr. Khrushchev's speech as propaganda only.

Senator Richard Neuberger of Oregon announced that Stevenson should be the 1960 Democratic nominee for President. Stevenson issued the following statement on September 18, 1959[115]

Senator Neuberger is very kind to me and I am grateful for the continued confidence of such a fine American. I have repeated to him, however, that I am not a candidate for the Democratic nomination for President in 1960. And in answer to his question I told Senator Neuberger that accordingly I do not want my name to appear on the primary ballot in Oregon this spring. He appreciates my position and I hope my friends in Oregon will respect my wishes.

To Walter Lippmann[116]

September 22, 1959

Dear Walter:

I am off in a few minutes — to spend your birthday rendezvousing with Mr. K[hrushchev]. in an Iowa cornfield!

Please know, dear friend, how much my thoughts tomorrow will be of you. There will be envy in them, for more and more it seems to me the only thing worth setting one's self to in this business of ours is trying to increase the traffic in truth and raise a little the level of public understanding; and you leave all the rest of us feeling so second-rate at it.

God bless you for all you do and all you are and will be.

With great affection,

ADLAI

When Stevenson was in Moscow in 1958, he had suggested to Premier Khrushchev that he should visit an Illinois corn farm, and in the New York Times Magazine, July 5, 1959, *Stevenson had described a "Tour for Khrushchev — The Real America." After conferences in Washington, D.C., with President Eisenhower and members of the Senate Foreign Relations Committee, Khrushchev visited farms at Coon Rapids, Iowa. Roswell Garst, a specialist in hybrid corn seed who owned a farm there*

[115] The text is from a handwritten copy.
[116] The original is in the Lippmann papers, Yale University Library.

and who had studied Soviet agriculture, was the host. Stevenson lunched with Khrushchev and afterward told reporters that he was encouraged by the premier's views on disarmament.

To Doris Fleeson

September 25, 1959

Dear Doris:

I don't know what the devil happened in Coon Rapids. Did you get caught in the rapids or by the coons? At all events, you didn't get caught by me and I am disappointed. I didn't know there were so many attractions around there, but I must learn never to discount the Russians.

Yours,

To Lady Barbara Jackson

September 30, 1959

Dearest Barbara:

You may remember that I talked to you last spring about doing a general review of my foreign policy views for *Foreign Affairs,* and later I sent Ham Armstrong[117] a speech I had given at the University of Illinois for his reaction as to whether it was adaptable, in his judgment, to what he had in mind. A copy of the speech is enclosed — and you will recognize it! He wrote back at that time and I enclose a copy of his letter of June 3 commenting on this speech. I suspect what he says about not overwriting economic development reflects a growing view in this country, i.e. that it is no longer controversial. But surely there is much to say about our deficiency in language facilities, the necessity for other countries participating for effective cooperation with our allies (something that Eisenhower has now embraced)[,] new machinery, like the Economic Development Bank, which we have now proposed at the Monetary Fund meeting, etc. Most of all I think a firm, positive statement that the disparity in living standards is the most important single fact, and then developing the argument that it is to win the respect and confidence of the poor peoples in the Communist system as the best method of relieving their poverty is the supreme struggle of the future. But I think he is right about rearguing the need for economic development.

His current letter of September 10, which I have shamefully neglected due to the usual horrors of my schedule, suggests other areas for special

117 Hamilton Fish Armstrong, editor of *Foreign Affairs.*

[364]

treatment and development. Out of my meeting with Khrushchev (clipping enclosed), I had the distinct impression that they are eager to reduce the arms burden and increase trade. They are not unrelated, of course. Any large decrease in defense spending would force us to look for other markets — even theirs! — so I think major emphasis should be put on the pursuit of disarmament, which in the nuclear phase has no precedent with the past failures to control conventional weapons. Whether it is too naive to talk about the total disarmament program he advance[d] I am not sure — to be followed, of course, by an international police force of some kind to protect the little from the weight of the big.

Reunification of Germany on any terms mutually acceptable seems impossible, and I think K[hrushchev]. has made that repeatedly clear. But what is his purpose? Is it fear; or is it their purpose to orient the industrial complex of Germany toward the East and away from us? A disarmed, neutralized Germany sounds all right (regardless of Adenauer's screams), but it could be very dangerous because its industrial power is a more potent factor in the Communist plan than its military power, even when rearmed.

And then, of course, there is the Middle East, Asia, China, etc. As to the latter, I suggested in a radio interview, which has been widely quoted,[118] that we should not be leading the opposition, twisting arms, gouging eyes, etc., to keep them out of the UN; that in fact there would be advantages to admission to the UN and being called to account before the bar of world opinion constantly. I have been attacked for this "dereliction, softness, stupidity," etc., by all the usual editors, including the [Chicago] Sun-Times and Daily News, but I think maybe something thoughtful should be included on this, not necessarily committing myself to a policy but inviting attention to considerations other than sentimentality and prejudice by China's conduct.

All this sounds to me, as I dictate it, like a melange of half digested thoughts, and I am sure it will read even worse. At all events, I wanted you to have these letters from Ham Armstrong, and as the time is so dreadfully short (and so is mine) to inquire if you thought you could put together anything thoughtful and considered by the end of October which I could rework in early November to meet his deadline for the January issue, which you will note, by the way, is to be circulated in the Book-of-the-Month Club and will have large circulation.

Borden is back in Cambridge . . . and looking for a job; John Fell is in New York and in good form; Adlai is working too hard — and Nancy

---

[118] See, for instance, the Chicago *Daily News*, September 22, 1959.

is having another baby! We all talk of you — and so does everyone else. Jane [Dick] seems as good as ever, and as for me, well, I have lost about three pounds since you left and I am still at it, and horribly harrassed by the rising political clamor along with the usual diversions.

I hope you are serene, and know you are. I hope you are well, and I know you are beautiful.

Love to all,

Carl Sandburg wrote Stevenson, "You wear well. You are kept deep in many hearts."

To Carl Sandburg

September 30, 1959

Dear Carl:

Bless you for that little note! I am glad to hear that I "wear well"; I thought I was worn out!

I hope you will let me know and save a moment if you are plotting a midwestern campaign for this winter.

Affectionate regards,

To Tom Dammann[119]

October 1, 1959

Dear Tom:

. . . I did have a good time in Iowa last week and am enclosing a copy of an article I wrote for the New York Times.[120] I don't recommend it but it does sum up some of my thoughts.

I was misquoted about recognizing China — as usual. What I said was that I felt that the United States should not take the leadership in opposing China's admission to the U.N. I think you are familiar with the pressure we bring on our allies to back up our position on China and while I can see perfectly good reason for our abstaining when it comes to a vote on admission, I don't see why we should go out of our way to alienate our friends. As you may have noticed, all of the Scandinavian countries supported admission in the last vote and I suspect that they will be joined by more next year.

[119] A young California rancher who had been active, with his wife, in Stevenson's 1956 campaign and whose father, John F. Dammann, a Chicago lawyer, was an old friend of Stevenson.

[120] "Tour for Khrushchev: The Real America," *New York Times Magazine*, July 5, 1959.

I have not seen your father lately but I'll talk up the European trip when next we meet. . . .

Sincerely,

To Lady Mary Spears

October 8, 1959

Dear Mary:

It was Borden who passed through London during your absence — and was, by the way, most disappointed to miss you. He had several days there and I had hoped so much that he might spend part of them with his beloved relatives.

. . . I had a happy, lazy summer, with more play than work for the first time in a long while. But since I have been home it has been hell again and that distasteful climate stretches as far ahead as I can see. The horizon for next year approaches faster than I like to contemplate and seems to include more and more politics. Three years ago, after the 1956 election, it seemed impossible that I might even be discussed let alone involved again. I am going to do my best to discourage both!

I saw Bobby and Deirdre[121] here not long ago and they are now comfortably settled in Cambridge [Massachusetts] I hear. My boys are well, and Adlai's wife Nancy is going to have another baby in April. It all seems rather hurried to me, but I guess that is one thing I can't manage! My nephew Timothy Ives has also just had his third child in about five years of marriage. I am beginning to wonder if we are developing some new family habits.

Much love to you all,

To Robert M. Hutchins[122]

October 8, 1959

Dear Bob:

I hope you were serious about some purple prose on red hot problems from your cool blue head!

Ever,

---

[121] Stevenson's nephew Robert S. Pirie, who was a first-year student at Harvard Law School, and his wife.

[122] President of the Fund for the Republic and former chancellor of the University of Chicago.

To Richard J. Daley

October 9, 1959

Dear Dick:

I had a talk the other day with Dan Walker[123] who, as you know, is among other things President of the Democratic Federation of Illinois. He worked with me in Springfield after serving as law clerk to Chief Justice [Fred M.] Vinson at the U.S. Supreme Court. In recent years he has been active in the Committee on Illinois Government and, while a young man, he is an old Democrat!

Dan has been giving some thought to running for office but is only interested if he can have the support and confidence of the regular organization. Before making any decisions he would like to have a talk with you at your convenience and if you could see him sometime, I would be very grateful. I think this is the kind of man who is certain to grow in public esteem and whom the party can use.[124]

Thanks for your thought of the World's Series — and me![125]

Yours,

To Ralph McGill[126]

October 21, 1959

Dear Ralph:

I have just seen your column "Adlai Sees His Program Adopted."[127] Thank you for saying some of the things so few seem to remember. But in 1956 it was not McCarthy but Nixon and Ike who "hotly attacked" my plea for us to take the initiative in nuclear arms control. And that is only one of the things I said in 1956 which were ridiculed — especially by Nixon — with such ugly inference, and which he is now saying himself, cf. Soviet economic development, Soviet economic competition in the new, poor countries, etc.

[123] A young Chicago lawyer who had been Stevenson's assistant during his governorship.
[124] In the 1972 Democratic primary, Walker won the gubernatorial nomination, defeating the candidate supported by Daley, and won the governorship of Illinois in the general election.
[125] Mayor Daley had sent Stevenson tickets for a World Series game at Comiskey Park.
[126] The original is in the possession of Mrs. Ralph McGill.
[127] Atlanta *Constitution*, October 9, 1959.

Ho Hum! — adult education is so slow, especially with unprincipled adults!

Yours,
ADLAI

To Thomas K. Finletter

October 27, 1959

Dear Tom:

I am distressed that I didn't have a proper opportunity to talk to you about the article[128] and the National Committee problems while in New York.

However, I did talk to [John Kenneth] Galbraith and [Arthur] Schlesinger in Cambridge about the possibility of having something ready in the way of a declaration of our dedication to peace and its relentless pursuit for the next meeting of the DAC [Democratic Advisory Council] in anticipation of some more saber-rattling by you know who.[129] They thought well of the idea; and I think it imperative to get a firm grip on the garments of that lady with the olive wreath and, if possible, snatch a few tail feathers out of the dove. I am afraid, however, that Nixon and Eisenhower have just about defeathered that pretty bird already.

Perhaps you could add your wicked pen to the professionals and come up with something that would give us at least a hold on the hem of the peace garment.

Yours,

To Arthur Schlesinger, Jr.

November 2, 1959

Dear Arthur:

Marietta [Tree] seems troubled lest you think I am really interested in the nomination again. Evidently I did not make myself clear about Oregon and the devices I have been put to to keep out of that primary — which my friends might even win and thus invite more attention to the draft possibility. She also fears that you took literally some crack I evidently made about Bill Blair's heart "belonging to Daddy." I have told all my friends — who have asked — to go to work for "the candi-

[128] The editors have been unable to identify this article.
[129] Professor Galbraith writes that Stevenson refers to Dean Acheson. Letter to Carol Evans, March 29, 1972.

[369]

date of their choice." That includes my partners and Marietta, who is active for Hubert Humphrey, I gather. And I think I told *you* that a long time ago. If I didn't, I do so herewith!

I wish circumstances had permitted a better talk at Cambridge, because I would like your advice — on how not to get nominated! I know when I have had enough. But I enjoyed the dinner party, and I am most grateful to you and the beloved Marian.[130]

Yours,

P.S. I have to speak to the Institute of Life Insurance at a luncheon at the Waldorf in New York on November 6. I am told this represents more capital than any group in the world. The members are the senior executives of the large life insurance companies. Have you any positive ideas about what we tell business at this time, and with no holds barred — by a man who is *not* running for office?

Professor Seymour Harris sent Stevenson a typescript of a book on economics and politics in the 1950's.

To Seymour E. Harris

November 10, 1959

Dear Seymour:

I am just back from another journey and have at long last had an opportunity to review your recent letters and also to have a look at your book on Eisenhower's economics — whatever they are!

I was very much interested in your article "Prosperity Without Armaments" and I am returning it herewith as requested. I see that it has been printed in Sunday's New York Times[131] and I only hope that I didn't hold on to it too long. It is a really fine piece of work and your general conclusions coincide with my views — as you so well know! When I saw Khrushchev in Iowa I kept asking him what he had found in America that surprised him most and his answer always was that for the first time he believed America could make the adjustments required with a disarmament program.

. . . I have leaved through the book — it is a monumental work that I am delighted to have any connection with. I am glad that the quotations of mine seem to stand the test of time — but gladder still that most of them originated with you! There are a few changes that I could

130 Mrs. Schlesinger.
131 "Can We Prosper Without Arms?" *New York Times Magazine,* November 8, 1959.

suggest for the Credentials but I gather that you have already reworked it and perhaps you could send on the revised version at your convenience.[132] If you could give me a little time to examine the book further I may have some additional suggestions. My problem is still one of finding time to find the time, but then you know me better than most!

Cordially yours,

To Miss Carol Evans[133]

November 13, 1959

CE — 4 copies marked "1st draft" — send one in mail to Walter Rostow[134] — with this letter —

Dear Walt — Here is a first painful draft of the article for Foreign Affairs. I have not read it over and am obliged to go away on business again. If you could read it and let me have your comments & corrections by telephone (collect!) come Wednesday afternoon I would be most grateful. I have to go to N.Y. at noon on Thu[r]sday and have promised this wretched thing to Ham Armstrong Friday morning.

Your notes were most helpful — as you will see!

Sincerely,

Also send a carbon to Hamilton Fish Armstrong —

Dear Ham — Here is a first draft of the article. I have not read it over since its painful birth over the week end and was obliged to go away again before it was typewritten. But I thought it might save time if you saw it even in this first draft and could make any changes before I saw you Friday morning.

Sincerely,

To Mrs. Ernest L. Ives[135]

November 20, 1959

RE: HELEN D. STEVENSON TRUST

Dear Buffy:

In 1930, at Mother's request, I prepared a Trust for you, as you know, and have served as co-Trustee for the past 30 years. Now that the Trust

---

[132] A revised version was published as *The Economics of the Political Parties* (New York: Macmillan, 1962).

[133] This handwritten letter is in the possession of Miss Evans.

[134] Walt W. Rostow, professor of economic history at Massachusetts Institute of Technology.

[135] The original is in the possession of Mrs. Ives.

has been moved from Chicago to Bloomington and the Pantagraph stock is about to be removed from the Trust assets, what remains to be done is largely the routine investment and reinvestment of the balance of the Trust property, which is in stocks and bonds. With Timmy [Ives] and the bank both in Bloomington, I believe he can handle this quite as well as I could, and I would like to be spared the further inconvenience and responsibility. Hence I have suggested my resignation and have written the bank and Timmy as per the enclosed copies.

Let me know if you have any objection.

Love,
ADLAI

P.S. I am quite sure you realize that no fees have ever been paid to me either as lawyer or as Trustee, nor do I want any. Moreover, I am willing to continue if you think it of any importance.

Author Vincent Sheean sent Stevenson a copy of a letter he had written to Under Secretary of State Robert D. Murphy expressing deep regret that Mr. Murphy was retiring from public service. Mr. Sheean observed that India's policy of noninvolvement was quite similar to Washington's advice in his Farewell Address. Mr. Sheean told Stevenson that he was sending him a copy of his new book, Nehru: The Years of Power *and observed that when Nehru died there would be a vacuum in moral authority in the world. He expressed the hope that such authority would pass to an American: "The* auctoritas *of Cicero and of Caesar Augustus."*

To Vincent Sheean

November 23, 1959

Dear Jimmy:

Thank you for that splendid letter to Bob Murphy. I was fascinated by your comparison of Washington's foreign policy views as revealed in the Farewell Address and Nehru's. Of course you are quite right; we have often urged our fellow countrymen to try to understand neutrality in terms of our own history. To remind them of the similarity of Nehru's and Washington's views should make it more understandable.

And thank you for coming to see me. I wish we could have a long quiet evening instead of an office lunch with its impatient undercurrents. Perhaps I can find you in New York some time.

I look forward to your book and am more grateful than I can tell you for the inscription, and I want to hear more about the auctoritas of the great Romans. Maybe the vacuum of moral authority in the West is our greatest weakness. But can there be such authority without some political or spiritual overlordship? And of course ours is an age of fragmented authority of state and religion. But more of this when we meet again.

Cordially,

J. Carroll Cone, assistant vice president of Pan American World Airways, wrote that Stevenson would be the strongest Democratic candidate in 1960.

To J. Carroll Cone

November 25, 1959

Dear Carroll:

I should have acknowledged your splendid letter long before this. It touched me deeply and reminded me vividly of your loyalty and infinite services in the past.[136] I hardly need tell you that the continuing confidence of old friends — who should have learned better — is the most gratifying aspect of my public career and of the present discussion of my further availability. It makes it all the harder to tell dear friends that I am quite sincere about my feeling that we should look elsewhere for our new leadership.

I am afraid our party has a lot of work to do before we take over the Executive Branch again, and I know you will always be in the forefront of the battle. I hope I can do my part as well.

With best wishes and everlasting thanks, I am

Cordially yours,

Allan Nevins, president of the American Historical Association, invited Stevenson to attend the association's annual dinner, to be held in Chicago. He wrote that a Stevenson-Kennedy ticket would be the best one for 1960, but he warned that it would be a hard campaign, since the majority of the people were in a lethargic mood.

---

[136] Mr. Cone had worked closely with Senator George Smathers and former Senator Earle Clements on the Senatorial Campaign Committee in 1958 and was a member of the finance committee of the Democratic Advisory Council.

[373]

To Allan Nevins

November 30, 1959

Dear Allen:

Of course I would be delighted to come to the American Historical Association's annual dinner at the Conrad Hilton on December 29, and the best of it will be to see you and my old friend Isaiah Berlin[137] again.

I am going to skip lightly over the courteous and charitable things you have said about me and 1960. I have found the perfect pattern for living, and I hope I can go on living this way. And to that end I am prepared, if I can, to frustrate — even you!

I must say that I agree most emphatically with your judgment about the state of mind in the country. I suspect it will make it no easier for Democrats next year.

With warm wishes, and my thanks for your thought of me,

Cordially yours,

Stevenson was in New York City from December 5 to December 10, 1959. He delivered two speeches, attended a meeting of the Field Foundation, and visited old friends. On December 7, 1959, he presided and spoke at the Democratic Advisory Council dinner in honor of Mrs. Franklin D. Roosevelt.[138]

This is not the first time I've introduced myself. One night long ago in Southern Illinois, at a small political rally, the chairman failed to appear and I had to introduce myself. It was the best introduction I ever had.

But tonight I am going to spare you — except to say that I am a former assistant to the Secretary of the Navy, a former assistant to the Secretary of State, a former delegate to the United Nations, the only living former Governor of Illinois, and the only living former unsuccessful Democratic candidate for President. You see I am both venerable — and *former!*

And that's the way I like it. There is something very relaxing and agreeable about being a "former" — you're not nervous, self-conscious

---

[137] Fellow of All Souls College and Chichele Professor of Social and Political Theory at Oxford University.
[138] The text is based on a typewritten copy.

or trying to please anyone. When the photographer says "smile please," you can just be yourself and scowl. You can even introduce yourself!

You see I have always been a bride and never a bridesmaid and I like my new position.

Another thing I've been is "Titular Leader" of the Democratic Party. I've never been sure what the job is, but I am sure I don't like the title: It reminds me of a small, unpleasant and noisy bird. Which is another reason I'm very much in favor of a Democratic President and a new honest to goodness leader of the Democratic Party. We've had enough "titulars."

Speaking of song birds and noise: This dinner is another Democratic record — 18 speakers! And we promise to be out of here by tomorrow noon — when I have to speak in this hotel to the Institute of Life Insurance — in street clothes.

But this is more than a dinner honoring Mrs. Roosevelt in the year of her 75th birthday; it is also a 1960 Democratic style show — and every one of the models is required to keep within his time so as not to impinge on the radio time of Mrs. Roosevelt and President Truman at the end. It was rudely suggested that if *I* could keep within my time — anyone could!

There are almost as many people to thank for this dinner as there are speakers to follow — first, all of you whose investment tonight of over $100,000 in the Democratic Advisory Council will help elect the next President of the United States.

. . . Why, you may ask, all this work for the Democratic Advisory Council? We must all remember that Presidential elections are no longer what they once were. They are not decided between the Convention and election day, and I can testify from personal experience that it is almost impossible to really inform the people about intricate issues from convention to election.

Campaigns now go on for four full years. The Republicans have seized on this more than we have. Their campaign for 1960 started the day after election day in 1956, and they have been hard at work ever since.

Moreover the Republican campaign is well financed and skillfully managed in all the modern arts of persuasion. The Democrats have to have something to counter this. It is particularly difficult because we are not in control of the White House and have but little of the media of mass communication on our side. It is not reasonable to expect the majority leadership in the Senate and House to carry the whole role of opposition. They have a different function. Above all, they have the job of making our Constitution work under conditions of divided responsibilities between the Executive and Legislative branches. And so the opposition must find some more voice elsewhere. This is what the Democratic Advisory Council is doing.

It is their job to bring to the attention of the public the shortcomings of the Republican Administration, to state the issues in which the Democratic party believes, and in general to stimulate that great role of debate so that the American people can make a free and informed choice.

The people, especially in a time such as this when so many are prosperous, bemused and complacent, will not choose wisely as between the two parties unless we can put to them our Democratic case.

This is what the Democratic Advisory Council was organized to do — just three years ago. And this is what this experimental institution in our political system has done surprisingly well, in my judgment, in its brief and troubled life — thanks to the leaders of our party — from President Truman to Mrs. Roosevelt — and to the thinkers and intellectuals around the country who have given gratuitously and so generously of their time and thought and convenience to the Council.

But none of us has given this new enterprise of the democracy of America more heart and courage and purpose than our guest of honor tonight — Mrs. Franklin D. Roosevelt.

For more than 30 years her stature and esteem the world over have steadily grown, which is the more remarkable when we recall that she began at the top — as the wife of the Governor of New York and then the President of the United States.

The pages of history are enlivened by the occasional appearance of an unusual woman who has had vast impact on her times. Almost always they have been ladies of singular charm — alas, not always of singular virtue! The despotic intrigues of many a Chinese Empress come to mind, while half the world away Helen launched her thousand ships, Cleopatra's conspiracies brought down Egypt's throne, the inspired Joan led her army of France to victory, and Marie Antoinette triggered a revolution. In the lives of these "First Ladies," we see reflected the values of their worlds and times.

How blessed we are that our beloved guest of honor is the representative by whom we are proudest to have posterity judge us — whether we deserve it or not! Flamboyant adjectives applicable to other ladies of history — "despotic," "conspiratorial," "frivolous," and so on — how absurd they sound in conjunction with our gentle "Mrs. R."

Yet "gentle" isn't the proper adjective either, unless one understands that here is gentleness of strength, not weakness; of courage, of integrity — yes, even of indignation and passion — the gentleness that is born of simplicity, forthrightness, conviction and compassion.

By her own statement, Mrs. Roosevelt was not born to be a leader — a beloved world figure. But there is a prophetic story told about her when she was five years old. While visiting Sorrento with her family, she went for a donkey ride (perhaps that was prophetic, too!). When she saw that the feet of the little boy who led her donkey were sore and tender she jumped off and put him on and walked home. From that day to this, when her indefatigable travels on behalf of world peace — and the Democratic party — are made by jet, not donkey, and her compassion encompasses the globe, she has walked with the less fortunate, and devoted her enormous talents and energies to working for justice, happiness and harmony for all humanity.

If the future belongs to those who greatly care, I believe the present belongs to those who greatly love. Both belong to "Mrs. R." Because she has loved greatly, she is greatly loved. Congressman [John A.] Blatnik of Minnesota told me of an incident that took place in the 1956 campaign on the Mesabi Iron Range, which its mixed-immigrant population proudly calls "The Little United Nations." Owing to a severe blizzard and icy roads, her arrival in the little mining town was delayed, but in the waiting crowds jamming the main street no one budged. As it grew darker and colder, John Blatnik urged an old Polish woman standing next to him to wait indoors. He translated her reply to me: "No, thank you, sir, when mine eyes shall have beheld her I shall be warmed all over."

And I myself have seen people in the streets of Europe in the hard, cold, hungry days after the war doff their hats, bare their heads, and kneel, as she passed by.

Mrs. Roosevelt has never dammed up her love for her fellow men behind the old and formidable barriers of nationality, color, creed or class. Nor has she ever hesitated to comfort the afflicted though it meant afflicting the comfortable.

It is little wonder, then, that as citizens first and Democrats second we who are here tonight, and millions around the world, are more truly her captives than those any ancient despot could command. Her courage has inspired us, her honesty and simplicity have humbled us, and her compassion has warmed the heart of the world. She has served our great tradition greatly!

And, finally, we may safely predict at the age of 75 that she will never grow old, because, as the poet said, the wise never grow old; their minds are nursed by living by the bold light of day.

[377]

This is December 7 — Pearl Harbor Day. The challenge confronting us now, 18 years later, is more complicated and in some ways even more exacting, more demanding of understanding and daring. Mrs. R., like her great husband, knew the full meaning of that dire day eighteen years ago; so also she perceives like few of us the full meaning of today, and the full price of peace!

For 1960 is more than the 44th running of the Presidential sweepstakes. We've had elections in war time, even in civil war, in depression and agony. But this is the first time since our rise to power that the United States has been seriously challenged — our national security, our democratic convictions, our economic institutions — every dimension of life, power and influence.

Just as a hundred years ago tonight, on the eve of the Civil War, we entered the decade of the sixties that proved decisive to our Republic, so in this century we are entering the same decade — on the eve of trials equally decisive. That we are in this position is the fault of history; that we are in an unfavorable position may in part be the fault of all of us; but that our people hardly know it and hardly care is the fault of the Eisenhower Administration — which has only now begun to act as if it knew it!

And that, above all else, is why there must be a Democratic President!

I see little sign of any challenging approach in positive terms to our problems at the present time. In the most radical and revolutionary epoch of man's history, the dominant concerns of our leadership have been almost wholly defensive. We have not been urged and spurred on by the positive opportunities of world-building and nation-building inherent in our position as the most fabulously endowed people mankind has ever seen. On the contrary, our foreign policy has been dominated by fear of communism, our domestic policy by fear of inflation. Economic assistance programs have been "sold" to the American people chiefly as a means of checking the communists, never as our creative part in extending our technological revolution to the rest of mankind. The spur to our exploration of the solar system has not been our restless desire to extend the boundaries of human knowledge. It has been the irritation of seeing the Russians hit the moon first.[139] Our interest in greater excellence in research and education flared up not because we want every free citizen to exercise to the full his innate talents and capacities, but because the Russians are producing more scientists and technologists than the West.

Even where we accept the Soviet challenge — as I assume we do in

139 Lunik II, the first object sent by man to another cosmic body, landed an instrument container on the moon on September 13, 1959.

defense, science and education — our sense of urgency is yet not sufficient to override our obsessive fear that, in some way, in spite of having a Gross National Product of almost $500 billion and a per capita income almost twice as high as any other country's, we are staring bankruptcy in the face.

The time has come to put an end to this unnatural timidity. And I am sure that if our political leadership defines the tasks with clarity and conviction, we will approve what is necessary to fulfill our national purpose whatever the sacrifice. The recompense will be to see American society once more the pacesetter in human affairs, to see freedom once more the great challenger on the human scene.

For this, surely, is the crux. An attitude of unadventurous conservatism cannot stand for long as the creative image of freedom. I tremble for our future — and for the world's future — if growth, thrust, initiative and the vast new frontiers of science are felt to be the prerogative of Communist discipline and drive — if "the shot heard around the world" has been silenced by the shot around the moon.

Freedom is not an ideal, it is not even a protection, if it means nothing more than freedom to stagnate, to live without dreams, to have no greater aim than a second car and another television set — and this in a world where half our fellow men have less than enough to eat. Today not rhetoric but sober fact bids us believe that our present combination of complacency and apprehension, of little aims and large fears, has within it the seed of destruction, first for our own community, and then for the larger hope that, as science and technology bring the nations inescapably together, freedom, not tyranny, will be the organizing principle of the society of man.

Within the United States are the moral and material elements of new purpose and the achievement of new goals. The country is ready and time is wasting. It is the task of National leadership to marshal our will and point the way. It is the task of the Democratic party.

On December 10, 1959, Stevenson flew to South Carolina to spend a holiday at the home of Mrs. Marshall Field.

To Mrs. Ernest L. Ives[140]

December 14, 1959

Dear Buffy — Thanks for your letter.

. . . This has been a pleasant, healt[h]y interlude of nature and exercise. Tomorrow I go to Wash. on law business, then on to New York

[140] This handwritten letter is in E.S.I., I.S.H.L.

for the firm year end meetings, and to Chicago Sunday [December 20] probably to get ready for Christmas.

I will remind [Bill] Blair to get a room for you & Ernest at Los Angeles;[141] (*two* rooms might be difficult) near me, altho I don't expect to go, *confidentially*.

Love —

ADLAI

On December 22, 1959, Newsday *published a letter that John Steinbeck had written Stevenson. Stevenson wrote the following introduction to the letter.*

On a hot June day last summer I visited John Steinbeck and his wife in an ancient cottage in Somerset. He was hard at work on a book about King Arthur and the Round Table, a legend that has fascinated him since childhood. After lunch — a fine fresh salmon! — he took me to see "the true Camelot" — the site of King Arthur's court. A narrow sunken roadway passed straight up the side of a conical wooded hill through ridges and wide ditches, the remains of the outer and middle fortification that then circled the hill.

Pausing to rest in the shade of the great beech trees, the sound of bells from the village church in the valley suddenly filled the glade with medieval magic. With John's help it wasn't long before I saw a Knight of the Round Table on his great charger, his lance erect and armor flashing in the dappled sunlight, ride slowly past up the steep ascent to Camelot and the King.

On the broad uneven summit listening to Steinbeck I could see a castle rise out of the mossy stone and shimmering heat. Was it Camelot? Who knows? There are six "true" Camelots in England. But long before King Arthur, it was clearly a Roman fortress and signal hill. To the West lay Cornwall and the ancient tin mines; to the East rose the ridge where Alfred stopped the Danes; to the North lay the Bristol Channel, and the Vale of Avalon, and Glastonbury in whose ruined abbey legend has it that King Arthur and Queen Guinevere were buried side by side, how long ago no one knows.

Here surrounded by all the ghosts — Druid, Saxon, Roman, Norman, English — John Steinbeck talked about the Arthurian legend and its symbolism of the recurrent need in times of confusions and doubt for moral authority and direction. He talked of its meaning for us today, of the everlasting struggle between simple goodness and clever evil, and

141 For the Democratic Convention.

the hunger for purity and ennobling purposes after intervals of corruption of the spirit of man.

So when many months later he came back home to our wealth, moral flabbiness, uncertainty and TV scandals, it is easy to understand why he wrote me this letter on Guy Fawkes Day, November 1959.

ADLAI STEVENSON

Professor Stuart Gerry Brown wrote Stevenson on December 23, 1959, that he was at a loss about what he should say when he was asked to address organization meetings of Stevenson-for-President clubs. Robert J. Donovan, in the Chicago Sun-Times, *November 20 1959, wrote: "Democratic supporters of Adlai E. Stevenson are stepping up the pace of their efforts to capture a third presidential nomination for him in 1960." The New York* Times, *November 22, 1959, reported that along with the organization in Wisconsin, there were loosely coordinated draft Stevenson groups in Ohio, Oregon, Washington, California, Missouri, Texas and Washington, D.C. Earl Mazo reported in the Chicago* Sun-Times, *November 30, 1959, "Stevenson devotees reportedly are preparing to undertake much work in his behalf — with a minimum of hoopla — after Stevenson leaves soon for an extended trip to South America."*

In addition to the activities of James Doyle in Madison and others around the country, including Joseph Smolen, a Wisconsin trade union leader, by late November, 1959, a group of prominent citizens and close friends of Stevenson, started a covert operation under the name Russell D. Hemenway and Associates, 745 Fifth Avenue, New York City. Mr. Hemenway, a New York City advertising executive, was a leader in Democratic reforms causes and a member of the anti-Tammany Committee for Democratic Voters. Among the leaders in this group were Thomas K. Finletter, Agnes Meyer, Ruth Field, Arthur B. Krim, Adele Levy, Robert Benjamin, Roger Stevens, and John Shea. Their first activity, conducted by Russell D. Hemenway and Eleanor Green, was to determine areas of pro-Stevenson strength.

To Stuart Gerry Brown

December 30, 1959

Dear Stuart:

I am sending you a copy of an article I have recently written for FOREIGN AFFAIRS.[142] Please don't feel that you have to read it or

---

[142] "Putting First Things First — A Democratic View," *Foreign Affairs*, January, 1960. It was reprinted in *Putting First Things First: A Democratic View* (New York: Random House, 1960), pp. 3–26.

comment. As to the latter, one gets so much perfunctory and favorable comment that I would appreciate some candid criticism.

I appreciate your letter of last week. I think you know my position — that I will not lift a finger for the nomination; indeed, don't want it. But I do want desperately a Democratic President. If the present euphoria goes on much longer it may be too late. I think others are more likely to be elected than I.

I wish we could have a talk some time, and I am planning to go to South America in February for two months of law business, travel and just plain exile. If not before, I shall see you when I return.

Cordially yours,

To Seymour N. Chase[143]

January 4, 1960

Dear Mr. Chase:

I have just seen a report in the Washington Star of December 30 carrying a purported quotation from you as President of the "District Draft Stevenson Committee" regarding Senator Humphrey's announcement of candidacy.

While I am sure you realize that I am most anxious to keep out of the primaries everywhere and do not wish to appear — even through the action of loyal friends — to be seeking the nomination. However, Mr. [Bill] Blair informs me that you and others of the District seem to be determined to go ahead with this unwelcome project.

However, I am sure you will understand my distress that anything should be said offensive to Senator Humphrey, an old and dear friend who has been extremely helpful to me when *I* was seeking the nomination.

While I wish it were possible to persuade you to discontinue your efforts on my behalf, I am sure you will be both circumspect and affirmative in any comments you make about other Democratic candidates as Chairman of a Committee bearing my name.

With kind regards, I am

Cordially yours,

[143] A Washington lawyer and president of the Draft Stevenson Committee of the District of Columbia.

To Vincent Sheean

January 4, 1960

Dear Jimmy:

I have pondered your letter — and with it admired your learning, style and conviction. Surely you have made much of your tastes and talents, and this must give you great comfort.

Auctoritas, as an expression of something we understand but don't often identify, fascinates me, and I suppose you are right that it settles on few people outside of public office. And when it does, as in the case of [Dr. Albert] Schweitzer, I suppose it commands only relatively small bands of the faithful.

I understand, too, what you are saying to *me.* And I shall not refuse a request to serve. The point is that I feel that I *have* already responded and also that there are others with better claims for that reason. Moreover, they want *auctoritas* more than I! I wish I had such "clumsy and insufficient" words as you have. Maybe I could make myself clearer.

With all good wishes, I am

Cordially yours,

P.S. I am sending you a copy of an article I wrote recently for FOREIGN AFFAIRS.

To Lady Mary Spears

January 7, 1960

My dear Mary:

Thank you for your sweet letter. Actually, I don't think our political situation is quite as bad as Walter Lippmann told you. Nixon is not "popular" in the usual sense. He is very much a politician's politician and I suspect there is extensive uneasiness and mistrust in people's hearts about him. God knows, there ought to be! However, there is no doubt that Eisenhower's sudden excess of energy and total reversal of the Dulles rigidity has given the Republicans a new lease on life and the better of the "peace" issue — as of now! That one day the press can applaud Dulles for rigid "firmness" and the next day praise Eisenhower's flexibility in the "search for peace" is a measure of our current scene. But I am used to that.

As for myself, I have tried to make it clear, consistently, for three years that I was not seeking and did not want the Democratic nomination again. I have little doubt that the party will accommodate me in this respect!

I was glad to hear that Michael[144] is getting along well and I hope you have a useful and not too tiring journey to Ghana. Barbara [Jackson] will be here soon and is coming to a birthday party for me in Lake Forest in early February (my 60th — horrors!).

With much love and best wishes to Louis,[145] I am

Devotedly,

P.S. I am sending you a copy of an article I wrote recently on foreign policy which I hope may have some effect on my party's posture in the forthcoming Congress — but I doubt it!

Senator John F. Kennedy wrote that he had heard that someone had told Stevenson that Kennedy was unhappy over the voting on the vice presidential nomination in 1956 and was saying that Stevenson had been unfair and had helped another candidate. Kennedy assured Stevenson that he never had said any such thing. Moreover, Kennedy said, his consideration for the nomination had been beneficial to him ever since.

To John F. Kennedy

January 8, 1960

Dear Jack:

Thanks for your letter. But please don't worry; I was sure the professor was confused. I will be in Washington, staying with Dr. Paul B. Magnuson at 3121 "O" Street, telephone Federal 3-5165, from Thursday afternoon, January 14 to Saturday evening, January 16. I would be delighted to see you if at all convenient.

Cordially,

P.S. You're doing fine!

Mrs. R. J. Heffernan, Stevenson's old friend from Bloomington, wrote him and urged him to state the reasons why Vice President Nixon would not be a good President.

144 Her son.
145 Her husband, General Sir Louis Spears.

To Mrs. R. J. Heffernan

January 12, 1960

My dear Amy:

. . . It was a wonderful letter, and I loved it. Moreover, you are quite right about Nixon. People just don't like him or trust him — and for good and obvious reasons. But, as you say, it will take more than vague misgivings to head him off after the buildup and whitewash of years and with more and better to come. It seems to me unthinkable that a man with his background of slander, abuse, innuendo, expediency and resort to all the most devious political devices should ever occupy an office which we have tried for generations to exalt in the esteem of young people and the world. However, strange things are happening here and elsewhere. I suppose, in this age of confusion, tastes, morals, standards and beliefs it is no longer easy to change much of anything but the pace, and maybe Nixon serves us right! I suppose you have or will read Costello's book about him.[146] I have not, but I am told it is excellent.

I envy you and wish I were rocking on your front porch!

Affectionately,

Senator Richard Neuberger wrote Stevenson that he and his wife, Maurine, considered him the "greatest American" they had ever known. He added that he had just written an article, "Adlai E. Stevenson: Last Chance," for the February, 1960, issue of Progressive.

To Richard L. Neuberger

January 12, 1960

Dear Dick:

Bless you for that sweet letter. And how I wish I saw more of you and dear Maurine.

I think it an imposition for *The Progressive* or any other magazine to be asking you to do pieces on me or anybody else. But I am glad you did! — as long as it doesn't get me into trouble.

Cordially and gratefully,

---

[146] William Costello, *The Facts about Nixon: An Unauthorized Biography* (New York: Viking, 1966).

At four o'clock on the afternoon of Saturday, January 16, 1960, Stevenson met with Ambassador Mikhail Menshikov at the Soviet embassy in Washington. Afterwards he prepared the following memorandum of their conversation.

January 25, 1960

A few days previous to this meeting Ambassador Menshikov telephoned me in Chicago that he had some presents that he wished to deliver from Premier Khrushchev, and also some messages. He suggested that he come to Chicago. I told him I was to be in Washington the following week and would be glad to call at his Embassy.

After the usual pleasantries about health, family, and the usual caviar, delicacies, fruit and drinks, Menshikov removed from his pocket a carefully folded sheaf of notes written in ink on small paper and spoke to me something as follows. (I hesitated for a week before making any record of this curious conversation.)

Before returning last week from Moscow, he had spent considerable time alone with Premier Khrushchev. He wishes me to convey the following: When you met in Moscow in August 1958, he said to you that he had voted for you in his heart in 1956. He says now that he will vote for you in his heart again in 1960. We have made a beginning with President Eisenhower and Khrushchev's visit to America toward better relations, but it is only a beginning. We are concerned with the future, and that America has the right President. All countries are concerned with the American election. It is impossible for us not to be concerned about our future and the American Presidency which is so important to everybody everywhere.

In Russia we know well Mr. Stevenson and his views regarding disarmament, nuclear testing, peaceful coexistence, and the conditions of a peaceful world. He has said many sober and correct things during his visit to Moscow and in his writings and speeches. When we compare all the possible candidates in the United States we feel that Mr. Stevenson is best for mutual understanding and progress toward peace. These are the views not only of myself — Khrushchev — but of the Presidium. We believe that Mr. Stevenson is more of a realist than others and is likely to understand Soviet anxieties and purposes. Friendly relations and cooperation between our countries are imperative for all. Sober realism and sensible talks are necessary to the settlement of international problems. Only on the basis of coexistence can we hope to *really* find proper solutions to our many problems.

The Soviet Union wishes to develop relations with the United States on a basis which will forever exclude the possibility of conflict. We believe our system is best and will prevail. You, Mr. Stevenson, think the same about yours. So we both say, let the competition proceed, but excluding any possibility of conflict

Because we know the ideas of Mr. Stevenson, we in our hearts all favor him. And you (Ambassador Menshikov) must ask him which way we could be of assistance to those forces in the United States which favor friendly relations. We don't know how we can help to make relations better and help those to succeed in political life who wish for better relations and more confidence. Could the Soviet press assist Mr. Stevenson's personal success? How? Should the press praise him, and, if so, for what? Should it criticize him, and, if so, for what? (We can always find many things to criticize Mr. Stevenson for because he has said many harsh and critical things about the Soviet Union and Communism!) Mr. Stevenson will know best what would help him.

The presentation concluded with questions about "Mr. Stevenson's rival," meaning Vice President Nixon, and repeated declarations of desire not "to interfere in an American election," together with many sober statements about the profound "interest" of the Soviet Union, and of all countries, in the American election. The protestations about non-interference were interspersed throughout the presentation, which I did not interrupt. The distaste and mistrust of Nixon was expressed cautiously but clearly. The Ambassador made a gesture of sad resignation about the Khrushchev-Nixon altercation in the model kitchen at the Trade Fair in Moscow last summer; if not saying, at least implying, that Khrushchev had not realized that such an irrelevant dialogue recorded on television would be shown and taken seriously in the United States, to the great political advantage of Nixon.

While it was not included in the formal presentation of Mr. Khrushchev's message, it was apparent that they were quite aware of the effect on the Presidential election of the Summit Conference and Eisenhower's visit to Russia; that a "success" would resound to the benefit of the Republican candidate which seems to leave them in some dilemma.

Mr. Menshikov concluded by saying that this interview was the best evidence of the confidence reposed in me by the Premier and his colleagues and that he had no misgivings about my keeping it in confidence.

At the conclusion, I made the following points:

(1) My thanks for this expression of Khrushchev's confidence.

(2) My thanks for this proffer of aid.

(3) However, I was not a candidate for the nomination and did not expect to be a candidate for the Presidency in 1960.

(4) My grave misgivings about the propriety or wisdom of any interference, direct or indirect, in the American election, and I mentioned to him the precedent of the British Ambassador and Grover Cleveland.[147] (He in turn implied that President Eisenhower was not above intervention in the British election last fall;[148] nor Dulles in behalf of Adenauer as [against?] the Social Democratic party in Germany.)[149]

(5) Finally, I said to him that even if I was a candidate I could not accept the assistance proffered. I believe I made it clear to him that I considered the offer of such assistance highly improper, indiscreet and dangerous to all concerned.

In thanking Khrushchev for his expressions of my respect for my "realism and understanding of the Soviet Union" I said that I hoped that I *did* have some understanding beyond the ordinary, and that I was sure Menshikov and Khrushchev had come to understand the U.S. much better, about which I found so much ignorance in the Soviet Union.

I said that I was aware of some of the difficulties of the Soviet Union, especially with respect to China. At this point, Menshikov said with a wry smile: "Yes, we may be allies again."

His manner was extremely amiable but very serious during his presentation of Khrushchev's message, which was done in a low voice, in a parlor adjoining the family dining room on the third floor. On two

---

[147] During the presidential campaign of 1888, the British minister, Lionel Sackville-West (later Lord Sackville), answered a letter, ostensibly from a naturalized citizen of British birth asking for whom he should vote, by recommending Cleveland. The letter was published, and amid furor over foreign interference in American politics, the minister was dismissed.

[148] On Eisenhower's trip abroad in August, 1959, he participated with Prime Minister Macmillan in a discussion at 10 Downing Street that covered the summit conference and other topics in international affairs and that was broadcast over radio and television. The British general election was scheduled for October 8. See the New York *Times*, September 1, 1959.

[149] Chancellor Konrad Adenauer, facing strong challenges in the election of 1953, pled with Dulles to meet with the Russians, and Dulles agreed only because he thought it would strengthen Adenauer's position. However, the Russians balked at setting a date, and when it became obvious that no meeting would take place before the German elections, Dulles took the more direct step of endorsing Adenauer, saying at a press conference on September 3, 1953, that Russia's enforced partition of Germany was a "menace to the peace" and that if Adenauer was not reelected it would be disastrous for Germany and the cause of peace. Adenauer's coalition won a sweeping victory in the election three days later, but Dulles's remarks were denounced by Social Democrats and others in Germany as blatant foreign interference in domestic politics. See the New York *Times*, September 4, 1953.

occasions when a waitress appeared with food, etc., he interrupted his conversation.

On January 22, 1960, I wrote Mr. Menshikov the attached letter.

To Mikhail Menshikov

January 22, 1960

My Dear Mr. Ambassador:

I am most grateful to you and Premier Khrushchev for the splendid gift you delivered to me at the Embassy in Washington last week. So much delicious Russian caviar and wine may not be good for me — but I like it! I hope you will extend my very warm thanks to Premier Khrushchev, and also my best wishes for his health and happiness in the New Year and the New Decade. That the year and decade will see ever closer and constantly improving relations between our great countries is my highest hope, and I am sure you and Mr. Khrushchev have similar sentiments about our common future.

The confidence expressed in me during our conversation and Premier Khrushchev's interest in my views were flattering, and I wish I could thank him in person. But I must repeat that I will not seek the nomination for President again and that I do not expect to be the candidate of the Democratic party this year. Even if I was, however, I would have to decline to take advantage in any way of the confidence and good will I am happy to enjoy among your compatriots. I am sure you and Premier Khrushchev will understand, and I hope respect, my feelings about the proprieties in the circumstances we discussed, and I trust that my re-action will not be misconstrued as discourteous or ungrateful.

With renewed thanks to you and the Premier, together with my hope that we may have further talks from time to time, I am

Cordially yours,

William Attwood, whose close friendship with Stevenson began during their 1953 trip through Asia, the Middle East, and Europe, took a leave of absence from Look *to help prepare speeches for Stevenson. In December, 1959, Attwood, Stevenson and Senator Mike Monroney discussed the approaching election. Monroney urged Stevenson to deliver a series of major speeches and thereby set the tone of the presidential campaign. From his own experiences in the 1956 primaries, Stevenson knew that broad basic issues became obscured by local issues and the exigencies of campaigning against a member of one's own party.*[150]

[150] After Senator Monroney saw them off at the Washington airport, Stevenson and Attwood discussed the idea further. Thomas K. Finletter also talked to Attwood

Stevenson told Attwood that he did not know what would happen at the convention, but in case the convention deadlocked and he was nominated, "I ought to be ready. I suppose I'm too old to change my ways of campaigning, but I do want to be better organized this time."[151]

On January 20, 1960, Attwood told Stevenson he would take leave from Look *"not to help him get the nomination but to help defeat Nixon." He seemed gratified, though harried and distracted as usual, and outlined the themes of five speeches he planned for the spring."*[152]

To William Attwood[153]

January 25, 1960

Dear Bill:

Excellent men for sharp verbal work in the Senate are Senators Gene McCarthy, Mike Monroney, John Pastore and Warren Magnuson. Why not a profile on Nixon by [John] Steinbeck or John Hersey? I haven't yet forgotten the job the latter did on [Bernard] Baruch.[154]

I think the operation needs someone with a sense of the ridiculous and who isn't afraid of bloodshed. You know what I mean — "He is a man of no character and we are going to prove it."

One of the most useful things that could be done for the Democrats would be to get some action on the bill for equal television time for the Presidential candidates. The "heavies" on the TV Committee include the above: Monroney, Pastore and Magnuson in the Senate, and Mack[155] in the House. I can't understand why nobody said a word about the "high cost of quail" after the President flew his enormous jet to Alden Jones' farm in Georgia for a week-end of quail shooting.

---

and wrote Stevenson on December 29, 1959, that Attwood "sees the great opportunities of a powerful campaign which would strike at the basic issues in a new and powerful way."

[151] William Attwood, *The Reds and the Blacks: A Personal Adventure* (New York: Harper & Row, 1967), p. 2.

[152] *Ibid.,* p. 3. Attwood later wrote: ". . . In addition to assembling speech material for the Governor, I was also circulating around Washington and Madison Avenue at this time (with his blessing) suggesting to Democratic friends (who had no Presidential ambitions) that while others were contesting primaries, they should start the job of undermining Nixon *before* the campaign started. This was an example of how the Governor's paramount concern in 1960 was always: how to beat Nixon in November. His torment over the convention was that he wasn't sure who had the best chance. . . ." Letter to Walter Johnson, April 27, 1971.

[153] The original is in the possession of Mr. Attwood.

[154] "Profile: The Old Man," *New Yorker,* January 3, 1948, pp. 28–37; January 10, 1948, pp. 30–40; January 17, 1948, pp. 30–41.

[155] Representative Peter F. Mack, of Illinois.

When I saw that campaign picture of "Dick and Pat" I was reminded of Lincoln's remark about a man he didn't appoint Post Master — "I don't like his face." And when the man's sponsors said that a man wasn't responsible for his face, Lincoln said: "After 40 every man is responsible for his face," — or something like that.

I hope you don't mind if I occasionally belabor you with brain throbs. Or are they convulsions?

Yours,
ADLAI

Julian P. Boyd, editor of The Papers of Thomas Jefferson, *urged Stevenson to accept an invitation to deliver the Founder's Day address at the University of Virginia on April 12 after his return from Latin America.*

To Julian P. Boyd

January 25, 1960

Dear Julian:

I will be back in my office in New York on next Thursday, the 28th. If by that time you have worked out any of the details we discussed, please call me by telephone. I am getting more and more hesitant about accepting this commitment. However, if I do I thought the enclosed might suggest something that could be included in the draft speech, i.e., that all positive Presidents, like Jefferson, have introduced proposals which have not contributed to unity but to division — and progress! I keep thinking of the extremities to which this administration has gone to constantly reassure the people and satisfy their creature wants at the expense of realism about our national purpose. As you well know, the theme is peace and the rhetoric is unconditional surrender to the Russians. Of course peace on these terms is impossible. But if you try to face the realities you are charged with appeasement and being soft on communism.

You may also find a speech that Allan Nevins gave here at the American Historical Association interesting on this general subject. I think of all this in connection with the forthcoming Presidential campaign and the relevance of Jefferson today. I suspect you will agree that we have little to look forward to from Nixon but a continuation of the sedatives and half truths which satisfy the majority of people.

Cordially yours,

[391]

Gerald W. Johnson recommended that Stevenson be sure to visit specific historic places in Latin America. He also urged him to write an article analyzing Vice President Nixon.

To Gerald W. Johnson

January 27, 1960

Dear Gerald:

I am mortified that I have an accumulation of letters from you, all unanswered — but not unnoticed. I regularly cannibalize your letters for speeches and utterances — and will persist in this larcenous habit!

Your suggestions about South America are excellent — and I mean that! I am sure that all American visitors there see the usual and obvious and few touch their historical pride.

Actually, as I think you know, my objective is not to teach but to learn, not to lecture but to listen. I feel so woefully ignorant about this vast and growing continent that I have wanted for a long time to see it intimately. Meanwhile, I have been everywhere else instead.

I wish we could have a talk about the unfolding pattern of politics. Somehow, even the possibility of the Republican hope as a tenant of the White House makes me profoundly uneasy and unhappy — and not because he is a Republican. I wonder if character has been emphasized enough in this public debate of qualifications of candidates for the Presidency. Or is "character" a Madison Avenue creation nowadays?

Ever yours,

Stevenson wrote Prime Minister Jawaharlal Nehru urging him to deliver the A. Powell Davies Memorial Lecture. Mr. Nehru declined and explained that India had so many pressing problems that he could not get away. Moreover, he explained that writing speeches was extremely time-consuming for him and that he did not have the time available to do it.

To Jawaharlal Nehru

February 5, 1960

My dear Mr. Prime Minister:

I was delighted to have your most thoughtful letter of January 18. Of course we are all disappointed that you cannot deliver the A. Powell Davies Memorial Lecture, but I must confess that I cannot begin to understand how you manage to do even a fraction of what you do, so none of us are surprised, and we hope our invitation has not caused you any unnecessary thought and concern.

As for travels about the world, I agree most emphatically with your view that the first claim on your time and energy is India and that the world will profit more from progress there than from ceremonial visits to other lands. Moreover, I must add that I likewise share your concern for the trying task and time of preparing suitable speeches. I suspect that you have not yet fallen victim to the Western practice of ghostwritten utterance, and I pray you never do!

It seems to me that too much of official utterance in the West bears the unmistakable mark of impersonal preparation and spurious authenticity.

I had only yesterday a glowing report of an interview with you from Barbara Ward (Lady Jackson), who carries India's economic torch high during her visits to this country each year, and recently, too, I had a most interesting and enlightening meeting with B. K. Nehru[156] in Washington. I am sure you know the respect he commands universally. In this country we watch India with increasing and gratifying attention and hopefulness — and admiration for your leadership.

With all good wishes and prayers for your health and success, I am

Cordially yours,

Mr. and Mrs. Edison Dick, Mr. and Mrs. Edward D. McDougal, Jr., and Mr. and Mrs. Hermon Dunlap Smith held a party on Saturday, February 6, the day after Stevenson's sixtieth birthday.

To Mr. and Mrs. Edward D. McDougal, Jr.[157]

February 8, 1960

Dear Kate and Ed:

Before going on my long journey I want to say thanks again for joining in the festivities and helping to launch me so successfully on my 7th Decade. It was really quite painless!

I am not only moved by everyone's generosity, but profoundly grateful for the much needed and exquisite Baccarat goblets. Henceforth all drinks, both spirituous and otherwise, will flow more freely than usual

---

[156] Commissioner General for Economic Affairs in the Indian government and later ambassador to the United States, 1961–1968.
[157] The original is in the possession of Mr. McDougal.

on St. Mary's Road. So come on over this spring and enjoy them with me.

Many many thanks — and love to you both.

Yours,
ADLAI

William Attwood suggested that in the speech at the University of Virginia, in addition to emphasizing the need for action on all fronts after years of drift and deception, Stevenson should add something like the following: "You have had the honor twice and would not ask for it again. You want to see the strongest candidate nominated — the one with the best chance of beating Nixon. Should the convention decide that you are that man, you would naturally take on the job. But you honestly don't expect it and would not be disappointed if someone else were chosen. You will support any vigorous, liberal candidate — the only kind who could win — with all your heart and energy and would be glad to serve in his administration. Meanwhile, you will speak out in the weeks ahead on the issues that the Republicans have chosen in order to expose the campaign deception that they are preparing. . . ."

To William Attwood[158]

February 8, 1960

Dear Bill:

I have just seen your letter of February 1. I doubt that I will want to use the speech at the University of Virginia for a personal political declaration. I am afraid it is much more an occasion for philosophical talk. But I shall have countless opportunities to say the sort of thing you suggest before the TV cameras and press. I think realism versus self deceit; education for responsibility rather than for election, and the sort of thing that is calculated to remind people that we can't practice democracy without knowing the facts of their situation is more indicated and will have Jefferson antecedents. My biggest indictment of the Eisenhower administration is "deceit."

The role of the opposition material sounds just right, but we have to face the fact that there are different philosophies between the Republicans and Democrats and that divided government with an Executive and Congress of different parties is hopelessly frustrating, etc. Perhaps it also suggests why the British Parliamentary system is better.

As I read on in your letter, I see that you have the deception point well in mind as well as the decline in our position and the confusion of influence with affluence, etc.

[158] The original is in the possession of Mr. Attwood.

It might be well if you had for me in advance of my arrival in New York a few statements which you thought were appropriate at that time both as to my own plans and also summarizing my view of what the Republicans have done to us. I will doubtless have something more to say about South America.

> Yours,
> ADLAI

To William Attwood[159]

February 8, 1960

Dear Bill:

I enclose some excerpts from a letter from Agnes Meyer just as I am leaving, which certainly state, as she often does, what I would *like* to do.[160] What I would like to do falls far short usually of what I do, however.

I am enclosing a copy of a letter to Dick Bissell. I don't know whether you know him. He is an "old" government servant from Roosevelt times; served briefly as one of the original top men at the Ford Foundation and has gone back to government as a top assistant to Allen Dulles.[161] I value him as a brain, as a liberal, as a writer, and as an old friend, who has recently sent me messages about his "availability" for party service.

I think it might be a good idea when you are in Washington to see him, to talk generally about his view of things, political and foreign, and what needs saying and doing. I don't think you can go much beyond that unless it would be to solicit volunteer help in any respect that you need.

I would also hope you might find an opportunity to talk with Barry Bingham some time. He is a thoughtful fellow, hears a lot and knows a lot of people, all of which you know. He was here for my birthday party this week and knows you are going to do this work for Agnes.[162] He comes to New York occasionally and also to Washington.

I had hoped to have a much more useful talk with you before I left, but I have been hard put to it these last days to make my escape.

I think some of this talk of Mrs. Meyers might be suitable "hard stuff" for the Virginia speech, although it may well be in a philosophical and

---

[159] The original is in the possession of Mr. Attwood.

[160] Mrs. Meyer wrote that Stevenson was the titular head of the Democratic party whether or not he was a candidate, and that it was his duty to explain to the public the deceptions practiced by the Eisenhower Administration. When he returned from his trip to Latin America, she said, he had to use all his resources to save the country.

[161] Director of the Central Intelligence Agency.

[162] Mrs. Meyer was financing Attwood's work for Stevenson.

historical vein that precludes this kind of talk. I assume you will have a draft for me at the American Embassy at Caracas not later than our arrival there on April 1st. If one is available still earlier so much the better, but I rather doubt I will be able to get to work on it much before that. And I rather doubt I will have enough strength left to do any work on it then!

Yours,
ADLAI

To Dr. Albert Schweitzer

February 8, 1960

My dear Dr. Schweitzer:

Your letter came during the Christmas holidays and I found it both comforting and disturbing — comforting because it was reassuring proof that your mind and heart are as vigorous as ever. But I was disturbed because you find so little that is bright and encouraging in your vision of the world. While I have been immeasurably provoked by our failure to reach a comprehensive agreement in nuclear testing at Geneva and get started with inspection, I do find comfort in the fact that we are still negotiating and, indeed, I understand on the threshhold of agreement. Is that not an important first step and a breach in the long and dreadful arms limitation deadlock?

As to these journeys of chiefs of state and the illusory impression of progress toward peace, I *quite* agree with your estimate. Moreover, one must view the effect on this institution of the Presidency of this experiment with personal diplomacy with anxiety. Surely, the President can't play all the instruments in the band and do justice to his constitutional task of leadership. But for all I know, conditions have been precarious enough to warrant what President Eisenhower has done and what Khrushchev is now doing — again.[163]

I think your estimate of the situation between the Soviet and the West is about right, and I look for little progress toward political settlements as long as the positions remain rigid. Nor can I dismiss the Soviet misgivings about German rearmament and missile installations.

Here in America we still have much to learn. While everyone declares solemnly that peace is his heart's desire and our most important national issue, they are also quick to denounce any accommodation with the Russians as appeasement or softness. I am afraid that most Americans think of peace as peace on our terms and unconditional surrender by

163 A summit meeting was being planned for June, 1960, in Paris.

the Soviet. Nor do our politicians or press do much to erase this naivete.

But, even worse, I am afraid we Americans have a great deal of mythology and self-deceit to penetrate before the realities of the world are clear and reason restored. I think it has been this tendency to constantly reassure our people that all is well and that the present uneasy and precarious situation is peace.

I wish very much that I could take advantage of your invitation to come to Lambarene. There is so much to talk about and so little time.

I pray that you continue well and will find other opportunities to let me have your views. But please don't despair. We are struggling with darkness here and I wish I felt that the Russian leaders were doing as much there.

Sincerely yours,

To Nikita S. Khrushchev

February 8, 1960

My dear Mr. Khrushchev:

Ambassador Menshikov has forwarded your thoughtful letter and birthday greetings. I am grateful indeed, and even crossing the milestone of 60 I find quite painless — at least until younger people start pulling out chairs for me to sit down! And let me thank you also for the welcome and splendid gift of Soviet wine and spirits which Mr. Menshikov delivered to me in such a beautiful case.

Your letter brought back happy memories of our visit last summer at Mr. [Roswell] Garst's farm. I, too, count it a most useful conversation, and I only regret that we have so little opportunity to exchange views about ways and means of improving the prospects for peace and the well being of all peoples. But when so much depends on so few, surely there is cause for hope that reasonable men can act reasonably.

It seems to me that arms limitation is still the most promising area for progress following the nuclear test agreement that I trust will soon be reached in Geneva — a goal that has long been dear to me, as you know. I am sure you will agree that we must go on from there to explore broader areas of cooperation.

I see that you are soon to commence further travels. I, too, am on the eve of a journey through South America — but I don't expect to work as hard as you! I shall try to remember that I have passed 60 — but will you?

Sincerely yours,

Part Five

Trip to Latin America

On February 9, 1960, Stevenson flew to Mexico City to begin his tour of twelve Latin American countries. He was accompanied by former Senator William Benton; Carleton Sprague Smith, of the Brazilian Institute of New York University; William McC. Blair, Jr., and his son John Fell Stevenson.

After Stevenson's death, Mr. Benton wrote: "I knew that the world had lost not merely its best interpreter in the continuing fight for peace; it had lost its 'first gentleman.' It was in Latin America that I learned, more abundantly than I can say, how much he deserved this title, in small matters as in large. And it was in Latin America that I realized fully the extent, and even more the intensity – the depth and sincerity – of the world's admiration for Adlai Stevenson, as the very conscience of the American people."[1]

Stevenson kept a handwritten diary of his trip. Some of this material the editors have selected for inclusion here. Frequently Stevenson wrote only a partial sentence – with names, a phrase, or a fact to remind him of what had been said or what he had done. While such jottings were useful to him, they are too fragmentary to be of value to anyone else. The editors have omitted such material. We include occasional letters and postcards that he wrote.

Mr. Benton dictated a much fuller report on the trip, and he made this available to the editors. Mr. Benton also published The Voice of Latin America in 1961 and a revised edition of this book in 1965 (a Harper Colophon book). We cite the revised edition. Mr. Benton wrote: "Throughout the trip, Governor Stevenson was infinitely patient. The entire two-month-long journey was a great personal triumph for him. He seems known to almost every Latin American. He was besieged everywhere by admiring crowds seeking autographs, bows, handshakes and smiles. Though we traveled strictly as private citizens, his appear-

---

[1] "Ambassador of Good Will in Latin America," in As We Knew Adlai: The Stevenson Story by Twenty-two Friends, edited and with preface by Edward P. Doyle, foreword by Adlai E. Stevenson III (New York: Harper & Row, 1966), p. 200.

ances became a triumph also for the United States; he symbolizes, in his learning, his wisdom and wit, his urbanity, oratory and his humane qualities, the characteristics the Latin Americans most value in their intellectuals and political leaders."[2]

When Stevenson left Chicago on February 9, 1960, he issued the following statement.

My journey to Latin America is one of a learner, for I have never had the opportunity to travel widely among our Portugese and Spanish-speaking neighbors. I also have some business to transact in several countries for American clients, and some old Latin American friends to visit.

I think all North Americans want to know a great deal more about our neighbors. Latin America is crucial to the United States and the free world. Rapid changes are taking place there and we are at the dawn of a more democratic era. But standards of living must be raised, illiteracy combated.

Latin America has many achievements — and some problems, as we all have. Among them are the population rise, inflation, the shortage of capital and confidence, economic and political instability, and fluctuating export prices. As we all know, some countries have suffered from dictatorship and corruption. I want to understand these problems better.

The political, economic and cultural ties between North and South America are long and strong. We want to be, and must be, good neighbors. By history and deep commitment we Americans, North and South, are on the side of the democratic forces we all hold dear: freedom, honest elections and integrity in political life. I hope to return from this trip a much better citizen of the hemisphere.

Excerpts from Stevenson's diary follow.

Part I — February 9–25, 1960 — Mexico, Guatemala, Costa Rica, Panama, Colombia, Ecuador

Feb. 9

. . . *Arr. Mexico City 8:30 P.M. — met by Amb. Hill*[3] *& staff & govt. people. Press conf[erence]. photos TV in great disorder. To Del Prado Hotel — plans & chat with Overseas Press Club group.*

[2] *The Voice of Latin America*, p. xvii.
[3] Robert C. Hill, U.S. ambassador to Mexico.

Already impressed with growth and modernization   after 24 years!
since last visit to Mexico — with Ellen.[4]

Feb. 10 — Wed. 8:45 A.M.!
Spoke to 250 of Embassy staff on lawn. Then briefing. One party
domination for many years — now stable and growing explosively.
Changes in US-Mex relations marked. More friendliness and understand-
ing. Presidential visits. Appalled by ignorance of L-A in U.S.![5] *Our*
largest consulate general! 600 000 tourists & $600 million spent. 50 000
Americans residing in Mex[ico]. Very limited reporting of L-A news
in US press except for the spectacular stuff. Mexico not in constant
crisis as in Brazil.
1960 — 150 ann[iversary]. of indep[endence]., 50th yr. of rev-
ol[ution]. Great objectives: land reform — breaking up large estates
& reducing foreign control.
Land reform not very successful from production [standpoint], but
program still active; large distribution under Mateos.[6] *Plan has greater*
mobility than serf, *moves to city and up into middle class, thus being*
consumers to support industrial growth. Small land owners not so
efficient — money lenders, crooked pols [politicians], poor credit facili-
ties. Only about 2% tillable; need fertilizer and irrigation.
Since 1938 Permex has controlled oil industry — one of objectives
of revol. Whether & how successful not important — sacred Rys [rail-
ways] in govt. hands long time. . . .
Mining industry stalled by taxation — if adjusted Mex capital may
participate & also beneficiate more ores here & use in industry.
Power — mixed private & public. Can't raise rates to attract capital
to expand Mateos proposes to double kw prod —from 2½ to 5 in 6 years.
Black[7] *prepared to loan large amt — $250 million — if rates raised;*
Mateos terminated interview quickly. Hopes to borrow elsewhere. Mex
[illegible] at end of borrowing capacity. Contracts made by govt. half
of program for expansion with French & American electrical mfgrs.
getting larger shares. *Cos. fighting with opposition rather than ideas.*
Policy of govt. — Mexican majority of stock. Large US cos. negotiating
on minority basis. Celenesa biggest — In Mfg. & services Cos. also more

---

[4] For Stevenson's visit to Mexico in 1936, see *The Papers of Adlai E. Stevenson,*
Vol. I, pp. 320–323.

[5] Passages printed here in roman type are underlined in Stevenson's diary. The
editors have been unable to determine when or why these passages were underlined.

[6] Adolfo López Mateos, president of Mexico, 1958–1964.

[7] Eugene R. Black, president of the International Bank for Reconstruction and
Development.

Mex. participation. US has ¾ of the 1.2 of foreign investment. Foreign partic[ipation]. still less than 10% of overall investment. . . . Cardenas[8] against increasing foreign investment.

Socializing tendency derives in part from Marxist influence in School of Economics of Univ.

. . . Political *briefing . . . Situation of & with Mexico unique. Role of history important to Mexicans. Revolution is guiding factor — was & is very* Mexican — against the Rich, the Foreigners & the Church. Its aim was to tear down, not build up. *Hence years of chaos — violent ambitious ruthless & often able men dominated from 1912 to '34. Affected our rights & interests;* [*Catholic*] church as defender of status quo was at war with state. *Climax in 1926 when churches were closed. Since 1934 Gen. Cardenas took office — vigorous rep*[*resentative*]. *of leftist spirit, land reform, labor organization; oil expropriation. Looked as tho on border of communism. Didn't happen; fun.*

Oligarchy of power — small group of pols [politicians] then control of party & army — have ruled ever since.

In form a repres[*entative*]. democracy; in fact a one party state & dictatorship. *Have institutionalized revolution — having attained pol*[*itical*]. *aims could go on to social aims.*

Each Pres. considered creature of his predecessor. Gives Ex. Pres. great influence. Cardenas has great hold on poorer classes. Aleman[9] on business community.

Effect of political stability is also a weakness — no healthy, vigorous opposition & political life. One result is corruption — *improve personal fortune. The bite — the cut — the rake off — mordida — universal in L.A.*

. . . *Little acc't taken that one party system is a real defect.*

Defended on ground that it is all inclusive — as expression of will of people is totalitarian. Descendant of Vice regal system. *Quite incompatible with our ideas.*

. . . *Our relations best they have ever been.* No serious *problem. But no treaties, joint defense.[10] We are worried about our soft underbelly. Mex. says no foreign troops which are necessary to protect approaches to SAC* [*Strategic Air Command*] *bases in SW from Pacific.*

. . . *Relations best ever — but requires constant effort — suspicion latent.* Revolution — socialist at 20, capitalist at 40 — reactionary at 60 — Harvard men.

8 Former President Lázaro Cárdenas (1934–1940).
9 Former President Miguel Alemán (1946–1952).
10 Mexico refused to enter into military agreements with the United States after 1950, when the U.S. made such agreements with many Latin American countries. See Edwin Lieuwen, *Arms and Politics in Latin America* (New York: Praeger, 1961).

. . . Influence of Castro with students in LA enormous! *45,000
students at Univ. of Mex. — tuition $16! Power of youth!*
    . . . *Education Mexico's biggest need; 18% of budget.*
Little danger of communism in L.A. except Bolivia.
*Should increase power of OAS [Organization of American States]
& effectiveness — less talk, more facts. Too many meaningless resolutions.*

Don't intervene with Trujillo.[11] *Support any movement to increase
democ. & protect human rights. Don't give any help; moral condemnation.*

*After the briefing at the United States embassy, Stevenson went to a
luncheon given by Foreign Minister Manuel Tello.*

*Luncheon by Tello at Foreign Office with . . . [Rufino] Tamayo —
greatest artist who lives mostly in Paris — and other prominent Mexicans.*
    *Usual fancy Foreign Office food & 3 wines — at lunch! Speeches —
made successful crack about item on menu — Profiteral — in connection
with U.S. investment "Profit over all."*
    Not much impressed with Tello. Old Foreign Office hand.
    *After lunch Tamayo took us to see his murals in the Belles Artes;
huge & very Mexican. Confess they don't please me very much but some
of his painting is fine.*
    Reception at Embassy Residence — 900 guests! Mob scene. . . .

Feb. 11 — Mexico City
    *Off to Pueblo [Puebla] by Embassy plane with J. F. [John Fell]
& Carleton Smith. Greeting by American residents — textiles, power.
Casa Cola! Marvellous churches —* Rosario chapel one of sights of
hemisphere. Indian work remarkable. Hidden convent. *Lunch at home
of some Americans.*
    *Chalula [Cholula] — Church for every day of year! — incredible how
they built so many churches — and such immense ones! Good restoration
going on after many years of anti clericalism.* . . .

*On February 12, Stevenson had a lengthy session with Minister of
Education Torres Bodet, and following that a meeting with Minister*

[11] Generalissimo Rafael Leonidas Trujillo Molina, dictator of the Dominican
Republic from 1930 until his assassination on May 30, 1961. In January, 1961, the
OAS voted to impose economic sanctions against the Trujillo government.

of Finance Ortiz Mena. After these conferences he visited the cathedral in Mexico City and then lunched with a group of Mexican businessmen. In the afternoon he had a second meeting with President Lopez Mateos. According to Stevenson's diary, the president was strongly in favor of Latin American disarmament but had "no disposition to take" the leadership on the issue. The president also expressed the hope that the United States would pay more attention to Latin America. Stevenson then wrote in his diary:

Brisk, tough, somewhat oblique man of ambition & energy. Said first tasks — Education and electric power. . . .

To dinner at Dr. Carillo Flores, Rector of Univ. 20–30 guests — Ex Pres. Aleman (biggest fortune from Presidency — "but he invests it in Mexico!") Dr. Adolfo Carso[12] *of Monte Alban fame, now head of Indiginous Institutes to help living conditions of Indians . . . leaders of intellectual, musical, arts, political & professional life.*

Pretty very Mexican house overlooking city. Charming old father, Julian Carillo, famous composer. Full blooded Indian!

Fancy Mexican dinner.

To St. Valentine's Day Ball at Jockey Club with Ambassador Hill for blind charity. Could have been anywhere. Short speech — recalling that it was Lincoln's Birthday. So — to bed!

Feb. 13

Overcast — take off in Govt. plane to Oaxaca delayed. Big Press Conference — good questions. Made big plea for S A [South American] disarmamant as example to world. Press extremely friendly — Emphasis economic — cf Why doesn't U.S. increase sugar quota from Mex? Some ignorance of their own protective tariffs & global U.S. responsibilities.

Talks with Ex-Mayor O'Dwyer[13] *(Stevenson man!). . . .*

To central market — vast and efficient — en route to airport. Off for Oaxaca several hours late with Mrs. Mary Elmendorf of CARE (wife of Dean of Mexico City College) and Dr. Carlos Maguin, archeologist from University.

Past volcanoes — greeting by officials & sad stories about all the plans made for our earlier arrival — band, children, dances etc.

12 Alfonso Caso, a noted Mexican archaeologist who from 1931 to 1943 was involved in the excavation of Monte Albán, the ancient capital and ceremonial site of the Zapotecs in Oaxaca.

13 William O'Dwyer, mayor of New York City from 1946 to 1950 and ambassador to Mexico, 1950–1952, who had become a resident of Mexico.

By motor to Monte Alban with horde of tourismo & officials. Incredible site on top of mountain — Zapatec [Zapotec] architecture more mighty & majestic than I had expected!

On 40 miles to Mitla — amazing geometric ornamentation of Mixtec culture — later than Zapatec (Everyone still speaks Zapatec in area).

Firecrackers and rockets greeted us in village square. (Loudest I ever heard!) Marimba band; presentation ceremonies of sewing machine, mid-wife kit, tools etc. Speeches all around; then to Mayor's Office (stocky little Indian) for rounds of local Mescal — like Tequila. Then inspection of mobile medical unit operated by CARE — and visit to museum of Zapatec. . . .

Back to Oaxaca in time for dances in court yard of city Hall — formerly monastery. Elaborate speech of welcome by leading lawyer of state followed by dancing — Indian, Spanish & Mestizo in costumes — with splendid band playing from balcony. Huge long table around court & tamale dinner after presentation of gifts of pottery, headdress and Oaxaca dagger engraved with my name, date and local saying "Don't kill me with the blade; it is too dull. Kill me with a kiss beneath my shawl"!

Bitterly cold — and home to bed — just in time for violent chill — at excellent Hotel Victoria.

Feb. 14

To jewelers to see reproduction of Monte Alban incredible "jewels" — which we saw in the museum yesterday.

Bill Benton bot about everything in sight — as usual!

To really remarkably beautiful and deserted monastery church — decoration of ceilings and alters more elaborate than anywhere except possibly Portugal.

Off to Merida in our govt. plane. And I hope to come back to Oaxaca again — !

Merida — by motor, after welcome by officials to Uxmal — about 40 miles — ruins of classical, early Mayan — 800–1000 AD — by many considered the most delicately beautiful of Mayan culture.

Reminded of An[g]kor Wat by these enormous structures covered by scrub jungle for centuries. . . .

Much good talk about Mayan history — including Charles Wicke from the Mexico City College dig at Yogul, near Mitla.

Dinner at "native" night club — restaurant in Merida & night at Hotel Merida!!

Work on the scores of thank you letters.

[407]

Feb. 15
To . . . — excavation of 500 AD *ruins by Nat[ional]. Geo[graphic].
— Tulane team headed by Dr. Wyllys Andrews (Bloomington mother!)
This site is* enormous *&* by far largest and oldest discovered yet. Goes
back to 2000 BC& changes much of historical assumptions about
Mayans.
   Visited temple of the dolls & Senator 1400 feet deep where skin
divers have brought up much material. . . .*
   Long drive to Chichen Itza . . . and much fascinating talk about
similarities *of Mayan & Indonesian languages & decoration; Egyptian
papyrus possibly linking Egypt & Yucatan & differences between Mayan
Indians & other American–Bering Strait Indians. Also how this thin,
rocky soil sustained such large and advanced populations — and why!*
   Chichen Itza — all you expect — but the bloody Toltec influence not
as attractive to me as the Mayan or Mixtec.
   *Lunch at Mayaland Hotel — wonderful mural of life & corn in dining
room! — more sightseeing. "Observatory" — Mayans had found true
north! Mayan classical more attractive to me than Toltec-Mayan and
plumed serpent motif of warlike Toltecs.
   . . . Back to Merida . . . dinner, walk around main square — letter
& bed — dead!*

Feb. 16
   *Up early; visit to Governor, Mayor etc & usual elaborate courtesies.
Visit to nice little museum — and farewell to these charming, friendly
smiling Mexicans — with thanks to all the* American money & archae-
ologists who have restored everything in Yucatan — with no visible
acknowledgement. Guatemala City . . . *Visit to President [Miguel]
YDIGORAS FUENTES who was elected in an upset after assassination
of [President] Castillo Armas. Gentle, quiet, humorous little man who
— the President of the Assembly — told me at lunch "had divided the
country — between the disappointed and the surprised" —*
   *After centuries of dictatorship & strong govt. since Spanish Captain
General most people expected and many wanted him to be a dictator
too.* Instead he has introduced democratic institutions — and now a
really free press proves it by attacking him & his family; a free judiciary
sends no one to jail; and everyone who is not in the gov't & on the
payroll conspires to overthrow the gov't!
   *Financial trouble — coffee price low — wants to sell more sugar to
U.S. If economy bad — unrest & trouble.
   . . . Gift of books re Guatemala & Mayans. Delightful man with*

[408]

rare touch of genuine greatness but probably not forceful or ruthless enough for these infant democracies.[14]

. . . Lunch with US Amb[15] *— Pres of Assembly, Chief Justice & head of US [United?] Fruit [Company] Complaints about large bureaucracy & few trained people.*

Country's needs, like all of them, — hospitals, medicines, schools, water supply.

65% illiterate — To educate must first learn Spanish — living as the Mayans.

. . . Visit to excellent, light, airy museum — beautifully arranged.

Over mountains & lakes to San Salvador — and press [conference] — & on to Costa Rica — arriving San Jose 7:15 P.M. in private Costa Rican plane — full of passengers!

Official welcome — also Pepe Figueras[16] *former Pres. & one of really significant democratic leaders of hemisphere. Dinner at Embassy Residence. . . .*

Feb. 17 —

Visit to President Echandi[17] *— and cabinet.* Wants more tax inducement by U.S. on investment *— also U.S. assume ⅔rds of maintenance of Inter-Am[erican] Highway when completed. Amb. agrees during early years while traffic bldg. up.*

. . . Briefing at Embassy . . . about Cuba & Carib[bean]. area — communist conspiracy. . . .

[Cuban] Embassies have secret radio, pouch for transferring funds etc. USSR does not have diplomatic network in L.A. — Cuba does! — has replaced every diplomat, many old career officers tossed out and desperate. . . .

. . . Visit to excellent museum of primitive cultures — amusing pottery figures & lovely painted bowls etc. No great structures like Maya. . . .

Visit to Univ[ersity]. — new — fine — ultra modern wooden-concrete bldgs. — met with faculty and students from Kansas City univ. taking 3rd year there.

Huge reception at brother in law of Pepe Figueras — refugees from

[14] Mr. Benton wrote in his diary: "President Ydigoras impressed Governor Stevenson and me with his candour, his competence, and his seeming capacity for leadership."

[15] John C. Muccio, U.S. ambassador to Guatemala.

[16] José Figueres, president of Costa Rica, 1953–1958.

[17] Jiménez Mario Echandi, president of Costa Rica, 1958–1962, who represented the coalition groups in opposition to President Figueres.

Nicaragua & Santo Domingo; Morgan Philips, Sec. of Br[itish]. Labor Party, and all of Pepe's former cabinet and principal followers.

State dinner at Presidential Palace — with leading citizens, 2 Vice Presidents, all Ex-Presidents invited. Arrived on time & drank for 1½ hrs before dinner! Splendid menu, beautiful table in ugly, tasteless house. Wonderful plant in center!! Pres. Brisk bright, humorous, without Pepe [*Figueres*]'s democratic passions. Preoccuped with econ. develop. — businessman type — philosophical about politics. . . .

Wife — beautiful in this country of beauties — in kitchen overseeing the dinner.

At 12 P.M. we started [for] La Lucha (The fight!) — Pres Pepe Figueras' home and sisal plantation in the mountains. Arrived after hair raising trip over rugged mountain road driven by Pepe who talked incessantly about civil war in C[osta] R[ica] which he led & which restored const[itutional]. democracy after 8 years of coalition of extreme right who wanted to make money & communists who wanted power. . . .

Stories of Somoza's[18] *tortures in Nicaragua — squeezing testicles, a favorite. Trujillos brutalities.* "That these things could be happening in mid-twentieth century." *We agreed and went to bed at 2 A.M. a little sick with his long recitation of our stupidities in L A & toleration of these bastards so long.*[19]

February 18

Slept till 9:30! Beautiful tropical mountain scenery. Very rugged; rope factory; idyllic setting; sweet, pregnant wife Karen, Danish-Am; charming bright eyed children. Incessant & fascinating talk from this eloquent, passionate, gentle, sensitive man who hates tyranny & injustice as no one I've ever met!

"What all S A wants is opportunity to develop themselves. So must limit investment from outside so as not to discourage growth of local wealth — otherwise jealousy, tension & agitation about econ. imperialism. Want investment of something more than money; that develops country & people who come to stay and participate.

18 Luis Somoza-Debayle, president of Nicaragua, 1956–1963.

19 Mr. Benton wrote in his diary: "Don Pepe seems to be one of Costa Rica's leading personalities. He is closely allied with the liberal movements throughout Latin America. . . . Don Pepe's principal interest in Governor Stevenson's trip . . . is to see to it that the Governor is properly guided so that he will understand the importance of the liberal and progressive forces in the various countries we visit — and will be properly allied with them. Dr. Figueres sees the great issue of Latin America as that of the 'dormant people' struggling to break the chains which have bound them — struggling upward towards the sun, towards a more perfect position and a better life."

"Latin Am has not been civilized by the New Deal. And Am[erican] business men think of the small L A economic hierarchy as the equivalent of the Am. business community."[20]

. . . Long drive back to San Jose in time for press conference and farewells and plane for Panama at 7 P.M.

Met in hot sticky Panama — with flood of memories of my exciting days here in early 1942.[21] Met also by Govt. protocol, U.S. Amb. etc., & off to the Embassy with Julian Harrington,[22] old friend from Hong Kong, and his artist Irish wife.

Place chattering with anxiety over renewal of violence about flying flag.[23] Conf[erence]. with Amb. & CIA man at huge Embas[s]y residence where J. F. [John Fell] & I stayed — very comfortably! . . .

Feb 19 — Panama

Up early to see excellent restoration of Old Panama — sacked & massacred by [Captain Henry] Morgan in 1671. Trip around with Ambassador — visited lock in Canal. Then to Pres. of Panama — White cranes in court yard. 300 lb protocol officer! Pres [Ernesto] de la Guardia short, swarthy, direct, simple little man. Term expiring. Said he would reaffirm U.S. rights [in Canal Zone] if could fly Panama flag & sensed resentment at exclusive life of Americans residing in Zone.[24]

[20] Mr. Benton wrote in his diary of this talk with Figueres: "The problem is made very difficult for the United States, he warns, because we must seek 'to protect the Latin American countries from their own oligarchies.' He concedes that business has changed greatly, and for the better, within the United States. This is not true in Latin America. When North American business men come to South America and meet the rich and entrenched business and social leaders, they may like to think they are meeting their own counterparts. But 'the rich oligarchies of South America are not like the successful and wealthy business leaders of the United States.' "

[21] For Stevenson's visit to the Canal Zone as part of his inspection tour of U.S. naval bases in the Caribbean in June, 1942, as official representative of the Secretary of the Navy, see *The Papers of Adlai E. Stevenson*, Vol. II, pp. 52–54.

[22] U.S. ambassador to Panama. For Stevenson's visit with Harrington in 1953, when Harrington was U.S. consul general in Hong Kong, see *The Papers of Adlai E. Stevenson*, Vol. V, pp. 72–76 *passim*.

[23] On November 3, 1959, a mob of two thousand Panamanians tried to enter the Canal Zone to plant a Panamanian flag there, but police repelled the attack with tear gas and clubs. Later, demonstrators directed violence against U.S. agencies and personnel in Panama and tore down the flag of the U.S. embassy. Attempts to restore cordial relations culminated in President Eisenhower's controversial order of September 17, 1960, that the Panamanian flag be flown alongside the U.S. flag in the Canal Zone as "visual evidence of Panama's titular sovereignty" over the area.

[24] Mr. Benton wrote in his diary that President de la Guardia "complains about the two sharp and distinct communities, Panamanian and American. He says he knows 'high officers' who have served for three years in the Canal Zone — who have never been in Panama City. . . . Later the Governor [Stevenson] and I chatted

Press conf. at Embassy: [I] *Said*
1. *OK on flag if Panama reaffirms 1903 treaty rights of US.*[25]
2. *Titular sovereignty includes consid[eration]. of all Panama complaints.*
3. *Break down segregation of U.S. residents.*
4. *Clarify confusion of authority bet[ween] Amb., Gen'l commanding forces, and Gov. of Zone.*[26]
5. *May be future some form of internationalization. OAS* [*Organization of American States*] *takeover. Also move to Zone — rename it District of Americas.*

Latter inserted because Panama hates idea of internationalization. But great fear of nationalization pressure mounting. Sure I pleased no one; but think proposals sensible & serious.

Off for Medillin [Medellín], *Colombia, big industrial center developed almost since war. Now being surpassed by Cali. Fine, growing city. Little of historical interest. . . .*

. . . Presentation of key to city and decree by Mayor & City Council. . . .

While in Medellín, Stevenson received a cablegram from his law partner, Newton Minow, saying that the New York Times, February 18, 1960, had published a dispatch from its correspondent in Costa Rica quoting Stevenson as having said that "the amount of money being spent" on Senator John F. Kennedy's presidential campaign "is phenomenal, probably the highest amount spent on a campaign in history. And I'm not sure that Kennedy planned it that way." Mr. Minow also reported that Stevenson was reported as saying that it was "somewhat arrogant" of Senator Kennedy to announce that he would not accept the vice presidential nomination. Mr. Minow added that Senator Kennedy was "very upset."[27] Stevenson sent the following cablegram to the managing editor of the Times.

---

about the cleavage between the two communities and we feel it is deeply regrettable."

[25] The 1903 treaty between Panama and the United States included the phrase "as if the United States were sovereign."

[26] Mr. Benton wrote in his diary that the president of Panama complained about the "divided authority" he faced in dealing with the United States. "There are three top officers — the Governor General of the Canal Zone (General [William E.] Potter); the Commander of U.S. Forces in the Canal Zone (General [Ridgely] Gaither; and the U.S. Ambassador (Julian Harrington). . . . Ambassador Harrington later confirmed to Governor Stevenson and me that this is indeed a most serious problem."

[27] See *Newsweek*, February 29, 1960, for a comment on the incident.

To Turner Catledge

February 19, 1960

UNAUTHORIZED QUOTES BY YOUR CORRESPONDENT IN COSTA
RICA VERY EMBARRASSING AND INACCURATE. HAVE JUST TELE-
PHONED MY PARTNER WILLARD WIRTZ, CHICAGO AS FOLLOWS:
I AM ASTONISHED BY THE NEW YORK TIMES STORY AND NEITHER
AUTHORIZED NOR MADE ANY SUCH STATEMENTS. STOP. IN RESPONSE
TO A QUESTION BY A COSTA RICAN AT A RECEPTION I AGREED THAT
IF THE TIME MAGAZINE STORY ABOUT SENATOR KENNEDY'S CAM-
PAIGN WAS CORRECT, IT WOULD BE VERY EXPENSIVE AND MIGHT
CREATE SYMPATHY FOR HIS OPPONENTS STOP.

ADLAI STEVENSON

Feb 20 — Medillin
Visit to two textile mills . . . [and] Hospital.
Average wages 10–15 pesos per day — $1.50 to $2.00.
*Interminable luncheon at Country Club (very fine — and expensive!
— golf, tennis, pool.) given by Governor. Speeches.*
Meeting with large group of Am[erican]. business people. Competi-
tion from Germany — better credits or prices or both![28] *Help! Help!*

Feb 21 —
Off to Bogota in President's *plane. Very swank.* Arrived in time for
bullfight. Dominguin & Ordonez, Caceras, Vasques. Two dedicated to
me! Tumultuous greeting by crowd! Almost mobbed![29]

---

[28] Mr. Benton wrote in his diary: "The American community . . . is greatly
interested in American laws which will give assistance to American industry in its
competition overseas with the Italians, French, West Germans, Swiss and others."

[29] John Fell Stevenson wrote Natalie Owings on February 22, 1960: "Yesterday
we were fortunate enough to arrive in Bogota in time to see Luis [Miguel] Dominguin
and [Antonio] Ordonez . . . the two greatest bullfighters in the world now . . .
took 300 pictures . . . Ordonez got two ears, Dominguin only one. . . .
"Dad too, caused quite a sensation at the Plaza de Toros. When he arrived the
whole crowd cheered. Two of the fighters, Dominguin and Caceres, dedicated their
bulls to him, a ceremony indicated by the throwing of their hat to Dad to be kept
during the fight.
". . . Following the fight there was a terrible mob scene centered around Dad.
Everyone wanted autographs. . . . Dad was protected by about five policemen,
one of which fell over the edge into the ring. People were throwing their wine skins
for Dad to have a squirt; one soggy thing hit me flat in the face. The crowd
followed all the way to the hotel. . . ."

On February 22 Stevenson attended a briefing at the United States embassy where he heard a good deal about the violence that characterized Colombian political life. In 1948 after the assassination of a Liberal party leader rioting broke out. The Conservative party, which was in office, used the army to drive Liberals from their farms. The Liberals retaliated by forming guerrilla bands and seizing Conservatives' property. Many people fled to Bogotá and other large cities for protection. In 1957 the Liberals and Conservatives joined forces and removed General Gustavo Rojas Pinilla from the presidency. The two parties agreed to alternate the presidency and divide all government offices evenly. In 1958 Alberto Lleras Camargo became the Liberal party president and he offered amnesty to all bandidos *who would turn in their weapons. While he accomplished much, some violence still remained. Estimates of how many Colombians had died by 1960 ranged up to 300,000.*

In addition to a discussion of the political turmoil, Stevenson was told that few of the rich used their wealth in a socially responsible way. Despite this, Stevenson learned, President Lleras Camargo was trying to push agrarian reform and stir social consciousness.

*Stevenson and his party lunched that day with a number of leaders of business and government. "Incredible," he wrote in his diary, "mon-*strous cathedral cut out of salt 500 feet underground in worlds largest salt mountain — Deeply impressive — scented with rotting potatoes stored in mine!*"*

Later that day Stevenson met with President Lleras Camargo. The president emphasized that there was nothing as important as resettling people, who had fled to the cities during the violence, on unused government-owned land. Funds were needed for credit facilities, roads, and schools. The president also told Stevenson that the feudal life of Colombia was "preserved in education and agriculture."

That evening Stevenson had time to answer some correspondence. Frank Karelsen, who was active in the liberal group in New York politics, had urged Stevenson to support Senator Hubert Humphrey. Many Stevenson supporters, because they believed that he might be a candidate, were withholding contributions to Humphrey, he remarked. Mr. Karelsen recommended that Stevenson announce that he would not accept the nomination even if drafted.

To Frank Karelsen[30]

February 22, 1960

Dear Frank:

I must write you hurriedly because the carnivorous courtesy of the

[30] The original is in the possession of Mr. Karelsen.

people along my path leaves me no time for correspondence and little for sleep!

I have your interesting letter of February 12, and, of course, I share your views about the importance of beating Nixon. I also share, and have for many years, your warm regard for Hubert; and I would urge you, as I have so many of my friends, not to "withhold your financial support," as your letter says, from him or any of the Democratic candidates on my account. I have issued statements for the past two years urging my friends to support the candidate of their choice because I was not a candidate and would not be.

But, I cannot comply with your request that I announce that "I would not accept the nomination even if drafted." Indeed I hope *no American* in *good health* will *ever* make such a statement, just as I hope no American will refuse to serve his country when called upon. As you know, I have expressed and written views of this kind going back to 1952, when I was sorely tempted to make such a statement because of my consuming desire to finish my job as Governor of Illinois.

Perhaps in reflection you might even agree with me that while I am glad to avoid political meetings and any covert or overt politicking, and *even leave the country, I cannot*, nor *should* ANYONE, do what you have suggested, unless circumstances of health or strength justify it.

Forgive this hurried dictation and rest assured that I understand your motive and personal goodwill and loyalty, for which I am humbly grateful!

> Cordially yours,
> AES

To Carol Evans[31]

February 22, 1960

Dear Carol:

I have your letter of February 16, and by all means send Worth Bingham[32] and his bride an E. B. [*Encyclopaedia Britannica*] Atlas for a wedding present. . . . Also, please notify Mrs. [Franklin D.] Roosevelt that I will not return until the 11th of April and barely in time to meet a speaking engagement at the University of Virginia; hence, I cannot accept her invitation to join her on the television program on the 10th. You might say that I am having trouble keeping up with my correspondence during this frantic and homicidal journey.

[31] This handwritten letter is in the possession of Miss Evans.
[32] Eldest son of Mr. and Mrs. Barry Bingham.

I assume you know my plans to return to New York from Barbados in time to meet the engagements in Charlottesville. . . .

> Yours sincerely,
> AES

P.S. I wish there was time to tell you about all that has happened together with an estimation of my prospects for survival! . . .

On February 23 Stevenson started the day with a meeting with trade union leaders from the two union confederations. They told him that while sixty per cent of industrial labor was organized, most workers were in agriculture and there was little organization there. They admitted that there had been some Communist infiltration in some unions. It was hard to combat, they explained, because poverty was rampant and also because of "reactionary industrial leaders" who fought unionization.

The remainder of the day was spent in sightseeing and conversations with government officials. The next day Stevenson visited the University of the Andes and discussed this experiment in private, nondenominational higher education with Jaime Samper, the rector, and Ramón de Zubiria, the assistant rector.[33] From there Stevenson went to the National University where he received an honorary degree. Benton wrote: "I believe Governor Stevenson startled some in his audience. . . . He said, 'Businessmen are economic servants for their people. When capital is built it must not be locked up, or spent in luxury for a few, but must be devoted to the further development of the country.'"[34]

Following the ceremonies a group of students asked Stevenson for an interview. After talking with them they proposed he should see some of the slums of Bogotá and particularly the areas where refugees were living. During the tour the students, particularly their spokesman, Guillermo Mannetti, described the civil war and criticized the lack of social consciousness among rich Colombians. The students were also highly critical of the reactionaries in the Conservative party.

Late that afternoon the bullfighter Luis Miguel Dominguín called on Stevenson and then accompanied him to a reception given by Eduardo Zuleta Angel, who had been a colleague of Stevenson's at the London meeting in 1945 of the Preparatory Commission of the United Nations.

---

[33] See Benton, *The Voice of Latin America*, pp. 138–140, for a description of this university.

[34] *Ibid.*, p. 180.

Following the reception, Stevenson held a press conference. He wrote in his diary: "Nothing eventful. Questions asked — will Dems. pay more [attention] to So Am? Price of bananas? Help!"

That hectic day was concluded with a dinner in his honor at the presidential palace. Before dinner the president escorted Stevenson and Benton on a tour of the palace. After the dinner the president spoke in both Spanish and English and Stevenson responded in English. Mr. Benton wrote in his diary: "Governor Stevenson had been making notes throughout the dinner and throughout the speech — as he always does, and then spoke with ease, with wit, with originality — and emotionally moving, with material closely keyed to his audience. One remark . . . that he made in his speech, 'As Lincoln said, a nation cannot live half slave and half free; and Franklin Roosevelt said, we cannot live half boom and half bust; and so I say that the Hemisphere cannot continue in peace and prosperity — while it is half rich and half poor.' "

By the time Stevenson returned to the hotel it was 2 A.M., and he wrote the following letter.

To Mrs. Ronald Tree[35]

February 25

M — A lovely Trollopian week for a *you!* a fantastic stereoptican week for me! Letter has arrived. . . . This afternoon awarded Doctor of Laws and Political Science, Honoris Causa, before the Rector Magnifi cus, Presidenta de la Consuliatura, Excellentissimo Arzobispo, Ministras del Despacho, Excellentissimos Embazadores, Senores Conciliarias, Decanas, Professores, faculties, friends and students of El Universidad Nacional de Bogota — following two passionate orations in Spanish about my virtue, scholarship, statesmanship, philosophy, magnanimity and wit. And so it has been a couple of times a day (but the stigmata is not showing *yet!*) I followed with a ponderous oration prepared this A.M. — mostly with scissors and paper clips. And now — 2 A.M. as usual — I'm in bed after a state dinner with the President and 100 guests in the great hall of Senor Bolivar's palace, where the President's eloquence quite unnerved me. Before dinner we drank in the room where the conspiracy on Bolivar's life took place — led by the President's great grandfather! And then he took me to the small room at the back of the palace where Bolivar jumped out the window while the lovely Manuela delayed the conspirators with her artifices and his ADC, Ferguson, an Englishman died defending the door.

Later — at that point I must have fallen asleep; and now its another

[35] This handwritten letter is in the possession of Mrs. Tree.

night and I'm back from the last fiesta in Bogota to pack for the usual 8 AM takeoff for Quito. I took Luis Miguel Dominguin, the bull fighter, with me this evening, and what an engaging, sensitive, slight, dignified young man he is. Small wonder Ava Gardner, Betty Bacall and all the rest flipped — to borrow a word from the young. So did John Fell — whom Luis insists on taking back to Spain to convert into the great matador Americano! He dedicated his bull to me in the Plaza de Toros Sunday — while the crowd howled — and then proceeded to dispatch him with stunning grace and glory.

But — whats the use — adventures multiply with such rapidity that reporting is hopeless. There's only *one* remedy! Yet I wonder if I'll ever want to travel again if this South American primary ever ends! Each day I resolve to cut the pose and find a sensible compromise, and each day it seems to get worse. But I suppose it can't all be like Columbia [Colombia] — pray God — for here I seem to be a national hero and they're "all Democrats"! . . .

Feb 25 — Bogotá

"Thank yous" for books, letters; visit to *incredible* collection of pre Columbian gold in National Bank. Finer than anything we say [saw] in O[a]xaca or Yucatan. Have 7000 pieces, overlooked by Spaniards! And think what they must have gathered and melted down!! Most of it cast, not hammered.

Bot some pieces in a store — [William] Benton, I mean! — for some lady!

Interminable delay at airport for plane to Quito — Anything worse than 2 hour farewells with protocol officers. . . .

Off to Quito at last — with very fond memories of Columbia, charming people, desperate problems, great President and a fair bet.

P.S. Visited at Hotel early this AM by large deleg[ation]. of farmers from Tolema [Tolima] (fine Gov.) Very touching, very humble & ignorant. Made hesitant speeches — praising Castro & US etc! . . .

During his first day in Quito, Stevenson talked with President Camilo Ponce Enriquez, who pointed out the need to raise living standards and the welfare of the mass of the people. The president described the Communist influence emanating from Cuba as a threat all through South America. They examined the opportunities for the investment of United States capital. At the close of the meeting they discussed the failure of newspapers to publish adequate news about Latin America.

[448]

Next Stevenson called on the rector of the Central University and met with faculty and students. One student observed that a basic problem in South America was that large military appropriations diverted funds from education. Stevenson replied that in Mexico and in each country visited thereafter he had urged Latin America to lead the world in disarmament.

Then Stevenson and his party dined with the vice president. Stevenson wrote in his diary: "Excellent dinner. No speeches!"

On February 26, former President Galo Plaza took Stevenson on a tour of the Monastery of St. Augustine and then to the American School (mainly for Ecuadorian students), which Plaza had helped found. From there they drove into the countryside to lunch at the home of Galo Plaza's sisters. Stevenson wrote in his diary: "Beautiful valleys! Highly cultivated. Fine dairy herds. . . . Lunch at San Luis — beautiful gardens, waterfall, Holstein . . . dairy herd, flowers, ponds, and handsome hacienda house behind great wall. Glorious lunch — even peach pie & ice cream in our honor."

On his return to Quito, Stevenson conferred with the foreign minister and then met with a large group of trade union leaders. Stevenson wrote in his diary: "Answered questions — all courteous and friendly personally for 1½ hours. Talked about USSR & Communism. Many bursts of applause. First meeting with labor a prominent American ever held — great success according to Embassy!!"

On February 27 the Stevenson party flew to Guayaquil. He wrote in his diary:

Guayaquil — sprawling, ugly, mouldy city of ½ million surrounded by noisome slums. They say this is height of rainy and worst season. I hope so! Nice, able consul, Ward Allen (from Copenhagen in '58) just arrived. Saw town with Governor who wants US help for his appalling housing and sanitation problem. Cocktail party in Consul's unfurnished house for his staff. Fine new consulate office with bachelor quarters on top for girls & unmarrieds. Good hotel — Humboldt. Some anxiety about communism among the miserable & unemployed. Large urban migration from highlands for jobs & "better life."

The Stevenson party was delayed in Guayaquil and was not able to get a plane for Lima, Peru, until 5:30 A.M. on February 28. After arriving in Lima at 8:30 A.M., Stevenson met with the leaders of three of Peru's political parties and several intellectuals, including the rector of the

[419]

University of San Marcos. They emphasized that Peru wanted to main-tain a constitutional democracy and was tired of dictators. There was considerable criticism of the United States for its support of dictators in Latin America. The need to raise living standards and to expand schools was discussed, as was the failure of the rich to give money to support education — "still in feudal age," Stevenson noted in his diary.

The remainder of the day Stevenson spent on a yacht cruising to the guano islands off the coast of Peru. On February 29, after a briefing at the United States embassy, Stevenson called on the acting president, Luis Gallo Parras (the president was in Europe). They discussed — as Stevenson had in Ecuador — a boundary dispute between Peru and Ecuador. Since the vice president felt Stevenson had received incorrect information in Quito, he explained Peru's position to him. Stevenson then called on the acting foreign minister, Luis Alvarado Garrido (the foreign minister was in Europe with the president).

Then Stevenson had a lengthy talk with Prime Minister Pedro Beltrán. The prime minister spoke of the need of improving the situation among Peru's Indians, who were largely illiterate and who lived in isolated seclusion. But he felt that time was short, since the "landless Indians" were now waking up and revolution was "not far off." Congress, dom-inated by the rich families, did not see this, the premier added.

After lunch in one of the most luxurious men's clubs in the world as the guest of Dr. Victor Andres Belaunde, Peru's permanent representa-tive at the United Nations, Stevenson visited the slums of Lima, a five-minute drive from the club. He noted in his diary that he found "about the worst squalor & filth I've ever seen."[36] Following the tour of the slums and a hospital for children, Stevenson dined with the premier in his huge old family home.

Tuesday March 1 — Lima —

Up at 5 A.M. in dark for Cusco [Cuzco]. Joined by Dr. Alberto A. Giescke, American, former Rector of U[niversity] of Cusco, great archeologist — now 76.

Paper work smothers Peru — "papeleo" — defeats all projects. Could do a lot for housing, land reform & education themselves by raising taxes, simplifying admin[istrative]. procedures, squeezing out the ap-palling graft. . . .

Spectacular flight thru snow peaks to Cusco (11 340) in beautiful

---

[36] John Fell Stevenson wrote Natalie Owings: ". . . I joined Dad for a tour of the slums. . . . I have seen slums in Calcutta, Hong Kong & Karachi & I thought I had seen everything. But, this was worse, it was hell on earth. . . ."

valley on top of Andes, Capital of Inca Empire. Greeting by officials. . . .

By car to ferrocarril — narrow guage [gauge] — up the Urumbamba
[Urubamba] valley — Sacred valley of Incas — across magnificent rich
wide valley covered with cows and sheep, thru narrow perpendicular
gorges more mighty than El Capitan & Yosemite. Indians high crowned
white straw hats; miserable poverty, thatched adobe on perpendicular
pole huts. Very dirty, no apparent sense of cleanliness, refuse all around,
guinea pigs all over, mangy dogs, no chimneys. No better than the worst
of darkest A[frica]!

Live as serfs on haciendas; get some land to cultivate, pigs, work 3
days a week for landlord, no money.

After 3 hours dismount, cross raging muddy Urubamba & zig zag
up mountain side in busses to Machu Pichu — incredible lost city of
Incas — evidently used for religious rites; only female skeletons (Vestal
Virgins) found. Marvellous masons. Stones fit so perfectly — can't get
knife between them. Dispute as to date. 1100–1400? Enormous stones.
How did they move 100 ton stones? . . .

Saw my first Vicuna — tied to a stake! Large liquid black reproachful
eyes.

One of greatest sights on earth — not as impressive structures as
Mayan — but setting of verticle mountains & wild scenery — majestic.
No rain — blue skies, great white clouds — in middle of rainy season!

Wed. Mar 2 — Machu Pic[c]hu
Woke up in black fog & rain at 6. Down mountain from little hotel
with singing chauffeur — in Quechua (keshwa) & Spanish from Peru,
Argen[tina], Chile & Bolivia!

Down the narrow guage, in sunshine, to . . . [a] great fortress of
Incas. More mag[nificent]. stone work. Never taken by Spaniards —
Incas folded up due to prophesy of white man with fair hair & blue eyes
who would come to rule the Incas. [Plus] Guns — horses

How did conquistadores get thru the Andes to Cuzco!!

To Cuzco in time for lunch. . . .
USSR broadcasting 1 hour a day in Quechua (Keshwa). Peasants —
Indian & mestizo — restless. Then, 4 or 5 years at most before there will
be a revol. USSR never mentions communism — just "days of oppressors
are numbered" stuff.

Dr. Geiseke took us to huge Inca empire — Inca fortress surrounding

[421]

hill top above city. Monstrous 100 ton stones, beautifully fitted in 3 concentric walls. Used as quarry by Spaniards to build their city. Llama train passed on way back to Indian village in mts. Temple of Sun — only Inca foundation of perfect stone work remains; Spanish church on top badly damaged in 1950 earthquake. Town all built on Inca foundations! Saw several Spanish churches & usual oversized cathedral — houses of conquistadores. . . .

Visit to Prefect — large, able, smiling man — more than ceremonial [visit]. Trying to raise wages — too low to live on at 30¢ a day for common labor! When hydro[electric project] done & tunnel & generator finished cheap power will attract industry to Cuzco — which certainly illustrates neglect of country for capital. Higher town wages will force up wages on haciendas — believes in land reform — tax unused land, break up over sized haciendas, credit facilities for Indians, regrets end of U.S. surplus disposal aid; *only dried milk now.*

. . . Reception at Bi-National [Cultural] Center — teaching English — 750 students during year. [Edward G.] Bernard, Am. from Vermont, & pretty girl only Americans [on the staff]; some Peruvian teachers. Supported largely by student fees (knowing English means better jobs — guides, hotel clerks, Lima etc) as well as hope for study in U.S. (Do we make mistake by requiring so much English of L.A. students for admission instead of picking best & giving intensive language training before they go?)

Touching evening in large room covered with US pictures — scenery — sports, industry — (too much play: beach beauties, sports & fun!) — Lincoln, Wash[ington]., Franklin — and Ike on walls! Chinese-Peruvian Pres[ident]. of directors of Bi-Nat Center made long flattering speech to audience of local dignitaries, all USIS [United States Information Service], ECA [Economic Cooperation Administration] etc, University people & students who could squeeze in. Then presented [me], after another speech with a "certificate"; another speech — then flowers — our colors & theirs. . . . My speech — laboriously translated. Dancing in native costumes (fast disappearing even here!) curious flat saucer shaped hats for women very pretty. Indian villages individualistic — dancing ditto. . . .

Pres[ident] of Cuzco Club indignant that I wouldn't [go?] there with him afterward. To hotel thru streets. . . .

Why do all Spanish colonial plazas & streets echo every sound all night — and why must I always have the best (and worst!) corner room! Not a wink of sleep in spite of pills — due to altitude & breathing trouble.

Stevenson and his party took an early plane flight on March 3 and reached Lima in time to lunch with British Ambassador Berkeley Gage and his wife. (Stevenson had known Gage when he was consul general in Chicago.) That afternoon Stevenson held a press conference. He noted in his diary: ". . . large . . . poor questions. Very polite. No heckling. Ques[tions]. about US Economic imperialism."

After the press conference the Cuban ambassador called on Stevenson and stated that the Castro government "would be very pleased" to have Stevenson visit Cuba. Then Stevenson had a conference with Fernando Belaunde Terry, who was one of the defeated candidates in the presidential election of 1956. He argued that the situation in Peru could not wait for the "orthodox" solutions that the present government had proposed. There was need immediately, he said, to divide up the great landed estates among the landless farmers, to establish credit facilities for the poor, and to build housing for the slum-dwellers.

Shortly after this interview, Stevenson wrote in his diary:

20 students from [University of] San Marcos arrive — just as I am dressing for FM's [Foreign Minister's] dinner at country club ½ hour away. Can't find my pants! Spent ½ hour in bath robe (!) talking with them — mostly communist. Leader cold, expressionless, thin ascetic looking "professional student" — at Univ. 8 years — organizing for communists. All law, economics or medical students. Anti Americanism evident; mostly economic questions — Why does USSR loan at 2½% & U.S. much higher? Why do we pay such low prices for Peru goods? Lead, zinc, sugar discrimination. Is Cuba revol[ution] communist? [Why does the U.S. support] *Dictators.* (I always reply by condemning dictatorship of right or left. Only gov't we can approve is one representing freely expressed will of people; and one that can be changed by some expression peacefully — without force) *They began to smile a little; some (Apristas?)* [37] *shook hands warmly when I had to leave. . . .*

Large banquet of F M [Foreign Minister] at big elegant "country club" really a plush hotel where they wanted me to stay. 50 govt. &

[37] The American Popular Revolutionary Alliance, founded in the 1920's by a group of students who opposed foreign imperialism and the oligarchy of the rich that ran Peru. The party called for land reform and better treatment of the Indian population. Although denounced as communist, it was an indigenous radical Peruvian movement. It became a powerful political force but it could never win control of the government in the face of the resistance by the oligarchy and by the army. In 1948, after an attempted rebellion, it was outlawed. In 1956, APRA supported the conservative presidential candidate, banker Manuel Prado. After Prado was elected he legalized the APRA party and included some of its members in his cabinet, but by 1960 most of them had been dropped from the cabinet.

*big shots "very representative list" according to [U.S.] chargé [Jack]
Neal. Sat between old Belaunde & Beltran — more philosophy from
former and from latter. [Beltrán being quoted] Why do I do this job
when I don't need to?* . . . *Only 4–5 people at table know revol.
imminent here.*

. . . *Beltran seems to clearly see* imperative necessity to close gap
between few very rich & masses of poor quickly. Has great faith that
Indians will do well given a chance — credit, land. *Can't make out just
what he thinks about land reform. [He is] Unclear about breaking up
big estates. Said he went often to Barriadas [slums.] Everyone seems
impressed that I went there — meet press — all good — about whole
visit "You are Peru's favorite American." Thought, first, Mexicans, then
Costa Ricans, then Columbians — then Ecuadorians and now Peruvians
most endearing! — but top drawer handful obviously not in touch.* Reminded of "Rocket A"[?] — and how fast the revol came there.
[I] *Made good speech — talked about gulf bet[ween]. rich & poor
— sacrifice — "arms limitation." (don't talk of "disarm[ament]" in these
military clique countries!) — and left for hotel with guests all applauding
at doorway.*

Friday Mar 4 — Off early for Chili [Chile] —
(*on their airline after our experience with Panagra!*) *1600 miles due
south to Santiago. Argentine & Chili beauty queens for fellow passengers! Embassy staff — officer from President & faithful Dr. Giesecke
to see us off.* . . . .
Santiago *on big broad flat plain at foot of arid mountains — looks
like Lima — large — European city — cosmo[politan]. — Hotel Carona
14 stories — very fine.* Beautiful women! *Usual ceremonial welcome at
airport — Ike gone 2 days.*[38] *People clapped.*

*At the briefing at the United States embassy there was a discussion
of the numerous political parties, including the Radicals, the Christian
Democrats led by Eduardo Frei,*[39] *and the Socialist grouping (Frente
Acción Popular) headed by Senator Salvador Allende.*[40] *In addition
there was a discussion of the organized labor force and Communist*

[38] President Eisenhower had visited Chile from February 29 to March 2, 1960,
as part of a ten-day goodwill tour of Latin America.
[39] Later elected president of Chile, in 1964.
[40] An avowed Marxist who became president of Chile in 1970 and was murdered
by the military in 1973.

influence within it, rampant inflation, and the concentration of land-ownership in the hands of a small percentage of the population.

That evening Stevenson dined at the United States embassy residence. He wrote in his diary: "Usual talk of commies, politics & US! Ike's trip evidently great personal triumph. Can't understand very well after all the mistakes and criticism; everyone evidently disliked Nixon personally in these politically sophisticated & European culture countries. But Ike is a war hero!"

On March 5, Stevenson had breakfast with a former Department of State official who, according to Stevenson's diary, had resigned when he discovered that the policy of the Eisenhower Administration was to make Latin America safe for United States business. There had been too much support of dictators under Eisenhower, Stevenson was told. President Jorge Alessandri was described as being to the right of the late Senator Robert A. Taft.

Later that morning Stevenson met for two and a half hours with some fifty students from the National University and the Catholic University. In their speeches of welcome to Stevenson, the students developed the points they had written in a letter to President Eisenhower when he was in Chile.[41] The letter described the "merciless exploitation" of Latin America by European and North American capitalists, discussed the need for "just prices" for Latin American commodities, criticized United States support of dictators, and charged that the United States had not encouraged the economic integration of Latin America or "collaborated decisively" in the industrialization of Latin America. The politics of the status quo, the students stated, were inadequate.

In the discussion that followed, as the students expressed their impatience with existing conditions, Stevenson remarked: "I trust this will always be so, for the idealism of today is the best hope for the practice of tomorrow." One student stated that capitalism was not right for Latin America since so few people reaped all the benefits. Communism, however, he explained also was no solution because of its tyranny and loss of human dignity.

Stevenson replied: "What are the alternatives to Communism? You've said capitalism is not a solution. If you mean that without capital you will have no capitalism, I agree that it isn't a solution. But I am confident that as capital is formed, and above all reinvested in Latin America, capitalism will serve a valuable purpose. Your problem is this: if governments are unstable, if your economies are stagnant, capital

---

[41] See the New York *Times,* March 2, 1960, for the text of the letter and President Eisenhower's reply.

will take refuge elsewhere. . . . Where there is little private capital available, certainly you must use any available government capital. If some recoil at the thought of government capital, don't include me. I'm one American who is not afraid of the word 'planning'!"[42]

Stevenson agreed with the students that the mass of the people in Latin America did not benefit sufficiently and that the rich paid too little in taxes. When he was asked if he did not believe that United States firms operating in Chile should plow more of their profits back into the country, Stevenson said the point was arguable but that it would be a good idea for wealthy Chileans to invest more in Chilean businesses rather than to put their money in Swiss and United States banks.

One student insisted that the United States should promote democracy instead of supporting dictators on the pretense that they were "anti-Communist."

Stevenson concluded by saying that the United States had its New Deal in the 1930's and that Latin America needed its own New Deal. He added: "The decade we are entering is perhaps the most perilous in history. We need moral and practical hemispheric solidarity. History teaches us we can do much for one another, but what our countries do for ourselves is decisive."[43]

Stevenson wrote in his diary:

Stayed 2½ hours with students; not sure I handled it very well but Embassy people seemed delighted. First time anyone had met them.

After meeting with students — to top of mountain where original Spanish town was established — visit to slums — on old dog track! Talked with jolly "Alcalde" [mayor] — after great anxiety of Embassy chaperone! Bad — but not as bad as Lima. . . .

Stevenson lunched with Gerry Robichaud, Latin American correspondent of the Chicago Daily News, who wrote in his newspaper (March 12, 1960): "He has been on an endless round of visits with presidents, foreign ministers and numerous other high government officials, student groups, business and labor leaders, opposition political chieftans and many more. Wherever he has been, Stevenson has been front-page news from the time of his arrival until his departure."

After the luncheon, Stevenson wrote in his diary:

[42] Benton, "Ambassador of Good Will in Latin America," pp. 206–207.
[43] Ibid., pp. 207–208.

Left with Hernan Santa Cruz — old friend from UN — now FAO[44]
for L.-A. by car for hacienda *of Pedro Ibanez, Pres. of State Bank —
2 hour drive. Splendid fruit farm — drove around in English dog carts
behind fine teams. Great old hacienda once owned by family who lived
always in Paris — usual story. Now connected to peaches, pears, plums
— shipped all over world. Tea on lawn — with watermelons! — like
English country house. Charming worldly people of the feudal aristocracy. . . . Fine dinner — enormous lobsters from Juan Fernandez —
Robinson Crusoe's island!*

*Sunday, March 6 — San Felipe to Zapallar to Cochagua to Santiago.
[Chilean] Air Force helicopter arrived on field in front of house at
breakfast — such excitement! Tenants and families goggle eyed.
([William] Benton stayed in Santiago for weekend to work.) J.F., [Bill]
Blair & [Carleton] Smith & I took off with Ibanez for visit to Valparaiso
and Vina del Mar — the great port of Chili & suburb resort on sea
founded by British merchants long ago —* and landed on a cricket ground
adjoining race course just as Sunday cricket match was starting. Big
Englishman stepped forward — "Glad to see you again, Sir; last time
was in Singapore — wasn't it!" *Tour of towns with rich friend of Ibanez
in Cadillac — visit to Univ[ersity]. of Santa Marta. . . .*

*The Stevenson party returned to Santiago that evening. The next day,
March 7, Stevenson had a lengthy talk with Raul Prebisch, director of
the United Nations Economic Commission for Latin America. Prebisch
asserted that the major goal of the United States in Latin America
should be to help improve the living standards of the lower half of the
population. He said that the rate of economic growth was poor — only
about one per cent per year — because the rate of savings was low, the
land tenure system was a serious handicap, there was a lack of trained
manpower and an insufficient use of manpower, and everywhere there
was a misuse of capital. "Look at the way the high-income groups live in
Latin America," he added. There had to be an introduction of steeply
graduated income taxes on high incomes in order that this money could
be used for government-designated aims.*
*Prebisch observed that in some countries there was the belief that the
free play of economic forces would bring development. State intervention was necessary, he contended, to avoid the feeling of frustration in*

[44] The Food and Agricultural Organization of the United Nations.

the younger generation. But state planning was resisted, because to the oligarchies it was associated with agrarian reform, higher taxes and structural changes in the economy that would unleash new social forces.[45]

Prebisch asked why the progressive elements in Latin America no longer believed in the United States as they had when Franklin D. Roosevelt was President. The progressive elements in Latin America wanted land reform, control of monopoly, a free press, proper taxation, and free unions, Prebisch observed, but the United States preached the importance of "private foreign capital." This had "no appeal," Stevenson noted in his diary. "Planning of economy only way to strengthen local initiative. . . . Thorough revision of U.S. ideas vital!"

After the meeting with Prebisch, Stevenson called on Foreign Minister Germán Vergara and Finance Minister Roberto Vergara. Stevenson, as William Benton noted in his diary, "pitched into the subject of disarmament." The Chileans responded by discussing their border dispute with Argentina over three islands near the Strait of Magellan. Stevenson was asked to speak to the Argentine government about arbitration of the dispute. There was some discussion of the financial needs of Chile to achieve economic development, and then the meeting adjourned for a formal luncheon given by the foreign minister in the exclusive Union Club. Mr. Benton wrote in his diary: "I don't know of any clubs in the United States comparable to these in expensive architecture, ornateness and luxurious appointments."

Later that day Stevenson and Benton met with President Jorge Alessandri for an hour. Stevenson wrote in his diary: "Unsmiling — large — tall — Mussolini look — voluble, high loud squeaky voice. Attack[ed] Marxist[s], demagogues, [Eduardo] Frei, Ch. Dems. [Christian Democrats]."

The president told Stevenson and Benton that Chile would sponsor a Latin American conference on disarmament. But Chile wanted an agreed-upon accounting on defense expenditures. He added that the United States in distributing economic aid should give preference to those countries which did not purchase armaments. They talked about land reform and the president made it clear that he did not contemplate breaking up the big private estates — only distributing government land.

The president attacked Senator Eduardo Frei, saying, "God made men with defects," according to Mr. Benton's diary. Then he added, "We won't ever be able to construct a political system with the virtues

[45] See Benton, *The Voice of Latin America*, pp. 21, 24–25.

both of democracy and communism." Stevenson interjected, "Unfortunately men will continue to look for it!"

As the conference ended, President Alessandri warned Stevenson that
he had spoken in confidence. William Benton wrote in his diary that
Stevenson replied: "I don't quote Presidents." Later Benton complained
to Stevenson that there was a general absence of candor in interviews
with government officials. Stevenson replied that Alessandri had been
among the most candid. Benton wrote in his diary: "I had the feeling of
far greater candor in many of my interviews in the Soviet Union."

On March 8, before the Stevenson party left Santiago, a number of
leaders of the opposition to President Alessandri in the Chilean Congress called on Stevenson. The first to speak stated that Chile needed
land reform and then capital. He criticized rich Chileans for not investing in Chile and Stevenson agreed with him. The speaker also insisted
upon the need for foreign capital.

After another speaker had finished, Stevenson observed that the two
speakers seemed to attack private capital from abroad on the one hand
and then to ask for more of it. He said that since there was not enough
government capital available for the task, Chile would make a mistake
to slam the door on private capital. A bit later in the discussion, Stevenson said flatly, according to Mr. Benton's diary: "If you permit old and
unjust differences to continue, it seems to me this is your fault and not
ours."

When this meeting was completed, the Stevenson party flew for a
vacation to Pucón in southern Chile. John Fell Stevenson wrote Natalie
Owings on March 8, 1960: "At last we have slackened our harassed pace
& are stopped for 2½ days at a lovely lake in Southern Chile. . . . We
fished all day today."

Stevenson wrote a number of letters while in Pucón.

To Mrs. Edison Dick[46]

March 9, 1960

. . . Tomorrow we get up early early — as always! — but this time
not to meet the opposition leaders, or the students, or the labor leaders,
or catch a plane, or see a market, or write up any notes — but to go
FISHING!! Floating down an Andean stream casting for huge rainbow
trout — up to 10 lbs! — with a Chilean guide, lunch on the bank with
other intrepid anglers like J. F. Stevenson, sensation of the Latin-Inca
social season, W. Blair, who will be reading last week's N.Y. Times, and
W. Benton who will be — talking — of course! But — what the hell! —

[46] This handwritten letter is in the possession of Mrs. Dick.

to tell you about this murderous and magnificent adventure would keep me up all night — also as usual! — and the whole purpose of coming here — thanks to a plane furnished by the President — was to get some rest before this hospitality goes to my head and I begin to think I'm Simon Bolivar! — (and I mistake some elegant feudal lady for Manuela!).*

. . . And now to bed, lest my lure lose its cunning in the morning, and then on and on and on this endless journey — which seems to be having one desired effect — my political fortunes are evaporating — Best to Eddie[47] and the Round Hill tennis courts! —

ADLAI

* If you are not acquainted with Bolivar's girl — Manuela — you should be!

To Mrs. Eugene Meyer[48]

March 10, 1960

Dear Agnes —

Yes, I *was* quite hurt by the Post article.[49] As I've told you all along, I have never expected to be nominated again since 1956 and have done everything short of refusing a nomination to avoid it — including leaving the country for long stretches. (And I couldn't, literally, be much fu[r]ther away than I am at this moment!) So if it doesn't come I don't want people to think I expected it and am disappointed. The article gives just that impression — that I really *want* it and even have a *"strategy"* to get it.

However, lets not cry over that, and the article *does* remove any doubt that I would accept if drafted. I could never understand that uncertainty after what I've said and done before. Nor can I understand the people who have been saying "Adlai is doing just the right thing, the only thing he can do," and are now saying "If Adlai doesn't DO something pretty soon, show some interest, get busy, it will be too late." I suppose this curious confusion of counsel, which is very evident in the mail coming thru to us, is due to the rising fortunes of young Jack Kennedy. As soon as the polls — those masters of our fate! — begin to change then everybody says I should *"do"* something. I could reply that if they don't like the situation — which I predicted a year ago, why

---

47 Mr. Dick.
48 This handwritten letter is in the Agnes Meyer files, Princeton University Library.
49 "Adlai Really Desires to Be Nominee Again," Washington *Post*, February 25, 1960. The article stated: "He wants the chance for once to run against someone other than an obvious winner. . . . He is banking on a deadlock — and a draft."

don't THEY do something. Jim Doyle of Madison Wis. *is* doing something, I hear, *and very intelligently,* but wholly without my authority. You should know him if you don't.

I was disturbed to hear that you are still coughing and I'm glad you're going to Florida. I hope you'll see my sister, Mrs. Ernest Ives; tho, on second thought, I don't think she'll be at Captiva Island during March. But *please* take care — you're *good* but no Eleanor Roosevelt!! I agree that she's past any understanding; and she breaks *my* heart too. But her power isn't from abstinence; I'm sure its from God, because she seldom does anything for *herself.* "My country is the world. My countrymen are all mankind."

Mary Lasker told me about Lyndon [Johnson]'s visit and his distress that the "NY liberals" didnot "understand" him. But she wasn't taken in by his sudden conversion. She does, of course, find him very useful and helpful in her health lobbying work, and in return tries to help him in little ways.*

I am curious about your talk with Kennedy. I can't believe it can yield much information you don't already have about him and his ambitions. From all I hear, and it isn't very much, what with the incessant and relentless pressures of this journey, I gather he may have the nomination sewed up if he wins the Wisconsin primary handsomely. (Down with polls and primaries, say I!!!) So I should doubt if he cared to talk about second choices at this time. But do let me hear what he says.

We've taken refuge for a couple of days to catch up on the paper work and sleep in this lovely place in southern Chili, en route to Buenos Aires by way of Bariloche, Mendoza and Cordova. The Argentine government is sending a plane, as the others have, thereby easing travel time and enabling me to see far more of the countries than I otherwise could. We "did" Valparaiso and Vina del Mar by helicopter.

Yesterday I fished a wild stream around the foot of a snow clad smoking volcano in a rowboat for 10 hours — my only "day off" in more than a month. The skillful boatmen maneuvered us thru a score of wild rapids between banks of bamboo, festooned with wild fuschia and dripping with ripening blackberries! As for the fish — well I guess I'm a natural conservationist — and not a killer like my friend AM!! I thought about you and how you would have loved the whole crazy day — and probably *survived* it better than I!

The journey has been immensely satisfactory — and the more I see of

---

* Besides I suspect, but don't know, that she would like to stop Kennedy because of Catholic indifference to medical research and her experience with them in Congress and elsewhere.

South America the better I like your title — "Educate or Perish"[50] (save me a copy!) My reception all along has, of course, been blanketed in the U.S. press by Ike's trip, plus the usual indifference of the U.S. press to what I do abroad. But my welcome has been a long lost brother's — and the embassies have "used" me unmercifully with the tough groups — labor leaders, students, intellectuals — besides the endless interviews with Pres., foreign mi[ni]sters, cabinet and the ghastly dinners and lunches with their inevitable excess of food, wines and speeches!

I've survived somehow, tho there has been little *fun*, and regret that I'm always in the position of defending my country when often my heart isnt in it. As in most of the rest of the world if our people really knew how we have come to look to the young leaders of the future down here, no presidential campaign would be necessary. The Rep[ublican]. program has been to make So. Am. safe for American business, and little else, but now it is changing and the amiable golfer's smiles and earnest banalities in a war hero's nise [mise] en scene has raised their hopes again. But, God, what a legacy he and Dulles have left the next President — and if its Nixon — a figure of positive contempt — I fear for our "hemispheric solidarity," so called.

Bless you, beloved Agnes — and keep me informed and yourself in form! Much love — ADLAI

After their rest in southern Chile, the Stevenson party flew to Mendoza and then to Córdoba in Argentina and on March 15 arrived in Buenos Aires. During the next four days, Stevenson's schedule was as crowded as in the other countries visited, so much so that his diary for Argentina became extremely sketchy. There was a briefing at the embassy of the United States, where it was emphasized that it was quite incorrect to speak of United States relations with Latin America. Instead, the relations were with twenty quite different countries. There was discussion of former President Juan Perón and his control over all aspects of the society, which was now being ended by President Arturo Frondizi. Part of the briefing analyzed the way Argentina was trying to attract foreign capital.

Stevenson visited the foreign minister, Dr. Diógenes Taboada, and lunched with President Frondizi. He also had a lengthy conversation with the minister of the economy, Alvaro C. Alsogaray who took him on a tour of department stores and markets to demonstrate how he was trying to reduce prices to consumers. Stevenson visited the minister of the interior, Alfred Vitalo, who said, according to William Benton's

50 The editors have been unable to identify this title further.

diary, that the major problem of the United States here was "to regain the confidence of Latin America." President Franklin D. Roosevelt, he observed, had won the spiritual and psychological confidence of Latin America. A visit like Stevenson's, he continued, would have "tremendous repercussions" because it "seems disinterested" and dramatized the "human element." This, he added, was "more important than aid."

After visiting the "dreadful slums" in Buenos Aires, Stevenson spent a day at the summer resort of Mar del Plata. He wrote in his diary: "End of summer; still large crowds on beaches. Almost mobbed walking along beach — 'Viva Stevensohn.' 'Stevensohn Para Presidente' etc. Genial, gay & oh so friendly."

On March 19, before leaving Buenos Aires for Montevideo, Uruguay, Stevenson held a press conference. According to the Associated Press, when asked whether he would accept a draft for the presidential nomination, he replied, "I will have to cross that bridge when I come to it. But I do not expect to come to it. It happened once, but it is very unlikely to happen again."[51]

Shortly after reaching Montevideo, Stevenson was driven to a ranch where there was a barbecue and gaucho dancing and singing in his honor. He wrote in his diary: "To bed, dead, at 2.30 A.M."

On Sunday, March 20, Stevenson discussed Uruguay with Ambassador Robert Woodward and members of his staff. He attended a soccer game, and afterward the ambassador held a reception at which Stevenson talked with political leaders of the country.

The next day Stevenson met with the members of the National Council. (Between 1951 and 1966 Uruguay placed executive power in this council of nine rather than in an individual president). Then he talked with the foreign minister, Lieutenant Homero Martinez Montero, who called him a symbol of the "maturity of U.S. policy & understanding of social problems." Later that day after a press conference, he flew to São Paulo, Brazil.

While he was in Montevideo with his father, John Fell Stevenson wrote the following as a partial description of a day of his father's schedule.[52]

ACT ONE

Scene 1: Hotel Bed Room, South American City
            Time 8:00 A.M.
       The telephone rings, Dad lifts his eye shade off, rolls over and

[51] Chicago *Sun-Times*, March 20, 1960.
[52] The original is in the possession of John Fell Stevenson.

answers it. Puts the receiver back, yawns sharply and lies back a moment as though reflecting his next move.

Then he throws the covers back, puts his feet on the floor, stops a moment, and then disappears into the bathroom, yawning as he goes.

Scene 2: Hotel Sitting Room

Time 8:20 A.M.

Bill Blair has come into the room in a light tan suit, with several file folders under his arm and the day's newspapers. He puts some papers down on the desk and sorts out others — then listens to see if there is movement in the bedroom. There is.

There is also a jingling of dishes heard coming down the hall. A knock at the door "Permizo?" [*sic*] and in rolls a table covered with breakfast for four people. The waiter bustles around the room arranging the table and chairs. Blair thrusts some pesos in his hand. He smiles broadly and departs.

Voices are heard in the hall (the door is open). They sound timid, as though uncertain whether or not to enter.

Blair hears them and goes to the door, still with a folder under his arm. He ushers in 3 young men and greets them cordially. They are obviously ill at ease and are dressed with particular care, though simply.

One speaks English better than the others and is clearly the spokesman for the group. He says he hopes they are not early and Blair says no, "the Governor will be out in just a moment." He asks them to sit down and start their breakfast — melon, scrambled eggs, toast, jam, and coffee.

They sit down hesitantly.

Suddenly the bedroom door flys [*sic*] open. Dad's head pops out, glances around quickly, and the door is closed again.

The boys have almost upset their breakfast trying to get to their feet. As the door closes they look at each other quizzingly. Blair reassures them and they sit down and start to eat their melon, slowly and stiffly.

The bedroom door opens again and this time Dad bursts forth in a dark blue suit. He is smiling broadly. The students are on their feet. As they shake hands they are soon smiling too, and then they are all seated and laughing about something Dad has said. He attacks his melon vigorously and fires off questions and jokes in between — and through mouthfulls [*sic*]. The boys hardly touch their breakfast. They concentrate intensely on Dad, as though afraid of missing something, that might cause them embarrassments.

They answer his questions slowly at first, telling about their positions at the university, what they study, and what their problems are.

Soon they loosen up and are volunteering all kinds of information and opinion.

Blair eases things at first, too, by making some introductory comments in a humorous vein. He then leaves the room.

By 9 o'clock Dad has completely consumed his breakfast, most of the toast on the table, and has learned all about what the students think on the problems of their country and what their complaints are about the United States.

The students haven't yet finished their melon and are a bit confused because they haven't, or are not sure whether or not they have, asked the questions they had so carefully planned.

Blair comes into the room silently and says "we must be going now." Dad has a briefing at the embassy at 9:15.

Dad asks if everyone is ready. Blair answers him that they are ready and waiting down in the lobby. Dad gets up wiping his mouth. Shakes hands again with the boys, thanks them. Blair ushers them to the door and they leave in good spirits.

Dad is back in his bedroom.

JFS strolls in, blue searsucker [*sic*] suit, unshined shoes, camera bag.

Blair says "you just missed the best picture of the trip!"

JFS: "Thanks for telling me in time . . . What?"

B: "Your father and the students — Marvelous!"

JFS: "Oh. Where is he?"

B: "Guess," (with a glance to the bedroom, or John)

JFS: "What do we do now?"

B: "Look at your schedule — *really*."

JFS: "Thanks —"

Dad rushes in — "John Fell, we must go." Blair is already leading the way out the door.

DAD: "Oh, John Fell get my key. It's in my room somewhere."

END OF ACT ONE

The students could be a Union delegation, a group of reporters, or any of a number of people that you have to see in each country. . . . The whole day would run into a book!

On March 22 Stevenson attended a briefing at the United States consulate where the rapid industrialization of São Paulo was explained. He lunched with the directors of the American Chamber of Commerce, had a conference with the governor of the state of São Paulo, and received a key to the city from the mayor. That evening Mr. and Mrs.

*Hickman Price, old friends of Stevenson's, gave a dinner dance in his
honor. Margaret Price had been a member of the Democratic National
Committee for Michigan in 1952 and was vice chairman in 1960. Mr.
Price, a businessman, was director of Mercedes-Benz of Brazil. Stevenson wrote in his diary: "All the talk about industrial development — and
are they proud! And why not! This is the most successful & modern
area of all L.A. . . . To bed at 2.30 A.M.!"*
Stevenson spent part of March 22 catching up on correspondence.

To William Attwood[53]

March 22, 1960

Dear Bill:

This is the first moment I have had to dictate for days. I have your
lists of March 1 and March 11, and I assume by this time you are
informed about my return to Idlewild around midnight April 10 from
Barbados. I think a press conference around noon the following day
would be convenient, and in the afternoon I must leave for Charlottesville.

. . . Your draft of the statement for the press on arrival is, I think,
very good. I may want to alter it somewhat to reduce the emphasis on
new speaking, and I presume we can have it duplicated in New York
before the press conference.

I also may want to answer the inevitable question about the nomination somewhat along the lines of the enclosed.

I was troubled about the stories in connection with your work for me
but have concluded to say nothing in accordance with your suggestion,
pending my return.[54] Also I have seen none of the newspaper stories,
save the one in the Wall Street Journal. If you have to make any further
statements, I think the emphasis had better be on [my] fitness* for the
office and your anxiety to further that result, even at personal inconvenience and without my solicitation or even approval. Otherwise, I think

* I hope you understand this, I don't make it very clear! I was hoping
you might say (a) the election is critical, (b) AES is the best man
(???), (c) you want to help him get elected and some likeminded
people are helping you do what you can.

53 The original is in the possession of Mr. Attwood.
54 When Attwood took a leave of absence from *Look* to draft speeches for Stevenson, the Associated Press stated: "Signs mounted Monday that Adlai E. Stevenson
intends to wage an active but soft-sell campaign for a third Democratic presidential
nomination." Chicago *Sun-Times*, March 15, 1960. And the *Wall Street Journal*,
March 15, 1960, observed that "well-heeled Democratic 'liberals' . . . stand ready
to finance this off-beat campaign."

I shall be in a most ambiguous and inconsistent position if it appears that you are ghost writing and actively cooperating with me. I hope you agree on this sort of emphasis rather than personal identification.

The journey has been tiring but extremely informative and also disquieting. During this administration, on most of this continent, we have made every possible mistake — almost. Things are turning for the better now, post Dulles. My own welcome has been more cordial than I had foreseen, and I have found another continent where I have a higher proportion of supporters than in the USA! Our party is intact, and I have material for books, not articles! How to condense it for the Look piece worries me, but under your subtle guidance I am sure we can do it somehow.

I hope you and Sim[55] and the children are well.

Yours,

AES

P.s I haven't followed things at home very well, but I gather Stevenson is fast fading as a Democratic alternative to worry about! . . .

On March 23, Stevenson was flown to a cattle ranch owned by International Packers. The next day he met with trade union leaders and visited two automobile factories and then flew to Rio de Janeiro. "Rio as beautiful as advertised," he noted in his diary. After a briefing by Ambassador John Moors Cabot and members of his staff, Stevenson went to his hotel. He wrote in his diary: "Suite of 5 huge rooms and two gold fitted marble bathrooms. Thank God I'm a guest of state!"

During the next few days Stevenson held conferences with government officials, labor leaders, writers and businessmen. He wrote in his diary that President Juscelino Kubitschek "Spoke most graciously about my fatherhood of his ideas and his Democratic partisanship."

On March 29 Stevenson flew to the new capital, Brasilia. He wrote in his diary: "Nothing here 4 years ago! . . . What wonders genius of man and the purpose of the leaders hath wrought — in the wilds of Brazil. And if this is the city of the future — I like it."

On March 31, after a press conference, Stevenson flew to Caracas, Venezuela. The flight was delayed and as a result he did not arrive in Caracas until 2 A.M. on April 1. After a briefing at the embassy of the United States, Stevenson had a long talk with President Rómulo Betancourt, who discussed the land reform program initiated by his administration. The president then had his cabinet members and legislative

55 Mrs. Attwood.

[437]

leaders to a luncheon in honor of Stevenson. "All Venezuelans evidently passionate Democrats and Stevenson fans!" he wrote in his diary.

The next day he had a lengthy meeting with Foreign Minister Ignacio Luis Arcaya Rivero. He told Stevenson that the common people of Venezuela and Latin America did not trust United State business, and he added that when Latin America wanted technical assistance the United States tried to tie this in with private United States business enterprises. He characterized President Eisenhower's speeches on his tour of Latin America as "those of a traveling salesman for American business." The foreign minister discussed what was taking place in Cuba and stated emphatically that Fidel Castro was not a Communist. He also criticized attacks on Cuba in United States newspapers as wholly unfair.

After this conference, Stevenson attended a luncheon with leading Venezuelan businessmen followed by a meeting with leaders of the United States business community. That afternoon he toured the slums of Caracas with President Betancourt's daughter, Señora Virginia Pérez.

The next day Stevenson visited a large iron mine on the Orinoco river. The following day he flew to Trinidad to talk with Prime Minister Eric Williams, and on April 5 he arrived in Barbados for a brief vacation with Mr. and Mrs. Ronald Tree.

Stevenson wrote the following article, "Our Plight in Latin America," for Look, *November 22, 1960.*

I was in Latin America last spring at the same time as President Eisenhower. I traveled through twelve countries in eight weeks. The President went to four countries in ten days.[56] He came back optimistic. I came back deeply concerned.

I am concerned because Latin America is in social and political revolution — like most of the evolving regions of the world.

I am concerned because, in a region rich in resources, half the people are hungry, half don't sleep in beds, half are illiterate.

I am concerned because the population increase is the fastest in the world and is outstripping production.

I am concerned because of our ignorance about our Latin neighbors and because of the anti-Americanism I found, in spite of their moving welcome to me.

And I am concerned that if they don't achieve their desire for a better economic and political life, we may find enemies, not friends, on our doorstep.

[56] The President had visited Brazil, Argentina, Chile, and Uruguay during his goodwill tour from February 24 to March 3, 1960.

José Figueres, ex-president of Costa Rica and a gallant democratic leader of the hemisphere, said to me, "There is now only a 50-50 chance of saving South America." The nonpolitical patriot who is prime minister of Peru, Pedro Beltrán, put it this way: "With millions of landless Indians and the miserable masses in our slums waking up, violence is not far off. We have perhaps five years to raise the standard of living."

(Those Latin urban slums are as horrible as any I've walked through from Hong Kong to Johannesburg; and many of the Indians of the Andes live in a subhuman squalor, little better than the naked pygmies of central Africa.)

In July, the Eisenhower Administration suddenly proposed a $500 million "Marshall Plan"[57] to help Latin America help itself with land reform, roads, housing, health, education and development — something that brisk, dynamic President Juscelino Kubitschek of Brazil has been pleading for in his "Operation Pan America" for the past two years. Unfortunately, the timing could not have been worse. The suspicion is widespread that if it had not been for Fidel Castro and Nikita S. Khrushchev, Washington would still be deaf.

We can be sure that Cuban agents are crowing that it is Castro who has brought these good things to his Latin brothers. And the Latin brethren may understandably be asking if abuse of the United States together with a Communist threat is the only way to get consideration in Washington.

The new aid program is a step in the right direction, albeit very late and little. The only way to immunize the rest of Latin America to the Cuban virus is to improve its social, political and economic health. It is a grave mistake for us to underestimate the popularity of the Cuban Revolution throughout South America. "Any hope of a better social order raises echoes among the impoverished," the foreign minister of Ecuador told me. The crushing of dictators, the expulsion of foreign influence and the giving of land to the landless have been potent programs south of the border since the Mexican Revolution 50 years ago. In Cuba, Castro has given thousands of peasants small parcels of land to use, if not to own. The *patrón* (boss) is gone; the peasants think they have a new status, and, for the moment at least, they are living as well as or better than before. They may be supporting Castro long after the revolution has been suffocated by the Communists, long after the urban population has felt the pinch and turned away from the new tyranny.

Castro's Communist methods have revolted the thoughtful people of

---

[57] For a discussion of the background to this forerunner of the Alliance for Progress, see Milton S. Eisenhower, *The Wine Is Bitter: The United States and Latin America* (Garden City, New York: Doubleday, 1963), pp. 8–11.

Latin America. But he caught the imagination of the masses. I will long remember the large delegation of peasant farmers who came to see me in Bogota. Humble and poor, they made hesitant, touching speeches of thanks for my visit, of hope for better coffee prices and innocently concluded with praise for the United States — and Castro!

Dr. Alberto Lleras Camargo, the remarkable and wise president of Colombia, asked us to think of the Cuban Revolution not as just an attack on the U.S., but as a Soviet effort to disrupt the Inter-American system by appealing directly to the people of Latin America — exploiting their poverty, illiteracy and discontent by attacking our postwar attention to Europe and "neglect" of them.

By now, all the old Cuban ambassadors have been replaced by aggressive young revolutionaries; as a result, Russia, which has only three embassies and one legation below the border, now has a base of operations in every country. With Communist aid and trade increasing and influence spreading, most Latin leaders would be more concerned at Communist propaganda transmitters in Cuba than rocket bases. Already, the Communist bloc is broadcasting over 120 hours a week to Latin America, including even an hour a day in Quechua, the language of the Andean Indians. The broadcasts don't mention communism or collectivization; instead, they preach land reform, social justice, progressive taxation, industrialization. "The days of the oppressors," they say, "are numbered."

Until Castro came to power, few people thought a Communist regime possible in Latin America. The shock that it *is* possible has suddenly awakened us to the fact that we had better know more about these Latin neighbors we have taken for granted too long.

The first thing to realize is that Latin America is not a unit like the United States. Among its twenty countries are great diversities — of development, climate, economy and race. Chile and Argentina have almost no Indians or Negroes. Others have few pure whites. Some are small; Brazil is huge and soon will be one of the great powers of the world.

Generalization is difficult and dangerous. But most countries of Latin America do have some things more or less in common — one-commodity economies, low per capita income, dependence on exports, a power oligarchy and feudal social structure, and a growing, dangerous chasm between the few rich who usually run the country and the many voiceless poor who are getting restless. The rich have little social conscience or responsibility. Tax evasion is standard practice. And corruption — the bite, the cut, the bribe — is endemic and as old as the plazas and palaces of colonial days.

Constitutional government is still largely an unsatisfied aspiration, after 150 years of revolution and tyranny. Inflation is common. Chile, Argentina and Peru are making heroic efforts to control it, but last year the cost of living in Brazil rose 50 per cent. Labor organization is mostly primitive. Education in most countries is inadequate and outdated at all levels; politically minded students seem virtually to run the universities. And with the encouragement of the United States, too much money is spent on armies that are more useful for internal politics than for external defense.[58]

Development is explosive in some places. In Sao Paulo, I could see from my room eight large buildings going up. But generally speaking, the growth rate is low, due to the low rate of savings and the misuse of land, manpower and capital.

The final similarity is a fortunate one. The nations of Latin America in most cases are now blessed with strong, dedicated, democratic leadership, men who want to put through the necessary social reforms and contain the revolution while there is yet time. I talked with them all and was deeply impressed with their sincerity and purpose. They know that what all Latin America wants intensely is economic development to raise the standard of living, and they are deeply disturbed by the obstacles. Can they overcome the obstacles? And how?

These are questions that concern the United States. They are intertwined with the dwindling good will inherited from Franklin D. Roosevelt's "Good Neighbor" policy. Nowadays, some Latins joke about it: "We are the good; you are the neighbor."

It is foolish for us to attribute anti-Americanism just to Communist agitation. Baiting the United States long antedates Castro and the Communists. The criticisms that I heard most often are these:

1. The Eisenhower Administration has been basically concerned with making Latin America safe for American business, not for democracy. It has supported and decorated hated dictators. One U.S. Cabinet officer, it is pointed out, even went to Buenos Aires to visit Juan Perón and compared him to Abraham Lincoln.

2. Our businessmen are said to be interested only in the profits they can make, not in the country and its development. They don't learn the language and don't come to stay, like Europeans. They are patronizing and think their way of doing things is the only right way.

3. Our Government is blamed for neglecting Latin America since the war. "You give money for development to neutrals and even enemies," I was told, "but won't even loan money to us, your faithful allies." Latin

[58] See Edwin Lieuwen, *Arms and Politics in Latin America* (New York: Praeger, 1961).

Americans complain of our "banker mentality" and say that when we do make loans, it is only due to pressure or fear of communism: "By the time we have been through the bureaucracy in Washington, we are too exhausted to say thank you."

4. America is blamed for the low prices and the price fluctuations of copper, coffee and other products that cause alternating boom and depression — mostly the latter. (Mainly due to falling export prices, Latin American nations lost $700 million in 1959, which is more than the total investment of foreign capital in that year.) For all our talk of competition and free enterprise, Latin American critics say, we tax their copper and put import quotas on their lead, zinc, sugar and oil.

5. Finally, there is a psychological irritation. Our neighbors must look to us for protection and assistance. A famous Chilean author said to me that Latin Americans like to blame us for their failures, because it is easier than correcting them; and the Communists channel the resentments and frustrations into hostility against a big, rich, obvious target.

The list of grievances is long. Many of them are ill-founded and easily answered — especially the attacks on American business, which contributes so heavily to the success or failure of our policy in Latin America. We can be proud of most present-day American businessmen in Latin America. They are becoming more interested in Latin values and more understanding of the diversities of philosophy and spirit. But ways will have to be found, such as partial ownership of these companies by local nationals, to integrate American firms into the national economies, so that their continued growth will be welcomed and not provoke more nationalism.

But what concerned me most was that, despite their deep belief in political liberty and individual freedom, so many of the progressive elements and the younger people of Latin America seemed to be impressed by Soviet economic achievement. Yet what they wanted for their countries has already been achieved by capitalism in the United States, from land distribution to progressive taxation and social-welfare legislation — and without loss of personal freedom.

Why do the progressives and young people overlook the obvious advantage of our system?

First, our incessant preaching about free enterprise and private foreign investment does not appeal to the Latin American imagination in these times of mounting pressure. An opposition leader in Peru said to me, "The situation won't wait for orthodoxy."

Second, "free enterprise" does not mean in Latin America what it does to us. There, it is generally advocated by those who are against progress — land reform and industrialization, the use of the tax system to redistribute income, improving social legislation, controlling monopolies and encouraging honest labor organization.

We should realize that we are not always loved and respected in Latin America. The reception Vice-President Richard M. Nixon got there should have been sufficient warning.[59] We need not have waited for Castro and Khrushchev to convince us that there is urgent need for a new approach to our neighbors.

Once the United States and its sister republics begin to cooperate in earnest, I have no doubt our relations will quickly improve. The problems themselves can be tackled only by the Latin Americans. *They* will have to take the bold, brave, difficult steps to achieve better land use and distribution, better housing and better education at all levels. *They* will have to clear away the ghastly slums that surround every city. *They* will have to reform taxation and tax collection, cut corruption, reduce the waste on arms, increase the rate of savings and narrow the gap between rich and poor.

In short, Latin America will have to make its own New Deal. But we, in the meantime, can do much to help.

We can loudly and clearly declare that we believe free and democratic societies are capable of providing rising standards of living and that we are prepared to prove it in co-operation with those who will help themselves.

We can propose, not a "Marshall Plan" for Latin America, but a *marshaling* plan — to marshal the available resources of the hemisphere for a carefully planned and sustained attack on economic stagnation and those old scourges — illiteracy, poverty and hunger — that we have all but banished from North America and that must now be banished from South America.

I repeat: *They* must do it. But we can help, first with surveys and the essential planning on a national and regional scale; second, with financing on a long-term basis of sound projects broad enough to assure progress; and third, with technical skills, experts and teachers in everything from agriculture to unionization.

What would it cost? Raúl Prebisch, the distinguished Argentine executive secretary of the United Nations Economic Commission for Latin America, estimates that to increase the rate of growth per year to 3 per cent per capita [annum?] — the rate in most Latin American countries is far below that — would require an annual increase in foreign investment of nearly $2 billion. This should rapidly decrease after a few years,

[59] For Mr. Nixon's discussion of the hostile reception he encountered in Caracas, see his *Six Crises* (Garden City, New York: Doubleday, 1962), pp. 183–234.

as domestic savings rise — and rise they must, or the effort would be largely wasted.

We don't know whether public and private investment on this scale in Latin America is practicable, even with the aid of Europe and other friends of freedom. Competing demands for aid are huge and urgent in other parts of the world. But, clearly, the United States must quickly give priority to the social revolution in Latin America and to its economic progress.

The most enlightened Latins can no longer be convinced that it is still the 19th century and that laissez-faire economics, the free market and foreign private investment — without concerted national and international action — are all that is necessary. On the other hand, a vigorous policy of industrialization, agrarian improvement and loans to enable the private Latin entrepreneur to compete — to do what his foreign counterparts are doing — would have the wide popular appeal we so urgently need. Stimulated with financial and technical help, private enterprise in Latin America would become a vital force in economic development.

Latin Americans claim special treatment for their special position as our nearest neighbors, sharing our common European heritage. If this means new regional arrangements, such as a common market, we should be prepared to make them. If it means efforts to stabilize the price of their exports, we should be prepared to try to work it out. And we should think of what we do in Latin America not as philanthropy, for as our production expands we will soon need a larger market in Latin America for our goods.

At the moment, the historical and psychological advantage is on our side in Latin America. The people's passion for political liberty and individual freedom has been clearly shown in the fight against dictatorships. This fight is almost won — for the present at least — but we need something that can continue to channel the common efforts and aspirations of Latin Americans. Until Castro laid the cold war on their doorstep, they had been more spectators than participants in the great struggle of this century. If Communist influence is growing, it is not just because of propaganda about "economic imperialism" and "capitalist oppression." It is growing because it does offer economic and social objectives, and in spite of the fact that it does not satisfy the political ideals of Latin America.

I believe we must appeal to the minds and hearts of Latin Americans with the idea that these same economic and social objectives can be reached within a free and democratic system — by concerted action, theirs and ours, to fully mobilize private initiative.

But first the gap in communications between our continents must be closed. We have too little information about each other, and too much misinformation. For a month during my travels, I never saw an American newspaperman. At no point could I find a single-volume biography of Lincoln in Spanish. Yet the Russians and Chinese are flooding all the countries with books and even send their magazines by airmail.

There has been too much government-to-government politeness. It is time for business and labor leaders, scholars, artists and politicians to have more contact. We must multiply such exchanges and draw closer as people as well as governments, for we in the United States have much to learn as well as teach.

Perhaps the most important change we have to make is in the attitude of our Government toward our Latin neighbors. They want to be — and they should be — treated as partners in the "American Commonwealth," not as dependents. The nations of Latin America have a proud history and culture, great resources and vitality. They are important members of the world community and have been our fast friends in time of trouble. They should be consulted on the issues that affect them as well as us.

As leader of the hemisphere, the United States should voice the common ideals of all the Americas — fighting together for a common cause. Latin American nations have not always felt, of late, that the cause was common.

At a state dinner in the Casa Rosada in Buenos Aires, an eloquent toast ended with words I won't forget: "The balance between East and West is precarious. Latin America and Africa can tip the scales."

Part Six

The Democratic Nomination
for President and the 1960
Campaign

William Attwood joined Stevenson in Barbados to help him prepare his speech for the University of Virginia. While Stevenson was in Latin America, there had been considerable comment in United States newspapers about the growing support for his nomination.

Mary McGrory in her syndicated column described the draft Stevenson clubs and noted that they were securing signatures to present to convention delegates.[1] Doris Fleeson in her syndicated column discussed a public opinion poll conducted in California which showed that either Stevenson or John F. Kennedy could carry the state against Vice President Nixon.[2]

On March 28 a public opinion survey conducted by Louis H. Bean was released to the press. Based on 1,800 interviews in four cities, it showed Stevenson receiving 54 per cent of the vote and Nixon 46 per cent.[3]

On April 5 Marquis Childs wrote in his syndicated newspaper column that Stevenson had been received in Latin America "with remarkable interest and curiosity. Twice defeated for the presidency, holding no public office for nearly eight years, he has nevertheless remained a symbol of what American leadership can mean in intellect, idealism and courage. It is because he has continued to symbolize these same qualities for millions of Americans that, despite all his disclaimers, he must still be considered a candidate for the Democratic nomination."[4]

[1] Chicago *Daily News*, March 16, 1960.
[2] Chicago *Daily News*, March 24, 1960.
[3] See the Chicago *Daily News*, March 28, 1960. The poll had been arranged by Russell Hemenway and his associates. According to Donald Murray, "Stevenson himself, Hemenway felt, needed a psychological stimulant to jar him loose from the consistently passive and discouraging role he had elected to follow." "Patronage and the Draft in the Nominating Process: A Case Study of the Stevenson Organization at the 1960 Democratic National Convention" (unpublished mimeographed master's thesis, Brooklyn College, 1962), p. 11. Stuart Gerry Brown has noted that the areas chosen for polling were "safe" for Stevenson. Interview with Walter Johnson, November 15, 1972.
[4] Chicago *Sun-Times*, April 5, 1960.

On April 11, 1960, Stevenson made the following statement at a press conference in New York City.

My position is exactly the same as it has been since November 1956 and has been expressed squarely and repeatedly.

I am not a candidate for the Democratic nomination. While I have never said that I would refuse the nomination, another draft at the convention has seemed to me out of the question.

I do intend, however, to keep on speaking as clearly as I can on public questions and in support of the Democratic party. I think its victory in November is imperative to the country's welfare, and this trip to Latin America has strengthened that conviction.

If what I do is misinterpreted by some as political self-promotion, the alternative of keeping completely still is too much for me. As for recent newspaper stories about hiring ghost writers, I have suffered from the do-it-yourself habit too long to look or hope for relief now.

In response to a question, he said that he had no knowledge of any combination of his supporters with those of Senator Humphrey as a "holding operation" against Senator Kennedy. "I am against a stop-Kennedy or stop-anybody movement," Stevenson stated. He also observed, "If I said I would accept a draft I'd be courting it; if I said I would not, I'd be a draft evader."[5]

On April 12, 1960, Stevenson delivered the Founder's Day address at the University of Virginia. "When he had finished," William McGaffin wrote, "Stevenson had produced an address so full of his old-time eloquence, wit and turn of phrase that it reminded his friends of 'the 1952 Stevenson.' . . . A single speech . . . has put him back in the runnning for 1960."[6] Senator Mike Monroney wrote later: "The speech was to set the tone of the subsequent Democratic assault on the Republican administration."[7]

[5] For comments on Stevenson's return, see, among others, "Stevenson Comes Ashore," *Time*, April 25, 1960; "Would Adlai Gladly?" *Newsweek*, April 25, 1960; Mary McGrory, "Return of the Native," *America*, April 30, 1960.

[6] Chicago *Daily News*, April 16, 1960.

[7] "The Plot against Adlai," in *As We Knew Adlai: The Stevenson Story by Twenty-two Friends*, edited and with preface by Edward P. Doyle, foreword by Adlai E. Stevenson III (New York: Harper & Row, 1966), p. 246.

JEFFERSON AND OUR NATIONAL LEADERSHIP[8]

This is the fifteenth anniversary of the death of Franklin D. Roosevelt at Warm Springs, Georgia. It was at Warm Springs, after he had been crippled by paralysis, that he said, "We will build a cottage here and begin a new life."

To build a cottage and begin a new life seems to me a peculiarly Jeffersonian idea, for that is what he helped to do in this country, and that is what he wanted for the world. I was reminded of this in South America, from whence I have just returned. When Jefferson was Ambassador to France in 1787, he met a young Brazilian patriot who was seeking aid for their struggle for independence. Jefferson explained to Senhor da Maia that he had no authority to discuss such a delicate subject, but that while the very young government of the United States could not get involved, the American people could and should be concerned with Brazil's freedom. He made a distinction between the acts of governments and the acts of private citizens, who played such a significant part in the independence struggle in Latin America.

I like to think about that talk long ago in a little French provincial inn and of what Jefferson may have said to the eager young Brazilian. Historians have long since released Jefferson from the narrow partisan and states' rights prisons that could never confine his universal dimensions. And he must have revealed that his great hope, as expressed in some magnificent letters, was not to extend our national power but to spread the dominion of our national ideals: "May it be to the world," he wrote, "what I believe it will be (to some parts sooner, to others later, but finally to all) the signal of arousing men . . . to assume the blessings and security of self-government."

South America must have been much in his mind when he wrote that. And I wonder if he didn't also warn the young Brazilian student about the evils of the European social order as well as the colonial system of that time; how, as he put it, "they have divided their nations into two classes, wolves and sheep." While he loved Europe, he was horrified by a system in which, in words he quoted from Voltaire, every man was either the hammer or the anvil.

"Cherish therefore," Jefferson wrote, "the spirit of our people, and keep alive their attention. Do not be too severe upon their errors, but reclaim them by enlightening them. Once they become inattentive to

[8] The text is from the *Virginia Quarterly Review*, Vol. 36, No. 3 (Summer, 1960), pp. 337–349.

public affairs, you and I, and Congress and . . . judges and governors shall all become wolves."

Jefferson today would, I suspect, scent some wolves and prescribe a large dose of enlightenment to keep alive "the people's attention." To be sure, the agrarian society that delighted him is a lost world, and he would have been dismayed by the urban, industrialized, automated society in which we live today. But he would have understood that, as the population swelled from five million to 180 million, it brought profound changes; that with the machine age would come tremendous pressures toward impersonalized conformity. For Jefferson knew full well that the world does not stand still. "The earth," he said, "belongs always to the living generation," and, "Nothing is unchangeable but the inherent and inalienable rights of man."

So Jefferson today would be plunged into a battle that was familiar to him, even though the terrain is different. The challenge of free men to stay free in a swiftly-changing world would absorb all his energies. As he fought for the Bill of Rights in his own lifetime, so would he be fighting today for their application to all Americans. What mattered to him, as to all liberals, was the extension of freedom and the rights of the individual. And he would be shocked to hear his name invoked in defense of doctrines no longer designed to extend civil rights, but to curtail them.

He would, I think, be quick to remind the Americans of today that they cannot take their freedom and security for granted, that they can no longer indulge in the comfortable illusion, as one historian put it, that "history does not happen to us." For we are no longer far removed from the tidal waves of history, and the common culture and convictions of the Western world are challenged as they have not been since Islam's challenge to Christianity hundreds of years ago.

I also believe that Jefferson would be deeply disturbed by the slowness with which this reality is sinking in. Not only has our society become infinitely more complex, but life itself has become infinitely more perilous. Not long ago, I visited Dr. Albert Schweitzer in his jungle hospital in equatorial Africa. He told me he thought this the most dangerous period in all human history. Why? Because, he said, man is no longer controlled by nature. He has learned to control the elemental forces — before he has learned to control himself.

To one who spent a dauntless, restless lifetime in the service of his fellow-men, some other symptoms of our times would also be profoundly disturbing. Jefferson thought of democracy as a moral principle. What of our public morals today? He knew how hard it was to win and preserve freedom. But the freedom many people want today is freedom from responsibility. Jefferson toiled night and day to serve his country. But in our time, millions of Americans are so indifferent to public affairs that they don't even bother to vote.

We can hear him pleading again: "Cherish the spirit of our people, and keep alive their attention . . . by enlightening them." Would he not say to us — man your defenses, and reaffirm your faith in salvation by works? Would he not say — strengthen the morals and might of your society to meet and master the new challenge of tyranny? Would he not say — rise up to the altitude of man's peril to prevent forever the thermonuclear tragedy?

What would he say about leadership? Jefferson's whole philosophy was based on belief in the ability and decency of the average man. But would he not caution us to beware of easy options, of beguiling promises, and of men on horseback? Would he not remind us again that any dominant group would, if given a chance, exploit the people? (The way beekeepers do to bees, was the way he put it.) Would he not decry our anti-intellectualism and the cult of the lowest common denominator at a time when terrible and dangerous decisions have to be made?

There is no doubt in my mind where Jefferson would stand. He was — to use a contemporary term — an egghead, and proud of it. "Of all the charges brought against me by my political adversaries," he said on leaving the Presidency, "That of possessing some science has probably done them the least credit. Our countrymen are too enlightened themselves to believe that ignorance is the best qualification for their service." He would see that our national leadership has not prepared us for the tasks of this searching century; that it has not summoned us to our duty; that it has not, in his words, "kept alive our attention." Too often — and I wish I could call Jefferson as a witness — our leadership has been hesitant and half-hearted, and has concealed from us the nature and dimensions of the crisis.

Such failure of leadership and communication touches the roots of the idea of democratic society. Our system of government was founded, as Jefferson declared, "not in the fears and follies of man, but on his reason, on his sense of right, on the predominance of the social over his dissocial passions." For the people can neither grant nor withhold consent on rational or just grounds unless they are informed — enlightened, to use his word. Government by concealment, by soothing assurances rather than candid communication, cannot be long tolerated if our system is to endure.

Concealment of the true nature of the crisis — even assurances from a Secretary of State, as late as 1956, that Communism is "a gigantic failure" — has been accompanied by an attitude on the part of our leaders that seems almost to equate discussion with disunity and criticism with disloyalty. And this history of truth trifling and misrepresentation goes way back to the talk about "liberating" Eastern Europe, "unleashing" Chiang Kai-shek, "Communists in government," and a long procession of impostures born of political expediency and cynical salesmanship.

But these impostures also derive from misunderstanding or disrespect for our system — from a vague feeling that the best kind of government is one in which the people turn their hopes and fears over to a kind of caretaker for the national welfare and conscience, to a benign chief magistrate who countenances little criticism and comforts the people with good news or none. This concept of leadership is in sharp contrast to Jefferson's conviction that the people must be kept attentive by enlightening them, and that democracy needs the fertilization of dissent if it is not to wither like a plant without water.

But if what I have been saying seems too contemporary for a memorial lecture, my excuse is that these attitudes about leadership are not new. Thomas Jefferson knew them well. Indeed, they represent one of the two enduring polarities of thought around which our political life has centered. What distinguished the Federalists, the Whigs, and in our day the Republicans from the party that Jefferson founded is that their leaders never really trusted what he called "the good sense of the people." Instead, they felt that the business of government should be left in the hands of those who believed they knew best.

This distinction was perceived by Tocqueville more than a hundred years ago. He called it a division "between two opinions which are as old as the world . . . the one tending to limit, the other to extend indefinitely the power of the people." This is a moral issue that has always kindled strong feelings, and he concluded that whenever America lost this distinction dividing the two parties, "her morality . . . suffered by their extinction."

Jefferson, too, discerned a natural division of men into opposing parties in every free and deliberate society — with each taking his side according to his fear of or confidence in the good sense of the people. And although historical parallels are never exact, we can see similarities between the central issue of today — the right of the people to know — and the one that the nation faced in what Jefferson called "the momentous crisis" of 1800.

Then, too, the nation had recently experienced an effort to suspend political debate, a drift away from government through discussion and towards a curbing of criticism. Even Washington, a military and world hero, cautioned in his Farewell Address against those self-created societies that had fomented so much political dissent. He spoke warmly of respect for law and order, little upon the subject of liberties, and not at all upon the right to criticize. And at the close of the 1790's, this tendency reached its most extreme form in legislation, the alien and sedition laws, which sought, in the name of national security, to apply a checkrein to criticism of public officials.

To Jefferson, this tendency to stifle debate struck at the very heart of our idea of government by consent, the moral foundation on which government rested. That is why I think he would be dismayed at today's public-relations techniques which are designed to smother political debate with images, slogans, and catchwords. In 1952, you remember, it was "Communism and Corruption" and "I shall go to Korea." In 1956, it was "I like Ike" and "Peace, Progress, and Prosperity." And in 1960 it will probably be something about "seven wonderful years" — or, more accurately, "seven comfortable years"!

But, whatever the slogans that are being tooled for us this year, those who trust the good sense of the people must report the facts and raise the questions the people must answer. In Jefferson's phrase, they must "cherish the spirit of our people," even though they will no doubt be accused of "gloom and doom," extravagance, hysteria, socialism. For, as Jefferson once said, "No experiment can be more interesting than that which we are now trying, and which we trust will end in establishing the fact that man may be governed by reason and truth. Our first object should therefore be to leave open all the avenues to truth."

In the months ahead, I hope we will open up the avenues to many truths, avenues that have been obscured too long. The people have a right to know why we have lost our once unquestionable military superiority; why we have repeatedly allowed the Soviets to seize the diplomatic initiative; why we have faltered in the fight for disarmament and the only true security; why we are not providing our children with the education to which they are entitled; why — nearly a century after the Fourteenth and Fifteenth Amendments — all of our citizens have still not been guaranteed the right to vote; why we spend billions of dollars storing surplus food when one third of humanity goes to bed hungry; why we have not formulated a development program geared to the worldwide passion for economic growth; why we have failed to win the confidence and respect of the billions of impatient people in Asia, Africa, and Latin America; why millions of Americans lead blighted lives in our spreading urban slums; why we have fewer doctors per capita than we did fifty years ago and pay more for our medical care than ever before; why we spent more money last year on tranquilizers than on space exploration, and more on leisure than on learning; why the richest nation in the history of the world cannot support the public services and facilities we must have, not only for world power but for national growth and opportunity.

The people have a right to know — and their leaders have a duty to tell them — the truth about the nature of our crisis and the dimensions of the problems that will have to be faced by the next Administration. We are entering a decade of great decisions affecting our nation, our civilization, and our very survival as human beings — a decade as fateful for the Republic as the great decade that began with Jefferson in 1800, and the one that began with Lincoln just a hundred years ago, in 1860. And one of the first of these decisions will be to select leadership that will help us fully understand our choices and our dangers, and how to cope with them. The task of leadership is heavier than any autocrat's, because in the decade of the 1960's democracy and the slow process of public persuasion must match the efficiency of central planning and the swiftness and certainty of dictatorial decision. Our chief executive will have to be a man who agrees with Franklin Roosevelt's definition of the Presidency as "pre-eminently a position of moral leadership," and who deeply believes, as Jefferson did, that "the spirit of liberty, when conducted by public virtue, is invincible."

Jefferson was this kind of President. In 1800, we as a nation were a defenseless confederation standing at the mercy of two great world powers. Yet this was the nation that Jefferson proclaimed to be the strongest on earth, not because of its military might or its productive capacity — for it had little of either — but because its people believed profoundly in a moral purpose from which they could not be swayed, even when men in office sought to curb their energies and suppress their criticisms.

Jefferson believed that the American revolution belonged to all mankind. "The inquiry which has been excited by our revolution, and its consequences," he said, "will ameliorate the condition of men over a great portion of the globe." There was no lethargy in 1800, no confusion about our values or objectives. Excitement was in the air, for we stood as a nation at the head of a crusade for freedom that was just beginning to unshackle humanity from the servitude of centuries. Jefferson brought the nation back to a sense of its proper mission.

And that is the essence of the task of leadership today — to bring the nation back to a sense of its proper mission. Today we are no longer poor and defenseless. We are by far the richest nation on earth and, until recently, the most impregnable. Yet, ironically, our actions have been timid and irresolute. Our leaders talk of freedom — and embrace dictators. We do not act as frightened as we did during the shameful McCarthy era. But to millions of people just emerging from feudalism

or colonialism we still look like a nation that has forgotten its revolutionary heritage and moral purpose, and that prefers the political status
quo, business profits, and personal comforts to the traditions on which
our republic was founded.

Rich and endowed as we are, the dominant concerns of our leadership have been almost wholly defensive. Our foreign policy has been
dominated by sterile anti-Communism and wishful thinking, our domestic policy by fear of inflation and mistrust of government. We offer aid
less to help others than to shield ourselves. We have been reassured on
the one hand that America has never been stronger or more prosperous
or more respected in the world; and on the other hand we have been
warned that in spite of a gross national product of $500 billion bank-
ruptcy stares us in the face if we divert any more of our wealth from
private self-indulgence to the urgent task of meeting the challenge of a
totalitarian society, already growing faster than ours, whose leaders are
determined to remake the whole world in their own image.

And our leaders tell us in effect that if we can just balance the budget
and produce more consumer goods, the Soviet challenge will somehow
disappear!

This is dangerous deception. It is impossible to spend years traveling
around the world, as I have, without a disquieting awareness of the
thrust and purpose of Soviet society. Its leaders believe in their revolution as the leaders in the American Revolution believed in theirs. They
are confident that it will sweep the world, that collective man in a
collective state is the ultimate unfolding of human destiny. Their agents
are everywhere. No effort is too great that may help to realize their
goals; and no corner of humanity is too insignificant to those who believe the whole human race is destined to become one in Communist
brotherhood.

And beyond Russia, in a nation that our leaders pretend does not
exist, there is an even greater thrust of power and purpose by 650,000,-
000 Chinese under a system even more disciplined and under leaders
even more dedicated to the triumph of their fanatical dream.

Our own leaders have deceived us by underrating the magnitude of
the crisis. But haven't we, as a people, also deceived ourselves? The
harsh verdict of history will be, I think, that our nation was quiescent
and complacent, content with illusions; that we failed to insist, through
our press and other agencies of opinion, that all the avenues to truth be
kept open.

Our strength does not lie in the iron discipline of the state. Nor does it
lie in the balance of a budget. It does not even lie in the productive
capacity of our farms and factories. These are merely instruments of

power, and we must wield them to accelerate our growth. In the final analysis, as Jefferson said, our national strength lies "in the spirit and the manners of the people." And late in life, he reflected upon the good fortune that "the full experiment of a government democratical, but representative, was reserved for us." And then he added, "and is *still* reserved for us" — knowing that we would never be a perfected society and should never think of ourselves as one.

The experiment, he knew, could never be concluded. Political action alternates endlessly between the great poles of attitude that determine policy. Periods of high purpose and endeavor yield to periods of complacency and relaxation, eras of energy and innovation are supplanted by eras of static timidity, stages of high public virtue are succeeded by stages of moral confusion, long years of struggle over mountainous terrain are followed by years of slumber in green valleys.

We are emerging — we must emerge — from one of these valleys today — with leaders who will have the courage to tell us the truth, the heart to inspire us, and the energy and wisdom to show us the way. Early this year Richard Nixon admitted that a crisis provokes demands that the President "lead the people up to the mountain top." And he added that this was the easy way, but not often the wise way.

Mr. Nixon is wrong. It is the wise way. But it is not the easy way.

And today, Jefferson would not understand why anything should stop us from showing this restless inquisitive world — only now beginning to sense its common humanity — that our free civilization is just as vigorous as the Soviet civilization, and that we Americans are just as capable of great deeds as we were when our frontier was not the wilderness of space but the wilderness of our own continent beyond the Alleghenies.

"We are never permitted to despair of the commonwealth," said Jefferson. And to do so today would be the ultimate treason, the last refuge of the faithless. But hope, in the face of universal and revolutionary change, cannot be sustained by platitudes and pieties. Publicity photographs are no substitute for making decisions; personal appearances in foreign capitals, for the hard work of imaginative diplomacy. Nor can we longer let our fears and mistaken priorities deter federal action where federal action is needed on defense, on education, on civil rights, on housing and slums, on industrial strife, on farm income and surpluses, on water resources, on the cost of medical care — on all the problems that affect the strength and well-being of the whole nation.

These have been tranquil, comfortable years, but the great decisions have been postponed. This is why the year 1960, like the year 1860 and the year 1800, is one in which the issues transcend all the usual political passions of a quadrennial election. This year we will be making a choice between two approaches. We shall have to decide whether to go on putting private consumption first or shift the first priority to our public needs. Not long ago, the Chairman of the President's Council of Economic Advisers[9] said, "As I understand our economy, its ultimate purpose is to produce more consumer goods. This is the objective of everything we are working at; to produce things for consumers."

This preference for private indulgence to public need is a far cry from the ideals expressed by Thomas Jefferson. So long as this kind of thinking prevails in our leadership, America will continue to entice talented young people into entertainment rather than teaching; into high-priced psychiatry rather than low-cost public health. And America, as a nation, will be the weaker for it.

We can no longer pretend that the challenge of the twentieth century can be met with better detergents and more toothpaste — with private opulence and public squalor. It can only be met with better education and more attention to our public needs.

To say that our system of liberty is so fragile that it cannot keep up the pace in this great contest of national power; to say that with a $500 billion economy the nation will be imperiled if it devotes a somewhat larger share of its resources to public purposes — is the language of those who fought Jefferson in 1800. It is the language of those who fought Roosevelt's great initiative, the New Deal, at another time of decision nearly thirty years ago. It is the language of those who have no confidence in the good sense of the people.

But our national character has not deteriorated beyond repair in this period of leaderless lassitude. Whatever their condition, Jefferson believed in the capacity of the people to rise to greatness once they know, once they are told, once they are summoned. In 1800 he brought a drifting nation back to a sense of its proper mission, not for the sake of any narrow, selfish nationalism, but for those maxims of a free society that Lincoln reaffirmed in 1860.

So now he would call upon this still young, still vigorous nation to rouse itself and resume the everlasting work of preserving "the blessings and security" of self-government.

Jefferson's power — his leadership — did not come just from the fact that he was a philosopher-statesman and that, in Henry Adams' phrase, he dared to legislate for all humanity. Rather his power lay in his unshaken confidence in the capacity for good in human beings, a confidence based not on fatuous illusions but on a clear, hard-headed realization that only on such a foundation could "the last best hope of earth" endure.

[9] Raymond J. Saulnier.

Jefferson's use of the power of the Presidency communicated a respect for the intelligence as well as the virtue of the people. As the avenues to truth are opened up, he would expect the people to understand the gravity of the issues and the decisions that lie before them. This is the Jeffersonian mission — the sacred obligation that confronts all Americans who honor his name today — the overwhelming challenge, the exciting opportunity, to show the world that the American revolution still belongs to all mankind.

Stevenson's speech was broadcast nationally by the American Broadcasting System. The day he spoke, the university newspaper, the Cavalier, *ran a full-page advertisement endorsing him for the Democratic nomination. Before he spoke he visited some old houses in Albemarle County, where some of his forebears had lived. He lunched with Mr. and Mrs. Francis L. Berkeley and wrote the following autograph inscription in Mrs. Berkeley's copy of* Friends and Enemies: What I Learned in Russia.[10]

For Helen Berkeley —

And I enjoyed Charlottesville
and Albemarle County
more than Moscow and
the USSR!

ADLAI E. STEVENSON

Stevenson returned to Chicago on April 14, 1960. That day newspapers described the launching in New York City of groups to get more than a million signatures on petitions urging that he be drafted. Asked about this at a press conference at the Chicago airport, Stevenson replied: "I don't know the people who have been quoted in this connection, but I am flattered if there are people who think well of me." Asked to comment on former President Harry S. Truman's recent remark that Stevenson's nomination would weaken the party's chance of winning, he replied: "Mr. Truman's position is always entitled to careful consideration."[11]

[10] The original is in the possession of Mrs. Berkeley.
[11] Chicago *Sun-Times*, April 15, 1960; Chicago *Daily News*, April 14, 1960.

To Mrs. Eugene Meyer[12]

April 14, 1960

Dearest Agnes:

I am back only this afternoon from Latin America via New York and Charlottesville. I worked like the devil on the speech in Barbados and enclose a copy. It was by no means as good as I wanted or had hoped, and I felt also that it was too harshly political for the occasion. But the reaction has been good, nor has there been audible criticism of the taste, at least yet! [William] Attwood flew all the way to Barbados, although I gave him no encouragement and wish he had not come — for no better reason that I could find than to take my copy back a few hours sooner for mimeographing. I am afraid he is a little impetuous and also lacks both judgment and experience, but certainly his heart is right and he has talents which should be useful. I only wish he was operating more on a party basis than personal, but I suspect this is difficult in the circumstances.

I had a most successful press conference in New York — felt relaxed and in good humor — the morning after my return (at 3.00 A.M.!) and before going on to Charlottesvillle. I also enclose a copy of a statement I made about politics and Latin America. The conference with all networks and a hundred press went on for well over an hour, and I really enjoyed it. Charlottesville was what we call a "full schedule," and from there I went back to New York for a day's work before returning here.

I have laughed and laughed at the account of your "crazy crew" and I pray that you are still afloat, happy and well. I was never more envious of a cruise in the Greek Islands. Even a couple of days at home in this political clamor makes South America and that long, brutal journey the more agreeable. But I have a new granddaughter and she is a perfect antidote to politics and pressure![13]

There is much to report, but I am sure you are getting it from many sources and I am not going to bedevil you with repetition.

With much love from your reluctant candidate and devoted friend.

Affectionately,

P.S. I am hoping that I can cancel my trip to England in mid-May. I have had enough travel for a bit and would like to enjoy the spring here for the first time in a long while. Meanwhile I will look forward to your return and a full account of your adventures on condition that you give me at least an hour on Latin America.

A.E.S.

[12] The original is in the Agnes Meyer files, Princeton University Library.
[13] Katherine Randolph Stevenson, born April 5, 1960.

To William Attwood[14]

April 16, 1960

Dear Bill:

I write this with distress because of my affection and respect for you — but I am afraid I no longer have any choice but to sever any "editorial" relationship.[15]

You know, I am sure, how badly I felt about the original announcement that you were going "to write speeches" or something for me. I assume you must have felt that I didn't want you to come to Barbados or to Charlottesville after that. And now I have two reports from the latter place of audible remarks "I [Attwood] wrote half the speech; [Julian] Boyd the other half" — or to that effect — and "Lawrence (or some news man) is angry because Stevenson changed *my* speech."

Frankly I've never had any experience of this kind before and, even if these reliably reported statements were true, they grossly violate the conventions that I assumed you knew. *So please don't write or draft anything more for me.* I'll be in N.Y. April 25–26 and perhaps we can talk then about what you *can* do — along the lines I originally suggested to Mrs. Meyer — that would be useful to the party, whoever its nominee.

The mass and mess that awaited me here is shocking and I must go back to New York on pressing business almost at once with almost no chance to reflect on "opposition." Ruth [Field] telephoned that she was bringing some notes from you. Thanks! And I'm sure they'll be helpful if I ever see them. When I'll get at the *Look* piece, God knows, but not before near the end of the month, I fear.

I am sorry to have to write this — *really* sorry — and I hope you will be able to understand why I must act quickly and decisively lest the public be further confused, not to mention myself!

With warm thanks for the loyalty, conviction and anxiety to help "the cause" which I know has animated you — Love to Sim[16] —

Yours hurriedly,

ADLAI

[14] This handwritten letter is in the possession of Mr. Attwood.

[15] Mr. Attwood writes that shortly thereafter, Stevenson changed his mind and resumed their "editorial" relationship. Letter to Walter Johnson, February 4, 1969.

[16] Mrs. Attwood.

To Luther H. Hodges

April 18, 1960

Dear Luther:

Thanks for your letter and the enclosure, which interested but did not surprise me. I am sure I have grossly underestimated the depth of the feeling. That religious prejudice exists in our country I am sure every infant realizes; but the extent of it I am afraid many adults don't, myself included. What with the race issue, and the liberal-conservative division, if we now have to carry the further burden of a religious division, I am afraid it may be a serious handicap to our party's chances.

So I deeply deplore the emergence of the religious conflict, both for its own sake and for its implications for the party. I think Jack Kennedy is a fine young man and that it's a pity that he has to defend himself against this sort of thing. Likewise, I think it's a pity that Hubert Humphrey must be the beneficiary of anti-Catholicism, as Jack is the beneficiary of Catholic solidarity. On my return from more than two months abroad, I was beset in New York by party people of all stripes to make a declaration on this subject before the situation degenerates further in the West Virginia primary. I am tempted to do so, but every time I open my mouth they say: "See, he's running for President hell-bent."

Bloc voting of various kinds is normal and inevitable in American politics: to some degree, labor, farmers, business, racial groups have voted together either within parties or between parties. We have lived with such factions since the nation was born in the 18th century. What we cannot live with is an attempt to polarize the vote around the two great Christian sects within our nation. I am confident that the candidates will present themselves as individuals in West Virginia, focusing on the issues and problems of the nation. I think it essential that everyone involved in the West Virginia and the other primaries follow the candidates' lead. But will they? I am afraid they won't.

Do you think I could usefully say something like this: I am confident that the vast majority of Americans are interested in the men, in the issues, and the nation's problems, and not the church in which they pray. I wish to request all of those who have supported me — and still attend my words — to make their assessment in the primaries in these unifying terms and make it clear that they will not share in any tactics which, at home, can only serve to weaken our party while, at the same time, they weaken the image of our country when its influence and unity is critically important.

I don't know quite why I am carrying on this way, but your letter, as usual, struck a responsive chord. Forgive me!

Yours,

On April 22, 1960, Stevenson spoke to the American Society of Newspaper Editors in Washington, D.C.[17]

As my two honorable friends[18] and I share this platform, it will no doubt cross the minds of some of you that we have something in common; we are demonstrably and obviously out of office! However, like George Orwell's[19] pigs, some of whom were more equal than others, I will yield to no one in my claim that I am more out of office than they are.

This is partly due to the fact that they are in Parliament and are the chosen leaders of their parties, and confidently expect at some point to take over the political leadership of their nations. And I do not. But it is also due to the fact that while they are out of office, I am out of an office which probably did not exist in the first place. I defy anyone to improve on this.

I never liked the title "Titular Head"; it always reminds me of an agitated and unattractive little bird. And to be "Titular Head" of the Party which does not occupy the White House is to be almost as much of a ghost as those who are popularly supposed these days to write all our speeches. You have no position, no office, no authority, no staff, no salary and no responsibilities, save perhaps to help pay off the last election debt.

Moreover, any vestigial claim to party leadership is disputed — very naturally, I may say — by Congressional leaders in their legislative role. On them falls, it can be argued, the full brunt of opposition if their party is out of power. They take up the essential dialogue of criticism and investigation. They harry and attack. They prepare the positions from which, four years later, a new campaign can be launched to capture the seat of executive power.

But parties out of office are at best a loose alliance of jealously independent politicians with an eye on the next election and even the Presidential nomination. Our American party system has more pluribus than unum in it and except for the purposes of Presidential campaigns is

17 The text is from a press release.
18 Hugh Gaitskell, head of the British Labour Party, and Lester B. Pearson, leader of the Liberal Party in Canada.
19 Author of *Animal Farm* (1946), a satire on Stalinist Russia.

really a multi-party system in two party dress. So to have an acknowledged leader a party has to have a President.

And latterly we have fallen into a new dilemma. For the first time in our history, we have had seven years of divided power. The President does not command a majority in Congress. He can only secure action with the concurrence, indeed the close cooperation of the opposition. If, to use a British phrase, the Queen's government is to be carried on, they are obliged to abandon in part the roles of critics and watchdogs and become partners in transacting the great business of the state.

This is all the more essential at a time when the challenges of the times are vast. But the result of divided government is to blunt the issues, confuse responsibility, and in some measure muzzle the opposition upon whose vigor the vitality of our system in great measure depends.

One consequence of this unexpected development in our traditional system is surely to enhance the need for some spokesman or office or organ which can speak for the party in its extra-congressional and national life, however loosely organized it is. And it is here, I believe, that the titular head of the party has a continuing responsibility to attempt to focus issues and participate in the great debate.

Of course, he does not stand alone. There are other party leaders outside Congress with as much or greater resonance. And to further help fulfill this role the Democratic Advisory Council was created after the 1956 election and has contributed much thoughtful partisan comment on public affairs. (Indeed, if our current Presidential contests are correct in their hint that Presidents are to be picked from steadily younger age groups, who knows — by the year 1990, we may confidently expect that the next Republican President will be checked and balanced by no less than four vigorous and determined ex-Democratic Presidents — a new hazard added to that already appalling office!)

It is not only the mechanics of our division of powers and the new fashion in ticket-splitting that has complicated the role of the opposition in America. There is evidence enough to suggest that public opinion at large is not too enamored of the critical approach. We are, I think, witnessing something new here in the democracies of the West. In the past, critics of social evils, of obvious injustice or privilege or oppression could mobilize behind their protest something like a majority vote. Most people were poor and oppressed and helpless. The vote was their first instrument to register their protest, the first force, other than violence, given them to redress their wrongs. But our modern mass electorates are verging on the comfortable — and to many freedom has come to mean freedom from political responsibility. "Don't let them take it away" —

with all its connotations of conservatism (and distasteful memories for me), is more appealing than "Let's build a better world." The engine of social progress has run out of fuel — the fuel of discontent. I suspect all three of us here today have found how difficult it is to struggle for change and challenge and reform as the waves of affluence and the high tide of consumption break over the modern electorate.

The style of our age reinforces a quiescent mood. It is a style framed by consumption and designed to increase it. Clearly if you want to sell something, you don't first make the customer mad at you. The voices wooing us from the ether and the screen, telling us of what we owe ourselves, of the admiration we shall excite and the prestigious groups to which we shall belong, and the high executive posts to which we shall succeed — strengthened with so and so's breakfast foods, ennobled with so and so's cosmetics, invigorated with so and so's whiskey — these are voices telling us of ease and success and the smiling side of life. It is not always life as we know it. But it is life as we may wish it or think it ought to be.

And the temptation is overwhelming to indulge in the "soft sell" and wrap up the critical issues of the atomic age and the Communist challenge, of residual poverty, old age, urban decay, racial minorities, under the bright labels of "peace" and "prosperity." Go further and tie a tag on those who still raise a critical voice, of "disloyalty," of "lack of confidence," of "selling our great country short," and under all the slogans and half truths the vigor of the virtue of self-criticism may be washed away.

I do not believe free government can survive on less than the truth. In the first place, democracy depends upon an unforced consensus of public opinion. In the short run, no doubt, agreement can be reached on the basis of some passion or prejudice or deception. But they cannot last. As Lincoln reminded us, you cannot fool all the people all the time. The only long term assurance of democratic unity is attendance to the facts, respect for reality, an abiding devotion to truth, "to cherish," as Jefferson said, "the spirit of the people."

Again, truth is the only possible operating principle for an open society. Perhaps dictators with all their capacity to control and blinker can govern for long periods on the basis of deception. The Soviets have contrived to keep alive a concept of an encircling hostile capitalist coalition that blinds their people and endangers world peace. But they must use every formidable means of censorship to do so. And how long will that last against disarmament with inspection and all the other mounting pressures toward an open society in this shrinking world?

And so it goes. Any government in the West which opts for deceit must sooner or later opt for control and censorship as well. We had an icy premonition of this risk during our shameful [Senator Joseph] Mc-Carthy interlude. His myths of universal conspiracy and ubiquitous disloyalty were quickly translated into blacklists, spying and informing, administrative and academic purges and other repellent symptoms of totalitarianism.

But our great need for truth lies in the fact that nowhere else can men and nations find genuine security. We all know in our personal lives that there is no greater danger to our health and sanity than delusions about ourselves, our significance or our status. And so it is with nations. They must command the facts about their strength, their resources, their standing, their risks and their opportunities. Otherwise, they have no means of judging policy, estimating risks or steeling themselves for decision. A nation that disregards truth puts its very survival in question.

So I think the role of the opposition is not just to oppose as Senator [Robert] Taft used to say, but to expose — to shed light on what has been obscured by the incumbents. In the stress of day to day business, all governments face the temptation to push the unsuccessful or the unattractive issues under the rug. All, at one time or another, succumb. So the opposition must engage in a perpetual and vigorous process of national housecleaning. Congressional investigation, public debate, personal pressure and inquiry all play their part. The rugs are shaken. The issues reappear and the administration itself is helped to perform better by facing, not evading, the difficult decisions.

Naturally, the effectiveness of this activity depends upon the honesty of the opposition's own endeavors. If we ask that government should not rely on prejudice or delusion or deceit, equally its critics must eschew these weapons. If I may illustrate the point from recent experience in Washington, I would say that the opposition had an obligation to expose a lot of fictions about our foreign and domestic situation that have grown up in recent years. And as for investigating committees under opposition leadership, many recent and useful contributions come to mind:

Senator Paul Douglas' Joint Congressional Economic Committee's disclosures of waste in the Defense Department.[20]

Senator [Estes] Kefauver's exposures of exploitation in the drug industry.[21]

[20] Study with special reference to excess prices and stocks, January 28–30, 1960. See *Congressional Record Daily Digest*, 86th Congress, Second Session, Vol. 106 — Part 16, pp. D5, D35, D38, D40.

[21] See Joseph Gorman, *Kefauver: A Political Biography* (New York: Oxford University Press, 1971), pp. 340–341.

Congressman Oren Harris' disclosure of the Adams-Goldfine relation-ship,[22] the television scandals[23] and shabby ethics in the regulatory agencies.

Congressman John Moss' investigation of governmental secrecy.

Senator Henry Jackson's studies of the Soviet challenge and our short-comings.[24]

Senator [J. William] Fulbright's Foreign Relations Committee has provided us outstanding regional studies.[25]

How few would know about the inner workings of our defense pro-gram or our economy, or the conduct of our foreign policy if it were not for such responsible opposition.

Traditionally the opposition has sought to smoke out corruption. Chairmen of regulatory commissions who accept benefits from those they are supposed to regulate, presidential assistants with dubious busi-ness associates, high officials exploiting office for private gain — all these are legitimate targets. But I would hope that in the next campaign neither party will lay claim to some special brand of political purity and that none of the contestants will suggest that "the mess in Washington" is made uniquely by men of one political complexion. To uncover cor-ruption is part of our service to truth. To tie a political tag on it is not.

There is another kind of opposition that doesn't meet the test but is very effective for discrediting the party in power. A classic example was the variety of Republican views on foreign policy at the end of the Truman administration. They ranged all the way from the interna-tionalia of [Senator Henry Cabot] Lodge and [Senator Irving] Ives, through the Asia first doctrines of [Senator Robert] Taft and [Senator William] Knowland, to the Fortress America isolation of Mr. [Herbert]

22 In 1958 the House Subcommittee on Legislative Oversight charged that Bernard Goldfine, a Boston businessman who had cases pending before federal agencies, had given Sherman Adams, chief assistant to President Eisenhower, a vicuña coat and had paid the cost of his hotel stays in several cities. Concerned Republicans, fearing that this publicity would affect the outcome of the congressional elections adversely, forced Adams to resign on September 22, 1958.

23 The House Subcommittee on Legislative Oversight had begun hearings in October, 1959, into alleged rigging of television quiz shows. Charles Van Doren, Herbert Stempel, and others at first denied and then testified that winning con-testants on NBC's *Twenty-one* were supplied with answers in advance and told when to lose, and similar allegations were directed at other quiz shows. The former contestants were charged with perjury and received suspended sentences.

24 For references to this investigation and those of regulatory agencies and gov-ernmental secrecy, see *Congress and the Nation, 1945–1964* (Washington, D.C.: Congressional Quarterly Service, 1965), pp. 1738–1739, 1757–1758, 1770.

25 See, for instance, *Study of U.S. Foreign Policy*, Senate Report No. 118, March 19, 1959, 86th Congress, 1st Session; *Study of Foreign Policy*, Senate Report No. 1027, January 18, 1960, 86th Congress, 2nd Session.

Hoover.[26] It represented no coherence, no party responsibility, but it bewildered the voters and insured an attack on the administration from some direction all the time. Having a fist full of policies and even issues may help the party out of power and be smart politics. But is it responsible; is the party ready and able to govern?

If the opposition owes it to our free system to operate within the limits of good sense, good taste and fair play, I would like to suggest similar standards for the government too. The temptation to resent outside criticism when you are "on the job" is, I know, immense. The critics appear to be incompetent bunglers with no intimate knowledge of the complexities and difficulties, simply trying — so you darkly suspect — to make everything more difficult. Yet I do not believe our system can work well unless the government concedes to the opposition some at least of the attributes of good faith.

This meeting of the A.S.N.E. reminds me of another example, because it was here just four years ago that I proposed suspension of the testing of the big nuclear bombs, to stop the headlong progression of lethalness and break the arms race deadlock.[27] I do not believe these sober suggestions deserved the rude obloquy heaped on them by even the President and the Vice President — especially since these gentlemen have subsequently agreed to a testing moratorium, but only after Russia took the lead and got the credit.

Similarly I do not believe that my warnings of Russia's growing economic strength back in 1956 and earlier should have been dismissed — as they were by the Vice President — as aid and comfort to the enemy and evidence of my disbelief in our economic system.

I could cite many other examples just from my own brief but brutal political experience. When you can't answer something, make a counter charge to discredit your opponent and divert attention is an old technique. But is it responsible, especially at the level of great national issues? In short, we must be able to attack and probe and criticize without incurring instant accusations of bad motives, bad faith and insufficient patriotism. These debase and distort the great debate upon which the vitality of our system depend.

If the people are complacent and unconcerned about the good health of our system the press must share the blame. I am not concerned with the Republican partisanship of the press, but I am profoundly con-

[26] See Walter Johnson, *1600 Pennsylvania Avenue: Presidents and the People, 1929–1959* (Boston: Little, Brown, 1960), chaps. 28, 29.

[27] For Stevenson's speech to the American Society of Newspaper Editors on April 21, 1956, see *The Papers of Adlai E. Stevenson*, Vol. VI, pp. 110–121.

cerned with its respect for the party system and its obligation to help make it work effectively.

Large sections of opinion are skeptical of politicians and political opposition needs to be reinforced about specific evils or virtues. I am even going to resist any temptation to berate you for unequal treatment of Republicans and Democrats in the news. Nor will I mention your ill-concealed zeal at certain sacrificial festivals of recent years. Instead I just want to exploit today's mood of mutual forgiveness and charity by reminding you that a responsible press can be a great help to the opposition by giving it an adequate hearing. And there have been two recent hopeful signs of objectivity: the *New York Post,* a Democratic paper, exposed the indiscretions of a Democratic Borough President in New York City;[28] and a Republican paper, the *New York Herald-Tribune,* exposed the indiscretions of the Republican Chairman of the Federal Communications Commission.[29]

And if responsible news reporting is essential to an effective opposition, an irresponsible or frivolous press obstructs the system and diverts the public. A good example came to me in Latin America this winter. I took time out somewhere to read a collection of American papers of the week of February 15. Khrushchev was in India. Mikoyan was in Cuba. The French exploded their atomic bomb. The latest Chinese production figures were released. An antiquated school building in New York collapsed. The Geneva talks on bomb testing were making some progress. If the Generals testifying in Washington were right, our country was in second place militarily. Eisenhower said he was puzzled that some people were worried.

All these events were important to us and to our children. Yet the big news in most of those American dailies that week was: When will Jack Paar make up his mind?[30] And when that burning question was finally resolved, Dr. Finch's murder trial took over the front pages.[31]

[28] As a result of an "exclusive" article by William Haddad in the New York *Post,* December 15, 1959, Manhattan Borough President Hulan E. Jack suspended himself in January, 1960. He was finally convicted in December, 1960, of conflict of interest and conspiracy for having allowed a real estate operator, Sidney J. Ungar, to pay a $4,400 bill for remodeling Jack's apartment at a time when Ungar was seeking a $30 million slum clearance contract from New York City. See *Time,* January 25, March 28, December 19, 1960; New York *Post,* March 3, 1960.

[29] John C. Doerfer, who had been under attack by Democrats for his alleged laxity in dealing with rigged quiz shows and other deceptive practices in television, was disclosed to have accepted favors from an industry executive. He resigned one week later, on March 10, 1960. See the article by David Wise, New York *Herald Tribune,* March 3, 1960.

[30] On February 11, 1960, Jack Paar walked off the stage during his *Tonight* show to protest NBC's censorship of some of his program material. He said he did not know whether he would return.

[31] Dr. Bernard Finch was being tried in California on charges of murdering his

The Government, the ins, then, must be measured by the same standards of responsibility as the opposition, the outs. And the press must call 'em as it sees 'em, not as it would like to see 'em. For make no mistake about it, the essence, the key to free society lies in the strength and critical effectiveness of the opposition. It is our proud claim that the only society that is truly tailored to the stature of man is a free society. But why is this? Why should we not say that man needs a good society or a moral society, or even, Heaven help us, an adjusted society? Why do we seek freedom first and why is the principle of a critical opposition part of its essential operation?

The answer, I think, is to be found in our deepest insights into man's sublime but divided nature, in the paradox of his needs and capacities and the perpetual drama of his struggle to realize his nature to the full. We are born to grow into truth by experience, by learning and failing and learning again. Truth is not a birthright. We are not born to it as we are to appetite or mobility. We have to seek it and learn it, and this is precisely our freedom. It is not a vain search, for truth can be known. But it *is* a genuine search.

Since, then, we are bound to err in our search for truth, error must be made real to us. Our mistakes cannot be left unchallenged, or our own search for truth will be checked. Nor have we any right to be silent when we see error, for we are inhibiting others' growth in the truth. It is this sense of truth made available to all by rational inquiry, by searching question, by honest criticism, by refusing nothing to the probing intellect, that is one of the glories of our way of life.

And it therefore should not surprise us that only in the West has the dialectic of truth and error come to be incorporated directly in the processes of government — administration and opposition, between them checking, correcting, revising, and even in the attack assisting each other to their moments of political truth. Indeed, our party system which grew up virtually undesigned and unplanned, first in Britain and then in America, seems almost a spontaneous product of our profound and subtle realization that truth is an unfolding and a discovery, a child of human trial and error — never an inheritance, never a possession, never an unearned right.

True, this dialectic depends upon the *honest* pursuit of truth. Reason is the instrument of our search, not passion or ambition or prejudice — or folly. And since we are prone to all these things, opposition as a principle of our political life represents another of our insights into the nature of man.

---

wife. The first trial resulted in a mistrial, the second in a hung jury, and a third trial was planned.

In spite of all his gifts and powers and aspirations, it is not good to tempt a man beyond his strength. Our virtue, like our truth, is not a heritage but a struggle. No moral achievement is entirely safe, for each day we face again the choice of doing as well or doing better — or doing much worse.

In this striving, it is a matter of experience that some strains are almost too great for human fortitude — and of these strains, none is more testing than that of prolonged and unquestioned power.

I am aware, indeed I might almost attest the truth, of the rephrasing of Lord Acton's dictum: "All power corrupts; being out of power corrupts absolutely." What is certain is that the possibility of alternating the government — which only the acceptance of opposition secures — is essential to the health of both — to those who govern and to those who would. If succession to power is the consequence of successful criticism, this fact in itself should sober the critics, keep their attacks within the limits of the practicable, weight them with the sense of coming responsibility, weaken the pull of the lunatic fringe.

And for the government itself, the certain knowledge of accountability checks the arrogance and insensitiveness, the opportunism and the greed which the vista of unopposed authority creates. But if succession to power is also sometimes the consequence of dishonest and irresponsible criticism, then the whole democratic system is corrupted and enfeebled. So I think the press has a special responsibility to police the duel and enforce the standards of political performance and accountability.

All this, I know, is likely to be forgotten in the heat of the fight, at the height of the partisan struggle, and above all in the big show of the Presidential election. But it is essential to the health of our great commonwealth that the dependence of each party on the other in some real measure for its honesty, its vigor, its thrust and its purpose, should never be wholly lost to sight.

The chorus of political rhetoric will be rising in the months to come. We shall not be mincing words on either side. Yet to every honest man in the fight the politicians must be ready to say: "My brother, my other self — *mon semblable, mon frère* — together we are building the liberty and strength of the Republic, together we are creating the conditions under which men can be governed and still be free."

Mrs. Eugene Meyer wrote Stevenson, April 22, 1960, praising his speech at the University of Virginia and observing that he was now not only "a" candidate but "the" candidate for many people. He had to continue to think of himself, she continued, as "the most responsible statesman of your party and your nation." She urged him not to go to England; it would appear frivolous, since his business was the welfare and the future of humanity. She concluded the letter by declaring that on her return from her cruise in Greece she intended to organize a campaign for his nomination.

To Mrs. Eugene Meyer[32]

April 27, 1960

My dear Agnes:

I was so happy to have your cheerful letters and the reports of your progress and gaiety. . . .

I was in Washington last week to speak before the American Society of Newspaper Editors — copy enclosed. I dined delightfully with the Grahams[33] and found them all well and the children glorious. On Sunday I did "Meet the Press," but without the same satisfaction as the appearance before the editors, which was a great success, thanks more to interpolated humor than the script, I fear. On Monday I spoke in New York to a large off-the-record group about Latin America.[34] So you will see that your friend has not been exactly disengaged!

We reached the same conclusion about my business trip to England, and unless a possible emergency develops, I am not going to go and will promptly cancel my commitment to speak to the Pilgrim Society and the English Speaking Union there. This kind of suggestion is more than welcome — especially when it confirms my own uneasy conclusions!

I must settle down now to my groaning desk and also get two pieces completed for *Life* and *Look*.[35] And there are two more speeches on the 12th and 13th which afflict me — one at a formidable conference at the University of Chicago on world tensions, and the other at the centennial of Northwestern University, which I think is supposed to be about freedom and the usual stuff. I am not sure how I'm going to get it all done — and also enjoy the spring, which has burst with sudden fury on the prairies.

I must also report that I felt obliged to rearrange my understanding with Bill Attwood. Somehow a lot of reports got out that he was going

---

[32] The original is in the Agnes Meyer files, Princeton University Library.

[33] Philip Graham, publisher of the Washington *Post,* and his wife Katharine, Mrs. Meyer's daughter.

[34] The editors have been unable to identify this group.

[35] "Extend Our Vision — To All Mankind," *Life,* May 30, 1960; "Our Plight in Latin America," *Look,* November 22, 1960.

to write speeches for me. As I am sure you realize, any such rumors both contradict my political policy and also my literary policy, so I have asked him to refrain from drafting anything, and that I will call upon him from time to time for research aid if needed. I just can't be left in any public ambiguity about ghost writing and political plotting. He came to Barbados, as you evidently insisted, although it was quite unnecessary, and of course has tried to be most helpful.

I had a talk with him in New York yesterday and told him that I thought he could well return to my original proposal, which was to plan the intellectual content of a Democratic campaign for this year and select the issues and even prepare materials; that to do such a job would require a great deal of consultation with many people and would, I believe, be of immeasurable potential value to the candidate, whoever he might be. I suspect that Bill got diverted from this original concept somewhat because of the cross-purposes involved — yours to nominate me, and his to defeat Nixon. I hope you will not worry about all this, and if you have more precise notions as to what he should be doing, of course you must let him know, as he is really your employee and at your service. I don't mean to imply that materials won't be useful to me and that I can't make some use of him. *But I must cut clean and decisively any idea that he is filling a new political role for me individually.*

I shall look forward to a talk with you promptly on your return. I do not think I will be in the East at that time, and perhaps we can talk by phone when convenient for you. Please give my love to the Finletters.[36]

Affectionately,
ADLAI

Vincent Sheean urged Stevenson to tell the American people that he was not satisfied with the qualifications of the Democratic candidates and that he was prepared to govern and lead and had no ambition except to serve the people.

To Vincent Sheean

April 27, 1960

Dear Jimmy:

I just can't tell 'em all those things. Some of it I truly believe, but I also dread the thought of ever having to go through the ordeal again. I hope you will understand and talk to me about it sometime when our paths converge. . . .

Yours,

[36] Mr. and Mrs. Thomas K. Finletter were on the cruise with Mrs. Meyer.

Peggy Lloyd, the daughter of Mr. and Mrs. Glen A. Lloyd, Liberty-ville neighbors of Stevenson, wrote him from school asking for material for a term paper.

To Peggy Lloyd

April 28, 1960

My dear Peggy:

I am mortified that I have not answered your letter long before this, but I have been away and it has come to the top of my heap only now. Please forgive me!

I wish I could tell you something about myself that would be interesting and helpful for your term paper. Actually, I'm afraid the sorry fact is that I am not very interesting. I was raised in a small town in central Illinois and went off to school in the East. Afterward, I wanted to be a newspaper man but I ended up as a lawyer. And once I had decided that I really wanted to be a lawyer, and a good one, the war came along.

After the war, I thought the most important thing I could do was to help with the peace — making it and keeping it. So I worked in diplomacy and in the United Nations for several years.

And then, just as I was going back to resume my career as a lawyer, something happened! I was diverted into politics by an invitation to run for Governor of our state. And then I ran for President twice, as you know. Then, at long last, I resumed my law practice, which I find very agreeable and which takes me traveling around the world a great deal.

But most of all I enjoy the little farm next to you.

Affectionately,

To Dore Schary[37]

May 6, 1960

Dear Dore:

Thank you for your letter and the suggested statement. I am loath to disagree with you, but I find it hard to understand why people are expecting me to make a "decision." I hear it everywhere, but nobody tells me what the decision is.

I have said repeatedly that I would not seek the nomination, and I won't. Beyond that I see no occasion for going. As I said in New York on the day I returned from Latin America, if I said I would accept a

[37] Hollywood producer and director and a strong supporter of Stevenson since 1952. The original is in the possession of the State Historical Society of Wisconsin.

draft, it would be quickly interpreted as seeking a draft, and of course I am not going to say that I wouldn't run if drafted, because I have said and written, going back ten years, that a man has no right to do that if his health permits, any more than he has a right to refuse to be drafted in the Army.[38]

But I am sure you know all of this, anyway, and I only hope that on reflection you will conclude that I have no real choice but to do what I have been doing, and do it consistently — courting nothing, evading nothing. Moreover, that's the way I feel. I know I can write you in this confidence, and I would welcome a chance to talk with you.

All good wishes.

Yours,

ADLAI

Senator Stuart Symington wrote that he had just read a column in which Ralph McGill described him as unfriendly to Stevenson. Mr. Symington assured Stevenson that this was not true.

To Stuart Symington

May 10, 1960

Dear Stu:

Thanks for your letter. I had not seen the McGill column; but even if I had I would have thought no more of it than I do of the many bits and pieces I get about unfriendly relations with Lyndon Johnson, Jack Kennedy — and Harry Truman. I haven't seen anything about strained relations with my sons — yet!

This is divide and conquer season, which is all the more reason for not being divided — *and conquered!*

I'll worry about you and me when something happens between us. It hasn't, and I don't believe it ever will.

Good luck!

Sincerely yours,

As part of the centennial celebration of Northwestern University, the Northwestern Law School sponsored a conference on Individual Freedom and Public Debate. Stevenson spoke on May 13, 1960.[39]

[38] For Stevenson's attitude toward his draft in 1952, see *The Papers of Adlai E. Stevenson,* Vol. IV, pp. 3–23.

[39] The text is from a press release.

I wish the words were mine, on this marking of its 100th Birthday, to express at all adequately my feelings toward the Northwestern Law School. I took my law degree here from Dean Wigmore[40] and his faculty. I was permitted thereafter to join, if only in occasional fashion, the faculties of Dean Green[41] and Dean Havighurst.[42] I have found here stalwart support for my postgraduate extracurricular activities. For thirty-four years now I have enjoyed the warmth of this company.

Surely I am the largest debtor this school will ever have. And words are poor recompense — unless you will accept them, Dean [John] Ritchie [III], on behalf of your faculty, as suggesting the grateful thanks not of one, but of many whose hearts hold full realization of a debt to this school and this faculty.

I turn to the subject of today's conference with a little of the farmer's feeling about spring plowing: the job is important, but the terrain is familiar and there is little chance for originality. We feel, to be sure, concerns about our political liberties, about the subject of this Conference: Individual Freedom and the Public Debate. Yet we realize that the answer to most of these concerns lies in the fact that we are here today to honor a school which has for a whole century nourished and been nourished by the freedom of public debate.

A similar thought came to me a few days ago at the annual meeting of the Newspaper Editors in Washington where I discussed "The Opposition" — along with the former Canadian Premier, Lester Pearson, and Hugh Gaitskell, leader of "Her Majesty's opposition." Now it may be that the newspaper editors had assembled this collection of "outs" as an exhibit of the corollary of Lord Acton's dictum: that all power corrupts; and being out of power corrupts absolutely. Yet as I sat there I found myself musing that in a different part of the world the three of us would today be exiles, or worse.

Political freedom is probably measurable in any system of government by the role accorded the opposition. Surely in this country today this role is a vital and vigorous one. "It's time for a change" is our most time honored campaign slogan. Even our laws of slander and libel give the candidate for office special license. I may entertain certain reservations about the proposition that any boy in America can grow up to be President, but we will not count lightly the blessing of our free political forum, at least so far as the rights of candidacy and the rights of free debate are concerned.

[40] John Henry Wigmore, dean of the school from 1901 to 1929.
[41] Leon Green, dean from 1929 to 1947.
[42] Harold C. Havighurst, dean from 1948 to 1957.

Yet the freedom to vote — not to debate but to decide — is of course the more vital factor.

We are still two steps short of the achievement of this freedom.

The continued withholding of the franchise from those living in the District of Columbia is an anachronism.

Even more serious is the continued denial of the right to vote to many Negroes. The Civil Rights Act passed by Congress last month is important for its re-affirmation of the principle that any discrimination against voters because of their race violates the federal law.[43] But the truth of the matter is that this statement of obvious principle is so cluttered up with procedural paraphernalia that few additional Negro voters are likely to be able to register and vote — unless the Civil Rights Act of 1960 is administered with an unfamiliar vigor.

I do not speak of this as a partisan matter. This grievous default of democracy has crossed party lines. Its correction is a national, not a partisan or sectional, purpose.

The Emancipation Proclamation came three years after the founding of this School. A glorious way to meet the centennial challenge of this great Law School — Individual Freedom and the Public Debate — if by the Centennial of that Proclamation no person affected by that debate was denied his voice in it.

It is appropriate to look for a moment, perhaps a little beyond today's discussion, to what is happening in those parts of the country where this problem of racial conflict has been most acute. It almost surpasses belief that last Tuesday, in the 184th year of this democracy, an American was convicted by a court and sent to prison for the "crime" of eating at the same table with other Americans.[44]

Yet I suppose another development in the South today is more significant than anything the Congress has done and more meaningful than all that has been said or can be said by those of us who feel strongly about this subject. I refer to the recent emergence of the policy and program of direct economic action through nonviolent and responsible means.

The so-called "sit-in" movement reflects a new sense of direction, of

[43] The 1960 act (74 U.S. Statutes at Large 86) extended the powers of the Civil Rights Commission. It also authorized the Department of Justice to enter a federal court in behalf of persons who have lodged a complaint with a U.S. attorney that they had been denied the right to register to vote. If the court determined that a pattern of discrimination existed, the court was empowered to appoint referees to hear complaints, and each referee could enroll any legally qualified person who could demonstrate that he had attempted to register and had been refused.

[44] Robert F. Williams, leader of the National Association for the Advancement of Colored People in Monroe, North Carolina, was convicted on May 10, 1960, of trespassing charges arising out of a drugstore sit-in. He was sentenced to a ten-dollar fine or thirty days in jail and placed on one year's probation. See the New York *Times*, May 11, 1960.

purpose and self-confidence. This quiet but insistent assertion of the simple right to be treated like everybody else may well offer the largest promise of effectiveness.

You wonder whether it may work out in the long run that proper race relations in this country may come about more through economic than moral and legal pressure. More is involved in this development than boycotts of stores by men and women subjected to the humiliation of being treated as human beings so long as they stand up, but not when they sit down. There is reflection here, too, of the much broader importance of any large group to the economy of any area. There can be no general prosperity where many are poor, backward and ignorant. To deny opportunity is to deny growth, not only culturally and politically, but economically as well. The clear economics of the free society are that equality of being is essential to a person's achievement of his full capacity, and to his ability to make his full contribution.

The thought is offensive that what is good should come about just because it is good business, or that what is right must be won by lonely people sitting patiently on stools at lunch counters. It is as citizens, not customers, that men and women are entitled to their rights of citizenship and dignity. Our purpose must be as broad as Dean O'Meara[45] has so simply put it: "America is equal opportunity or it is nothing; not equal opportunity as regards this or that, but equal opportunity in every area of American life."

Returning to the matter of the public debate, I suggest that the hard problems — save in these two areas — are not so much problems of freedom as they are of achieving the responsibility which is freedom's price. We do so much better at honoring the Bill of Rights than in respecting the Bill of Duties which is written between its lines. And part of the problem is that while freedom can be protected by law, responsibility cannot be enforced.

No argument or bill of particulars is required in support of the proposition that too few of the participants in the public debate measure their freedoms by its responsibilities. In politics we know the debaters fall short of the standard of absolute candor, of the truth. Too many citizens — the deciders — fall short of the standard of full responsibility — of exercising an informed judgment and sometimes even participating at all.

The elements of this problem were listed by Sir James Bryce fifty years ago, in his lectures at Yale.[46] One he called "excessive partisanship"; a second, the "sin of indolence" — the failure of citizens to inform

---

[45] Joseph O'Meara, dean of the Notre Dame University law school.
[46] *The Hindrances to Good Citizenship* (Yale Lectures on the Responsibility of Citizenship; New Haven: Yale University Press, 1909).

themselves on public issues and their indifference to the privilege of voting.

Bryce thought partisanship was a hindrance to good citizenship when allegiances to political parties transcended loyalty to the nation. But a greater concern today I think would be excessive loyalty to any grouping smaller than what Justice Holmes called "the one great club to which we all belong." Today we are more familiar with the tendency to vote on the basis of identification with one economic group or another, one race or another, one social grouping or another, and, of course, even on sectional location. And this year we have heard loud talk — which I trust will now be stilled — about a Catholic-Protestant division in the electorate.[47]

It is easy to say that there is something amiss in the public debate when it presents a voter with no stronger reason for his vote than what he thinks serves his own economic, religious or racial status.

But hasn't it always been that way? Hasn't freedom of the franchise for most people been freedom to vote self-interest, or to follow the crowd, his crowd? And yet now, when the lines drawn in these same terms are so much less marked than they used to be one wonders if there isn't some hope that the debate could be sharpened and narrowed to illuminate choices more precisely and thereby weaken, if not break, the iron shackles of conformity and "group think" — and to make more meaningful the freedom we are talking about.

Bryce's other point is what he called the "sin of indolence." Today in even a larger sense than fifty years ago the problems the nation and the world face have grown big and complex: the testing of nuclear bombs, economic aid for undeveloped countries, budgets in the tens of billions, the control of interest rates and inflation, complicated parity prices, matching grants for social services like education — even espionage in the stratosphere! It becomes increasingly easy to throw up your hands, decide "to let George do it," vote for lower taxes and for whoever says what you want to hear, or even for whoever goes to the same church.

The welcome acceptance for the easy option and the lullaby and the salesman is assured in any society, let alone ours, where we spend per capita almost as much on advertising to multiply the private wants of our people as we do in educating them to seek a fuller, wiser and more satisfying civic existence. With the super-market as our temple, self-satisfaction our habit, the political half truth our standard, and the

---

[47] On May 10, 1960, Senator John F. Kennedy had decisively defeated Senator Hubert H. Humphrey in the primary election in West Virginia despite its overwhelmingly Protestant population.

singing commercial our background music, are we likely to elevate the public debate and exalt the meaning of individual freedom? Are we likely to fire the world with an irresistible vision of America's great purpose and inspiring way of life?

Yet John Adams said that at the time of the American Revolution never more than a third of the colonists really wanted independence. Probably even less cared to make the exertion independence demanded. A third were loyal to the King, and the rest were inert and uncommitted.

So the condition of our public discourse and individual freedom today is hardly one for despair or even much discouragement. And it is arguable that after the shocks and rigors of the 1930's and '40's, we as a nation needed a period of relaxation — though I would note that the Russians and the Chinese after far greater shocks have had no opportunity for a cozy nap. Now, however, we have had our rest, and I sense the stirring of a new vitality, curiosity and concern for the realities of our situation. The reasons are various: in business groups the whiff of effective foreign competition; in those concerned with home affairs, the farm situation, the schools, the deteriorating cities, the proliferating rural slums of tomorrow, the contrast between private opulence and public squalor — and most of all, the widely shared suspicion that we have been misled and that the United States has lost pace while the rest of the world is moving ahead, and that something ought to be done.

Today's problems are not beyond people's capacity to understand and decide. The sin of citizen indolence is not an original sin; rather it is a natural weakness. And where there is human weakness there is always exploitation. So it is with the public debate. The heart of the problem of Individual Freedom and the Public Debate is whether the leaders of this debate will *permit* its judges to decide the great issues which they are able and willing to decide. Or will they so mislead them they can't decide or even identify the real issues.

We are told that people are content and comfortable, and want no challenge; that everyone is complacent — except me! We are told there is no sense of crisis, that things will have to get worse before anyone can start talking effectively about making them better. But this is only because there is too little trying, too little hard distasteful truth and too much soft sell and comforting reassurance.

The essential conditions of responsible public debate, the essential elements in recognizing people's divine right to decide, are not difficult either to state or to honor. They include honest statement of the facts of our problems, our needs, our opportunities. They include temperate argument of the different means to ends for the most part agreed upon. They include a larger re-emphasis of the national purposes which are the democracy's unifying force.

No one suggests that this debate be conducted in the language of a great romance. Yet surely there is no excuse for the kind of push-button political warfare that automatically releases prejudice and stifles reason.

Why must a proposal to extend the Social Security Act to provide medical care for older people face the false charge of "socialized medicine" — a hollow echo of the cries of "socialism" and "cruel hoax" that came twenty-five years ago when the Social Security Act was first adopted. Here is a matter of urgent human needs, of important economic decisions. The real issues are the kind Arthur Goldberg,[48] respected graduate of this law school, pointed out this week when he suggested that the alternative to coverage of this need through the Social Security program would undoubtedly be a union demand for such protection through collective bargaining. This is the kind of choice the public should be considering and making instead of having its mind confused, its attention distracted, by false issues and weary tocsins of the past.

So I think the sin is less of voter indolence than of the public debaters' distortion, and I am optimistic that things are getting better.

There must be no underestimating, however, the increasingly difficult and demanding circumstances of our discourse. There are the obvious factors of geographical remoteness of many new areas of Americans' concerns, and the ever finer intricacies of the answers in an ever more complex society. In our difficult system of government by persuasion and the reaching of public consensus we are at a disadvantage with the closed, secret societies. The dictatorships have the advantage of celerity, certainty and secrecy in policy formation and execution. We must develop an equivalent efficiency consistent with democracy.

Perhaps the most important new dimension in democratic debate and decision-making is the need for perspective and foresight.

In his chapter on foresight, Alfred North Whitehead speaks of the astounding survival power of insect societies.[49] "We can," he notes, "observe insects performing elaborate routine actions whose purposes they cannot possibly understand, which yet are essential either for their own individual survival or for race survival." But, he adds, "these insect

---

[48] A Chicago lawyer specializing in labor law; later associate justice of the Supreme Court under President Kennedy and Stevenson's successor as ambassador to the UN, under President Johnson.

[49] "On Foresight," introduction to Brett Donham, *Business Adrift* (New York: McGraw-Hill, 1931).

societies have one great characteristic in common. They are not progressive." They exercise no significant foresight.

Whitehead goes on to point out that it is progressiveness that sets man's civilization apart from insect societies; that the condition of progress is foresight; that less was demanded in this respect when notable changes took place over long periods of time because they depended on physical causes; that until very recently "the time span of important change was considerably longer than that of a single human life." Our thinking was bent by the assumption that each generation would "substantially live amid the conditions governing the lives of its fathers and (would) transmit those conditions to mould with equal force the lives of its children." But today, as Whitehead said, "we are living in the first period of human history for which this assumption is false."

Can we exercise public foresight? This will mean that the public debate must be made the instrument for weighing the needs of the next generation for educated minds against the desires of the present generation for lower taxes. It will have to make us see a future water shortage even while today the lawn sprinklers are running free. We will have to be made to see the white race in terms of its future minority status. We must be qualified to calculate the present risks of stopping nuclear bomb tests against the risks of proliferating and spreading the means of extinction.

It is so easy to look back and see how, even when the demands and the price were so much less, men have been blinded by passion and prejudice that led to cruel injustice, how our ancestors stumbled from one catastrophe to the next, how often men of courage and foresight were ignored or persecuted. The charge on those who participate in the public debate today — as debaters or deciders — is that knowing this history they know too that no counsel, no argument, no decision, can any longer be measured by its immediate effect; that it is right or wrong by tomorrow's measuring rather than today's; and that our tomorrows come now in minutes rather than in centuries.

The idea long ascendant in the West has been that the individual will is the supreme arbiter of human destiny. Our basic proposition has been that "everybody" is smarter than "anybody." This basic proposition is challenged today, and we know we are at a critical moment in the long triumphant history of individualism.

We know, too, that we face this challenge only with what is in us. There are no laws to be passed enforcing responsibility. Democracy is a fabric woven from enforceable freedoms and unenforceable responsibilities. We can, at meetings such as this, send up our prayers that the public debate will be turned from pettifogging and bickering, unrealities and half-truths, which breed dissension; that it will be directed instead to finding the central national purposes which transcend narrow group interests, that it can be an instrument for catching that "great beat that is in the hearts of all human circumstance and of all human feelings."

Yet we know that such discussion as ours today is useless except as we may be reminded of what is so clear and obvious in terms of our precepts. Nor could there be a better time than today for critical and constructive thought about our responsibilities as participants in the public debate.

Our country has suffered a severe injury in the last few days.[50] On the very eve of the Summit Conference, the President has been acutely embarrassed — just as he leaves to take his place at one of the historic incidents in the great struggle of this century — the contest for the undecided masses of the world who will one day weight the scales decisively. In these next history laden days the leaders of the world will consider how to make sure there will be a world. And the President must have our prayers and support.

One of the issues on the conference table at Paris will be the controlling of nuclear bomb tests. This issue has taxed the capacity of people for full understanding of a problem which still seems almost unreal, defying the reach of our minds and even our imaginations.

Yet the basic elements in this issue are not beyond the people's competence. I wish they had been debated out when the proposal to cease these tests was first made in 1956. If they had been, there would not be today the doubt, the uncertainty, the divided counsels that still becloud this subject in our country and may still imperil ratification of any agreement we might reach.

The President should go before the world next week armed with the full strength of this nation's deepest convictions undeterred by voices of timidity or by any threat of partisan division.

I believe I know something of the people on this issue. I have followed with close attention the conflicting claims about the various risks involved, about the possibilities of detection, about the monitoring and inspection systems that are required. And I believe there is almost universal desire, here and abroad, that some way be found to halt the development of nuclear weapons; to establish the principle of international inspection; to break the arms race deadlock and to press on with

---

[50] An American U-2 spy plane had been shot down while on a reconnaissance flight over Russian territory. For details of the incident and its repercussions, including its effects on the summit conference, see the editorial introduction immediately following (pp. 485–488, below).

disarmament — which is now the only hope of security and peace for the long run. I wish more earnestly than I can convey that the United States had been leading the way toward total disarmament from the beginning. And I believe confidently that the people of this country will support the fullest measure of accord in Paris.

What I have thought to say here is that essential to the service of freedom by the public debate is to serve its highest purpose — which is man, and the civilization he has created. For that civilization these are visionary days in every field. We have unlocked the atom. We are laying bare the secrets of man's heredity. New infinite vistas have opened in space, new infinite abysms are opening backward in time. We have seen a rocket hit the moon. We know its dark face. Our astronauts wait to venture on a journey more mysterious than the quest of the Golden Fleece. We are adding a city a day to the world's population. How can we be content in such an age to keep our political thinking and discourse within the narrow bonds of class or race or even nation? How can we permit outdated ideology to obscure our identity as citizens of a common world larger than our borders?

Just as you are doing here at Northwestern Law School in this Conference on Individual Freedom and Public Debate, our Western peoples must think and speak, again and again, for man and for the human city. In doing so, they save freedom and debate itself; they save not only themselves but their adversaries too.

On May 5, 1960, Nikita Khrushchev announced that on May 1 an American plane had flown over Soviet territory and had been shot down. The Department of State replied that "an unarmed plane, a U-2 weather research plane based at Adana, Turkey, piloted by a civilian had been missing since May 1," and added that it was possible the plane had accidentally violated Soviet airspace. On May 6 the Department of State again denied that any American plane had ever deliberately violated the Soviet border.

On May 7, Khrushchev announced that the pilot, Francis Gary Powers, had been captured alive and had given details of the flight. Khrushchev added that the Soviet Union had parts of the plane. The Department of State responded on May 7 by issuing a statement, cleared by President Eisenhower, that "there was no authorization for such flights as described by Mr. Khrushchev. . . . Nevertheless, it appears that in endeavoring to obtain information now concealed behind the Iron Curtain a flight over Soviet territory was probably undertaken by an unarmed civilian U-2 plane." The statement continued, "It is

[485]

certainly no secret that, given the state of the world today, intelligence collection activities are practiced by all countries and postwar history certainly reveals that the Soviet Union has not been lagging behind in the field. . . . It is in relation to the danger of surprise attack that planes of the type of the unarmed civilian U–2 aircraft have made flights along the frontiers of the free world for the past four years."

On May 9, Secretary of State Christian Herter stated: "In accordance with the National Security Act of 1947, the President has put into effect since the beginning of his Administration directives to gather by every possible means the information required to protect the United States and the Free World against surprise attack and to enable them to make effective preparations for their defense. Under these directives programs have been developed and put into operation which have included extensive aerial surveillance by unarmed civilian aircraft, normally of a peripheral character but on occasion by penetration." Later in the statement Herter declared, "The Government of the United States would be derelict to its responsibilities not only to the American people but to free peoples everywhere if it did not, in the absence of Soviet cooperation, take measures as are possible unilaterally to lessen and to overcome this danger of surprise attack. In fact the United States has not and does not shirk this responsibility."

A summit conference of the leaders of the United States, the Soviet Union, France, and the United Kingdom had been scheduled to convene in Paris on May 16, 1960, and afterward President Eisenhower was to visit the Soviet Union. At the first meeting of the four leaders, Mr. Khrushchev termed the U–2 flight "provocative" and "aggressive." The only thing that would save the conference, he insisted, was for the United States government to condemn the provocative action, pledge to refrain from such actions in the future, and punish those responsible.

President Eisenhower replied that "these activities had no aggressive intent but rather were to assure the safety of the United States and the free world against surprise attack." He stated that the Soviet leaders were under the misapprehension that flights would continue. "In point of fact, these flights were suspended after the recent incident and are not to be resumed."

When Khrushchev asked if the President meant "temporary suspension," Eisenhower said that the flights were suspended "indefinitely" but that he could not bind his successor in the White House.[51] Khrushchev withdrew his invitation to Eisenhower and subsequently refused to con-

<hr>

[51] *Events Incident to the Summit Conference,* Hearings before the Senate Committee on Foreign Relations, U.S. Senate, 86th Congress, 2nd Session, May 27, June 1, 2, 1960.

tinue the talks, despite attempts by British Prime Minister Harold Macmillan and French President Charles de Gaulle to persuade him to participate.

The U-2 incident and the collapse of the summit conference had widespread ramifications, including the question of presidential control over the Administration. Another result was its impact on the attempt to draft Stevenson for the nomination. Theodore H. White wrote:

> Over the previous eight years, Adlai Stevenson had become the most clear and eloquent voice on foreign policy in the Democratic Party. By his travels, by his writings, by his speeches, by the simple seepage of his ideas, he had, in good season and bad, outlined a picture of the world and the direction of American movement that, though frequently abused on first enunciation, had become so accepted as to have become a cliche of everyone's thinking by the spring of 1960. The strengthening of the UN, the cessation of bomb testing, the reorganization of the Atlantic Alliance, the search for a modus vivendi with the Soviet Union in Europe — all these positions, first pioneered by Stevenson, were now the common utterance of all Democratic speakers.
>
> Thus, when in May of 1960 American policy in the outer world crumbled and a new architecture seemed necessary Democrats high and low, who had been neutral and indifferent before, suddenly took note of Stevenson again. His unauthorized headquarters in Washington now rang busily with telephone messages from governors and senators, from volunteers and contributors. Across the country, the leaderless troops of his 1952 and 1956 campaign began to stir. If he would lead they would march. But would he lead? . . .[52]

On May 12, 1960, at the Conference on World Tensions at the University of Chicago, Stevenson stated:

In spite of all the rhetoric of the past few days, no one questions the necessity of gathering intelligence for our security. The Russians, of course, do the same, and they have a great advantage because of their addiction to secrecy, while our countries are virtually wide open to all the world's spies. But our timing, our words, our management must and will be sharply questioned. Could it serve the purpose of peace and mutual trust to send intelligence missions over the heart of the Soviet Union on the very eve of the long awaited Summit Conference? Can the

[52] *The Making of the President, 1960* (New York: Atheneum, 1961), pp. 118–119.

President be embarrassed and national policies endangered at such a critical time by an unknown government official?

Four days later Stevenson testified before a Senate committee on the need of legislation requiring television networks and stations to provide free time for debates by major party presidential candidates. Stevenson had been advocating this in speeches, letters, and articles before he testified to the Senate committee.[53] The television-radio "debates" between Senator John F. Kennedy and Vice President Richard M. Nixon were made possible when this legislation was subsequently adopted by Congress. Stevenson delivered the following statement before the subcommittee on May 16, 1960.[54]

MR. STEVENSON. Mr. Chairman and members of the committee, I appreciate the opportunity to make a statement uninterrupted and then I will be happy to attempt to answer any questions that you choose to ask me.

Mr. Chairman and members of the committee, while I am not an expert in the field of public relations or even in campaigning, as I think my record has proven [laughter], I appreciate very much the invitation of your committee to appear here in support of a proposal, calculated, I believe, to help to furnish the American people with the knowledge which is prerequisite to an intelligent exercise of their duty as electors in a free society. What I have to say will be brief and merely suggestive of why I approve this or similar legislation.

I am happy to share with you my experience as a candidate for President and my views on a subject that I think has not attracted the attention its importance warrants.

I come here also at this time with a sense of urgency in view of the imminent decision which Americans will have to make in November. I believe your action on this bill may well contribute heavily to whether that decision is wisely made, and in our system that means by voters who have some understanding of the real choices and issues and by voters who have had some opportunity to make an appraisal of the candidates.

53 See, for example, "Choice by Hullabaloo," *This Week,* February 28, March 6, 1960; New York *Herald Tribune,* March 6, 1960.

54 Hearings before the Communications Subcommittee of the Committee on Interstate and Foreign Commerce, U.S. Senate, 86th Congress, 2nd Session, on S. 3171. Questions by subcommittee members and Stevenson's answers, which followed his statement, have been omitted here.

I doubt if ever before in history have so many men and women, living over so wide an area, been expected to participate in choosing from among men they do not know, two national leaders to whom they will entrust such a large measure of their destiny. I doubt further if the issues with which these leaders will have to deal have ever been more complex and fateful.

To suggest comparison with the usual questions to which our fore-bears expected the candidates to devote hours of public debate illus-trates this growing complexity. Compare the argument over free coinage of silver with today's problems of fiscal and monetary policy, or the debate over the size of the standing army or the fortification of Guam with that over the missile gap. Consider what issues faced by previous generations had the implications of nuclear arms development and dis-tribution. And doesn't agricultural overproduction produce more baffling problems than underproduction?

To hear the candidate discuss the great issues of an earlier America, people rode all day by buggy or wagon; they waited for hours for the candidate's train; they stood in the sun and rain and listened. They wanted to know about the issues and where the candidate stood.

Today's citizens seem to have less time and taste for political contro-versy, but certainly the need for enlightenment and considered partici-pation is no less. And they are entitled to demand: Who is this man? How does he look? What does he believe? What is his idea of America's future and its place in the world? How will he use the power of the Presidency, and for what ends? Does he deal in facts, and discuss issues frankly, or does he prefer generalities and platitudes? He may declare for education, but is he for better schools; for health, but does he favor medical insurance; for free enterprise, but will he seek to restrain monopoly; for prosperity, but has he a program to restore depressed areas; for peace, but will he press for negotiated settlement of differ-ences? How deep are his convictions? How considered his views? How honest his attitudes?

All of these matters seem directly related to the bill before you, for the technology of our civilization is equal to its problems. We have the means, through television, to bring the candidates for President and Vice President face to face with virtually all Americans for the first time. They can sit down with 40 million families often enough and for long enough periods to discuss the questions which are critical to our sur-vival and our leadership in the world. But only the Congress can make that possible.

The political parties, the Congress, and the television industry share responsibility, I suppose, for the fact that television has contributed far less than it could to the people's understanding of the issues or knowledge of the candidate's position.

Network television time has become almost prohibitively expensive. For example, one hour of prime TV time on all networks this fall may cost over $400,000, or over $6,000 a minute.

The party with the largest campaign fund will provide its candidate more time on television than his opponent. He is seen and heard more times by more people. He gains an advantage, and democracy suffers from the unequal contest.

The cost of television also produces a frantic determination to squeeze the maximum number of votes from the investment. The almost unbelievable complexity of television scheduling has long since made necessary the services of the professional advertising agency in national campaigns. Drawing on their broad experience and unquestioned success in selling soap, cereal, and deodorants, it isn't surprising that the advertising agencies recommend the jingle, the spot announcement, and the animated cartoon. So the American voter, faced with issues of life and death, is solicited in song to "Vote for Dan, the man with the plan." This kind of presentation.

There are, of course, television broadcasts of speeches by the candidates in normal campaigns. These are sometimes not much more useful, however, to the voter than the jingle. Presidential campaign ritual requires that the candidate be shuttled from coast to coast as many times as possible, assuring maximum physical exhaustion, and minimum opportunity to prepare his statements. The result is the ever greater use of the ghost writer and the ever greater difficulty of knowing the candidate himself. Because his time is scheduled around personal appearances, it is the television broadcast which must be fitted in, often at the last minute and in unsuitable circumstances.

The result is that the candidate is usually seen and heard addressing a rally of the party faithful. This means a lengthy introduction of the candidate by a person whose views on his qualifications are both predictable and irrelevant, with diminished time for the candidate. It also means the audience expects that a certain amount of time be devoted to the assertion, if a Democratic rally, that the Democratic Party is the party of the people, or if a Republican rally, that Republicans are patriotic savers and Democrats socialistic spenders.

The bill before you seeks to bring more order, more intelligent discussion into the present confusion and showmanship of presidential campaigns, by providing the environment in which such discussion can occur. What would it accomplish? As the chairman has said, the pending bill would insure that both political parties would be given an equal opportunity to present their candidates and their programs to the American people on television.

Second, it would insure that the candidates of both parties would have an adequate amount of time to discuss the most important issues facing the Nation, regardless of the size of their party budgets.

Third, it would provide 30 minutes for each presidential candidate, scheduled consecutively, thus giving the voters a better opportunity to make a direct comparison between the candidates. If the candidates will take full advantage of this arrangement, and agree in advance upon the issues to be discussed on each of these programs, the people could have the benefit of a truly useful discussion of some of these difficult, intricate questions. I think that this discussion and subsequent performance would thereby become more responsible.

In the fourth place it would assure that these programs could be seen by the maximum number of people by requiring that they be scheduled in the prime viewing hours, and by requiring simultaneous broadcast on all stations in a given time zone. This would give a nationwide coverage never before possible.

Such a series of programs, in the fifth place, on predetermined dates, would make it possible to organize the campaign around the candidates' appearance on them, and would give priority to the most important function of the campaign — to inform the people of the candidate's views on the public issues with which he will have to deal if he is subsequently elected.

I would make one recommendation for a major change in the present bill. I believe that one program of, say, 1½ hours each week is preferable to two programs of 1 hour each, and that even one program of 1 hour each week would be quite adequate. Over an 8-week period, this would give each candidate time for eight 30-minute speeches, or a total of 4 hours of television time. Scheduling the first week's program on Sunday, the second week's program on Monday, and so forth, would entail the minimum disruption of station schedules and insure that no commercial program would be canceled more than once.

I might interpose there to say I am sensitive to this subject of cancellation of commercial programs. I remember the 1956 campaign when our Democratic Party's advertising agency purchased 5 minutes off of a very popular program, then I went on and said something, and the first telegram I received said, "I like Ike, and I love Lucy; drop dead." [Laughter.]

I wholeheartedly endorse the purpose of section 2(e) of the bill, in requiring that time made available be utilized only by the candidate. There is certainly no public interest in providing free time for a political party to present Fred Waring and his Pennsylvanians, or a collection of Hollywood starlets at a political rally. The time is for the responsible use of the candidate himself; the purpose is not to entertain but to enlighten, to raise the quality of these great quadrennial discussions about our country's policy and its management.

I would also suggest, if the time available to each presidential candidate is reduced to one-half hour per week, that no change be made in the provision permitting the candidate for Vice President to use two of the eight half-hour periods made available. Certainly, the burdens of the President are now obviously such that he must share them with the man chosen by the people to succeed him in the event of his death — and thus the man they judge to be fully qualified for the Presidency. If the candidate for Vice President is to be the President's principal deputy, it is important that the people have as adequate a basis on which to judge his qualifications as they have to judge those of the candidate for President himself.

Before closing, Mr. Chairman and gentlemen, I would like to discuss some of the grounds which have been suggested for opposition to, or at least apprehension about, this legislation. Some who are in complete sympathy with its purposes are concerned over the effect of the eligibility requirements on third parties. As I understand it, the bill requires that broadcasters make free time available only to the presidential candidate of a political party whose candidate in the preceding election was supported by not fewer than 4 per cent of the total popular votes cast. The practical effect of this requirement is that only the candidates of the Democratic and Republican Parties would be eligible for free television time in this year's election. A third party organized this year would have to get 4 per cent of the popular vote in 1960 to have its candidate eligible for free time in 1964.

I believe that this is a sensible provision. Our two-party system has evolved more than a century and a half, and the realities of our political system are such that no third party is going to elect its candidate for President in the first election after its organization. Nor is it likely to elect its candidate in the second election after its organization if in its first attempt it was supported by less than 4 per cent of the popular vote. It is obviously impractical to make free time available to a dozen presidential candidates which may emerge and often have in our political past.

I believe that the results which would be achieved through this legislation can be accomplished in no other way. Representatives of the television industry have insisted that the networks are anxious to provide adequate time, and that no legislative compulsion of this kind is required. I believe this view is unrealistic.

Even if the networks are prepared to sell prime time to the political parties, which they are not obligated to do, this does not correct their unequal ability to purchase it. It does not simplify the problem of dealing with a number of networks and dozens of individual stations, nor eliminate the difficulty of scheduling anything like nationwide coverage. It does not insure the responsible use of the time purchased by the political parties. Moreover, such offers of cooperation are always made with the unstated reservation that it be on the networks' own terms. For example, I understand that one network has recently announced that it will only sell time on an exclusive basis, and not for programs to be broadcast simultaneously by a competitor.

The networks and stations are effectively prevented from making free time available to the candidates of the major parties by the provisions of section 315, that the chairman just discussed and you are all familiar with, of the Federal Communications Act, which would require that equal time be made available to any minor party which demanded it. Before time for a series of speeches or debates could be provided, this section would have to be amended to relieve them of the obligation to provide equal time to other parties. Thus, legislation would be necessary in any event. I understand that there was strong opposition in the Congress last year to a general exemption of political debates from the equal-time requirement. Even if such an exemption were confined to the presidential campaign, we would still confront a confusion of opinion about the proper form, time, and manner of using the exemption, compounded by the inevitable differences between the two parties.

One network has proposed to meet this problem by making time available to the major candidates on a news interview program, which is already exempt from the equal-time requirement. NBC Television proposes to reschedule "Meet the Press" on Saturday night for the 8 weeks prior to the election and devote it exclusively to interviews with the candidates. This is certainly an interesting and inviting proposal. However, it obviously is not a substitute for the candidate's discussing deliberately and in his own way the issues which he regards as most important. In short, while a useful proposal, it bears little relation to the problems to which this legislation is, I believe, addressed.

The television station operates pursuant to a temporary license to use assigned frequencies only so long as its operation is in the public interest. It is required to make available a reasonable amount of time for public service programs, and its failure to do so is grounds for revocation or refusal to renew its license. To require 8 hours every 4 years for a particular type of public service programing would involve preemption of three one-hundredths of 1 per cent of each station's total broadcast time during that period, or one one-hundredth of 1 per cent of each station's prime time.

Finally, gentlemen, I find no criticism of this measure is more unjustified, it seems to me, than the charge that it is Government interference with free speech. Rather, it represents a guarantee of free speech. The freedom of speech which our Nation's founders fought to preserve was more than the right of a peddler on Boston Common to hawk his oysters without restraint. It was the right of public discussion of political issues. Their devotion to it was not to an abstract right, but born of conviction that full discussion of alternatives was prerequisite to an intelligent choice between them. The same conviction motivates the sponsors of this bill. They propose only to insure the free access to the means of communication which will permit that discussion to take place in the full view of all our citizens.

So I would urge the Congress to say to the political parties and the television industry:

> We reclaim for a few hours every 4 years the public airwaves. We owe it to our system of government to give the voters — now numbering more than 100 million and beyond the physical reach of any candidate — a chance to hear the issues discussed and make their choice with knowledge of the facts.

If I may, I should like to conclude with a quote from the article[55] I wrote last winter that the chairman referred to in his opening remarks, an article written out of a feeling of importance and anxiety to get a further public consideration of this matter, and I am happy to say that this public consideration has now taken place.

Television —

I said —

today is the most powerful medium available to candidates for public office. Such a useful means of mass communication must be conserved for the improvement of the democratic dialogue, not allowed to encourage its debasement. During the 1956 campaign I was urged by some of my advisers to challenge President Eisenhower to a debate. I did not, for I feared the challenge would be misunderstood, would be taken as a gimmick. What I am proposing now is no gimmick; it is the establishment of what I hope will become a national institution, a great debate for the Presidency.

55 "Choice by Hullabaloo."

I don't mean a debate in the literal collegiate sense of that word; I mean rather a sustained discussion. Only television can establish such a forum any longer. I propose that it provide a quadronnial clearing of the air by the use of the air.

Such sustained serious discussion on all networks would reach all of the people directly. It would require effort on their part, mental effort, and I know of no better cure for apathy. It would end the financial problem that TV now presents to the parties. It would end the tendency to reduce everything to assertions and to slogans. It would diminish the temptation of politicians to entertain, to please, to evade the unpleasant realities. It might even help to restore what we seem to have lost — our sense of great national purpose.

I ended, then:

For in the long run it may turn out that the direction we give to political television is one of the great decisions of the decisive decade of the 1960's.

Thank you, Mr. Chairman, and members of the committee for your patience.

Stevenson's testimony and the significance of the proposed law were overshadowed by the U–2 incident and events that day in Paris which ended the summit conference. Stevenson, Speaker of the House of Representatives Sam Rayburn, Senate Majority Leader Lyndon B. Johnson, and Senator J. W. Fulbright, chairman of the Senate Foreign Relations Committee, sent the following cable to President Eisenhower in Paris on May 16, 1960.

As leaders of the Democratic party of the United States we earnestly urge you to convey to Premier Khrushchev the views of the opposition party in your country that he reconsider his suggestion for postponement of the summit conference until after the national elections in this country. We feel that total failure of the conference and increasing mistrust on both sides will be serious and deeply disturbing to the whole world.

All of the American people earnestly desire peace, an end to the arms race and ever better relations between our countries. We ask you as the leader of this nation to see that these views are conveyed to Mr. Khrushchev.

Stevenson returned to Chicago after his May 16 meetings in Washington, D.C. Ben W. Heineman, chairman of the board of directors of the

Chicago and Northwestern Railway Company, wrote Stevenson that what disturbed him most about the U-2 was the "inflammatory nature of the lie" the United States government had told. If the pilot had not been captured, Heineman added, most people would have accepted the version that it was an unarmed weather plane skirting the Russian border on a "well-known and publicized weather mission" which was "shot down mercilessly by the Russians," a "lie designed to confirm both American and foreign opinions of Russian bestiality."

To Ben W. Heineman

May 17, 1960

Dear Ben:

I am much interested in your letter, and I confess I had the same kind of shocked feeling about the handling of this incident, with the un-equivocal statement followed by the abject confession. I am sure it has had consequences around the world that we will not perceive here, and includes the reactions you felt, misgivings about our good faith and reliability and mirth and ridicule.

But here we will forgive and forget it all too soon, content with "too bad we wuz caught!"

I wish I saw you more often.

Cordially yours,

On May 19, 1960, Stevenson spoke at a dinner meeting of the Democratic party of Cook County.[56]

It appears that this year's campaign will be waged under the darkest shadows that ever hovered over the world — the mushroom clouds of a nuclear war that no one wants. This terrible danger — and how to avert it — will and should overshadow every other issue.

For the chances of a more stable world, which seemed to be brightening, have been rudely reversed by the breakdown of the summit conference in this historic week.

Premier Khrushchev wrecked this conference. Let there be no mistake about that. When he demanded that President Eisenhower apologize and punish those responsible for the spy plane flight, he was in effect asking the President to punish himself. This was an impossible request, and he knew it.

[56] The text is from the Chicago *Daily News*, May 20, 1960. Typographical errors have been corrected by the editors.

But we handed Khrushchev the crowbar and sledgehammer to wreck the meeting. Without our series of blunders, Mr. Khrushchev would not have had a pretext for making his impossible demand and wild charges. Let there be no mistake about that either.

We sent an espionage plane deep into the Soviet Union just before the summit meeting. Then we denied it. Then we admitted it.

And when Mr. Khrushchev gave the President an out by suggesting that he was not responsible for ordering the flight, the President proudly asserted that he was responsible.

On top of that we intimated that such espionage flights over Russia would continue.

(At this point if Khrushchev did not protest he would be condoning our right to spy — and how long could he keep his job that way?)

Next we evidently reconsidered and called off the espionage flights. But, to compound the incredible, we postponed the announcement that the flights were terminated — just long enough to make it seem we were yielding to pressure, but too long to prevent Mr. Khrushchev from reaching the boiling point.

And, as if that wasn't enough, on Sunday night when there was still a chance that De Gaulle and Macmillan could save the situation, we ordered a world-wide alert of our combat forces!

Is it reasonable for suspicious Russians to think such a series of mistakes could only be a deliberate effort to break up a conference we never wanted anyway?

We Democrats know how clumsy this administration can be. We are not likely to forget the fumbles that preceded the Suez crisis on the eve of the 1956 election.

Nothing, of course, can justify Mr. Khrushchev's contemptuous conduct, especially after President Eisenhower had announced that our espionage flights had been called off. But his anger was predictable, if not his violence.

How would we feel if Soviet spy planes based in Cuba were flying over Cape Canaveral and Oak Ridge?

And also we could predict with certainty his efforts to use the situation to split the Western Alliance and intimidate the countries where our bases are situated.

Republican leaders are now saying that in this grave crisis we must all rally round the President in the name of national unity.

Our respect for the Presidency will find us joined in salute to President Eisenhower upon his return. We resent deeply and bitterly the gross affront to the President and his office.

There is no question about national unity in a time of crisis. But errors must be corrected, and we must not forget that the opposition party also has an obligation to our country and to our allies whose security is also involved.

It is the duty of responsible opposition in a democracy to expose and criticize carelessness and mistakes, especially in a case of such national and world importance as this. We must see to it that we profit from such grave mistakes and misfortunes.

It is particularly regrettable that this happened in an election year. And we can already predict what the Republicans will tell the people in the months ahead.

They will say that President Eisenhower's patience and dignity in Paris scored a diplomatic triumph by exposing Khrushchev's insincerity.

They will say that the Russians are hoping that a "softer" Democratic President will be elected in November.

They will tell the people that a vote for the candidate the Russians distrust is a vote against appeasement.

It will be our duty, it will be the duty of all thoughtful, concerned citizens to help retrieve the situation and to face the hard, inescapable facts; that this administration played into Khrushchev's hands; that if Khrushchev wanted to wreck the conference our government made it possible; that the administration has acutely embarrassed our allies and endangered our bases; that they have helped make successful negotiations with the Russians — negotiations that are vital to our survival — impossible so long as they are in power.

We cannot sweep this whole sorry mess under the rug in the name of national unity. We cannot and must not. Too much is at stake.

Rather we must try to help the American people understand the nature of the crisis, to see how we got into this predicament, how we can get out of it, and how we get on with the business of improving relations and mutual confidence and building a safer, saner world in the nuclear age.

For in this age, unprecedented in human history, all of us, Americans and Russians alike, have one common enemy. The enemy is the danger of war.

We must defeat the enemy together.

Despite his hysterics last night, Mr. Khrushchev says he still believes in peaceful progress by negotiation.

Let us hope he proves it and let the United States come into the United Nations not content with the ordinary speeches, not content with the usual anti-Russian majority votes, but with constructive, positive, affirmative proposals to restore the hope of peace.

To those who will see nothing but Russian vice and American virtue, to those who will cry appeasement to any acknowledgment of our mistakes, I say that this is the toughest kind of common sense.

For there is no future for any of us in a spiraling arms race propelled by mounting suspicion and distrust on both sides.

The fact that Khrushchev seems to have lost his temper in Paris makes it all the more important that we not lose ours — or our heads.[57]

In April, 1960, shortly after Stevenson's speech at the University of Virginia, Mike Monroney, Jr., Tom Finney, Jr. — Senator Mike Monroney's administrative assistant — and Washington lawyers George Ball and John Sharon had opened a Washington headquarters under the name of Russell Hemenway & Associates, to stimulate a Stevenson draft. Senator Monroney was persuaded by them to lead the operation.

They were in communication with James E. Doyle, of Madison, Wisconsin, who had for months been in touch with political leaders around the country. The Washington office also maintained close contact with a fund-raising group in Los Angeles headed by Dore Schary.

On May 19, 1960, after Stevenson testified before the Senate Subcommittee regarding the need for free radio and television time for debates between the two major party candidates, he talked with Senator Lyndon B. Johnson. According to Senator Monroney, who was present, Johnson warned Stevenson that he "might yet be the nominee of the Democratic party."[58] After an interview with Stevenson on November 14, 1960, Stuart Gerry Brown wrote:

> Johnson indicated his disapproval of Kennedy's candidacy and observed that he would not then be stopped unless AES became a candidate and "went out and got himself some 400 delegates." Johnson seemed to think that Stevenson could readily obtain support to this extent. The combination of Johnson and Stevenson delegates would then be more than enough to stop Kennedy. It was clear that Johnson was interested in the nomination for himself, but the suggestion was that should he fail to obtain it he would support AES. Stevenson told Johnson that he was not a candidate, would not be a candidate, and thus could not expect to have 400 delegates. AES indicated that he would not endorse Kennedy at that time, in order

[57] Vice President Nixon, through his press secretary, expressed "shock" at Stevenson's speech. Chicago *Daily News*, May 20, 1960. The Chicago *Tribune* criticized Stevenson in an editorial on May 21. The Chicago *Sun-Times* on May 21 called Stevenson's speech "an attempt to divide the nation." James A. Farley denounced Stevenson as "the apostle of appeasement." New York *Times*, May 22, 1960.
[58] "The Plot against Adlai," p. 249.

to give all candidates as good a chance as possible, but that he could not otherwise participate in the pre-election maneuvering.[59]

After talking with Senator Johnson, Stevenson met with Senator Monroney and some others advocating his nomination. Monroney wrote: "We levied our demands: that he provide the voice of leadership for the Democratic party, that he do nothing to handicap our effort to secure his nomination. We asked more, but to these two he agreed."[60]

That same day James E. Doyle, at the suggestion of Bill Blair, sent a memorandum to Stevenson analyzing the strength of the candidates for the nomination. Doyle stated that the chance for Senator Kennedy's nomination was now very strong. Only if Kennedy failed, and he and the forces allied with him decided at the convention to go for Stevenson "vigorously and enthusiastically," could Stevenson be nominated. In pencil Stevenson wrote in the margin opposite that sentence: "Johnson told AES on 5/16 that his votes would go to AES."

The Doyle memorandum concluded that assuming he judged Kennedy worthy of the presidency, Stevenson should be prepared to support Kennedy at a time when such support would be decisive. Doyle suggested possibly June 1 for such a statement, but he added "perhaps not so soon."

To James E. Doyle[61]

[no date]

Dear Jim:

Thanks for this VERY helpful analysis. I have heard from all of the parties — and most everyone else! — and I think your judgment is accurate & sound. That I agree with it is perhaps irrelevant but comforting to me!

Yours —
AES

P.S. I doubt if I should do anything as early as *June 1*.

---

[59] This handwritten memorandum is in the Stuart Gerry Brown papers, Syracuse University Library.

[60] "The Plot against Adlai," p. 250.

[61] This handwritten note is in the possession of Mr. Doyle. It is written on the bottom of Mr. Doyle's letter of May 16, 1960.

To Arthur M. Schlesinger, Jr.[62]

May 21, 1960

Dear Arthur:

You were so good to write me about Jack Kennedy's views that I am sending you this report on our talk at Libertyville this morning — written hurriedly as the airplane approaches La Guardia.

He came for breakfast en route from Oregon to Cape Cod for his birthday (43rd — hush! hush!) party; looked fine & fit (Mirab[i]le dictu), and happy of course to be finished with the damn primaries. He defends them now on but one ground, I gathered: an opportunity to get known all over the country and I think he makes a good point, if not good enough to convince me!

He *seemed* to feel that my reaction to the summit bungling was correct and that we shouldn't, either for the country or the party, let this one be buried in maudlin mush. But I will wait to see what he *does* with interest.[63]

He felt that Nixon would take the tough guy with Khrushchev line now; that he *had* to, and his strategy would be to put us on the defensive as the soft on communism party. I have hoped for this, and that we can get some generalship and coherence to handle it effectively — thus recapturing the peace issue — and also getting the country in a posture to save the alliance, restore confidence & perhaps sometime make some progress toward peace in fact!

As to the campaign, Jack reviewed *all* the states and said he was still short 80–100 votes probably; that I (AES) was strong especially in Oregon, Wash, Calif, Colo, Pa. etc. — that I could help him and he wanted the help without specifying *when*.

I explained that I wanted to be consistent & did not feel therefore that I could come out for him *now*, but that he could be sure that I would not be a party — overtly, covertly etc. — to any "stop Kennedy" movements; that I had been approached — and HAVE I! — with that proposal and had emphatically & unequivocally rejected the overtures; that, further, I would, as in the past (cf. [Washington] D.C.) do NOTHING to encourage "Draft Stevenson" movements which could embar[r]ass or weaken him. (And I think my speech here the other night on facing the

---

[62] This handwritten letter is in the Schlesinger papers, John F. Kennedy Library.
[63] On May 24, 1960, Senator Kennedy questioned the timing of the U-2 flight over the Soviet Union just before the summit conference. If elected President, he declared, he would continue the ban on U-2 flights. Chicago *Sun-Times*, May 25, 1960. Kennedy was the only candidate publicly to support Stevenson's position.

realities of the summit debacle has probably effectively taken care of *that!*)

The meeting was entirely satisfactory from my point of view and I cannot say he seemed disappointed or surprised about my attitude — and certainly not elated! The only sensitive point I felt was his response to some remark I made about Johnson & the importance of his cooperation if K was elected. Here the reaction was sharp & certain — that there was only *one* way to treat Lyndon now — *Beat* him! that he would come along after the election, etc. etc. etc.

There was *no* talk about Secy of state or deals. "If I can't make it," he said, "we'll have to reappraise the situation at that time," but no reference or hint about supporting me. There were several references to "the same people" are "your friends and mine."[64]

I can add that he seemed *very* self-confident & assured & much tougher and blunter than I remember him in the past. We talked a little about the release from the Osservatore Romano, which *shocked* me (as Nixon would say!) and he said if necessary he would repudiate, or some such word, publicly the idea of any such dictation on influence in political affairs.[65] I offered to help, as a Protestant layman, on that if I could.

[64] Stuart Gerry Brown wrote: "JFK took this opportunity to ask AES directly for his support for the nomination. He urged that the only alternative to himself was then LBJ [Senator Lyndon B. Johnson], and took the position that AES could not possibly favor this course. JFK said that an AES endorsement would unite the liberals, bring an end to the LBJ threat, and lead to a harmonious convention with a head start against Nixon. AES indicated that he understood the position but could not agree with it. He told JFK that he had given his word to LBJ not to intervene (see AES interview #1), and that he had spoken similarly to Symington. He said that as leader of the party he thought it improper for him to be anything but neutral, at least until the convention itself. He did not rule out the possibility that he would endorse JFK at the convention. Finally, he told JFK that he feared an endorsement by him of JFK would look to the public at large and the leaders and candidates in the party as though a deal had been made. (AES told us that JFK never hinted at a deal for Secretary of State. But his people had been making suggestions along this line to [Bill] Blair, etc. for some time, so that it was quite unnecessary for JFK to mention it — as well as being too crude. But AES seemed fairly clear that he would indeed have had assurance of the appointment if he had endorsed JFK at this time). JFK was bitterly and obviously disappointed at the attitude of AES, though he, of course, professed to understand it. AES says that at this time the possibility that he himself might be drafted, and that to endorse JFK would scuttle the movement being made by his friends, played only a very minor part in his thinking. . . ." Handwritten notes on a conversation with Stevenson, March 29, 1961, in the Stuart Gerry Brown papers, Syracuse University Library. The discrepancy between what Stevenson wrote Schlesinger and what he later told Brown about the meeting with Kennedy probably stems from the fact that Schlesinger was supporting Kennedy for the nomination.

[65] On May 17, 1960, the Vatican newspaper, *L'Osservatore Romano*, stated that the Roman Catholic Church had a responsibility and duty to guide its members in both private and political affairs. The pronouncement was explicitly directed to all

And I think — and HOPE that I left him with a feeling of great good will, determination not to hinder, and no doubt about my preference & anxiety to *help* in any way if he is nominated.

He did not use the "liberals stand together" argument; indeed didn't argue at all & was totally correct. As I conclude this I guess the only faint misgiving about the meeting I have is that he may not fully appreciate some of *my* difficulties & how easy it has been & would be [to] give some impetus to a movement for myself which would be largely at his expense & with some of the people he mentioned with such confidence as '*his*.' But perhaps that's hardly surprising in *view* of *his* difficulties.

Caution! Poison! — La Guardia below, *I hope!*

ADLAI

On April 16, 1960, Mrs. Clifton Utley, as midwest director of the Institute of International Education, brought a visiting French journalist, Robert Boulay, to Libertyville to meet Stevenson. According to Mr. Boulay, they talked alone for nearly an hour. On May 14, 1960, the Paris-Presse-L'Intransigeant *published Mr. Boulay's account of the talk. The heading of the story read:*

I SPENT AN AFTERNOON WITH A POSSIBLE
SUCCESSOR TO EISENHOWER
Adlai Stevenson Told Me:
"The Americans ought to quit Berlin and
Europe, if they wish to make an atomic peace."

On May 17, 1960, William H. Stoneman cabled a story from Paris to the Chicago Daily News *which began: "A startling statement by Soviet Premier Khrushchev expressing hope that he could do more business with one of Ike's successors than with Ike himself is being connected by imaginative Europeans with an interview recently given to a French newspaperman by Adlai Stevenson."*

On May 24 Senator Everett M. Dirksen inserted the article in the Congressional Record *and accused Stevenson of not only being "soft" toward the Soviet Union but also actually torpedoing the summit conference with his statements to Boulay. Dirksen stated: "Mr. Khrushchev would have been a fool not to consider postponement of the conference*

members of the Church everywhere in the world and thus had the potential of placing Senator Kennedy in an embarrassing situation.

*for six or eight months — that is, after election day — on the theory that
he might be dealing with a gentler, more tractable, less firm President."*[66]

*Stevenson, in a statement issued May 24, denied that he had granted
Boulay an interview and said that the statements attributed to him did
not remotely reflect his views on foreign policy.*[67]

Scores of visitors from all over the world come to my house. I believe
this man, Mr. Boulay, came with several Chicago friends of mine on a
week-end afternoon this spring. He never asked for an interview and I
never gave him one. What he has reported about my opinions is gro-
tesque. I have often expressed the opinion in this country and abroad
that the Allies must stand firm in West Berlin and make no change in
the Allied position until agreements to improve the situation, which are
satisfactory to all, can be reached.

The Frenchman asked me about discussion of the future of Europe in
the United States and I doubtless said that all the proposals discussed
abroad were discussed here too — withdrawal of occupying forces of
both sides from Germany and Eastern Europe, unification and free
elections in both Germanies, a demilitarization zone, the Rapacki Plan,[68]
etc.

The young journalist has evidently written that I was in favor of all of
these proposals, whether contradictory or not. The most charitable
interpretation of such irresponsibility is that his understanding of my
English was as bad as mine of his French. A less charitable interpretation is that a foreign journalist, masquerading as a friendly guest in my
home, has written without my permission or knowledge and attributed
opinions to me without any verification or even relevance to what I
said.

I am happy to say that I have never encountered such journalistic

[66] Alice Widener, in "L'Affaire Stevenson," *U.S.A.,* June 17, 1960, reprinted the
original story and many of the subsequent charges and countercharges. See also the
Chicago *Sun-Times,* May 29, 1960; the Chicago *Daily News,* May 26, 1960; the
Reporter, June 9, 1960.

[67] In a speech to the Chicago Council on Foreign Relations on May 26, 1960,
Stevenson insisted that the Boulay "interview" was never "requested, never granted,
and never authorized." He observed that if Mr. Boulay or Senator Dirksen "really
wanted my views on West Berlin they are readily available in my utterances and
articles." He specifically called attention to his January, 1960, article in *Foreign
Affairs,* reprinted in his recently published book, *Putting First Things First: A
Democratic View* (New York: Random House, 1960).

[68] A proposal, first made in 1957 by Polish Foreign Minister Adam Rapacki, to
create a zone in Central Europe in which nuclear weapons would be prohibited,
comprising all of Germany, Poland, and Czechoslovakia.

irresponsibility and discourtesy here or abroad before, and I have been interviewed in virtually every country in the world.

To Newton N. Minow[69]

May 31, 1960

Having no public relations management, couldn't you in your way make it clear that *not* coming out for K[ennedy]. is consistent with the policy of four years, and fair to the others; and that I won't be party to any "stop K. movements."

It is discouraging to read about my "entourage" all the time always in terms of "to come out for K. or not to come out — to help *myself* get the nomination." Couldn't someone suggest that I never had any intention of "coming out" for anyone — or stopping anyone and it is unrelated to any "draft Stevenson" movement and exactly consistent with what I've been doing for four years — keeping out of everyone's way and not being a candidate myself.

A.E.S.

Copies to:
Bill Wirtz
Bill Blair
E. D. McDougal
Lloyd Garrison
T. K. Finletter
A.E.S. III

On May 26, 1960, Senator Hubert Humphrey inserted Stevenson's article "National Purpose: Stevenson's View" (*New York* Times, *May 26, 1960*) in the Congressional Record (*pp. 11144–11147*). He wrote Stevenson that there was no wonder why millions of Americans wanted him to be President and that he should stop writing articles like this if he did not want to be President.

To Hubert H. Humphrey

June 1, 1960

Dear Hubert:

I have just seen your letter and the Congressional Record. I am grateful indeed that you thought well enough of that piece in Life to

[69] A copy of this office memorandum is in the possession of Edward D. McDougal.

insert it in the Record. But who is that fellow you talked about with such soaring eloquence? Surely not the Stevenson we know!

I yearn to see you, and I am distressed that you had no time during your visit to the Textile Workers. Meanwhile, I repeat — I am *not* a candidate! — and I don't like primaries!!

Yours,

P.S. . . .

To Dr. Albert Schweitzer

June 2, 1960

Dear Dr. Schweitzer:

I was delighted to have your letter . . . and I can think of nothing I would rather do than come to visit you in Lambarene for a few days of *tranquil* talk. Tranquil talk has become so infrequent in our Western political society and the atmosphere of the cold war is, I suspect, a reflection of the malaise that afflicts us all — suspicion and impatience.

I am flattered that you envision my active political participation again in public affairs in this country. Actually, after running for President twice I am sure you will understand why I view that possibility again with something less than enthusiasm. Moreover, I see little prospect that the party will turn to me in view of the aggressive ambitions of others. However, I hope to be able to exercise some influence over the direction of our affairs, especially in the foreign field where I am afraid we still suffer from many illusions, even as the Communists suffer many illusions about us. With things as they are, the prospect of a visit to you at this time seems most remote, but I shall bear it in mind hopefully. We all need your quiet counsel and depth of vision. I am sure the Russians need it, too, and I wish they were getting it.

With profoundest respect, I am

Cordially yours,

Stevenson went to Boston to appear on a television program with Mrs. Franklin D. Roosevelt. While there, he spent an evening with Mr. and Mrs. Arthur M. Schlesinger, Jr. Mr. Schlesinger was working for Senator Kennedy's nomination.[70]

[70] See his *A Thousand Days: John F. Kennedy in the White House* (Boston: Houghton Mifflin, 1965), p. 35.

To Mr. and Mrs. Arthur M. Schlesinger, Jr.

June 7, 1960

Dear Arthur and Marion:

It was a lovely evening! I felt guilty that I had imposed on you on such an important family feast day, but you made me content and comfortable and I enjoyed it very, very much. . . .

I wish if any wandering Schlesingers were travelling this way during the summer they would take refuge in my prairie cabin. It would be a delight for me.

Arthur — I have been reflecting a little about our talk and find myself getting more provoked by the feeling I get from the Kennedy camp that I should do this or that to help if I expect any consideration later for myself. I have refrained from saying this until now, but I think I will say it to you before you leave for Europe, and say it no more to anyone!

I have always felt in a way responsible for Jack's recent political progress. After all, I had a lively regard for him as a classic example of the best in our new party leadership. For that reason, and also because of the importance of retrieving the Catholic defectors, I wanted him, as you know, to be my vice presidential candidate in 1956, or at least I wanted him to have every chance of being the candidate. Hence, I asked him to nominate me, as you will recall, and thereafter, in view of Kefauver's withdrawal and endorsement of me, I threw the vice presidency open to the convention (Ed Plaut[71] notwithstanding!), thinking that Kennedy's chances would be at least good. As a result of the convention in 1956 he had a quickly earned national reputation and identification which he has exploited most effectively. Would it have been as easy to exploit it in this campaign year had I chosen to be a candidate or done anything to encourage my friends to promote a third candidacy? In short, I have felt that I launched him, in a sense, on the national scene and have conscientiously kept out of his way since not to impede or embarrass his progress, and have spoken about him in a flattering way at every opportunity. With all this in mind, I have found the talk from his camp, albeit not from him, quite aggravating.

Do let me have any advice that comes to you before your departure and any inspiration that overtakes you in Europe. And have a good time too!

Affectionately and gratefully,

[71] Unable to identify.

Look, in its June 7, 1960, issue, published an article by Harry S. Truman entitled "How Stevenson Let Me Down." Among other things, Truman stated that in 1952 he had flown to the Chicago convention and told the leaders that Stevenson was the logical candidate. "As a result, he received the nomination," Truman concluded. To correct this distortion of the historical record, Walter Johnson wrote a letter to the editor, which Look *published July 19, 1960.[72] A copy of the letter was sent to Stevenson. The only public statement Stevenson issued about the article was, "I respect President Truman if not for his memory of events."[73]*

To Walter Johnson[74]

June 7, 1960

Dear Walter:

Bless you for writing that letter to LOOK. It also served to confirm my recollection. I cannot explain the Old Man, but I am sure that the fact that he did not have anything to do with the nomination after having pleaded with me so often to be a "candidate" has irked him ever since and even persuaded him that he was responsible. I wish I had a good story at hand constantly!

Yours,
ADLAI

Hundreds of volunteer Stevenson for President groups had sprung up by June 1960. Irving Kupcinet wrote in the Chicago Sun-Times, *May 22, 1960, "The boom for Adlai Stevenson is growing more torrid." The Stevenson-for-President Committee of New York launched a petition campaign and ran a full-page advertisement in the New York* Times, *Sunday, May 22, 1960. The next day the formation of the Illinois Committee for Stevenson was announced. On May 25 the Washington headquarters that had been functioning for more than a month, under the leadership of Senator Mike Monroney, George W. Ball, Mike Monroney, Jr., and John Sharon, became a public operation. James Doyle agreed to be campaign manager, although this was not made public until June 22, 1960.*

---

[72] See also *The Papers of Adlai E. Stevenson*, Vol. IV, p. 5.
[73] Chicago *Sun-Times*, May 25, 1960.
[74] The original is in the possession of Walter Johnson.

To Lady Barbara Jackson

June 9, 1960

Dearest Barbara:

So much is happening that I can't begin to report properly or even to give you a savor of the developing storm. I have tried not to antagonize the Kennedy people but it is not always easy. They seem to coin rumors to serve their ends and exercise seductive coercion on delegates right and left with consequences that are sometimes provoking and frequently effective!

Your letters have been a comfort and I only wish their author was here. But I have gulped down all your news and enchanting pictures of life in Ghana and the life and thought of the Jacksons.

I wish it were possible to reflect a little with you by mail about what is going on in the world and the feeling I have that Khrushchev is trying desperately to hold his own position at home and sustain confidence in his era of good feeling policy. But why they have to be so obtuse about American politics while trying to influence it baffles me. I think it must reflect in part on [Ambassador] Menschikov [Menshikov] to communicate properly what I am sure he must know or else Khrushchev, who is no fool, as we know, must be under constant duress.

The 'draft Stevenson' movement has gathered momentum of late in various cities about the country, but I doubt if it can stem the Kennedy tide which has followed the primaries and the incessant work of his huge teams that operate on delegates individually. It is all the same with me, as you know, and I will certainly be relieved when it is over and I can relax again. I have to speak once more, on the 23rd of this month, to the Illinois State Bar Association, and I had thought to talk a little about neo-McCarthyism and the problem of conducting a proper, sensible discussion of foreign policy in an atmosphere of epithets and accusations of appeasement, "soft" on Communism, etc. If you have any ideas, send them along. I may also pick up some of your Rutgers material which I never used. I had to cancel the engagement. Of course, I may change the whole thing according to developments. Basically, I wanted to use this interval to try to get national thinking focused on the foreign policy discussion and exploit the interest aroused by the summit collapse.

Rockefeller[75] is raising hell and it won't be long before his detestation for Nixon begins to show, I suspect, but the GOP is rallying with unmis-

[75] Nelson A. Rockefeller, Republican governor of New York.

takable signs of unity behind Sir Richard the brave and bold, and a leopard can't change his spots.

I wish there were time for more, or indeed time for something.

Much love to all,

To Mrs. Thomas K. Finletter

June 9, 1960

Dear Gay:

Thanks for your letter, but to announce that I am a candidate is just what we agreed long ago at Chelsea[76] I would not do, and I really can't do it now. That I will accept a draft — yes — who wouldn't or couldn't! But to actively seek the nomination for a third time is quite inconsistent with the position I have taken for so long, and it would make me feel also quite out of character.

I hope you will understand and forgive me.

Affectionately,

To Dwight D. Eisenhower

June 9, 1960

Dear Mr. President:

At a time when it still seemed possible to resume negotiations between East and West at the Paris gathering of Heads of State, we sent you a message to be forwarded to the Soviet Government. The purpose of our message was to make certain that the Soviet Government did not miscalculate the position of the opposition Party in the United States and, on account of such a miscalculation, postpone negotiations among the Heads of State.

On June 2, the Soviet Premier transmitted a reply to our message. We believe there is no need to dwell on his gross distortion of what actually occurred at the Summit, or on the sorry spectacle of the Soviet Premier's behavior at Paris.

There is, however, one aspect of his intemperance upon which we would comment for transmittal by you to the Soviet Premier, if you deem it advisable. We refer to his remarks in Paris, Berlin, and Moscow which were directed at our forthcoming Presidential election.[77] We are

[76] Chelsea Plantation, the South Carolina home of Mrs. Marshall Field. For Stevenson's vacation there with the Finletters, see *The Papers of Adlai E. Stevenson,* Vol. VI, p. 374.

[77] In East Berlin on May 20, 1960, Premier Khrushchev stated that his country would not attempt to change the existing situation in West Berlin until after the

shocked, as all Americans must be, that the Soviet Premier would meddle in an American election for the apparent purpose of coping with his own domestic problems. We suggest that Mr. Khrushchev mind his own business and we Americans mind ours. The American people will choose their next President on the basis of his views and record and their own judgment. They do not now and never have needed the unsolicited advice of the Soviet Premier.

With renewed assurances, Mr. President, of our esteem,

Yours faithfully,

LYNDON B. JOHNSON

SAM RAYBURN

J. WILLIAM FULBRIGHT

ADLAI E. STEVENSON

Mrs. Eugene Meyer offered to make a contribution to help defray expenses for Stevenson's staff to answer all the fan mail he was receiving, and she suggested that he talk to William L. McFetridge of the Chicago American Federation of Labor, who was close to Mayor Richard J. Daley.

At about the time this letter was written, Theodore H. White visited Stevenson at Libertyville. He described how Stevenson analyzed the problems at home and abroad. "It was the Adlai Stevenson and the clear voice for which Americans in search of leadership were aching," White wrote. Then the conversation was interrupted by a lengthy phone call from New York. Stevenson was told that Eleanor Roosevelt was about to insist that he declare publicly whether he sought the nomination. White wrote:

> But he felt his position was clear. He had stated it over and over again. He felt the Party *must* beat Nixon, the country would be unsafe in Nixon's hands. Thus, if the Party called on him to serve, he would serve as citizen or as leader or as nominee. But the Party had given him the chance twice. He would not demand it again, nor would he reach for it. Nor would he declare himself out of the race. He was not trying to stop anyone, or help anyone — why was not all this clear?

American presidential election. His statement implied that he wanted to ensure that he would not have to deal with President Eisenhower, who was under pressure from U.S. militarists. He indicated no preference for any presidential candidate but suggested that he would be willing to discuss the matter with whoever won the election. See the New York *Times,* June 3, 1960.

[*511*]

For an hour there in the sun he tried to resolve these turbulent thoughts into some clear answer that Eleanor Roosevelt could make public; and the telephone rang from Washington and again from New York, and one had the sense of a distant clamor calling for executive leadership. Yet he would not act. He would wait.[78]

To Mrs. Eugene Meyer[79]

June 9, 1960

Dear Agnes:

Thanks for your letter. Of course we would be delighted to have the money and can always find a way to use it, but I am not sure what our situation is. Blair is only now back from a trip abroad and I will tell him to expect some supplemental funds in case we need more help or have other incidental expenses due to the current troubles.

I am bewildered by all of the calls and incessant clamor for some kind of a declaration of *candidacy*. I have written today something I will send to Mrs. Roosevelt if she asks me, which I think should resolve any doubt, but I doubt if it resolves anything else, because I think Kennedy probably has enough votes to be nominated anyway.

With respect to your inquiry about Mr. McFetridge, my recollection is that he is a partisan Republican, although he plays pretty close to the Democratic organization in Cook County.

Affectionately,

ADLAI

I have been deeply grieved by all the press over Arthur Schlesingers letter.[80] I know the circumstances and <u>pray</u> it will be mentioned no more by any of *my* friends.

AES

If you send money I think your idea of sending it to me and to William McBlair, Jr is a good one — but you've done so much already please don't feel you must do any more!

AES

---

[78] *The Making of the President, 1960*, pp. 121–122.

[79] The original is in the Agnes Meyer files, Princeton University Library. The two postscripts are handwritten.

[80] Schlesinger, Henry Steele Commager, John Kenneth Galbraith, and others sent a letter to liberals throughout the country, urging support for Senator Kennedy. See the Chicago *Sun-Times*, June 8, 1960. When Mrs. Meyer heard of the letter, she announced to the press, "They are absolutely unrealistic as politicians and absolutely disloyal as friends." Chicago *Daily News*, June 10, 1960.

Mrs. Franklin D. Roosevelt considered Stevenson the only "mature person" among those possible for the 1960 nomination. In April, 1960, she had urged Governor G. Mennen Williams of Michigan and Walter Reuther, president of the United Automobile Workers of the World, not to endorse Kennedy.[81]

On June 10, 1960, Mrs. Roosevelt announced that she was joining some of her friends in a plea to convention delegates to nominate Stevenson. The collapse of the summit conference convinced her, she stated, that the country needed the wisdom, maturity and experience of Stevenson. She urged Senator Kennedy to accept the vice presidential nomination.

To Mrs. Franklin D. Roosevelt[82]

June 10, 1960

My dear Mrs. Roosevelt:

This is quite unrelated to the statement which I have just read, and which has left me a little shaken. Knowing me as well as you do, how you can say such nice things so often confounds me! — but more of that later.

Meanwhile, I have a message from Mary Lasker saying you do not plan to go to the convention. While I doubt very much if I become involved out there, I would think as a Democrat that your presence is important, symbolically and actually. Moreover, I hope you will reconsider and plan to be there. If there is any question about suitable rooms I am sure we can take care of that very well, or perhaps you will be staying with friends.

Affectionately and hurriedly,

ADLAI

To Mrs. Arthur Schlesinger, Jr.

June 13, 1960

Dearest Marian:

Bless you for that sweet letter. I am distressed by all that has happened, and that I should be the cause of any embarrassment to Arthur whom I love as dearly as ever, as I am sure you both know. I think we will all survive the present distemper.

[81] See Joseph P. Lash, *Eleanor: The Years Alone* (New York: W. W. Norton, 1971), pp. 285, 286.
[82] The original is in the Franklin D. Roosevelt Library, Hyde Park, New York.

How I wish the blessed Schlesingers were invading my premises this summer!

Much love,

On June 13, 1960, Mrs. Franklin D. Roosevelt issued the following statement to the press.[83]

On Friday of last week I telephoned Mr. Stevenson because of a mis-understanding which seemed to exist, both on the part of Professor Schlesinger and Professor Commager and of Chairman [Paul] Butler of the National Democratic Committee as to whether he would be a candidate or not, and I asked to clarify his position for me. I quote his statement here:

"I am deeply affected by what you have said of me but I do confess that your request that I 'clarify my position' presents some difficulty.

"I realize that under present circumstances even a restatement of what has been said before may be given unintended and un-warranted interpretation.

"I have as you know, taken no part in Presidential politics for the past three years. And I do not now intend to try to influence the nomination in any way by 'endorsing' anyone or trying to 'stop' anyone, or by seeking it myself.

"I have not made and will not make any 'deals' with anyone.

"I am not, as you recognize in your statement, a 'declared candidate.' This leaves only the question, again in your terms, of 'shirking public responsibility.'

"I have declined repeatedly to comment on questions about a 'draft.' I think I have made it clear in my public life, however, that I will serve my country and my party whenever called upon."

From this statement, I think you will find it clear that he is a candidate, since there is a sizeable number of people who are asking him to accept the responsibility of being the candidate for the Democratic party in the next Convention. . . .[84]

People feel the need of maturity and have confidence in Adlai Stevenson, and are asking him to run again. I will have to confess

[83] The original is in the Franklin D. Roosevelt Library, Hyde Park, New York.
[84] The New York *Times*, June 13, 1960, carried the headline "Stevenson: Not Candidate. Mrs. Roosevelt: Yes He Is." Doris Fleeson wrote: "Mrs. Roosevelt came through for her friends again. The best working politician in the trade secured from Adali Stevenson the 'will serve' statement about his candidacy he was unwilling to give anyone else." Chicago *Daily News*, June 14, 1960. On June 12, 1960, the St. Louis *Post-Dispatch* had endorsed Stevenson as the "ablest and best fitted" for the presidency.

that I personally would not ask him to run because I think being twice defeated and now running in all probability against a man who will make the campaign as disagreeable as possible, is something no one can ask a person to do, but Mr. Stevenson has answered my query for clarification of his position in exactly the way I thought he would, and I stress again his words "I think I have made it clear in my public life, however, that I would serve my country and my party whenever called upon."

To Mrs. Franklin D. Roosevelt[85]

June 13, 1960

My dear Mrs. Roosevelt:

I have no words to tell you how your endorsement has moved this "tired old face." I will have more to say about that when I see you.

Meanwhile, I must also say that I am anxious about your reaction to my statement that "I am not a candidate." Obviously this is what I had to say, because it is true, and to be consistent with all I have said for the past three and a half years — i.e., that I will not seek the nomination at the convention. I suppose the confusion arises over availability to serve if called upon and being a candidate, which means to seek, if my understanding of the word is correct. I do not want people to feel I have altered my position of not seeking and yet readiness to serve if called upon.

I need not add that this letter is not for the public eye but to explain to you my attitude lest I have appeared ungracious.

With all my thanks and much love,

Yours,
ADLAI

Arthur Krock described in the New York Times, June 14, 1960, the meaning of the word candidate as defined by Noah Webster, "a candidate is one who offers himself, or is put forward by others." Krock wrote there was no evidence that Stevenson rejected Webster until June 12, 1960, when he stated: "I will not seek the nomination for President at the 1960 Democratic convention — therefore I am not a candidate."[86]

[85] The original is in the Franklin D. Roosevelt Library, Hyde Park, New York.

[86] In an undated handwritten letter to Mrs. Edison Dick, Stevenson wrote: ". . . Now try to tell me from time to time simply and quickly what you think I'm doing wrong and right, more importantly the former, for you're objective. I don't know what the recent criticism you refer to is; there is so much! But what interests me most is to keep the record clear that I'm not and never have been a 'candidate'

Krock observed: "Stevenson is taking on the highest authority in etymology as well as Mrs. Roosevelt, a combination against which mere intrepidity cannot possibly prevail." Stevenson clipped this column to the following note to Mrs. Roosevelt.

To Mrs. Franklin D. Roosevelt[87]

June 15, 1960

My dear Mrs. R —
    I surrender!!

With love —
ADLAI

To Mike Monroney, Jr.

June 17, 1960

Dear Mike:
    Thanks for your letter and for the enclosures, which I have not seen and give me a much better impression of the extent of this activity.[88] It all makes me a little uncomfortable, but also reminds me how much I owe to you and your father for resurrecting my political corpse!

Cordially yours,

To Harvey Curtis Webster[89]

June 21, 1960

Dear Mr. Webster:
    I enjoyed our talk on the telephone, and I have also read with much interest your telegram and the excellent statements you have prepared. However, you must forgive me if I feel obliged to decline to make any further statements. I really feel that more statements do not clarify but only contribute to the abuse. Ever since November 1956 I have repeatedly said I would not seek the nomination again and I have repeatedly left no doubt that I would also respond to my party's and country's call,

---

for the nomination — and some steps are being taken in N.Y., at least to correct that confusion. . . . Evidently 'draft' and 'availability' etc. are words that have seldom been used in our politics which is accustomed only to people who *want* an office. Do you suppose the time will ever come when no [one] dares seek nomination for President — and the party seeks him? I hope — I doubt. . . ."

87 This handwritten note is in the Franklin D. Roosevelt Library, Hyde Park, New York.

88 The Washington Draft Stevenson operation.

89 Chairman of the Stevenson Committee of Kentucky.

so I can't believe it is necessary to repeat it and contribute to the feeling that I have now changed my stance and I am an active candidate.

I hardly need add that I am deeply flattered that people like yourself would spend so much of their time, energy and money promoting me for the nomination — for a third time. I should think you would all be really fed up with me by this time!

Cordially yours,

Mrs. Eugene Meyer wrote Stevenson describing her speaking in California to the draft Stevenson groups.

To Mrs. Eugene Meyer[90]

June 21, 1960

Dear Agnes:

I hear you got off to Saratoga after all. I am back now after a couple of hectic days in New York on business. Some time I hope when it is convenient you will call me on the telephone, preferably at Libertyville, in the evening or early morning and let me bring you up to date — or rather you bring me up to date!

Later: I have now just found your recent letters, and also read the advertisement in Monday's Times[91] flying back from New York this afternoon. I think all the advertising has been extremely good and certainly the reports I hear from all sides about the rallies in the New York area and elsewhere in the country touch my torpid old heart. I thought the story of the young people who solicited with a tin cup and then left it sitting on the street corner in New York when they had to return to work and found $15 in it when they came back in the evening almost incredible.

I really haven't tried to follow the delegate count and you may be right, although I have a feeling that our young friend may get enough delegates lined up to make it on the first ballot. I really don't know and find strength in the fact that I don't seem to care. I am afraid this will make you angry. But it gives me a confidence about what I say and do.

[90] The original is in the Agnes Meyer files, Princeton University Library.
[91] A full-page advertisement placed in the New York *Times*, June 20, 1960, by a Stevenson for President committee with E. F. Roosevelt as honorary chairman. The headline read: "These 142 delegates may determine the next leader of the free world. We urge them to heed the growing demand for ADLAI E. STEVENSON."

I share your shock at the easy way Republicans rationalize their support of Nixon. The whole process has started all over again and I have no doubt that by the time the Republican press has done its work he will look more pure and righteous than the saints. But I am used to that and don't in the least despair about a Democratic victory. If we don't get a change pretty soon I dread to think of the further deterioration of our prestige and its implications for the future. I have a feeling that some of this is beginning to come through to the people.

I also find in the mail your checks and your advice about handling the fan mail. We have taken steps in the latter direction and the money will be extremely helpful in connection with that and some inevitable abnormal political expenses.

I hope you are slowing up a bit. From all I hear I gather that your activity has been relentless!

Affectionately,
ADLAI

P.S. I loved the quote from Thomas Mann — and how true it is!

John Steinbeck wrote Stevenson a number of lengthy letters — the Stevenson Letters, he called them — analyzing personalities and events in a pungent style.[92]

To John Steinbeck

June 21, 1960

Dear John:

The "Stevenson Letters" will be my most precious legacy — to literature, political science, history — and my children. Or would you prefer a library? Which one? Anyway, keep it up. You lift my heart — and I think you must be better when you are not working than when you are working. Or is it catching flounders? Whatever it is, I wish I were doing it with you.

Instead I am struggling with my mail, my visitors, my law business, my travels, my speeches, and all that is unimportant. As to politics, I don't struggle, I sit and let the tides rise and fall. I suspect by election time they will have fallen low enough to leave me secure, private, disen-

[92] For a discussion of their relationship, see Sanford E. Marovitz, "John Steinbeck and Adlai Stevenson: The Shattered Image of America," *Steinbeck Quarterly*, published by the English Department, Ball State University, Muncie, Indiana, Vol. 3, No. 3 (Summer, 1970), pp. 51–62.

gaged — and available for a visit to Sag Harbor and a conference with the Lily Maid[93] about her Knight.

So — let the dam break and please don't repair it.

Yours. . . .

p.s. Yes, as you say, I'd rather be Right than Nixon, too.

To Gerald Johnson

June 21, 1960

Dear Gerald:

I appreciate your recent jottings. I hardly know what I am expected to do. I must have made it clear four years ago that while I will not seek the nomination after having had it twice I will not decline it if the party wants me. Why this is called "indecisive" or "confusing," etc. etc. I cannot for the life of me understand.

I have to speak at the Democratic fund-raising gathering briefly the night before the Convention opens, and also I will be called on for a speech (not an acceptance speech!) during the convention. If Gerald Johnson has any elevating contributions for those utterances they would be more than welcome.

Bless you, my dear friend, and please don't feel that I was deeply wounded by the defection of The New Republic.[94] Affection, after all these years, would come as a surprise!

Cordially yours,

To Lady Barbara Jackson

June 21, 1960

Dearest Barbara:

Your letter of June 4 has just come and I have lifted liberally, as always, but just when and where I shall use it I don't know. Have no fear, however, that I will find an early occasion to, especially the idea of exploiting Nixon's impetuosity. Here the papers all over the country are blossoming with full page "draft Adlai" advertisements and children are filling tin cups with pennies and young people "madly for Adlai" are circulating petitions. Meanwhile, Mrs. Roosevelt and I have declared a tacit truce to our dignified duel over my status. Even [Arthur] Krock has entered the act with a Webster's definition that includes "one offered by others for public office." I could send you sheets of clippings,

93 Mrs. Steinbeck.
94 The magazine endorsed Senator Kennedy.

cartoons and the usual spawn of wickedness and weariness. Instead, I will just enclose a couple of recent letters from John Steinbeck which [will] give you a few moments of amusement. I somehow manage to maintain my unconcern with little difficulty, in spite of the defection of Arthur Schlesinger, Kenneth Galbraith, et al, who are doing no more than I urged them to do long ago. The effect, however, has been to lay a triumphant call to other liberals and the denunciations fly thick and fast, while A. and K. have "crept out of the country," in Julie Jeppson's[95] idiom. Marion [Marian] Schlesinger has joined the pro-Stevenson forces with a loud declaration, and Stevenson is highly amused and languid at Libertyville. Kennedy's tactics are coercive, but effective, and if he is nominated, as I suspect he will be, all will be well, but if he slips the victims will turn on him like wolves, I fear. He has made an excellent foreign policy speech[96] and verbally handles everything well. But the entourage is ruthless and tough beyond the virtues in that word, I fear.

But all this I am sure you know from even better informed sources than I.

Tell Robert [Jackson] that I have been quite out of touch with the aluminum business since Reynolds went to England a month ago. They urged me to come with them but I could not leave the country what with the work load and the unfinished piece for Look.[97] The latter, by the way, is still unfinished. Indeed, I haven't even "cracked a book" since I returned from South America. But, of course, that has not deterred me from speaking pompously on several occasions, including the Council on Foreign Relations in Chicago and New York. The country is lovely, the weather dreadful, and the fever chart wild. We all miss you!

Love,

William Attwood had a lengthy conversation with Senator and Mrs. John F. Kennedy on June 14. On June 17 he prepared a memorandum for Stevenson on this meeting.[98] Kennedy said that his conversation with Stevenson on May 21 had been "rather unsatisfactory." He could not understand why Stevenson, if he did not want the nomination him-

---

95 Mr. Schlesinger's secretary. Schlesinger and Galbraith were abroad.
96 Senator Kennedy, speaking before the Senate on June 14, 1960, had proposed that the United States restore its international leadership by reevaluating its non-communicative policy toward China and had urged new talks with the Soviet Union.
97 "Our Plight in Latin America," *Look,* November 22, 1960.
98 This memorandum is in the possession of Mr. Attwood.

self, refused to endorse him. Kennedy said that a deadlock was an unlikely possibility but even if it did occur, Stevenson could not count on support from Lyndon Johnson, who did not like either Stevenson or Kennedy. Furthermore, he emphasized that Stevenson could not expect Kennedy support unless Stevenson supported him first.

Attwood remarked that many people thought a Stevenson-Kennedy ticket offered the best choice of defeating Nixon. Attwood wrote: "Kennedy then emphatically stated that anyone who still thought he would take second place was deluding himself. . . . I suggested that it would be hard to refuse the Vice-Presidential nomination if the Convention selected him. He replied that he would refuse it."

Later in the conversation Kennedy asked Attwood for his "objective" opinion as to whether Stevenson or Chester Bowles would make the best Secretary of State. Attwood wrote Stevenson: "I naturally replied that you were the only possible choice, and he pointed out that he had said as much on several occasions. . . . Kennedy went on to say that you and he had been hurt by your criticism of the Summit fiasco but that he still felt you would be an asset to him politically as Secretary of State — if you were interested. . . ."

Attwood concluded the memorandum: "The total impression I was left with was a mixture of cockiness and uncertainty, a consuming drive to win and a total absorption in political strategy. And I feel sure that much of what he said was intended to get back to you."

When Stevenson read the memorandum he said to Attwood: "How could I ever go to work for such an arrogant young man?"[99]

On June 22, at the suggestion of William Attwood, Walter Johnson (who had been cochairman of the 1952 Draft Stevenson Committee)[100] accompanied Attwood to Libertyville. Johnson wrote the following memorandum of part of the conversation.

Bill started the conversation by informing Adlai about a telephone call from John Sharon. Sharon reports (1) Mike Monroney and Governor [David] Lawrence were planning to have breakfast in Washington on June 23; (2) Jim Doyle has been put in charge as chairman of all draft groups across the country. The headquarters for these non-delegates will be separate from a political headquarters that Monroney is trying to open at the Biltmore [Hotel].

[99] William Attwood, *The Reds and the Blacks: A Personal Adventure* (New York: Harper & Row, 1967), p. 7.
[100] See Walter Johnson, *How We Drafted Adlai Stevenson* (New York: Alfred A. Knopf, 1955).

(3) The Monroney group challenged Kennedy's figure of 709 delegates and figures at best he has only 609.

I then explained to him that for months I had been receiving letters from people I didn't know from all over the country asking what they could do for Stevenson. I told the Governor that I always answered these people telling them to keep it up and to get in touch with Jim Doyle, [and] more recently with the Illinois Committee [to draft Stevenson] led by Victor di Grazia. I then explained that I was not directly involved in any of this draft movement because, as he well knew, the 1952 draft had been honest and I felt that if I became identified with the 1960 group, people would charge both Stevenson and Johnson with having been dishonest in 1952 and 1960. Then I told him about the New York City committee, the opening of their new headquarters on June 20th, and Mrs. Roosevelt's press conference there. I explained to him how beautifully she handled the question of why you weren't a candidate. She explained to the press that you had the experience, the brains, the wisdom, and then she paused and said the humility to be President. She then said, you see, he is not a candidate in the ordinary sense because, being a man of humility, he doesn't think he is the only person who can save the world. Then she added, in her own inimitable way with the charm of a great lady but with the devastating knife she can put in, that the others who were so avidly campaigning lacked — and then she paused and then said — shall we say they lack sensitivity. Adlai was very pleased about this report.

I then said that New York has 6,000 volunteers and is calling 6 public meetings this week. I then explained that Mrs. Marshall Field, I, and the four organizing chairmen of the Illinois Committee were signing an ad for next Monday's *Daily News* and *Sun Times*. He suddenly looked at me and said, "Well, why are you doing this? Have you been organizing all this? You and a few of your friends?" I immediately explained to him that I and a few of my friends like Mrs. Field were not responsible for the groups that have sprung up over the last few months but particularly mushroomed since the U–2 incident. I explained to him that I wasn't interested in talking to him as a personal friend, that as an historian I would analyze this as the demand of literate Americans (and many of the leaders of these organizations, I explained, were young business and professional people) for leadership; that they were sick and tired of the way we had drifted in the 1950's. They wanted no more postponement of great decisions that had to be made. They had, therefore, turned to him as the man who could lead the nation. He seemed to be convinced by my statement, seemed to indicate some bewilderment over his strong appeal, but by no means did he display any dislike about its being done. At this point, Bill said that some of the heads of the draft-Stevenson committees were running into opposition from people who said well, he is not a candidate. Adlai leaned back in his chair, closed his eyes, and held his throat with his hand. Then he said, "Why can't these people understand my position? I said when I got back from Latin America I wasn't a draft evader. I said in 1952 the office should seek the man. I wrote in the introduction to my 1952 speeches the same thing." Bill and I immediately jumped in and said that people forgot and some people don't read. Adlai said he could go no further than what he had said, that he was not a draft evader.

At this point I shifted the conversation and asked him what he planned to say at the $100 a plate dinner Sunday night before the convention. The candidates are speaking and so is Adlai. I urged him to do something comparable to his speech of welcome in 1952 and develop, after he made five or six points about the Eisenhower administration postponing great decisions, moving on to the spirit of America which he developed so well in the Tabernacle Speech in Salt Lake in 1952.[101] This suggestion appealed to him, and Bill agreed to rough out an outline for that talk. Then we talked about the strategy on the balloting. He said he had given a great deal of thought to it, that at some point on the second or third ballot it is conceivable that he should probably throw his strength to Jack, if that seemed to be demanded at the time. He then went on to say that he was deeply concerned that if Jack didn't get it, Lyndon didn't get it, and the balloting went on to the eighth or ninth time, he would be nominated amid blood in a badly divided party. At this point I urged him to discuss at great length with Dave Lawrence Dave's analysis of the convention strategy. At that moment in the conversation, he seemed sympathetic to the idea. Then I explained to him that I just didn't see how Jack Kennedy could win the presidency. I expressed the fear that the above-ground and below-ground campaign against Jack would be disastrous, and I thought much of the Catholic hierarchy would do their best to injure Jack. Bill concurred at this point. I also said that Lyndon could not win the presidency, that a considerable loss would occur in the big cities if he were on the ticket. Bill and I both said that if Jack began to fade on the third ballot there had to be a bridge between the supporters of Stevenson and Jack personally. It couldn't be Adlai, we said, but we both thought Lawrence was the only possibility.[102]

[101] See *The Papers of Adlai E. Stevenson*, Vol. IV, pp. 158–163.

[102] Although Johnson did not record it in the memorandum, at approximately this point in the conversation, Stevenson observed that Kennedy was bright and able but too young and unseasoned for the presidency; Symington was simply not qualified; Lyndon Johnson was too regional a candidate to be a strong contender against Nixon. Johnson then said to Stevenson: "Look, Governor . . . You can't have it the same way [as in 1952]. It's utterly impossible. . . . Now, since you feel

Bill then referred to his memorandum of conversation with Kennedy about four days before [June 17], a copy of which Adlai has read. (Bill now has the copy read by Adlai, and the pencil marks on it, certain things underlined, and question marks are Adlai's. It is a very significant document.)[103]

At dinner we chatted a while about some of our amusing incidents on our trip around the world together,[104] and then Bill pushed again on the idea of a meeting with Dave Lawrence. Adlai now said he didn't see how he could do it. Such a meeting might leak out and make him look like a hypocrite, and so we dropped it.

The Governor was in good form, most interested in what we had to say, and I am convinced in no mood to throw a monkey-wrench into what had taken place. On the drive back Bill and I agreed that the first order of business was for Bill to call John Sharon that night so Monroney could be filled in on the conversation for their breakfast[105] on the 23rd, and if possible, Monroney be convinced by Sharon that they should phone Stevenson at Libertyville and simply say they were coming out. In our opinion, such a move on their part would conform to his conception of the office seeking the man, as he would be in no way initiating it.

To Marya Mannes[106]

June 24, 1960

My dear Marya:

I have your letter of June 22. It troubles me, because it reflects an attitude I hear expressed so often these days — and also because it is from you! First, let me say that I have always felt that in theory, at least, no one should seek his party's nomination for the Presidency; that an office so exalted and so impossible to fill should be beyond the presump-

---

the way you do about the other candidates, it seems to me it's beholden upon you to lift the telephone, call Dave Lawrence, call Mike Monroney . . . invite them to come out. . . . Tell them that you really do want this thing, that you're not going to campaign for it, but do want it." Stevenson said, "No, no, I can't do that." Walter Johnson, interview for Columbia University Oral History Project, June 16, 1966.

Johnson also stated in that interview: "It was quite clear to me that what he really wanted was to be drafted again, the same way he'd been drafted in 1952, with no real effort on his part. Effort means that you have to make commitments, and strings. He wanted to be drafted." See also Kenneth S. Davis, *The Politics of Honor: A Biography of Adlai E. Stevenson* (New York: Putnam, 1967), pp. 423–424.

[103] Mr. Attwood was unable to locate the copy bearing Stevenson's marks.

[104] See *The Papers of Adlai E. Stevenson*, Vol. V.

[105] With Governor David Lawrence.

[106] Author and staff writer for the *Reporter*.

tions or conceits of men; that to assert one's competence, indeed superior qualifications, for that office was a reflection of excessive ambition and arrogance and presumption.

But this attitude, I know, is not common, and I have no doubt that men will always seek the office instead of the office seeking the man. At all events, feeling that way, I have found it difficult to assert with any confidence that I was endowed above all other Democrats with the qualifications for this austere office. Having led the party twice, once by draft and once by desire, I have felt that it was hardly proper and becoming that I should seek that privilege again. If the party wants me, they can have me, of course. If, as you say, "the desire must be urgent and urgently expressed," then I am confronted with the further difficulty that I have taken the position consistently since 1956 that I would not seek the nomination again.

I hope you can understand at least some of this and forgive me for my reticence. It would be nice to talk about it — and other things, besides!

Cordially yours,

Harry Ayers, of the Anniston, Alabama, Star, *sent Stevenson a copy of an editorial endorsing him for the nomination. The editorial was critical of Senator Everett M. Dirksen and others for charging that Stevenson was appeasing the Soviet Union.*

To Harry M. Ayers

June 24, 1960

My dear Friend:

Every time I read an editorial from the *Anniston Star* my heart leaps. And then I have to read it again to be sure it is me!

If one of these days I burst from a distended ego, I hope you will feel guilty. But I like it! As for the nomination, I am beset from all sides by people who want me to be "an active candidate." I confess I don't understand it, nor the presumption, conceit and self-confidence in anyone who could ask his party to entrust him with the responsibility of the most difficult office on earth — for a third time.

I sent you a recent speech. When I think of the right wing Republican record before Pearl Harbor, their use of the word "appeasement" is sheer impudence. Telling Mr. Khrushchev about our politics is like trying to tell a blind man what a rainbow is like. It is all very difficult, and our positions are crumbling one by one around the world. Meanwhile, Eisenhower's popularity is rising. Ho Hum!

Cordially yours,

Mrs. Cyrus Eaton wrote that she and her husband had just returned from a trip to Central and Eastern Europe. People in those countries, she observed, regarded him as a great hope for the future. Mrs. Eaton was a delegate to the forthcoming Democratic National Convention.

To Mrs. Cyrus S. Eaton

June 28, 1960

Dear Mrs. Eaton:

Thank you so much for your letter and the fascinating report of your journey behind the Curtain. I am pleased, of course, that they trust me in those countries — and that you do too!

I do not share the thoughtless attitude of so many Americans that not to be feared, hated or mistrusted in the Communist countries is a breach of public honor. But in time we will learn that we must live, do business and compete with these countries, probably for years to come, and that to command respect and confidence will become indispensable to better relations. Somehow we seem to even confuse better relations with approval or adoption of each other's systems. I think that only maturity born of experience is going to solve these attitude problems and replace the black and white simplicities which you describe so well with the gray realities.

I hope to see a certain delegate from Ohio in Los Angeles!

Cordially yours,

On June 30, 1960, Stevenson attended a fund raising party in Washington, D.C., to help pay off the deficit from Senator Hubert Humphrey's primary campaign. Stevenson was met at the airport by several hundred supporters waving signs and shouting, "We need Adlai badly." Reporters asked him if he would object to having his name placed in nomination. He replied: "On the basis of my experience so far, I don't think it would make any difference whether I had any objection. No, I don't really."

Earlier, according to Chicago *Sun-Times correspondent Carleton Kent, Senator Mike Monroney predicted that Stevenson, who had refused to call himself a candidate, would have his name placed in nomi-*

nation and would win "after six, eight, or nine ballots." When asked if Stevenson had approved of this decision, Monroney replied: "We didn't ask, but I'm certain if his name is put in, he'll not ask for equal time to withdraw it."[107]

On June 29, 1960, the New York Post endorsed Stevenson for the nomination, stating: "At this critical moment, we believe the greatest single act of reassurance the Democratic Convention can offer to the country and the universe is the nomination of Adlai Stevenson for President and John F. Kennedy for Vice President."

To Dorothy Schiff[108]

July 5, 1960

My dear Dorothy:

I am a very lucky man! Many kind things have been said and written about me, some deserved and more undeserved. There have been some harsh and ugly, bitter ones, too, but they seem unimportant in contrast. And never more so than after a second reading of the editorial endorsement of Schiff and Wechsler![109]

I had thought to telephone you both to thank you, but on second thought I concluded to do it this way and not risk the excessive emotion. Somehow as I get older I get more sentimental — and especially about friends that have been so loyal, charitable and helpful for so long.

I will cherish this editorial always as a precious reminder of my momentary political resurrection in 1960. After reading so many political obituaries, your endorsement is all the more gratifying — if not convincing, especially to delegates!

I wish we could have a good talk sometime — all three of us. I won't even try to convince you that it is *not* the best ticket. And I *will* try to convince you that I am grateful beyond measure that you think so.

Yours,

P.S. It suddenly occurs to me that you will both be in Los Angeles and maybe we can foregather there.

---

[107] Chicago *Sun-Times*, July 1, 1960.
[108] Publisher of the New York *Post*.
[109] James Wechsler, editor of the New York *Post*.

To Norman K. Winston[110]

July 5, 1960

Dear Norman:

I have been disturbed to learn that Estes Kefauver faces a hard, close fight in the August 4 Democratic Senatorial Primary in Tennessee.

I am disturbed because Senator Kefauver has been such an effective champion of sound, progressive national policies during the past two decades, and also because of some policy positions espoused by his opponent. Kefauver's defeat would mean not only the loss of a courageous, liberal Democrat, but also would be a setback for all that is most hopeful in the South.

I understand that money to defeat Estes is flowing into Tennessee from the special-interest groups who would welcome his removal from the Senate. He urgently needs financial support to counter this massive effort.

I would not write you, and a few other close friends who have been so generous to me on many occasions, were I not convinced that Estes' contest is really significant.

If you care to contribute to his campaign — and I hope you will want to if you have not already done so — please send your contribution to me at my office, here in Chicago, and I shall pass it along immediately to Estes.

Cordially yours,

P.S. I am really embarrassed to be imposing on you — again!

To Lady Barbara Jackson

July 8, 1960

Dearest Barbara:

I had thought to write you a long, wise letter before this — to thank you for the piece for the Convention, and to bring you up to date on a myriad of matters, all critical and unimportant! I am enclosing a series of utterances on arrival at the airport, where some five or ten thousand shouting, banner waving, undaunted Madlys for Adlais will greet me, and for Democratic dinners to follow. The major speech which I shall have to deliver at the end of the Convention, I have not been able to do much about. And here your manuscript will be extremely helpful. I must also do "Face the Nation" Sunday afternoon and a myriad of other trying chores.

110 A New York City housing and real estate developer.

As for the Convention itself, I have little doubt that Kennedy will be nominated, perhaps promptly. I have tried hard to keep aloof from any possible accusations of stop-movements and at the same time not chill the demonstrations of wide popular confidence and support which should be valuable in the campaign to follow. Anxieties about Jack's youth and religion are arising, but they will not suffice to head off a nomination, in my judgment. I pray that they won't suffice to head off an election, either. I have no doubt, however, that Nixon will conduct a high-road low-road campaign against him and that there will be much ugliness before it's over.

. . . I will report again from Los Angeles if that mad house permits. Meanwhile, much love, and a caress for the "magnifikent"!

Yours,

On Friday, July 8, Stevenson taped an interview with CBS in his law office in Chicago.[111]

QUESTION: Governor Stevenson, on the eve of your traveling to the Democratic Convention there are certain questions which seek an answer. Why, sir, haven't you sought the nomination?

ANSWER: I felt that after the 1956 campaign it wasn't fitting and proper that I should ask my Party, which had given me its highest honor twice to run against General Eisenhower in two campaigns — that I should ask for a third nomination. It seemed to me that the proper, appropriate thing for me to do was to stand aloof, step aside and let the Party decide what it wished to do in the future without any intervention on my part.

QUESTION: Without any intervention, sir, do you expect to be drafted, and if you were, would you accept a draft?

ANSWER: I think I have made it clear that I will serve my Party if called upon in any capacity that I can. As Presidential nominee I was in the same position in 1952 when I didn't seek the nomination and was drafted. I don't expect a draft. I think it's quite unlikely that anyone in our country can be drafted twice.

QUESTION: That you believe is unlikely.

ANSWER: I think it's unlikely, quite unlikely.

QUESTION: What, then, is all of your reaction to this great surge of

[111] Punctuation has been supplied by the editors.

Stevenson sentiment that has shown up around the country in the past month — the Draft Stevenson movements and the petition signings?

ANSWER: I had no idea that there was such an extensive grass-roots support and confidence in me still, and it's been deeply moving, deeply touching and very gratifying. I've read my political obituary so many times that to discover that I was still alive politically was a great relief. So I hope very much that this enthusiasm and support and goodwill that has been generated in these grass-roots Draft Stevenson movements can be — will be — rallied around our candidate of the Democratic party, whoever he may be in the forthcoming campaign.

QUESTION: Speaking of whoever the candidate . . .

ANSWER: Would you give me an opportunity to express my gratitude to all of these enthusiastic people who have given me such comfort and such confidence.

QUESTION: Whoever that candidate might be, Governor, will you expect to join in any stop Kennedy or stop Johnson movement once you are at the Convention?

ANSWER: No, under no circumstances. The only stop movement in which I propose to join is the stop Nixon movement.

QUESTION: That's as far as you intend to go?

ANSWER: Indeed.

QUESTION: What political part do you expect to play in the Convention?

ANSWER: I don't know what political part I will play in the Convention or what opportunity I will have. I suspect I will speak to the Convention at its end after the ceremonies conclude. I have felt that my role in this pre-Convention period as long as I wasn't a candidate, as long as I wasn't seeking delegates, was to concentrate on the issues, to encourage if I could a thoughtful discussion of the important problems that our country confronts which it will have to debate and discuss — and I hope intelligently and I hope thoughtfully — in the ensuing campaign this summer, because we are, at one of the watersheds of history, in one of the great crises of our national life.

QUESTION: You told me some months ago, sir, that the Republican campaign would be conducted on the items of peace and prosperity. Do you believe that you could effectively battle those Republican ——

ANSWER: Well, I think the item of the Republican platform of peace has been pretty well shattered by the bungling and the fumbling of the

Republican Administration in the past few weeks, something I think that a good many people have been aware of for a good long while, which has become now fairly transparent. As to prosperity, I hope very much that our country can continue prosperous. As to what the Republicans propose to do in the campaign, I don't know where they propose to put their emphasis. There are, of course, many many issues of infinite importance that we will have to confront. The rate of growth in the country, which the Vice President has derided as unimportant, I think is extremely important.

QUESTION: This is the increase in percentage that you are . . .

ANSWER: Yes, yes, of our economic development. Likewise the problems that we have to confront with respect to a greater unity in the Western world, which has been badly shattered by these recent developments. The problems of education, the problems of health, the problems of social security, medical assistance to the old, the extent to which we use our national resources for the social welfare requirements of the country, which has been somewhat neglected in these recent years. These are important decisions. The extent to which we are prepared to compete with the Russians, with the Communist bloc, in trade, in economic development, in the underdeveloped countries, in research, education and science. All of these fields are going to require great exertion by this country. Somebody must present this issue and present it clearly — give the American people a clear, precise understanding of what they confront. I've felt that this was my role and this is what I have tried to do.

QUESTION: You believe, then, that the Democratic nominee, whoever he may be, will have to present these issues in an understandable and extremely decisive manner?

ANSWER: Yes, and I hope we can get the Republicans engaged in the controversy — the Republican nominee.

QUESTION: Up till now, Governor, you have indicated that you choose to show no preference for any of the Democratic front-runners before Convention time. In fact, in December you described your position as one of vertical neutrality, but said, however, that you reserved the right to change your mind. Are you still holding that right in reserve?

ANSWER: Oh, yes, surely.

QUESTION: Or are you about to exercise it?

ANSWER: No, I haven't any present intention of exercising it, but I surely will preserve that right.

[531]

QUESTION: You still will preserve the right to change your mind?

ANSWER: Yes.

QUESTION: Thank you very much, Governor.

ANSWER: Not at all. It's been a great privilege to talk with you.

Among the early arrivals in Los Angeles to organize the Draft Stevenson campaign were James Doyle, John Sharon, Tom Finney, Jr., Mayme Miller, Thomas Morgan, Victor de Grazia, and Tedson Meyers.[112]

On July 5 Doyle announced to the press that neither Kennedy nor Johnson could win the nomination. Stevenson had, he said, enough first ballot strength to win on a later ballot. The next morning Stevenson appeared on the NBC Today television program and observed that his nomination was "possible but not probable." He stated: "I have not been in touch with Mr. Doyle for, I suspect, something more than six months, so that I am not at all familiar with what the distribution of the ballot is, or prospects for, as Mr. Doyle would suggest, my nomination in Los Angeles. . . . I perhaps should be more informed, but I am not."[113]

761 votes were required for the nomination. On the weekend before the convention opened, the Stevenson supporters estimated that Kennedy had 600 certain votes, Johnson had between 450 and 500, and Symington perhaps 100 or 150. The strategy of the Draft Stevenson people was to deadlock the convention. In order to achieve this, it was necessary that the states with favorite sons — Minnesota, New Jersey, Kansas, Iowa, and California — hold firm through the first ballot and not go to Kennedy. Moreover, on July 9, Illinois and Pennsylvania were still uncommitted.[114]

Stevenson flew from Chicago to Los Angeles on Saturday, July 9. The weather was bad, the plane had to stop at Las Vegas to refuel, and he arrived in Los Angeles three hours late. On the plane, Stevenson read a New York Times story which referred to his "confused" position. He then wrote out in longhand a one-page statement which he handed to Willard Wirtz, saying, "This is what I want to say at the airport." Wirtz questioned the advisability of "one more statement." Stevenson did not issue the statement.[115]

112 See Murray, "Patronage and the Draft in the Nominating Process," for a description of the people involved and the strategy they planned to guide thousands of volunteers and meet with delegates.

113 New York *Post*, July 6, 1960.

114 White, *The Making of the President, 1960*, p. 158.

115 The original is in the possession of Mr. Wirtz. It bears his notation that "this is exactly the way the Governor viewed the whole affair."

Every day I read strange stories about what I am doing.

Well, I don't see why my position is so hard to understand.

I'm not doing anything. And I don't see why it was improper for me not to seek a third nomination on the one hand, or improper to say on the other hand that of course I would run if nominated — and run hard because it is so important to win this time.

I thought and still do that it would be presumptuous and selfish to ask for a third chance after two defeats.

And I thought and still do that no one in good health could or should refuse to run if nominated.

I have tried for 3 years to avoid talking about a draft so as not to instigate one.

But evidently some Democrats think it improper to stand aside and that I should actively seek the nomination again. I am sorry we disagree on the proprieties. Perhaps in my shoes they would see more merit in modesty.

Then, still on the plane, Stevenson took up a draft of "Notes for Informal Remarks at Los Angeles Airport" which had been prepared on the basis of Stevenson's discussion with Wirtz earlier in the week and which was largely a direct reflection of Stevenson's specific suggestions. From this draft, Stevenson wrote out in longhand two pages of notes from which he spoke at the Los Angeles airport, where a crowd of people (estimated by the police as between 5,000 and 10,000) who had waited several hours gave him a tumultuous welcome. Wirtz recorded in his files at the time that "these notes are almost precisely what the Governor said in the conversation earlier in the week."[116]

NOTES FOR INFORMAL REMARKS
AT LOS ANGELES AIRPORT

You make it hard for me to speak.

There came to me once before, under very different circumstances, Lincoln's confession once that he was too old to cry but he hurt too much to laugh. Well, I don't really *hurt* at all right now — but we better start *laughing* so I won't embarrass myself all over the place.

You can't know what is in my heart.

---

[116] Instead of using Stevenson's two pages of notes, which are too sketchy to be intelligible to the reader, the editors decided to use the draft "Notes for Informal Remarks at Los Angeles Airport." Both documents are in the possession of Willard Wirtz.

And yet maybe you can. For I suspect that many of you here have been together before.

That was when our Republican friends — and I use that phrase loosely! — were talking about its being "time for a change." What irony the years have wrought. In a period of the most revolutionary change the world has ever known, the one thing that has stood stock still, dead in its tracks, was the administration in Washington.

And in 1956 they said theirs was the peace party and Ike its prophet. But now all is in disarray — and America is groping in the tinder dry ruins of their peace.

I guess they've been trying to decide which club to use. There was another Republican administration, you remember, that built a foreign policy around the injunction to "speak softly but carry a big stick." The modern version is "Don't talk about problems while putting." Or, perhaps, "U-2 can make a foreign policy."

This year they have changed their slogan a little. Now they say "it's time for a changer" — and they have their man: Revolving Richard, who has changed so many times he doesn't know whether he's coming or going. Well, we do. He's going!

Your being here today makes me think — more seriously — of something Woodrow Wilson once said when he was greeted as you have greeted me. I don't remember it exactly, but it was along these lines: that "Great outpourings like this are not in compliment to an individual; they are the demonstration of a purpose. And all I have to say is that, whoever may be the Democratic candidate for the Presidency, I pray God he may be shown the way not to disappoint the expectations of such people."

And when you say here today, by being here, that we have a common purpose, I can only say in reply that I will do always all I can to serve that purpose.

We believe together that politics is important business — worth giving up a Saturday afternoon for, and a lot more besides.

Partly, I suppose this is because we want to be part of something bigger than we are — to give ourselves meaning. We see Democracy as a restless, demanding, animate ideal. We want to do our part to make it work — for us as individuals, and for the country and for the whole world.

It's partly, too, I guess, because we realize — especially today — that the whole future depends on political decisions here in the United States. We want to make these decisions, and not have them made for us. We don't want to see this society of ours drifting. We don't want to be shipwrecked on other people's reefs. We know this is the 20th Century; that we need the world, but that the world needs us, too, and our way of finding the right answers together — as a people.

But I feel a speech coming on — and you know how dangerous this is!

Thank you for coming here. You give me a warmth of feeling I cannot express — and a very big lump in my throat. I am proud to be a native son of California and an Angelino!

Saturday evening Stevenson attended a party in his honor given by Mrs. Eugene Meyer. Among those present were Mrs. Franklin D. Roosevelt, Mrs. Albert Lasker, Mr. and Mrs. Barry Bingham, Mr. and Mrs. Thomas K. Finletter, Senator and Mrs. Mike Monroney, Tom Finney, John Sharon, Mrs. Edison Dick, Senator Joseph Clark, Miss Genevieve Blatt, Mrs. Harriet Welling, Mrs. Ronald Tree, and Mr. and Mrs. Philip Graham.[117]

Shortly after midnight, Governor David Lawrence of Pennsylvania met with Stevenson for a two-hour conversation. Just prior to this meeting some of Stevenson's friends urged him to tell Lawrence that he would announce his candidacy. Lawrence had been an important figure in the 1952 draft, had stated many times that Stevenson was the best qualified person to be President in 1960, and up to this July 10 meeting had held the Pennsylvania delegation uncommitted.

Stuart Gerry Brown interviewed Stevenson about this conversation and wrote: "AES thought the entire conversation consisted of explanations by Lawrence as to why he was coming out for Kennedy despite his preference for Stevenson.[118] *Lawrence said that he had been subjected to great pressure by the Kennedy forces and by Kennedy supporters in his own organization, especially Congressman [William] Green of Philadelphia."*

Brown asked Stevenson "if he detected in the conversation any suggestion that Lawrence was trying to invite some hint by AES that he wished Pennsylvania support — if perhaps this possibility was what had caused the great length of the conversation — AES said that the idea had not occurred to him, but that looking at the situation in retrospect,

[117] For a description of the party, see Katie Louchheim, *By the Political Sea* (Garden City, New York: Doubleday, 1970), pp. 86–87.

[118] In an interview with Lawrence on June 13, 1961, Lawrence told Robert Lewis Piper that he had advised Stevenson that Illinois's vote for Kennedy meant there was no hope for him. Lawrence added, "I told him that he should nominate Kennedy, but he said that he wouldn't. He said he couldn't let down all those people who had come out to Los Angeles to work for his nomination; he couldn't let them down." A copy is in the Stuart Gerry Brown papers, Syracuse University Library.

it was possible. For his own part, AES told Lawrence that he was not a candidate, was not seeking delegates, was grateful to his friends for their efforts, and did not expect to be nominated, though he would, of course, accept it if it should happen."[119]

On Sunday, July 10, the Illinois delegation caucused (Stevenson was not present). Then Mayor Richard J. Daley announced to the press that Illinois would cast forty-nine and a half votes for Kennedy, two for Stevenson, one uncommitted, and the balance for Senator Stuart Symington.

Meanwhile that day, Tom Finney described to Stevenson the full range of the activities being undertaken in support of his nomination. "Successively and hour by hour other old friends whom he had first brought into politics but who now marshaled independent political power pressed him to act," Theodore H. White wrote.[120]

On Monday morning, after the Pennsylvania caucus, Lawrence announced that his state would cast sixty-four votes for Kennedy, eight for Stevenson, and the rest were scattered. Minnesota meanwhile heard Eleanor Roosevelt and Senator Herbert Lehman plead for Stevenson, but the delegation could not decide. Governor Orville Freeman was to place Kennedy in nomination and Senator Eugene McCarthy was to place Stevenson in nomination.

On Tuesday morning California caucused and decided to cast thirty-one and a half votes for Stevenson and thirty and one-half for Kennedy. Theodore H. White wrote: "Now for the first time (although too late), the Stevenson forces had a cluster for maneuver; their belated, leaderless, but spectacular last-minute exertions had begun to pay off."[121]

On Tuesday Stevenson spoke to the Minnesota delegation, which was ready to break for him, but again he would not summon them to vote for him. Later that afternoon he visited the convention floor to take his seat in the Illinois delegation, and spectators in the galleries and the delegates alike erupted. The arena became a bedlam, with the people in the balconies roaring, "We want Stevenson." Willard Edwards wrote in the Chicago Tribune, July 13: "He was pushed, dragged, pulled, yanked, and hauled along, almost losing his feet. His face was crimson and he was bathed in perspiration while maintaining a fixed smile which sometimes was replaced by a scared expression."

The permanent chairman of the convention permitted the demonstra-

---

[119] "Notes on a Conversation with Adlai E. Stevenson, November 14, 1960," in the Stuart Gerry Brown papers, Syracuse University Library.
[120] The Making of the President, 1960, p. 163.
[121] Ibid., p. 162.

tion to proceed for ten minutes and then called on "the delegate from Illinois" to come to the rostrum.[122]

After thanking the delegates for their welcome, Stevenson quipped: "After getting in and out of the Biltmore Hotel and this hall, I know who you are going to nominate. It will be the last survivor."[123]

At 12:15 Wednesday morning Stevenson spoke to a group of New York delegates. He reiterated what he had said so many times before. He had received the nomination twice and he would not be "so immodest as to ask for it again." One Stevenson supporter in the New York delegation who attended this meeting wrote later that Stevenson had not helped the situation with his polite but insistent refusals to seek the nomination.

On Wednesday, as the nominations began, thousands of Stevenson supporters marched outside the convention hall and inside the galleries filled up with Stevenson banners and placards. "Certainly the high point of drama in the Los Angeles Convention was the placing in nomination of Adlai E. Stevenson by Senator Eugene McCarthy of Minnesota," Theodore H. White wrote. "In magnificent voice, holding the crowd with the rhythm of his cry, toying with the crowd, letting it respond when he asked questions, McCarthy pleaded for Adlai Stevenson. 'Do not reject this man,' he pleaded. 'Do not reject this man who has made us all proud to be Democrats. Do not leave this prophet without honor in his own party.' "[124]

Before the nominations began, Stevenson placed a call to Mayor Daley. He had been under pressure from Mrs. Roosevelt, Senator Monroney, Senator Lehman, Thomas K. Finletter, and others, to make an appeal for support from his home state, which was controlled by Daley. Stevenson reiterated his position as a non-candidate but agreed to make the call and express the concern of Mrs. Roosevelt[125] *and others that in*

[122] Stuart Gerry Brown wrote: "As he approached the rostrum, physically set upon by his well-wishers, he sensed that he could probably exploit the opportunity in such a way as to greatly enhance his own candidacy. He says that his chief thought was that this would be immoral and a betrayal of his own principles, since no other candidate had a similar opportunity." Interview with Stevenson, March 29, 1961, in the Stuart Gerry Brown papers, Syracuse University Library.

[123] Many people, including Senator Eugene McCarthy, told Brown that this statement cost Stevenson the nomination. "AES thinks that this may be so, but he has no regrets," Brown noted. Ibid.

[124] *The Making of the President, 1960*, p. 165.

[125] After Kennedy was nominated, Mrs. Roosevelt was exasperated by Stevenson's having neither told her to stop her efforts nor ever clearly urged her to go ahead. When Mrs. Roosevelt held a press conference before the nomination, Stevenson introduced her and then left the room. Lash, *Eleanor: The Years Alone*, pp. 293, 296.

view of the fact that his name was to be placed in nomination, there should be some Illinois support for him. When Stevenson reached Daley, "Daley again asserted that he could do nothing for him since he had not been a candidate, but said that he 'would see what could be done.' It was clear to AES, however, that Daley had been all along a chief bulwark of Kennedy strength and would stand firm, as he did. Stevenson was of the opinion that even at the last moment Daley had the power to shift the Illinois delegation — at least a great part of it — from Kennedy to Stevenson, had he wished to do so."[126]

Theodore H. White wrote that in view of Daley's position any real hope of a Stevenson candidacy ended. Stevenson supporters left Los Angeles "some in sorrow and some in bitterness," according to White. "Yet neither sorrow nor bitterness was warranted. . . . Stevenson as an agent of American politics had left behind him such an infection as no other defeated aspirant for the Presidency ever left. He had left behind the virus of morality in the bloodstream of both parties; there was a permanent monument to him in the behavior and attitude of the victorious candidate; and also of his antagonists, the Republicans."[127]

On the first ballot, Kennedy won with 806 votes. Johnson received 409; Symington, 86; Stevenson, 79½; and there was a scattering of votes for others. When the first ballot ended, the nomination was made unanimous.

On July 15, Stevenson introduced the Democratic presidential nominee to the Convention.[128]

I have come to say goodbye — but not farewell.

This is not the end of a journey. It is a beginning — a new and splendid beginning for the Democratic party and for America. And it is my privilege to present the leader of that new beginning, chosen here in Los Angeles in accordance with our time-tested practices.

As I look about me I am sure that never before have so many ex-candidates assembled. Their number seems to me symbolic of the difference between the Democratic and Republican parties — we Democrats believe in an economy of abundance, not scarcity!

Far and wide people struggling to plant the tender seeds of democ-

---

[126] Stuart Gerry Brown, "Notes on a Conversation with Adlai E. Stevenson, November 14, 1960," in the Stuart Gerry Brown papers, Syracuse University Library. In *The Making of the President, 1960,* Theodore H. White gives a different version of the telephone conversation with Daley (p. 167), as does Irv Kupcinet in "Kup's Column," Chicago *Sun-Times,* July 15, 1960.

[127] *The Making of the President, 1960,* p. 168.

[128] The text is from a press release.

racy have followed the stirring drama enacted here in Los Angeles. They have seen how our party system works. And they have noted how yesterday's competition for party leadership becomes today's solidarity for party victory.

Twice I have been the beneficiary of this last and glorious hour of the nominating process of the Democratic party. And twice my spirit has been enriched by the confidence of millions of Americans. But the spontaneous outpouring of labor, loyalty and love in the past few weeks and, finally, here in Los Angeles has been the most enriching experience of my life.

I have no words to express my thanks; but I do have words to express my hopes — my hope that all of you who have lifted my heart will share my enthusiasm for this new beginning for the Democratic party and for our country; my hope that everyone of you will join me in making this new beginning a reality in the election next November.

For too long our nation has been groping in a mist of uncertain values. Now, at last, we have the promise of deliverance — the promise of a return to the realities of our times, the promise of the clarity of direction and the magnanimity of purpose which have illuminated America's proudest hours.

We have spoken at the Convention our disquiet, our distress about the place of America today in the eyes and minds and hearts of the world.

These past years of quiet drift have been years of quiet decline. Softly our country has slipped even closer to national peril.

Even through the din and clamor of the Convention we have been dimly aware of new crises in the Congo and in Cuba, new turbulence in the world, new threats from the Kremlin.

Let no one think that this rush of trouble is all purely a natural calamity, beyond our control and beyond our responsibility. Many things are indeed beyond our control; but many more are the direct product of our own unwillingness to identify and confront the hazards of this revolutionary age.

The headlines of today are the heritage of yesterday. They are angry symptoms which our nation dare not longer ignore — from which we can no longer avert our eyes. The time is long overdue not alone for searching self-examination, but for prompt, bold action.

To declare our ideals of equality, of justice, of peace is not to achieve them; that has been the tragic error of this epoch of illusion. To achieve an ideal is to face the hard actuality of choice and to conquer the hard necessity of decision.

We rejoice that we no longer have to argue with the Republicans over the great social reforms which we used to call the New Deal. And we rejoice, even more, that "internationalism" and the principle of collective security in this shrinking world is no longer a partisan dispute in America.

But we still see children growing up in slums, we still see children jammed into stifling classrooms, we still see older people whose needs go unmet, we still see some among us who are denied their birthright because of their race.

And we still see peace and the survival of our ideals of freedom and justice and order in the world more elusive than ever, after these listless, comfortable years of illusion.

Revitalizing our purposes, resuming our responsibilities, will demand great strength of arm, of head, of heart. But our nation cannot rest — our people will not rest — on the march toward that distant day when no one rattles a saber, where all dwell without fear, where the struggle is not to frighten and to enslave men, but to liberate their decency and to vindicate their dignity.

Just eight years ago on a similar occasion I said:

". . . more important than winning the election is governing the nation. That is the test of a political party — the acid, final test. When the tumult and the shouting die, when the bands are gone and the lights are dimmed, there remains the stark reality of responsibility in an hour of history haunted with those gaunt, grim specters of strife, dissension and materialism at home, and ruthless, inscrutable and hostile power abroad."[129]

Tonight the world is darker, the task of governing greater. But with "realism and responsibility" for our motto, America will become again what we once were, the guiding star of the hopes of free men.

The moments of American greatness have been those when its leaders have awakened the strength that lies in no one man, in no government, but in people.

Today we stand for peace, for an end to the strategy of terror, for making the world safe for disarmament. There must be enlisted in their cause the full strength of people's commitment to human values and moral principles.

It is that strength that we ask you to give us as we meet here in Los Angeles tonight — a united political party, on the threshold of a great campaign to awaken our country, to restore her purpose, to exercise her responsibility.

We have just spoken our pride and our thanks to one of the two men

[129] See *The Papers of Adlai E. Stevenson*, Vol. IV, p. 18.

who will lead us — that distinguished and talented veteran in the vital business of making democracy work — Lyndon B. Johnson of Texas.

Now we pledge our fealty to the man who above all others will be, in these next years, the instrument of our highest purpose.

He is a man brave and strong in his own right.

He is a man who embodies the hopes of the generation which is rising to power in the world.

He is a man whose passion for peace was bred in the agony of war.

And this man, too, has shown that capacity to draw forth the inborn goodness of mankind, the unquenchable power for good in people which no dictator can match or meet or long deny.

His devotion to the ideals of liberal democracy assures our nation swift and steady progress toward the full promise of our American heritage. His nomination restores the best hopes of the American past — the hope of vision, the hope of vitality, the hope of victory.

He will lead our people into a new and spacious era, not for us alone, but for our troubled, trembling world. And he will do it with the vigorous support of all of us who have fought our party's battles in the past — and who have lived to fight again.

The Democratic party proudly presents to the nation, to the world, to the future, our next President, John F. Kennedy.

After the Democratic Convention, Stevenson visited in Santa Barbara, San Francisco and Lake Tahoe, where he was the guest of Mr. and Mrs. Edward Heller, who had been his friends and staunch supporters since the 1952 campaign.

To Mr. and Mrs. Edward Heller[130]

July 25, 1960

My dear Hellers —

Nebraska below — Illinois ahead — Borden in the steerage — and Marietta [Tree] in the afterglow of Reno and Gary Cooper!![131] I don't know whether a new movie star has been born, but I'm sure an old political star is content and happy and refreshed — thanks to the Heller Tahoe Treatment! — and his son, Borden, is also babbling about the "opportunities" in California!

---

[130] This handwritten letter is in the possession of Adlai E. Stevenson College, University of California, Santa Cruz.

[131] Mrs. Tree played a bit part in a movie with Clark Gable — not Gary Cooper — then in production in Reno.

Thank you — my dear and patient friends — for that glorious and restorative interlude and for taking in my tribe. As for the latter, my only anxiety is that John Fell has tasted the DELIGHTS of life in California prematurely! But your kindness and Ed's counsel to him will, I'm sure, be the happiest introduction a young man ever had to that state where I left a part of my heart long ago.

There was much to say about the future — the long, meaningful future — of our country and our party — but somehow it didn't seem just the time to try to say it. So forgive me if I was "repressed" — as the psychologists say — and another time we'll have a good talk about the things that matter.

Goodbye — thanks from us both — and long may you wave!

Affec —

ADLAI

P.S. . . .

PPS . . .

PPPS . . .

To Dore Schary[132]

July 25, 1960

Dear Dore:

The first thing that greeted me in Santa Barbara was "GOOD BYE, GOOD NIGHT, GOD BLESS— THE VOLUNTEERS." I have a feeling I know the author. I also have a feeling that the author has been good and gallant beyond my powers to express gratitude.[133]

When I reflect on the ovations, demonstrations and emotional earthquakes that tortured the police and the delegates in Los Angeles there always seems to emerge from that swirling mass the noble mien of Dore Schary — sometimes with a whip in hand, sometimes a manuscript, sometimes with a megaphone — and always with a smile.

I am afraid I was a lousy draftee — but I am sure no one had a better time — or has been so overpaid in love and loyalty.

Thank you, my dear friend, and I hope it won't be long before we can

---

[132] The original is in the possession of the State Historical Society of Wisconsin.

[133] Mr. Schary wrote: "The Guv was, of course, referring to all that took place in California during the '60 Convention. The 'volunteers' were people who knocked themselves out to make a wish and a dream come true. . . . Other candidates may have had better organization, a more aggressive candidacy, but none had a constituency that loved them as much as we loved Adlai Stevenson during those hot July days in 1960. The Governor knew this and when he saw the sign that had been prepared to greet him in Santa Barbara, he knew it came from us — and by us I mean all of us." Letter to Carol Evans, May 28, 1971.

have some joyous post mortems and perhaps even a little explanation of your magic and magnificent alchemy.

Yours,
ADLAI

P.S. Much love to Miriam.[134] I hope she survived the crisis as well as I have!

To David Lawrence

July 26, 1960

Dear Dave:

It was good to see you in Los Angeles. With the Convention behind us, I, too, look forward to the campaign which we *must* win! As an old and close friend — in politics and out! — you know as well as anyone else the depth of my conviction that the security of our future was never more dependent on a Democratic victory in November. I will do my best to enlist support for our leaders and our program. And if there were a chance to do a little campaigning with one David Lawrence — nothing would please me more!

Sincerely yours,

Bill Mauldin, cartoonist for the St. Louis Post-Dispatch, wrote Stevenson that he had set a standard by which "they're going to be measuring candidates for a long, long time."

To Bill Mauldin

July 27, 1960

Dear Bill:

Bless you, my dear friend, for that letter — and for your special contribution to those years of loyalty that all but drowned me in Los Angeles.

It is comforting — really — to have you say that my behavior was not too exasperating or confusing to my friends. I felt that I had no other course; that to seek a third nomination would be impertinent.

I wish we could meet once in a while. My old friends are far more important to me than I am to them.

Cordially yours,

134 Mrs. Schary.

To Mrs. T. S. Matthews

July 28, 1960

My dear Martha:

Thanks for the last and the one before the last. They give me feelings both good and different from the usual suffocating sentimentality of my correspondents.

I am content. I thought it impertinent to seek a third nomination, and I did not. But the outpouring of love and loyalty across the country and in the streets of Los Angeles and at the convention surprised and moved me. I count myself a very rich man indeed. That so many people should have wanted the nomination for me after two defeats adds to my contentment.

Of course I will campaign for the "ticket." How much and where and when I don't yet know. But I am leaving today to see Kennedy and talk it over. Beyond the campaign I have no assurances of any kind nor can I ask any. He repeatedly indicated during the primary campaign that he would want me for Secretary of State. But there has been no technical commitment nor am I quite confident yet whether our views coincide sufficiently.

Meanwhile, there is a campaign to fight and an election to win. It would [will] be tough, rough and dirty — and unenlightening — I fear. If you have any moments of ugly realism in that rustic retreat,[135] please translate them into glorious, soaring prose and send them along at once — what America should mean, what America does not mean, etc. etc. Imagine my telling you!

And some day let's do get tight in a quiet place. You talk about politics and I will talk about poetry. It will be nice dozing in the sunlight.

Fond regards,

To Lady Mary Spears[136]

July 28, 1960

Dearest Mary:

Please don't be too upset. I thought it impertinent to ask for a third nomination. But the outpouring of love and loyalty and the demonstra-

[135] Mr. and Mrs. Matthews were in Spain.
[136] The original was in the possession of General Sir Louis Spears at his death on January 27, 1974. His correspondence is now in the possession of Churchill College, Cambridge University.

tions and support across the country and at Los Angeles have been a rich reward for my services. The Kennedy operation was, as you know, powerfully financed and organized and prolonged and the consequences were virtually inevitable. But Kennedy is an able man and there should be no possible question in your mind about his superiority to Nixon — one of the few people in my life I really deeply distrust and dislike.

Kennedy has asked me to come to see him this week and I have no doubt he will want me to campaign most extensively this fall. Beyond that I have no present information about his intentions. But my campaigning this fall brings to mind the possibility that you might write some bits and pieces about America which I can use and which would contribute to our perspective, especially of the world scene and America's role. We are certain to have a brutal campaign, with Nixon travelling the high road and all his supporters the low road of the [Joseph] McCarthy type, accusing us of being soft on communism, appeasement, etc. Do send along anything you can that you think needs saying.

With affectionate wishes to you and Louis [Spears].

Devotedly,
ADLAI

To Lady Barbara Jackson

July 29, 1960

Dearest Barbara:

I am dictating this hurriedly at Agnes Meyer's en route to Hyannis to see Kennedy. It will be followed, I hope, by a proper letter soon.

Yours of July 14 distressed me. There is a note of anguish on your mind about the state of the world, about Robert [Jackson]'s illness and your own discontent with your book.[137] I pray that he has really recovered. I wish I understood more about his condition. I can imagine that after so many years in that climate and post[138] there must be an accumulation of fatigue, both physical and psychological.

I am sure you are right about the deterioration in America's position but here it is little known or understood. The Republican Convention has drowned the country in reassurances and it is apparent that the Republican campaign will be pitched in the theme that all is well as could possibly be, that any criticism by the Democrats is either unwarranted or malicious and certainly anti-American, probably somehow related to Communist sympathy.

---

[137] *India and the West* (New York: Norton, 1961).

[138] Sir Robert Jackson had been stationed in Ghana since 1953.

Kennedy is going to send me out to campaign very actively. After consultation with Mrs. Roosevelt, Senator Herbert Lehman et al I am planning to agree to eight major speeches, two in California, two in New York, Philadelphia, St. Louis, Denver and somewhere else. Doubtless more will be added later. I will concentrate on foreign policy, of course. I will badly need the "Stevenson people" who number several million and who are a little disaffected at present for a variety of reasons. He will, of course, try to delay any indication about the Secretary of State and may not want me at all, also for a variety of reasons. But in any event I must and want to help as best I can even without assurances on that score.

I expect you will have to stick to your MS. now but if any time becomes available for writing you know how helpful it is. I will have no staff save for Bill Wirtz and [William] Attwood and perhaps some contributions here and there on an ad hoc basis. Hence any material that you can send me will be most precious.

I am going up to Maine next week for a few days with Walter Lippmann and Tom Finletter and then back to Libertyville by the 7th or 8th of August. Please let me know what your situation is and will be through October when you can. I wish it included travel in this direction instead of Australia!

With much love

P.S. Nancy [Stevenson] and all the boys were in Los Angeles and we had a glorious time there. I suspect I was the most relaxed person there. While the draft movement came to a predictable end the outpouring of love and loyalty was surprising and moved not only me!

On July 31, Stevenson spent four hours with Kennedy at Hyannis Port, Massachusetts. At a joint press conference, Stevenson appealed to his backers to give the "same vigorous support" to Senator Kennedy that they had given him. Kennedy observed: "I hope, Adlai, they give me the same vigorous support they gave you in Los Angeles."

Stevenson stated that the Eisenhower-Nixon Administration had lost the initiative diplomatically and "put our people to sleep." "The big issue," he asserted, "is how to live in the world without surrendering to communism and without war."[139]

Stevenson suggested to Kennedy that after months of campaigning he would need to be brought up to date on foreign policy if elected. The senator asked Stevenson to prepare such a report for him. Arthur M.

[139] New York *Times*, August 1, 1960.

Schlesinger, Jr., who visited with Kennedy a few days later, wrote that Kennedy was "rather impressed" with his conversation with Stevenson. "He apparently found general agreement on foreign affairs and was quite surprised by AES's shrewdness on campaign problems." Kennedy told Schlesinger that he wished he had more rapport with Stevenson, that "Stevenson obviously had it with Jacqueline; but he always was conscious of strain when he and Stevenson were in direct contact."[140]

Stevenson and Kennedy did not discuss whether he would become Secretary of State. Kennedy told Schlesinger, "I would not ask him to help me now if I did not think of him as playing a role in the future."

Stevenson stayed at Chatham, Massachusetts, with Mrs. Loring Underwood, her daughter Lorna (who had been a close friend when Stevenson attended Harvard Law School), and Lorna's husband, George Sagendorph.

To Mrs. George Sagendorph[141]

August 3, 1960

My dear Lorna —

A reunion and recall of almost 40 years in a howling hurricane is something I won't forget! It was a glorious interlude. With your blessed mother at the head of the table and you girls all about I thought time had stood still. And for you I think it has!

You were sweet to take me in and on this tour of one night stands Chatham and the beloved Underwoods compensates for all the difficulties.

I don't know (and really don't much care!) if the forget me nots worked! I spent most of the day with the Kennedys, found it agreeable, their mood optimistic & efficiency high. I think he expects rather more campaigning of me than I had in mind for this fall. We shall see. Please give much love to your mother & all the family — and so many, many thanks to you and George —

Affec —

ADLAI

---

[140] Letter, Schlesinger to Mrs. Ronald Tree, August 8, 1960; Schlesinger, *A Thousand Days*, pp. 66–67.

[141] This handwritten letter is in the possession of Mrs. Sagendorph.

To James E. Doyle[142]

August 3, 1960

Dear Jim:

I had thought to telephone you long before this but I have been constantly on the move since Los Angeles and have been doing one-night stands in Santa Barbara, San Francisco, Lake Tahoe, Libertyville, New York, Mt. Kisco, Osterville, Chatham, Hyannis, Mishaum Point, Amenia — and on and on. Please get no wrong impression that I have started to campaign for the nomination after the convention!

But I shall be back in Chicago and Libertyville by the 8th or 10th. I hope thereafter it will be convenient for you and your lady to come down for a night with me and a good long talk. I promise not to try to tell you how grateful I am for all you did and how patient you were with me. But there are futures to talk about too!

Yours,

To Mrs. Franklin D. Roosevelt[143]

August 7, 1960

My dear Eleanor —

Before the convention several people around the country sent money to my office "for expenses." For awhile we returned the checks. Toward the end some of the contributors became insistent and we made a "Los Angeles Fund."

We have used the money to pay the travel expenses of several principals in the Draft movement and it makes me feel much better.

The outpouring of loyalty and love moved me deeply, as you know. I can't repay them for what they *did*. But in a few cases at least I *can* repay them for what they *spent* — with this money which is not mine any way.

So I am enclosing a check for $1000 for your travel and for David Gurewitsch's.[144] *Please* keep it; do with it as you will. I'll feel a mite better — even if I can *never* thank you for my "finest hour."

I had a long and frequently interrupted talk at Hyannisport a week ago. He wanted suggestions on how to meet the youth and inexperience

[142] This letter was dictated over the telephone from Maine, where Stevenson was vacationing.
[143] This handwritten letter is in the Franklin D. Roosevelt Library, Hyde Park, New York. It was written from Maine.
[144] Mrs. Roosevelt's physician and close friend.

charge, and asked me to campaign for him which I will do, of course, if not as much as his managers may want. There was no hint of his plans about the State Department and I said nothing. He was much concerned about New York — the Negro and Jewish vote especially — and how to get the reform group, the independants and Stevenson people, to really work for him. His interest and concentration seemed to be on organization not ideas at this stage, which I suppose is proper.

I will be back in New York in mid-September but I hope to be in touch with you before that — or when you get back. I wish you were *really resting* this summer!!

With so much love and gratitude —

ADLAI

To John Fell Stevenson[145]

August 7, 1960

Dear John Fell —

I am here for a few days visiting Ruth Field. . . .

Mr. & Mrs. Finletter and Mr. & Mrs. Barry Bingham are also here. The weather is fine; also tennis and sailing, but the water is icy cold! Yesterday I sailed with Ruth and her capta[i]n (she has a big cruising motor boat that sleeps 6) in a sail boat race. Running with the wind they all put out spin[n]akers — red, blue, striped, solid etc for all the world like Hankö in Norway. We were about 5th of 15 as we approached the finish — when we piled up on a hidden rock! and that was the ignominious end of our race.

I had a talk with Kennedy who wants me to campaign extensively but hinted nothing about his future plans as far as I am concerned. After visiting in several other places I am anxious to get home now and get back to work — and to see you.

. . . I am so eager to see you! and so glad you evidently like S.F. [San Francisco]. . . . I'm going back[146] on Tuesday. I'll be there continuously I *think* until about Sept 10 when I start campaigning first in Wis, then NY. Please let me know your dates at home as early as possible.

Love
DAD.

---

[145] This handwritten letter is in the possession of John Fell Stevenson. It was written from Dark Harbor, Maine.
[146] To Chicago.

To Eugene McCarthy[147]

August 10, 1960

Dear Gene:

Last night I listened again to your nominating speech. Someone sent me a record of it, and I am told it sells for $25.00. I could not value it more if it were purest gold.

I think it is the most eloquent utterance I have ever heard — at least since Newton Baker's League of Nations speech back in 1924.[148] Certainly it was for me my "finest hour" and the pinnacle of a long and varied career. That I could number among my supporters for a third nomination for President one who is destined for such universal respect is my most enduring gratification. I only regret, like Garfield, that the nominator did not become the nominee.[149]

I wish you and Abigail[150] were going to stay a night with me in Libertyville some time soon — and bring the girls.

Affectionate regards to you both.

Yours,
ADLAI

To Mike Monroney, Jr.

August 10, 1960

Dear Mike:

If there were decorations for gallantry above and beyond the call of political duty you should be festooned with medals! Certainly few have labored longer for a poor cause than you — and I am inordinately grateful. That I should have been blessed with the counsel of one Mike Monro[n]ey is more than I had a right to expect. To have had you in addition makes me not only very proud but profoundly grateful. And I hope our collaboration will continue — in more fruitful causes!

With affectionate regards, I am

Cordially yours,

---

[147] The original is in the possession of Mr. McCarthy.
[148] See *The Papers of Adlai E. Stevenson*, Vol. I, pp. 149, 490.
[149] James A. Garfield, who placed Senator John Sherman in nomination at the 1880 Republican Convention, received the nomination on the thirty-sixth ballot.
[150] Mrs. McCarthy.

To Mrs. Marshall Field

August 11, 1960

Dearest Ruthie:

Please excuse this hurriedly dictated letter. I got home according to schedule after a strange and wonderful visit with my Yugoslav and American relatives[151] in Camden [Maine] and a mad dash to the Bangor airport which Zlatko, the violinist, couldn't find, having lived in Camden only twenty years! At Libertyville and Chicago I was greeted by an appalling accumulation of work, visitors, etc. etc. And now I am deep under water *again!*

. . . I hardly need to tell you what a glorious, gay and restful interlude that was. Surely *your* harbor and Dark Harbor is as happy a refuge as I have ever found — and I'll be back!

Hurriedly and affectionately,

To Lady Barbara Jackson

August 11, 1960

My dear Barbara:

I have your note of August 2 on my return after a couple of weeks of one night stands in the East in New England. What awaits me here has left me in a state of black depression. I can't seem to get on top of my mail, my visitors, my phone calls and, of course, the article on South America is still in the pre-reading, let alone writing stage. Meanwhile, my time is almost gone and I am desperate — also as always! I will have to speak a lot this fall, although confine it largely to major engagements, but there will be more of those than I can do well. With Bill Wirtz's help I have tried to draft a letter to some of my former contributors and enclose a draft. . . . It will at least give you a little idea of what I have been thinking about, or perhaps more accurately what Wirtz has been thinking about for me! I also enclose an editorial from the Sun-Times which results from a talk I had with them the other day. I wish I had a Felixstowe[152] where I could creep off for some real escape and do some thinking, reading and writing, but I have foresaken all hope. Which, of course, makes any contributions from you even more welcome than ever — something I can say of no one else!

---

[151] Zlatko Balokovic, a well-known Yugoslav violinist, was married to Ellen Stevenson's aunt.

[152] A resort on the coast of Suffolk, England, where Lady Jackson had attended school.

Please send me any material you can, saying the things that you think need saying from where you see us. I want to talk this autumn not only sensibly and with dignity but also with an eye to my foreign audience, which seems to be large and attentive still.

Very confidentially, Kennedy has also eagerly accepted my suggestion that some study be commenced of the problems that he will face and the steps he must take, both after the election and after the inauguration, to lay hands on our foreign policy. I have put George Ball in charge of an extremely small and secret working party on this project and enclose a copy of a preliminary outline which may be of possible interest to you. For obvious reasons I want no publicity about this.

We are largely preoccupied now with [Fidel] Castro and the Congo. At last the administration is waking up to the necessity of doing something about Latin America. It is also a late and lamentable response to Khrushchev's penetration in Cuba. But the Congo is something else, and here the feeling seems to be that the UN is our only hope for the survival of order and reason.[153] Whether we are cooking up any post pacification policies I don't know and rather doubt. From what little I have heard, even Lumumba seemed to be an unknown to our State Department. And what little I have heard from people in New York who met him there has increased my fears. If there are things we should be saying and doing about Africa now, and especially in this campaign, I would welcome them particularly. Certainly your line that Africa is politics not economics for decades to come epitomizes the situation. But what do we do to aid the politics? . . .

I won't go on now; indeed I can't. But short of a visit to Libertyville, words from Felixstowe would be my greatest blessing.

Devotedly,

To John Sharon

August 11, 1960

Dear John:

I had hoped for an opportunity to see you before this, and I count this a poor way of thanking you for your relentless, effective and anonymous promotion of your non-candidate this spring and summer. I have

[153] In July, 1960, shortly after the Congo became an independent republic, two of its provinces declared themselves independent of the central government headed by President Joseph Kasavubu and Premier Patrice Lumumba. Lumumba appealed to the UN for military aid to cope with the ensuing troop mutinies and separatist disturbances, and on August 12, Secretary-General Dag Hammarskjöld led UN troops into Katanga province. The UN troops remained until June, 1964, but unrest and fighting continued for several years thereafter.

heard from so many people about your superhuman efforts, and if what happened at Los Angeles was a tribute to your energy and sleepless resourcefulness it was also for me a most enduring and unforgettable event in my hectic career.

Thank you, my dear friend, and let us continue to collaborate — in more fruitful causes!

Cordially yours,

To Mr. and Mrs. A. S. Mike Monroney

August 11, 1960

My beloved Monroneys:

I am just back after a couple of weeks of one night stands through the East and New England, caucusing and cackling, and on top of the appalling pile is that blessed post card from the HF Bar Ranch.[154] It brings back the past and it also brought you back and more recently vivid memories.

I can't thank you for "my finest hour," but I can and will remember it forever and ever. We all know that a few people come through the mists of the mind very clearly in one's life, brilliantly illuminated by disinterest, unselfishness and genuine motives. So it is with both of you. I will always marvel at your persistence and skill in harnessing the affection and loyalty throughout the country which burst at Los Angeles.

How I wish we could talk about all these stirring events. And that reminds me that there is agitation afoot for a history of this curious phenomenon — the draft movement — and that you will doubtless be interviewed at length in due course. By whom and when, however, I don't know.

But I *do* know that I should like an interview with both of you at Libertyville after the session.[155]

Affectionately,

To Mrs. Eugene Meyer[156]

August 12, 1960

My dear Agnes:

My one night stands through the East culminated with three lovely

---

[154] A ranch in Buffalo, Wyoming, where Stevenson stayed several times during his youth. See *The Papers of Adlai E. Stevenson*, Vol. I, pp. 36–38; John Bartlow Martin, *Adlai Stevenson of Illinois: The Life of Adlai E. Stevenson* (Garden City, New York: Doubleday, 1976), pp. 50, 82.

[155] Of Congress.

[156] The original is in the Agnes Meyer files, Princeton University Library.

blue and white Maine days at Ruth Field's with the Finletters and the Binghams and a gay house party. Now I am back here submerged again.

I find your letters and also have had a talk with Attwood.[157] I think you have done the right thing. He wants to and should work for Kennedy, and you should be relieved of further expense and should make any contribution to him [Kennedy] directly and not by this indirect means. Just what he will be able to do for me I don't know, but I am sure he can be helpful from time to time, and meanwhile I will try to develop other resources here, although it will not be easy. But I can do much more of my own work than in the past if I can only get on top of the ghastly accumulation on top of my desk and get the wretched article for Look written.

As for a real holiday, I have given up hope.

I can see from your letters that you are on top of everything again and as busy as ever. But please don't drink up all the 1928 champagne or the 1832 brandy. I'll be back!

. . . I know what you mean about the lack of spirit. I find it everywhere, but I suspect that will change as the battle advances. Kennedy called me yesterday to warn me about Bowles pulling out of the race in Connecticut and evidently to reassure me about the Secretary of State business.[158] I haven't the remotest idea what he has in mind. I am not sure *he* does. But we shall see. I also wanted to give Phil Graham some material about what I was doing for him. I wish I knew what Phil was up to.

Love,
ADLAI

P.S. . . .

P.P.S. And why don't you come to Libertyville and see where all your things are!

The recipient of the following letter — like so many other California admirers of Stevenson — was reluctant to work for Kennedy unless the candidate promised to make Stevenson Secretary of State.

---

157 William Attwood worked on the Kennedy campaign staff and then, in September, joined Stevenson's speaking tour to arouse Stevenson supporters to work for Kennedy.
158 Chester Bowles, instead of running for reelection to Congress, campaigned for Kennedy. He was later made Undersecretary of State by Kennedy.

To Bennet Skews-Cox

August 13, 1960

Dear Bennet:

I told you by telephone in San Francisco that I would keep you informed about developments. I had a long talk with Jack Kennedy and his entourage on Cape Cod, but I cannot report any hint on the matter that interests you especially. I really don't know what he has in mind, but he seemed most eager for my counsel on many aspects of the campaign and my active participation, and certainly I will help him as best I can, regardless of my future relationship, if any. I wish I could be more reasuring, but I cannot.

I will be in California during the fall and will hope for a talk with you then.

With all good wishes, I am

Cordially,

Stevenson wrote to several persons, including Archibald MacLeish, author John Hersey, and Herbert Agar, former editor of the Louisville Courier-Journal, *seeking their help in the forthcoming campaign.*

To Archibald MacLeish[159]

August 13, 1960

Dear Archie:

There has been descending on me these past two or three weeks the chill of realization that I face still another round of political forensics this fall — and worse prepared this time even than before. Twelve years now of almost constant utterance have left me distressingly barren of new words, new formulas, new ideas.

As nearly as I can now tell there will be as many as a dozen "major" speeches — perhaps more — to be made between Labor Day and the "first Monday after the First Tuesday . . ." And I am totally unequipped for them in terms of either staff or inspiration.

This is *not* a request for a speech draft — although I face shamelessly the possibility of being reduced to that later. My thought is rather to suggest to you here some of the preliminary thoughts I have had about

[159] The original is in the MacLeish papers, Library of Congress.

the prospect I face, with the hope of getting your reactions to them. And I do not conceal the fact that on previous occasion I have shop-lifted directly and liberally from your answers to similar communiques!

My purpose during the campaign will, of course, be to muster support for the ticket particularly among any who may have doubts I am in a position to assuage. I think of three groups to whom I may perhaps be able to speak with some special persuasiveness: the "Stevenson people" (who may perhaps be identified in terms of their a-political idealism regarding public affairs — more school teachers than labor leaders, for example — and the people marching *outside* the Arena at Los Angeles); those who feel as strongly as I do about the need for developing an affirmative foreign policy with at least a healthy measure of disregard for adverse domestic political reactions; those who may be at least subconsciously affected by the Republican talk about "youth." Are there others?

I suppose I will be talking more about foreign affairs than anything else. Is there some way of anticipating and meeting the "appeasement" and "soft on Communism" reactions? I want to hit the Truth business *hard* — both in terms of attack on the Eisenhower-Nixon policy of bland deceit about our situation and the difficulties which lie ahead and all around. How to counteract the Republican decision to exploit every statement that can be distorted into a suggestion that we are a "second rate nation" — even where the context of the statement includes full recognition of our infinite potential? And I should like to avoid as much as possible seeming always to be insisting that we have to put on a hair shirt. But isn't it right that we must not let ourselves be scared out of this?

What affirmative suggestions can be made in the foreign affairs field to dramatize the ideas? I do not want, though, to compromise the conviction that most of the "right" answers in this area are not dramatic, but depend rather on the better doing of fairly obvious things.

So far as discussion of disarmament is concerned, isn't there a proper emphasis suggested by my phrase, "making the world safe for disarmament"? Surely this is at least as much a matter of reducing the causes of war as the means of war; neither will be effective without the other; and "reducing" either is practically meaningless except in terms of steps toward complete elimination; we can never be half safe.

Turning to the domestic issues: I think there can be no compromising of the fact that we must do a great deal more on the education, health, old age, housing, etc. fronts. I assume that the official campaign position will have much of Seymour Harris and [John Kenneth] Galbraith (except for his sales tax)[160] in it. But how do we put our proposals so that they are no more exposed than is necessary to the distorted "fiscal irresponsibility" charge?

There is the question of how much — and what — I should say about the Republican candidate. What do you think?

There will be repeated occasion in every speech to indicate my support of Kennedy. I find myself wondering particularly about the best ways of counteracting whatever effect the "youth" charge may be expected to have — for this seems to be utterly unfounded.

These are no more than notations of what would occur to you anyway. And I will welcome, perhaps more than anything else, your more constructive suggestions of what newer approaches I should be taking.

And now if you wish to drop this in the wastebasket, please do so. And certainly don't let me intrude beyond your own interests on either time or energy. My position of intellectual and oratorical bankruptcy is perpetual, but sometimes even that is now wholly apparent to the audience — and I don't want to impose, especially on incorrigible friends.

Much love to Ada.[161]

Ever yours,
ADLAI

Mrs. Shirley Forbes, who had worked for Stevenson in California in 1956 and had worked hard for his nomination at the 1960 Los Angeles Convention, wrote that after Kennedy was nominated she would have sold out for a Knowland button and a glass of absinthe. But, she remarked, Stevenson's speech to the convention restored her to the human race. She wrote: "I am still marvelling at your ability to lift John Kennedy with the strength of your integrity from the position of pain and indignity [in] which we, your aficionados, had put him; your infinite finesse in infusing him with your dignity and wisdom that we might join in the fight for which, following his nomination, we had been reluctant and of which we had felt cheated." She added that perhaps power — which she saw as the ultimate Kennedy value — was perhaps a greater force than love. Unhappily, she continued, she would now teach this to her students. She concluded that she was going to a school for Sorcerers and Enchantresses "so that I may some day dialectically materialize you."

[160] John Kenneth Galbraith differed from the orthodox liberal view of the sales tax as a regressive and therefore undesirable tax, feeling that despite this it was better for the states to have such a tax than to be forced to curtail services for lack of the revenue it provided.

[161] Mrs. MacLeish.

To Shirley Forbes[162]

August 15, 1960

My dear Shirley —

How you can write — and feel — and *love!* I'm *glad* you didn't sell out for "a Knowland button & a glass of absinthe"; and I'm *elated* that I had something to do with your rejoining the human race. Because you are immensely human, and so am I!

Please, please don't give those boys *power* as a substitute for *love.* There *is no* substitute here below, and there above. And if you do — then there *will* be "an invisible curtain between us" — So there!

But you *won't*, because you *can't;* but you *can* impart, communicate, love and compassion, and even a *meaning* to "America" that you can't touch, chew, ride in, wear, watch or put in the freeze[r]. And your meditations "can never become presumption," tho my replies — snatched from moments on airplanes like this one — *can*, and, alas, have!!

I apologize — but please keep on "tempting" me — and *loving* me — and *you* don't need a school for sorcerers and Enchantresses!

Gratefully — fondly —

A DLAI

On August 13, 1960, Sara Roosevelt, the thirteen-year-old daughter of Mr. and Mrs. John Roosevelt, fell from a horse and died of a brain hemorrhage.

To Mrs. Franklin D. Roosevelt[163]

August 15, 1960

My dear Mrs. Roosevelt —

I've heard the sad news about your granddaughter and send you this belated note of sympathy and love. With all you have to bear and do this further misery — just when you should be feeling peaceful and relaxed — seems grossly unfair.

You have more love and devotion than anyone alive; and I know that *sustains* you. I only wish that *mine* could somehow comfort you and

162 This handwritten letter is in the possession of Mrs. Hamlin Dunlap Smith, the former Shirley Forbes. It was written in pencil aboard a plane between Youngstown and Chicago.

163 This handwritten letter is in the Franklin D. Roosevelt Library, Hyde Park, New York.

ease your burdens. I like to think you would promptly let me know where and when I could ever help — because —

I love you very much,

ADLAI

Mrs. John B. Currie, an ardent supporter of Stevenson since 1952, asked him if a news story that he had delayed for forty-eight hours before refusing to place Kennedy in nomination was accurate. She reported that she had written Edward R. Murrow after his TV comments on the convention: "Stevenson gave us something to brag about, something to be proud of, something to believe in and follow to the barricades if necessary. We joined the party because he was in it." Mrs. Currie concluded her letter to Stevenson: "And we thought it might help sometimes to know that there are, in Cornwall [Connecticut], two people who recognize the warmed-over Stevensoniana in the speeches of both parties. . . . They haven't begun to catch up to what you said in 1952, and the New Frontier . . . owes more than a little to the New America. We remember."

To Mrs. John B. Currie[164]

August 16, 1960

Dear Bethia:

Heavens, woman, you're making me feel a little unmanageable too! Tell John to start worrying!

And — in case you're *really* interested — I did not keep Kennedy waiting 48 hours about nominating him. I kept him waiting — *if at all* — only overnight until I could find and consult with my principal "drafters" — Senators [Mike] Monroney, [John] Carroll, [Eugene] McCarthy, etc. They insisted on putting me in nomination again and felt I could not "let down" my friends all over the country by nominating Senator Kennedy.

But you are right that I wanted to be neutral with all the contestants and did so with considerable dexterity for difficult months of pressure from all sides.

And you are also right that while I thought it impertinent to ask for the nomination a *third* time, I would have accepted a draft and "run like crazy mad" — as you put it in that eloquent Currie idiom!

I loved that letter to Ed Murrow. You've said many beautiful things

---

[164] The original is in the possession of Mrs. Currie.

[559]

about me — but nothing finer. I have copied it and will keep for my old age and reflections — and both will be welcome!

I am glad you recognize the kinship between some recent and less recent utterances. Few did — but "warmed-over Stevensoniana" pleases me immensely — and all the more for your recognition of it too. I *was* amused when I read that Kennedy and Nixon had both taken Stevenson's speeches to the conventions with them.

The black-faced sheep are fine. I hope you are, and that the visit together isn't permanently postponed. I would even welcome John!

Thanks — and long may you wave —

ADLAI

To John F. Kennedy

August 17, 1960

PERSONAL AND CONFIDENTIAL

Dear Jack:

May I suggest that if your representatives are discussing details of your debates with Nixon that you give some thought to an agreement to exclude any extended discussion of Berlin because of the manifest delicacy of that situation. It is difficult to say anything very constructive about a settlement in Berlin without embarrassing future negotiations. Beyond a declaration of our intention to preserve our rights and do our duty lies the temptation to assert greater rigidity and inflexibility than the other fellow. Yet any discussion envisioning the possibility of permanent division of Germany, for example, would cause violent reaction in West Germany where such a thought is political poison for either party, as you know.

What I am trying to say is that it would be discreet not to take any chances on limiting the freedom of future discussion. And I suspect you agree that it is likely, at least at present, that the new President will be quickly confronted by Khrushchev's demands for new negotiations on Germany. He should not be hobbled by his "campaign oratory" and should be free to consider any and all positions with our allies. There are, as you know, some possibilities.

I "unilaterally" took a similar position in September 1956 — that I would not discuss Suez because the situation was "too delicate," although I was aching to have at 'em. A month later came the disaster and Eisenhower was the beneficiary of my restraint. So I write you with misgivings and diffidence.

Don't bother to acknowledge this. You are doing fine, if only the special session [of Congress] does not embarrass us — and I have had reassuring reports about aid from Mrs. Roosevelt and other old friends of mine.

Sincerely yours,

To George W. Ball

August 24, 1960

Dear George:

The enclosed memorandum on the Atomic Energy Agency may be of no interest, but I think it belongs with the post-election documents more than in my waste basket!

I'm also enclosing a letter from Peter Grothe of Senator Humphrey's office relating to his proposal for a "Peace Corps" and for bringing more cultural groups to this country from the under-developed areas. Perhaps this should go in your lesser ideas file.

Yours,

To John Steinbeck[165]

August 29, 1960

Dear John:

Our luncheon visit I am afraid has only stimulated an appetite that can never be satisfied, but I am grateful for even that short, good sample.

I told you that I had agreed to do an interview on "morals or something." I find on reference to the letter from the Ladies Home Journal that the discussion is about "strengthening the American character and stimulating the civic virtues in our society." Quoting further: "In almost every statement of issues and problems, mention is made of this need, but with very little development. Won't you help us to answer the question specifically? How can the sense of humor, or virtue, be taught or 'caught,' and by what institutions? What is wrong with American life that we seem unable to inculcate these virtues?"

It sounds to me as though "the winter of our discontent"[166] is on the same theme. If you could find time to give me a few reflections I would be grateful indeed. I suspect, however, that this is a pretty lightheaded discussion and hardly worthy of your thought. So if I hear nothing I shall not be surprised.

I called your daughter to thank her for her charming letter and the

---

[165] The original is in the possession of Mrs. John Steinbeck.
[166] The title of the novel which Mr. Steinbeck published the following year.

proffer of a ride to Sag Harbor.[167] The latter may have to wait another year, unhappily. She sounded a little bereft but steady and purposeful.

My love to the fair Elaine,[168] whose letter has charmed me all over again.

Yours,
ADLAI

John Fischer wrote that many of Stevenson's most ardent supporters were refusing to support Kennedy. He urged Stevenson to deliver a ringing speech "pointing out that a politically mature citizen owes his first allegiance to an ideal and a cause, rather than to an individual."

To John Fischer

August 29, 1960

Dear Jack:

Thanks for your letter of August 19. I am sorry I didn't see it ten days ago, but I find my mail quite beyond control.

I emphatically agree with you about my loyal and sulking friends. They must be animated somehow. I have tried with many, individually, but the earliest speeches must carry some thought of that kind. I wonder if you could put down your ideas of how to do it for me. Maybe I could use it in speeches I have to make, beginning in New York on the 14th, and then in the West.

Hurriedly,

To William Benton[169]

August 30, 1960

Dear Bill:

I have been leading a dog's life of late and find it wholly impossible to keep up with the mail — let alone do any writing for the campaign. And still more remote is thinking about the State Department in case Kennedy has anything in mind for me there. If he has I haven't heard about it!

I have finally written a little piece for Look on Latin America, copy of which has been sent to you. The manuscript of your piece for the

---

[167] The Steinbecks' home on Long Island.
[168] Mrs. Steinbeck.
[169] The original is in the possession of the estate of William Benton. See note 12 to Part Two, above.

[*Encyclopaedia Britannica*] Year Book and your letter of the 17th requesting critical comment has now come. I have dipped into the manuscript here and there and I am immensely pleased with what I have read. While anyone can pick away at another's work, I would find it hard to make any broad, sound, useful, critical comment — at least on the basis of what I have read. Rather, I am tempted to say I think you have reduced the volumes we brought back to something useful and extremely well done.

I am tempted to share John Howe's[170] view that perhaps it should be put into book form for early publication now that interest in South America is mounting with such rapidity.[171] Scarcely a year ago you could not sell an article on South America to the magazines. Now they can't get enough of them — thanks to Messrs. Castro and Khrushchev.

Please understand that I am only deferring a careful reading of the manuscript until I can get my head above water — if ever.

If it isn't too much to ask of you, I hope you will let me have your views on reorganization in the State Department in connection with some work I must do for Kennedy for the post-election period. Also, I would certainly welcome anything you can send me which will be helpful for speech material, especially in the foreign policy field this autumn. I am having more than the usual staff trouble — indeed, I have none except for dear old Bill Wirtz, who stands by faithfully.

. . . Thank dear Helen[172] for her card; and you don't know how often I have yearned for escape to the Baltic — or anywhere else.

Yours,
ADLAI

To Walter P. Jones[173]

September 2, 1960

Dear Walter:

I am presuming to send on to you a speech I made last night for the American Bar Association in Washington.

There were in attendance some 1500 British judges and lawyers, and the speech was addressed to them. It attracted very little attention in the press, but I would like you to have a copy and also to understand what I was trying to say: One, the British view the presidential alternatives with equal distress, although for very different reasons. Second, my

---

170 Mr. Benton's assistant for over thirty years.
171 It was published as *The Voice of Latin America* in 1961.
172 Mrs. Benton.
173 Editor of the McClatchy Newspapers, Sacramento, California.

intent was to reassure them that a Democratic Administration would want to draw closer to the British. But, third, the Anglo-American association must not peril the broader Western community relationship. Fourth, we can meet the competition of the East only by marshalling all of the resources of the West.

In other words, I was trying to reassure the British about the objectives of a Democratic Administration and also reassure our Continental allies that our reliance must be on the larger community. You know, I am sure, what misgivings the Germans and French have had about exclusive Anglo-American relations.

Just why I write all this I hardly know. Perhaps it is because I have been meaning to write you anyway to say that I am coming to California the end of the month on behalf of the ticket, and that I am hoping very much to be able to see you when I am there — to talk about the Party, and the candidates — what I think and what I know. I shall want even more to hear what you think and know.

I shall arrive in San Francisco on the 25th or 26th, and if possible will hope to see you there.

Cordially yours,

Carbon copies to: Miss Alicia Patterson, *Newsday*
       Robert Lasch, St. Louis *Post-Dispatch*
       Agnes Meyer
       Barry Bingham, Louisville *Courier-Journal*

Mrs. Eugene Meyer wrote Stevenson on September 3 praising his September 1 speech — "To read English again in a political address, what a relief!"

To Agnes Meyer[174]

[probably September 5, 1960]

Dearest Agnes —

Thanks so much for your Labor day letter & the Amalgamated speech. Struggling with my writched load I marvel more and more at your eloquence and creativity. What a gal! and what a help to me! I'll hope to see you at St. Regis Wed — but fear I must campaign for Van der Huval[175] in the late afternoon. Much love —

ADLAI

[174] This handwritten postcard is in the Agnes Meyer files, Princeton University Library.
[175] William J. vanden Heuvel, Democratic candidate for Congress.

P.S. Now just heard that Mike Monroney is $19,000 in debt from Los Angeles. Horrors!

To David K. E. Bruce

September 5, 1960

Dear David:

I was in Washington last week and talked at length with Jack Kennedy, Paul Nitze, George Ball and others about the confusion that has arisen since Kennedy appointed Nitze, yourself and some others to study "national security." Kennedy was at pains to make it quite clear to me that this was related to national security problems and not "foreign policy," in so far as they can be divided. He added, further, that he thought of it as an avenue towards the restoration of bipartisanship.

He was earnest in his request that the exploration of post-election foreign policy problems which you and George Ball and a few others have been working on should proceed; that he counted heavily on our conclusions for immediate direction after the election. I have been worried lest you might be confused and feel that these were wholly duplications.

Affectionate regards to Evangeline.[176]

Yours,

Carbon copy: To George Ball

To Mrs. T. S. Matthews

September 12, 1960

My dear Martha:

Thank you for those precious letters and your "thoughts on America." Obviously the Elder Stateswoman of Denia[177] is indispensable to my enlightenment, and I hope she will send along more and more reflections.

. . . As to your speculation on Mr. Kennedy's plans for me, if any, I can contribute no hint.[178] Meanwhile, however, I shall do my best to

---

[176] Mrs. Bruce.

[177] A Mediterranean seaport town in Spain where Mrs. Matthews was staying.

[178] Kennedy replied to those who insisted that Stevenson be named Secretary of State that Stevenson had met with him at Hyannis Port, that they had discussed international affairs, and that Stevenson would play an important part in the campaign. One such letter, to Robert Dickholtz, of Altadena, California, concluded: "However, you will appreciate that I cannot at this time select members of a cabinet. To designate one member would open up pressures to make other appointments. . . . I do expect, however, that Mr. Stevenson will have a significant role in our future affairs."

elect the ticket and campaign extensively. The alternative appals and revolts me. And, lest you misunderstand, the requests by Kennedy in person to campaign everywhere are urgent. I think he is beginning to fully appreciate the situation and yesterday his brother came to my house at Libertyville.

So I have not abandoned you. Nor do I know just what to do about you! Which, of course, has not deterred me from making countless speeches of late, but I am not going to bother you with the manuscripts.

I much appreciated your remarks about the UN and I am really moved by your perception of the potentials.[179] Indeed, I have just written a hurried piece for the New York Times Magazine section next Sunday on the eve of Khrushchev's arrival.[180] But the point is not that I deprecate the organization or its importance, but that I simply don't want to work there myself. Perhaps it is because I don't like to carry other people's briefs any more.

The gallant Tom[181] has arrived and we had an all too brief session in New York. I am sure he will be helpful, and I hope I can see something of him during the autumn.

With much love and my hope for more of the same,

Yours,

To Willard Wirtz and William Mc C. Blair, Jr.

MEMORANDUM TO WIRTZ AND BLAIR, SEPTEMBER 13, 1960

(1) I think I should be prepared in California to hit concisely and hard the "no difference" between candidates' attitude on the basis of the difference between the parties, their philosophy and record. Perhaps there was a speech on this in 1956, or have been speeches by others later, that could be condensed and made effective.

(2) In Dallas Nixon said that he was against Federal aid for teachers' salaries, against closing the tax loophole for oil depletion; and against meaningful negotiation with the Russians (he said we should make no concessions, and of course there could be no meaningful negotiations without mutual concessions).

He said that everything was fine, that the U.S. was strong enough economically and militarily and has lost neither prestige nor influence in the world: and that he is the best man to keep it that way. "We have kept the peace without surrender"; and "the job of the next President

---

[179] The editors do not have a copy of Mrs. Matthews's letter.
[180] "Why the World Looks to the U.N.," *New York Times Magazine*, September 18, 1960.
[181] Mr. Matthews.

will be to keep the peace without surrender and extend freedom throughout the world."

With no more perception of the state of the world and the U.S. and of the prospects for peace, if the country is left to him he will be saying that we have kept the peace without surrender long after we are isolated and alone.

As far as extending freedom, the Communists have done the extending in the past few years.

(3) In Lippmann's piece in the Sun-Times of September 13 his theme is what I have been trying to state since the beginning, and I think it should be the basis of most of what I say in the West. But there should be amplification of the "decline of American power and influence" by illustration.

A.E.S.

Stevenson had told Mrs. Eugene Meyer that he did not know whether he wanted to be Secretary of State for Kennedy. She insisted he must want it. She wrote that she had not been firm enough with him over the necessity of his being nominated for President. "You yourself said to me: 'Had I wanted it, I could have taken it away from him' — meaning Kennedy." Mrs. Meyer added that she blamed herself for not influencing him more to want it, but she would not make that mistake regarding his possible appointment as Secretary of State.

To Mrs. Eugene Meyer[182]

September 20, 1960

Dear Agnes:

I neglected to show you my wallet, which is uncommonly splendid for Stevenson equipment!

I have just read your letter of the 16th and really regret that you haven't fully understood my state of mind. It has nothing to do with "shilly-shallying" and a great deal to do with conditions in which it would be possible to work for or with anyone. Perhaps it is because I am more concerned with what you term "the sake of the country" than my "own sake." But perhaps we can talk of that another time. Meanwhile, please don't express to anyone the misgivings I expressed to you in confidence.

---

[182] The original is in the Agnes Meyer files, Princeton University Library.

I am touched by your offer of help, before and after. I look forward to [William] Attwood's return, although I doubt if I will need too much speech writing. I certainly need a lot of miscellaneous editorial assistance, research and ideas.

It sounds to me as though you had undertaken a formidable schedule and I regret that we don't overlap on the Coast. Perhaps you could stop off here going or returning, for a brief visit.

Don't worry about our finances — at least not yet. I think we can manage, although these long, nonproductive periods are a little tough on my firm. The travel for three or four of us[183] will be expensive but I hope to unload most of this on the National Committee.

With much love,

ADLAI

To Lady Barbara Jackson

September 20, 1960

Dearest Barbara:

I am heartsick that the squirrel cage never slows down long enough for a proper letter. It hardly slows down long enough to digest your superb contributions to my (a) literary (b) political (c) intellectual — enlightenment. But they are very welcome, indeed, and seep into every utterance. Indeed, the Truth and Dealing with K[hrushchev]. pieces will be the backbone of two quasi-political lectures at the University of California at Berkeley and UCLA. I leave Friday for ten days in Washington, California and Colorado. Already I have campaigned in Wisconsin, Minnesota, New York and Illinois. And when I return from the West I shall go back to New York, New Jersey, Pennsylvania, North Carolina, etc. etc., returning to the West Coast again before the end, with some intermediate stops, I suppose. I have undertaken more than I had planned originally, and if my spirit and involvement ever lag the thought of Nixon quickly restores them.

Somewhere along the line I hope to find two or three days for conferences about the post-election and post-inauguration foreign policy problems. I promised Kennedy some time ago that I would try to suggest steps he could take to lay firm hands on our foreign affairs and give our country a new direction promptly in case he is elected. The impetus of decisive action at the outset and during the first "hundred days" of the new Congress would give his administration a momentum which would last a long time.

I can't predict a Democratic victory with any certainty yet. The reli-

183 Attwood, Blair, and Wirtz accompanied him.

gious issue has reared its ugly head and I am amazed at the naivete of politicians who thought it was buried in West Virginia. On balance it will probably prove expensive, but Kennedy has been getting some excellent breaks by the excesses of Norman Vincent Peale, et al.[184] (I have said with some effect that the difference between St. Paul and Peale is that Paul is appealing and Peale is appalling.)

Also, the Republican press use the "experience" factor with regard to Nixon constantly, and perhaps effectively. If you have some of your gently homicidal sarcasm for that nonsense, it would be welcome, by the way.

I am glad you are going to send along the China piece,[185] although I am not positive just when or where it will fit in. It reminds me, however, that some more education on the subject of our minority position in the world might be helpful. X% of the people cannot go on forever using Y% of the production; we must be prepared for changes and not be immobilized and enfeebled by obsolete attitudes, etc. etc.

The Nixon campaign, as you know, seems to have come down to (a) "all is well," and (b) "Don't change administrations in this perilous period (to which we have brought you)." I think we could make more of the kind of people Nixon would attract to Washington and those who will be attracted to Washington by a new Democratic administration. I have also thought to try to do a little more about the Atlantic Community and Council idea, how and why we must concert our policies, our brains and resources in the great struggle. But somehow General De-Gaulle has a way of disunifying us every time I talk about subordinating national interests! Peace is the really big issue. The Democratic presentation (mostly Kennedy's and mine) has been the deterioration of American power and influence and its restoration. I have also tried to talk about disarmament. But Kennedy hammers incessantly on (a) lost prestige abroad; (b) we can be no stronger abroad than we are at home; and (c) religion. His horde of speechwriters is in despair. They seem to get the press releases but not the speeches!

[184] The Reverend Norman Vincent Peale headed a group of Protestant clergy and laymen to discuss religious issues in the campaign. Their lengthy statement of September 7, 1960, said, among other things: "The key question is whether it is in the best interests of our society for any church organization to attempt to exercise control over its members in political and civic affairs. While the current Roman Catholic contender for the Presidency states specifically that he would not be so influenced, his church insists that he is duty-bound to admit to its direction. This unresolved conflict leaves doubt in the minds of millions of our citizens." New York *Times*, September 8, 1960.

[185] Lady Jackson had offered to outline her ideas about Western aid to Asia in general and her belief that China could be contained and her influence undermined by surrounding her with strong and flexible open societies like those of Japan and India.

But I always find your own thoughts about what needs saying more elevating and wholesome than mine.

But I have gone on too long. Forgive me; and please don't feel compelled to work for the Democrats when the Jacksons come first! I pray that you will not overdo and that all goes well with Robert [Jackson] and Robin.[186]

Love,

During September, William V. Shannon and others wrote various columns about the efforts that were being made to get Kennedy to announce that he would appoint Stevenson Secretary of State. Shannon referred in one column to some of "Kennedy's personal entourage" resenting Stevenson's "allowing his name to go before the convention." Stevenson wrote a longhand memorandum to Wirtz.

To Willard Wirtz

[no date]

MEMORANDUM TO BILL WIRTZ

Shannon should be told (1) that *I* have *never* pressed for Sec. State; (2) that by 1956 and keeping strictly *out of his way* since, I made K's nomination possible, so if there is no gratitude there should be! (3) that it is by no means certain that I would accept if asked — until quite clear on policies and attitudes; (4) that "the Stevenson people" may or may not be important in the campaign, but the pressure is understandable [i.e. the surest way to get them is to make clear now his intentions — as Eisenhower did re Dulles in '52.][187] (5) "Allowing his name to go before the Convention" — I asked Monroney repeatedly *not* to put my name in nomination. He insisted for reasons you know.

A.E.S.

To Harry Golden[188]

September 23, 1960

Dear Harry:

I'm sorry that I've delayed acknowledging your most interesting letter — or should I say confession? My excuse is that I have been traveling and talking incessantly as usual! Your letter disturbed me not a little,

---

186 Their son.
187 This phrase is in brackets in the original.
188 The original is in the possession of Mr. Golden.

but surprised me not at all. Coming from central Illinois, I have always feared that religion was bound to be an issue. And I think you *really* knew it too, regardless of that bold face you put on it. I have also felt that if bigotry became too obvious, it could backfire to Kennedy's benefit. And now it appears, thanks to Norman Vincent Peale, that may be happening. I'm not sure. What do you think?

Incidentally, I was looking the other day through some old speeches I made in 1957 and I came on the following:

"The 1952 campaign was marked with revelations about the financial condition of the candidates. 1956 was marked by revelations about their physical condition. What next? Spiritual revelations? Well, nothing would surprise me — even the news that Nixon is in constant communication with Abraham Lincoln, or that he tried to step aside in favor of Norman Vincent Peale."

I expect to be in North Carolina on October 21st or 22nd, in Durham and Winston-Salem, and would, of course, like nothing better than to see you again.

Cordially,
ADLAI

William Attwood, after traveling as a member of Kennedy's campaign staff in California and Texas during mid-September, wrote: "But one disturbing revelation of this September trip was that the Stevenson cultists were still sulking. They weren't out ringing doorbells or licking envelopes for Kennedy. Most were passive; some were even planning to sit out the election. There were plenty of them, and nobody but Adlai could crank them up." *Attwood joined Stevenson on his tour of the West in late September. He wrote:* "All the Stevensonians wanted was just to hear Adlai himself say he was really for Jack."[189]

Attwood recalled: "In Sacramento (good Stevenson territory) [Bill] Wirtz and I drafted a speech that let Nixon have it with all barrels — something Kennedy himself correctly refrained from doing. Stevenson liked it but wondered if it wasn't perhaps too rough. We resolved his doubts by saying it had already been released to the press. And the crowd, most of them still flaunting Adlai-For-President buttons, roared with delight as he poured it on. But when he left the hall and met the reporters outside, a voice in the dark asked, 'Governor, since when have you become Jack Kennedy's hatchet man'? And that was the last time he delivered that speech."[190]

[189] *The Reds and the Blacks*, pp. 9–10.
[190] Ibid., p. 10.

[571]

To Dag Hammarskjöld[191]

October 5, 1960

Dear Mr. Secretary:

On October 17th Mr. and Mrs. Harry Oppenheimer are dining with me in New York, together with two or three other friends who have familiarity with South Africa. You will identify Mr. Oppenheimer as the son of Sir Ernest Oppenheimer and the head of the huge Anglo-American Company, which includes De Beers and large gold, diamond and other industrial enterprises.

If by any chance you are free for dinner, I can promise to release you very early. I think you might enjoy meeting this remarkable young man who has been such a daring and liberal leader in the industrial and political life of his country. I am sure he would enjoy meeting you very much.

I hardly need to add that in recent weeks millions of Americans have become your devoted and respectful adherents — or should I say millions more.[192]

Cordially yours,

P.S. If dinner is impossible, perhaps Mr. Oppenheimer could call on you in the ensuing week while he is in New York. I think a talk with him would be helpful in view of your forthcoming trip to South Africa.

Stevenson campaigned in New York beginning in mid-October, then flew to North Carolina to speak.

To Lady Barbara Jackson

October 28, 1960

Dearest Barbara:

Two hours ago I arrived in my office in Chicago after another fortnight of incessant travel and utterance in the East and South. I found the Ian Gilmores,[193] of London, awaiting me and enough neglected work to smother Nixon. (What a wonderful idea that would be — to get rid of him and the work too). But the best of all was another note from

---

191 Secretary-General of the United Nations.

192 Stevenson refers to Hammarskjöld's leadership of the UN military mission to the Congo.

193 Ian Gilmour, former editor of the *Spectator,* and his wife, the daughter of the Duke of Buccleuch and Queensberry.

you. I wish I knew or could learn how you do it — write, travel, create, correspond — and think. I suppose a woman would think of a few other things such as minding babies, husbands, help and schedules.

Anyway, I have long since surrendered to your talents as well as your charms, as well you know, but I wish to hell I could write a proper letter to you some time before I can't write it at all. Or perhaps that day has already arrived!

The material is *all* helpful and useful. We chew it up and distribute it around, use it in fragments and chunks, and thank God for it. I go now to Oregon and California for the windup. And the windup looks like an easy victory for Kennedy. But it will be as much a defeat for Nixon as a victory for Kennedy. Nixon has come through much as you foretold, with diminishing confidence and enthusiasm even among the Republicans. Their foolish insistence that all is well with the world and our prestige never better, etc. etc., has crumbled before emerging facts — all equally visible four years ago! Even the New York Times has had to face the realities of this sad world at last — albeit with limited enthusiasm.

The debates (my proposal, as you know) have paid off heavily for Kennedy, and there is no surer way to lose confidence in Nixon than to see him, which was also forseeable.[194] With the recession advancing apace Kennedy has had another break. And, finally, with the anti-Catholics overdoing it even that handicap has been neutralized to some extent.

I have had wildly enthusiastic crowds and find the Stevensonians still emotional and moving. Most of them are staying with the party and many of them working actively for Kennedy and the ticket. A handful are irreconcilable and are recommending "Vote No on November 8 and keep the White House empty for another four years." In many places they have "Stevensonian for Kennedy" bumper tags and similar devices. My own efforts have been unqualified, and I assume will not be overlooked or underestimated in the Kennedy camp. But I can assure you that the candidate's "foreign policy advisers" neither see, hear nor advise the candidate! I think he has been extricated from his appalling blunder about Cuba[195] and, in short, is in excellent shape and riding a

---

[194] The candidates took part in four debates broadcast over nationwide television and radio on September 26 and October 7, 13, and 21, 1960. Many observers believed that Kennedy benefited greatly from the increased national exposure and that he had an advantage over Mr. Nixon in television "presence."

[195] On October 20, 1960, Kennedy issued a statement attacking the Eisenhower Administration for its complacency about Communism in Cuba and asserting: "We must attempt to strengthen the non-Batista democratic anti-Castro forces in exile, and even in Cuba itself, who offer eventual hope of overthrowing Castro. Thus

rising tide. But what to do after the election? The problems that are arising all around the horizons are staggering. But who knows more about that than you! And I hope we can talk about them — preferably this evening.

And now, farewell, while I pack for Portland and another endurance contest.

With much love and endless thanks for your letters and manuscripts.

Ever,

P.S. If you have ideas as to the priority problems a new President should be prepared to meet I would love to know how you rate them. And I also wish you were here to help me do a speech for the Commonwealth Club in San Francisco on the balance of payments and a growing free world economy.

P.P.S. . . .

Stevenson campaigned for Kennedy in Portland, Oregon, on October 30 and 31, and on November 1 introduced Kennedy at a rally in Los Angeles.

To Mrs. Ronald Tree[196]

[no date]

M — I've just arrived in this familiar place after a) triumphant affair in Portland & (one of the *best speeches!*) — preceded by a TV show and followed by a $50 "supper" fund raiser, b) a sleepless night at the dear Corbetts,[197] c) a beefsteak breakfast at 8 chez Corbett d) a hotel breakfast with 200 "business people" cum speech e) a TV press conference with Maurine[198] for 45 minutes, f) a speech to convocation at Reed College g) greetings to the Kennedy Hqrs, h) ditto to the Woodworkers of America i) lunch with faculty of Portland Univ cum speech and (J) speech to convocation of Portland Univ!!!

---

far these fighters for freedom have had virtually no support from our Government." However, from classified reports he was receiving from the Central Intelligence Agency, Kennedy was aware that the United States was training "fighters for freedom" for a planned action against Cuba. The statement was widely criticized, and Kennedy spoke no more of Cuba during the campaign. Arthur M. Schlesinger, Jr., asserts that the statement was issued without Kennedy's having seen it. *A Thousand Days*, pp. 74–75.

196 This handwritten letter is in the possession of Mrs. Tree. It was written from the Beverly Hills Hotel, November 1, 1960.

197 Portland attorney Alfred Corbett and his wife.

198 Maurine Neuberger, widow of U.S. Senator Richard L. Neuberger and a candidate for his seat.

But Maurine was delighted; and Wayne Morse flew out from the UN[199] to introduce [me] and went overboard in a burst of passionate oratory — "I had converted him to the Dem[ocratic] party;[200] *every* Dem in Oregon was a Stevensonian; I was high on his list of the 25 greatest Dems etc!" (I guess he's running for re-election already!). . . .

Jane [Dick] telephoned — this minute — to report rising agitation and indignation that I had not been invited to the Chicago rally[201] Friday — T.V. program by a Chicago commentator tonight. Ho Hum! I wish I were there — you were here — . . .

Stevenson spoke in San Francisco, November 3–4, and made his final speech of the campaign at Fresno on November 5.

To Mrs. Ronald Tree[202]

November 6, 1960

M —

Fresno last night was a happy end — in a flood of love and excitement. The introducer a mad fanatic, member of the Calif[ornia] legislature & the best speaker I've encountered in 2 mos. of this travail. After the rally — an endless crushing buffet supper with my finest faithful financially. And back to S[an] F[rancisco] by charter plane at 2 AM!

Now Chicago is beneath & I'm dropping this in the airport to send Jane [Dick]'s letter re the Chicago rally to which I wasn't invited, thinking it would interest you — and because I wanted to send you something. . . .

---

[199] Senator Morse was a member of the United States delegation to the United Nations General Assembly.

[200] Senator Morse was a Republican member of the Senate from 1945 until he resigned from the party in 1952 in protest over Eisenhower's nomination. He was reelected as a Democrat in 1956.

[201] A Democratic rally to be held in Chicago Stadium.

[202] This handwritten letter is in the possession of Mrs. Tree.

Part Seven

Ambassador-Designate to the
United Nations

On November 8, 1960, John F. Kennedy was elected President in the closest election since 1916. For the next few weeks there was speculation as to what role Stevenson might be called upon to play in the Kennedy Administration. At some time during this period, he wrote the following notes.[1]

1. Decisiveness — As *Gov. of Ill.* so decisive and effective (with a Rep[ublican] legislature) that he was drafted for Pres — after he had refused Truman's request that he be a candidate (because he was a candidate for Governor) which Truman never could forgive him for.
2. Competance — Lifetime interest in foreign affairs; extensive writing and publication abroad; travel and acquaintance unequalled in Dem[ocratic] Party's experience here and abroad in diplomacy during and after war. Knows Russia and Russians. Record of being right and in advance of general thinking going back to support of aid for Britain activity before last war. Seven years experience in Fed[eral] Gov[ernment]. in Agriculture, Navy and State Depts. going back to 1933.
3. Influence, respect, popularity — unequalled abroad by any American, including Ike!
4. Position at home. Twice nominee virtually without opposition. Respect evidence by draft movement culminating in Los Angeles ovations — after keeping out of politics completely, except for DAC [Democratic Advisory Council] for four years and out of the country much of time.
5. What has he done for me — J.F.K.?[2] Between 60–75 speeches in 12

[1] This handwritten document is in the possession of Mrs. Ronald Tree.
[2] For an assessment of the importance of Stevenson's activity in support of Kennedy during the campaign and its effect on the outcome of the election, see Kenneth S. Davis, *The Politics of Honor: A Biography of Adlai E. Stevenson* (New York: Putnam, 1967), pp. 441–443.

states during campaign. Host and speaker at fund raising affairs. Gave JK first national prominence by invitation to nominate AES in 1956 and throwing Vice Pres[idential nomination]. open to give him chance without offending Kefauver's followers. Keeping out of the contest and strictly neutral for 4 years; doing *nothing* to encourage draft.

To Robert F. Kennedy[3]

November 9, 1960

Dear Bobby:

Sure, and it's a glorious day!

I don't know who should receive applications for personal appointments, but I am taking the liberty of forwarding to you this application from Captain [W. V.] Pratt for appointment as a Naval Aide to the President.

Captain Pratt was a very young officer who commanded the Secretary of the Navy's yacht, the "Sequoia" in the early days of the last war. I lived on the ship with Colonel Frank Knox a good deal and had a warm regard for Lt. Pratt at that time. I have not seen him since — until he delivered this letter at my house the other night.

With best wishes,

Cordially yours,

Paul Ziffren wired Stevenson on the evening of November 9 that the Democratic party's victory was "the victory of a party created largely in your image and thru your efforts."

To Paul Ziffren[4]

November 10, 1960

Dear Paul:

Thanks for your wire and I know that you as much as anyone were responsible for what happened. And I hope what happened elsewhere happened in California, too, but I gather it is close.[5]

3 Younger brother of John F. Kennedy and manager of his presidential campaign.
4 The original is in the possession of Mr. Ziffren.
5 The outcome of the election in California was uncertain for more than a week after November 8, owing to a widespread use of paper ballots and the delay in tabulating absentee votes caused by the state's law that permitted ballots mailed at the last minute to be counted if received as much as four days after the election. See "California Seeks a Vote-Count Aid," New York *Times*, November 20, 1960,

If I helped in any way I am well rewarded.
With warmest good wishes to you and Mickey,[6]

Cordially,
ADLAI

To John F. Kennedy[7]

November 11, 1960

Dear Jack,

I wish I could ease your burdens. I know the anxieties and decisions that torment you — and I'm afraid this report won't make things any easier.

Do you remember the story about Lincoln when the White House corridors were crowded with job seekers, even the family living quarters, and the doctor told him he had a light case of small pox. "Open the door," he said, "and let 'em all in. At last I've got something I can give every one."

Yours,
AES

To John F. Kennedy

November 11, 1960

Dear Mr. President:

Last July at Hyannisport you commissioned me to prepare suggestions about the foreign policy problems you would confront after *election* and after *inauguration*.

I have asked John Sharon, from the Washington office of my long time friend and former associate, George W. Ball, to deliver this *confidential* report.[8] I emphasize *confidential* for obvious reasons. Therefore, I am sending only one copy. Additional copies can, of course, be delivered promptly. Also, the names of other contributors to the report can be furnished on request. But it has been reviewed by Senator Fulbright, Chester Bowles and David Bruce, with general approval.

My basic purpose has been to suggest steps to enable you to quickly

---

p. 54. There were approximately 260,000 absentee ballots cast, and Mr. Nixon eventually won the state by fewer than 36,000 votes out of a total of more than 6.5 million after early returns seemed to indicate a narrow Kennedy victory.

[6] Mrs. Ziffren.

[7] This handwritten letter is in the Theodore C. Sorensen papers, John F. Kennedy Library.

[8] A copy of this report is in the Adlai E. Stevenson papers, Princeton University Library.

lay firm and decisive hands on our foreign relations and give them new and certain directions. Due to my campaign schedule for the past two months I have not been able to spend as much time on this report as I had expected. The document has infirmities in emphasis, is uneven in treatment, and I apologize for its length.

I suggest two broad *new* lines of policy – in the field of foreign economic policy, and for nuclear cooperation within NATO – and also a new emphasis on disarmament.

At a time when Cuba, the Congo and Laos concentrate attention on the grave problems of the world south of the Equator, the emphasis on strengthening the Atlantic Community may seem disproportionate, but I believe that it is indispensable to solving the pressing problems of the less developed countries.

There is too much detail in the report on sharing the nuclear deterrent and not enough on disarmament and on East-West negotiation. There is almost no discussion of Soviet trade inroads by barter and price cutting and the competitive consequences. Nor do I reach satisfactory conclusions as to how the United States aid programs can more effectively stress economic development instead of military cooperation – a result I recommend.

Also, some of the statements sound more emphatic and categorical than my convictions warrant.

Appendix D on organization of the State Department is not complete or adequate and is included only to bring some matters to your attention. In my opinion the single most important problem as always in government, is personnel, and your conclusions at Wittenberg College on October 17th[9] are correct: senior positions should be filled "with the best talent in both parties, giving preference to those willing to commit themselves to stay on the job long enough to apply what they learn," and "campaign contributions will not be regarded as a substitute for training and experience for diplomatic positions."

Nor have I expressed my feeling that a delegation of authority in the field more commensurate with responsibility will attract more capable men. Good men are not content to sit at the end of a cable line waiting for orders from country desks. I think more country planning should be done in the field and carried out by the people who make the plans.

The report also fails to recognize that the problems of the underdeveloped nations are less military and economic and more social and political in nature. I think we can make more effective use of the ex-

---

[9] In a speech at Wittenberg University in Springfield, Ohio, Kennedy outlined the principles of ethical conduct his Administration would follow to restore moral leadership in the White House. See the New York *Times,* October 18, 1960.

perts, sociologists, anthropologists, historians, etc., with which our country is richly endowed.

Finally, I equate in importance the economic effort of the "western" countries with their military defense. After Sputnik in 1957, President Eisenhower and Secretary Dulles asked me to help prepare for the critical NATO Council meeting in Paris. While serving in the State Department at that time I repeatedly urged them to put their emphasis on this and submitted proposals for an organizational approach. I am happy to say that the Organization for Economic Coordination and Development (OECD) has now emerged — three years later — and the report includes some recommendations in regard thereto.

While they are not worth your reading, I am enclosing an article on Africa written more than a year ago, before the independence of the Congo, and an article on Latin America, written months ago but published by *Look* only this week because it was so critical of the administration.

I appreciate this opportunity to record some of my views, and I will, of course, be available at your convenience.

Respectfully yours,

To Thomas G. Corcoran[10]

November 14, 1960

Dear Tommy:

Bless you for that engaging letter. The years have not withered any of that wit and poetry and wisdom which I learned to admire so long ago — when we were very young!

Yes, I agree that the "debates" had an incalculable effect on the election and will in the future. If I had a part in it I am proud. And I haven't forgotten the source of the idea or who nudged me along.

So, as one quartermaster to another, here's hoping for a moment of philosophy together some time soon.

Yours,

[10] A Washington lawyer who had held various positions in the New Deal and was for many years one of President Roosevelt's most influential advisers.

To Lewis M. Stevens[11]

November 14, 1960

Dear Lew:

Thank you for your letter.

. . . I don't know what Kennedy has in mind as far as I am concerned, if anything. And I am pleased and flattered that you share the views of so many about the State Department. I am sure letters from you, Dick Dilworth,[12] Dave Lawrence and Matt McCloskey would be helpful. But I have not felt like encouraging anything of that kind myself and I don't wish to embarrass him.

I shall look forward to a talk with you somewhere, and soon, I hope.

Cordially yours,

Cyrus Eaton wired Stevenson that he had made a "mighty contribution" to the Democratic victory. He subsequently wrote that he would be in Moscow and offered to carry a word of greeting from Stevenson. Stevenson replied from his New York City law office.

To Cyrus S. Eaton

November 17, 1960

Dear Mr. Eaton:

Your telegram of November 9 pleased and flattered me. I am grateful indeed.

And now I have your letter of November 1 and I welcome your offer to pay my respects to Messrs. Khrushchev, Mikoyan and Gromyko. I was especially disappointed to miss an opportunity to speak with the Premier while he was in New York this fall. As you know, I was otherwise engaged! I hope you will tell the Premier that I look forward hopefully and confidently to improved Soviet-American relations, and that I am sure that with good will and sincere purpose on both sides we can now move toward a safer, saner world.

I envy you your journey and wish I could be with you. Please give my regards to Mrs. Eaton.

Cordially yours,

Stevenson vacationed at the Kingsland, Georgia, home of Mr. and Mrs. Harry Guggenheim and then at the South Carolina home of Mrs.

[11] A friend of Stevenson's since Princeton days who was active in Pennsylvania Democratic politics and had been chairman of the state's Volunteers for Stevenson in 1952 and 1956.

[12] Richardson Dilworth, mayor of Philadelphia.

Marshall Field. He wrote the following letter while at the Guggenheims'.

To John F. Kennedy

November 22, 1960

Dear Jack:

I am taking the liberty of reporting some conversations with callers in New York last week as of possible interest to you.

U.S.–Soviet Relations. On Wednesday, November 16, Ambassador Menshikov brought me a "long message" from Khrushchev. I have had several such messages from K since I visited him in the U.S.S.R. in 1958. The substance was as follows:

K sends you (Stevenson) greetings and regrets that he did not see you in New York during the General Assembly. He says that your activities toward better relations, lessening tensions, are very much appreciated and will always have support in Moscow, etc.

K[h]rus[h]chev sees a better possibility for fruitful action now, especially in relation to disarmament. He has high hopes that we can reach understandings. *War must be avoided.* He does not wish to argue about who is stronger, but to reach understandings and cooperate.

Disarmament would settle — basically — everything. It is K's first priority. He agrees we cannot do it overnight, but should lay foundations by agreements "at the top." He urges discussion off the record by letter and representatives — not on the rostrum with the world as audience. Mr. K. deems it advisable to use not only official channels, because official language has so many "reservations." He wants informal talks with representatives of the new president there or here. When "on the rostrum" we have to repeat "old accusations."

Khrushchev hopes for agreement on nuclear testing "in a short time" after President Kennedy's inauguration. He asked me to tell President Kennedy that the time is coming when it will be "easier to reach an understanding and that he has a sincere desire to do so."

After questioning, Menshikov said K's basic position on disarmament was enunciated in his concluding speech before the U.N. That is not an "ultimatum," however, and "he is ready to hear the other side." If we reach a basic agreement that our objective is complete and general disarmament, any disagreements "can be settled," and they will agree to "any" inspection and control.

As on several previous occasions with me, Ambassador Menshikov became ambiguous when questioned about the form and formality of "basic agreement on disarmament." In response to my request, he agreed to give me the fundamentals of basic agreement in the Soviet view. He then asked me to suggest how to do something more effective on all outstanding questions, of which disarmament was the most important to them.

With respect to Berlin — he said the proposals for internationalization of both Berlins was impossible. With respect to China — he said "they could not be helpful" in connection with renunciation of China's claim to Taiwan and that the Chinese would never accept the idea of "two China's." But on the "expansion" of China elsewhere, the Russians would be "glad to help."

Several times he quoted K as wishing me to know that "of course we had different views but they should not endanger the peace," as Mr. Nixon seemed to insist.

Latin-America. My visitor was a friend of fifteen years, Hernan Santa Cruz of Chile, deputy director of F.A.O.[13] for Latin America and a "liberal." He said the situation was explosive; social unrest and stagnant economy. Last year population increased .6 per cent and average per capita income declined .03 per cent. Per capita food production declined 4 per cent and is now lower than before the war. Foreign investment decreased $300 million.

"The new administration in the U.S. should make clear at outset that it is concerned first of all with the *people* of Latin America, not just the ruling classes and American business. The Bogota meeting was a beginning, a first recognition by U.S. of the causes and cures for social unrest. The U.S. should favor economic and political integration in Latin America as in Europe. The U.S. should say clearly that it expects taxation and land reform. The Communists are opposing integration and aggravating nationalism, which offers the U.S. an opportunity."

"The non-Communist countries should be prepared to invest $2 billion dollars annually for five years on a rising scale, following pre-investment surveys by the new bank, the U.N. Special Fund, the OAS and ECLA."

Guinea. You may have heard from Bill Foster[14] about the efforts to persuade Sekou Toure[15] to postpone agreement with the U.S.S.R. on building the Konkure dam until after your administration is in office.

For more than five years I have been concerned with economic development in West Africa. Stanley Osborne, president of Olin-Mathieson, which has a large investment in Guinea, came to see me, as he often does, to report that he has assured Sekou Toure that U.S. aid in financ-

13 The Food and Agriculture Organization of the United Nations.
14 William C. Foster, vice president of Olin Mathieson Chemical Corporation.
15 Seko Touré, first president of the Republic of Guinea.

ing the dam will be given prompt and sympathetic attention by the new administration. He said he felt he had to say this — even without authority — in order to induce President Sekou Toure to delay his pending agreement with the Communists.

Forgive this hurried dictation from the "piney woods" of Georgia.

Sincerely yours,

To George W. Ball

November 29, 1960

Dear George:

On Wednesday, November 23rd, I sent to Senator Kennedy at Palm Beach a letter summarizing some talks I had with visitors in New York during the previous week, namely, Ambassador Menshikov of the U.S.S.R. and Hernan Santa Cruz of the F.A.O. I have had no acknowledgement.

Ambassador Menshikov has insisted on seeing me again and I enclose a hasty summary of our talks here in New York yesterday and today. If Senator Kennedy has arranged any way to handle foreign visitors, I wish you would inform me. I would be happy to route Mr. Menshikov to whomever he designates. I have not felt, however, that I could refuse to see him when he was bearing a "personal message" from Khrushchev.

Perhaps you could deliver the enclosure to Senator Kennedy if he cares to see it — although it contains little that is new — and explain my predicament with a view to instructions either to continue conversations with Menshikov or direct him to someone else.

Sincerely yours,

REPORT ON CONFERENCE WITH AMBASSADOR MENSHIKOV, NOVEMBER 28, 1960, AT 575 MADISON AVENUE, NEW YORK CITY

Menshikov advised me that he had informed Khrushchev of our previous conversation and had received a long reply which he proceeded to translate from voluminous notes in Russian. A tight condensation follows.

Mr. Khrushchev says he has read with great interest and special satisfaction about Stevenson's hope that pressing problems can be settled and relations improved between the U.S. and the U.S.S.R. Stevenson's activities in that direction will be met with gratitude and support from "their side." A frank exchange of opinions will always help toward finding ways of settling pressing issues between our countries.

A lot of such issues and questions have piled up. Desiring to begin an exchange of opinions, Mr. Khrushchev wishes to outline some views of the Soviet on questions touched upon at our last talk.

I. *DISARMAMENT*

Mr. Khrushchev agrees with all those who consider this the most important problem. It should be settled without delay. Peace or war depends on how this can be peacefully solved.

Since an atmosphere of confidence does not exist between our countries Mr. Khrushchev believes that we should not sit passively by, but should roll up our sleeves and attack the problems — remembering that measures toward disarmament will help disperse suspicions.

He says that the U.S.S.R. wishes to find a "way out of this stalemate." When the development of most destructive weapons has reached such unprecedented levels, general and complete disarmament is the only way out. Experience shows that a partial approach complicates achievement of agreement, and partial measures mean maintaining the war potential. Partial measures do not settle the main problem or eliminate the threat of war.

So agreement on general and complete disarmament is the only way to end production of fissionable materials.

The United States proposal of ending production of fissionable materials makes sense only if nuclear weapons are simultaneously destroyed and their future use prohibited.

If we are serious about disarmament and the danger of nuclear war, we must take the following steps:

1) Stop production.
2) Prohibit use.
3) Destroy nuclear weapons, so that fissionable materials can only be used for peaceful purposes.

However, the U.S.S.R. is not against partial steps where they contribute to ultimate disarmament, cf. the reduction of the armed forces by the U.S.S.R. The U.S.S.R. has insisted that all testing and development be stopped.

Negotiations on the test ban convince Khrushchev that the United States is to blame for no agreement in order to continue the possibility of further tests and give the U.S. an advantage in the control system. He thinks that the United States, by threatening resumption of tests, is trying to force the U.S.S.R. to make concessions and conclude a treaty which will be favorable to Western arms and intelligence services while the arms race goes on.

The U.S.S.R. cannot agree to an unequal position damaging its security

So it is necessary to begin by working out basic principles of general and complete disarmament. The views of the U.S.S.R. were put forth at the recent General Assembly. It is not seeking unilateral advantages but is striving to reach acceptable agreements and is ready to consider any constructive proposals.

If the West will agree to general and complete disarmament, then the U.S.S.R. will accept any control and inspection worked out by the West.

It is obvious that on every phase of disarmament the control should be established to correspond to the needs.

The U.S.S.R. proposes a special session of the [UN] General Assembly in March or April on disarmament alone. Such a meeting will contribute to the mutual trust which is so indispensable. It will not be possible to work out details but only the main principles of a treaty and assign the details to a committee on disarmament. The present committee should be enlarged to include five neutral nations and work out a treaty on general and complete disarmament pursuant to the "foundations, terms of reference or directives" of the General Assembly.

It is important that neutral states participate in great international issues.

II. *GERMANY AND BERLIN*

The only practical way to liquidate tension and stabilize the situation in Europe is peace treaties with the two German states. But if the United States is not ready to recognize East Germany it would be acceptable for our country to decide whether to sign one treaty or two treaties. The U.S.S.R. is prepared to sign two treaties.

The essence of the peace treaties is recognition of the unalterability of the present boundaries of Germany and the existence of two German states. Any peace treaty must also solve the question of West Berlin.

In West Berlin the U.S.S.R. proposes to make de jure what already exists de facto. Thereby nobody loses anything, and no one gains at the expense of the other side. At the same time such a settlement would improve relations, and would remove mistrust and suspicion in Europe about West Germany.

If the United States does not like the Soviet draft of a peace treaty, it is ready to discuss an American draft. Possibly we have proposals of our own concerning the treaty. We are convinced that a "common language" can be found on every provision assuming there is no question about German boundaries.

The abnormality of the situation in West Berlin is recognized by everybody. It would be "incorrect to complicate the question by any groundless talk about joining West Berlin with West Germany because the U.S.S.R. does not consider West Berlin a part of West Germany" (this seemed to be a reference to the corridor proposal). Mr. Khrushchev dismissed the idea of treating East and West Berlin as a single city by saying that it would be "incorrect to introduce the question of East Berlin because it is an organic part and capital of East Germany." "The U.S.S.R. thinks the proposal to transform West Berlin into a free city is the best solution because it gives due regard to the protection and freedom of citizens of West Berlin. We do not propose to change the social and economic order in West Berlin or its close ties with West Germany."

West Berlin should not (a) permit subversive activities and hostile propaganda against East Germany and other Socialist countries, and (b) participate in blocs of a military-political nature.

The United Nations and the four powers should give "wide and efficient guarantees not to interfere with the free city and its ties with the outside world."

Taking into account considerations of prestige, perhaps there should be a transition period before a final decision on the creation of a free city, in the form of a temporary agreement for a strictly limited time. This is subject to discussion.

Mr. Khrushchev also wants to bring to my attention the unstable situation in West Berlin where life depends on the relations of the four powers and on the relations between the two Germanys. "For instance, a breach of the trade agreement by West Germany would provoke retaliatory measures which would be grounds for banning shipments from or to the federal republic. Such justified and logical measures would affect West Berlin also. This example shows how ripe the time is to work out a new status for West Berlin."

III. *COLONIALISM.*

The U.S.S.R. believes that the colonial system has outlived itself but that the process of liberation has not been completed.

The U.S.S.R. is not seeking any advantage in this connection. "All we are doing is to help these countries get and keep their independence. We call upon the United States to do likewise."

"From your extensive travels, Mr. Stevenson, you know these countries need scientific, economic and technical assistance and do not want to be the arena of sharp conflict between the great powers for spheres of influence. We believe our two countries could help to normalize relations in these regions."

———————

At the conclusion of our talk Mr. Menshikov asked for my comments and I reported that I saw hope in what he had to say about disarmament, but the repetition of their views about Berlin was not encouraging. I added that the talk about ending colonialism was of course propaganda as it had virtually ended already.

Ambassador Menshikov asked if he could see me again during the evening to continue our talk. When I said it was impossible he said he would wait over to see me the next day.

A.E.S.

REPORT ON CONFERENCE WITH AMBASSADOR MEN-SHIKOV, NOVEMBER 29, 1960, AT 575 MADISON AVENUE, NEW YORK CITY

Mr. Menshikov asked for my reflections on Mr. Khrushchev's message. We had a rather fruitless talk about Khrushchev's insistence that the Western powers agree to general and complete disarmament first before discussion of the phases and details of disarmament and control.

Menshikov quoted Khrushchev as saying: "If the Western powers agree to carry out general and complete disarmament, the Soviet Union is ready to accept Western proposals on international control. If a decision is taken on total and universal disarmament and on the destruction of weapons, we shall be ready to accept any controls. Let the Western countries prepare the proposals, we will accept them * * * any proposals they wish to submit. But if the West insists on control and inspection first, then we think that its objective is not disarmament but intelligence — to find out what the Soviet Union has."

After some discussion of the meaning of the resolutions adopted by the United Nations on general and complete disarmament he urged me to compare proposals at the U.N. this fall with the United States proposals at Geneva last summer; that I would find "great differences" because there had been no agreement by the West to the basic principle of general and complete disarmament.

He concluded by asking for my comments on Mr. Khrushchev's proposals at the U.N. I agreed to read them carefully and see him again on my next trip East.

A.E.S.

On November 23, 1960, President-elect Kennedy wrote that Steven-son's foreign policy reports were "informative and helpful. They are excellent and will be most useful." He added that he had phoned John Sharon that morning to ask Stevenson's help on other matters as well. According to a memorandum from Sharon to Stevenson, November 23, 1960, Kennedy asked that task forces be established to study Latin America, Africa, the United States Information Agency, and foreign economic policy.

To John F. Kennedy

December 1, 1960

Dear Jack:

Thanks for your note of November 23. I am glad you found the foreign policy discussions helpful — in spite of the manifest haste of their preparation.

I have met with John Sharon and George Ball and submitted some possible names for the "task forces" which I understand you asked John to organize. I am, of course, ready to assist them further.

Please let me know if I can be of further help to you at any time. You have more than reasonable anxieties — what with a new administration, a new baby[16] — and Illinois![17]

Sincerely yours,

To Mrs. John F. Kennedy

December 1, 1960

Dear Jackie:

Now that the tumult and shouting are dying down — at least I hope they are for your sake — I just want you to know how delighted all of us here are for Jack, Jack Jr. — but most of all for you!

Cordially yours,

Philip Noel-Baker wrote from London that had the Democratic Con-vention been held in Europe with delegates from its states, Stevenson

---

[16] John F. Kennedy, Jr., was born on November 25, 1960.

[17] Illinois Republicans were considering a challenge of the election results in view of the closeness of the vote (Kennedy won by fewer than 10,000 votes out of over 4.7 million cast) and allegations of voting irregularities. On November 30, 1960, Republican Governor William G. Stratton suggested that the state's Electoral Board, of which he was head, might refuse to certify Kennedy's election because of "considerable evidence of fraud," particularly "downright fraud and graft" in the Chicago voting. New York *Times*, December 1, 1960.

would have been nominated on the first ballot. It was assumed in Britain, he wrote, that Stevenson would be Secretary of State. If not, and he was offered the ambassadorship to the United Nations, Noel-Baker added, it would fill other nations with great hope if he accepted the post.

To Philip Noel-Baker

December 6, 1960

Dear Philip:

Your letter of November 5th has just reached me — from Helen Gahagan Douglas. I am flattered and pleased no end that the Europeans were voting for me — again.

As to my future, while I have had some communication with Kennedy subsequent to the election it has all been indirect and pertaining to policy and program. I have had no personal discussion about service in his administration.

I note with interest what you say about the UN and I heartily agree. I must also add in candor that I would go back to those familiar precincts and trials only with reluctance. Besides, I think that there is much even outside the government that I could still do to be useful.

However, we shall see.

I have had some interesting talks lately about disarmament with the Russian Ambassador, and I hope you will let me know when you are next going to be here. Your information during the campaign about the true state of affairs of the Labour Party was most reassuring — and I needed reassurance!

With all good wishes for a happy Christmas, I am

Cordially yours,

To Lady Mary Spears

December 7, 1960

My dear Mary:

Thanks for your letter. I hope for the best for the future with our new administration. But Kennedy was elected by a minority of the votes and faces appalling accumulated difficulties. I wish the mandate was clearer, but it was evident that his youth and religion almost saved Nixon. Certainly no more unpopular figure than the latter has run in many a day.

It is premature to foresee with certainty what will happen, but I think he will organize his administration with one certain purpose — to be its undiluted leader.

I wish you were coming over here and we could have a good talk, but perhaps I will have that opportunity there.

Affectionately,

On December 6, 1960, President-elect Kennedy and Bill Blair conferred in Washington, D.C. According to notes that Stevenson wrote down after Blair told him about the conversation, Kennedy stated that he was "not prepared" to appoint Stevenson Secretary of State. It would be too "controversial" an appointment and he did not want to start his Administration on a "note of controversy." The closeness of the election, Kennedy explained, and the "belligerence" of the Republicans would make relations with Congress difficult. Kennedy stated that his decision was no reflection on Stevenson's "qualities or capabilities." He repeated that it was taken because the appointment would be too "controversial."

Kennedy mentioned that he was considering Senator J. W. Fulbright, David K. E. Bruce, and Dean Rusk for the post. Kennedy told Blair that he wanted Stevenson as ambassador to the United Nations.

In Stevenson's notes about the Kennedy-Blair talk, there are jottings that probably were made after Blair telephoned. It is not clear whether these were Stevenson's own views or comments from various people with whom he discussed the appointment. He wrote, for instance, "Would I feel more frustrated out than in? — If after year could retire if not being effective & have subordinated my own interests — been good soldier as usual. If say no — not prepared to take lesser job — bad sport? If say no — 6 mos. may feel frustrated — something may jeopardize whole UN."

A few sentences later there is a comment on Kennedy's statement that Stevenson's appointment as Secretary of State would be too controversial: " 'Controversial' poppycock — Closeness very reason for being Sec State — would bring confidence he needs."

On December 8, 1960, when Stevenson conferred with Kennedy in Washington, the President-elect formally offered him the post of ambassador to the United Nations with cabinet rank. Stevenson deferred acceptance since, among other things, he wanted to know who would be Secretary of State.[18] *At a press conference after the meeting, Kennedy stated: "I can think of no American who would fill this responsibility with greater distinction. . . . The Ambassadorship and the Mission to*

[18] Arthur M. Schlesinger, Jr., *A Thousand Days: John F. Kennedy in the White House* (Boston: Houghton Mifflin, 1965), pp. 134–135.

the United Nations must be strengthened. . . . The Ambassador to the United Nations . . . must play a greater role in policy making as well as in representing our foreign policy views at the United Nations in New York. . . . The job is part of the Cabinet and it is my hope, if Governor Stevenson accepts the position that he will attend Cabinet meetings and will serve as a strong voice in foreign policy over its entire range."

Stevenson told the reporters that he shared Kennedy's views of the importance of the position but that he had not accepted it pending a further talk.[19]

Stevenson made the following notes. It is not clear whether they were written before the meeting with Kennedy, during the meeting, or after it.

Talk with JK — 12/8

I'll be Frank — Expected Sec State — Something of value to you and country. Administration — policy making — not representation — my interest.

Most difficult assignment — 99 nations — in trouble everywhere. Soviet attack — budget — Africa, China, colonial identification, disarmament, Aid, Cuba-Congo. Save UN! — will depend on U.S. Have used up good will on China.

All policies affect UN — made *here* [Washington] — stuck *there* [New York].

Cabinet? — policy making — Asst Sec'y hardly adequate — Strong enough to fight battles.

What policy participation? *Name* — have in Wash — bureau —

Ans. charges — freedom of action

More senior help & money — if necessary. Need 2 or 3 top pros — Russians Social

Sec — Under Sec — pol — Econ — Defense — Disarmament — *Ball*[20]
        Statement   German   letters re Alsop[21]

On December 10, 1960, Stevenson phoned Kennedy at Palm Beach, Florida. According to Stevenson's handwritten notes these were the "Conditions — given to JK by phone."

[19] New York *Times*, December 9, 1960. When Stevenson balked at accepting the ambassadorship to the UN, Kennedy told him "not to worry; as President, he would guarantee any stipulations Stevenson wanted to make about the UN job." Schlesinger, *A Thousand Days*, p. 134.

[20] George W. Ball, whom Kennedy appointed Under Secretary of State.

[21] Stevenson refers to either Stewart or Joseph Alsop, but the editors are unable to explain the other references in this line.

1. Adm recognizes UN as center of our foreign policy (needs strengthen[in]g — USSR attack)

1A Some voice in policy making. No important decisions without an opportunity to express my views. How? Upgrade asst Secy?[22] firmer base in Dept?

2. At least a veto on appointments to his staff in Wash. & N.Y.

3. When NSC [National Security Council] considers foreign policy matters should have option to attend.

4. To win support of less developed & smaller powers — hold more conf[erences] at all levels under auspices of UN (Disarm[ament] c[ommi]ttee of 10 with Sec[retary] Gen[eral]) One way to counter Soviet attack on UN

5. Increase the portion of our aid channeled thru UN.

6. Our pol[icy] is to end the cold war as soon as possible. Our aid directed not against anyone or system.

8. Strengthen mission by assigning several senior officers.

9. Adequate quarters & representation allowances.

10. Reconsideration of composition of Gen[eral] Ass[embly]. deleg[ation]. to insure more experience competance & continuity ($\frac{1}{2}$ of our deleg. had no dip[lomatic]. exp[erience]. ag[ainst]. toughest team K[hrushchev] could send)[23]

    but to create conditions in which countries can keep them indep[endent], improve living st[andar]ds and reduce illiteracy poverty etc. *Pro* improvement rather than *anti* Comm[un]ist.

11. Will be consulted about organization and direction of our disarm[ament]. efforts. Negotiations should be resp[onsibility]. of Sec State — not head of disarm. agency.

12. Something to say about machinery of coordination between State & Defense. Many decisions by Defense embarrassing of late at UN.

On December 11, 1960, Kennedy and the newly appointed Secretary of State, Dean Rusk, phoned Stevenson from Florida. Stevenson made the following notes of the conversation.[24]

Notes on Negotiations with Senator Kennedy — regarding UN post

    . . . I have something to say about Job before I could accept it

    1. $\overline{\overline{My}}$ tastes & experience — executive, administrative & creative —

22 The Assistant Secretary of State for International Organization Affairs.
23 Stevenson refers to the 1960 delegation to the General Assembly.
24 For a further discussion of this document, see *The Papers of Adlai E. Stevenson,* Vol. VIII.

not legislative or representational. Don't know whether I can do this job or will care for it, but willing to try if JK & Sec want me to — *and* are sympathetic to following suggestions

1. Member of Cabinet.
2. Option to attend NSC when foreign policy matters considered.
3. Should be in mainstream of policy making. No important decisions without opportunity to express views. How? a) Restore traditional position of "counsellor" to Sec'y level — Amb. to UN is 'senior adviser' to Secy extending beyond UN.
4. Free hand with staff in Wash & N.Y. — or at least a veto We can find someone who is [illegible] satis.
5. Assign 3 deputies to Ambassadorial rank to N.Y.
6. Chief of Mission & senior members of staff — adequate quarters & representation allowance. Congress*
7. Better coordination between State & Defense on UN matters. Yes[25]
8. Clear definition of attitude toward UN & conceptual idea of mission. UN center of our foreign policy. Will use it more — not just occasionally in desperation as [John Foster] Dulles did.
   a) To preserve UN as center of our foreign policy ag[ainst]. Soviet attacks
   b) Create feeling that we want to end the cold war as soon as poss[ible]. To win the support of less developed countries
      (1) Channel more of our aid thru UN. Point when UN can't absorb.
      (2) Hold more conferences at all levels under UN auspices.
   c) Our aid not just anti Comm[un]ist but pro improvement of st[andar]d. of living literacy, health, etc.

9. I'll be consulted about organization and direction of disarmament. Negotiations should be resp. to *Sec State*.

Arthur Dean[26] — long patient neg[otiator?].
Bill Foster[27]

* Have to appropriate funds?

[25] It is not clear whether "Yes" here indicates agreement by Kennedy and Rusk.

[26] Partner in the New York law firm of Sullivan & Cromwell, representative of the U.S. and other nations at the Panmunjom negotiations and later special U.S. ambassador to Korea, and U.S. representative at the UN conference on the law of the sea. Kennedy appointed him ambassador to the nuclear test ban talks in Geneva and later to the Geneva disarmament talks, and in 1963 appointed him consultant to advise the director of the U.S. Arms Control and Disarmament Agency.

[27] Kennedy appointed Mr. Foster to head the Arms Control and Disarmament Agency.

10. US should get on offensive not just defensive: For example —
we should press USSR to speed econ dev[28]

    a. Join [World] Bank & [International Monetary] Fund & DLF
[Development Loan Fund]?

*On December 12, 1960, when Stevenson's acceptance of the ambassa-
dorship was announced to the press, B. K. Nehru, Indian ambassador to
the United States, wired Stevenson that the "United Nations could not
be in better hands."*

To B. K. Nehru

December 12, 1960

Dear Mr. Nehru:

Thank you so much for your very kind and thoughtful telegram. You
encourage and comfort me — and I need it!

I shall hope for another visit with you very soon.

Cordially yours,

To Jonathan Daniels

December 12, 1960

Dear Jonathan:

Thanks for those kind things you said about me to Bill Blair.[29]

I have undertaken this tough assignment at the UN with the hope
that I can contribute something in a trying and dangerous time for us
and that organization. It is not just what I had envisioned for my
concluding service.

Yours,

Murray Kempton, in the New York Post, *November 2, 1960, after
describing Stevenson's introduction of Kennedy at Los Angeles on
November 1, wrote: "I suppose the Democrats need him now for very
little except mopping up operations like this one. . . . But let us never
forget that if a light still rises above this dreary land, it is because for so
long and so lonely a time this man held it up." The editor of the* Post
sent Stevenson a copy of the column.

---

[28] Stevenson refers to the economic development of underdeveloped nations.

[29] Mr. Daniels had written that Stevenson was "just about the ablest spokesman
on foreign affairs we have around."

To James A. Wechsler

December 12, 1960

Dear Jimmy:

I am mortified that your letter of November 2 has come to my desk on December 12. But that is about par for my correspondence course this fall. You were good to send me that exquisite column of Murray Kempton's. If I have held anything aloft that wonderful guy aided and abetted by his editor and colleagues have held me aloft.

Bless you, my dear friend.

Cordially yours,

Under Secretary Andrew W. Cordier, Dag Hammarskjöld's executive assistant at the United Nations, wired Stevenson: ". . . We look forward to the great contribution that you will make in this major center of world foreign policy. . . ."

To Andrew W. Cordier

December 14, 1960

Dear Andy:

Thank you so much for your thoughtful telegram. It encourages me! And knowing something of the task I need encouragement. Perhaps if I knew any more about it I wouldn't be in it!

I shall look forward to working with you again and also to getting some counsel from you very soon.

Cordially yours,

On December 14, 1960, Stevenson and Dean Rusk conferred in New York City. At a joint press conference afterward, Rusk stated that Stevenson would "play a key role in the formulation of foreign policy." Rusk added that the new Administration would want Stevenson's "full counsels in the formulation of foreign policy." When a reporter asked Stevenson whether the "key role" had been a factor in his acceptance of the post, he replied: "This is the first time I've heard of it, and I think it's a very nice phrase."

In reply to a question, Stevenson said that he did not believe the Soviet Union could wreck the United Nations. "It is our hope," he added, "that the UN will be a factor to end the 'cold war' and not aggravate it."[30]

To Harry L. Golden[31]

December 17, 1960

Dear Harry:

I have had a lot of wires in the last few days asking me to do this or that, or thanking or damning me for that or that, but the best of all was yours to Newt Minow[32] — as usual! Some day I hope we can talk a little about this "tremendous opportunity." I agree that there is a tremendous opportunity, but there are also hazards, frustrations and dangers ahead which disturb me mightily. In undertaking this task I feel I am "doing my duty" — and how! — but that has its rewards too.

I pray that you are well and that somehow some time I can begin to convey the better vision of our country to the news peoples that you do.

All good wishes — and Merry Christmas!

Cordially yours,

ADLAI

To Robert F. Kennedy

December 19, 1960

Dear Bobby:

It will be nice seeing you at those cabinet meetings[33] and I am really delighted at the prospect. You have had a remarkable career and I don't doubt this is another step upwards.

With warmest good wishes to you and Ethel,[34]

Cordially,

Mrs. Bessie Moore, who had been one of Stevenson's teachers when he attended school in Bloomington, wrote him, enclosing an article describing her son, who made his living raising queen bees for sale.

---

[30] New York *Times*, December 15, 1960.
[31] The original is in the possession of Mr. Golden.
[32] The editors do not have a copy of this telegram.
[33] He had been appointed Attorney General.
[34] Mrs. Kennedy.

To Bessie Moore

December 20, 1960

My beloved teacher and friend:

I have been in the East most of the time since the election and have only now been able to read your letter, which cheers me and grieves me at the same time. I am distressed that you have been ill so much this year and are deprived of the joy of Christmas giving. But your faith and courage and your belief in life shine out all the more clearly in all you say, and I am thankful again to have had the guidance of such a spirit in my boyhood days.

With the new and appalling job that confronts me, and so few days in which to finish up my law work and prepare for my duties at the UN, I have very little chance to enjoy the Christmas season this year, but at least I am going to have a day or two in Bloomington with as much of the clan as we can assemble. My three grandchildren (Adlai, Lucy and Katie) and Buffie's three (Alison, Sandra and Timothy) — none of them older than four years — are a perpetual delight to us all.

And thank you for the interesting article about your son and his fascinating occupation. I am returning it herewith. It makes me happy to know that you have such fine sons, and that you have them near you. Mine are scattered around and I don't see them as much as I would like. But Adlai is here in Chicago, and I will soon be near Borden, who has moved to New York. John Fell, however, has taken up his abode in San Francisco. He is still in the real estate business. My travel plans all seem to be in the other direction at present, but I hope that one of these days I can visit him — and you, too!

I am leaving my law firm early in January and shall be in New York most of the time after that. Beginning January 20th, I shall be living at the Waldorf Towers in New York, but I hope I can get home to Liberty-ville occasionally.

I pray that the New Year will bring you brighter skies and fresh strength, my dear friend, and that you will continue to remember

Your affectionate

To Dean Rusk

December 21, 1960

PERSONAL AND CONFIDENTIAL

Dear Dean:

Further in regard to my talks with Ambassador Menshikov, I am enclosing the following for your information:

1) My report to Senator Kennedy of a talk with Ambassador Menshikov on November 16.
2) My report of conferences with the Ambassador on November 28 and 29.
3) A document left with me by the Ambassador at our most recent talk in New York on Thursday, December 15.
4) A letter from Harrison Salisbury and accompanying memorandum of his conversation with Menshikov in New York on the same date, December 15.

In my last talk — December 15th — the note of anxiety to proceed with disarmament persisted. He asked me specifically to review the Soviet proposals submitted to the General Assembly by Mr. Khrushchev on September 23rd and to "give him my reaction to these proposals." He protested for the second or third time that these proposals had never been published in United States newspapers. He did not talk to me about a summit meeting, as he evidently did to Mr. Salisbury, but the same note of urgency, perhaps slightly muted, was evident if not articulate.

He repeated the fear that partial disarmament and control would be for the purpose of espionage, not disarmament. He was optimistic about a nuclear test agreement, hopeful about general and complete disarmament, and discouraging about China and any concessions on Taiwan. At the conclusion of our meeting, he asked for another and for my "thoughts on Germany, Berlin and Africa." The theme of our conversation was his anxiety to talk unofficially and informally in order to understand each other's positions.

Perhaps we should talk about how to handle future discussions. I should also like to exchange views with you about the Assistant Secretary for United Nations Affairs and the delegation in New York. I could meet you in Washington Monday, January 2, or Tuesday, January 3. Thereafter I will be in New York until January 8th.

Warm regards.

Yours,

To Dean Rusk

December 22, 1960

Dear Dean:

I talked yesterday with Chester Bowles[35] and told him something of the progress of my thinking. We concluded that it would be well, subject to your convenience, for me to meet you in Washington to review things right after the first of the year. I could be there all of January 3rd and the morning of January 4th if that is possible for you and Chester.

What with the year end problems of a scattered law firm, a scattered family, and scattered affairs of all kinds — I've been a little scattered myself! Hence my progress has not been great, but I shall have some thinking to report.

Merry Christmas, and my best wishes for the year that awaits you.

Yours,

Senator Wayne Morse, who was a member of the 1960 United States delegation to the United Nations General Assembly, wrote Stevenson that the declining prestige of the United States at the United Nations among African and Asian delegations had to be stopped. There were key people in the Department of State and in the United States mission in New York City who were out of touch with colonial issues involving Spain, Portugal, and the Union of South Africa, he wrote. He urged Stevenson not to appoint any of these people to the mission. (He did not, however, name them in his letter.) Morse mentioned that he was preparing a report for the Senate on the mistakes the Department of State was making at the United Nations.

To Wayne Morse

December 28, 1960

Dear Wayne:

Thank you so much for your letters, which have been enormously helpful to me. I appreciate more than I can tell you your anxiety to inform me before I make any changes.

I had in mind the possibility of appointing only a few top level people — a new Assistant Secretary in Washington and a couple of Ambassadors or senior officials for the Mission in New York. After I

---

[35] Mr. Bowles had been appointed Under Secretary of State.

[603]

have been there a while I suspect there will be other changes I will want to make, and your warning is comforting confirmation.

Do you suppose I could see your report to the Senate in advance? I may be in Washington for a day or so next week, but can always be reached best through this office.

I have been appalled by the mistakes we have made this past fall in the UN and I begin to wonder if there's going to be a UN for me to go to!

Yours,

P.S. I think what I'm trying to say is that I would like your confidential evaluation of the attitudes and prejudices of the individuals in the Department and the Mission to whom you refer.

A.E.S.

To Theodore C. Sorensen[36]

December 30, 1960

Dear Mr. Sorensen:

In response to your telegram of December 24 requesting suggestions for the Inaugural [Address] by December 31, I will confine my comments to foreign affairs. Due to a myriad of other pressing "priorities" just now, I have had little time for this, but my first reaction is that it would be well for Senator Kennedy to include the following:

1. A frank acknowledgement of the changing equilibrium in the world and the grave dangers and difficulties which the West faces for the first time.

2. The assertion that our objective is the peace, the progress and the independence of all people, everywhere. We want to end, not prolong the cold war. Hence, all-out support of the UN, (a) as the protector of the new nations against involvement in the cold war; (b) as the ideal instrument for fostering economic development; (c) as the agency which will have to be strengthened in order that it may be able to keep the peace and enforce world law.

3. An unequivocal commitment to disarmament.

4. Recognition that the first order of business is to halt the proliferation of nuclear powers and to reduce the ever growing danger of war by accident.

5. An unequivocal commitment to the Western defensive alliance to deter aggression and keep the peace.

---

[36] Chief speechwriter for Senator Kennedy and later special counsel to the President.

6. Definition of the ultimate goal of world-wide cooperation on the part of the industrialized nations toward lifting the living standards of the under-privileged peoples. However, so long as the Communists want to compete instead of cooperate, an assumption of leadership in organizing the resources of the non-Communist industrialized nations in a multilateral cooperative effort to win the non-military cold war. (Perhaps a note of approval and hope for the OECD would be helpful).

7. Recognition of a special U.S. responsibility for Latin America.

8. A disavowal of the Republican proposal to reduce foreign *economic* aid and a pledge to increase it, as possible, provided other industrialized nations do their share (especially Germany).

9. A desire to liquidate overseas military bases as fast as progress toward disarmament makes this possible.

10. Eagerness to reduce tensions by negotiation in the hot spot areas (Germany, the Taiwan Strait, the Middle East, Congo, Cuba, Laos).

11. *Perhaps* a conditioned hint of re-examination of our China policy to advance controlled disarmament and reduce the danger of war in Asia.

The main thing, of course, is to create the impression of new, bold, imaginative, purposeful leadership; to de-emphasize the bi-polar power struggle; and to emphasize the affirmative approaches to peace. (In this connection, what about a proposal to put all space exploration under UN control?)

You are doubtless familiar with my report to Senator Kennedy and the recommendation of an omnibus bill to gather our aid agencies together for unified direction. Because I think this most important I would like Jack to mention it, although the State of the Union [Message] may be a more appropriate time for programmatic proposals.

I have not been able to articulate all of this, but enclose some hurried paragraphs which are an attempt to cover at least some of the points, including some passages which are probably quite inappropriate for his address.

I'm afraid this may all be too hurried to be helpful. I will be in Washington (at FEderal 3–5165) Tuesday and part of Wednesday of next week, in case I can be of any help.

Sincerely yours,

Blind carbon copies to: Dean Rusk and Chester Bowles

Stevenson sent the following material — he entitled it "Some Miscellaneous Paragraphs" — to Dean Rusk, Chester Bowles, and Theodore Sorensen, on December 30, 1960.

We will support the growth of democracy everywhere, not only by fulfilling our own Bill of Rights at home, but by supporting their self-government wherever men are still under the yoke of involuntary foreign domination.

We will do this not because of anything the Russians may say or do, but because it is right, because it is what the world has been waiting for from us, because it is what the best traditions of America require.

———

The material and spiritual advancement of the underdeveloped world and of all mankind is the primary business on the world's agenda. This is what the world is thirsting for. It is because we have so largely neglected this in our preoccupation with the military problem of stopping Communism that we have so largely lost touch with the minds and hearts of the more than two billion human beings who are neither Russians nor Americans.

The Russians, too, have begun to underrate our basic strength and purpose. Let there be no mistake about either. We have not seen one form of colonial control superceded simply to see another far more iron and implacable system take its place. The only reason for not playing the Russian game of infiltration and pressure is that we are trying to substitute another pattern for it — a pattern new to history — and that is the pattern first announced by President Woodrow Wilson — the pattern of genuine self determination under which all nations, great and small, have the right *not* to be ruled by others and to mark out their own way of life without interference.

The latest General Assembly has been one long illustration of the need to keep in the closest and most cordial touch with the new nations feeling their way to effective independence and to make clear to them that our one aim is to restrict the cold war, to keep Great Power rivalries out of Asia and Africa and Latin America, and to convince them that it is Communist infiltration, not the ghost of Western colonialism, that threatens their autonomy in the future. We cannot expect them to be actively on our side. Why should they be? We do want them to be vigilantly and intelligently on the side of their own freedom and integrity.

———

The foreign policy of the United States can be stated very shortly, and very positively: it is peace, with justice.

The ultimate evil in the world is not the danger of war or even war itself, but the denial of justice.

The real test of the Soviet desire for world peace is whether the Soviet leaders are willing to live under world law. Are they willing to see such world law vested in the United Nations? Are they willing to subscribe to those principles of world justice that can prevent threats to the peace and well-being of the world community?

These questions must be put to the Soviet leaders not in a belligerent spirit but with utmost good faith, for it is as much to the interest of the Russian people as it is to the interest of the American people — indeed to the interest of all people everywhere — that some way be found to end the present madness.

The prospect of drawing one third of humanity through the sound barrier of modernization has in it a sense of a new frontier, of a new great field of human endeavor where our best efforts and skills, our best plans and talents can be drawn on to the full, creating a new sense of direction in our own society, a new era of hope for the emergent peoples, and above all a new pattern of cooperation and common effort to underpin world peace.

At present, there are barriers in the way of opening up this great new frontier. There is the unfinished business of racial equality at home. We are held back by supposed contradictions between public and private enterprise in our aid programs — whereas in truth both forms of enterprise are needed and each complements the other. We are hindered by our continuing lack of a clear, long term strategy for world investment and world growth. So much of our work is still provisional — to stop the Communists, to plug a hole, to meet a crisis. We lack a grandly moving, forward looking perspective which sees the work as a generation's achievement and dedicates a generation to the task.

But we can overcome such handicaps. We can organize a sustained and systematic attack upon the poverty of the world and in doing so I believe we shall discover that even America of the pioneers did not offer such scope, such excitement, such dedication to those who engaged in the new adventure of building a decent home for all mankind.

We must raise the standards by which we live in this most splendid and happy land. Not in creature comforts, but in the goals of our national life.

No nation in all history from the days of Greece and Rome has survived the poison which creeps into its life-blood when the pursuit of ease and comfort becomes its goal.

The disease is most dangerous for it works unseen. And the nation falls before another whose vigor has not been sapped, whose men and women have gone forward with grim and steady steps, heedless of privations, austere and resolute and dedicated.

New opportunities and new powers demand new policies and new ideas. A world of supersonic flight, instant communication and potential atomic catastrophe needs instruments of cooperation which go beyond narrow frontiers and parochial interests. We cannot be content to project beyond our frontiers little but rockets and the threat of destruction. We need to replace our human neighborhood of potential death with a full human neighborhood of common work and cooperation. We have only embryonic institutions in this field so far. We cannot allow our instruments of war to outpace the instruments of peace and construction.

Self delusion has betrayed us too often of late. We must seek the truth about our affairs. But obviously it takes courage to seek and say the truth if it is greeted by charges of disloyalty and appeasement. By this means we all become a country of the blind.

In America we are accustomed to thinking of colored people, both Negroes and Orientals, as racial minorities in our midst. But in the world as a whole it is we, the white peoples, who are a racial minority. Two-thirds of the 2,800,000,000 people in the world are colored. If we choose to deny equal rights to our minority, we can expect that as the colored peoples of the earth grow stronger they will do the same to theirs.

This is not a problem we can leave for future generations to solve. It has overtaken us. We are facing it this year in the United Nations, and we will face it next year, and every year for the rest of our lives.

My strength is only what I can draw from those who share the vitalizing hope for a better world, from those whose dream is not of what America was or is but of what she will be — and who will work, will sacrifice, to make this dream come true.

The present aimless disunity of Western society is no match for the ruthless, purposefulness of Communism. Until we are jolted out of our complacency, self-satisfaction and self delusion we will continue to lose ground. We must reaffirm not only our economic and technical concern, but our intellectual, moral and spiritual solidarity with the great areas of Asia, Africa and South America.

To John Fell Stevenson[37]

December 31, 1960

Dear John Fell:

I'm sorry we missed each other at Christmas. I was glad to have your letter and the news of your happy weekend at Squaw Valley. Bloomington was a little dreary, enlivened largely by your cousin Jill Merwin[38] and her new husband, who is a very nice guy, and a passionate bull fighting fan who envies your acquaintance with Dominguin.

My new job is going to be difficult. The roof is falling in at the UN just as I arrive,[39] but it will keep me busy for a little longer. I shall have to add some more senior people to the Mission, and in time some junior ones, too. I wish you were going to be in New York to lend me a hand now and then. Perhaps Borden can be dislodged from his desk in Wall Street. I don't see how he can afford the apartment any longer, and have asked him to move in with me. Somehow he seems reluctant!

As I wrote you, let me know if you have anything really good to invest in. Adlai, at the moment, is tempted by a hotel in Antigua. . . .

Love,
DAD

To Ellen Borden Stevenson

December 31, 1960

Dear Ellen:

I have located the sleigh bells and the black bear sleigh rug, and asked Adlai to deliver them to you. If the time comes when they are no longer useful, I hope you will return them, as I am sure the children will have an opportunity to use them very soon with the old sleigh.

Sincerely yours,

---

[37] The original is in the possession of John Fell Stevenson.

[38] The oldest daughter of Mr. and Mrs. Loring Merwin. She had recently married Rollin Montelius.

[39] Differences over UN policies in dealing with the continuing crisis in the Congo led several nations to withdraw their troops from the UN force there during December, 1960. Secretary-General Hammarskjöld sought new directives from the assembly, but the debate ended in an impasse on December 21.

To Lady Barbara Jackson

January 4, 1960

Dearest Barbara:

I have such an accumulation of neglected letters from you — and almost everyone else! I had thought to send you a detailed account of late events long before this, but everything is as usual, i.e. much too much for me to handle and compose myself for a proper report.

There is some disquiet about the large conservative Republican influence in the new Administration, but Kennedy seems to be enjoying the usual honeymoon with the press, enhanced by his "non-partisan competence" test for major positions. There are unkind words from some Democrats who feel that maybe taking positions and being "controversial" is precisely what we need. But who am I to say? The new formula seems to work — at least for the present.

As time goes on and the bugs begin to emerge from the rugs, one gets more and more anxious about our future. Everywhere you look, deferred decisions and neglected opportunities and past errors await the new Administration. I have many comforting moments about my own decision to lift no finger to seek the nomination again!

As for me, I will take over in New York after the Inauguration, with offices at 2 Park Avenue and spacious living quarters in the Waldorf Towers. The task is appalling, in view of the sad decline in American prestige and influence in this past year. The staff will need much strengthening. I have valid expectations of full cooperation from Kennedy and Rusk on that score, but some continuity for the resumed session of the General Assembly will be necessary, and any changes may have to be gradual. The effect, of course, will be disappointing to many who will expect the whole brave new team of players to dash onto the field behind me.

I get some comfort out of the growing realization of the difficulties we are in and the mistakes we have made. You doubtless have seen some of the newspaper stories about the troubles I will inherit. I enclose a charitable bit by Eric Sevareid in case you did not see it.

Your arrival will be none too soon, and I hope you come fully equipped with the rescue equipment. By that time, I will be sinking fast, I have no doubt.

We have worried about you and your health and Robert [Jackson]'s much in the past few months. By we, I mean the legions of your devoted. Moreover, I am sure the news from Africa can hardly be reassuring. Only the other day I had more news about the aluminum companies losing heart in Guinea, and signs of a crack in the hopeful front in Ghana. . . . Will all be best under the new dispensation? Let us pray.

Devotedly,

P.S. I wanted to comment on a thousand things you've written me, and about all that comes to the top of my head at the moment is that snatching the fat out of the fire is a blistering job!

A.E.S.

To Chester Bowles

January 7, 1961

Dear Chester:

Three small items of business:

A letter from Jo Forrestal, 5 Mespil Road, Dublin, Ireland, James Forrestal's widow who has lived for years in Ireland, tells me that she aspires to be Ambassadress to that lovely green land.

If anything comes of the Peace Corps idea, I hope that the proper people will not overlook the possible availability of Harold Taylor, 35 Ellison Avenue, Bronxville, New York. You will recall him as former President of Sarah Lawrence College, and an extremely bright alert man who has a way with younger people. I enclose a letter from him for what it may be worth and which can give you more information.

You will recall that I talked to you on the phone about Charles F. Darlington. I enclose a biographic sketch of this rather exceptional man and would most earnestly urge its careful consideration for an Ambassadorial post. His French is as good as his English, and he has long government experience — and he would be interested in a French-African post, such as Dakar, or Brazzaville, or ? His wife is most attractive and intelligent. Years ago she was Executive Director of the Chicago Council on Foreign Relations when I was its President. I would *really* rate this prospect for your more difficult and critical posts very high. . . .[40]

Sincerely yours,

[40] Mr. Darlington was appointed ambassador to Gabon.

To Joseph Pois[41]

January 12, 1960 [1961]

Dear Joe:

I had fervently hoped to be present today at the luncheon honoring you,[42] but instead I will be presiding over what is left of my law firm! You may have read in the papers what the administration has done to the firm and, inasmuch as I am leaving myself tomorrow and my partners are being picked off at the rate of about one a day, I wanted to have a farewell luncheon with them.[43]

My only regret is that I can't join you and your friends. I think you know of the affection I have for you and my indebtedness to you for all that you did for me — but more importantly for the State of Illinois — when you served with my administration. Since then you have contributed in numberless other ways to a better life for your fellow citizens and your community. You have enriched it greatly by having been here and you leave behind countless friends and admirers, of whom I am proud to be one.

Good luck — and all best wishes.

Cordially yours,

To Richard J. Daley

January 13, 1961

Dear Dick:

If and when there is a vacancy in the post of National Committeewoman, I hope consideration will be given to Jane Dick. I think you know what a loyal worker she has been over the years under circumstances which have not been easy for her. With her children all married now she has plenty of time, but more important, the enthusiasm and energy to do a job for the Party — and for you.

Cordially,

[41] Vice president and treasurer of the Signode Steel Strapping Company of Chicago and formerly director of the Illinois Department of Finance during Stevenson's governorship.

[42] Mr. Pois was leaving Chicago to join the faculty of the University of Pittsburgh, and a group of his friends were holding a farewell luncheon.

[43] Bill Blair was to be ambassador to Denmark; Willard Wirtz had been appointed Under Secretary of Labor; and Newton Minow was to be chairman of the Federal Communications Commissions.

P.S. It was good of you to come to that farewell party yesterday.[44] I was flattered!

TELEPHONE CONVERSATION WITH PRESIDENT ELECT JOHN F. KENNEDY, JANUARY 13, 1961

s: I have a couple of things I wanted to mention to you. I want to put in a word for my friend, Tom Finletter, for that NATO post, again.[45]

K: Yes. That looks all set. . . .

s: (Re: Mission in New York — Economic and Social Council)
I have had a lot of communications from Sarge[46] regarding Phil Klutznick.[47] I like him, and I think I can use one senior Jew without too much trouble with the Arabs. But I would like to feel it along a little bit before I do that. I have asked him to come in — if he will accept the rank of Minister rather than Ambassador — but if he doesn't want to do this — I could talk to Dean [Rusk] about this and after a course of time we could up-grade the position.

K: I don't think anyone ought to get mad about being a Minister — I wouldn't give it a moment's thought — I would say Minister — if he is a good man, but not Ambassador. — Leave an "out" on it. Just say I understand the problem and we will see what we can do.

s: On that New York Situation, the people I have signed up so far: Harlan Cleveland.[48]

K: Fine.

s: I am going to talk to Dean — Jack Bingham[49] and Francis Plimpton,[50] a senior lawyer in New York of my generation. He is an ex-

[44] On January 12, 1961, the Chicago branch of the American Association for the United Nations held a reception in Stevenson's honor.
[45] Kennedy appointed Mr. Finletter ambassador to the North Atlantic Treaty Organization.
[46] Kennedy's brother-in-law, R. Sargent Shriver, who was in charge of recruiting top personnel for the new Administration.
[47] Philip M. Klutznick, commissioner of the Federal Public Housing Authority, 1944–1946, and alternate delegate to the United Nations, 1957. Kennedy appointed him representative to the UN Economic and Social Council with the rank of ambassador.
[48] Dean of the Maxwell Graduate School of Citizenship and Public Affairs, Syracuse University. Kennedy appointed him Assistant Secretary of State for International Organization Affairs.
[49] Jonathan B. Bingham, a member of the New York law firm of Goldwater & Flynn. Kennedy appointed him U.S. representative on the UN Trusteeship Council.
[50] Francis T. P. Plimpton, who became Stevenson's senior deputy ambassador to the UN.

tremely able fellow and will add stature to the Mission. Also Charles Noyes[51] who was with me in London and San Francisco — a fellow with long familiarity with the Mission and its work and I think he can help in managing the Mission. That is all I have — plus Klutznick. I haven't got a senior ambassador — Ellsworth Bunker[52] is not up to it.

— I will try to get Harry La Bouisse[53] — Pete Collado.[54]

k: Would you take La Bouisse?

s: Yes — I would like to have him as my senior deputy to do representational work. — and with Plimpton on Security Council.

k: I will talk to Rusk about that and — we could ask Collado — and if Collado is interested in ICA [International Cooperation Administration], o.k. and let La Bouisse go to New York.

s: Well, I am not sure. But I will mention the alternative to Dean — because he told me he wanted La Bouisse if he could get him.

s: I want to mention a word for another old friend, Jonathan Daniels. You probably know him well.

k: I just met him. He seems bright, but I don't know whether he would be right for this.

s: I don't know your alternatives.

k: One of the alternatives is Pat Weaver.[55] He used to be head of NBC — rather vigorous, no political connections, but he has ideas.

s: I don't know how much government experience or world vision he has, but Daniels was in the White House with Truman — has run a fine newspaper in Raleigh. A sophisticated man — has written good books. I am sure you would like him. . . . He has a lot to recommend him.

s: I had a visitor today who talked about Cuba and I am going to send some notes to you down there, with a copy to Rusk.

k: Fine.

---

51 A consultant to the Rockefeller Brothers Fund. He became counselor to the U.S. mission to the UN.

52 Ambassador to India.

53 Henry R. Labouisse, a consultant to the International Bank for Reconstruction and Development. Kennedy appointed him director of the International Cooperation Administration and later ambassador to Greece.

54 Emilio G. Collado, a director and former treasurer of Standard Oil Company of New Jersey.

55 Sylvester L. Weaver, Jr., chairman of the board of McCann-Erickson Corporation, International.

s: This person is a well known writer and has been in and out of Cuba and he has some ideas for your administration that I think ought to be thought about

k: Right.

s: May I ask about Mrs. Roosevelt — member of the delegation — adjourned session of the General Assembly in March?

k: Fine, if she would.

s: Not full time, but I think she would be flattered to be invited to be a delegate — would make good impression on Africans and Asians.

k: Right.

s: Now, regarding Mrs. R's position — there's Mary Lord,[56] Mary Price,[57] Mrs. E. Anderson,[58] Gladys Tillette,[59] Marietta Tree. Marietta has a fine standing regarding race relations, and endearing ways with the Africans.[60] Should I discuss with Dean?

k: I would say Marietta and Mrs. Tillette. I think Mrs. Tillette is full of zip. I don't know — maybe we could give the place to her for a year or something — then maybe Marietta. I think Mrs. Tillette first, Marietta second. Is Marietta British?[61]

s: No, I think she has independent status.

k: Is she an American citizen?

s: Yes. I never talked to her about this thing — she is a great friend — but I haven't wanted to say anything until I was prepared to say something.

k: Whatever your final judgment is — I would say I thought she was an extraordinary woman when I met her.

s: Maybe we could use them both.

k: Fine. I would put them ahead of all the others. . . .

s: I talked to Rusk and Chester [Bowles] several weeks ago urging them to suggest to you or discuss with you sometime what seems to

[56] Mrs. Oswald Bates Lord, U.S. delegate to the UN General Assembly, 1959–1960.

[57] Margaret Price (Mrs. Hickman Price, Jr.), a member of the Democratic National Committee and vice chairman of the Democratic Committee for Michigan.

[58] Eugenie Anderson, ambassador to Denmark, 1949–1953, and later minister to Bulgaria, 1962–1965.

[59] Mrs. Charles W. Tillett, Democratic National Committeewoman from North Carolina. She became an alternate delegate to the UN fall session in 1961 and U.S. representative on the Commission on the Status of Women.

[60] Mrs. Tree became U.S. representative to the UN Human Rights Commission and a member of the U.S. mission to the UN.

[61] Mrs. Tree was American but was married to a British subject.

me the most important first thing that this administration has to do —
and that is to discover what is in K[hrushchev]'s mind, if possible.
There's only one way I know of and this would be by direct talks in
Moscow without formality by somebody who is not the diplomatic
agent but someone who corresponds to Khrushchev's concept of
power. That is, a political figure rather than a diplomatic one; someone who would go there after the inauguration as your emissary to
review the situation and exploit what opportunities there may be. I
think it is important to find out what his troubles are — as well as to
explore with him ours. I am told one trouble of his may be his health
— which we don't know anything about. Extremists in the Presidium
and China — and what he has to deal with. I think we will not find
anyone easier to deal with than K is. I think it is important to find out
whether he wants to expand the cold war — if we make proposals on
general and complete disarmament — how are we going to proceed — does he want an effective U.N., or is he determined to destroy
it? — I know how he reveals himself in conversation — and it could
be this could determine quite a good deal, especially if he wants to do
business. — What we want to do is to discover some means of creating a favorable world order and we must explore the kind of thing we
could do — for example, if they would make a gesture of releasing the
B–47 pilots[62] we could with grace make a gesture in their direction. It
would be helpful if Zorin[63] at the U.N. got some new instructions
and we could have a more profitable meeting in the Spring than we
had in the Fall. I think they have been taking the initiative too long
now. This would recapture the world's imagination which is one of
the first jobs to be done — and I don't think we can do it by being too
cautious. I think this is one of the things that you should talk over — I
haven't been able to get Dean.

к: We should talk about the desirability of bringing Thompson[64] home
right away to report, then we can talk to him and see what best way
we can proceed from there.

к: Who would be the best one to talk to K?

s: I think the unhappy thing is the best one is me. But I haven't wanted
to suggest this and it would come at an awkward time — but I would

---

[62] An American RB-47 reconnaissance plane had been shot down by a Russian
fighter plane over Soviet territorial waters on July 1, 1960, and two of the crew of six
had been taken alive. The Russians announced that the flyers would be tried and
rejected demands to release them or even to allow the Red Cross access to them.
Kennedy announced at his first news conference, on January 25, 1961, that the
U.S.S.R. had freed the two men.

[63] Valerian A. Zorin, Soviet ambassador to the UN, 1960–1962.

[64] Llewellyn E. Thompson, Jr., U.S. ambassador to the Soviet Union.

do this if it were deemed wise and helpful — and I would put other things aside. The alternative would be [W. Averell] Harriman — he has disadvantages in view of the fact that he always insists on talking — and has difficulty in hearing.

I think it would be best to send someone K knows and with whom he has had dealings before — someone he would be quite sure would represent you — someone influential — not just a personal diplomat.

K: Good. We will have a chance to talk before we come to a final judgment on this?

K: And — again — I would prefer Mrs. Tillette — if only a year and put Marietta in another spot and let her move up then. We haven't got many Southerners in this.

K: I'll see you at the inauguration and then the Cabinet luncheon.

S: I had a call from the Senate [Foreign Relations] Committee to come down next Wednesday so I'll be there then.

On January 17, 1961, Stevenson left Chicago to appear before the Senate Foreign Relations Committee and to attend the inauguration of President John F. Kennedy on January 20. Stevenson then went to New York City to assume his position as the Permanent Representative of the United States to the United Nations.

Acknowledgments

We are most grateful to Adlai E. Stevenson's sister, Mrs. Ernest L. Ives, for her infinite patience and considerate help at all stages in the preparation of this volume.

Professor Stuart Gerry Brown, Mrs. Ernest L. Ives, Edward D. McDougal, Jr., Newton N. Minow, William McC. Blair, Jr., and W. Willard Wirtz have read all or portions of the manuscript.

Little, Brown and Company, Mrs. Eugene Meyer, Mrs. Marshall Field and the Field Foundation, Mr. and Mrs. Harold Hochschild, Arnold Picker, Robert S. Benjamin, Newton N. Minow, James F. Oates, Jr., Francis T. P. Plimpton, Benjamin Swig, Philip M. Klutznick, Mrs. John Paul Welling, William McCormick Blair, the late R. Keith Kane, Simon H. Rifkind, Wilson W. Wyatt, the late William Benton, the late Daggett Harvey, Mr. and Mrs. Edison Dick, William McC. Blair, Jr., Lloyd K. Garrison, J. M. Kaplan, Jerrold Loebl, Hermon D. Smith, Edward D. McDougal, Jr., Glen A. Lloyd, Mr. and Mrs. Gilbert Harrison, Irving B. Harris, Edwin C. Austin, Archibald Alexander, Jacob M. Arvey, Paul Ziffren, Frank Karelsen, George W. Ball, C. K. McClatchy, Maurice Tempelsman, Barnet Hodes and Scott Hodes, generously provided funds to defray the editorial expense of this volume.

Roger Shugg of the University of New Mexico Press and Ned Bradford of Little, Brown and Company have been constant in their encouragement.

William E. Dix, Alexander P. Clark and Mrs. Nancy Bressler, of Princeton University Library; Paul Edlund of the Library of Congress; Phyllis Gustafson; Roxane Eberlein; Linda Inlay and Adele Sugawara have been most helpful. Louis B. Cella, of Elmhurst, Illinois, kindly sent us his collection of newspaper clippings.

WALTER JOHNSON
CAROL EVANS
C. ERIC SEARS

Index

219, 241, 253; on Soviet equality in power, 219–220, 279, 457; on U.S. "defensiveness," 263, 325, 328, 330, 378; on China, 289–290, 365, (as "number one problem") 274, 297, 319, 457; on giving testimony when called upon, 300; on importance of Asia to U.S., 314; on "political relevance of moral principle," 321–333; on brotherhood, 322–325 *passim*, 329–330, 473; on "paralysis of will" vs. dedication, 325–333; on virtue, 330–332; on continuing education, 339–340 (*see also* education); on party organization, 340–343; on role of "opposition party," 375, 464–472, 477, 498, 510; on serving if chosen, 383, 394, 415, 430, 476, 511–519 *passim*, 523, 533; on British Parliamentary system, 394; on "hemispheric solidarity," 426, 432, 445; on religious prejudice, 463, 480; on national unity in time of crisis, 497–498; on seeking presidency, 524–525 (*see also* AND PRESIDENTIAL CAMPAIGNS, *above*); on democracy, 534, 606; on U.S. foreign policy: "peace, with justice," 606 (*see also* foreign policy; North Atlantic Treaty Organization (NATO); State, U.S. Department of); on "racial minority," 608

WRITINGS:

diary: attempt fails, 23; Washington (one day), 114–116; Europe–Russia trip, 226–253 *passim*, 278–280, 281–285; Latin American trip, 401, 402–428 *passim*, 433, 437, 438

notes: of visits to Dr. Schweitzer, 32–33; for "A Year After Suez," 62–64; on pre-NATO State Department mission, 97–98; for New York press conference on Quemoy and Matsu, 289–290; "for Informal Remarks at Los Angeles Airport," 533–535; on possible role in Kennedy Administration, 579–580; on UN ambassadorship, 594, 595, 596–598

book reviews: in *New Republic*, of *The Lunatic Fringe* (Johnson), 47; in *New York Times Book Review*, of *Elm Street Politics* (Mitchell), 340–343

books, articles, reports, etc.: The New America, 53n; "My Visit to Dr.

Schweitzer at Lambarene Summer of 1957," 56–57; article for *Optima*, reprinted in *Sunday Times* (London), 62; refuses to write about South Africa, 62; "Preliminary Memorandum re: U.S. Position at North Atlantic Treaty Council Meeting in December 1957," 100–103; "Memorandum Number 3, NATO Heads of Government Meeting," 127–132 (*see also* Dulles, John Foster); handwritten proposed changes in Eisenhower speech, 133n; "Dual Education Problem: School and Home" (*New York Times Magazine*), 182n; comments (in letters) on *Only in America* (Golden) and *Special for Today* (Block), 197, 295; on Soviet economic challenge (unidentified article), 215–216; articles for NANA, later published as *Friends and Enemies: What I Learned in Russia*, 232, 294, 304n, 334n, 337–338, 460, (conclusions quoted) 274–279; mentions articles on USSR and Khrushchev, 283, 294, 300; essay (for Miami *Daily News*) on 1959 prospects, 318, 319–320; *An Ethic for Survival* (collected speeches), 321n; "This Time We Might Get Licked" (*New York Times Magazine*), 337; promises jacket copy for *The Coming Political Breakthrough* (Bowles), 358; "Tour for Khrushchev — The Real America" (*New York Times Magazine*), 363, 366; articles for *Foreign Affairs*, later reprinted in *Putting First Things First: A Democratic View*, 364, 371, 381, 383, 384, 504n; on "Camelot" (introduction to Steinbeck letter, for *Newsday*), 380–381; "Our Plight in Latin America" (*Look*), 438–445, 473n, 520, 551, 554, 562, 583; "Extend Our Vision — To All Mankind" (*Life*), 473n; "Choice by Hullabaloo" (*This Week*), 488n, 494n; "National Purpose: Stevenson's View" (*New York Times*), 505, (*Congressional Record reprints*) 505–506; "Why the World Looks to the U.N." (*New York Times Magazine*), 566n; AES sends copy of his article on Africa to Kennedy, 583; "Report(s) on Con-